INGENIX®

SAVE MORE and qualify for REWARDS when you order at IngenixOnline.com.

AF772735

HERE ARE THE TOP THREE REASONS TO PLACE YOUR ORDER ONLINE:

1. Save an additional 5% when you order online*—use source **FOBW7.**
2. Get rewards for every $500 you spend at Ingenix Online with our eSmart program.**
3. Experience a quick, hassle-free purchase process with streamlined checkout options.

ingenix esmart
ingenix online frequent buyer program

Get rewards when you order online.

Ingenix eSmart is a program designed to reward our best Ingenix Online customers. If you are a registered online customer and qualify to participate**, all you have to do is use the returning customer checkout option for your web purchases every time you shop online. We keep track of your purchases. Once you reach $500, we send you a FREE product—it's that easy!

If you are not yet registered, go to IngenixOnline.com and register right away so we can get you started with the Ingenix eSmart program.

Are you part of our Medallion program?

Ingenix Online has enhanced options for you, for a hassle-free, streamlined purchase and account management experience!

To view your enhanced online account options, simply register with us at IngenixOnline.com. You will then be able to easily place orders from your Price List, get access to your purchase history, track shipments, change your profile, manage your address book and much more.

Could you benefit from an easy, quick way to consolidate orders for your company?

The Ingenix web-based consolidation tool is designed to streamline the purchasing process and enhance your productivity. For more information log into your account or visit www.ingenixonline.com/orderconsolidation.

(*) Additional 5% savings offer valid online, cannot be combined with any other offer and is not applicable to Partner accounts. Bookstore products, package items, eLearning products, Academy Credential Study Guides, online exams, Worker's Compensation items and conferences not included. For Medallion accounts, we compare the Price List discounts against the offer discounts and honor the better of the two.

(**) eSmart program valid for Ingenix customers who are NOT part of Medallion or Partner Accounts programs. You must be registered at Ingenix Online to have your online purchases tracked for rewards purposes. Shipping charges and taxes still apply and cannot be used for rewards. eSmart reward offers valid online only.

100% Money Back Guarantee

If our merchandise* ever fails to meet your expectations, please contact our Customer Service Department toll-free at 1.800.INGENIX (464.3649), option 1, for an immediate response. *Software and Data File: Credit will be granted for unopened packages only.

SAVE 5% when you order at www.ingenixonline.com (reference source code FOBW7)

or call toll-free 1.800.INGENIX(464.3649), option 1.

Also available from your medical bookstore or distributor.

FOBA7

INGENIX.

Four simple ways
to place an order.

Call

1.800.ingenix (464.3649), option 1. Mention source code FOBA7 when ordering.

Mail

PO Box 27116
Salt Lake City, UT 84127-0116
With payment and/or purchase order.

Fax

801.982.4033
With credit card information and/or purchase order.

Click

www.ingenixonline.com
Save 5% when you order online today—use source code FOBW7.

ingenix*e*smart
ingenix online frequent buyer program

GET REWARDS FOR SHOPPING ONLINE!
To find out more, visit IngenixOnline.com

eSmart program available only to Ingenix customers who are not part of Medallion, Gold Medallion or Partner Accounts programs. You must be registered at Ingenix Online to have your online purchases tracked for rewards purposes. Shipping charges and taxes still apply and cannot be used for rewards. Offer valid online only.

100% Money Back Guarantee

If our merchandise* ever fails to meet your expectations, please contact our Customer Service Department toll-free at 1.800.ingenix (464.3649), option 1 for an immediate response.
*Software: Credit will be granted for unopened packages only.

Customer Service Hours

7:00 am - 5:00 pm Mountain Time
9:00 am - 7:00 pm Eastern Time

Shipping and Handling

no. of items	fee
1	$10.95
2-4	$12.95
5-7	$14.95
8-10	$19.95
11+	Call

Order Form

Information

Customer No. ____________ Contact No. ____________

Source Code ____________

Contact Name ____________

Title ____________ Specialty ____________

Company ____________

Street Address ____________
NO PO BOXES, PLEASE

City ____________ State ______ Zip ______

Telephone (   ) ____________ Fax (   ) ____________
IN CASE WE HAVE QUESTIONS ABOUT YOUR ORDER

E-mail ____________ @ ____________
REQUIRED FOR ORDER CONFIRMATION AND SELECT PRODUCT DELIVERY.

Ingenix respects your right to privacy. We will not sell or rent your e-mail address or fax number to anyone outside Ingenix and its business partners. If you would like to remove your name from Ingenix promotion, please call 1.800.ingenix (464.3649), option 1.

Product

Item No.	Qty	Description	Price	Total

Subtotal ______

UT & VA residents, please add applicable Sales tax ______

(See chart on the left) Shipping & handling charges ______
All foreign orders, please call for shipping costs

Total ______

Payment

○Please bill my credit card ○MasterCard ○VISA ○Amex ○Discover

Card No. | | | | | | | | | | | | | | | | | Expires ______ | ______
MONTH YEAR

Signature ____________

○Check enclosed, made payable to: Ingenix, Inc. ○Please bill my office

Purchase Order No. ____________
ATTACH COPY OF PURCHASE ORDER

INGENIX®

Insurance Directory

Largest and most complete listing of insurers

2007

Publishers Notice

2007 Insurance Directory is designed to be an accurate and authoritative source regarding coding and every reasonable effort has been made to ensure accuracy and completeness of the content. However, Ingenix makes no guarantee, warranty, or representation that this publication is accurate, complete, or without errors. It is understood that Ingenix is not rendering any legal or other professional services or advice in this publication and that Ingenix bears no liability for any results or consequences that may arise from the use of this book. Please e-mail all correspondence to the Ingenix customer service department at customerservice@ingenix.com or call 1.800.INGENIX (464.3649), option 1.

Acknowledgments

Mike Goleman, *Product Manager*
Ralph Wankier, MBA, *VP Product Management*
Karen Schmidt, BSN, *Technical Director*
Lynn Speirs, *Senior Director, Editorial/Desktop Publishing*
Stacy Perry, *Manager, Desktop Publishing*
Lisa Singley, *Project Manager*
Lauri Gray, RHIT, CPC, *Clinical/Technical Editor*
Kerrie Hornsby, *Desktop Publishing Specialist*
Jean Parkinson, *Editor*
Joleen Scott, *Editorial Assistance*
Sharon Walter, *Editorial Assistance*
Katie Ericson, *Editorial Assistance*
Flora Bernard, *Editorial Assistance*

Copyright

First printing, August 2006

Made in the USA.

ISBN 978-1-56337-691-7

Our Commitment to Accuracy

Ingenix is committed to producing accurate and reliable materials. To report corrections, please visit www.ingenixonline.com/accuracy or email accuracy@ingenix.com. You can also reach customer service by calling 1.800.INGENIX (464.3649), option 1.

Technical Editors

Lauri Gray, RHIT, CPC
Ms. Gray is a clinical technical editor for Ingenix, a position she has held for the past eight years. She has more than 25 years experience in health information management. She began her career as a medical records supervisor in a multispecialty clinic and then shifted to the managed care industry where she was employed as a contracting and coding specialist for a major HMO. Ms. Gray has extensive experience in physician coding, claims adjudication processes, third-party reimbursement, and fee schedule development. She is a member of the American Academy of Professional Coders (AAPC) and the American Health Information Management Association (AHIMA).

Contents

Introduction

The 2007 *Insurance Directory* is a comprehensive reference of more than 5,000 listings for all United States, Puerto Rico, Virgin Islands, American Samoa, and Guam insurance companies that process claims. Ingenix structures this publication to offer providers, payers, and employers a ready reference of insurance companies' addresses, phone and fax numbers, and the types of claims they process. Each listing in the *2007 Insurance Directory* provides the user with easily identifiable icons to identify the types of claims processed by individual insurance companies (e.g., medical, dental, vision, HCPCS Level II codes, and Medigap policies). Ingenix makes every effort to assure the validity and accuracy of the *2007 Insurance Directory* by personally calling each insurance company listed to verify and update the information published.

In addition to specific company information, the *2007 Insurance Directory* is updated with an extensive introduction explaining insurance claims policies and procedures that are new for the year. For example, the *2007 Insurance Directory* outlines the steps for completing the form required for Medicare Part B reimbursement (CMS-1500) and provides a copy of the standard Electronic Data Interchange (EDI) enrollment form that must be completed prior to submitting electronic media claims to Medicare. Ingenix also gives you the most current information regarding national identification programs for health care providers and health care organizations.

The *2007 Insurance Directory* continues and enhances popular standard features such as the state-by-state listing of private payers, the addresses and phone numbers of individual state insurance commissioners, and the companies that utilize HCPCS Level II codes.

Insurance Directory 2007

Places of Operation

Whether it's a private payer claim, workers' compensation claim, or other government claim, the *2007 Insurance Directory* provides the information you need for getting claims to the right place. The *2007 Insurance Directory* also directs you to the electronic addresses of third-party administrators (TPAs) for quick on-line assistance with your claims questions.

HCPCS, Medigap, Prior Authorization Identifiers

The *2007 Insurance Directory* identifies a greater number of companies that accept HCPCS Level II codes and a greater number of payers offering Medigap policies. HCPCS and Medigap can be defined as follows:

- HCPCS (pronounced "hick-picks") is an acronym for Healthcare Common Procedure Coding System. *Current Procedural Terminology* (CPT), copyright American Medical Association and updated on an annual basis, is HCPCS Level I. HCPCS Level II national codes are developed by the Centers for Medicare and Medicaid Services (CMS) and are used to report medical services and supplies not specifically identified in the CPT book, including drugs administered by injection and durable medical equipment. HCPCS codes are required for reporting most medical services and supplies provided to Medicare and Medicaid patients, and are often required for private payer reimbursement. Payers that require HCPCS Level II codes are identified with the icon .
- A Medigap policy, as defined by CMS, is a health insurance policy or other health benefit plan offered by a private company to those entitled to Medicare benefits. The policy provides payment for Medicare charges not payable due to deductibles, coinsurance amounts, or other Medicare and Medicaid imposed limitations. Payers offering Medigap policies are identified with the icon .
- Prior authorization is a cost-control procedure used by insurers to discourage over prescription of diagnostic tests, pharmaceuticals, and services (e.g., physical, speech, and behavioral therapies). The procedure requires the physician's or insurer's advance approval of the tests, drugs, and services. Without prior authorization, the stipulated items would not be reimbursed by the plan and the patient would be responsible for payment. Prior authorization is identified with the icon .

Electronic Claims Capability

The *2007 Insurance Directory* continues to identify the payers that accept electronically filed claims. HIPAA requires that payers have the capability to receive claims electronically to reduce the costs and administrative functions of health care tracking and reimbursement. The Administrative Simplification Provisions of HIPAA apply to payers and providers and affect all health claims and equivalent encounter information (professional, institutional, and dental). Some entities are not required to comply with the electronic claims mandate including those with no means of electronic claim submission capability, facilities with 25 or fewer full-time employees, and physician practices with 10 or fewer full-time employees. Payers that accept electronic claims are identified with the icon 🖳.

Because the majority of claims are now filed in electronic format, the *2007 Insurance Directory* provides more detailed information on electronic claims media. This information as well as the standard information required at a minimum in each carrier, DMERC, and fiscal intermediary (FI) Electronic Data Interchange (EDI) Enrollment Form can be found in the Claims Processing chapter.

Revised CMS-1500

The standard claim form (CMS-1500), used when submitting paper claims, has been updated to accommodate National Provider Identifiers (NPI). The current CMS-1500 (12-90) form is being replaced with the revised form designated as the CMS-1500 (08-05). The revised form is being phased in over a four month period beginning October 1, 2006. For Medicare claims, the 12-90 or 08-05 versions may be submitted as of October 1, 2006 until January 31, 2007. Effective February 1, 2007, however, only the 08-05 version will be accepted by Medicare contractors. At this time, it is not known when commercial payers will begin accepting the 08-05 version.

Detailed information on the changes as well as a copy of the revised form is included in the *2007 Insurance Directory*.

Note: Insurance information changes rapidly, and while Ingenix attempts to provide the latest information possible, there will be new information Ingenix must hold until the next printing or edition of the *Insurance Directory*.

Claims Processing

The term "claims processing" describes the course of submitting a claim to the payer and subsequent adjudication. Understanding how this process works allows physicians and staff members to file claims properly and leads to maximum and timely reimbursement. In addition, this knowledge will allow you and your staff to serve as a resource to patients in understanding this process.

Patient Information

Before filing any claim, you need to obtain clear, accurate information from your patients. A good patient information (PI) form is the key to this aspect of claims submission. The PI form should include such basic items as the policy name and number, insured's name, dates of coverage, and secondary insurance information. While this information is a good place to start, it is by no means all of the information required by most insurers. Providing as much information as possible will reduce the insurance company's need to contact your office. Avoiding unnecessary contact will reduce the costs of claims processing and hasten your payment

You may also wish to preregister new patients over the phone or, if time permits, through the mail. Having a shortened version of your PI form for phone registrations could be valuable.

Patient information must be updated regularly. Most offices verify the information at each visit. If you work in a multiple physicians' office or clinic, establishing a uniform information policy makes everyone accountable for current and correct patient data.

Patient information forms follow the same basic pattern, but each differs by the type of patient your office might encounter. Each form is titled with the targeted group's name. If your office has some special information needs or you wish to include additional instructions, consider using the back of the form. If your practice has a high volume of Medicare patients, you may want to consider two separate forms—one for Medicare patients and another for non-Medicare patients. These forms could be printed on different colored paper for easy identification.

Primary vs. Secondary Coverage

Households with dual incomes often have more than one insurer. You must determine which is the primary and which is the secondary insurance company. For commercial plans, the subscriber's or insured's insurance company is always primary for the subscriber. In other words, the husband's insurance company is primary for him and the wife's insurance company is primary for her. However, the primary insurance company for any dependents is determined by the insureds' birthdays, the primary insured being the individual whose birthday is first during the year. This is often referred to as the "birthday rule." For example, if the husband's birthday is October 15, 1965 and the wife's birthday is March 1, 1967, the wife is primary for their dependents because her birthday is first during the year (year of birth is ignored). Therefore, obtaining a date of birth for both subscribers is important.

Assignment of Benefits and Release of Information

If you haven't already done so, consider adding an assignment of benefits statement to your patient information form. It should state that the patient has agreed to have insurance payments sent directly to the physician and that medical information can be released to the patient's insurance company. A signed copy of this assignment submitted with a claim helps ensure at least partial payment from most commercial insurers. Assignments also reduce collection expenses. An alternative, lifetime assignment of benefits, should nearly eliminate the need to obtain a signature after each date of service; however, there are a few payers who require a current signature with each claim.

If your office participates with Medicare, remember that an assignment of benefits and a release of billing are still necessary. To avoid the hassle of obtaining updated signatures, you may want to obtain lifetime assignment agreements and a commercial insurer's yearly signature agreement. Most commercial payers accept the yearly signature agreement form, but it is not applicable to the Medicare patient.

Determining Coverage

Ideally, a patient's insurance coverage should be verified before any nonemergent service is rendered. This policy shouldn't apply exclusively to new patients. Established patients may have changed employers, gotten married or divorced, or may no longer be covered by the policy that was in effect during their last visit.

When a new patient appointment is made, stress that the patient must present a current insurance identification card. However, a copy of the card does not guarantee eligibility. You may want to take the pertinent information over the phone to verify benefits before the patient arrives. The law requires Medicaid patients to provide current proof of eligibility with each visit, and requesting this information from all patients can be done in a pleasant manner without alienating anyone.

During the visit, photocopy insurance cards and place the copies in the patient's record. Always check and highlight the eligibility dates as well as coverage information. Many offices have a policy that the first visit is always paid at the time of service, with the exception of Medicare, Medicaid, and any contractual arrangement your office may have with an individual payer. Payment for the first service allows you time to verify coverage prior to additional treatment.

The Claim

The most important document for correct reimbursement is the insurance claim form. Other information, such as operative reports, chart notes, and cover letters may establish medical necessity, but the claim itself sets the stage.

There are two types of claims media, paper and electronic. Legislation has been in effect for several years that requires claim submission of HIPAA compliant electronic format for facilities with more than 25 full-time employees and physician practices with more than 10 full-time employees. The legislation also requires that all payers, including small health plans, have the capability of accepting claims in HIPAA compliant electronic format.

With commercial insurance companies, you may submit the claim directly to the payer or provide your patient with the necessary information to submit the claim. If you've signed an agreement with Blue Cross/Blue Shield or with an HMO or PPO, you are probably required to send the claim directly to them. Medicare now requires that you submit all Medicare claims directly to the carrier, whether you participate or not.

If patients pay at the time of service, you may wish to provide an itemized statement or superbill attached to a claim form that they can submit to their insurance company. This arrangement works well for office services, but surgical services are usually more accurately reimbursed if you bill your hospital and surgical services directly to the payer.

For electronic media claims, all health care providers and health plans are required to use the ASC X12N 837 which is the standard HIPAA format. An overview of the ASC X12N 837 is described in the Electronic Claims section of this chapter.

The standard claim form (CMS-1500), used when submitting paper claims, has been updated to accommodate National Provider Identifiers (NPI). The current CMS-1500 (12-90) form is being replaced with the revised form designated as the CMS-1500 (08-05). For Medicare claims either the 12-90 or 08-05 versions may be submitted as of October 1, 2006 until January 31, 2007. Effective February 1, 2007, however, only the 08-05 version will be accepted by Medicare contractors. At this time, it is unknown as to when commercial payers will begin accepting the 08-05 version.

In the past, offices were given a great deal of latitude with claims submission, but today the insurance industry (both government and private) demands greater uniformity, making it even more important to understand how to complete the fields of the claim form accurately.

While Medicare is requiring use of the CMS-1500 (08-05) effective February 1, 2007, some of the revisions, particularly those regarding the NPI, should be provided if available but will not be required to be completed until May 23, 2007, which is the deadline for every provider to have an NPI.

Revisions to the CMS-1500 (08-05) form are detailed later in this chapter.

Electronic Claims

The percentage of electronic claims submitted in HIPAA compliant format to CMS has steadily increased in recent years and now exceeds 85 percent. There are a number of advantages to electronic claim submission. These are detailed on the CMS website and include:

- Faster payment is made on HIPAA compliant electronic claims. HIPAA compliant electronic claims can be paid after 13 days while paper claims and electronic claims that are not HIPAA compliant cannot be paid for at least 27 days.
- Electronic transactions are cost effective, and reduce the opportunity for error.
- Electronic claims lower administrative, postage, and handling costs associated with paper claim submissions.
- Online receipt or acknowledgment is provided eliminating delays due to "lost" claims.
- Standardized formats reduce administrative costs since one format will meet all current billing requirements and is accepted by all Medicare contractors as well as many third-party billers.
- Standardized electronic claims submission and COB exchange and remittance receipt reduce system costs.
- Remittances are sent to a provider-preferred location.
- Claim status and eligibility information is available in 24 hours or less.
- Electronic funds transfer (EFT) can have accounts receivable revenue in the provider's bank, drawing interest, in two working days after payment. Paper checks can take as long as one week to process.

Electronic Claim Submission Using ASC X12N 837

The Administrative Simplification Provisions of the Health Insurance Portability and Accountability Act (HIPAA) of 1996 mandated that the Secretary of Health and Human Services (HHS) establish uniform standards for electronic health care transactions that would reduce the administrative costs in the health care industry. HIPAA focused on the following five areas:

- Electronic Data Interchange (EDI): the electronic transfer of information in a standardized format including enrollment, eligibility, payment and remittance advice, claims, health plan premium payments, health claim status, and referral certification and authorization
- Code Sets: the data elements used to document the reason a patient is seen and the services and supplies provided
- Identifiers: used to identify health care providers, health plans, employers, and patients
- Security: standards developed for all health plans, clearinghouses, and providers to protect the confidentiality and integrity of all medical information during all stages before, during, and after the transmission
- Privacy: standards that protect the patient's personal health information and define when and how it is appropriate to disclose this information

Even though the majority of providers are required by law to submit claims electronically in HIPAA compliant format, Medicare implemented a contingency plan in October 2003 that permits some providers to continue sending pre-HIPAA format electronic claims. This measure is temporary. Effective July 1, 2004, claims submitted electronically that are not HIPAA compliant are treated like paper claims and cannot be paid for at least 27 days.

A final rule published in the August 17, 2000 *Federal Register* acted on the standards of electronic health care transactions, as well as established the medical data sets (code sets) that are suitable for electronic transaction. All health care providers and health plans are required to use the ASC X12N 837 for submitting electronic health care claims (hospital, physician/supplier, and dental), and have the option of using a health care clearinghouse to satisfy the HIPAA standard requirements. The ASC X12N 837 was also selected as the standard for the institutional claims (hospital, nursing facilities, and similar inpatient institutions) and replaces the UB-92 format developed by CMS for Medicare claims.

At first glance the ASC X12N 837 format may appear daunting because the format has hundreds of fields and hundreds of pages of instructions. However, there are two things to keep in mind when familiarizing oneself with this format. First, the five level hierarchical looping format has been designed to maximize efficiency. The five levels include: billing provider, subscriber, patient, claim level, and line item. When claims data is sorted using this structure, providers only need to complete those lower levels of the claim that differ. Often this will include only the claim level and line item data. Second, upon review of the usage field it should be noted that not all fields are required (R).

The majority of fields have been designated for situational (S) and optional (O) data. While some claim types may require completion of the situational fields and some payers may require completion of some of the optional fields, not all of these fields will need to be completed for all claim types or for all payers.

The implementation guides and formats for the ASC X12N 837 standards are not included in this book. They can be obtained from the Washington Publishing Company, 806 W. Diamond Ave., Suite 400, Gaithersburg, MD. The guides are also available at no cost through the Washington Publishing Company on the Internet at http://www.wpc-edi.com/hipaa/.

It is important to check this website and the CMS website regularly for any changes to the standards because the code sets approved may change once HHS formalizes the choice of diagnostic and procedural coding systems.

Electronic Data Interchange (EDI) Enrollment Form

Electronic Data Interchange (EDI) forms are available from your local CMS contractor. The agreement is required from each provider of health care services, physician, or supplier that intends to submit electronic media claims (EMC). In addition, a separate EDI form is required for each CMS contractor that is billed. So, if claims are submitted to both a Part B physician contractor and a DMERC, a separate EDI enrollment form will be required for each. New EMC billers must obtain a form from each contractor to be billed, complete and sign the form, and submit it to the designated local contractor. The *2007 Insurance Directory* contains a copy of the standard information required at a minimum in each carrier, DMERC, and FI EDI enrollment form. Additional information is available in the *Medicare Claims Processing Manual* (Pub 100-04), chapter 24, section 20.

Electronic Data Interchange (EDI) Enrollment Form

A. The provider agrees to the following provisions for submitting Medicare claims electronically to CMS or to CMS' carriers, DMERCs, or FIs:

1. That it will be responsible for all Medicare claims submitted to CMS by itself, its employees, or its agents.
2. That it will not disclose any information concerning a Medicare beneficiary to any other person or organization, except CMS and/or its carriers, DMERCs, FIs, or another contractor if so designated by CMS, without the express written permission of the Medicare beneficiary or his/her parent or legal guardian, or where required for the care and treatment of a beneficiary who is unable to provide written consent, or to bill insurance primary or supplementary, to Medicare, or as required by State or Federal Law.
3. That it will submit claims only on behalf of those Medicare beneficiaries who have given their written authorization to do so, and to certify that required beneficiary signatures, or legally authorized signatures on behalf of beneficiaries, are on file.
4. That it will ensure that every electronic entry can be readily associated and identified with an original source document. Each source document must reflect the following information:
   - Beneficiary's name,
   - Beneficiary's health insurance claim number,
   - Date(s) of service,
   - Diagnosis/nature of illness, and
   - Procedure/service performed.
5. That the Secretary of Health and Human Services or his/her designee and/or the carrier, DMERC, FI, or other contractor if designated by CMS, has the right to audit and confirm information submitted by the provider and shall have access to all original source documents and medical records related to the provider's submissions, including the beneficiary's authorization and signature. All incorrect payments that are discovered as a result of such an audit shall be adjusted according to the applicable provisions of the Social Security Act, Federal regulations, and CMS guidelines.
6. That it will ensure that all claims for Medicare primary payment have been developed for other insurance involvement and that Medicare is the primary payer.
7. That it will submit claims that are accurate, complete, and truthful.
8. That it will retain all original source documentation and medical records pertaining to any such particular Medicare claim for a period of at least six years, three months after the bill is paid.
9. That it will affix the CMS-assigned unique identifiere number (submitter identifier) of the provider on each claim electronically transmitted to the carrier, DMERC, FI, or other contractor if designated by CMS.
10. That the CMS-assigned unique identifier number identifier (submitter identifier) constitues the provider's legal eectronic signature and constitutes an assurance by the provider that services weree performed as billed.
11. That it will use sufficient security procedures (including compliance with all provisions of the HIPAA security regulations) to ensure that all transmissions of documents are authorized and protect all beneficiary-specific data from improper access.
12. That it will acknowledge that all claims will be paid from Federal funds, that the submission of such claims is a claim for payment under the Medicare program, and that anyone who misrepresents or falsifies or causes to be misrepresented or falsified any record or other information relating to that claim that is required pursuant to this Agreement may, upon conviction, be subject to a fine and/or imprisonment under applicable Federal law.

13. That it will establish and maintain procedures and controls so that information concerning Medicare beneficiaries, or any information obtained from CMS or its carrier, DMERC, FI, or other contractor if designated by CMS, shall not be used by agents, officers, or employyees of the billing service except as proviced by the carrier, DMERC, or FI (in accordance with §11 06(a) of the Social Security Act (the Act).
14. That it will research and correct claim discrepancies.
15. That it will notify the carrier, DMERC, FI, or other contractor if designated by CMS, within two business days if any transmitted data are received in an unintelligible or garbled form.

B. The Centers for Medicare and Medicaid Services (CMS) Agrees To

1. Transmit to the provider an acknowledgement of claim receipt.
2. Affix the carrier, DMERC, FI, or other contractor if designated by CMS, number as its electronic signature, on each remittance advice sent to the provider.
3. Ensure that payments to providers are timely in accordance with CMS' policies.
4. Ensure that no carrier, DMERC, FI, or other contractor if designated by CMS, may require the provider to purchase any or all electronic services from the carrier, DMERC, of FI or from any subsidiary of the carrier, DMERC, FI, other contractor if designated by CMS, or from any company for which the carrier, DMERC, or FI has an interest. The carrier, DMERC, FI, or other contractor if designated by CMS, will make alternative means available to any electronic biller to obtain such services.
5. Ensure that all Medicare electronic billers have equal access to any services that CMS requires Medicare carriers, DMERCs, FIs, or other contractors if designated by CMS, to make available to providers or their billing services, regardless of the electronic billing technique or service they choose. Equal access will be granted to any services the carrier, DMERC, FI, or other contractor if designated by CMS, sells directly, or indirectly, or by arrangement.
6. Notify the provider within two business days if any transmitted data are received in an unintelligible or garbled form.

NOTICE:
Federal law shall govern both the interpretation of this document and the appropriate jurisdiction and venue for appealing any final decision made by CMS under this document.

This document shall become effective when signed by the provider. The responsibilities and obligations contained in this document will remain in effect as long as Medicare claims are submitted to carrier, DMERC, FI, or other contractor if designated by CMS. Either party may terminate this arrangement by giving the other party thirty (30) days written notice of its intent to terminate. In the event that the notice is mailed, the written notice of termination shall be deemed to have been given upon the date of mailing, as established by the postmark or other appropriate evidence of tansmittal.

C. Signature:
I am authorized to sign this document on behalf of the indicated party and I have read and agree to the foregoing provisions and acknowledge same by signing below.

Provider's Name ______________________________

____

Title ______________________________

Address ______________________________

City/State/Zip ______________________________

By ______________________ ______________________
Signature Printed Name

Title ______________________________

Date ______________________________

CMS-1500

The following information is a step-by-step guide through the CMS-1500 claim form.

The current version of form CMS-1500 (12-90) has been revised to allow reporting of the National Provider Identifier (NPI). The revised form is referred to as the CMS-1500 (08-05). The revised form is being phased in over a four month period. For Medicare claims, the 12-90 or 08-05 versions may be submitted beginning October 1, 2006 until January 31, 2007. Effective February 1, 2007, however, only the 08-05 version will be accepted by Medicare contractors. At this time, it is not known when commercial payers will begin accepting the 08-05 version. Because the deadline for providers to obtain an NPI is May 23, 2007, completion of those sections related to NPI information should be provided if available but will not be required until May 23, 2007.

Among the revisions:

- Appropriate NPI language has been added to items 17 and 17a and additional information must be collected by the provider in order to complete this field.
- New item 17b is introduced and defined allowing for additional information regarding a referring source.
- Item 17a and/or 17b is required when a service was ordered or referred by a physician. Effective May 23, 2007, and later, 17a is not to be reported but 17b MUST be reported when a service was ordered or referred by a physician.
- Information on surrogate UPINs has been removed.
- The six service lines in item 24 have been divided horizontally to accommodate submission of both the NPI and legacy identifier during the NPI transition and to accommodate the submission of supplemental information to support the billed service. The top portion in each of the six service lines is shaded and is the location for reporting supplemental information. It is not intended to allow the billing of 12 service lines. At this time, the shaded area is not used by Medicare. Future guidance will be provided on when and how to use this shaded area for the submission of Medicare claims.
- Item 24d has been revised so that the form has the ability to capture up to four modifiers on the same line. Previously, modifiers had to be split between multiple lines.
- Item 24i of form CMS-1500 (08-05) will require entering the ID qualifier 1C in the shaded portion.
- Introduction of item 24j, a new item that must be completed. CMS has also provided clearer instructions as to what PIN should be identified when services are performed as an incident to service. Prior to May 23, 2007, enter the rendering provider's PIN in the shaded portion. In the case of a service provided incident to the service of a physician or nonphysician practitioner, when the person who ordered the service is not supervising, enter the PIN of the supervisor in the shaded portion. Effective May 23, 2007 and later, do not use the shaded portion. Beginning no earlier than October 1, 2006, enter the rendering provider's NPI number in the lower portion. In the case of a service provided incident to the service of a physician or nonphysician practitioner, when the person who ordered the service is not supervising, enter the NPI of the supervisor in the lower portion.
- There is no item 24k on form CMS-1500 (08-05).
- Appropriate NPI language has been added to items 32 and 33.
- New items are introduced in 32a, 32b, 33a, and 33b. These fields allow for more detailed data collection for HPSA billing, where services where rendered, where the provider of the service is located (if different from where performed such as in the case of home health and durable medical equipment providers)

These guidelines reflect the latest changes at the time of printing. This information is also contained in the *Medicare Claims Processing Manual* (Pub 100-04), chapter 26. For the most current information including any changes since the date of printing of the *2007 Insurance Directory*, the online manual can be reviewed at http://www.cms.hhs.gov/manuals/104_claims/clm104c26.pdf.

Information required for both the 12-90 and 08-05 versions is included. Information specific to the 12-90 version is identified as (12-90) following the item number. Information specific to the revised 08-05 version is identified as (08-05) following the item number and new/changed information is bolded and in italics.

Items 1-13

Patient and Insured Information

Item 1

Show the type of health insurance coverage applicable to this claim by checking the appropriate box, e.g., if a Medicare claim is being filed, check the Medicare box.

Item 1a

Enter the patient's Medicare Health Insurance Claim Number (HICN) whether Medicare is the primary or secondary payer. This is a required field.

Item 2

Enter the patient's last name, first name, and middle initial, if any, as shown on the patient's Medicare card. This is a required field.

Item 3
Enter the patient's 8-digit birth date (MM | DD | CCYY) and sex.

Item 4
If there is insurance primary to Medicare, either through the patient's or spouse's employment or any other source, list the name of the insured here. When the insured and the patient are the same, enter the word SAME. If Medicare is primary, leave blank.

Item 5
Enter the patient's mailing address and telephone number. On the first line enter the street address; the second line, the city and state; the third line, the ZIP code and phone number.

Item 6
Check the appropriate box for patient's relationship to insured when item 4 is completed.

Item 7
Enter the insured's address and telephone number. When the address is the same as the patient's, enter the word SAME. Complete this item only when items 4, 6, and 11 are completed.

Item 8
Check the appropriate box for the patient's marital status and whether employed or a student.

Item 9
Enter the last name, first name, and middle initial of the enrollee in a Medigap policy if it is different from that shown in item 2. Otherwise, enter the word SAME. If no Medigap benefits are assigned, leave blank. This field may be used in the future for supplemental insurance plans.

Note: Only participating physicians and suppliers are to complete item 9 and its subdivisions and only when the beneficiary wishes to assign his/her benefits under a Medigap policy to the participating physician or supplier.

Participating physicians and suppliers must enter information required in item 9 and its subdivisions if requested by the beneficiary. Participating physicians/suppliers sign an agreement with Medicare to accept assignment of Medicare benefits for all Medicare patients. A claim for which a beneficiary elects to assign his/her benefits under a Medigap policy to a participating physician/supplier is called a mandated Medigap transfer.

Medigap. A Medigap policy meets the statutory definition of a "Medicare supplemental policy" contained in §1882(g)(1) of Title XVIII of the Social Security Act (the Act) and the definition contained in the NAIC Model Regulation that is incorporated by reference to the statute. It is a health insurance policy or other health benefit plan offered by a private entity to those persons entitled to Medicare benefits and is specifically designed to supplement Medicare benefits. It fills in some of the "gaps" in Medicare coverage by providing payment for some of the charges for which Medicare does not have responsibility due to the applicability of deductibles, coinsurance amounts, or other limitations imposed by Medicare. It does not include limited benefit coverage available to Medicare beneficiaries such as "specified disease" or "hospital indemnity" coverage. Also, it explicitly excludes a policy or plan offered by an employer to employees or former employees, as well as that offered by a labor organization to members or former members.

Do not list other supplemental coverage in item 9 and its subdivisions at the time a Medicare claim is filed. Other supplemental claims are forwarded automatically to the private insurer if the private insurer contracts with the carrier to send Medicare claim information electronically. If there is no such contract, the beneficiary must file his/her own supplemental claim.

Item 9a
Enter the policy and/or group number of the Medigap insured preceded by **MEDIGAP, MG, or MGAP.**

Note: Item 9d must be completed if the provider enters a policy and/or group number in item 9a.

Item 9b
Enter the Medigap insured's 8-digit birth date (MM | DD | CCYY) and sex.

Item 9c
Leave blank if a Medigap PayerID is entered in item 9d. Otherwise, enter the claims processing address of the Medigap insurer. Use an abbreviated street address, two-letter postal code, and ZIP code copied from the Medigap insured's Medigap identification card. For example:

1257 Anywhere Street
Baltimore, MD 21204

is shown as "1257 Anywhere St MD 21204."

Item 9d
Enter the 9-digit PAYERID number of the Medigap insurer. If no PAYERID number exists, then enter the Medigap insurance program or plan name.

If the beneficiary wants Medicare payment data forwarded to a Medigap insurer under a mandated Medigap transfer, the participating provider of service or supplier must accurately complete all of the information in items 9, 9a, 9b, and 9d. Otherwise, the Medicare carrier cannot forward the claim information to the Medigap insurer.

Items 10a through 10c
Check "YES" or "NO" to indicate whether employment, auto liability, or other accident involvement applies to one or more of the services described in item 24. Enter the State postal code. Any item checked "YES" indicates there may be other insurance primary to Medicare. Identify primary insurance information in item 11.

Item 10d
Use this item exclusively for Medicaid (MCD) information. If the patient is entitled to Medicaid, enter the patient's Medicaid number preceded by MCD.

Item 11
THIS ITEM MUST BE COMPLETED, IT IS A REQUIRED FIELD. BY COMPLETING THIS ITEM, THE PHYSICIAN/SUPPLIER ACKNOWLEDGES HAVING MADE A GOOD FAITH EFFORT TO DETERMINE WHETHER MEDICARE IS THE PRIMARY OR SECONDARY PAYER.

If there is insurance primary to Medicare, enter the insured's policy or group number and proceed to items 11a-11c. Items 4, 6, and 7 must also be completed.

Note: Enter the appropriate information in item 11c if insurance primary to Medicare is indicated in item 11.

If there is no insurance primary to Medicare, enter the word "NONE" and proceed to item 12.

If the insured reports a terminating event with regard to insurance that had been primary to Medicare (e.g., insured retired), enter the word "NONE" and proceed to item 11b.

If a lab has collected previously and retained MSP information for a beneficiary, the lab may use that information for billing purposes of the non-face-to-face lab service. If the lab has no MSP information for the beneficiary, the lab will enter the word "None" in Block 11 of Form CMS-1500, when submitting a claim for payment of a reference lab service. Where there has been no face-to-face encounter with the beneficiary, the claim will then follow the normal claims process. When a lab has a face-to-face encounter with a beneficiary, the lab is expected to collect the MSP information and bill accordingly.

Insurance Primary to Medicare. Circumstances under which Medicare payment may be secondary to other insurance include:

- Group Health Plan Coverage:
  —Working aged
  —Disability (Large Group Health Plan)
  —End Stage Renal Disease
- No Fault and/or Other Liability
- Work-Related Illness/Injury:
  —Workers' compensation
  —Black lung
  —Veterans benefits

Note: For a paper claim to be considered for Medicare secondary payer benefits, a copy of the primary payer's explanation of benefits (EOB) notice must be forwarded along with the claim form. (See Pub. 100-05, *Medicare Secondary Payer Manual*, chapter 3.)

Item 11a
Enter the insured's 8-digit birth date (MM | DD | CCYY) and sex if different from item 3.

Item 11b
Enter employer's name, if applicable. If there is a change in the insured's insurance status, e.g., retired, enter either a 6-digit (MM | DD | YY) or 8-digit (MM | DD | CCYY) retirement date preceded by the word "RETIRED."

Item 11c
Enter the 9-digit PAYERID number of the primary insurer. If no PAYERID number exists, then enter the complete primary payer's program or plan name. If the primary payer's EOB does not contain the claims processing address, record the primary payer's claims processing address directly on the EOB. This is required if there is insurance primary to Medicare that is indicated in item 11.

Item 11d
Leave blank. Not required by Medicare.

Item 12
The patient or authorized representative must sign and enter either a 6-digit date (MM | DD | YY), 8-digit date (MM | DD | CCYY), or an alphanumeric date (e.g., January 1, 1998) unless the signature is on file. In lieu of signing the claim, the patient may sign a statement to be retained in the provider, physician, or supplier file in accordance with chapter 1, "General Billing Requirements." If the patient is physically or mentally unable to sign, a representative specified in chapter 1, "General Billing Requirements" may sign on the patient's behalf. In this event, the statement's signature line must indicate the patient's name followed by "by" and the representative's name, address, relationship to the patient, and the reason the patient cannot sign. The authorization is effective indefinitely unless the patient or the patient's representative revokes this arrangement.

Note: This can be "signature on file" and/or a computer generated signature.

The patient's signature authorizes release of medical information necessary to process the claim. It also authorizes payment of benefits to the provider of service or supplier when the provider of service or supplier accepts assignment on the claim.

Signature by Mark (X). When an illiterate or physically handicapped enrollee signs by mark, a witness must enter his/her name and address next to the mark.

Item 13

The signature in this item authorizes payment of mandated Medigap benefits to the participating physician or supplier if required Medigap information is included in item 9 and its subdivisions. The patient or his/her authorized representative signs this item, or the signature must be on file as a separate Medigap authorization. The Medigap assignment on file in the participating provider of service/supplier's office must be insurer specific. It may state that the authorization applies to all occasions of service until it is revoked.

Note: This can be "signature on file" and/or a computer generated signature.

Items 14-33

Provider of Service or Supplier Information

Reminder: For date fields other than date of birth, all fields shall be one or the other format, 6-digit (MM | DD | YY) or 8-digit (MM | DD | CCYY). Intermixing the two formats on the claim is not allowed.

Item 14

Enter either an 8-digit (MM | DD | CCYY) or 6-digit (MM | DD | YY) date of current illness, injury, or pregnancy. For chiropractic services, enter either an 8-digit (MM | DD | CCYY) or 6-digit (MM | DD | YY) date of the initiation of the course of treatment and enter an 8-digit (MM | DD | CCYY) or 6-digit (MM | DD | YY) date in item 19.

Item 15

Leave blank. Not required by Medicare.

Item 16

If the patient is employed and is unable to work in current occupation, enter an 8-digit (MM | DD | CCYY) or 6-digit (MM | DD | YY) date when patient is unable to work. An entry in this field may indicate employment related insurance coverage.

Item 17

Enter the name of the referring or ordering physician if the service or item was ordered or referred by a physician.

The term "physician" when used within the meaning of §1861(r) of the Act and used in connection with performing any function or action refers to:

1. A doctor of medicine or osteopathy legally authorized to practice medicine and surgery by the State in which he/she performs such function or action;
2. A doctor of dental surgery or dental medicine who is legally authorized to practice dentistry by the State in which he/she performs such functions and who is acting within the scope of his/her license when performing such functions;
3. A doctor of podiatric medicine for purposes of §§(k), (m), (p)(1), and (s) and §§1814(a), 1832(a)(2)(F)(ii), and 1835 of the Act, but only with respect to functions which he/she is legally authorized to perform as such by the State in which he/she performs them;
4. A doctor of optometry, but only with respect to the provision of items or services described in §1861(s) of the Act which he/she is legally authorized to perform as a doctor of optometry by the State in which he/she performs them; or
5. A chiropractor who is licensed as such by a State (or in a State which does not license chiropractors as such), and is legally authorized to perform the services of a chiropractor in the jurisdiction in which he/she performs such services, and who meets uniform minimum standards specified by the Secretary, but only for purposes of §§1861(s)(1) and 1861(s)(2)(A) of the Act, and only with respect to treatment by means of manual manipulation of the spine (to correct a subluxation). For the purposes of §1862(a)(4) of the Act and subject to the limitations and conditions provided above, chiropractor includes a doctor of one of the arts specified in the statute and legally authorized to practice such art in the country in which the inpatient hospital services (referred to in §1862(a)(4) of the Act) are furnished.

Referring physician — a physician who requests an item or service for the beneficiary for which payment may be made under the Medicare program

Ordering physician — a physician or, when appropriate, a nonphysician practitioner who orders nonphysician services for the patient. See Pub 100-02, *Medicare Benefit Policy Manual*, chapter 15 for nonphysician practitioner rules. Examples of services that might be ordered include diagnostic laboratory tests, clinical laboratory tests, pharmaceutical services, durable medical equipment, and services incident to that physician's or nonphysician practitioner's service

The ordering/referring requirement became effective January 1, 1992, and is required by §1833(q) of the Act. All claims for Medicare covered services and items that are the result of a physician's order or referral shall include the ordering/referring physician's name. ***See Items 17a and 17b below for further guidance on reporting the referring/ordering provider's UPIN and/or NPI. The following services/situations require the submission of the referring/ordering provider information:***

- *Medicare covered services and items that are the result of a physician's order or referral;*
- *Parenteral and enteral nutrition;*
- *Immunosuppressive drug claims;*
- *Hepatitis B claims;*
- Diagnostic laboratory services;
- Diagnostic radiology services;
- Portable x-ray services;
- Consultative services;
- Durable medical equipment;
- ***When the ordering physician is also the performing physician (as often is the case with in-office clinical laboratory tests);***
- ***When a service is incident to the service of a physician or nonphysician practitioner, the name of the physician or nonphysician practitioner who performs the initial service and orders the nonphysician service must appear in item 17;***
- ***When a physician extender or other limited licensed practitioner refers a patient for consultative service, submit the name of the physician who is supervising the limited licensed practitioner.***

Item 17a (12-90)

Enter the CMS assigned UPIN (the NPI will be used when implemented) of the referring/ordering physician listed in item 17.

When a claim involves multiple referring and/or ordering physicians, a separate CMS-1500 shall be used for each ordering/referring physician.

Contractors use the following surrogate UPINs for physicians who have not been assigned individual UPINs. Claims received with surrogate numbers will be tracked and possibly audited.

- Residents who are issued a UPIN in conjunction with activities outside of their residency status must use that UPIN. For interns and residents without UPINs, use the 8-character surrogate UPIN RES00000
- Retired physicians who were not issued a UPIN may use the surrogate RET00000
- Physicians serving in the Department of Veterans Affairs or the U.S. Armed Services may use VAD00000
- Physicians serving in the Public Health or Indian Health Services may use PHS00000
- When the ordering/referring physician has not been assigned a UPIN and does not meet the criteria for using one of the surrogate UPINs, the biller may use the surrogate UPIN "OTH00000" until an individual UPIN is assigned
- The UPIN must be entered in item 17a for hepatitis B claims

Note: This field is required when a service was ordered or referred by a physician.

Item 17a (08-05)

Enter the CMS assigned UPIN of the referring/ordering physician listed in item 17. ***The UPIN may be reported on the form CMS-1500 until May 22, 2007, and MUST be reported if an NPI is not available.***

NOTE: Field17a and/or 17b is required when a service was ordered or referred by a physician. Effective May 23, 2007, and later, 17a is not to be reported but 17b MUST be reported when a service was ordered or referred by a physician.

When a claim involves multiple referring and/or ordering physicians, a separate form CMS-1500 shall be used for each ordering/referring physician. ***All physicians who order or refer Medicare beneficiaries or services must report either an NPI or UPIN or both prior to May 23, 2007. After that date, an NPI (but not a UPIN) must be reported even though they may never bill Medicare directly. A physician who has not been assigned a UPIN shall contact the Medicare carrier. Refer to Pub 100-08, chapter 14, section 14.6 for additional information regarding UPINs.***

Item 17b (08-05)

Enter the NPI of the referring/ordering physician listed in item 17 as soon as it is available. The NPI may be reported on the form CMS-1500 (08-05) as early as October 1, 2006.

NOTE: Field17a and/or 17b is required when a service was ordered or referred by a physician. Effective May 23, 2007, and later, 17a is not to be reported but 17b MUST be reported when a service was ordered or referred by a physician.

Item 18

Enter either the 8-digit (MM | DD | CCYY) or 6-digit (MM | DD | YY) date when a medical service is furnished as a result of, or subsequent to, a related hospitalization.

Item 19

Enter either a 6-digit (MM | DD | YY) or an 8-digit (MM | DD | CCYY) date patient was last seen and the UPIN (NPI when it becomes effective) of his/her attending physician when an independent physical or occupational therapist submits claims or a physician providing routine foot care submits claims. For physical or occupational therapists, entering this information certifies that the required physician certification (or recertification) is being kept on file.

Enter either a 6-digit (MM | DD | YY) or an 8-digit (MM | DD | CCYY) x-ray date for chiropractor services (if an x-ray, rather than a physical examination was the the method used to demonstrate the subluxation). By entering an x-ray date, and the initiation date for course of chiropractic treatment in item 14, the chiropractor is certifying that all the relevant information requirements (including level of subluxation) of *Medicare Benefit Policy Manual*, Pub. 100-02, chapter 15, are on file along with the appropriate x-ray and all are available for carrier review.

Enter the drug's name and dosage when submitting a claim for Not Otherwise Classified (NOC) drugs.

Enter a concise description of an "unlisted procedure code" or an NOC code if one can be given within the confines of this box. Otherwise an attachment shall be submitted with the claim.

Enter all applicable modifiers when modifier 99 (multiple modifiers) is entered in item 24d. If modifier 99 is entered on multiple line items of a single claim form, all applicable modifiers for each line item containing modifier 99 should be listed as follows: 1=(mod) where the number 1 represents the line item and "mod" represents all modifiers applicable to the referenced line item.

Enter the statement "Homebound" when an independent laboratory renders an EKG tracing or obtains a specimen from a homebound or institutionalized patient. (See Pub. 100-02, *Medicare Benefit Policy Manual*, chapter 15, "Covered Medical and Other Health Services," and Pub. 100-04 *Medicare Claims Processing Manual*, chapter 16, "Laboratory Services from Independent Labs, Physicians and Providers," and Pub. 100-01 *Medicare General Information, Eligibility, and Entitlement Manual*, chapter 5, "Definitions," respectively, for the definition of "homebound" and a more complete definition of a medically necessary laboratory service to a homebound or an institutional patient.)

Enter the statement, "Patient refuses to assign benefits" when the beneficiary absolutely refuses to assign benefits to a participating provider. In this case, no payment may be made on the claim.

Enter the statement, "Testing for hearing aid" when billing services involving the testing of a hearing aid(s) is used to obtain intentional denials when other payers are involved.

Enter the specific name and dosage amount when low osmolar contrast material is billed, but only if HCPCS codes do not cover them.

Enter either a 6-digit (MM | DD | YY) or an 8-digit (MM | DD | CCYY) assumed and/or relinquished date for a global surgery claim when providers share postoperative care.

Enter demonstration ID number "30" for all national emphysema treatment trial claims.

Enter the PIN (or NPI when effective) of the physician who is performing a purchased interpretation of a diagnostic test. (See Pub. 100-04, chapter 1, section 30.2.9.1, for additional information.)

Method II suppliers shall enter the most current HCT value for the injection of Aranesp for ESRD beneficiaries on dialysis. (See Pub. 100-04, chapter 8, section 60.7.2.)

Item 20

Complete this item when billing for diagnostic tests subject to purchase price limitations. Enter the purchase price under charges if the "yes" block is checked. A "yes" check indicates that an entity other than the entity billing for the service performed the diagnostic test. A "no" check indicates "no purchased tests are included on the claim." When "yes" is annotated, item 32 shall be completed. When billing for multiple purchased diagnostic tests, each test shall be submitted on a separate claim form CMS-1500. Multiple purchased tests may be submitted on the ASC X12 837 electronic format as long as appropriate line level information is submitted when services are rendered at different service facility locations. See chapter 1.

Note: This is a required field when billing for diagnostic tests subject to purchase price limitations.

Item 21

Enter the patient's diagnosis/condition. With the exception of claims submitted by ambulance suppliers (specialty type 59), all physician and nonphysician specialties (i.e., PA, NP, CNS, CRNA) use an ICD-9-CM code number and code to the highest level of specificity for the date of service. Enter up to four codes in priority order (primary, secondary condition). An independent laboratory shall enter a diagnosis only for limited coverage procedures.

All narrative diagnoses for nonphysician specialties shall be submitted on an attachment.

Item 22

Leave blank. Not required by Medicare.

Item 23

Enter the Quality Improvement Organization (QIO) prior authorization number for those procedures requiring QIO prior approval.

Enter the Investigational Device Exemption (IDE) number when an investigational device is used in an FDA-approved clinical trial. Post Market Approval number should also be placed here when applicable.

For physicians performing care plan oversight services, enter the 6-digit Medicare provider number ***(or NPI when effective)*** of the home health agency (HHA) or hospice when HCPCS code G0181 (HH) or G0182 (Hospice) is billed.

Enter the 10-digit Clinical Laboratory Improvement Act (CLIA) certification number for laboratory services billed by an entity performing CLIA covered procedures.

When a physician provides services to a beneficiary residing in a SNF and the services were rendered to a SNF beneficiary outside of the SNF, the physician shall enter the Medicare facility provider number of the SNF in item 23.

Note: Item 23 can contain only one condition. Any additional conditions should be reported on a separate form CMS-1500.

Item 24 (08-05)

The six service lines in section 24 have been divided horizontally to accommodate submission of both the NPI and legacy identifier during the NPI transition and to accommodate the submission of supplemental information to support the billed service. The top portion in each of the six service lines is shaded and is the location for reporting supplemental information. It is not intended to allow the billing of 12 service lines. At this time, the shaded area is not used by Medicare. Future guidance will be provided on when and how to use this shaded area for the submission of Medicare claims.

Item 24a

Enter either a 6-digit (MM | DD | YY) or an 8-digit (MM | DD | CCYY) date for each procedure, service, or supply. When "from" and "to" dates are shown for a series of identical services, enter the number of days or units in column G. This is a required field.

Return as unprocessable if a date of service extends more than one day and a valid "to" date is not present.

Item 24b

Enter the appropriate place of service code(s) from the list provided in section 10.5. Identify the location, using a place of service code, for each item used or service performed. This is a required field.

Note: When a service is rendered to a hospital inpatient, use the "inpatient hospital" code.

Item 24c

Medicare providers are not required to complete this item.

Item 24d

Enter the procedures, services, or supplies using the CMS Healthcare Common Procedure Coding System (HCPCS) code. When applicable, show HCPCS code modifiers with the HCPCS code. ***The form CMS-1500 (08-05) has the ability to capture up to four modifiers.***

Enter the specific procedure code without a narrative description. However, when reporting an "unlisted procedure code" or a "not otherwise classified" (NOC) code, include a narrative description in item 19 if a coherent description can be given within the confines of that box. Otherwise, an attachment shall be submitted with the claim. This is a required field.

Return as unprocessable if an "unlisted procedure code" or an NOC code is indicated in item 24d, but an accompanying narrative is not present in Item 19 or on an attachment.

Item 24e

Enter the diagnosis code reference number as shown in item 21 to relate the date of service and the procedures performed to the primary diagnosis. Enter only one reference number per line item. When multiple services are performed, enter the primary reference number for each service; either a 1, or a 2, or a 3, or a 4. This is a required field.

If a situation arises where two or more diagnoses are required for a procedure code (e.g., pap smears), the provider shall reference only one of the diagnoses in item 21.

Item 24f

Enter the charge for each listed service.

Item 24g

Enter the number of days or units. This field is most commonly used for multiple visits, units of supplies, anesthesia minutes, or oxygen volume. If only one service is performed, the numeral 1 must be entered.

Some services require that the actual number or quantity billed be clearly indicated on the claim form (e.g., multiple ostomy or urinary supplies, medication dosages, or allergy testing procedures). When multiple services are provided, enter the actual number provided.

For anesthesia, show the elapsed time (minutes) in item 24g. Convert hours into minutes and enter the total minutes required for this procedure.

For instructions on submitting units for oxygen claims, see chapter 20, section 130.6 of the *Medicare Claims Processing Manual* (Pub 100-04).

Note: This field should contain at least one day or unit. The carrier should program their system to automatically default "1" unit when the information in this field is missing to avoid returning as unprocessable

Item 24h

Leave blank. Not required by Medicare.

Item 24i (12-90)
Leave blank. Not required by Medicare.

Item 24i (08-05)
Enter the ID qualifier 1C in the shaded portion.

Item 24j (12-90)
Leave blank. Not required by Medicare

Item 24j (08-05)
Prior to May 23, 2007, enter the rendering provider's PIN in the shaded portion. In the case of a service provided incident to the service of a physician or nonphysician practitioner, when the person who ordered the service is not supervising, enter the PIN of the supervisor in the shaded portion.

Effective May 23, 2007 and later, do not use the shaded portion. Beginning no earlier than October 1, 2006, enter the rendering provider's NPI number in the lower portion. In the case of a service provided incident to the service of a physician or nonphysician practitioner, when the person who ordered the service is not supervising, enter the NPI of the supervisor in the lower portion.

Item 24k (12-90)
Enter the PIN (the UPIN will be used when implemented) of the performing provider of service/supplier if the provider is a member of a group practice. When several different providers of service or suppliers within a group are billing on the same form CMS-1500, show the individual PIN (or UPIN when implemented) in the corresponding line item. In the case of a service provided incident to the service of a physician or nonphysician practitioner, when the person who ordered the service is not supervising, enter the PIN (or UPIN when implemented) of the supervisor in item 24k.

Item 24k (08-05)
There is no Item 24k on this version.

Item 25
Enter the provider of service or supplier Federal Tax I.D. (Employer Identification Number) or Social Security Number. The participating provider of service or supplier Federal Tax I.D. number is required for a mandated Medigap transfer.

Item 26
Enter the patient's account number assigned by the provider of service's or supplier's accounting system. This field is optional to assist the provider in patient identification. As a service, any account numbers entered here will be returned to the provider.

Item 27
Check the appropriate block to indicate whether the provider of service or supplier accepts assignment of Medicare benefits. If Medigap is indicated in item 9 and Medigap payment authorization is given in item 13, the provider of service or supplier shall also be a Medicare participating provider of service or supplier and shall accept assignment of Medicare benefits for all covered charges for all patients.

The following providers of service/suppliers and claims can only be paid on an assignment basis:

- Clinical diagnostic laboratory services
- Physician services to individuals dually entitled to Medicare and Medicaid
- Participating physician/supplier services
- Services of physician assistants, nurse practitioners, clinical nurse specialists, nurse midwives, certified registered nurse anesthetists, clinical psychologists, and clinical social workers
- Ambulatory surgical center services for covered ASC procedures
- Home dialysis supplies and equipment paid under Method II
- Ambulance services
- Drugs and biologicals
- Simplified Billing Roster for influenza virus vaccine and pneumococcal vaccine

Item 28
Enter total charges for the services (i.e., total of all charges in item 24f).

Item 29
Enter the total amount the patient paid on the covered services only.

Item 30
Leave blank. Not required by Medicare.

Item 31
Enter the signature of provider of service or supplier, or his/her representative, and either the 6-digit date (MM | DD | YY), 8-digit date (MM | DD | CCYY), or alphanumeric date (e.g., January 1, 1998) the form was signed.

In the case of a service that is provided incident to the service of a physician or nonphysician practitioner, when the ordering physician or nonphysician practitioner is directly supervising the service as in 42 CFR 410.32, the signature of the ordering physician or nonphysician practitioner shall be entered in item

31. When the ordering physician or nonphysician practitioner is not supervising the service, then enter the signature of the physician or nonphysician practitioner providing the direct supervision in item 31.

Note: This is a required field, however the claim can be processed if the following is true. If a physician, supplier, or authorized person's signature is missing, but the signature is on file; or if any authorization is attached to the claim or if the signature field has "Signature on File" and/or a computer generated signature.

Item 32 (12-90)

Enter the name and address, and ZIP code of the facility if the services were furnished in a hospital, clinic, laboratory, or facility other than the patient's home or physician's office. Effective for claims received on or after April 1, 2004, the name, address, and ZIP code of the service location for all services other than those furnished in place of service home—12.

Effective for claims received on or after April 1, 2004, on the form CMS-1500, only one name, address and ZIP code may be entered in the block. If additional entries are needed, separate claim forms shall be submitted.

Providers of service (namely physicians) shall identify the supplier's name, address, ZIP code and PIN when billing for purchased diagnostic tests. When more than one supplier is used, a separate form CMS-1500 should be used to bill for each supplier.

For foreign claims, only the enrollee can file for Part B benefits rendered outside of the United States. These claims will not include a valid ZIP code. When a claim is received for these services on a beneficiary submitted form CMS-1490S, before the claim is entered in the system, it should be determined if it is a foreign claim. If it is a foreign claim, follow instructions in chapter 1 for disposition of the claim. The carrier processing the foreign claim will have to make necessary accommodations to verify that the claim is not returned as unprocessable due to the lack of a ZIP code.

For durable medical, orthotic, and prosthetic claims, the name address, or PIN of the location where the order was accepted must be entered (DMERC only).

This field is required. When more than one supplier is used, a separate form CMS-1500 should be used to bill for each supplier.

This item is completed whether the supplier's personnel performs the work at the physician's office or at another location.

If a modifier is billed, indicating the service was rendered in a Health Professional Shortage Area (HPSA) or Physician Scarcity Area (PSA), the physical location where the service was rendered shall be entered if other than home.

If the supplier is a certified mammography screening center, enter the six-digit FDA approved certification number.

Complete this item for all laboratory work performed outside a physician's office. If an independent laboratory is billing, enter the place where the test was performed, and the PIN.

Item 32 (08-05)

Enter the name, address, and ZIP code of the facility if the services were furnished in a hospital, clinic, laboratory, or facility other than the patient's home or physician's office. Effective for claims received on or after April 1, 2004, the name, address, and ZIP code of the service location for all services other than those furnished in place of service home-- 12. Effective for claims received on or after April 1, 2004, on the form CMS-1500, only one name, address, and ZIP code may be entered in the block. If additional entries are needed, separate claim forms shall be submitted.

Providers of service (namely physicians) shall identify the supplier's name, address, and ZIP code when billing for purchased diagnostic tests. When more than one supplier is used, a separate form CMS-1500 should be used to bill for each supplier.

For foreign claims, only the enrollee can file for Part B benefits rendered outside of the United States. These claims will not include a valid ZIP code. When a claim is received for these services on a beneficiary submitted form CMS-1490S, before the claim is entered in the system, it should be determined if it is a foreign claim. If it is a foreign claim, follow instructions in chapter 1 for disposition of the claim. The carrier processing the foreign claim will have to make necessary accommodations to verify that the claim is not returned as unprocessable due to the lack of a ZIP code.

For durable medical, orthotic, and prosthetic claims, the name and address of the location where the order was accepted must be entered (DMERC only). This field is required. When more than one supplier is used, a separate form CMS-1500 should be used to bill for each supplier. This item is completed whether the supplier's personnel performs the work at the physician's office or at another location.

If a modifier is billed, indicating the service was rendered in a Health Professional Shortage Area (HPSA) or Physician Scarcity Area (PSA), the physical location where the service was rendered shall be entered if other than home.

Complete this item for all laboratory work performed outside a physician's office. If an independent laboratory is billing, enter the place where the test was performed.

Item 32a (08-05)
Enter the NPI of the service facility as soon as it is available. The NPI may be reported on the form CMS-1500 (08-05) as early as October 1, 2006.

Item 32b (08-05)
Enter the ID qualifier 1C followed by one blank space and then the PIN of the service facility. Effective May 23, 2007, and later, 32b is not to be reported.

Providers of service (namely physicians) shall identify the supplier's PIN when billing for purchased diagnostic tests.

If the supplier is a certified mammography screening center, enter the 6-digit FDA approved certification number.

For durable medical, orthotic, and prosthetic claims, enter the PIN (of the location where the order was accepted) if the name and address was not provided in item 32 (DMERC only).

Item 33 (12-90)
Enter the provider of service's/supplier's billing name, address, ZIP code, and telephone number. Enter the PIN, for the performing provider of service/supplier who is not a member of a group practice. This is a required field.

Enter the group PIN (or NPI when implemented), for the performing provider of service/supplier who is a member of a group practice.

Suppliers billing the DMERC will use the National Supplier Clearinghouse (NSC) number in this item.

Enter the group UPIN, including the 2-digit location identifier, for the performing practitioner/supplier who is a member of a group practice.

Item 33 (08-05)
Enter the provider of service/supplier's billing name, address, ZIP code, and telephone number. This is a required field.

Item 33a (08-05)
Effective May 23, 2007, and later, you MUST enter the NPI of the billing provider or group. The NPI may be reported on the form CMS-1500 (08-05) as early as October 1, 2006. This is a required field.

Item 33b (08-05)
Enter the ID qualifier 1C followed by one blank space and then the PIN of the billing provider or group. Effective May 23, 2007, and later, 33b is not to be reported. Suppliers billing the DMERC will use the National Supplier Clearinghouse (NSC) number in this item. Enter the PIN for the performing provider of service/supplier who is not a member of a group practice. Enter the group PIN for the performing provider of service/supplier who is a member of a group practice. Enter the group UPIN, including the 2-digit location identifier, for the performing practitioner/supplier who is a member of a group practice.

Place of Service Codes (POS) and Definitions
The Health Insurance Portability and Accountability Act of 1996 (HIPAA) became effective October 16, 2003, for all covered entities. Medicare is a covered entity under HIPAA.

The final rule, "Health Insurance Reform: Standards for Electronic Transactions," published in the *Federal Register*, August 17, 2000, adopts the standards to be used under HIPAA and names the implementation guides to be used for these standards. The ASC X12N 837 professional is the standard to be used for transmitting health care claims electronically, and its implementation guide requires the use of POS codes from the National POS code set, currently maintained by CMS.

As a covered entity, Medicare must use the POS codes from the National POS code set for processing its electronically submitted claims. Medicare must also recognize as valid POS codes from the POS code set when these codes appear on such a claim.

Medicare must recognize and accept POS codes from the National POS code set in terms of HIPAA compliance. Note special considerations for Homeless Shelter (code 04) as well as Indian Health Service (codes 05, 06) and Tribal 638 (codes 07, 08) settings, described below. Where there is no National policy for a given POS code, carriers may work with their carrier medical directors to develop local policy regarding the services payable in a given setting, and this could include creating a crosswalk to an existing setting if desired. However, carriers must pay for the services at either the facility or the nonfacility rate as designated below. In addition, carriers, when developing policy must ensure that they continue to pay appropriate rates for services rendered in the new setting; if they choose to create a crosswalk from one setting to another, they must crosswalk a facility rate designated code to another facility rate designated code, and a nonfacility rate designated code to another nonfacility rate designated code. For previously issued POS codes for which a crosswalk was mandated, and for which no other National Medicare directive has been issued, carriers may elect to continue to use the crosswalk or develop local policy regarding the services payable in the setting, including another crosswalk, if appropriate. If a carrier develops local policy for these settings, but later receives specific National instructions for these codes, the carriers shall defer to and comply with the newer instructions. (*Note:* While, effective January 1, 2003, codes 03 School, 04 Homeless Shelter, and 20 Urgent Care became part of the National POS code set and were to be crosswalked to 11 Office, this mandate to crosswalk has since been lifted as indicated above).

The National POS Code Set and Instructions for Using It

The following is the current National POS code set, with facility and non-facility designations noted for Medicare payment for services on the Physician Fee Schedule, as of October 1, 2005. This code set has changed to include a new code for a pharmacy setting, effective October 1, 2005. Note that codes 03, 04, 05, 06, 07, 08, 15, and 20 became part of the National POS code set effective January 1, 2003, and codes 13, 14, 49, and 57 became part of the National code set effective October 1, 2003. In addition, the description of code 14 (group home) was revised effective April 1, 2004.

Place of Service Code(s)	Place of Service Name	Place of Service Description	Facility (F)/Non Facility (NF) Designation
01	Pharmacy	A facility or location where drugs and other medically related items and services are sold, dispensed, or otherwise provided directly to patients.	NF
02	Unassigned	N/A	
03	School	A facility whose primary purpose is education.	NF
04	Homeless Shelter	A facility or location whose primary purpose is to provide temporary housing to homeless individuals (e.g., emergency shelters, individual or family shelters).	NF
05	Indian Health Service Free-standing Facility	A facility or location, owned and operated by the Indian Health Service, which provides diagnostic, therapeutic (surgical and non-surgical), and rehabilitation services to American Indians and Alaska Natives who do not require hospitalization.	Not applicable for adjudication of Medicare claims; systems must recognize for HIPAA
06	Indian Health Service Provider-based Facility	A facility or location, owned and operated by the Indian Health Service, which provides diagnostic, therapeutic (surgical and non-surgical), and rehabilitation services rendered by, or under the supervision of, physicians to American Indians and Alaska Natives admitted as inpatients or outpatients.	Not applicable for adjudication of Medicare claims; systems must recognize for HIPAA
07	Tribal 638 Free-standing Facility	A facility or location owned and operated by a federally recognized American Indian or Alaska Native tribe or tribal organization under a 638 agreement, which provides diagnostic, therapeutic (surgical and nonsurgical), and rehabilitation services to tribal members who do not require hospitalization.	Not applicable for adjudication of Medicare claims; systems must recognize for HIPAA
08	Tribal 638 Provider-based Facility	A facility or location owned and operated by a federally recognized American Indian or Alaska Native tribe or tribal organization under a 638 agreement, which provides diagnostic, therapeutic (surgical and non-surgical), and rehabilitation services to tribal members admitted as inpatients or outpatients.	Not applicable for adjudication of Medicare claims; systems must recognize for HIPAA
09-10	Unassigned	N/A	

Place of Service Code(s)	Place of Service Name	Place of Service Description	Facility (F)/Non Facility (NF) Designation
11	Office	Location, other than a hospital, skilled nursing facility (SNF), military treatment facility, community health center, State or local public health clinic, or intermediate care facility (ICF), where the health professional routinely provides health examinations, diagnosis, and treatment of illness or injury on an ambulatory basis.	NF
12	Home	Location, other than a hospital or other facility, where the patient receives care in a private residence.	NF
13	Assisted Living Facility	Congregate residential facility with self-contained living units providing assessment of each resident's needs and on-site support 24 hours a day, 7 days a week, with the capacity to deliver or arrange for services including some health care and other services.	NF
14	Group Home	A residence, with shared living areas, where clients receive supervision and other services such as social and/or behavioral services, custodial service, and minimal services (e.g., medication administration).	NF
15	Mobile Unit	A facility/unit that moves from place-to-place equipped to provide preventive, screening, diagnostic, and/or treatment services.	NF
16-19	Unassigned	N/A	
20	Urgent Care Facility	Location, distinct from a hospital emergency room, an office, or a clinic, whose purpose is to diagnose and treat illness or injury for unscheduled, ambulatory patients seeking immediate medical attention.	NF
21	Inpatient Hospital	A facility, other than psychiatric, which primarily provides diagnostic, therapeutic (both surgical and nonsurgical), and rehabilitation services by, or under, the supervision of physicians to patients admitted for a variety of medical conditions.	F
22	Outpatient Hospital	A portion of a hospital which provides diagnostic, therapeutic (both surgical and nonsurgical), and rehabilitation services to sick or injured persons who do not require hospitalization or institutionalization.	F
23	Emergency Room - Hospital	A portion of a hospital where emergency diagnosis and treatment of illness or injury is provided.	F
24	Ambulatory Surgical Center	A freestanding facility, other than a physician's office, where surgical and diagnostic services are provided on an ambulatory basis.	F (Note: pay at the nonfacility rate for payable procedures not on the ASC list)

Place of Service Code(s)	Place of Service Name	Place of Service Description	Facility (F)/Non Facility (NF) Designation
25	Birthing Center	A facility, other than a hospital's maternity facilities or a physician's office, which provides a setting for labor, delivery, and immediate post-partum care as well as immediate care of newborn infants.	NF
26	Military Treatment Facility	A medical facility operated by one or more of the Uniformed Services. Military Treatment Facility (MTF) also refers to certain former U.S. Public Health Service (USPHS) facilities now designated as Uniformed Service Treatment Facilities (USTF).	F
27-30	Unassigned	N/A	
31	Skilled Nursing Facility	A facility which primarily provides inpatient skilled nursing care and related services to patients who require medical, nursing, or rehabilitative services but does not provide the level of care or treatment available in a hospital.	F
32	Nursing Facility	A facility which primarily provides to residents skilled nursing care and related services for the rehabilitation of injured, disabled, or sick persons, or, on a regular basis, health-related care services above the level of custodial care to other than mentally retarded individuals.	NF
33	Custodial Care Facility	A facility which provides room, board and other personal assistance services, generally on a long-term basis, and which does not include a medical component.	NF
34	Hospice	A facility, other than a patient's home, in which palliative and supportive care for terminally ill patients and their families are provided.	F
35-40	Unassigned	N/A	
41	Ambulance - Land	A land vehicle specifically designed, equipped and staffed for lifesaving and transporting the sick or injured.	F
42	Ambulance - Air or Water	An air or water vehicle specifically designed, equipped and staffed for lifesaving and transporting the sick or injured.	F
43-48	Unassigned	N/A	
49	Independent Clinic	A location, not part of a hospital and not described by any other Place of Service code, that is organized and operated to provide preventive, diagnostic, therapeutic, rehabilitative, or palliative services to outpatients only.	NF
50	Federally Qualified Health Center	A facility located in a medically underserved area that provides Medicare beneficiaries preventive primary medical care under the general direction of a physician.	NF

Place of Service Code(s)	Place of Service Name	Place of Service Description	Facility (F)/Non Facility (NF) Designation
51	Inpatient Psychiatric Facility	A facility that provides inpatient psychiatric services for the diagnosis and treatment of mental illness on a 24-hour basis, by or under the supervision of a physician.	F
52	Psychiatric Facility-Partial Hospitalization	A facility for the diagnosis and treatment of mental illness that provides a planned therapeutic program for patients who do not require full time hospitalization, but who need broader programs than are possible from outpatient visits to a hospital-based or hospital-affiliated facility.	F
53	Community Mental Health Center	A facility that provides the following services: outpatient services, including specialized outpatient services for children, the elderly, individuals who are chronically ill, and residents of the CMHC's mental health services area who have been discharged from inpatient treatment at a mental health facility; 24 hour a day emergency care services; day treatment, other partial hospitalization services, or psychosocial rehabilitation services; screening for patients being considered for admission to State mental health facilities to determine the appropriateness of such admission; and consultation and education services.	F
54	Intermediate Care Facility/Mentally Retarded	A facility which primarily provides health-related care and services above the level of custodial care to mentally retarded individuals but does not provide the level of care or treatment available in a hospital or SNF.	NF
55	Residential Substance Abuse Treatment Facility	A facility which provides treatment for substance (alcohol and drug) abuse to live-in residents who do not require acute medical care. Services include individual and group therapy and counseling, family counseling, laboratory tests, drugs and supplies, psychological testing, and room and board.	NF
56	Psychiatric Residential Treatment Center	A facility or distinct part of a facility for psychiatric care which provides a total 24-hour therapeutically planned and professionally staffed group living and learning environment.	F
57	Non-residential Substance Abuse Treatment Facility	A location which provides treatment for substance (alcohol and drug) abuse on an ambulatory basis. Services include individual and group therapy and counseling, family counseling, laboratory tests, drugs and supplies, and psychological testing.	NF
58-59	Unassigned	N/A	

Place of Service Code(s)	Place of Service Name	Place of Service Description	Facility (F)/Non Facility (NF) Designation
60	Mass Immunization Center	A location where providers administer pneumococcal pneumonia and influenza virus vaccinations and submit these services as electronic media claims, paper claims, or using the roster billing method. This generally takes place in a mass immunization setting, such as, a public health center, pharmacy, or mall but may include a physician office setting.	NF
61	Comprehensive Inpatient Rehabilitation Facility	A facility that provides comprehensive rehabilitation services under the supervision of a physician to inpatients with physical disabilities. Services include physical therapy, occupational therapy, speech pathology, social or psychological services, and orthotics and prosthetics services.	F
62	Comprehensive Outpatient Rehabilitation Facility	A facility that provides comprehensive rehabilitation services under the supervision of a physician to outpatients with physical disabilities. Services include physical therapy, occupational therapy, and speech pathology services.	NF
63-64	Unassigned	N/A	
65	End-Stage Renal Disease Treatment Facility	A facility other than a hospital, which provides dialysis treatment, maintenance, and/or training to patients or caregivers on an ambulatory or home-care basis.	NF
66-70	Unassigned	N/A	NF
71	State or Local Public Health Clinic	A facility maintained by either State or local health departments that provides ambulatory primary medical care under the general direction of a physician.	NF
72	Rural Health Clinic	A certified facility which is located in a rural medically underserved area that provides ambulatory primary medical care under the general direction of a physician.	NF
73-80	Unassigned	N/A	
81	Independent Laboratory	A laboratory certified to perform diagnostic and/or clinical tests independent of an institution or a physician's office.	NF
82-98	Unassigned	N/A	
99	Other Place of Service	Other place of service not identified above.	NF

Special Considerations for Homeless Shelter (Code 04)
Note that for the purposes of receiving durable medical equipment (DME), a homeless shelter is considered the beneficiary's home. Because DME is payable in the beneficiary's home, the crosswalk for Homeless Shelter (code 04) to Office (code 11) that was mandated effective January 1, 2003, may need to be adjusted or local policy developed so that HCPCS codes for DME are covered when other conditions are met and the beneficiary is in a homeless shelter. If desired, carriers are permitted to work with their carrier medical directors to determine a new crosswalk such as from Homeless Shelter (code 04) to Home (code 12) or Custodial Care Facility (code 33) for DME provided in a homeless shelter setting. If a carrier is currently paying claims correctly, however, it is not necessary to change the current crosswalk.

Special Considerations for Indian Health Service (Codes 05, 06) and Tribal 638 Settings (Codes 07, 08)
Medicare does not currently use the POS codes designated for these settings. Follow the instructions you have received regarding how to process claims for services rendered in IHS and Tribal 638 settings. If you receive claims with these codes, you must initially accept them in terms of HIPAA compliance. However, follow your "return as unprocessable" procedures after this initial compliance check. Follow your "return as unprocessable" procedures when you receive paper claims with these codes. (Note that while these codes became part of the National POS code set effective January 1, 2003, Medicare contractors received instructions regarding how to process claims with these codes effective October 1, 2003, so that Medicare could be HIPAA compliant by October 16, 2003).

Special Considerations for Mobile Unit Settings (Code 15)
When services are furnished in a mobile unit, they are often provided to serve an entity for which another POS code exists. For example, a mobile unit may be sent to a physician's office or a skilled nursing facility. If the mobile unit is serving an entity for which another POS code already exists, providers should use the POS code for that entity. However, if the mobile unit is not serving an entity that could be described by an existing POS code, the providers are to use the Mobile Unit POS code 15. Apply the nonfacility rate to payments for services designated as being furnished in POS code 15; apply the appropriate facility or nonfacility rate for the POS code designated when a code other than the mobile unit code is indicated.

Paper Claims
Adjudicate paper claims with codes from the National POS code set as you would for electronic claims. (Prior to HIPAA implementation, Medicare contractors were instructed to also apply these requirements to nonstandard formats, effective January 1, 2003. However, it is not the purpose of instructions for this code set to determine how nonstandard formats are to be handled in a HIPAA environment, and this information should be expected from other instructions.)

Carrier Instructions for Place of Service Codes
If the physician bills for lab services performed in his/her office, the code for "Office" is shown. If the physician bills for a lab test furnished by another physician who maintains a lab in his/her office, the code for "Other" is shown. If the physician bills for a lab service furnished by an independent lab, the code for "Independent Laboratory" is used. Items 21 and 22 on the CMS-1500 must be completed for all laboratory work performed outside a physician's office. If an independent lab bills, the place where the sample was taken is shown. An independent laboratory taking a sample in its laboratory shows "IL" as place of service. If an independent laboratory bills for a test on a sample drawn on a hospital inpatient, it uses the code for "Hospital Inpatient."

For hospital visits by physicians, presume, in the absence of evidence to the contrary, that visits billed for were made. However, review a sample of physician's records when there are questionable patterns of utilization. Confirm these visits where the medical facts do not support the frequency of the physician's visits or in cases of beneficiary complaints.

If questioning whether the visit had been made, ascertain whether the physician's own entry is in the patient's record at the provider's office. Accept an entry where the nurses' notes indicate that the physician saw the patient on a given day. A statement by the beneficiary is also acceptable documentation if it was made close to the alleged date of the visit. Entries in the physician's records represent possible secondary evidence. However, these are of less value since they are self-serving statements. Exercise judgment regarding their authenticity. The policy requiring daily physician visits is not conclusive if, in the individual case, the facts did not support a finding that daily visits were made. If the place of service is not specified, then edit and review claims for missing place of service information.

If a claim lacks a valid POS code in 24b or contains an invalid POS in item 24b, return the claim as unprocessable to the provider or supplier using RA remark code M77. Effective for claims received on or after April 1, 2004, on the CMS-1500 form, if a claim contains more than one POS (other than Home—12), for services paid under the MPFS and anesthesia services.

If the place of service is not indicated and the carrier cannot infer the place of service from the procedure code billed (e.g., a procedure code for which the definition is not site specific or that can be performed in more than one setting), then return assigned services as unprocessable and develop for the place of service on nonassigned claims.

If the place of service is inconsistent with the procedure code billed, then edit for consistency or compatibility between the place of service and site-specific procedure codes.

If the place of service is valid but inconsistent or incompatible with the procedure billed (e.g., the place of service is inpatient hospital and the procedure code billed is office visit), then return assigned services as unprocessable and develop nonassigned services since the carrier typically will not know whether the procedure code or the place of service is incorrect in such instances.

If the place of service is invalid, edit for the validity of the place of service coding.

If the place of service code is not valid (e.g., the number designation has not been assigned or defined by CMS), return assigned services as unprocessable and develop for a valid place of service on nonassigned line items.

Claims Processing

Type of Service (TOS)

For submitting a claim to the Common Working File (CWF), use the following table to assign the proper TOS. The only exceptions are:

- Surgical services billed with the ASC facility service modifier SG must be reported as TOS F. The indicator F does not appear on the TOS table because its use is dependent upon the use of the SG modifier.
- Surgical services billed with an assistant-at-surgery modifier (80–82, AS) must be reported with TOS 8. The 8 indicator does not appear on the TOS table because its use is dependent upon the use of the appropriate modifier. (See Pub 100-4, *Medicare Claims Processing Manual*, chapter 12, "Physician/Practitioner Billing," for instructions on when assistant-at-surgery is allowable.)
- Psychiatric treatment services that are subject to the outpatient mental health treatment limitation should be reported with TOS T.
- TOS H appears in the list of descriptors. However, it does not appear in the table. In CWF, "H" is used only as an indicator for hospice. You should not submit TOS H to CWF at this time.
- When these specific transfusion medicine codes appear on the claim (86880, 86885, 86886, 86900, 86903, 86904, 86905, and 86906 that also contains a blood product (P9010-P9022)), they are paid under reasonable charge. When these services are to be paid under reasonable charge, use TOS 1. When paid under reasonable charge, tests are paid at 80 percent. Coinsurance and deductible also apply.

Note: For injection codes with more than one possible TOS designation, use the following guidelines when assigning the TOS:

When the choice is L or 1:

- Use TOS L when the drug is used related to ESRD
- Use TOS 1 when the drug is not related to ESRD and is administered in the office

When the choice is G or 1:

- Use TOS G when the drug is an immunosuppressive drug
- Use TOS 1 when the drug is used for other than immunosuppression

When the choice is P or 1:

- Use TOS P if the drug is administered through durable medical equipment (DME)
- Use TOS 1 if the drug is administered in the office

You may consider the place of service or diagnosis when determining the appropriate TOS. The descriptors for each of the TOS codes are:

Type of Service Indicators

0 Whole Blood
1 Medical Care
2 Surgery
3 Consultation
4 Diagnostic Radiology
5 Diagnostic Laboratory
6 Therapeutic Radiology
7 Anesthesia
8 Assistant at Surgery
9 Other Medical Items or Services
A Used DME
B High Risk Screening Mammography
C Low Risk Screening Mammography
D Ambulance
E Enteral/Parenteral Nutrients/Supplies
F Ambulatory Surgical Center (Facility Usage for Surgical Services)
G Immunosuppressive Drugs
H Hospice
J Diabetic Shoes
K Hearing Items and Services
L ESRD Supplies
M Monthly Capitation Payment for Dialysis
N Kidney Donor
P Lump Sum Purchase of DME, Prosthetics, Orthotics
Q Vision Items or Services
R Rental of DME
S Surgical Dressings or Other Medical Supplies
T Outpatient Mental Health Treatment Limitation
U Occupational Therapy
V Pneumococcal/Flu Vaccine
W Physical Therapy

For more information on CMS-1500 claim forms as well as information on where to purchase forms, please go to http://www.cms.hhs.gov/ElectronicBillingEDITrans/16_1500.asp#TopofPage. You can also find basic form completion instructions and print specifications for the CMS-1500 form in chapter 26 of the *Medicare Claims Processing Manual* (Pub.100-04).

Clean Claims

Claims submitted with all of the information necessary for processing are referred to as "clean" and are usually paid in a timely manner. Paying careful attention to what should appear on your claim form helps produce these clean claims. Now we'll discuss some of the common reasons that claims are denied. Being aware of common mistakes helps you avoid them. It's extremely important to read the communications you receive from insurers. Their information will often put you on the right track to correct your errors through resubmission.

Common Errors

- The patient's ID number is incorrect
- The patient's name and address does not match the insurer's records
- The physician's tax ID number, provider number, or Social Security number is missing
- There is little or no information regarding primary or secondary coverage
- The physician's or authorized person's signature is missing
- Dates of service are incorrect or do not relate to the claims information from other providers (hospital, nursing homes, etc.)
- Dates are not six or eight digits as required
- The fee column is blank or not itemized and totaled
- The patient information is incomplete
- The CPT, HCPCS Level II, and ICD-9-CM codes are invalid, or the diagnostic codes are not linked to the correct services, procedures, or supplies
- The claim is illegible

Standardized Claims Processing

The Administrative Simplification Provisions of the Health Insurance Portability and Accountability Act (HIPAA) (Title II) require the Department of Health and Human Services (DHHS) to establish national standards for electronic health care transactions and national identifiers for providers, health plans, and employers. It also addresses the security and privacy of health data. Implementation of these standards and encouraging the use of electronic data interchange (EDI) in health care will improve the efficiency of the nation's health care system, reduce the administrative burden on providers and health care plans, and save more than $30 billion over the next decade.

Under HIPAA, every health care provider will be able to use EDI standards for billing and other health care transactions, such as referrals and diagnosis reports. All health plans will be required to accept these standard electronic claims and all health care providers using electronic transmittals will be required to use the EDI standards. Providers that submit information by paper will not be affected by the rules. However, the health plans they bill are not prohibited from independently requiring the EDI standards for paper transactions as well.

Guidelines specify that transactions involving the following types of information exchanges between health care plans, clearinghouses, and providers are subject to EDI standards:

- Health care claims and equivalent encounter information
- Health care payment and remittance advice
- Coordination of benefits
- Health care claim status
- Enrollment or disenrollment in a health plan
- Eligibility for a health plan
- Referral certification and authorization
- Health insurance plan premiums

Since October 16, 2003, the majority of health plans, providers, and other entities have been required by law to be in compliance with the HIPAA electronic transactions standards. The only exceptions being certain types of claims, such as those related to demonstration projects and roster billing of Medicare covered vaccinations, and providers with no capability for electronic claim submission and those with less than 25 full-time employees (facilities) and 10 full-time employees (physician practices). This legislation further stipulated that, electronic claims were no longer to be processed if they were in a format other than the HIPAA format. However, in October 2003 Medicare implemented a contingency plan permitting some providers that bill electronically to continue sending pre-HIPAA format electronic claims. This contingency plan stipulated that after July 1, 2004, electronic claims submitted in a pre-HIPAA format would not be eligible for payment after 13-days, but would be treated like paper claims and subject to the 27-day waiting period before being processed. CMS wants this contingency plan to end soon and is keeping a close watch on HIPAA compliance In August of 2005, CMS instructed contractors to begin setting the groundwork for preventing submission of legacy and pre-HIPAA claim formats. Contractors are expected to be able to enforce HIPAA electronic transaction standards within 30 days of being notified by CMS.

Standards and Code Sets

CMS has adopted the following standard medical data code sets:

- National Drug Codes (NDC): required for reporting drugs and biologicals. (In the *Federal Register* on May 31, 2002 a rule was proposed that would retract the adoption of NDC codes for reporting drugs and biologicals with the exception of retail pharmacy transactions that already use them)

- CDT-5: Current Dental Terminology (CDT): required for reporting dental services
- American Medical Association's CPT: required for reporting physician and other health care services
- Alphanumeric HCPCS Level II: required for reporting not only physician and other health care services, but also for supplies, equipment, substances, and other items used for health care services
- ICD-9-CM Volumes 1 and 2: required for reporting the following conditions: diseases, injuries, impairments, other health problems and their manifestations, and causes
- ICD-9-CM Volume 3: required for reporting diagnostic, preventive, therapeutic, or management procedures or actions provided by hospitals

CMS notes that the CDT-5 and CPT code sets are proprietary and that there are royalties for electronic use of them.

National Privacy Standards

With publication of a final rule in December 2000, HHS established regulations that protect the privacy of an individual's health information. The regulations are applicable to all medical records and health information that can be individually identified—that is, transmitted in any form. The regulations also grant individuals the right to control the disclosure of their health information and how it is used. Any improper use or disclosure of this information is subject to criminal and civil sanctions including civil monetary penalties, fines, and prison. All covered entities were required to be in compliance with the privacy standards as of April 14, 2004.

In general, the HIPAA regulations for the privacy of personal health information (PHI) require that an individual has the right to be notified as to the uses and disclosures of PHI that may be made by the covered entity. Legislation requires that a written notice of privacy practices be provided to patients. The notice must also explain the individual's rights and the covered entity's legal duties with respect to PHI. Covered entities should make every effort to obtain the patient's written acknowledgement that he/she received or received a copy of the privacy notice.

Security Standards

HHS proposed security standards for the protection of electronic health information systems on August 12, 1998. The final HIPAA security rules were released to the health care industry on February 20, 2003, but due to the 60-day period mandated by the Congressional Review Act and the 24 months mandated by the HIPAA statute, the security rules did not become effective until April 2005. Small health plans had until April 2006 to comply.

Understanding section 164.306 of the new security rules is crucial. This section is the heart of the new security rules and tracks the part of the HIPAA statute that governs security standards and safeguards. Covered entities must meet the four following security requirements specified in section 164.306(a):

- Ensure the confidentiality, integrity, and availability of all electronic PHI the covered entity creates, receives, maintains or transmits
- Protect against any reasonably anticipated threats or hazards to the security or integrity of such information
- Protect against any reasonably anticipated uses or disclosures of such information that are not permitted or required under the security rules
- Ensure compliance by its workforce

Standard Unique Employer Identifier

HIPAA also required the establishment of a national standard for employer identification to be used by covered health care providers, health plans, and clearinghouses for electronic health transactions. The final rule was published May 31, 2002, and as expected the standard selected was the employer identification number (EIN), already in use and assigned by the Internal Revenue Service (IRS). Compliance with this standard was required by July 30, 2004, for the majority of covered entities, with small health plans being required to comply no later than August 1, 2005.

National Provider Identifier

A final rule that established the national provider identifier (NPI) as the standard unique health identifier was published in the *Federal Register* on January 23, 2004. The NPI is an operational provider identification number that will replace the current unique physician identification numbers (UPIN) and local contractor provider identifications numbers (PIN). The NPI establishes a unique identifier for each provider to use on all bills, claim forms, and correspondence. CMS intends to use the NPI for all Medicare services. Additionally, TRICARE, the Department of Labor, the Department of Veterans Affairs, the Social Security Administration, and many state agencies have participated in the development of the NPI program with the intention of ultimately using the system. All providers will receive a 10-position NPI prior to implementation of this initiative.

The effective date of this final rule was May 23, 2005. All covered entities (except small health plans) are required to use NPIs for standard transactions no later than May 23, 2007. Small health plans have until May 23, 2008 to comply. Health care providers could begin applying for NPIs after the May 23, 2005, effective date of the final rule.

Additional Requirements for Health Plans

Health plans must permit the use of EDI standard transactions when requested to do so. They may not delay or reject a transaction because it is an EDI standard transaction. They may not reject a standard transaction on the basis that it contains data elements not needed or used by the health plan. They may not offer incentives to steer providers toward direct data entry transactions.

A health plan that operates a health care clearinghouse or requires a provider to use a health care clearinghouse to receive, process, or transmit a standard transaction may not charge fees or costs in excess of the fees or costs for normal telecommunications that the provider incurs when it directly transmits or receives a standard transaction to or from a health plan.

PREAUTHORIZATION

A preauthorization should supply and organize the information regarding a procedure's insurance coverage. Determining in advance the benefits and allowable provides you with reimbursement figures in advance. Under most circumstances you'll be able to discuss the deductible, copayment, and balance over and above the allowable with the patient prior to providing costly surgical services. Asking a few pointed questions of the patient and insurer will provide you with additional information regarding allowable, for example:

- How much is the deductible and has it been met for the current year?
- What is the allowable for the quoted procedure?
- What percent of the allowable will be paid?

Be prepared to answer questions regarding any proposed procedures and the diagnosis for each. In other words, have your CPT, HCPCS Level II, and ICD-9-CM codes ready.

Involve your patient when an insurer refuses to provide the information. Most patients don't like surprises in the form of a large unpaid balance after the insurance company has determined its benefits. Submitting your claim is the next (though not final) step toward receiving payment. Verify the insurance company's name and address before mailing the claim and you may save the time and aggravation of having it returned.

Claims Processing

CMS–1500 (12-90)

PLEASE DO NOT STAPLE IN THIS AREA

BAR CODE AREA

(APPROVED OMB-0938-0008)

HEALTH INSURANCE CLAIM FORM

PICA PICA

Carrier

MEDICARE (Medicare No.) MEDICAID (Medicaid No.) CHAMPUS (Sponser's SSN) CHAMPVA (VA File No.) GROUP HEALTH PLAN (SSN or ID) FECA BLK LUNG (SSN) OTHER (ID)

1a. INSURED'S I.D. NUMBER (FOR PROGRAM IN ITEM 1)

2. PATIENT'S NAME (Last Name , First Name, Middle Initial)

3. PATIENT'S BIRTH DATE MM DD YY SEX M F

4. INSURED'S NAME (Last Name, First Name, Middle Initial)

5. PATIENT'S ADDRESS (No., Street)

6. PATIENT RELATIONSHIP TO INSURED Self Spouse Child Other

7. INSURED'S ADDRESS (No. Street)

CITY STATE

8. PATIENT STATUS Single Married Other Employed Full-time Student Part-time Student

CITY STATE

ZIP CODE TELEPHONE (Include Area Code) ( )

ZIP CODE TELEPHONE (Include Area Code) ( )

9. OTHER INSURED'S NAME (Last Name, First Name, Middle Intial)

10. IS PATIENT'S CONDITION RELATED TO:

11. INSURED'S POLICY, GROUP OR FECA NUMBER

a. OTHER INSURED'S POLICY OR GROUP NUMBER

a. EMPLOYMENT? (CURRENT OR PREVIOUS) YES NO

a. INSURED'S DATE OF BIRTH MM DD YY SEX M F

b. OTHER INSURED'S DATE OF BIRTH MM DD YY SEX M F

b. AUTO ACCIDENT? PLACE (State) YES NO

b. EMPLOYER'S NAME OR SCHOOL NAME

c. EMPLOYER'S NAME OR SCHOOL NAME

c. OTHER ACCIDENT? YES NO

c. INSURANCE PLAN NAME OR PROGRAM NAME

d. INSURANCE PLAN NAME OR PROGRAM NAME

10d. RESERVED FOR LOCAL USE

d. IS THERE ANOTHER HEALTH BENEFIT PLAN? YES NO If yes, return to and complete item 9 a-d

READ BACK OF FORM BEFORE COMPLETING & SIGNING THIS FORM

12. PATIENT'S OR AUTHORIZED PERSON'S SIGNATURE I authorize the release of any medical information necessary to process this claim. I also request payment of government benefits either to myself or to the party who accepts assignment below.

SIGNED ____ DATE ____

13. INSURED'S OR AUTHORIZED PERSON'S SIGNATURE I authorize payment of medical benefits to undersigned physician or supplier for services described below.

SIGNED ____

Patient and Insured Information

14. DATE OF CURRENT MM DD YY — ILLNESS (First symptom) OR INJURY (Accident) OR PREGNANCY (LMP)

15. IF PATIENT HAS HAD SAME OR SIMILAR ILLNESS GIVE FIRST DATE MM DD YY

16. DATES PATIENT UNABLE TO WORK IN CURRENT OCCUPATION FROM MM DD YY TO MM DD YY

17. NAME OF REFERRING PHYSICIAN OR OTHER SOURCE

17a. I.D. NUMBER OF REFERRING PHYSICIAN

18. HOSPITALIZATION DATES RELATED TO CURRENT SERVICES FROM MM DD YY TO MM DD YY

19. RESERVED FOR LOCAL USE

20. OUTSIDE LAB ? YES NO $ CHARGES

21. DIAGNOSIS OR NATURE OF ILLNESS OR INJURY (RELATE ITEMS 1, 2, 3 OR 4 TO ITEM 24E BY LINE)

1 ___ . ___ 3 ___ . ___

2 ___ . ___ 4 ___ . ___

22. MEDICAID RESUBMISSION CODE ORIGINAL REF. NO.

23. PRIOR AUTHORIZATION NUMBER

24. A DATE(S) OF SERVICE From MM DD YY To MM DD YY	B Place of Service	C Type of Service	D PROCEDURES, SERVICES, OR SUPPLIES (Explain Unusual Circumstances) CPT/HCPCS MODIFIER	E DIAGNOSIS CODE	F $ CHARGES	G DAYS OR UNITS	H EPSDT Family Planning	I	J	K RESERVED FOR LOCAL USE

25. FEDERAL TAX I.D. NUMBER SSN EIN

26. PATIENT'S ACCOUNT NO.

27. ACCEPT ASSIGNMENT? (For govt. claims, see back) YES NO

28. TOTAL CHARGE $

29. AMOUNT PAID $

30. BALANCE DUE $

31. SIGNATURE OF PHYSICIAN OR SUPPLIER INCLUDING DEGREES OR CREDENTIALS *(I certify that the statements on the reverse apply to this bill and are made a part thereof.)*

SIGNED ____ DATE ____

32. NAME AND ADDRESS OF FACILITY WHERE SERVICES RENDERED (If other than home or office)

33. PHYSICIAN'S, SUPPLIER'S BILLING NAME, ADDRESS, ZIP CODE & PHONE #

PIN # GRP#

Physician or Supplier Information

Approved by AMA Council on Medical Services

Please Print or Type

APPROVED OMB-0938-0008 FORM CMS-1500 (12-90), FORM RRB-1500, APPROVED OMB-1215-0055 FORM OWCP-1500, APPROVED OMB-0720-0001 (CHAMPUS)

CMS–1500 (08-05)

1500

TEST VERSION – NOT FOR OFFICIAL USE

HEALTH INSURANCE CLAIM FORM

APPROVED BY NATIONAL UNIFORM CLAIM COMMITTEE 08/05

PICA   PICA

CARRIER

1. MEDICARE (Medicare #) MEDICAID (Medicaid #) TRICARE CHAMPUS (Sponsor's SSN) CHAMPVA (Member ID#) GROUP HEALTH PLAN (SSN or ID) FECA BLK LUNG (SSN) OTHER (ID)

1a. INSURED'S I.D. NUMBER (For Program in Item 1)

2. PATIENT'S NAME (Last Name, First Name, Middle Initial)

3. PATIENT'S BIRTH DATE MM DD YY SEX M F

4. INSURED'S NAME (Last Name, First Name, Middle Initial)

5. PATIENT'S ADDRESS (No., Street)

6. PATIENT RELATIONSHIP TO INSURED Self Spouse Child Other

7. INSURED'S ADDRESS (No., Street)

CITY STATE

8. PATIENT STATUS Single Married Other

CITY STATE

ZIP CODE TELEPHONE (Include Area Code) ( )

Employed Full-Time Student Part-Time Student

ZIP CODE TELEPHONE (Include Area Code) ( )

9. OTHER INSURED'S NAME (Last Name, First Name, Middle Initial)

10. IS PATIENT'S CONDITION RELATED TO:

11. INSURED'S POLICY GROUP OR FECA NUMBER

a. OTHER INSURED'S POLICY OR GROUP NUMBER

a. EMPLOYMENT? (Current or Previous) YES NO

a. INSURED'S DATE OF BIRTH MM DD YY SEX M F

b. OTHER INSURED'S DATE OF BIRTH MM DD YY SEX M F

b. AUTO ACCIDENT? YES NO PLACE (State)

b. EMPLOYER'S NAME OR SCHOOL NAME

c. EMPLOYER'S NAME OR SCHOOL NAME

c. OTHER ACCIDENT? YES NO

c. INSURANCE PLAN NAME OR PROGRAM NAME

d. INSURANCE PLAN NAME OR PROGRAM NAME

10d. RESERVED FOR LOCAL USE

d. IS THERE ANOTHER HEALTH BENEFIT PLAN? YES NO *If yes*, return to and complete item 9 a-d.

READ BACK OF FORM BEFORE COMPLETING & SIGNING THIS FORM.

12. PATIENT'S OR AUTHORIZED PERSON'S SIGNATURE I authorize the release of any medical or other information necessary to process this claim. I also request payment of government benefits either to myself or to the party who accepts assignment below.

SIGNED DATE

13. INSURED'S OR AUTHORIZED PERSON'S SIGNATURE I authorize payment of medical benefits to the undersigned physician or supplier for services described below.

SIGNED

PATIENT AND INSURED INFORMATION

14. DATE OF CURRENT: MM DD YY ILLNESS (First symptom) OR INJURY (Accident) OR PREGNANCY(LMP)

15. IF PATIENT HAS HAD SAME OR SIMILAR ILLNESS. GIVE FIRST DATE MM DD YY

16. DATES PATIENT UNABLE TO WORK IN CURRENT OCCUPATION MM DD YY FROM TO

17. NAME OF REFERRING PROVIDER OR OTHER SOURCE 17a. 17b. NPI

18. HOSPITALIZATION DATES RELATED TO CURRENT SERVICES MM DD YY FROM TO

19. RESERVED FOR LOCAL USE

20. OUTSIDE LAB? YES NO $ CHARGES

21. DIAGNOSIS OR NATURE OF ILLNESS OR INJURY (Relate Items 1, 2, 3 or 4 to Item 24E by Line)

1. ___ . ___ 3. ___ . ___

2. ___ . ___ 4. ___ . ___

22. MEDICAID RESUBMISSION CODE ORIGINAL REF. NO.

23. PRIOR AUTHORIZATION NUMBER

24. A. DATE(S) OF SERVICE From MM DD YY To MM DD YY	B. PLACE OF SERVICE	C. EMG	D. PROCEDURES, SERVICES, OR SUPPLIES (Explain Unusual Circumstances) CPT/HCPCS MODIFIER	E. DIAGNOSIS POINTER	F. $ CHARGES	G. DAYS OR UNITS	H. EPSDT Family Plan	I. ID. QUAL.	J. RENDERING PROVIDER ID. #
1								NPI	
2								NPI	
3								NPI	
4								NPI	
5								NPI	
6								NPI	

PHYSICIAN OR SUPPLIER INFORMATION

25. FEDERAL TAX I.D. NUMBER SSN EIN

26. PATIENT'S ACCOUNT NO.

27. ACCEPT ASSIGNMENT? (For govt. claims, see back) YES NO

28. TOTAL CHARGE $

29. AMOUNT PAID $

30. BALANCE DUE $

31. SIGNATURE OF PHYSICIAN OR SUPPLIER INCLUDING DEGREES OR CREDENTIALS (I certify that the statements on the reverse apply to this bill and are made a part thereof.)

SIGNED DATE

32. SERVICE FACILITY LOCATION INFORMATION

a. NPI b.

33. BILLING PROVIDER INFO & PH # ( )

a. NPI b.

NUCC Instruction Manual available at: www.nucc.org

OMB APPROVAL PENDING

Claims Processing

Monitoring Claims

A Day in the Life of a Claim

Once the payer has received a claim, the process of adjudication follows a well-established path. Hopefully, the claim will proceed unimpeded toward reimbursement, but along the way the claim may be stopped and returned to your office for lack of information. Let's look at this adjudication process so you know what to expect and how to speed up your payment.

The Claim Arrives

Upon receipt, each claim is dated and possibly microfilmed or photocopied. Electronic claims are filed into the beneficiary's electronic folder. If the payer uses an optical recognition scanner (OCR), any attachments, such as operative reports, cover letters, pathology reports, etc., are separated from the claim. You may save a few headaches by stamping your practice name, provider number, address, and phone number on all forms and attachments. The same information should be recorded for electronic claims. This helps the payer avoid losing the documentation necessary to pay the claim.

The Claims Adjudicator

The data are entered into the payer's computer system, and if the claim is "clean" (no problems) it's paid. But first, claims must pass through a series of edits to verify the patient's coverage and eligibility as well as check for medical necessity and noncovered services. If the claim requires additional information, also known as development, the insurer contacts either you or your patient. Let your patients know you're available to help them with questions. This contact for development is usually by mail, but it can also be by phone. Many problem claims are denied immediately or placed at the bottom of the pile due to lack of information. The best way to receive prompt and correct payment is to submit a clean claim. This is definitely a case where time well spent is money earned.

Occasionally, your office will submit a claim that contains all pertinent information needed for payment but requires examination by the payer's medical review department. This will delay your payment. However, if your office has a program for monitoring claims, you'll not only be watching your claims for timely payment, you'll also know where your claim is in the processing system when payment is delayed. Carefully tracking the progress of your claims will alert you to those unpaid claims that have been lost and need to be resubmitted.

Why Monitor?

Monitoring insurance submissions can significantly improve an office's cash and profit position because, as you track specific claims, you assure timely and appropriate payment. Leaving your claims to chance can cause problems that can easily be solved if brought to the processor's attention at first submission. Since some insurance companies have been found to commit errors on as many as 25 percent of all claims, monitoring should be an ongoing process. The payer may have neither the information nor the incentive to catch mistakes made in payment. When a patient receives an incorrect payment, the error may go unnoticed. An alert insurance clerk carefully monitoring reimbursement is the best safeguard against insurance company errors.

Once you've sent a claim, either on paper or electronically, you need a mechanism for following it through to reimbursement. Commonly, this takes four weeks to six weeks, but it may vary geographically or by payer. If your office uses computers, the software package should include a reporting system for tracking claims. You need to define "prompt payment" for the computer system. In other words, you have to tell the computer what you feel is a reasonable time delay before the computer alerts you that no payment has been received. Optimally, your computerized system allows you to set this parameter for individual payers.

One downfall of most computer systems is found in payment posting. Do you relate portions of a payment to each individual service or to the original service date? The former is generally referred to as "open item billing" and is considered a more accurate tracking method. Unfortunately, many offices don't use this capability, ultimately reducing the accuracy of claims tracking. If you lack the ability to track your claims via the computer, you will want to use a manual tracking system.

Tracking Systems

The Suspension File System

For nonautomated offices filing paper claims, it's wise to create a suspension file. Simply set up a series of files for a month at a time. Usually it's better not to mix claims that are current (less than 30 days) with claims more than 30 days. Depending on your practice, you may find it necessary to have a current file, a 30-day file, and a 60+-day file.

A practical method for creating your suspension file is to use three separate hanging files, each with four separate folders marked Week 1, Week 2, etc.—one folder for each week of the month. Mark the hanging files Month 1, Month 2, and Month 3. Place the current month's claims in the hanging file marked Month 1. Place the claims over one month old in the file for Month 2 and claims 60+ days old in Month 3. As each week goes by, roll the outstanding claims to the next file. Keep the claims in each file in alphabetic order to eliminate the time and energy spent looking for them when the payment is received.

Claims review should be given a high priority and a regularly scheduled part of your workweek. Insurance claims that are current, or have been filed in the current month, generally require no additional work until the Explanation of Benefits (EOB) and payment are received. Claims more than 30 days old should be reviewed for possible inquiries to the payer.

Make it a rule in your office that most inquiries are written. Notably, this rule applies to Medicare and Medicaid carriers, many of whom require their own forms. Some inquiries are most efficiently made by phone. For example, if a claim has been denied for a simple reason, without notification, a quick phone call is time well spent. If resubmission is the solution, always attach a note with the date, contact person's name, and a description of the conversation. This provides you with the documentation needed if you have to repeat this process.

Your office computer software program may provide you with a comment field or area for "collection" notes. If you don't have this luxury, keep hard copy files of your claims inquiries.

The Log System

An alternative to the suspension file is to record your claims information on a log sheet. When a claim is submitted, record the filing date, patient's name and chart number, account number, name and address of the payer, and the amount billed. The claim itself can be filed temporarily in either the patient's chart or an unpaid insurance file.

After all of the day's or week's claims have been recorded, leave a blank space to tag the claims submitted during that time frame. You may want to highlight those dates in a specific color for review in about three to four weeks.

As payments come in, pull the original claim form and compare it to the EOB. Record the amount paid along with any difference on your log sheet. Any notations such as "claim sent to review" or "claim denied for additional information" should be recorded in the status column.

INSURANCE CLAIM REGISTER

Filing Date	Chart Number	Patient's Name	Name & Address Where Claim Submitted	Amount Billed	Amount Paid	Difference	Status or Comment
7/30	1221	Matthew Kramer	First Insurance 1st Avenue, Newark, NJ 12345	$525.00			9/26 busy 9/27 busy 9/28 " "
8/30	1032	Mark Lane	Fine Insurance 2nd Avenue New Haven, CT 12346	$50.00	$40.00	$10.00	Pd. at 80% Pt. owes balance
8/30	1350	Luke Myers	Better Insurance 3rd Avenue New York City, NY 02111	$1,200.00	$700.00	$500.00	Requested review 9/23
8/30	1118	John Jacobs	Gold Insurance 4th Avenue Newton, WI 12456	$50.00			9/23 claim being processed today
8/30	1179	Mary Byer	Transaccident Insurance 5th Avenue New Hill, NC 24567	$50.00			9/23 no record of claim-resubmit
8/30	1098	Christi Wilson	County Farm Insurance 6th Avenue New Era, IA 45678	$125.00	$50.00	$75.00	$75.00 deductible; bill patient
8/30	1352	Rose Larsen	Last Insurance 7th Avenue New Hope, MS 56789	$1,500.00	$0.00		Sent to medical review 9/10

Understanding Explanation Of Benefits (EOB)

The EOB is the key to knowing what you were paid and why, but understanding what this document really means is sometimes not as easy as it sounds. An EOB has its own language: "applied to deductible," "above usual and customary," "patient co-pay," "allowable," and so on. Often hidden in this language is the explanation of what the patient is responsible for paying. Too many offices write off thousands of dollars of earned income each year because the EOBs are misunderstood or not carefully read.

Each EOB has its own format. Some are very confusing and may even lead the patient to believe he/she is not responsible for a balance. Knowing how to read an EOB can help you collect full reimbursement, including any balance owed by the patient.

It's frustrating, but payers sometimes change your CPT codes and pay you based on a CPT code different from the one you submitted. Watch these changes carefully, as many payment mistakes occur from simple data entry errors by the insurer. Read and learn from your EOB; you may be the one making a common coding error that could be easily corrected.

A wise tactic is to "volunteer" to review EOBs sent to your patients. Your help accomplishes two things: Assures that your office receives the payment, and you show your patients that you take an interest in their financial well-being.

Monitoring EOBs and comparing payments allows you to track your claims and tells you which claims have been sent for medical review. There's also the benefit of understanding why insurance companies pay the way they do.

Medicare Summary Notice

The Explanation of Medicare Benefits (EOMB) shares the same problem as the EOB: they are both confusing to the provider and the beneficiary. To resolve the problem, at least for Medicare beneficiaries, CMS has developed the Medicare Summary Notice (MSN). The MSN lists all claims filed during each month for each beneficiary. One type covers inpatient and outpatient facility services, another type includes all Part B physician and other services, and a third type covers durable medical equipment (DME). Each periodically carries messages pertinent to the beneficiary, such as the hotline for reporting fraud and abuse.

Common Payment Errors

There will be times when your diligent monitoring shows claim problems that are difficult to resolve. The following chart may help you determine what caused an incorrect payment.

Common Payment Errors

Result	Why?
✓ *A service is reduced.*	✓ *The adjudicator may have downcoded the claim for lack of documentation.*
✓ *Reimbursement is made at a much reduced rate.*	✓ *Possibly a data entry error. Compare the CPT code submitted to the code paid.*
✓ *Low or no reimbursement.*	✓ *Precertification was not completed.*
✓ *Low or no reimbursement.*	✓ *Insufficient documentation to establish medical necessity.*
✓ *Multiple units are paid as one unit.*	✓ *The insurer "missed" your number in the units column.*
✓ *The reimbursement for a procedure or service suddenly drops.*	✓ *This could mean a recalculation of allowables or an error. Phone the payer.*
✓ *Payment is not received.*	✓ *Claim is lost or "caught in the system." Begin your inquiry.*
✓ *Multiple procedures were not paid.*	✓ *The insurance company either ignored the additional procedures or lumped them in with the primary procedure.*

Insurance Payment Log

CPT Code	Payment	Payment	Payment	Payment	Payment
	$1,832	$1,600			
	$1,950				
47600	$1,250				
	$2,150				
	$2,000	$1,900			
	$2,460	$2,158			
47605	$2,833				
	$2,112				
	$2,150	$2,066			
	$2,380				
47610	$2,740				
	$2,950				

GATHERING INFORMATION

Most physicians' offices have contractual arrangements with government or private third-party payers. Many of these payers provide your office with a "fee schedule" or other type of payment information. Medicare payment is based on the Medicare Fee Schedule, also known as Resource Based Relative Value Scale or RBRVS. The locality-specific fees are available from CMS on their website or from other commercial sources such as Ingenix.

Another good source of information is available in those states that have developed a Relative Value Study (RVS) or fee schedule for their state workers' compensation payers. When using an RVS, these states usually pay at a set rate based on the relative value of a procedure multiplied by a dollar conversion factor. Workers' compensation rates based on a fee schedule usually provide the dollar value, sometimes called the maximum allowable rate (MAR) for the service.

As a rule, commercial insurers don't readily provide fee information, but it can be obtained. When a payment is received, record the amount in a payment log. For frequently billed payers, devote a column to each payer. List all procedures performed and be conscientious in keeping this information up-to-date. This helps you develop a UCR (usual, customary, and reasonable) reimbursement amount by payer for each procedure and service performed by your practice.

Information from a variety of sources helps you develop a fee schedule that is "in-step" with accepted relative values. It also helps you identify reimbursement errors. If you know your fee for a service is fair, low reimbursement indicates an error may have occurred in processing the claim.

When it's apparent an error has been made, don't hesitate to challenge the payment. Medicare and private payers will correct proven mistakes, when brought to their attention. Errors such as billing the wrong procedure code, omitting a procedure code usually billed with that service, or omitting a standard supply are acceptable reasons for resubmission. Payers usually require this resubmission in a timely manner.

Payment Rationales

Contrary to popular belief, most payers do follow logical mechanisms for reimbursing claims. Many insurers base payments on UCR amounts adjusted for specific geographic areas. Payers acquire this information from several sources and then adjust it to fit their needs in written policies. This UCR information is gathered within specific geographic boundaries though it is not broken down by specialty. Other payers gather their own data for the regions they service and base their payment on a percentage of the UCR charge they've established for your area.

Workers' compensation payers often use a straightforward relative value study chosen by that state. Payments are determined by multiplying a conversion factor, usually established by the state's industrial commission, against the relative value for the service.

HMO and PPO fee schedules are usually developed internally by each organization and are often published on request for their participants. These fee schedules are generally updated on a yearly basis.

Downcoding

Downcoding or recoding by an insurance company is another possible cause of reduced payments. Downcoding occurs when a payer either reviews a claim and determines that the code selected is not correct and a lesser valued code is substituted. It may also occur when the payer uses statistical frequencies to evaluate coding patterns and determines that the provider is oversubmitting higher valued codes. This occurs most frequently with evaluation and management (E/M) services. If the payer determines E/M levels are higher than the norm, the payer may downcode the services to the next lower level E/M service.

Recoding occurs most frequently when claims are submitted with deleted or nonexistent CPT codes. In this case, the payer may assign a current code. Obviously, you may not like the choice. The opposite may occur in billing workers' compensation. Many workers' compensation payers are RVS-based or based on the CPT code set from a previous year, and if your CPT code doesn't match the RVS code or code set being used, your code may be reassigned or denied. Knowing which coding systems and code sets your payers use helps you avoid these problems.

Inquiries, Reviews, and Appeals

Inquiries, reviews, and appeals are the final essential component to monitoring your payments whether you choose the suspension file or log system, or create your own method of tracking claims.

When your claims and EOB monitoring turns up an error (yours or the payer's), correct the claim and resubmit it for appropriate reimbursement. If this doesn't solve the problem, immediately appeal.

Claims Correction

When a claims error is discovered that could result, or already has resulted, in inaccurate reimbursement, send a corrected claim. Clearly mark this claim as a "CORRECTED BILLING—NOT A DUPLICATE CLAIM." Include a note describing the error, plus any additional documentation necessary to support your position. Don't be tempted to keep overpayments; bring it to the attention of the insurance company with a refund. Medicare does not look favorably on practices holding claim overpayments and will prosecute.

Medicare law contains two provisions dealing with liability for and recovery of overpayments that can be found in the *Medicare Claims Processing Manual*, Pub. 100-04, chapter 12, section 40.4 and also in the *Medicare Financial Management Manual*, Pub. 100-06, chapter 3, section 90.

Appealing Incorrect Payments

Before appealing a claim, whether with Medicare or a private insurer, notify the insurer in writing that an error has occurred. Many payers have a set time allowance for claims appeals and often print it on their EOBs. Don't let appeals slide. Actively monitor your claims and stay current with any appeals in progress.

One of the basic rules for appealing a claim is to always include a copy of the original claim, EOB or EOMB (or MSN), and any additional documentation necessary to provide evidence for the appeal. Cover letters are also effective for appeals and will "set the stage" with the claims reviewer. If you feel the payer has not responded to your complaint, don't give up—there are alternatives. Contact your state's insurance commissioner and send a clear, well-documented account of your dissatisfaction. Your argument carries greater weight if you have several examples of the problem from the same insurance company.

Appealing a Part B Medicare Claim

Medicare claims appeals have several levels supported by numerous regulations. The journey starts when either the physician or beneficiary disagrees with the carrier's determination as explained on the EOMB (or MSN). If the claim was assigned, only the physician can initiate the review. If the claim was unassigned, the beneficiary usually initiates the review or can stipulate in writing that the physician is authorized to act on his/her behalf.

The review request must come within 120 days of the date the notice of initial determination was made. The request needs to be submitted in writing. Requests for redetermination of Part B benefits are typically filed on the Form CMS-1964 Request for Review of Part B Medicare Claim. Forward the request to your carrier, prominently marked as a "review" to avoid denial as a duplicate claim. As with any review, include a copy of the claim, the EOMB (or MSN), and any information that will make the review determination possible. *Note:* Letters and telephone calls are considered to be inquiries not an appeal request.

Hearing Officer Hearing—If you've gone through the basic review steps and still disagree with the payer's determination, you may want to request a Hearing Officer (HO) hearing with a CMS-1965 form. The use of the form is not essential, as long as the information submitted follows Medicare regulations. To qualify, the amount in question must be at least $100. However, Medicare will allow you to batch claims with the same problem and procedure to equal the required $100 base. A provision of the Medicare Prescription Drug, Improvement and Modernization Act (MMA) of 2003 mandates that the amount in controversy (AIC) threshold be adjusted annually based on the increase in the medical care component of the consumer price index. If this adjusted amount is not a multiple of $10, the amount will be rounded to the nearest multiple of $10. The adjusted amount will be published annually in the *Federal*

Register. In addition to meeting the AIC threshold requirements, you must request the hearing within six months of the date the informal review decision was made. Make your request in writing and send it to your Medicare hearing officer or coordinator. Your request for an HO hearing will be pursued in one of three ways:

> *On-the-record (OTR) decision*. In an OTR decision, a hearing officer investigates all aspects of the claim. The physician does not testify unless oral testimony is deemed necessary. A hearing on record is often the most productive hearing procedure. The physician is advised of the officer's decision and a copy of the decision is forwarded to the local Medicare carrier for appropriate action.
>
> *Telephone hearing*. In a telephone hearing, the physician presents the case by phone to a hearing officer. Prior to the scheduled hearing, the physician is provided with information in the hearing officer's file. A careful study of this information may help avoid surprises. The physician is advised of the decision and a copy is forwarded to the Medicare carrier for action.
>
> *In-person hearing*. An in-person hearing is guaranteed by regulation to any claimant who requests it. The claimant and/or a representative presents oral testimony supporting the claim and challenging the information the fiscal intermediary or carrier used to deny the claim. Complete and well-organized records help present the best case possible.

Administrative Law Judge Review—If you are not satisfied with the HO hearing decision, the next level of review is the administrative law judge (ALJ) review. To qualify for an ALJ review, you must request a hearing within 60 days of the final HO hearing decision. Prior to October 1, 2002, the AIC was required to be at least $500. However, for claims in which the initial determination was made on or after October 1, 2002, the amount was reduced to $100 to be consistent with the amount required for Part A ALJ hearings. This amount is subject to AIC threshold adjustments as mandated by the MMA of 2003. For claims filed on or after January 1, 2006 the minimum amount is $110.

Department of Appeals Board Appeals Council Review—The Department of Appeals Board (DAB) appeals council is a division of the Social Security Administration (SSA) Office of Hearings and Appeals. A written request for council review must be made through the SSA within 60 days of the ALJ decision and at least $500 must be in dispute. The request must specify the issues and findings of fact and conclusion of law as well as the basis for contending that the findings and conclusion were incorrect. The SSA will contact the requester regarding regulations and protocol. At this level of appeal, retaining an experienced health care attorney should be considered, but is not mandatory.

U.S. District Court—A civil action must be filed in federal district court within 60 days of the mailing of the appeals council decision or its denial of a request to review an ALJ decision. A minimum of $1,000 must be in dispute for claims filed prior to January 1, 2005, $1,040 for claims filed from January 1, 2005 to December 31, 2005, and $1,090 for claims filed on or after January 1, 2006. An attorney is mandatory and the action must be filed in the federal district in which you either live or practice.

Appealing a Part A Medicare Claim
The process for appealing a Part A Medicare claim is similar to that of appealing a Part B claim. Requests for redetermination begin with the filing of the Form CMS-2649, Request for Redetermination of Part A Health Insurance Benefits. If the filing party is dissatisfied following the redetermination and the amount in controversy is at least $110 for claims filed on or after January 1, 2006 (subject to the AIC threshold adjustment), the party is entitled to a hearing before a federal ALJ. If the dissatisfaction continues after the ALJ's decision, the appellant may request the Department of Appeals Board (DAB) review the decision. The DAB may, on its own motion, review an ALJ decision. After DAB review or its denial of review, an appellant who is dissatisfied may file a civil action in the U.S. District Court for a review of the final administrative decision if the amount in controversy is at least $1,000 for claims filed prior to January 1, 2005, $1,040 for claims filed from January 1, 2005 to December 31, 2005, and $1,090 for claims filed on or after January 1, 2006.

Fostering a Spirit of Cooperation

Combative behavior toward a claims reviewer never works in your favor. Concentrate instead on developing a respectful working relationship with one person in each frequently billed insurance company. If you've worked with a particularly good reviewer, send your review requests to that individual's attention. Using the fax numbers found in the *2007 Insurance Directory*, you'll be able to send your request directly to that individual.

Measuring Your Success

One way of viewing the financial health of a practice is with an accounts receivable report. The age (30, 60, 90 days, etc.) of each unpaid balance should be calculated every month. Offices that develop good monitoring systems and collection plans find their outstanding accounts are more current. Receivables can also be influenced by the physician's specialty, type of practice, and participation agreements with insurance companies.

Periodically review your billing, monitoring, and collection policies. Don't hesitate to adjust them if necessary. Set goals for your accounts receivable and track them carefully. This will help you develop greater efficiency in your claims monitoring habits.

Collecting the remainder (co-insurance, deductible, and unpaid amounts) after the insurer has paid is also important. If you don't already have a good plan for collecting these balances, you should: (1) predetermine insurance coverage while patients are in your office and have them pay the anticipated remainder at the time of the service, and (2) regularly bill and follow up on all unpaid balances.

Summary

The claims monitoring process should include a system to:

- Label all attachments to claims with identifying information
- Actively monitor claims payments by comparing the EOB to the original claim
- Gather reimbursement data to help evaluate your fee schedule
- Resubmit claims if necessary to correct errors
- Avoid payer downcoding or coding changes by using current CPT, HCPCS Level II, and ICD-9-CM codes
- Follow the correct steps when appealing claims
- Frequently evaluate your office's billing and monitoring patterns

The Payers

Today's health insurance industry is comprised of many companies each with its own policies, rules, and regulations. The benefits available to groups or individuals vary and the definitions for medical exclusions and pre-existing conditions are almost certain to differ among comparable policies. This variability makes it difficult for a billing staff to predict an insurance company's response to a particular claim submission.

There are ways around the problem. First, get as much information as possible. The policyholder may be the best place to start. The policyholder should be aware of how his/her insurance plan works. But you might have to refresh his/her memory with the following questions:

- Are you aware of any exclusions?
- Is there an annual or lifetime maximum allowed under your policy?
- Is there a waiting period for the policy to take effect?
- Are there any coverage limitations based on a specific illness, such as mental disorders?

These variables and a policy's deductible and copayment create an endless number of challenges in preparing a claim.

Patients with dual coverage (more than one policy) present a special billing challenge. Generally, the primary payer will pay the full benefit (allowable less copayments and deductible) on an individual's plan. The secondary payer and payers providing supplemental coverage will pay an additional amount up to the allowable or contracted rate or the difference between the actual (billed) charge and the amount paid by the primary payer. The total of the combined payments from the primary and secondary payers should not exceed the total billed charges. When an overpayment occurs, contact the payers.

When setting standards for dealing with payers, a rule of thumb is to contact them directly for certain basic facts regarding claims submission. Record the information on 3x5 cards indexed alphabetically for quick reference. Try to get the answers from a supervisor or a provider relations person to help ensure accuracy of the claim processing information.

Payer Comparisons

The following sections discuss a variety of payers and payer types. This is a general discussion only. Specific information on payers and plans should be obtained directly from the payer. Specific information can be obtained by contacting the payer by phone or accessing the payer's website.

Blue Cross/Blue Shield Plans

Blue Cross is a nonprofit health organization providing hospital benefits. In most states, this plan has merged with its counterpart, Blue Shield, which offers physician services benefits to provide total health care coverage for its subscribers. Although all of the plans in the United States, Canada, and Puerto Rico are separate entities, they are coordinated through the national Blue Cross/Blue Shield Plan Association headquartered in Chicago.

Like Medicare, Blue Cross/Blue Shield plans have provider I.D. numbers and participating and nonparticipating provider arrangements. Most plans pay participating providers directly, and the providers agree not to bill the patient for the difference between the allowable and the fee.

Blue Cross/Blue Shield payments are subject to deductibles and copayments that vary according to the patient's plan. A tip: Your office should request a recent provider manual for your state's Blue Cross/Blue Shield plans. It is a good idea to obtain a current provider manual from all participating major health plans. This will be valuable to understanding how and why you are paid.

Health Care Service Plans (HSPs)

Health care service plans, typically operated by Blue Cross and Blue Shield Plans throughout the country, have provided health care coverage for many years. Although initially they acted like indemnity carriers, merely paying claims, many HSPs began to develop managed care products to compete with companies offering HMO, PPO, and EPO products. The products were not necessarily offered through the same organizations that operate the health care service plans.

TRICARE

TRICARE (formerly CHAMPUS) is a regionally managed health care program for active duty and retired members of the uniformed services, their families, and survivors. TRICARE brings together the health care resources of the Army, Navy, and Air Force and supplements them with networks of civilian health care professionals to provide better access and high quality service while maintaining the capability to support military operations.

TRICARE is available to military retirees and their families, survivors of all uniformed services who are not eligible for Medicare, and reservists.

TRICARE has three health plan options available: TRICARE Prime, TRICARE Extra, and TRICARE Standard. TRICARE Prime is a managed care option similar to a civilian health maintenance organization. TRICARE Prime offers fewer out-of-pocket costs than any other TRICARE option. TRICARE Prime enrollees receive most of their care from a military treatment facility (MTF), augmented by the TRICARE contractor's Preferred Provider Network. TRICARE Prime enrollees are assigned a primary care manager (PCM). TRICARE Extra is a preferred provider option. TRICARE Standard is a fee-for-service option.

Benefits and requirements vary based on the plan. Providers should consult the TRICARE website http://www.tricare.osd.mil/provider.aspx for detailed information on these three plans.

Health Maintenance Organizations (HMOs)
HMOs are the most common form of managed care. Generally, they incorporate a number of cost containment techniques to manage care, such as utilization management, development of provider networks, and financial incentives for both providers and members. HMOs must follow the requirements of P.L. 1301 of the Public Health Service Act and 43 CFR 417.100-417.109.

There are a number of models under which HMOs can be organized. HMOs can be staff model plans, Independent Practice Association (IPA), and Point-of-Service (POS).

Staff Model Plans
Staff model plans, also called group models, are HMOs that own the facilities and employ personnel to provide care to their enrollees. A staff model may provide all the services required by their members or they may provide only the more frequently utilized services and contract with other providers for less frequently utilized services such as cardiovascular surgery, burn care, and organ and tissue transplant services.

Independent Practice Association (IPA)
An Independent Practice Association (IPA) consists of physicians who have not combined their assets and liabilities and are not practicing in a truly integrated fashion. They maintain their separate practices and participate in the IPA as a means to contract with HMOs or other health plans. Providers may also see patients who are not enrolled in HMO plans. Where IPAs primarily contract with the HMO to provide services to the HMO's members, the HMO model typically is called the IPA model HMO.

IPAs are developed in two ways. Providers may market themselves as an IPA group and perform their own administrative functions, or payers may develop an IPA from a panel of contracted providers. Whether developed by the providers or a payer, provider members of the IPA should appoint a committee to meet with payer representatives to negotiate contracts, review financial performance of the plan, and settle payer-provider or provider-enrollee disputes. In addition, the committee should be responsible for sanctioning IPA providers and adding/deleting providers from the panel.

Point-of-Service Plan (POS)
A point-of-service health plan allows the covered person to choose to receive a service from a participating or nonparticipating provider, with different benefit levels associated with the use of participating providers. If a POS is purchased, a nonparticipating provider may cost the subscriber the deductibles and 30 percent of the remaining costs up to a set limit. When the costs exceed the limit, the HMO assumes the remaining expenses.

Point-of-service can be provided in several ways (and in various combinations):

- An HMO may allow members to obtain limited services from nonparticipating providers
- An HMO may provide nonparticipating benefits through a supplemental major medical policy
- A PPO may be used to provide both participating and nonparticipating levels of coverage and access

Preferred Provider Organizations (PPOs)
A Preferred Provider Organization (PPO) typically contracts on behalf of employer groups or other plans with hospital and physician providers at reduced rates. The hospitals and physicians participating in the preferred provider network generally are called either preferred or participating providers. Usually, there is an incentive to the patient to use a preferred provider. A patient who visits a physician who is not a preferred provider likely will have to pay a higher copayment or deductible. Providers offer discounts to PPOs in anticipation of achieving additional patient volumes or to minimize the chances that their patient volume will go to another provider.

Exclusive Provider Organizations (EPOs)
An Exclusive Provider Organization (EPO) is a variation of a PPO. EPOs contract with providers on a discounted basis, but enrollees must receive care within the network. EPOs, like PPOs, provide no penalties to providers if the patient opts to obtain care outside the network. Instead, the enrollee assumes responsibility for out-of-network costs.

Third-Party Administrators (TPAs) and Administrative Services Organizations (ASOs)
TPAs and ASOs are neither health plans nor insurers, but organizations that provide claims-paying functions for the clients which they service. Many self-insured groups, such as employers and union trusts, use TPAs or ASOs to manage and

pay their claims. In lieu of paying premiums to health insurers who would charge group premiums, these self-insured groups assume the risk of the provision of such services on their own, usually with some stop loss insurance. The self-insured group may contract directly with providers and it may use the services of a PPO. Although historically such TPAs and ASOs merely paid claims, their functions have expanded. Many have some function in the management of care. In addition, many self-insured groups were pioneers in PPO development, and thus a TPA or ASO may be paying claims based on discounted rates negotiated by a PPO on behalf of a self-insured group.

Single or Specialty Service Plans

There also are single or specialty service plans, such as health plans that provide services only in the mental health area or plans for vision and dental services. Plans for mental health were developed to slow the rising costs of care. Employer groups can contract with these specialty health plans for services that focus on mental health. Vision and dental plans often have been add-on or supplemental coverage to health plans. They vary greatly in the benefits and services that they offer, and represent another example of single specialty service plans.

Medicaid

Federal and state governments jointly administer Medicaid, a program that may go by another name in your state (e.g., Welfare, Title XIX, or Medi-Cal). Medicaid payers do share some characteristics. For example, payers are subject to the same federal guidelines, although there may be individual guidelines for claims submission. Each payer publishes a handbook that outlines and updates the Medicaid rules for that state.

The program issues each recipient an eligibility card that indicates coverage dates. Examine this card carefully to confirm coverage on the date of service. Coverage can change monthly so verify coverage frequently. This card also contains the ID number, which must be included on your claim. A photocopy of the Medicaid card should be placed in the patient's file.

Medicaid, Blue Cross/Blue Shield, and Medicare assign each physician and supplier a local provider number that must be printed in the appropriate box on the claim form. An obvious difficulty arises when a physician provides care to a patient residing in a different state. When this happens, make it a priority to apply immediately for a provider number in that state before submitting the claim. If your office is in a border town or close to a state line, apply for a provider number in both states.

Medicare

The Medicare program, created in 1966, was originally intended to provide health insurance benefits (both hospital and nonhospital) to people older than age 65. The program was expanded in July 1973 to include persons of any age who are entitled to monthly disability benefits for 24 consecutive months under Social Security or the Railroad Retirement program. Additionally, end-stage renal disease (ESRD) patients requiring hemodialysis or kidney transplant are eligible. The Centers for Medicare and Medicaid Services (CMS) was established in 1977 to administer this growing program and is headquartered in Baltimore with 10 regional offices.

As with Medicaid, each Medicare patient is issued an identification card listing a Medicare number and letter combination. The letter suffix identifies the patient's status, e.g., A (wage earner), B (wife of wage earner), D (widow). A complete listing is available from your local Social Security office.

The Medicare program is divided into four components. Part A covers hospital facility services (operating suites, hospital rooms, and supplies), skilled nursing facilities, home health services, and hospice care. Part B covers medical or nonhospital services such as office visits, outpatient surgery and supplies, etc. Part B is voluntary, with premiums deducted from the beneficiary's social security check, allowing the beneficiary to refuse this portion of the Medicare program and maintain only Part A coverage. Part C refers to managed care plans that provide Part A and B benefits to enrollees. Formerly called "Medicare+Choice," Part C has been renamed "Medicare Advantage." Part D refers to the new outpatient prescription drug benefit that was implemented in 2006, enacted under the Medicare Prescription Drug, Improvement, and Modernization Act (MMA) of 2003.

Both Part A and Part B have deductibles, but they're handled in different ways. Part A's deductible is based on benefit periods and may have to be satisfied for each hospitalization. The deductible for Part B is met yearly and renews each January 1. Under most circumstances, Medicare benefits are paid at 80 percent of the allowable and the patient is responsible for the remaining 20 percent if the claim is assigned. When a claim is unassigned, the patient is responsible for the entire amount remaining after Medicare makes its payment up to the limiting charge. When assignment is accepted, the supplier or physician cannot seek additional payment—beyond the Medicare allowable—from the beneficiary or co-insurer. Participating physicians can only submit assigned claims and always check "yes" in box 27 on the CMS-1500 form.

Medicare HMOs

Managed care organizations must apply with CMS for approval to offer this type of plan to Medicare beneficiaries. Once approved, the managed care organization receives a monthly premium payment based on the Adjusted Average Per Capita Cost (AAPCC) from CMS for each beneficiary enrolled under the Medicare risk plan. In return for these monthly premiums, the managed care organization assumes full financial responsibility for all covered services. All services normally covered by Medicare are included in the benefit plan, but the managed care organization has the option of enhancing these benefits to include items such as pharmacy and vision coverage. Generally, the managed care organization provides both basic Medicare coverage (80 percent of allowed charges) and supplemental coverage. When filing claims on Medicare beneficiaries enrolled in Medicare risk plans, the claim should be sent directly to the managed care organization. The managed care organization then adjudicates the claim at 100 percent of allowed charges, based on contract rates, thereby eliminating a step in the Medicare claims adjudication process. The allowed charges may be different rates negotiated with physicians and other providers specifically for Medicare HMO beneficiaries. Because the managed care organization has assumed full financial risk for all care provided to Medicare risk beneficiaries, the MCO strictly monitors all care provided. Therefore, it is crucial to follow all prior approval requirements mandated by the managed care organization to assure that claims will be paid.

Medicare Advantage

The Medicare Advantage Plan (formerly called Medicare+Choice) or Part C of the Medicare program modifies the method the federal government uses to establish capitation rates for Medicare beneficiaries enrolled in managed care plans. Under this program, eligible individuals may elect to receive Medicare benefits through enrollment in one of many private health plans choices beyond the original Medicare programs or plans not available through MCOs. A Medicare Advantage plan is required to provide their Medicare enrollees with those services that are covered under Medicare and available to other fee-for-service Medicare beneficiaries residing in the geographic area covered by the plan.

A Medicare Advantage Plan is required to issue a notice when it denies an enrollee's request for medical service, or whenever there is a request for payment for services already received. Information regarding two standardized appeal notices—Notice of Denial of Medical Services and the Notice of Denial of Request for Payment—were published in the *Federal Register* on June 8, 2000 and March 22, 2001.

Indemnity Plans

Even though MCOs dominate the health insurance market, many indemnity plans continue to exist. Usually, the indemnity carrier will pay the provider directly where the patient has assigned his/her benefits to the provider. Many of the indemnity carriers have attempted to include PPO like characteristics to reduce their costs.

Physician Hospital Organizations (PHOs)

A physician hospital organization (PHO) is created by a hospital and a physician organization, or physicians and physician groups, to assist in managed care contracting on behalf of the parties. The best PHOs include a physician organization that has its own structure, providing a means for reviewing pertinent issues both internal and external, such as contracts, payer disputes, or physician monitoring.

Management Services Organizations (MSOs)

A Management (or Medical) Services Organization (MSO) provides services to physicians and physician groups. It also may provide services to a hospital or hospitals. An MSO may acquire physicians' tangible assets and certain intangible assets, as with the PHO. An MSO, like a PHO, is generally not a provider or supplier of hospital or medical services for Medicare purposes. Goods and services provided by the MSO should be provided to the physicians and not patients, unless the MSO can practice medicine.

MSOs unable to employ physicians contract with them. MSOs might provide office space, equipment, furnishings, management information systems, nonprofessional and certain professional personnel, and services to physicians on a turnkey basis.

MSOs generally are good vehicles for physician recruitment because physicians can contract with the MSO to run their practices. The costs of opening and operating a practice can be offered by the MSO to the physicians on a flat fee, percentage, or hybrid basis.

State Children's Health Insurance Program (SCHIP)

Children who are not covered under a group health plan or other health insurance coverage are often eligible to participate in SCHIP if they meet the income and state-specific standards. Eligibility requirements vary from state-to-state, but in most states uninsured children 18 years of age and younger, whose families earn less than a state specific maximum, qualify for coverage.

For children in families with income at or below 150 percent of poverty, cost-sharing charges cannot exceed the limits for the medically needy under Medicaid. For children in families with income above 150 percent of the poverty line, cost sharing is on a sliding scale related to income, but the total annual cost-sharing for all children in the family cannot exceed 5 percent of the family's annual income.

Covered services vary from state-to-state, but at a minimum SCHIP covers:

- Physician visits
- Prescription medicines
- Hospitalizations
- Immunizations recommended by the Advisory Committee on Immunization Practices (ACIP) in accordance with the ACIP schedule

Workers' Compensation
All states require workers' compensation benefits to provide medical and disability coverage for employees who are injured, contract an illness or disease, or become disabled as a result of their employment. In most states, employers voluntarily provide these benefits, but the criteria for mandatory coverage vary. Some states require employers to carry workers' compensation coverage only if they hire a certain number of people.

The requirements for filing a claim also vary from state to state. In some states the claim is sent directly to a court or the workers' compensation office, while others want it sent to the employer or directly to the insurance carrier.

There does seem to be a common denominator for claims payment. The amount paid is based on an allowable for that service, and the physician doesn't bill the patient for an unpaid balance. When your practice accepts a workers' compensation case, you've essentially agreed to accept the allowable as payment in full.

Most programs do require an initial accident or medical report, a periodic progress report, and a final report if the patient is temporarily disabled and unable to return to work.

Helpful Terms

Adjusted Average Per Capita Cost (AAPCC)
AAPCC is the estimated average cost of Medicare benefits for an individual, based on the following criteria: age, sex, institutional status, Medicaid, disability, and end stage renal disease. CMS uses AAPCC as a guide to make monthly payments to risk and cost contractors.

Affiliation Period
An affiliation period is the length of time an HMO may make you wait before you can receive benefits. During this time, you cannot be charged a premium. Under HIPAA, an affiliation period may not last longer than two months (three months if you are a late enrollee), and it must begin on your enrollment date under the group health plan. As a result, if you switch to HMO coverage more than three months after your enrollment date, the HMO cannot impose an affiliation period on you. Affiliation periods are an alternative to pre-existing condition exclusions; an HMO cannot impose both, even on different individuals.

Alternative Delivery System (ADS)
This is a phrase indicating any health care delivery system other than traditional fee-for-service.

Average Length of Stay (ALOS)
The hospital establishes an average number of days stay for each type of admission. The number is derived from the simple formula: the total number of patient days divided by the total number of admissions for a determined period.

Certificate of Coverage (COC)
The COC describes the benefits included in an individual's health plan. State law requires that all individuals insured under a health plan receive a COC, as well as any employer offering a health care plan.

Church Plan
A church or other religious organization may establish a health plan for its employees.

Consolidated Omnibus Budget Reconciliation Act (COBRA)
COBRA is a federal law that allows and requires past employees to be covered under company health insurance plans for a set premium. This program gives individuals the opportunity to remain insured when their current plan or position has been terminated.

Coordination of Benefits (COB)
COB is a contract that applies when an individual is covered by more than one health care plan. This contract requires that all insurers coordinate the payment of benefits to eliminate the possibility of duplication and overpayment of benefits.

Date of Service (DOS)
This is the date that a health care service was provided to an individual under a particular health plan.

Duplicate Coverage Inquiry (DCI)
DCIs are requests made to insurance companies or medical providers to determine whether other medical coverage exists under another plan.

Durable Medical Equipment (DME)
DME is any equipment that usually can withstand repeated use, is useable at home, and is not beneficial to a person without an illness or injury. Splinting, orthopedic bracing, and wheelchairs are good examples of DME.

Eligible Individual
A person whose most recent coverage was under a group health plan and who may be eligible to purchase health insurance in the individual market regardless of prior health problems.

Employee Retirement Income Security Act (ERISA)
The law provides protections for individuals enrolled in pension, health, and other benefit plans sponsored by private sector employees. The Department of Labor administers the law.

Health Employer Data and Information Set (HEDIS)
HEDIS provides a set of performance measures for employers and other purchasers of health plans to understand and evaluate a health plan's performance.

Health Insurance Portability and Accountability Act of 1996 (HIPAA)
HIPAA amends the Internal Revenue Code of 1986 to improve portability and continuity of health insurance coverage in the group and individual markets. Among its provisions, HIPAA addresses access to long-term care services and coverage and the administration of health insurance.

Health Insurance Purchasing Cooperatives (HIPC)
A HIPC is a pool of purchasers that uses its large numbers of participants as leverage for negotiating with health care providers and insurers. Small employers and communities of individuals lacking large numbers of health care purchasers pursue HIPCs to minimize costs and increase negotiating power with providers and purchasers.

Independent Medical Evaluation (IME)
IMEs are independent examinations of a patient by an unbiased provider to resolve a dispute over an illness or injury incurred by the patient.

Individual Market
Individuals and their dependents not covered through a group health plan may be insured under an individual market plan.

Length of Stay (LOS)
This is the length of stay or number of days that an individual stays in an inpatient setting.

Medical Condition
A medical condition is any physical or medical condition resulting from an illness, pregnancy, or congenital malformation. Genetic information is not a medical condition.

Mental Health Parity Act (MHPA)
MHPA, enacted on September 26, 1996, prohibits a lifetime dollar limit on mental health benefits by a group health plan or health insurance coverage offered in connection with a group health plan. If the plan does impose a limit or annual limit on all medical and surgical benefits, the plan can only impose a comparable limit on mental health. If a group health plan offers two or more benefit package options under the plan, the requirements of MHPA apply separately to each option. MHPA makes clear that the requirements of the law apply to group health plans and health insurance issuers offering coverage under such plans, regardless of whether the mental health benefits are separately administered under the plan.

Ordering Physician
The ordering physician orders nonphysician services for the patient, such as diagnostic laboratory tests, clinical laboratory tests, pharmaceutical services, or durable medical equipment.

Out-of-Area (OOA)
OOA indicates services obtained by a covered individual outside the area where the individual is insured.

Participating Provider (Par)
The term has different meanings for different provider types. For physicians and other Part B suppliers, such as suppliers of durable medical equipment, prosthetics, orthotics, and supplies (DMEPOS), the term holds the meaning that the supplier of services will always accept assignment on claims submitted on behalf of a Medicare beneficiary.

When a supplier accepts assignment, the supplier agrees to bill the beneficiary only for any coinsurance or deductible that may be applicable, and accepts the Medicare payment as full payment. Suppliers, generally, have the option of "participating" in this regard. If they choose not to participate, they may still bill Medicare if they are enrolled, but may decide on a claim-by-claim basis whether to accept assignment. Certified providers, such as hospitals and home health agencies, are considered participating if they are enrolled in Medicare, and must follow Medicare rules for billing the program and beneficiaries.

Peer Review Organization (PRO)
A peer review is usually initiated by a physician group or insurance company to determine if the services provided are medically necessary, in the proper setting, and following professional norms and standards. These reviews are performed by PROs.

Referring Physician
A referring physician requests an item or service for the beneficiary. Payment may be made under the Medicare program.

Usual, Customary, and Reasonable (UCR)
UCR is a term indicating fees charged for medical services that are considered normal, common, and in line with the prevailing fees in the provider's area.

Waiting Period
In the individual market, a waiting period is the time between when the application is filed and coverage begins. In a group health plan, it is the time that must pass before a new employee becomes eligible for plan benefits. The waiting period generally starts on the date of hire.

Supplemental Insurance

Supplemental Insurance for Medicare

Many private insurance companies sell Medicare supplement (Medigap) insurance policies for the specific purpose of filling the "gaps" in Medicare coverage. Other supplemental coverage may also be available through an employer or union health plan. The American Association of Retired Persons (AARP) is another source of supplemental coverage. AARP member coverage may be for both hospital and nonhospital charges. AARP does not require an insurance form, only a copy of the benefits summary. The national headquarters for AARP is in Philadelphia, PA. Inquiries are handled at this single location for claims and the insurance program itself. Send claims to the following address:

AARP Health Care Options
PO Box 1017
Montgomeryville, PA 18936
800.523.5880

Though a benefit for the patient, supplemental insurance is added paperwork for your practice. Since the September 1, 1990 law requiring physicians to file all primary Medicare claims, many practices have felt the need to analyze their stance on filing supplemental insurance claims.

Your Medicare patients may subscribe to an additional policy with an automatic coordination of benefits. The provider must list the secondary coverage in the appropriate space on the CMS-1500 and Medicare does the rest of the work.

Medigap

"Gaps" in the original Medicare plan are costs that are not covered under Medicare, like deductibles and coinsurance. Medigap policies may pay for some or all of the Medicare coinsurance and copayment amounts, and some or all deductibles. Some standardized Medigap plans also pay for services not covered by Medicare, such as coverage for foreign travel or hospital stays after Medicare coverage is exhausted.

In most states, there are 10 standard Medigap plans available; some states offer alternative sets of standardized plans under a federal waiver.

Only the supplemental insurance coverage that has been privately purchased directly by the beneficiary meets the definition of a Medigap policy. The Omnibus Budget Reconciliation Act (OBRA) of 1990 requires all Medigap insurance policies to conform to minimum standards including loss ratio requirements, standardized benefit packages, and consumer protection requirements. Companies selling these policies cannot place conditions on the policy (such as an exclusion of benefits based on a pre-existing condition) or discriminate in the price of the policy because of health status, claims experience, receipt of health care, or medical condition.

To facilitate this process, OBRA created a mechanism to pay participating physicians directly for supplemental benefits. This process allows your Medicare carrier to send an Explanation of Medicare Benefits (EOMB) directly to the Medigap carrier. The Centers for Medicare and Medicaid Services (CMS) requires Medigap carriers to accept the EOMB (or MSN) as a replacement for the CMS-1500 form, eliminating the need for an additional claim. The Medigap carrier issues the payment for coinsurance, deductible, or other charges directly to participating physicians.

Conveying the Correct Information

When completing an electronic media claim or the CMS-1500 form, provide your Medicare carrier with the appropriate information. Refer to the *2007 Insurance Directory* section describing the CMS-1500 form for further instructions on paper claims. Refer to instructions in the ASC X12N 837 implementation guide for submission of supplemental insurance information on electronic claims.

Your local carrier may have special instructions regarding addresses, so watch for this information in carrier newsletters. If a patient has more than one Medigap policy, Medicare will send this payment information to only one of the carriers.

For participating physicians, the assignment of benefits on the claim form must authorize the payment to be made directly to your practice. In addition to the Medicare assignment of benefits, you must have a Medigap assignment of benefits.

Medigap carriers may require the assignment of benefits for this supplemental insurance to be carrier specific. You could add a statement to your current Medicare assignment of benefits stating:

I authorize payment of all medical benefits to apply to all occasions for primary and supplemental (Medigap) coverage to be paid to (physician's name). This assignment will remain in effect until revoked by me in writing.

A photocopy of this assignment is considered as valid as the original.

Once the claim has been processed, Medicare has 30 days to forward the EOMB or Medicare Summary Notice (MSN) to the Medigap carrier.

Participating physicians receive notification on the EOMB or an MSN stating that a copy has been sent to the Medigap carrier. Medicare will not forward an EOMB or an MSN to a Medigap carrier if the charges are denied as noncovered.

If you don't accept assignment on Medicare claims, either you or your patients need to submit claims directly to the supplemental insurance carrier to receive benefits. To assist your patients, present them with an itemized statement (at the time of service) and instructions, such as the following:

As of September 1, 2003, Dr. ____________ is required by law to submit your claim to Medicare. You will still receive an explanation of Medicare benefits (EOMB) from Medicare identifying any coinsurance and deductible in most cases. An exception to this is laboratory services, which have been billed separately to Medicare. When you receive your EOMB or Medicare Summary Notice (MSN), attach it to this itemized statement and forward both to your supplemental carrier. If we can assist you in billing your supplemental carrier, please notify our billing and insurance department.

These instructions may be preprinted on a separate sheet or on the back of your itemized statement. Stamp or print the following phrase on your statement: "Medicare has been billed for these charges." This prevents your patient from sending a duplicate bill to Medicare.

See the section "Payer Comparisons" for information about Medicare and Medicare Advantage programs.

Nonparticipating physicians treating Medicare patients who have secondary coverage through Medicaid must accept assignment on these claims. In most states, the Medicare carrier automatically transmits the forms to Medicaid for payment.

Insurance Commissioners

The following is a list of state insurance commissioners. They function as a source of appeal against commercial insurers just as the Medicare appeals process is set up to ensure fair treatment from Medicare payers (see chapter 2). To appeal to an insurance commissioner, carefully document the problems you are experiencing, particularly repeated problems with an individual payer. Forward this information to the appropriate office as listed on the following pages.

Alabama Dept of Insurance
201 Monroe St, Ste 1700
Montgomery, AL 36104
Mailing address:
PO Box 303351
Montgomery, AL 36130-3351
334.269.3550
www.aldoi.gov/

Alaska Division of Insurance
Juneau Office
9th Fl State Office Bldg
333 Willoughby Ave
Juneau, AK 99801
PO Box 110805
Juneau, AK 99811-0805
907.465.2515
Fax: 907.465.3422
TDD: 907.465.5437

Anchorage Office
Robert B. Atwood Bldg
550 W 7th Ave, Ste 1560
Anchorage, AK 99501-3567
907.269.7900
Fax: 907.269.7910
TDD: 907.465.5437
www.commerce.state.ak.us/insurance/

American Samoa Government
Insurance Commissioner
Pago Pago, AS 96799 USA
011.684.633.4116
Fax: 011.684.633.2269
www.samoanet.com

Arizona Dept of Insurance
Phoenix Office
2910 N 44th St, Ste 210
Phoenix, AZ 85018-7269
602.912.8449 or 800.325.2548

Tucson Office
400 W Congress, Ste 152
Tucson, AZ 85701
520.628.6370 or 800.325.2548
www.id.state.az.us

Arkansas Insurance Dept
1200 W Third St
Little Rock, AR 72201
501.371.2600 or 800.282.9134
Fax: 501.371.2618
www.state.ar.us/insurance/

California Dept of Insurance
Consumer Services Division
300 S Spring St South Tower
Los Angeles, CA 90013
Outside California: 213.897.8921
Within California only: 800.927.4357
TDD: 800.482.4833
www.insurance.ca.gov

Colorado Division of Insurance
1560 Broadway, Ste 850
Denver, CO 80202
303.894.7499 or 800.930.3745
Fax: 303.894.7455
TTY: 800.659.2656
www.dora.state.co.us/insurance/

Connecticut Insurance Dept
153 Market St, 7th Fl
Hartford, CT 06103
Mailing address:
PO Box 816
Hartford, CT 06142-0816
860.297.3800
Within CT only: 800.203.3447
Fax: 860.566.7410
www.state.ct.us/cid/

Delaware Insurance Dept
841 Silver Lake Blvd
Dover, DE 19904
302.674.7300 or 800.282.8611
www.state.de.us/inscom/

District of Columbia
Dept of Insurance, Securities and Banking
810 First St NE, Ste 701
Washington, DC 20002
202.727.8000
TTY/TTD: 202.727.1000
www.disr.washingtondc.gov

Florida Office of Insurance Regulation
200 E Gaines St
Tallahassee, FL 32399-0326
850.413.3140 or 800.342.2762
TDD: 850.410.9700
www.fldfs.com

Georgia Insurance and Safety Fire Commission
Two Martin Luther King, Jr Dr
West Tower, Ste 704
Atlanta, GA 30334
404.656.2070 or 800.656.2298
Fax: 404.657.8542
www.gainsurance.org

Government of Guam
Dept of Revenue and Taxation
Insurance and Banking
Building 13-1 Mariner Ave
Tiyan, Barrigada, GU 96913
671.475.1820
Fax: 671.472.2643
www.gov.gu/revtax/ins

Hawaii Dept of Commerce and Consumer Affairs
Division of Insurance
335 Merchant St, Rm 213
Honolulu, HI 96813
Mailing address:
PO Box 3614
Honolulu, HI 96811
808.586.2790
Fax: 808.586.2806
www.state.hi.us/dcca/ins/

Idaho Dept of Insurance
Boise Main Office
700 W State St, 3rd Fl
PO Box 83720
Boise, ID 83720-0043
208.334.4250
Fax: 208.334.4398

Coeur d' Alene Regional Office
2005 Ironwood Parkway, Ste 143
Coeur d' Alene, ID 83814
Consumer Affairs: 1.800.488.5725
Fax: 208.666.6849

Pocatello Regional Office
611 Wilson Street, Ste 3A
Pocatello, ID 83201
Consumer Affairs: 208.236.6411
Fax: 208.236.6351
www.doi.state.id.us/

Illinois Div of Insurance
Springfield Office
320 W Washington St
Springfield, IL 62767-0001
217.782.4515
Fax: 217.782.5020
TDD: 217.524.4872

Chicago Office
James R. Thompson Center
100 W Randolph St, Ste 9-301
Chicago, IL 60601-3395
312.814.2420
Fax: 312.814.5416
TDD: 312.814.2603
www.ins.state.il.us/

Indiana Dept of Insurance
311 W Washington St
Indianapolis, IN 46204-2787
317.232.2385
Fax: 317.232.5251
www.ai.org/idoi

Iowa Insurance Division
330 Maple St
Des Moines, IA 50319-0065
515.281.5705 or 877.955.1212
Fax: 515.281.3059
www.iid.state.ia.us/

Kansas Insurance Dept
Topeka Office
420 SW 9th St
Topeka, KS 66612-1678
785.296.3071 or 800.432.2484
Fax: 785.296.2283

Wichita Office
130 S Market St, Ste 1028
Box 3850
Wichita, KS 67201-3850
316.337.6010 or 800.432.2484
Fax: 316.337.6018
www.ksinsurance.org/

Kentucky Office of Insurance
215 W Main St
Frankfort, KY 40601
Mailing Address:
PO Box 517
Frankfort, KY 40602
502.564.6154 or 800.595.6053
Fax: 502.564.1650
TTY: 800.462.2081
www.doi.state.ky.us/

Louisiana Dept of Insurance
1702 N 3rd St
Baton Rouge, LA 70802
Mailing address:
PO Box 94214
Baton Rouge, LA 70802
225.342.5900 or 800.259.5300
www.ldi.la.gov/

Maine Bureau of Insurance
124 Northern Ave
Gardiner, ME 04345
Mailing address:
34 State House Station
Augusta, ME 04333-0034
207.624.8475
Within ME only: 800.300.5000
Fax: 207.624.8599
www.state.me.us/pfr/ins/inshome2.htm

Maryland Insurance Administration
525 St Paul Place
Baltimore, MD 21202-2272
410.468.2000 or 800.492.6116
TTY: 800.735.2258
www.mdinsurance.state.md.us/

Massachusetts Division of Insurance
One South Station, 5th Fl
Boston, MA 02110-2208
617.521.7794
TTD/TDD: 617.521.7490
www.state.ma.us/doi/

Michigan Office of Financial and Insurance Services
611 W Ottawa St, 3rd Fl
Lansing, MI 48909
Mailing address:
PO Box 30220
Lansing, MI 48909-7720
517.373.0220 or 877.999.6442
Fax: 517.335.4978
www.michigan.gov/cis

Minnesota Dept of Commerce
85 7th Place E, Ste 500
St. Paul, MN 55101
651.296.4026
Fax: 651.297.1959
TTY: 651.296.2860
www.commerce.state.mn.us/

Mississippi Insurance Dept
1001 Woolfolk State Office Bldg
501 N West St
Jackson, MS 39201
Mailing address:
PO Box 79
Jackson, MS 39205
601.359.3569
Within MS only: 800.562.2957
Out of state: 866.856.1982
www.doi.state.ms.us/

Missouri Dept of Insurance
301 W High St Rm 530
Jefferson City, MO 65101
Mailing Address:
PO Box 690
Jefferson City, MO 65102-0690
573.751.4126 or 800.726.7390
TTY: 573.526.4536
www.insurance.mo.gov

Montana State Auditor
Insurance Division
840 Helena Ave
Helena, MT 59601
406.444.2040 or 800.332.6148
TDD: 406.444.3246
www.sao.state.mt.us/

Nebraska Dept of Insurance
Terminal Bldg
941 "O" St, Ste 400
Lincoln, NE 68508-3639
402.471.2201
TDD: 800.833.7352
www.doi.ne.gov

Nevada Division of Insurance
Carson City Office
788 Fairview Dr, Ste 300
Carson City, NV 89701-5491
775.687.4270
Fax: 775.687.3937

Las Vegas Office
2501 E Sahara Ave, Ste 302
Las Vegas, NV 89104
702.486.4009
Fax: 702.486.4007
www.doi.state.nv.us/

New Hampshire Insurance Dept
21 S Fruit St, Ste 14
Concord, NH 03301
603.271.7973 or 800.852.3416
Fax: 603.271.1406
www.state.nh.us/insurance/

New Jersey Dept of Banking and Insurance
20 W State St
PO Box 325
Trenton, NJ 08625-0325
609.292.5360 or 800.838.0935
Fax: 609.292.2431
www.njdobi.org

New Mexico Insurance Division
PERA Bldg, 4th Fl
1120 Paseo de Peralta
Santa Fe, NM 87501
Mailing address:
PO Box 1269
Santa Fe, NM 87504-1269
505.827.4601
800.947.4722
Fax: 505.827.4734
www.nmprc.state.nm.us/insurance/ nshm.htm

New York State Insurance Dept

Albany Office
One Commerce Plaza
Albany, NY 12257
518.474.6600

Buffalo Office
Walter Mahoney Office Bldg
65 Court St
Buffalo, NY 14202
716.847.7618

Long Island Office
163 Mineola Blvd
Mineola, NY 11501
516.248.5886

New York City Office
25 Beaver St
New York, NY 10004
212.480.6400 or 800.342.3736

Oneonta Office
Road 4, Box 51E
Oneonta, NY 13820

Rochester Office
189 N Water St
Rochester, NY 14604
585.325.3274

Syracuse Office
620 Erie Blvd West, Ste 105
Syracuse, NY 13204
315.423.1102
www.ins.state.ny.us/

North Carolina Dept of Insurance
1201 Mail Service Center
Raleigh, NC 27699-1201
919.733.2032 or 800.546.5664

Eastern Regional Office
233 Middle St
PO Box 1691
New Bern, NC 28563
252.514.4813

Western Regional Office
537 College St
PO Box 1688
Asheville, NC 28802
828.251.6483
www.ncdoi.com/

North Dakota Dept of Insurance
State Capitol, 5th Fl
600 E Boulevard Ave
Bismarck, ND 58505-0320
701.328.2440 or 800.247.0560
Fax: 701.328.4880
www.state.nd.us/ndins/

Ohio Dept of Insurance
2100 Stella Ct
Columbus, OH 43215-1067
614.644.2658
Fax: 614.644.3743
www.ohioinsurance.gov/

Oklahoma Insurance Dept
Oklahoma City Office
2401 NW 23rd, Ste 28
Oklahoma City, OK 73107
Mailing address:
PO Box 53408
Oklahoma City, OK 73152-3408
405.521.2828 or 800.522.0071
Fax: 405.521.6635

Tulsa Office
4157 S Harvard, Ste 121
Tulsa, OK 74135
918.747.7700 or 800.728 2906
Fax: 918.747.7720
www.oid.state.ok.us/

Oregon Dept of Consumer and Business Services
Oregon Insurance Division
350 Winter St NE, Rm 440
Salem, OR 97301-3883
Mailing address:
PO Box 14480
Salem, OR 97309-0405
503.947.7980
Fax: 503.378.4351
TTY: 503.378.4100
www.cbs.state.or.us/external/ins/index.html

Pennsylvania Insurance Dept
1326 Strawberry Sq
Harrisburg, PA 17120
717.787.2317 or 877.881.6388
Fax: 717.787.8585
TTY/TDD: 717.783.3898

Philadelphia Regional Office
Room 1701, State Office Building
1400 Spring Garden St
Philadelphia, PA 19130
215.560.2630
Fax: 215.560.2648
TTY/TDD: 215.560.2471

Pittsburgh Regional Office
Room 304, State Office Building
300 Liberty Ave
Pittsburgh, PA 15222
412.565.5020
Fax: 412.565.7648
TTY/TDD: 412.565.2376
www.insurance.state.pa.us/

Puerto Rico Dept of Insurance
Cobian's Plaza Bldg
1607 Ponce de Leon Ave, Ste 23
Santurce, PR 00909
Mailing address:
Apartado 8330
Fernandez Juncos Station
San Juan, PR 00910-8330
787.722.8686
888.722.8686
Fax: 787.722.4400
www.ocs.gobierno.pr

Rhode Island Division of Insurance
233 Richmond St, Ste 233
Providence, RI 02903-4233
401.222.2246
Fax: 401.222.6098
www.dbr.state.ri.us/

South Carolina Dept of Insurance
300 Arbor Lake Dr, Ste 1200
Columbia, SC 29223
Mailing address:
PO Box 100105
Columbia, SC 29202-3105
803.737.6212
Fax: 803.737.6229
www.doi.sc.gov

South Dakota Div of Insurance
445 E Capitol Ave
Pierre, SD 57501
605.773.3563
Fax: 605.773.5369
www.state.sd.us/drr2/reg/insurance/

Tennessee Dept of Commerce and Insurance
Davy Crocket Tower
500 James Robertson Pkwy, Ste 500
Nashville, TN 37243-0565
615.741.2241
www.state.tn.us/commerce/

Texas Dept of Insurance
333 Guadalupe
Austin, TX 78701
Mailing address:
PO Box 149104
Austin, TX 78714-9104
512.463.6169 or 800.578.4677
TDD: 512.322.4238
www.tdi.state.tx.us/

Utah Dept of Insurance
3110 State Office Bldg
Salt Lake City, UT 84114-6901
801.538.3800 or 800.439.3805
Fax: 801.538.3829
TDD: 801.538.3826
www.insurance.utah.gov

Vermont Insurance Div
89 Main St, Drawer 20
Montpelier, VT 05620-3101
802.828.3301
Fax: 802.828.3306
www.bishca.state.vt.us/insurdiv/insur_index.htm

Virgin Islands Dept of Finance
No 76 Kronprindsens Gade
GERS Bldg, 2nd Fl
St. Thomas, USVI 00802
340.774.4750
Fax: 340.776.4028
www.gov.vi/

Virginia Bureau of Insurance
Tyler Bldg, 9th FL
1300 E Main St
Richmond, VA 23219
Mailing address:
PO Box 1157
Richmond, VA 23218
804.371.9741
Within VA only: 800.552.7945
TDD: 804.371.9206
www.state.va.us/scc/division/boi/index.htm

Washington Insurance Commission
Insurance Bldg
5000 Capitol Blvd
Tumwater, WA 98501
Mailing address:
PO Box 40255
Olympia, WA 98504-0255
360.725.7000 or 800.562.6900
Fax: 360.586.3535
TDD: 360.664.3154
www.insurance.wa.gov/

West Virginia Insurance Commission
Greenbrooke Bldg, Rm 403
1124 Smith St
Charleston, WV 25301
Mailing address:
PO Box 50540
Charleston, WV 25305-0540
304.558.3354
Fax: 304.558.4967
www.wvinsurance.gov

Wisconsin Office of the Commissioner of Insurance
125 S Webster St
Madison, WI 53702
608.266.3585 or 800.236.8517
Fax: 608.266.9935
TDD: 711 ask for 608.266.3586
www.oci.wi.gov/

Wyoming Insurance Dept
Herschler Bldg, 3rd Fl East
122 W 25th St
Cheyenne, WY 82002
307.777.7401
Within WY only: 800.438.5768
Fax: 307.777.5895
http://insurance.state.wy.us/

Workers' Compensation

Workers' Compensation laws are designed to ensure that employees who are injured or disabled on the job are provided with fixed monetary awards, eliminating the need for litigation. These laws also provide benefits for dependents of those workers who are killed because of work-related accidents or illnesses. Some laws also protect employers and fellow workers by limiting the amount an injured employee can recover from an employer and by eliminating the liability of coworkers in most accidents. State Workers' Compensation statutes establish this framework for most employment. Federal statutes are limited to federal employees or those workers employed in some significant aspect of interstate commerce.

In most cases, an individual must have a burden of proof to be entitled to workers' compensation benefits. Burden of proof involves providing the information to support the claim. Discovery is a formal way of obtaining information about the other side's case. Only limited discovery is available in workers' compensation cases. Documents that can be used in discovery include medical and hospital records, physician reports, and vocational counselor reports if provided to the other side at least 20 days before the hearing. Once the hearing begins, each side can introduce relevant evidence to prove its case.

Alabama
Department of Industrial Relations
Workers' Compensation Division
649 Monroe St
Montgomery, AL 36131
334.353.0900
800.528.5165

Alaska
Department of Workers' Compensation
Anchorage Office
PO Box 107019
Anchorage, AK 99510-7019
907.269.4980

Fairbanks Office
675 Seventh Ave, Station H2
Fairbanks, AK 99701-4586
907.451.2889

Fisherman's Fund
PO Box 25512
Juneau, AK 99802-5512
907.465.2766

Juneau Office
PO Box 25512
Juneau, AK 99802-5512
907.465.2790

State Employees Claims
Harbor Adjustment Services
900 W Benson Blvd, Ste 101
Anchorage, AK 99517
907.277.1377

American Samoa
Workers' Compensation
Office of Governor
Pago Pago, AS 96799

Arizona
State Compensation Fund of Arizona
3030 N Third St
Phoenix, AZ 85012-3068
602.631.2300
800.231.1363

Arkansas
Workers' Compensation Commission
324 Spring St
PO Box 950
Little Rock, AR 72203-0950
501.682.3930
800.622.4472

California
Division of Workers' Compensation

Anaheim Office
1661 N Raymond Ave, Rm 200
Anaheim, CA 92801-1162
714.738.4000

Bakersfield Office
1800 30th St, Ste 100
Bakersfield, CA 93301-1929
661.395.2723

Eureka Office
100 "H" Street, Ste 202
Eureka, CA 95501-0421
707.445.6518

Fresno Office
2550 Mariposa St, Ste 4078
Fresno, CA 93721-2280
559.445.5051

Goleta Office
6755 Hollister Ave, Ste 100
Goleta, CA 93117-3018
805.968.0258

Grover Beach Office
1562 Grand Ave
Grover Beach, CA 93433-2261
805.481.4912

Long Beach Office
300 Oceangate St, Ste 200
Long Beach, CA 90802-4339
562.590.5001

Los Angeles Office
320 W Fourth St, 9th Fl
Los Angeles, CA 90013-1105
213.576.7335

Oakland Office (Headquarters)
1515 Clay St, 6th Fl
Oakland, CA 94612-1402
510.622.2866

Oxnard Office
2220 E Gonzales Rd, Ste 100
Oxnard, CA 93036
805.485.2533

Pomona Office
732 Corporate Center Dr
Pomona, CA 91768
909.623.4301

Redding Office
2115 Civic Center Dr, Ste 15
Redding, CA 96001-2796
530.225.2845

Riverside Office
3737 Main St, Ste 300
Riverside, CA 92501-3337
951.782.4269

Sacramento Office
2424 Arden Wy, Ste 230
Sacramento, CA 95825-2403
916.263.2735

Salinas Office
1880 N Main St, Ste 100 & 200
Salinas, CA 93906-2204
831.443.3060

San Bernardino Office
464 W Fourth St, Ste 239
San Bernardino, CA 92108-4402
909.383.4341

San Diego Office
7575 Metropolitan Dr, Ste 202
San Diego, CA 94102-3660
619.767.2083

San Francisco Office
455 Golden Gate Ave, 2nd Fl
San Francisco, CA 94102
415.703.5011

San Jose Office
100 Paseo de San Antonio, Rm 241
San Jose, CA 95113-1482
408.277.1246

Santa Ana Office
28 Civic Center Plz, Ste 451
Santa Ana, CA 92701-4070
714.558.4121

Santa Monica Office
2701 Ocean Park Blvd, Ste 220
Santa Monica, CA 90405-5219
310.452.9114

Santa Rosa Office
50 "D" Street, Ste 420
Santa Rosa, CA 95404-4760
707.576.2391

Stockton Office
31 E Channel St, Rm 344
Stockton, CA 95202-2314
209.948.7759

Van Nuys Office
6150 Van Nuys Blvd, Ste 105
Van Nuys, CA 91401-3373
818.901.5367

Colorado
Division of Workers' Compensation
Tower 2, Ste 500
1515 Arapahoe St
Denver, CO 80202-2117
303.575.8700
888.390.7936

Connecticut
Workers' Compensation Commission

First District Office – Hartford
999 Asylum Ave
Hartford, CT 06105
860.566.4154

Second District Office – Norwich
90 Sachem Street
Norwich, CT 06360
860.823.3900

Third District Office – New Haven
700 State Street
New Haven, CT 06511-6500
203.789.7512

Fourth District Office – Bridgeport
350 Fairfield Avenue
Bridgeport, CT 06604
203.382.5600

Fifth District Office – Waterbury
55 W Main Street
Waterbury, CT 06702
203.596.4207

Sixth District Office – New Britain
233 Main St
New Britain, CT 06051
860.827.7180

Seventh District Office – Stamford
111 High Ridge Rd
Stamford, CT 06905
203.325.3881

Eighth District Office – Middletown
90 Court St
Middletown, CT 06457
860.344.7453

Office of the Chairman
Capitol Place
21 Oak Street, 4th Fl
Hartford, CT 06106
860.493.1500

Delaware
Workers' Compensation Commission

Milford Office
24 NW Front Street
Milford, DE 19963
302.422.1392

Wilmington Office
4425 N Market Street, 3rd Fl
Wilmington, DE 19802
PO Box 9954
Wilmington, DE 19809-9954
302.761.8200

District of Columbia
DC Department of Employment Services
Office of Workers' Compensation
64 New York Ave NE, Rm 2909
Washington, DC 20011
PO BOX 56098
Washington, DC 20002
202.671.1000

Florida
Division of Workers' Compensation
200 E Gaines St
Tallahassee, FL 32399-4220
850.921.6966

Georgia
State Board of Workers' Compensation
270 Peachtree Street NW
Atlanta, GA 30303-1299
404.656.3875
800.533.0682

Guam
Department of Labor – Workers' Compensation Commission
PO Box 9970
Tamuning, GU 96931-9970
671.647.4205

Hawaii
Department of Labor and Industrial Relations
830 Punchbowl St, Rm 209
Honolulu, HI 96813
808.586.9174

Idaho
Workers' Compensation
1215 W State St
PO Box 83720
Boise, ID 83720-0044
208.332.2100
800.334.2370

Illinois
Workers' Compensation Commission

Chicago Office
100 W Randolph St, Ste 8-200
Chicago, IL 60601
312.814.6611
866.352.3033

Collinsville Office
1014 Eastport Plaza Dr
Collinsville, IL 62234
618.346.3450
866.352.3033

Peoria Office
202 NE Madison Ave, Ste 201
Peoria, IL 61602
309.671.3019
866.352.3033

Rockford
200 S Wyman
Rockford, IL 61101
815.987.7292
866.352.3033

Springfield Office
701 S Second St
Springfield, IL 62704
217.785.7087

Indiana
Workers' Compensation Board
Government Center South
402 W Washington St, Ste W196
Indianapolis, IN 46204
317.232.3808

Iowa
Iowa Division of Workers' Compensation
1000 E Grand Ave
Des Moines, IA 50319-0209
515.281.5387
800.562.4692

Kansas
Div of Workers' Compensation
800 SW Jackson, Ste 600
Topeka, KS 66612-1227
785.296.2996
800.332.0353

Kentucky
Department Labor – Office of Workers' Claims
657 Chamberlin Ave
Frankfort, KY 40601
502.564.5550
800.554.8601

Louisiana
Office of Workers' Compensation Admin
1001 N 23rd St
Baton Rouge, LA 70802
PO Box 94040
Baton Rouge, LA 70804
225.342.7555

Maine
Workers' Compensation Board
27 State House Station
Augusta, ME 04333-0027
207.287.3751

Augusta Regional Office
24 Stone Street
Augusta, ME 04330
207.287.2308
800.400.6854

Bangor Regional Office
106 Hogan Rd
Bangor, ME 04401
207.941.4550
800.400.6856

Caribou Regional Office
One Vaughn Place
43 Hatch Dr
Caribou, ME 04736
207.498.6428
800.400.6855

Lewiston Regional Office
36 Mollison Wy
Lewiston, ME 04240
207.753.7700
800.400.6857

Portland Regional Office
62 Elm Street
Portland, ME 04101
207.822.0840
800.400.6858

Maryland
Workers' Compensation Commission
10 E Baltimore St
Baltimore, MD 21202-1641
410.864.5100
800.492.0479

Massachusetts
Workers' Compensation Advisory Council
600 Washington St, 7th Fl
Boston, MA 02111
617.727.4900

Michigan
Workers' Compensation Agency
General Office Bldg
1st Fl – B-Wing
7150 Harris Dr
Lansing, MI 48913
PO Box 30016
Lansing, MI 48909
313.456.2400
888.396.5041

Minnesota
Workers' Compensation Division
443 Lafayette Rd N
St Paul, MN 55155-4305
651.284.5005
800.365.4584

Mississippi
Workers' Compensation Commission
1428 Lakeland Dr
Jackson, MS 39216
PO Box 5300
Jackson, MS 39296-5300
601.987.4200

Missouri
Division of Workers' Compensation
3315 West Truman Blvd, Rm 131
Jefferson City, MO 65102-0058
PO Box 58
Jefferson City, MO 65102-0058
573.751.4231
800.775.2667

Montana
Montana State Fund
5 S Last Chance Gulch
Helena, MT 59601
PO Box 4759
Helena, MT 59604-4759
406.444.6500
800.332.6102

Navajo Nation
Workers' Compensation Program
PO Box 2489
Window Rock, AZ 86515
928.871.6389

Nebraska
Workers' Compensation Court
State House 13th Fl
1445 K St
Lincoln, NE 68508
PO Box 98908
Lincoln, NE 68509-8908
402.471.6468
800.599.5155

Nevada
Division of Industrial Relations
400 W King St, Ste 400
Carson City, NV 89703
775.684.7260

New Hampshire
Workers' Compensation Division
95 Pleasant St
Concord, NH 03301
603.271.3174

New Jersey
Division of Workers' Compensation
John Fitch Plz
PO Box 381
Trenton, NJ 08625-0381
609.292.2515

New Mexico
Workers' Compensation Administration

Main Office
2410 Centre Ave SE
PO Box 27198
Albuquerque, NM 87125-7198
505.841.6000
800.255.7965

Farmington Office
3535 East 30th St
Farmington, NM 87402
505.599.9746
800.568.7310

Las Cruces Office
1120 Commerce Dr, Ste B-1
Las Cruces, NM 88011
505.524.6246
800.870.6826

Las Vegas Office
2515-2 Ridge Runner Rd
Las Vegas, NM 87701
505.454.9251
800.281.7889

Lovington Office
100 West Central, Ste A
Lovington, NM 88260
505.396.3437
800.934.2450

Roswell Office
Penn Plaza Bldg
400 N Pennsylvania Ave, Ste 425
Roswell, NM 88201
505.623.3781
866.311.8587

Santa Fe Office
810 West San Mateo, Ste A2
Sante Fe, NM 87505
505.476.7381

New York
Workers' Compensation Board

Albany District Office
100 Broadway-Menands
Albany, NY 12241
518.486.7143
866.750.5157

Binghamton District Office
44 Hawley St
Binghamton, NY 13901
518.474.6670
866.802.3604

Brooklyn District Office
111 Livingston St
Brooklyn, NY 11201
607.721.8356
800.877.1373

Buffalo District Office
Statler Towers, 3rd Fl
107 Delaware Ave
Buffalo, NY 14202-2898
718.834.3752
866.211.0645

Executive Offices
100 Broadway-Menands
Albany, NY 14202-2898
716.842.2166

Hauppauge District Office
220 Rabro Dr, Ste 100
Hauppauge, NY 11788-4230
631.952.6000
866.681.5354

Hempstead District Office
175 Fulton Ave
Hempstead, NY 11550
516.560.7700
866.805.3630

Manhattan District Office
215 W 125th St
New York, NY 10027
718.291.6529
800.877.1373

Peekskill District Office
41 N Division St
Peekskill, NY 10566
212.932.2690
866.746.0552

Queens District Office
168-46 91st Ave
Jamaica, NY 11432
914.788.5775
800.877.1373

Rochester District Office
130 Main St W
Rochester, NY 14614
585.238.8341
866.211.0644

Syracuse District Office
935 James St
Syracuse, NY 13203
315.423.2932
866.802.3730

North Carolina
Industrial Commission
430 N Salisbury St
Raleigh, NC 27611
4319 Mail Service Center
Raleigh, NC 27699-4319
919.807.2501
800.688.8349

North Dakota
Workforce Safety and Insurance
1600 E Century Ave, Ste 1
Bismarck, ND 58503-0644
PO Box 5585
Bismarck, ND 58506-5585
701.328.3800
800.777.5033

Fargo Office
2601 12th Ave SW
Fargo, ND 58103-2354
701.298.4988

Northern Mariana Islands
Commonwealth of the Northern Mariana Islands
Caller Box 10,007
Saipan, MP 96950 USA
670.664.2200

Ohio
Bureau of Workers' Compensation
30 W Spring St
Columbus, OH 43215-2256
614.644.6292
800.644.6292

Oklahoma
Workers' Compensation Court
Tulsa Office
440 S Houston Ave, Ste 300
Tulsa, OK 74127
918.581.2714

Oklahoma City Office
1915 N Stiles Ave
Oklahoma City, OK 73105-5212
405.522.8600
800.522.8210

Oregon
Workers' Compensation Division
350 Winter St NE, Rm 27
Salem, OR 97301-3879
PO Box 14480
Salem, OR 97309-0405
503.947.7810
800.452.0288

Pennsylvania
Bureau of Workers' Compensation
1171 S Cameron St, Rm 324
Harrisburg, PA 17104-2501
717.772.4447
800.482.2383

Puerto Rico
Workers' Compensation Commission
Industrial Commissioner Office
GPO Box 364466
San Juan, PR 00936-4466
787.781.0545

Rhode Island
Division of Workers' Compensation
1511 Pontiac Ave, Bldg 69
Cranston, RI 02920
PO Box 20190
Cranston, RI 02920-0942
401.462.8100

South Carolina
Workers' Compensation Commission
1612 Marion St
Columbia, SC 29201
PO Box 1715
Columbia, SC 29202-1715
803.737.5700

South Dakota
Division of Labor and Management
Kneip Bldg, 3rd Fl
700 Governors Dr
Pierre, SD 57501-2291
605.773.3681

Tennessee
Workers' Compensation Division
Gateway Plaza, 2nd Fl
710 James Robertson Pkwy
Nashville, TN 37243-0661
615.532.4812
800.332.2667

Texas
Division of Workers' Compensation

Central Office
7551 Metro Center Dr, Ste 100
Austin, TX 78744-1609
512.804.4000

Abilene Office
1290 S Willis, Ste 102
Abilene, TX 79605-4064
325.695.4992

Amarillo Office
7112 IH-40 W, Bldg D
Amarillo, TX 79106-2503
806.351.1222

Austin Office
4616 W Howard Ln, Ste 130
Austin, TX 78728
512.933.1899
800.452.9595

Beaumont Office
Concord Square Office Park
6430 Concord Rd
Beaumont, TX 77708-4315
409.899.5589

Bryan/College Station
4001 E 29th St, Ste 185
Bryan, TX 77802-4211
979.268.6766

Corpus Christi Office
One Agnes Plaza Bldg
1231 Agnes St
Corpus Cristi, TX 78401-3266
361.883.2551

Dallas Office
American General Tower
6363 Forest Park Rd, Ste 900
Dallas, TX 75235-5443
PO Box 45790
Dallas, TX 75245-0790
214.350.9299

Denton Office
Dallas Dr Tech Center
625 Dallas Dr, Ste 475
Denton, TX 76205-7289
940.380.1400

El Paso Office
El Paso State Office Bldg
401 Franklin Ave, Ste 330
El Paso, TX 79901
915.834.7000

Fort Worth
6900 Anderson Blvd, Ste 200
Fort Worth, TX 76120-3011
817.446.4488

Houston East Office
Elias Ramirez Bldg
5425 Polk St, Ste 130
Houston, TX 77023
713.924.2200

Houston West Office
507 N Sam Houston Pkwy E, Ste 600
Houston, TX 77060
281.260.3035

Laredo Office
5420 Springfield Ave
Laredo, TX 78041
956.718.2040

Lubbock Office
22 Briercroft Office Park, Ste A
Lubbock, TX 79412-3089
806.744.4569

Lufkin Office
4415 S Medford Dr
Lufkin, TX 75901-5639
936.639.6425

Midland/Odessa Office
4500 W Illinois Ave, Ste 315
Midland, TX 79703-5486
432.699.1281

Missouri City Office
2440 Texas Pkwy, Ste 240
Missouri City, TX 77489
281.403.7050

San Angelo Office
622 S Oakes, Ste M
San Angelo, TX 76903-7013
325.657.0404

San Antonio Office
9514 Console Dr, Ste 200
San Antonio, TX 78229-2043
210.593.0070

Tyler Office
3800 Paluxy Dr, Ste 570
Tyler, TX 75703-1665
903.534.6250

Victoria Office
3001 N Cameron St
Victoria, TX 77901-3931
361.576.9612

Waco Office
801 Austin Ave, Ste 840
Waco, TX 76701-1937
254.755.7011

Weslaco Office
1108 Pike Blvd
Weslaco, TX 78596
956.447.4416

Wichita Falls
Pyramid Center
2910 Kemp Blvd, Ste 118
Wichita Falls, TX 76308-1040
940.767.2691

Utah
Division of Workers' Compensation
392 E 6400 S
Murray, UT 84107
PO Box 146610
Salt Lake City, UT 84114-6610
801.530.6800
800.446.2667

Vermont
Division of Workers' Compensation
National Life Bldg
Drawer 20
Montpelier, VT 05620-3401
802.828.2286

Virgin Islands
Division of Workers' Compensation
St. Thomas Office
53AB & 54AB Kronsrindsens Gade
Charlotte Amalie, St Thomas, VI 00802
304.776.3700

St Croix Office
302 King St
Fredriksted, St Croix, VI 00820
304.692.9390

Virginia
Workers' Compensation Commission
Central Office
1000 DMV Dr
Richmond, VA 23220
540.433.7701
877.664.2566

Fairfax Regional Office
3020 Hamaker Ct, Ste 100
Fairfax, VA 22030
503.934.0521

Harrisonburg Regional Office
41 Court Sq, Ste B
Harrisonburg, VA 22801
540.433.7701

Lebanon Regional Office
Rte 19 Center One
Lebanon, VA 24266
PO Box 98
Lebanon, VA 24266
276.889.7644

Manassas Regional Office
7900 Sudley Rd, Ste 619
Manassas, VA 20109
703.257.7994

Roanoke Regional Office
2149 Electric Rd
Roanoke, VA 24018
PO Box 21634
Roanoke, VA 24018
540.776.2700

Virginia Beach Regional Office
281 Independence Blvd
Pembroke One, Ste 600
Virginia Beach, VA 23462
757.552.1117

Washington
Department of Labor and Industries
PO Box 44001
Olympia, WA 98504-4001
360.902.4200
800.547.8367

West Virginia
BrickStreet Mutual Insurance Co
4700 MacCorkle Ave SE
Charleston, WV 25304
PO Box 3824
Charleston, WV 25338-3824
304.926.3400
800.498.2667

Wisconsin
Workers' Compensation Division
201 E Washington Ave, Rm C100
Madison, WI 53703
PO Box 7901
Madison, WI 53707-7901
608.266.1340

Milwaukee Office
State Office Bldg
819 N 6th St, Rm 330
Milwaukee, WI 53203
414.227.4381

Appleton Office
Fidelity Bank Bldg
1500 N Casaloma Dr
Appleton, WI 54913-8200
920.832.5450

Wyoming
Department of Employment
Workers' Safety and Compensation Division
1510 E Pershing Blvd
Cheyenne, WY 82002
307.777.7159

Using the Directory

FORMATTING

The format for the *2007 Insurance Directory* has been updated to make it more user-friendly. With more than 5,000 entries, the directory is formatted in a five-column-per-page style for easy reference. The entries are read alphabetically across the page with the first column identifying the national, state, U.S. territory, and international offices of each insurance company; the second column consists of icons, which represent the types of claims the insurance company processes; the third column the office address; the fourth column the office telephone/fax number; and the fifth column the email and web address.

All listings are alphabetized by company name and are printed in large, bold type. The national offices are listed immediately after the company name. Following the national office listings, you will find the state offices listed alphabetically. If more than one state in the alphabetical listing uses the same office, you will find those states listed together. For example, New Jersey, New York, and Pennsylvania are listed together in the first column under New Jersey Manufacturers Insurance Company, as the office located in West Trenton, New Jersey is central to all three locations. U.S. territory and international listings follow the states.

The addresses are printed in capital letters with no punctuation. This follows guidelines set by the U.S. Postal Service to facilitate more efficient electronic scanning. See Appendix A for acceptable abbreviations. We've also included the post office's recommendations for addressing envelopes.

Icons

To make the *2007 Insurance Directory* even more valuable, we verified the types of claims processed by each office and identified them with an icon. These icons represent the types of claims processed and the key is printed across the bottom of facing pages.

If no icon is given, the office is either a corporate office or an office that did not verify claims information when contacted.

- Casualty/Liability
- Dental
- Disability
- EMC – Electronic Media Claims
- HCPCS*
- H HMO
- Home Health
- Main Office
- Medical
- Medigap
- ℞ Pharmaceutical
- Prior Authorization
- Self-Insured
- TPA – Third-Party Corporation Administrator
- Vision
- Workers' Compensation
- No information given – company did not verify nonpublic information

* Although companies within the *2007 Insurance Directory* have indicated that they process HCPCS Level II codes, it is important to check that the particular plan being billed processes these claims.

STATE-BY-STATE INDEX

For your convenience, we've sorted all entries in the directory into a state-by-state index. The company name is listed once though there may be more than one office in that state.

21ST CENTURY INSURANCE GROUP

ARIZONA

6301 OWENSMOUTH AVE
WOODLAND HILLS, CA 91367-2286
PO BOX 2020
WOODLAND HILLS, CA 91365-2020

PHONE: (818) 704-3700
FAX: (818) 704-3796
TOLL FREE: (800) 211-7283

E-MAIL: INETCLAIMS@21ST.COM
WEB: WWW.21ST.COM

A & I BENEFIT PLAN ADMINISTRATORS

NATIONAL

1220 SW MORRISON STE 300
PORTLAND, OR 97205-2222

PHONE: (503) 224-0048
FAX: (503) 228-0149
TOLL FREE: (800) 547-4457
IN-STATE: (800) 547-4457

WEB: WWW.AIBPA.COM

A-PLUS BENEFITS

ARIZONA
COLORADO
NEVADA
UTAH
VIRGINIA
WYOMING

PO BOX 849
PLEASANT GROVE, UT 84062

PHONE: (801) 443-1090
FAX: (801) 443-1198

WEB: WWW.APLUSBENEFITS.COM

A+ AUTO & HOME INSURANCE — *SEE ALSO CALIFORNIA CASUALTY INSURANCE*

AAA INSURANCE CO — *AUTOCLUB SOUTH*

FLORIDA
GEORGIA

1515 N WESTSHORE BLVD
TAMPA, FL 33607-4505
PO BOX 31107
TAMPA, FL 33631-3107

PHONE: (813) 289-1325
FAX: (813) 289-1498
TOLL FREE: (800) 289-1325

WEB: WWW.AAASOUTH.COM

AAA MID-ATLANTIC INSURANCE GROUP — *KEYSTONE INSURANCE CO*

PENNSYLVANIA

TEN PENN CENTER
1801 MARKET ST STE 180
PHILADELPHIA, PA 19103

PHONE: (215) 399-1180

WEB: WWW.AAA.COM OR WWW.AAAMIDATLANTIC.COM

AAA OF MISSOURI

ARKANSAS
ILLINOIS
INDIANA
IOWA
KANSAS
LOUISIANA
MISSISSIPPI
MISSOURI

12901 N FORTY DR
ST. LOUIS, MO 63141

PHONE: (314) 523-7300
TOLL FREE: (800) 222-7623

WEB: WWW.AAAMISSOURI.COM

AARP HEALTHCARE OPTIONS — *UNITED HEALTHCARE CLAIMS DIVISION*

NATIONAL
PUERTO RICO
VIRGIN ISLANDS

PO BOX 740819
ATLANTA, GA 30374-0819

PHONE: (800) 227-7789
TOLL FREE: (800) 523-5800

WEB: WWW.AARPHEALTHCARE.COM

ABAS — *AMERICAN BENEFIT ADMINISTRATIVE SERVICES*

ALABAMA
ALASKA
ARIZONA
ARKANSAS
DELAWARE
DISTRICT OF COLUMBIA
FLORIDA
ILLINOIS
IOWA
KENTUCKY
LOUISIANA
MASSACHUSETTS
MICHIGAN
MISSISSIPPI
MISSOURI
NEBRASKA
NEVADA
NEW HAMPSHIRE
NEW MEXICO
OHIO
OKLAHOMA
PENNSYLVANIA
RHODE ISLAND
TENNESSEE
TEXAS
UTAH
WISCONSIN
WYOMING

1733 PARK ST STE 300
NAPERVILLE, IL 60563

PHONE: (630) 416-1111
FAX: (630) 416-9310
TOLL FREE: (800) 736-7872

WEB: WWW.ABASTPA.COM

ABC HEALTH PLAN — *THE INSTITUTE FOR URBAN FAMILY HEALTH*

NEW YORK	19 W 21ST ST 504 NEW YORK, NY 10010	PHONE: (212) 633-0815 FAX: (212) 620-0688 TOLL FREE: (800) 298-2420	E-MAIL: INFORMATION@ABCHEALTHPLAN.ORG WEB: WWW.ABCHEALTHPLAN.ORG

ABETON

OREGON	1618 SW FIRST AVE STE 450 PORTLAND, OR 97201	FAX: (503) 796-0749 TOLL FREE: (888) 822-3866	WEB: WWW.ABETON.COM

ABPA — *AMERICAN BENEFIT PLAN ADMINISTRATION*

NATIONAL	4040 MCEWEN STE 100 DALLAS, TX 75244	PHONE: (972) 980-1123 FAX: (972) 341-8097	WEB: WWW.ABPA-TPA.COM
ARIZONA	1430 E MISSOURI AVE STE B155 PHOENIX, AZ 85014	PHONE: (602) 264-1804	WEB: WWW.ABPA-TPA.COM
CALIFORNIA	4401 SANTA ANITA AVE EL MONTE, CA 91731	PHONE: (626) 732-2151	WEB: WWW.ABPA-TPA.COM
NEVADA	1830 E SAHARA AVE STE 305 LAS VEGAS, NV 89104	PHONE: (702) 650-6596	WEB: WWW.ABPA-TPA.COM
NEW MEXICO	4901 CHAPPELL DR NE ALBUQUERQUE, NM 87107	PHONE: (505) 881-3141 FAX: (505) 884-7968	WEB: WWW.ABPA-TPA.COM

ABS — *SEE ALSO AMERIBEN SOLUTIONS*

ACADEMY LIFE INSURANCE

NATIONAL	20 MOORES RD FRAZER, PA 19355	PHONE: (610) 648-5000 FAX: (610) 648-5308 OR (800) 392-8139 TOLL FREE: (800) 523-5625	WEB: WWW.ACADEMYLIFE.COM

ACADIA INSURANCE

CONNECTICUT *MAINE* *MASSACHUSETTS* *NEW HAMPSHIRE* *NEW YORK* *VERMONT*	1775 WILLISTON RD SOUTH BURLINGTON, VT 05407-9500 PO BOX 9500 SOUTH BURLINGTON, VT 05407-9500	PHONE: (800) 424-1001	WEB: WWW.ACADIAINSURANCE.COM
	195 SCOTT SWAMP RD FARMINGTON, CT 06032 PO BOX 4063 FARMINGTON, CT 06034	PHONE: (866) 382-0036	WEB: WWW.ACADIAINSURANCE.COM
	200 SALINA MEADOWS PKWY STE 250 SYRACUSE, NY 13212	PHONE: (866) 811-7722 FAX: (315) 350-2993	WEB: WWW.ACADIAINSURANCE.COM
	290 DONALD J. LYNCH BLVD MARLBOROUGH, MA 01752 PO BOX 9168 MARLBOROUGH, MA 01752	PHONE: (508) 786-6677 TOLL FREE: (888) 665-1170	WEB: WWW.ACADIAINSURANCE.COM
	ONE ACADIA COMMONS WESTBROOK, ME 04098-5010 PO BOX 9010 WESTBROOK, ME 04098-5010	TOLL FREE: (800) 773-4300	WEB: WWW.ACADIAINSURANCE.COM
	23 COMMERCE DR BEDFORD, MA 03110-6835 PO BOX 9526 MANCHESTER, NH 03108-9526	TOLL FREE: (800) 224-8850	WEB: WWW.ACADIAINSURANCE.COM

A

ACADIA UNDERWRITERS — *SEE ALSO ACADIA INSURANCE*

ACCESS ADMINISTRATORS, INC

TEXAS

7100 WESTWIND DR STE 115
EL PASO, TX 79912-1756
PO BOX 12609
EL PASO, TX 79913-0609

PHONE: (915) 581-8182
FAX: (915) 581-7537
TOLL FREE: (800) 854-2339

E-MAIL: CS@AHS-ACCESS.COM
WEB: WWW.AHS-ACCESS.COM

ACCIDENT FUND INSURANCE COMPANY OF AMERICA

ILLINOIS
INDIANA
IOWA
KANSAS
MICHIGAN
NORTH CAROLINA
SOUTH CAROLINA
TENNESSEE
WISCONSIN

232 S CAPITAL AVE
LANSING, MI 48901-7900
PO BOX 40790
LANSING, MI 48901-7990

PHONE: (517) 342-4200
TOLL FREE: (800) 888-0616

WEB: WWW.ACCIDENTFUND.COM

ACCIDENT HEALTH LIFE & GROUP INSURANCE

ALABAMA

8916 PKWY EAST
BIRMINGHAM, AL 35206

PHONE: (205) 833-1149

ACCORDANT HEALTH SERVICES, INC

NATIONAL

4900 KOGER BLVD STE 300
GREENSBORO, NC 27407-2710

PHONE: (336) 855-5870
FAX: (366) 852-7413
TOLL FREE: (800) 948-2497

WEB: WWW.ACCORDANT.NET

ACE GROUP — *SEE ALSO ESIS*

ACE USA WORKERS' COMPENSATION — *ESIS*

IOWA
KANSAS
MINNESOTA
MISSOURI
NEBRASKA
SOUTH DAKOTA

7007 COLLEGE BLVD STE 600
OVERLAND PARK, KS 66211
PO BOX 419310
KANSAS CITY, MO 64141-6310

PHONE: (913) 491-2000
FAX: (913) 491-2026
TOLL FREE: (800) 722-7451
IN-STATE: (800) 722-7451

WEB: WWW.ESIS.COM

ACH — *AMERICAS CHOICE HEALTHPLANS*

NATIONAL

PO BOX 922043
HOUSTON, TX 77292-2043

PHONE: (713) 895-3900
TOLL FREE: (800) 633-4227

WEB: WWW.ACHONLINE.COM

ACI — *SEE ALSO ADMINISTRATIVE CONCEPTS, INC*

ACMG, INC

OHIO

2570 TECHNICAL DR
MIAMISBURG, OH 45342-6110

PHONE: (937) 866-6660
FAX: (937) 866-8083
TOLL FREE: (800) 848-2264

WEB: WWW.ACMG-INC.COM

ACORDIA NATIONAL

NATIONAL

602 VIRGINIA ST E
CHARLESTON, WV 25301-2154
PO BOX 3262
CHARLESTON, WV 25332

PHONE: (304) 340-0253
FAX: (304) 353-8748
TOLL FREE: (800) 624-8605

WEB: WWW.ACORDIANATIONAL.COM

ACS BENEFIT SERVICES

NATIONAL

8025 N POINT BLVD
WINSTON SALEM, NC 27106
PO BOX 2000
WINSTON SALEM, NC 27102-2000

PHONE: (336) 759-2013
TOLL FREE: (336) 759-0404

WEB: WWW.ACSBENEFITSERVICESINC.COM

ACSTAR INSURANCE COMPANY

NATIONAL

233 MAIN ST
NEW BRITAIN, CT 06050-2350

PHONE: (860) 224-2000
FAX: (860) 229-1111

E-MAIL: INFO@ACSTARINS.COM
WEB: WWW.ACSTARINS.COM

ACUITY

ILLINOIS
INDIANA
IOWA
KENTUCKY
MICHIGAN
MINNESOTA
MISSOURI
NEBRASKA
NORTH DAKOTA
SOUTH DAKOTA
TENNESSEE
WISCONSIN

2800 S TAYLOR DR
SHEBOYGAN, WI 53081
PO BOX 58
SHEBOYGAN, WI 53082-0058

PHONE: (920) 458-9131
FAX: (920) 458-1618
TOLL FREE: (800) 242-7666
IN-STATE: (800) 242-7666

WEB: WWW.ACUITY.COM

ADMINASTAR FEDERAL, INC — *SEE ALSO MEDICARE - PART B CARRIERS*

ADMINISTRATION SERVICES, INC

ALASKA
IDAHO
MONTANA
OREGON
WASHINGTON
WYOMING

111 W CATALDO AVE STE 110
SPOKANE, WA 99201-3203
PO BOX 5434
SPOKANE, WA 99205-0434

PHONE: (509) 328-0300
FAX: (509) 328-8623
TOLL FREE: (800) 716-0300

E-MAIL: ASI@ADMIN-SERV.COM
WEB: WWW.ADMIN-SERV.COM

ADMINISTRATION SYSTEMS RESEARCH CORP — *ASR CORP*

NATIONAL

3033 ORCHARD VISTA DR SE STE 200
GRAND RAPIDS, MI 49546
PO BOX 6392
GRAND RAPIDS, MI 49516-6392

PHONE: (616) 957-1751
FAX: (616) 559-0916
TOLL FREE: (800) 968-2449
IN-STATE: (800) 968-2449

WEB: WWW.ASRCORP.COM

ADMINISTRATIVE CONCEPTS, INC — *ACI*

TEXAS

102 N LAKESHORE DR
ROCK WALL, TX 75087

PHONE: (972) 772-0707
FAX: (972) 722-9118
TOLL FREE: (800) 805-0622

WEB: WWW.ADMINCONCEPTS.COM

ADMINISTRATIVE ENTERPRISES, INC — *AEI*

ARIZONA

5810 W BEVERLY LANE
GLENDALE, AZ 85306-1800

PHONE: (602) 789-1170
FAX: (602) 789-9369
TOLL FREE: (800) 762-2234

WEB: WWW.AEIAZ.BIZ

ADMINISTRATIVE SERVICES, INC — *ASI*

FLORIDA

7990 SW 117TH AVE
MIAMI, FL 33183-3815
PO BOX 839000
MIAMI, FL 33283-9000

PHONE: (305) 595-4040
FAX: (305) 596-6820
TOLL FREE: (800) 749-1858

E-MAIL: INFO@ADMINSERV.COM
WEB: WWW.ADMINSERV.COM

ADMIRAL INSURANCE CO

NATIONAL		1255 CALDWELL RD CHERRY HILL, NJ 08034 PO BOX 5725 CHERRY HILL, NJ 08034-0524	PHONE: (856) 429-9200 FAX: (856) 429-8611	WEB: WWW.ADMIRALINS.COM

ADVANCE INSURANCE COMPANY

KANSAS		1133 TOPEKA BLVD SW TOPEKA, KS 66629	PHONE: (800) 530-5989 FAX: (785) 273-6121 TOLL FREE: (800) 530-5939	E-MAIL: FEEDBACK@ADVANCEINSURANCE.COM WEB: WWW.ADVANCEINSURANCE.COM

ADVANTAGE INSURANCE COMPANY — *WORKERS COMP FUND*

UTAH		392 E 6400 S SALT LAKE CITY, UT 84107 PO BOX 57929 SALT LAKE CITY, UT 84157-0929	PHONE: (801) 288-8905 FAX: (801) 284-8984 TOLL FREE: (800) 446-2667	WEB: WWW.WCFGROUP.COM

AEGON — *SEE ALSO TRANSAMERICA ASSURANCE CO*

AEGON MARKETING — *STONE BRIDGE LIFE INS*

NATIONAL		2700 W PLANO PKWY PLANO, TX 75075-8205 PO BOX 869090 PLANO, TX 75086	PHONE: (972) 881-6000 FAX: (972) 881-6782 TOLL FREE: (800) 692-5246	WEB: WWW.STONEBRIDGELIFE.COM

AEI — *SEE ALSO ADMINISTRATIVE ENTERPRISES, INC*

AETNA DENTAL

NATIONAL		PO BOX 847 BLUE BELL, PA 19422	TOLL FREE: (800) 872-3862	WEB: WWW.AETNA.COM
ALABAMA		PO BOX 14096 LEXINGTON, KY 40512	TOLL FREE: (800) 872-3862	WEB: WWW.AETNA.COM
ALASKA *ARIZONA*		PO BOX 14027 LEXINGTON, KY 40512	TOLL FREE: (800) 872-3862	WEB: WWW.AETNA.COM
ARKANSAS		PO BOX 14096 LEXINGTON, KY 40512	TOLL FREE: (800) 872-3862	WEB: WWW.AETNA.COM
CALIFORNIA *COLORADO*		PO BOX 14027 LEXINGTON, KY 40512	TOLL FREE: (800) 872-3862	WEB: WWW.AETNA.COM
CONNECTICUT *DELAWARE* *FLORIDA* *GEORGIA*		PO BOX 14096 LEXINGTON, KY 40512	TOLL FREE: (800) 872-3862	WEB: WWW.AETNA.COM
HAWAII *IDAHO*		PO BOX 14027 LEXINGTON, KY 40512	TOLL FREE: (800) 872-3862	WEB: WWW.AETNA.COM
ILLINOIS *INDIANA*		PO BOX 14096 LEXINGTON, KY 40512	TOLL FREE: (800) 872-3862	WEB: WWW.AETNA.COM
IOWA *KANSAS*		PO BOX 14027 LEXINGTON, KY 40512	TOLL FREE: (800) 872-3862	WEB: WWW.AETNA.COM
KENTUCKY *LOUISIANA* *MAINE* *MARYLAND* *MICHIGAN*		PO BOX 14096 LEXINGTON, KY 40512	TOLL FREE: (800) 872-3862	WEB: WWW.AETNA.COM
MINNESOTA		PO BOX 14027 LEXINGTON, KY 40512	TOLL FREE: (800) 872-3862	WEB: WWW.AETNA.COM

MISSISSIPPI	PO BOX 14096 LEXINGTON, KY 40512	TOLL FREE: (800) 872-3862	WEB: WWW.AETNA.COM
MISSOURI *MONTANA* *NEBRASKA* *NEVADA*	PO BOX 14027 LEXINGTON, KY 40512	TOLL FREE: (800) 872-3862	WEB: WWW.AETNA.COM
NEW HAMPSHIRE *NEW JERSEY*	PO BOX 14096 LEXINGTON, KY 40512	TOLL FREE: (800) 872-3862	WEB: WWW.AETNA.COM
NEW MEXICO	PO BOX 14027 LEXINGTON, KY 40512	TOLL FREE: (800) 872-3862	WEB: WWW.AETNA.COM
NEW YORK *NORTH CAROLINA*	PO BOX 14096 LEXINGTON, KY 40512	TOLL FREE: (800) 872-3862	WEB: WWW.AETNA.COM
NORTH DAKOTA	PO BOX 14027 LEXINGTON, KY 40512	TOLL FREE: (800) 872-3862	WEB: WWW.AETNA.COM
OHIO	PO BOX 14096 LEXINGTON, KY 40512	TOLL FREE: (800) 872-3862	WEB: WWW.AETNA.COM
OKLAHOMA *OREGON*	PO BOX 14027 LEXINGTON, KY 40512	TOLL FREE: (800) 872-3862	WEB: WWW.AETNA.COM
PENNSYLVANIA *RHODE ISLAND* *SOUTH CAROLINA*	PO BOX 14096 LEXINGTON, KY 40512	TOLL FREE: (800) 872-3862	WEB: WWW.AETNA.COM
SOUTH DAKOTA	PO BOX 14027 LEXINGTON, KY 40512	TOLL FREE: (800) 872-3862	WEB: WWW.AETNA.COM
TENNESSEE *TEXAS* *VERMONT* *VIRGINIA*	PO BOX 14096 LEXINGTON, KY 40512	TOLL FREE: (800) 872-3862	WEB: WWW.AETNA.COM
WASHINGTON	PO BOX 14027 LEXINGTON, KY 40512	TOLL FREE: (800) 872-3862	WEB: WWW.AETNA.COM
WEST VIRGINIA *WISCONSIN*	PO BOX 14096 LEXINGTON, KY 40512	TOLL FREE: (800) 872-3862	WEB: WWW.AETNA.COM
WYOMING	PO BOX 14027 LEXINGTON, KY 40512	TOLL FREE: (800) 872-3862	WEB: WWW.AETNA.COM

AETNA U.S. HEALTHCARE

NATIONAL	PO BOX 1125 BLUE BELL, PA 19422	TOLL FREE: (800) 872-3862	WEB: WWW.AETNA.COM

ADDITIONAL COMMENTS: NATIONAL EXCEPT CALIFORNIA

ALABAMA	PO BOX 14079 LEXINGTON, KY 40512-4079	TOLL FREE: (800) 872-3862	WEB: WWW.AETNA.COM
ALASKA *ARIZONA*	PO BOX 14089 LEXINGTON, KY 40512-4089	TOLL FREE: (800) 872-3862	WEB: WWW.AETNA.COM
ARKANSAS	PO BOX 14079 LEXINGTON, KY 40512-4079	TOLL FREE: (800) 872-3862	WEB: WWW.AETNA.COM

CALIFORNIA	PO BOX 14089 LEXINGTON, KY 40512-4089	TOLL FREE: (800) 872-3862	WEB: WWW.AETNA.COM
	PO BOX 24019 FRESNO, CA 93779-4019	TOLL FREE: (800) 872-3862	WEB: WWW.AETNA.COM
COLORADO	PO BOX 981107 EL PASO, TX 79998-1107	TOLL FREE: (800) 872-3862	WEB: WWW.AETNA.COM
CONNECTICUT	151 FARMINGTON AVE HARTFORD, CT 06156-0002	PHONE: (860) 273-0123 TOLL FREE: (800) 872-3852	WEB: WWW.AETNA.COM
	PO BOX 981109 EL PASO, TX 79998-1109	TOLL FREE: (800) 872-3852	WEB: WWW.AETNA.COM
DELAWARE *DISTRICT OF COLUMBIA*	PO BOX 981106 EL PASO, TX 79998-1106	TOLL FREE: (800) 872-3862	WEB: WWW.AETNA.COM
FLORIDA *GEORGIA*	PO BOX 14079 LEXINGTON, KY 40512-4079	TOLL FREE: (800) 872-3862	WEB: WWW.AETNA.COM
HAWAII *IDAHO*	PO BOX 14089 LEXINGTON, KY 40512-4089	TOLL FREE: (800) 872-3862	WEB: WWW.AETNA.COM
ILLINOIS *INDIANA* *IOWA* *KANSAS* *KENTUCKY*	PO BOX 981107 EL PASO, TX 79998-1107	TOLL FREE: (800) 872-3862	WEB: WWW.AETNA.COM
LOUISIANA	PO BOX 14079 LEXINGTON, KY 40512-4079	TOLL FREE: (800) 872-3862	WEB: WWW.AETNA.COM
MAINE	PO BOX 981109 EL PASO, TX 79998-1109	TOLL FREE: (800) 872-3862	WEB: WWW.AETNA.COM
MARYLAND	PO BOX 981106 EL PASO, TX 79998-1106	TOLL FREE: (800) 872-3862	WEB: WWW.AETNA.COM
MASSACHUSETTS	PO BOX 981109 EL PASO, TX 79998-1109	TOLL FREE: (800) 872-3862	WEB: WWW.AETNA.COM

MICHIGAN *MINNESOTA*	PO BOX 981107 EL PASO, TX 79998-1107	TOLL FREE: (800) 872-3862	WEB: WWW.AETNA.COM
MISSISSIPPI	PO BOX 14079 LEXINGTON, KY 40512-4079	TOLL FREE: (800) 872-3862	WEB: WWW.AETNA.COM
MISSOURI *MONTANA* *NEBRASKA*	PO BOX 981107 EL PASO, TX 79998-1107	TOLL FREE: (800) 872-3862	WEB: WWW.AETNA.COM
NEVADA	PO BOX 14089 LEXINGTON, KY 40512-4089	TOLL FREE: (800) 872-3862	WEB: WWW.AETNA.COM
NEW HAMPSHIRE *NEW JERSEY*	PO BOX 981109 EL PASO, TX 79998-1109	TOLL FREE: (800) 872-3862	WEB: WWW.AETNA.COM
NEW JERSEY	PO BOX 981106 EL PASO, TX 79998-1106	TOLL FREE: (800) 872-3862	WEB: WWW.AETNA.COM
NEW MEXICO	PO BOX 14089 LEXINGTON, KY 40512-4089	TOLL FREE: (800) 872-3862	WEB: WWW.AETNA.COM
NEW YORK	PO BOX 981109 EL PASO, TX 79998-1109	TOLL FREE: (800) 872-3862	WEB: WWW.AETNA.COM
NORTH CAROLINA	PO BOX 14079 LEXINGTON, KY 40512-4079	TOLL FREE: (800) 872-3862	WEB: WWW.AETNA.COM
NORTH DAKOTA *OHIO*	PO BOX 981107 EL PASO, TX 79998-1107	TOLL FREE: (800) 872-3862	WEB: WWW.AETNA.COM
OREGON	PO BOX 14089 LEXINGTON, KY 40512-4089	TOLL FREE: (800) 872-3862	WEB: WWW.AETNA.COM
PENNSYLVANIA	PO BOX 981106 EL PASO, TX 79998-1106	TOLL FREE: (800) 872-3862	WEB: WWW.AETNA.COM
RHODE ISLAND	PO BOX 981109 EL PASO, TX 79998-1109	TOLL FREE: (800) 872-3862	WEB: WWW.AETNA.COM
SOUTH CAROLINA	PO BOX 14079 LEXINGTON, KY 40512-4079	TOLL FREE: (800) 872-3862	WEB: WWW.AETNA.COM

SOUTH DAKOTA	PO BOX 981107 EL PASO, TX 79998-1107	TOLL FREE: (800) 872-3862	WEB: WWW.AETNA.COM
TENNESSEE	PO BOX 14079 LEXINGTON, KY 40512-4079	TOLL FREE: (800) 872-3862	WEB: WWW.AETNA.COM
UTAH	PO BOX 14089 LEXINGTON, KY 40512-4089	TOLL FREE: (800) 872-3862	WEB: WWW.AETNA.COM
VERMONT	PO BOX 981109 EL PASO, TX 79998-1109	TOLL FREE: (800) 872-3852	WEB: WWW.AETNA.COM
VIRGINIA	PO BOX 981106 EL PASO, TX 79998-1106	TOLL FREE: (800) 872-3862	WEB: WWW.AETNA.COM
WASHINGTON	PO BOX 14089 LEXINGTON, KY 40512-4089	TOLL FREE: (800) 872-3862	WEB: WWW.AETNA.COM
WEST VIRGINIA	PO BOX 981106 EL PASO, TX 79998-1106	TOLL FREE: (800) 872-3862	WEB: WWW.AETNA.COM
WISCONSIN *WYOMING*	PO BOX 981107 EL PASO, TX 79998-1107	TOLL FREE: (800) 872-3362	WEB: WWW.AETNA.COM

AFFINITY HEALTH PLAN

NEW YORK	2500 HALSEY ST BRONX, NY 10461	PHONE: (718) 794-7700 FAX: (718) 794-7800 TOLL FREE: (866) 247-5678	E-MAIL: MEMBER@AFFINITYPLAN.ORG WEB: WWW.AFFINITYPLAN.ORG

AFFORDABLE BENEFIT ADMINISTRATORS, INC

NATIONAL	444 IRVING DR STE 202 BURBANK, CA 91504 PO BOX 10787 BURBANK, CA 91510-0787	PHONE: (818) 842-0147 FAX: (818) 842-0225 TOLL FREE: (800) 350-0148	WEB: WWW.BENEFITSABA.COM

AFLAC

NATIONAL	1932 WYNNTON RD COLUMBUS, GA 31999-7251	PHONE: (706) 323-3431 FAX: (877) 442-3522 TOLL FREE: (800) 992-3522 IN-STATE: (800) 992-3522	WEB: WWW.AFLAC.COM
ALASKA	341 W TUDOR STE 209 ANCHORAGE, AK 99503	PHONE: (907) 563-8244 FAX: (907) 562-3522	E-MAIL: AK@AFLAC.COM WEB: WWW.AFLAC.COM

AFLAC NEW YORK

NATIONAL	22 CORPORATE WOODS BLVD STE 2 ALBANY, NY 12211 PO BOX 15087 ALBANY, NY 12212-5087	PHONE: (518) 438-0764 FAX: (518) 438-0896 TOLL FREE: (800) 366-3436	WEB: WWW.AFLACNY.COM

AGA — *SEE ALSO AMERICAN GROUP ADMINISTRATORS*

AGENCY OF HUMAN SERVICE OF VERMONT

VERMONT	103 S MAIN ST WATERBURY, VT 05671	PHONE: (802) 241-2800 FAX: (802) 241-2897 TOLL FREE: (800) 287-0589 IN-STATE: (800) 250-8427	

AGENCY SERVICES, INC

TENNESSEE	8275 TOURNAMENT DR STE 350 MEMPHIS, TN 38125	PHONE: (901) 767-4271 FAX: (901) 685-9811 TOLL FREE: (800) 777-0988	WEB: WWW.AGENCYSERVICES.COM

AGIA, INC

NATIONAL	1155 EUGEUNA PL CARPENTERIA, CA 85020-4470	PHONE: (805) 566-9191 FAX: (805) 566-9091 TOLL FREE: (800) 782-7267	WEB: WWW.AGIA.COM
	4835 E CACTUS RD STE 410 SCOTTSDALE, AZ 85254 PO BOX 9060 PHOENIX, AZ 85068-9060	PHONE: (602) 870-4121 FAX: (602) 870-3026 TOLL FREE: (800) 782-7267	WEB: WWW.AGIA.COM

AGRI SERVICES AGENCY

NATIONAL	5001 BRITTONFIELD PKY EAST SYRACUSE, NY 13057-9201 PO BOX 4910 SYRACUSE, NY 13221-4910	PHONE: (315) 433-0100 FAX: (315) 433-2345 TOLL FREE: (800) 654-8840	WEB: WWW.DAILYLEA.COM

AHI-HEALTHLINK — *AFFILIATED HEALTHCARE*

NATIONAL	2 GREENWAY 502 HOUSTON, TX 77046	PHONE: (713) 914-3400	WEB: WWW.AHI-HEALTHLINK.COM
OKLAHOMA	3121 QUAIL SPRINGS PKY OKLAHOMA CITY, OK 73134	PHONE: (405) 848-1975	WEB: WWW.MAA-TPA.COM
TEXAS	11200 W HEIMER RD 700 HOUSTON, TX 77042	PHONE: (713) 782-4555	WEB: WWW.AHI-HEALTHLINK.COM
	7535 CANYON DR AMARILLO, TX 79110	PHONE: (713) 782-4555	WEB: WWW.AHI-HEALTHLINK.COM

AIG AMERICAN GENERAL — *SEE ALSO UNITED STATES LIFE INSURANCE CO*

AIG CLAIM SERVICES

ARKANSAS	TCBY TOWER 425 W CAPITOL STE 1600 LITTLE ROCK, AR 72201-3486 PO BOX 25972 SHAWNEE MISSION, KS 66225	PHONE: (501) 375-5040 FAX: (501) 375-5066 TOLL FREE: (800) 955-6520	WEB: WWW.AIGCS.COM

AIG CLAIM SERVICES, INC

NATIONAL	PO BOX 1822 ALPHARETTA, GA 30023	PHONE: (212) 770-0103 FAX: (212) 770-0101 TOLL FREE: (800) 603-1785 IN-STATE: (800) 603-1785	WEB: WWW.AIGCS.COM

ARIZONA	Workers Comp	2201 E CAMELBACK RD STE 400 B PHOENIX, AZ 85016-3431 PO BOX 25971 SHAWNEE MISSION, KS 66225	PHONE: (602) 468-8700 FAX: (866) 739-6983 TOLL FREE: (800) 456-1547	WEB: WWW.AIGCS.COM
CALIFORNIA	Workers Comp	PO BOX 85153 SAN DIEGO, CA 92186-5153	PHONE: (619) 688-3700 FAX: (619) 688-1704 TOLL FREE: (800) 736-6671 IN-STATE: (877) 802-5246	WEB: WWW.AIGCS.COM
	Workers Comp	2633 CAMINO RAMON STE 200 SAN RAMON, CA 94583-2174 PO BOX 5121 SAN RAMON, CA 94583	PHONE: (800) 428-0906 FAX: (925) 901-2342 TOLL FREE: (800) 473-7677	WEB: WWW.AIGCS.COM
	Workers Comp	ONE MACARTHUR PL STE 400 SOUTH COAST METRO, CA 92707-5944 PO BOX 1110 COSTA MESA, CA 92628	PHONE: (714) 436-5100 FAX: (714) 436-5126 TOLL FREE: (800) 642-4231	WEB: WWW.AIGCS.COM
DELAWARE DISTRICT OF COLUMBIA	Workers Comp	11311 MCCORMICK RD STE 200 HUNT VALLEY, MD 21031-8675	PHONE: (410) 316-8700 FAX: (410) 316-8712 TOLL FREE: (800) 654-1204 IN-STATE: (800) 638-3394	WEB: WWW.AIGCS.COM
FLORIDA	Workers Comp	100 N TAMPA ST STE 2550 TAMPA, FL 33602-5809 PO BOX 25477 TAMPA, FL 33622-5477	PHONE: (813) 218-3000 FAX: (813) 272-1122 IN-STATE: (800) 647-4767	WEB: WWW.AIGCS.COM
GEORGIA	TPA	2550 NORTHWINDS PKY 4TH FL ALPHARETTA, GA 30004-2241 PO BOX 1821 ALPHARETTA, GA 30023-1821	PHONE: (770) 870-2000 FAX: (866) 958-1211 TOLL FREE: (800) 448-9707 IN-STATE: (800) 448-9707	WEB: WWW.AIGCS.COM
HAWAII	TPA	196 KAMEHAMEHA AVE HILO, HI 96720	PHONE: (808) 935-7776 FAX: (808) 969-7471 TOLL FREE: (888) 208-2444 IN-STATE: (877) 533-2444	E-MAIL: AIGH@AIGHAWAII.COM WEB: WWW.AIGHAWAII.COM
	TPA	33 LONO AVE STE 100 KAHULUI, HI 96766	TOLL FREE: (888) 543-0440 IN-STATE: (800) 413-1711	E-MAIL: AIGH@AIGHAWAII.COM WEB: WWW.AIGHAWAII.COM
	TPA, Main Office	500 ALA MOANA BLVD BLDG 6 5TH FL HONOLULU, HI 96813	PHONE: (808) 543-0440 FAX: (808) 521-9501 TOLL FREE: (888) 208-2444 IN-STATE: (800) 413-1711	E-MAIL: AIGH@AIGHAWAII.COM WEB: WWW.AIGHAWAII.COM
	TPA	75-1015 HENRY ST KAILUA-KONA, HI 96740	PHONE: (808) 935-7776 FAX: (808) 969-7471 TOLL FREE: (888) 208-2444 IN-STATE: (800) 413-1711	E-MAIL: AIGH@AIGHAWAII.COM WEB: WWW.AIGHAWAII.COM
	TPA	98-1258 KAAHUMANU ST STE 102 PEARL CITY, HI 96782	PHONE: (808) 543-0440 FAX: (808) 521-2444 TOLL FREE: (888) 208-2444 IN-STATE: (800) 413-1711	E-MAIL: AIGH@AIGHAWAII.COM WEB: WWW.AIGHAWAII.COM
IDAHO	Workers Comp	200 N 4TH ST STE 206 BOISE, ID 83702	PHONE: (208) 384-0204 FAX: (866) 947-3318	WEB: WWW.AIGCS.COM
INDIANA	Self-Insured, Workers Comp	400 S 4TH AVE STE 400 LOUISVILLE, KY 40202-3442 PO BOX 1822 ALPHARETTA, GA 30023	PHONE: (502) 561-8700 FAX: (502) 589-2657 TOLL FREE: (800) 428-2422	WEB: WWW.AIGCS.COM
IOWA	Workers Comp	120 S CENTRAL AVE STE 300 CLAYTON, MO 63105 PO BOX 25971 SHAWNEE MISSION, KS 66225	PHONE: (314) 719-4000 FAX: (866) 739-6983 TOLL FREE: (888) 745-7819	WEB: WWW.AIGCS.COM
	Workers Comp, TPA	1401 50TH ST BLDG 2 STE 200 WEST DES MOINES, IA 50266 PO BOX 25588 SHAWNEE MISSION, KS 66225	PHONE: (515) 221-6800 FAX: (866) 854-4926 TOLL FREE: (877) 802-5246	WEB: WWW.AIGCS.COM

KANSAS	9401 INDIAN CREEK PKY BLDG 40 STE 1300 OVERLAND PARK, KS 66210 PO BOX 25588 SHAWNEE MISSION, KS 66225	PHONE: (913) 338-9200 FAX: (866) 854-4926 TOLL FREE: (877) 802-5246	WEB: WWW.AIGCS.COM
KENTUCKY	400 S 4TH AVE STE 400 LOUISVILLE, KY 40202-3442 PO BOX 1822 ALPHARETTA, GA 30023	PHONE: (502) 561-8700 FAX: (502) 589-2657 TOLL FREE: (800) 428-2422	WEB: WWW.AIGCS.COM
LOUISIANA	909 POYDRAS ST STE 1250 NEW ORLEANS, LA 70112 PO BOX 25971 SHAWNEE MISSION, KS 66225	PHONE: (504) 527-5600 FAX: (866) 739-6983 TOLL FREE: (800) 225-6130	WEB: WWW.AIGCS.COM
MARYLAND	11311 MCCORMICK RD STE 200 HUNT VALLEY, MD 21031-8675	PHONE: (410) 316-8700 FAX: (410) 316-8712 TOLL FREE: (800) 654-1204 IN-STATE: (800) 638-3394	WEB: WWW.AIGCS.COM
MICHIGAN	2601 COOLIDGE RD STE 200 EAST LANSING, MI 48823	PHONE: (517) 336-2100 TOLL FREE: (800) 875-5600	WEB: WWW.AIGCS.COM
NEVADA	101 CONVENTION CTR DR STE 1100 LAS VEGAS, NV 89109-2036 PO BOX 25971 SHAWNEE MISSION, KS 66225	FAX: (866) 739-6983 TOLL FREE: (800) 547-9475	WEB: WWW.AIGCS.COM
NEW JERSEY	ONE INTERNATIONAL PLZ STE 200 PHILADELPHIA, PA 19113 PO BOX 499 ESSINGTON, PA 19029-0499	PHONE: (610) 362-3100 FAX: (610) 362-3215 TOLL FREE: (800) 222-4309	WEB: WWW.AIGCS.COM
NEW MEXICO	7510 MONTGOMERY NE STE 204 ALBUQUERQUE, NM 87109-0000 PO BOX 25972 SHAWNEE MISSION, KS 66225	PHONE: (505) 888-0073 FAX: (505) 888-0060 TOLL FREE: (800) 472-2109	WEB: WWW.AIGCS.COM
NEW YORK	15 CORNELL DR 2ND FL LATHAM, NY 12110	PHONE: (518) 220-7200 FAX: (866) 958-1211 TOLL FREE: (877) 640-2450	WEB: WWW.AIGCS.COM
NORTH CAROLINA	4201 CONGRESS ST STE 455 CHARLOTTE, NC 28209	PHONE: (704) 553-5100 FAX: (704) 553-5220	WEB: WWW.AIGCS.COM
OHIO	400 S 4TH AVE STE 400 LOUISVILLE, KY 40202-3442 PO BOX 1822 ALPHARETTA, GA 30023	PHONE: (502) 561-8700 FAX: (502) 589-2657 TOLL FREE: (800) 428-2422	WEB: WWW.AIGCS.COM
OREGON	222 SW COLUMBIA STE 100 PORTLAND, OR 97201-6600 PO BOX 25972 SHAWNEE MISSION, KS 66225	PHONE: (503) 323-2500 FAX: (503) 323-2501 TOLL FREE: (877) 802-5246	WEB: WWW.AIGCS.COM
PENNSYLVANIA	1700 DOMINION TOWER 625 LIBERTY AVE PITTSBURGH, PA 15222 PO BOX 22035 PITTSBURGH, PA 15222	PHONE: (412) 393-3960 TOLL FREE: (800) 258-7152	WEB: WWW.AIGCS.COM
PENNSYLVANIA	ONE INTERNATIONAL PLZ STE 200 PHILADELPHIA, PA 19113 PO BOX 499 ESSINGTON, PA 19029-0499	PHONE: (610) 362-3100 FAX: (610) 362-3215 TOLL FREE: (800) 222-4309	WEB: WWW.AIGCS.COM
TENNESSEE	400 S 4TH AVE STE 400 LOUISVILLE, KY 40202-3442 PO BOX 1822 ALPHARETTA, GA 30023	PHONE: (502) 561-8700 FAX: (502) 589-2657 TOLL FREE: (800) 428-2422	WEB: WWW.AIGCS.COM

A

TEXAS	8144 WALNUT HILL LN 15TH FL DALLAS, TX 75231-4388 PO BOX 25974 SHAWNEE MISSION, KS 66225	PHONE: (214) 932-2600 FAX: (214) 932-2725 TOLL FREE: (800) 456-8533	WEB: WWW.AIG.COM
VIRGINIA	400 S 4TH AVE STE 400 LOUISVILLE, KY 40202-3442 PO BOX 1822 ALPHARETTA, GA 30023	PHONE: (502) 561-8700 FAX: (502) 589-2657 TOLL FREE: (800) 428-2422	WEB: WWW.AIGCS.COM

AIM MUTUAL INSURANCE COMPANY

MASSACHUSETTS	54 3RD AVE BURLINGTON, MA 01803 PO BOX 47070 BURLINGTON, MA 01803	PHONE: (781) 221-1600 FAX: (781) 270-5599 TOLL FREE: (800) 876-2765	E-MAIL: CLAIMS@AIMMUTUAL.COM WEB: WWW.AIMMUTUAL.COM

ALABAMA FINANCIAL POTENTIAL CENTRES, INC

ALABAMA	1560 MONTGOMERY HWY STE 210 HOOVER, AL 35216	PHONE: (205) 979-9907 FAX: (205) 979-9041 TOLL FREE: (877) 848-7234	E-MAIL: MSNOW@ALSTC.COM WEB: WWW.ALSTC.COM

ALAMANCE INSURANCE CO

NATIONAL	238 BURLINGTON INTERNATIONAL RD BURLINGTON, NC 27215	PHONE: (336) 586-2500 FAX: (336) 586-2867 TOLL FREE: (877) 434-2667	WEB: WWW.BURLINGTONINSURANCE.COM

ALASKA NATIONAL INSURANCE COMPANY

ALASKA *CALIFORNIA* *WASHINGTON*	1111 THIRD AVE STE 2600 SEATTLE, WA 98101-3219	PHONE: (206) 292-6360 FAX: (206) 343-4599 TOLL FREE: (800) 292-0588	E-MAIL: SEATTLE@ALASKANATIONAL.COM WEB: WWW.ALASKANATIONAL.COM
	7001 JEWEL LAKE RD ANCHORAGE, AK 99502-2825	PHONE: (907) 266-9227 FAX: (907) 266-9250 TOLL FREE: (877) 248-2642	E-MAIL: ANCHORAGE@ALASKANATIONAL.COM WEB: WWW.ALASKANATIONAL.COM
	601 CALIFORNIA STE 1000 SAN FRANCISCO, CA 94108 PO BOX 193970 SAN FRANCISCO, CA 94119-3970	PHONE: (415) 248-5030 FAX: (415) 248-5035 TOLL FREE: (866) 355-2642	E-MAIL: SANFRANSICO@ALASKANATIONAL.COM WEB: WWW.ALASKANATIONAL.COM

ALASKA TIMBER INSURANCE EXCHANGE

ALASKA	2417 TONGASS AVE STE 214 KETCHIKAN, AK 99901-5803	PHONE: (907) 225-9451 FAX: (907) 225-9454	WEB: WWW.ATIE-INS.COM

ALBERTA BLUE CROSS — *SEE ALSO BLUE CROSS CANADA*

ALEA NORTH AMERICA INSURANCE COMPANY — *ALTERNATIVE RISK*

CONNECTICUT	55 CAPITAL BLVD ROCKY HILL, CT 06067-3578	PHONE: (860) 513-4180 FAX: (860) 258-6725 TOLL FREE: (877) 775-8637	E-MAIL: ROCKYHILL@ALEAGROUP.COM WEB: WWW.ALEAGROUP.COM

ALFA INSURANCE CORP — *ALFA MUTUAL INSURANCE / ALFA MUTUAL GENERAL & FIRE INSURANCE*

ALABAMA	2108 E SOUTH BLVD MONTGOMERY, AL 36191 PO BOX 11000 MONTGOMERY, AL 36191-0001	PHONE: (334) 288-3900 FAX: (334) 394-3087 IN-STATE: (800) 392-5705	WEB: WWW.ALFAINS.COM

ALFA MUTUAL INSURANCE / ALFA MUTUAL GENERAL & FIRE INSURANCE — *SEE ALSO ALFA INSURANCE CORP*

ALI CARE, INC — *SEE ALSO AMALGAMATED LIFE & HEALTH INSURANCE CO*

A

ALICARE — *AMALGAMATED LIFE INSURANCE CO*

NATIONAL		730 BROADWAY NEW YORK, NY 10003 PO BOX 1431 NEW YORK, NY 10116	PHONE: (212) 539-5000	E-MAIL: GENERALINFO@ALICARE.COM WEB: WWW.ALICARE.COM

ALL STATE FLORIDIAN — *SEE ALSO ALLSTATE INSURANCE CO*

ALLEGIANCE BENEFIT PLAN MANAGEMENT, INC.

MONTANA		2806 S GARFIELD ST MISSOULA, MT 59801-7703 PO BOX 3018 MISSOULA, MT 59806-3018	PHONE: (406) 721-2222 FAX: (406) 721-2252 TOLL FREE: (800) 877-1122	WEB: WWW.ABPMTPA.COM

ALLIANZ INSURANCE COMPANY — *GLOBAL RISK INSURANCE COMPANY*

CALIFORNIA		2350 EMPIRE AVE BURBANK, CA 91504 PO BOX 7780 BURBANK, CA 91510-7780	PHONE: (818) 260-7500 FAX: (818) 260-7203 TOLL FREE: (800) 421-0504	WEB: WWW.AIC-ALLIANZ.COM

ALLIANZ LIFE INSURANCE CO OF NORTH AMERICA

NATIONAL
ALBERTA
AMERICAN SAMOA
BRITISH COLUMBIA
CANADA
GUAM
MANITOBA
MEXICO
NEW BRUNSWICK
NEW ZEALAND
NEWFOUNDLAND
NOVA SCOTIA
ONTARIO
PRINCE EDWARD ISLAND
PUERTO RICO
QUEBEC
SASKATCHEWAN
UK
VIRGIN ISLANDS

		5701 GOLDEN HILLS DR MINNEAPOLIS, MN 55416-1297 PO BOX 1344 MINNEAPOLIS, MN 55440-1344	PHONE: (763) 765-5386 FAX: (763) 582-6501 TOLL FREE: (800) 950-5872	WEB: WWW.ALLIANZLIFE.COM

ADDITIONAL COMMENTS: HQ - GLOBAL CO.

ALLIED ADMINISTRATORS, INC

NATIONAL		633 BATTERY ST 2ND FL SAN FRANCISCO, CA 94111-1405 PO BOX 2500 SAN FRANCISCO, CA 94126-2500	PHONE: (415) 986-6276 FAX: (415) 439-5857 TOLL FREE: (888) 877-8363	WEB: WWW.ALLIEDADMINISTRATORS.COM

ALLIED BENEFIT SYSTEMS, INC

NATIONAL		208 S LASALLE ST STE 1300 CHICAGO, IL 60604	PHONE: (312) 906-8080 FAX: (312) 906-8359 TOLL FREE: (800) 288-2078	WEB: WWW.ALLIEDBENEFIT.COM

ALLIED INSURANCE CO — *NATIONWIDE HEALTH PLANS*

CALIFORNIA		1601 EXPOSITION BLVD SACRAMENTO, CA 95815-5103 PO BOX 13200 SACRAMENTO, CA 95813	PHONE: (916) 924-4000 FAX: (800) 742-1341 TOLL FREE: (877) 234-2727	WEB: WWW.ALLIEDINSURANCE.COM
IOWA		1100 LOCUST DES MOINES, IA 50309	PHONE: (515) 508-4211 TOLL FREE: (800) 228-4011 IN-STATE: (800) 532-1436	WEB: WWW.ALLIEDINSURANCE.COM

ALLIED NATIONAL

NATIONAL		911 BROADWAY KANSAS CITY, MO 64105 PO BOX 419233 KANSAS CITY, MO 64141-6233	PHONE: (816) 474-1200 FAX: (816) 221-4638 TOLL FREE: (800) 825-7531	WEB: WWW.ALLIEDNATIONAL.COM

ALLMERICA FINANCIAL — *SEE ALSO HANOVER INSURANCE CO*

ALLSTATE INSURANCE CO

NATIONAL	2775 SANDERS RD NORTHBROOK, IL 60062-6127	PHONE: (847) 402-5000 FAX: (847) 402-0169 TOLL FREE: (800) 366-2953	WEB: WWW.ALLSTATE.COM
	740 CARILLON PKY STE 400 ST PETERSBURG, FL 33716-1105 PO BOX 42160 ST PETERSBURG, FL 33742	PHONE: (800) 309-1251 FAX: (727) 571-8229 TOLL FREE: (800) 877-4809	WEB: WWW.ALLSTATE.COM
OREGON	7632 SW DURHAM RD STE 200 TIGARD, OR 97224-7584	FAX: (503) 603-5969 TOLL FREE: (888) 442-6219	WEB: WWW.ALLSTATE.COM
UTAH	6056 S FASHION SQ DR STE 100 MURRAY, UT 84107-7356 PO BOX 57995 SALT LAKE CITY, UT 84157-0995	FAX: (801) 264-2140 TOLL FREE: (800) 662-5366	WEB: WWW.ALLSTATE.COM
WASHINGTON	18911 N CREEK PKY STE 201 BOTHELL, WA 98011-8030 PO BOX 3036 BOTHELL, WA 98041	FAX: (425) 424-1500 TOLL FREE: (800) 597-9001	WEB: WWW.ALLSTATE.COM

ALOHA CARE OF HAWAII

HAWAII	1357 KAPLOLANI BLVD STE 1250 HONOLULU, HI 96814	PHONE: (808) 973-1650 FAX: (808) 973-0726 IN-STATE: (800) 434-1002	E-MAIL: CUSTOMERSERVICE@ALOHACAREHAWAII.ORG WEB: WWW.ALOHACAREHAWAII.ORG

ALTERNATIVE RISK — *SEE ALSO ALEA NORTH AMERICA INSURANCE CO*

ALTERNATIVE RISK MANAGEMENT LIMITED — *ARM LTD*

NATIONAL	171 W WING ST STE 210 ARLINGTON HEIGHTS, IL 60005-1406	PHONE: (847) 394-1700 FAX: (847) 394-1770 TOLL FREE: (800) 392-1770	WEB: WWW.ALTRISK.COM

ALTICOR

NATIONAL	7575 E FULTON ST ADA, MI 49355-0001	PHONE: (616) 787-1000 FAX: (616) 787-4590 TOLL FREE: (800) 269-7[illegible]96	WEB: WWW.ALTICOR.COM

AMALGAMATED LIFE & HEALTH INSURANCE CO — *ALI CARE, INC*

NATIONAL	730 BROADWAY NEW YORK, NY 10030-9502	PHONE: (212) 539-5111 FAX: (212) 674-6679	

AMERAPLAN, INC

NATIONAL	22500 METROPOLITAN PKY STE 100 CLINTON TOWNSHIP, MI 48035-1928	PHONE: (586) 792-4000 FAX: (586) 791-0537 TOLL FREE: (800) 221-4254	WEB: WWW.AMERAPLAN.COM

AMERIBEN SOLUTIONS — *ABS*

NATIONAL	3449 E COPPER POINT DR MERIDIAN, ID 83642 PO BOX 7186 BOISE, ID 83707	PHONE: (208) 344-7900 FAX: (208) 424-0595 TOLL FREE: (800) 786-7930	E-MAIL: INFO@AMERIBEN.COM WEB: WWW.AMERIBENIECGROUP.COM

A

AMERICA FIRST INSURANCE

ARKANSAS *LOUISIANA* *OKLAHOMA* *TEXAS*	504 S SERVICE RD E RUSTON, LA 71270-3404 PO BOX 1300 RUSTON, LA 71273-1300	PHONE: (318) 255-2622 FAX: (318) 254-4522 TOLL FREE: (800) 372-4823	WEB: WWW.AMERICAFIRST-INS.COM

AMERICA FIRST INSURANCE CO

ARKANSAS *OKLAHOMA* *TEXAS*	3400 WATERVIEW PKY STE 200 RICHARDSON, TX 75080 PO BOX 833906 RICHARDSON, TX 75083	PHONE: (800) 443-2534 FAX: (972) 470-8700 TOLL FREE: (800) 443-2534	WEB: WWW.AMERICAFIRST-INS.COM

AMERICAN ADMINISTRATIVE GROUP

NATIONAL	1000 PLZ DR STE 300 SCHAUMBURG, IL 60173 PO BOX 156 CARY, IL 60013	PHONE: (800) 658-9777	WEB: WWW.AAGCORPORATE.COM
	4500 MERCANTILE PLZ STE 200 FT WORTH, TX 76137 PO BOX 619037 DALLAS, TX 76317	PHONE: (800) 658-9777 TOLL FREE: (800) 641-2214	WEB: WWW.AAGCORPORATE.COM

AMERICAN ADMINISTRATORS GROUP

TEXAS	222 W LAS COLINAS BLVD MILLENNIUM CTR STE 1600 IRVING, TX 75039	PHONE: (214) 574-2375 FAX: (214) 574-2338 OR (214) 574-2348	WEB: WWW.ICONBA.COM
	2002 W LOOP 289 WAYLAND PLZ STE 110 LUBBOCK, TX 79407-7701 PO BOX 53010 LUBBOCK, TX 79453	PHONE: (806) 473-3000 FAX: (806) 473-3030 TOLL FREE: (800) 658-9777	WEB: WWW.ICONBA.COM

AMERICAN AMBASSADOR CASUALTY CO — *GO AMERICA AUTO INSURANCE*

ILLINOIS	1100 ARLINGTON HEIGHTS RD STE 300 ITASCA, IL 60143-3176 PO BOX 7178 INDIANAPOLIS, IN 46207-7178	FAX: (317) 816-3508 TOLL FREE: (800) 876-3500	

AMERICAN BENEFIT ADMINISTRATIVE SERVICES — *SEE ALSO ABAS*

AMERICAN BENEFIT PLAN ADMINISTRATION — *SEE ALSO ABPA*

AMERICAN BENEFITS MANAGEMENT

ARIZONA, *FLORIDA*, *ILLINOIS*, *INDIANA*, *KENTUCKY*, *MICHIGAN*, *OHIO*, *PENNSYLVANIA*, *VIRGINIA*

	8310 PORT JACKSON AVE NW NORTH CANTON, OH 44720-7340 PO BOX 35008 NORTH CANTON, OH 44735-5008	PHONE: (330) 966-5500 FAX: (330) 966-5506 TOLL FREE: (800) 456-4002 IN-STATE: (800) 456-4002	WEB: WWW.AMERICANBENEFITS.ORG

AMERICAN CENTENNIAL INSURANCE CO — *INTERNATIONAL AMERICAN MANAGEMENT CO*

NATIONAL	3501 SILVERSIDE RD 203 NAAMANS BLDG CONCORD PLZ WILMINGTON, DE 19810-4910	PHONE: (302) 479-2100 FAX: (302) 479-2103	

AMERICAN COMMERCE INSURANCE CO

INDIANA	*OHIO*	*TENNESSEE*	
KENTUCKY	*OKLAHOMA*	*WEST VIRGINIA*	

	3801 SHARON PARK LN STE 150 SHARONVILLE, OH 45241-4118	PHONE: (513) 563-6800 FAX: (513) 554-6854	E-MAIL: CUSTOMERSERVICE@ACILINK.COM WEB: WWW.ACILINK.COM

AMERICAN COMMERCIAL BARGE LINES

ILLINOIS *INDIANA* *MICHIGAN* *WISCONSIN*	1701 E MARKET ST JEFFERSONVILLE, IN 47130-4717 PO BOX 610 JEFFERSONVILLE, IN 47131-0610	PHONE: (812) 288-0100 FAX: (812) 288-1720	WEB: WWW.ACBL.NET

AMERICAN COMMUNITY MUTUAL INSURANCE CO

ARIZONA	*INDIANA*	*MICHIGAN*	*NEBRASKA*
ILLINOIS	*IOWA*	*MISSOURI*	*OHIO*

	39201 SEVEN MILE RD LIVONIA, MI 48152	PHONE: (734) 591-9000 FAX: (734) 591-4628 TOLL FREE: (800) 991-2642	WEB: WWW.AMERICAN-COMMUNITY.COM

AMERICAN DENTAL CENTERS — *SEE ALSO AMERICAN MEDICAL & LIFE INSURANCE CO*

AMERICAN EMPIRE SURPLUS LINES INSURANCE CO

NATIONAL	580 WALNUT ST CINCINNATI, OH 45202-3226 PO BOX 5370 CINCINNATI, OH 45201-5370	PHONE: (513) 369-3000 FAX: (513) 369-3062	WEB: WWW.AESLIC.COM

AMERICAN FAMILY INSURANCE

ARIZONA	PO BOX 52048 PHOENIX, AZ 85072	PHONE: (602) 225-3740 FAX: (602) 225-3748 TOLL FREE: (800) 374-1111	WEB: WWW.AMFAM.COM
	225 N 45TH ST PHOENIX, AZ 85034-1901 PO BOX 52048 PHOENIX, AZ 85072	PHONE: (602) 225-3740 FAX: (602) 225-3748	WEB: WWW.AMFAM.COM
	5255 E WILLIAMS CIR TUCSON, AZ 85711 PO BOX 12750 TUCSON, AZ 85711	PHONE: (520) 747-9432 FAX: (520) 747-9830	WEB: WWW.AMFAM.COM
ARIZONA *COLORADO*	HOME OFFICE 6000 AMERICAN PKY MADISON, WI 53783-0001	PHONE: (608) 249-2111 TOLL FREE: (800) 374-1111	WEB: WWW.AMFAM.COM
COLORADO	9510 MERIDIAN BLVD ENGLEWOOD, CO 80112 PO BOX 3328 ENGLEWOOD, CO 80155-3328	PHONE: (303) 799-3515 FAX: (303) 799-1630	WEB: WWW.AMFAM.COM
IDAHO	408 S EAGLE RD STE 109 EAGLE, ID 83616	PHONE: (208) 938-6420 FAX: (208) 938-6421 TOLL FREE: (800) 374-1111	WEB: WWW.AMFAM.COM
	6340 S 3000 E STE 400 SALT LAKE CITY, UT 84121 PO BOX 71500 SALT LAKE CITY, UT 84121	TOLL FREE: (800) 374-1111	WEB: WWW.AMFAM.COM

IDAHO *ILLINOIS*	Casualty/Liability	HOME OFFICE 6000 AMERICAN PKY MADISON, WI 53783-0001	PHONE: (608) 249-2111 TOLL FREE: (800) 374-1111	WEB: WWW.AMFAM.COM
ILLINOIS	Casualty/Liability	1946 DAIMLER RD ROCKFORD, IL 61112-1008 PO BOX 7747 ROCKFORD, IL 61126-7747	PHONE: (815) 398-6684 FAX: (815) 398-9813 IN-STATE: (800) 374-0008	WEB: WWW.AMFAM.COM
	Casualty/Liability	20 N MARTINGALE RD STE 400 SCHAUMBURG, IL 60173-2275	PHONE: (847) 605-0660 FAX: (847) 605-9012	WEB: WWW.AMFAM.COM
	Casualty/Liability, EMC	4501 N STERLING AVE STE 300 PEORIA, IL 61615 PO BOX 3220 PEORIA, IL 61612-3220	PHONE: (309) 688-0653 FAX: (309) 688-9718 TOLL FREE: (800) 374-1111	WEB: WWW.AMFAM.COM
	Casualty/Liability	740 N LAKEVIEW PKY STE 100 VERNON HILLS, IL 60061 PO BOX 6750 VERNON HILLS, IL 60061-6750	PHONE: (847) 367-2510 FAX: (847) 367-2515 TOLL FREE: (800) 374-1111	WEB: WWW.AMFAM.COM
INDIANA	Casualty/Liability	900 E 96TH ST STE 100 INDIANAPOLIS, IN 46240 PO BOX 7093 INDIANAPOLIS, IN 46207	PHONE: (317) 842-0096 FAX: (317) 815-4402	WEB: WWW.AMFAM.COM
INDIANA *IOWA*	Casualty/Liability	HOME OFFICE 6000 AMERICAN PKY MADISON, WI 53783-0001	PHONE: (608) 249-2111 TOLL FREE: (800) 374-1111	WEB: WWW.AMFAM.COM
IOWA	Casualty/Liability	5500 WESTOWN PKY STE 180 WEST DES MOINES, IA 58266-5271 PO BOX 65630 WEST DES MOINES, IA 50265-0630	PHONE: (515) 223-1145 FAX: (866) 299-5539	WEB: WWW.AMFAM.COM
KANSAS	Casualty/Liability	7325 W TAFT WICHITA, KS 67209-2089 PO BOX 7703 WICHITA, KS 67209	PHONE: (316) 729-9600 FAX: (316) 729-9963	WEB: WWW.AMFAM.COM
	Casualty/Liability	1300 SW ARROWHEAD RD TOPEKA, KS 66604-4019 PO BOX 4384 TOPEKA, KS 66604	PHONE: (785) 273-5120 FAX: (800) 377-0021 TOLL FREE: (800) 374-1111	WEB: WWW.AMFAM.COM
KANSAS *MINNESOTA*	Casualty/Liability	HOME OFFICE 6000 AMERICAN PKY MADISON, WI 53783-0001	PHONE: (608) 249-2111 TOLL FREE: (800) 374-1111	WEB: WWW.AMFAM.COM
MINNESOTA	Casualty/Liability	1696 GREENVIEW DR SW ROCHESTER, MN 55902-1034 PO BOX 5829 ROCHESTER, MN 55903	PHONE: (507) 281-4144 IN-STATE: (888) 222-6326	WEB: WWW.AMFAM.COM
	Casualty/Liability, EMC	3601 18TH ST S STE 110 ST CLOUD, MN 56301-3758 PO BOX 1719 ST CLOUD, MN 56302	PHONE: (320) 253-6605 FAX: (320) 253-0915	WEB: WWW.AMFAM.COM
	Casualty/Liability	3920 NORTHWOODS DR ARDEN HILLS, MN 55112-6963 PO BOX 64885 ST PAUL, MN 55164	PHONE: (651) 483-8271 FAX: (651) 483-6501	WEB: WWW.AMFAM.COM
	Casualty/Liability	6131 BLUE CIRCLE DR EDEN PRAIRIE, MN 55343 PO BOX 59173 MINNEAPOLIS, MN 55440-0173	PHONE: (952) 933-4884	WEB: WWW.AMFAM.COM
MISSOURI	Casualty/Liability	1300 SW ARROWHEAD RD TOPEKA, KS 66604-4019 PO BOX 4384 TOPEKA, KS 66604	PHONE: (785) 273-5120 FAX: (800) 377-0021 TOLL FREE: (800) 374-1111	WEB: WWW.AMFAM.COM

MISSOURI — CONTINUED	11789 BORMAN DR ST LOUIS, MO 63146-4188 PO BOX 28408 ST LOUIS, MO 63146-0908	PHONE: (314) 991-0070 FAX: (314) 991-2935 TOLL FREE: (800) 374-0008	WEB: WWW.AMFAM.COM
	3130 S DELAWARE AVE SPRINGFIELD, MO 65804 PO BOX 10667 SPRINGFIELD, MO 65808	PHONE: (417) 882-6021 FAX: (800) 977-7210 TOLL FREE: (800) 374-1111	WEB: WWW.AMFAM.COM
	3600 AMAZONAS DR JEFFERSON CITY, MO 65109 PO BOX 1786 JEFFERSON CITY, MO 65102	PHONE: (573) 893-5600 TOLL FREE: (800) 374-1111	WEB: WWW.AMFAM.COM
	4802 MITCHELL AVE ST JOSEPH, MO 64507-2500	PHONE: (816) 364-1541 FAX: (800) 801-8045 TOLL FREE: (800) 374-0008	WEB: WWW.AMFAM.COM
	6301 JAMES A REED RD KANSAS CITY, MO 64133	PHONE: (816) 356-2100 FAX: (866) 539-6731	WEB: WWW.AMFAM.COM
MISSOURI NEBRASKA	HOME OFFICE 6000 AMERICAN PKY MADISON, WI 53783-0001	PHONE: (608) 249-2111 TOLL FREE: (800) 374-1111	WEB: WWW.AMFAM.COM
NEBRASKA	1300 SW ARROWHEAD RD TOPEKA, KS 66604-4019 PO BOX 4384 TOPEKA, KS 66604	PHONE: (785) 273-5120 FAX: (800) 377-0021 TOLL FREE: (800) 374-1111	WEB: WWW.AMFAM.COM
	9290 W DODGE RD STE 400 OMAHA, NE 68114 PO BOX 247043 OMAHA, NE 68124	PHONE: (402) 330-1010 FAX: (866) 589-7453 TOLL FREE: (800) 374-0008	WEB: WWW.AMFAM.COM
NEVADA	6775 EDMOND ST STE 300 LAS VEGAS, NV 89118	PHONE: (702) 733-5820 FAX: (702) 733-5961	WEB: WWW.AMFAM.COM
NEVADA NORTH DAKOTA	HOME OFFICE 6000 AMERICAN PKY MADISON, WI 53783-0001	PHONE: (608) 249-2111 TOLL FREE: (800) 374-1111	WEB: WWW.AMFAM.COM
NORTH DAKOTA	2829 S UNIVERSITY DR FARGO, ND 58103-6029 PO BOX 966 FARGO, ND 58107-0966	PHONE: (701) 280-1100 FAX: (701) 280-1102 TOLL FREE: (800) 374-1111	WEB: WWW.AMFAM.COM
OHIO	550 POLARIS PKWY STE 100 WESTERVILLE, OH 43082 PO BOX 6165 WESTERVLILE, OH 43082-6165	PHONE: (614) 794-9770	WEB: WWW.AMFAM.COM
OHIO OREGON SOUTH DAKOTA	HOME OFFICE 6000 AMERICAN PKY MADISON, WI 53783-0001	PHONE: (608) 249-2111 TOLL FREE: (800) 374-1111	WEB: WWW.AMFAM.COM
SOUTH DAKOTA	4009 W 49TH ST SIOUX FALLS, SD 57106-5221 PO BOX 5021 SIOUX FALLS, SD 57117-5021	PHONE: (605) 361-5000 FAX: (605) 361-5005 TOLL FREE: (800) 374-1111	WEB: WWW.AMFAM.COM
UTAH	408 S EAGLE RD STE 109 EAGLE, ID 83616	PHONE: (208) 938-6420 FAX: (208) 938-6421 TOLL FREE: (800) 374-1111	WEB: WWW.AMFAM.COM
	6340 S 3000 E STE 400 SALT LAKE CITY, UT 84121 PO BOX 71500 SALT LAKE CITY, UT 84121	TOLL FREE: (800) 374-1111	WEB: WWW.AMFAM.COM
	6340 S 3000 E STE 400 SALT LAKE CITY, UT 84121 PO BOX 71500 SALT LAKE CITY, UT 84171	PHONE: (801) 944-3620 FAX: (801) 944-3622 TOLL FREE: (800) 374-1111	WEB: WWW.AMFAM.COM

UTAH *WISCONSIN*	HOME OFFICE 6000 AMERICAN PKY MADISON, WI 53783-0001	PHONE: (608) 249-2111 TOLL FREE: (800) 374-1111	WEB: WWW.AMFAM.COM
WISCONSIN	3232 N BALLARD RD APPLETON, WI 54911 PO BOX 2639 APPLETON, WI 54912-2639	PHONE: (920) 739-5514 FAX: (920) 739-8407 TOLL FREE: (800) 374-1111	WEB: WWW.AMFAM.COM
	440 S EXECUTIVE DR BROOKFIELD, WI 53005-4280 PO BOX 2927 MILWAUKEE, WI 53201-2927	PHONE: (262) 784-9100 FAX: (262) 784-3828 TOLL FREE: (800) 374-1111	WEB: WWW.AMFAM.COM
	5209 RIB MOUNTAIN DR WASAU, WI 54401 PO BOX 530 SCHOFIELD, WI 54476-0530	PHONE: (715) 359-9487 FAX: (715) 359-5852 TOLL FREE: (800) 374-1111	WEB: WWW.AMFAM.COM

AMERICAN FAMILY MUTUAL INSURANCE — *AMERICAN STANDARD INSURANCE*

NEBRASKA	9290 WEST DODGE RD STE 400 OMAHA, NE 68114 PO BOX 247043 OMAHA, NE 68124	PHONE: (402) 330-1010 FAX: (866) 589-7453 TOLL FREE: (800) 374-1111	WEB: WWW.AMFAM.COM
UTAH	6340 S 3000 E STE 400 SALT LAKE CITY, UT 84121 PO BOX 71500 SALT LAKE CITY, UT 84171	PHONE: (801) 944-3620 TOLL FREE: (800) 374-1111	WEB: WWW.AMFAM.COM

AMERICAN FIDELITY ASSURANCE CO

NATIONAL	2000 N CLASSEN BLVD OKLAHOMA CITY, OK 73106 PO BOX 25523 OKLAHOMA CITY, OK 73125-0523	PHONE: (405) 523-2027 TOLL FREE: (800) 654-8489	WEB: WWW.AF-GROUP.COM

AMERICAN FINANCIAL GROUP — *SEE ALSO MID-CONTINENT GROUP*

AMERICAN FOREIGN SERVICE PROTECTIVE ASSOCIATION — *SEE ALSO FOREIGN SERVICE BENEFIT PLAN*

AMERICAN GENERAL FINANCE — *MERIT LIFE*

NATIONAL	601 NW 2ND ST EVANSVILLE, IN 47701 PO BOX 39 EVANSVILLE, IN 47701-0039	PHONE: (812) 424-8031 FAX: (800) 350-9582 TOLL FREE: (800) 325-2147 IN-STATE: (800) 325-2147	

AMERICAN GENERAL LIFE & ACCIDENT INSURANCE CO — *AMERICAN INTERNATIONAL GROUP INC*

NATIONAL	2000 AMERICAN GENERAL WAY BRENTWOOD, TN 37027-4525 PO BOX 1500 NASHVILLE, TN 37202-1500	PHONE: (615) 749-1000 FAX: (615) 749-2932 TOLL FREE: (800) 888-2452	WEB: WWW.AIGAG.COM

AMERICAN GENERAL PROPERTY INSURANCE CO

NATIONAL	AMERICAN GENERAL CTR 346 S NASHVILLE, TN 37202 PO BOX 1995 NASHVILLE, TN 37202	FAX: (615) 749-2620 TOLL FREE: (800) 321-2452	

AMERICAN GROUP ADMINISTRATORS — *AGA*

NATIONAL	101 CONVENTION CTR DR STE 200 LAS VEGAS, NV 89109	PHONE: (702) 893-3050 FAX: (702) 893-8397 TOLL FREE: (800) 842-4742	WEB: WWW.AMGROUPADMIN.COM

NATIONAL — CONTINUED		EMPIRE STATE BLDG 350 FIFTH AVE STE 2819 NEW YORK, NY 10118	PHONE: (212) 404-7800 FAX: (212) 760-1049 OR (212) 404-7805 TOLL FREE: (800) 826-5722	WEB: WWW.AMGROUPADMIN.COM

AMERICAN GUARANTY LIFE INSURANCE COMPANY — *SOUTHWEST*

TEXAS		7001 GRAPEVINE HWY STE 434 FORT WORTH, TX 76180 PO BOX 982005 FORT WORTH, TX 76182	PHONE: (817) 284-4888 FAX: (817) 284-4474 TOLL FREE: (800) 966-7491 IN-STATE: (800) 966-3712	WEB: WWW.TDI.STATE.TX.US

AMERICAN HARDWARE MUTUAL INSURANCE CO — *MOTORISTS INSURANCE GROUP*

ALASKA, ARIZONA, CALIFORNIA, COLORADO, CONNECTICUT, FLORIDA, GEORGIA, IDAHO, ILLINOIS, IOWA, KANSAS, LOUISIANA, MAINE, MASSACHUSETTS, MINNESOTA, MISSOURI, MONTANA, NEBRASKA, NEVADA, NEW HAMPSHIRE, NEW MEXICO, NORTH CAROLINA, NORTH DAKOTA, OHIO, OKLAHOMA, OREGON, RHODE ISLAND, SOUTH CAROLINA, SOUTH DAKOTA, TENNESSEE, TEXAS, UTAH, VERMONT, WASHINGTON, WEST VIRGINIA, WYOMING

		5605 GREEN CIR DR MINNETONKA, MN 55343-9058 PO BOX 435 MINNEAPOLIS, MN 55440-0435	PHONE: (952) 935-1400 FAX: (952) 935-7823 TOLL FREE: (800) 922-6757	E-MAIL: MINNETONKABRANCH@MOTORISTSGROUP.COM WEB: WWW.AMERICANHARDWAREINS.COM

AMERICAN HARDWARE MUTUAL INSURANCE COMPANY — *MOTORIST MUTUAL*

ALABAMA		8320 ALLISON POINT BLVD INDIANAPOLIS, IN 46250 PO BOX 503288 INDIANAPOLIS, IN 46250-8288	PHONE: (800) 876-4634 FAX: (800) 727-4634 TOLL FREE: (800) 876-4634	E-MAIL: INDIANAPOLIS.BRANCH@MOTORISTSGROUP.COM WEB: WWW.MOTORISTSGROUP.COM
ALASKA, ARIZONA, CALIFORNIA, COLORADO, CONNECTICUT, FLORIDA, GEORGIA, IDAHO, ILLINOIS		5605 GREEN CIRCLE DR MINNETONKA, MN 55343-9058 PO BOX 435 MINNEAPOLIS, MN 55440-0435	FAX: (952) 939-4374 OR (952) 939-4577 TOLL FREE: (800) 922-6757	
INDIANA		8320 ALLISON POINT BLVD INDIANAPOLIS, IN 46250 PO BOX 503288 INDIANAPOLIS, IN 46250-8288	PHONE: (800) 876-4634 FAX: (800) 727-4634 TOLL FREE: (800) 876-4634	E-MAIL: INDIANAPOLIS.BRANCH@MOTORISTSGROUP.COM WEB: WWW.MOTORISTSGROUP.COM
IOWA KANSAS		5605 GREEN CIRCLE DR MINNETONKA, MN 55343-9058 PO BOX 435 MINNEAPOLIS, MN 55440-0435	FAX: (952) 939-4374 OR (952) 939-4577 TOLL FREE: (800) 922-6757	
KENTUCKY		471 E BROAD ST COLUMBUS, OH 43215-3861	PHONE: (614) 232-1700 FAX: (614) 232-1730 TOLL FREE: (800) 876-2658	E-MAIL: COLUMBUSBRANCH@MOTORISTGROUP.COM WEB: WWW.MOTORISTSGROUP.COM
LOUISIANA MAINE MASSACHUSETTS		5605 GREEN CIRCLE DR MINNETONKA, MN 55343-9058 PO BOX 435 MINNEAPOLIS, MN 55440-0435	FAX: (952) 939-4374 OR (952) 939-4577 TOLL FREE: (800) 922-6757	
MICHIGAN		8320 ALLISON POINT BLVD INDIANAPOLIS, IN 46250 PO BOX 503288 INDIANAPOLIS, IN 46250-8288	PHONE: (800) 876-4634 FAX: (800) 727-4634 TOLL FREE: (800) 876-4634	E-MAIL: INDIANAPOLIS.BRANCH@MOTORISTSGROUP.COM WEB: WWW.MOTORISTSGROUP.COM

A

MICHIGAN — CONTINUED		471 E BROAD ST COLUMBUS, OH 43215-3861	PHONE: (614) 232-1700 FAX: (614) 232-1730 TOLL FREE: (800) 876-2658	E-MAIL: COLUMBUSBRANCH@MOTORISTGROUP.COM WEB: WWW.MOTORISTSGROUP.COM

MINNESOTA
MISSOURI
MONTANA
NEBRASKA
NEVADA
NEW HAMPSHIRE
NEW MEXICO
NORTH CAROLINA
NORTH DAKOTA
OHIO

		5605 GREEN CIRCLE DR MINNETONKA, MN 55343-9058 PO BOX 435 MINNEAPOLIS, MN 55440-0435	FAX: (952) 939-4374 OR (952) 939-4577 TOLL FREE: (800) 922-6757	
OHIO		471 E BROAD ST COLUMBUS, OH 43215-3861	PHONE: (614) 232-1700 FAX: (614) 232-1730 TOLL FREE: (800) 876-2658	E-MAIL: COLUMBUSBRANCH@MOTORISTGROUP.COM WEB: WWW.MOTORISTSGROUP.COM
OKLAHOMA *OREGON*		5605 GREEN CIRCLE DR MINNETONKA, MN 55343-9058 PO BOX 435 MINNEAPOLIS, MN 55440-0435	FAX: (952) 939-4374 OR (952) 939-4577 TOLL FREE: (800) 922-6757	
PENNSYLVANIA		471 E BROAD ST COLUMBUS, OH 43215-3861	PHONE: (614) 232-1700 FAX: (614) 232-1730 TOLL FREE: (800) 876-2658	E-MAIL: COLUMBUSBRANCH@MOTORISTGROUP.COM WEB: WWW.MOTORISTSGROUP.COM

RHODE ISLAND
SOUTH CAROLINA
SOUTH DAKOTA
TENNESSEE
TEXAS
UTAH
VERMONT
WASHINGTON
WEST VIRGINIA

		5605 GREEN CIRCLE DR MINNETONKA, MN 55343-9058 PO BOX 435 MINNEAPOLIS, MN 55440-0435	FAX: (952) 939-4374 OR (952) 939-4577 TOLL FREE: (800) 922-6757	
WEST VIRGINIA		471 E BROAD ST COLUMBUS, OH 43215-3861	PHONE: (614) 232-1700 FAX: (614) 232-1730 TOLL FREE: (800) 876-2658	E-MAIL: COLUMBUSBRANCH@MOTORISTGROUP.COM WEB: WWW.MOTORISTSGROUP.COM
WISCONSIN		5605 GREEN CIRCLE DR MINNETONKA, MN 55343-9058 PO BOX 435 MINNEAPOLIS, MN 55440-0435	FAX: (952) 939-4374 OR (952) 939-4577 TOLL FREE: (800) 922-6757	
WYOMING		5605 GREEN CIRCLE DR MINNETONKA, MN 55343-9058 PO BOX 435 MINNEAPOLIS, MN 55440-0435	FAX: (952) 939-4374 OR (952) 939-4577 TOLL FREE: (800) 922-6757	

AMERICAN HOME SECURITY LIFE — *SEE ALSO SECURITY NATIONAL LIFE INSURANCE CO*

AMERICAN INCOME LIFE INSURANCE CO

NATIONAL		1200 WOODED ACRES DR WACO, TX 76710-4436 PO BOX 2608 WACO, TX 76797-2608	PHONE: (254) 761-6400 FAX: (254) 741-5705 TOLL FREE: (800) 433-3405	E-MAIL: CONTACTUS@AILINS.COM WEB: WWW.AILINS.COM

AMERICAN INSURANCE ADMINISTRATORS

CALIFORNIA		3415 S SEPULVEDA BLVD STE 200 LOS ANGELES, CA 90034-6035	PHONE: (310) 397-7220 FAX: (310) 398-6105 IN-STATE: (800) 654-7942	

AMERICAN INSURANCE INDEMNITY CORP — *SEE ALSO FIREMAN'S FUND INSURANCE CO*

A

AMERICAN LIFECARE — *PRIVATE HEALTHCARE SYSTEMS*

ALABAMA
ARKANSAS
LOUISIANA
MISSISSIPPI
TENNESSEE

1100 POYDRAS ST STE 2600
NEW ORLEANS, LA 70163

PHONE: (800) 749-2298
FAX: (504) 681-3609
TOLL FREE: (800) 749-2298

E-MAIL: INFO@AMERICANLIFECARE.COM
WEB: WWW.AMERICANLIFECARE.COM

AMERICAN MAYFLOWER — *GE FINANCIAL SERVICE*

CONNECTICUT
FLORIDA
MARYLAND
NEW JERSEY
NEW YORK
RHODE ISLAND
VIRGINIA

622 THIRD AVE 33RD FL
NEW YORK, NY 10017

PHONE: (212) 672-4200
FAX: (212) 672-4299
TOLL FREE: (888) 265-5433

E-MAIL: AML1@GECAPITAL.COM
WEB: WWW.GEFINANCIALSERVICE.COM

AMERICAN MEDICAL & LIFE INSURANCE CO — *AMERICAN DENTAL CENTERS*

NEW YORK

35 N BROADWAY
HICKSVILLE, NY 11801-4236
PO BOX 546
HICKSVILLE, NY 11802-0546

PHONE: (516) 822-8700
FAX: (516) 931-1010 OR
(516) 822-5994
TOLL FREE: (800) 822-0004

WEB: WWW.AMLICO.COM

AMERICAN MEDICAL SECURITY

ALABAMA
ARIZONA
ARKANSAS
CALIFORNIA
COLORADO
FLORIDA
GEORGIA
ILLINOIS
INDIANA
IOWA
KANSAS
LOUISIANA
MARYLAND
MICHIGAN
MISSISSIPPI
MISSOURI
NEBRASKA
NEVADA
NEW MEXICO
NORTH CAROLINA
NORTH DAKOTA
OHIO
OKLAHOMA
PENNSYLVANIA
SOUTH CAROLINA
SOUTH DAKOTA
TENNESSEE
TEXAS
UTAH
VIRGINIA
WASHINGTON
WEST VIRGINIA
WISCONSIN

3100 AMS BLVD
GREEN BAY, WI 54313-9700
PO BOX 19032
GREEN BAY, WI 54307-9032

PHONE: (920) 661-1111
FAX: (920) 661-6161
TOLL FREE: (800) 232-5432

WEB: WWW.EAMS.COM

AMERICAN MINING INSURANCE CO, INC — *CGH INSURANCE GROUP*

ALABAMA
KENTUCKY
PENNSYLVANIA
TENNESSEE
VIRGINIA

3490 INDEPENDENCE DR
BIRMINGHAM, AL 35209-5604
PO BOX 660847
BIRMINGHAM, AL 35266-0988

PHONE: (205) 870-3535
FAX: (205) 870-3245
TOLL FREE: (800) 448-5621

WEB: WWW.CGHINSURANCE.COM

AMERICAN MODERN INSURANCE GROUP — *SEE ALSO MIDLAND CO*

AMERICAN NATIONAL — *SEE ALSO FARM FAMILY CASUALTY*

AMERICAN NATIONAL INSURANCE CO

NATIONAL

ONE MOODY PLZ
GALVESTON, TX 77550-7960

PHONE: (409) 763-4661
TOLL FREE: (800) 899-6806

WEB: WWW.ANICO.COM

A

AMERICAN NATIONAL PROPERTY & CASUALTY CO

NATIONAL

1949 E SUNSHINE ST
SPRINGFIELD, MO 65899-0001

PHONE: (417) 887-0220
FAX: (417) 887-1801
TOLL FREE: (800) 333-2860

WEB: WWW.ANPAC.COM

AMERICAN POLICY HOLDERS LIQUIDATING TRUST — *AIM MUTUAL INSURANCE COMPANIES*

MASSACHUSETTS
NEW HAMPSHIRE

54 3RD AVE
BURLINGTON, MA 01803
PO BOX 4070
BURLINGTON, MA 01803-0970

PHONE: (800) 876-2765
FAX: (781) 270-5599
TOLL FREE: (800) 225-3646
IN-STATE: (800) 225-3646

WEB: WWW.AIMMUTUAL.COM

AMERICAN PROGRESSIVE LIFE & HEALTH INSURANCE CO

CONNECTICUT
FLORIDA
NEW YORK
PENNSYLVANIA
SOUTH CAROLINA
VERMONT

SIX INTERNATIONAL DR
RYE BROOK, NY 10573-1068

PHONE: (914) 934-8300
FAX: (914) 934-9123
TOLL FREE: (800) 332-3377

WEB: WWW.UAFC.COM

AMERICAN PUBLIC LIFE INSURANCE CO

ALABAMA
ARIZONA
ARKANSAS
COLORADO
FLORIDA
GEORGIA
ILLINOIS
INDIANA
KANSAS
KENTUCKY
LOUISIANA
MISSISSIPPI
MISSOURI
NEVADA
NEW MEXICO
NORTH CAROLINA
OHIO
OKLAHOMA
OREGON
TENNESSEE
TEXAS
UTAH
VIRGINIA
WASHINGTON

2305 LAKELAND DR
FLOWOOD, MS 39232-9549
PO BOX 925
JACKSON, MS 39205-0925

PHONE: (601) 936-6600
FAX: (601) 939-0655
TOLL FREE: (800) 256-8606

WEB: WWW.AMPUBLIC.COM

AMERICAN RE-INSURANCE

NATIONAL

555 COLLEGE RD E
PRINCETON, NJ 08540-6616

PHONE: (609) 243-4200
TOLL FREE: (800) 255-5657

E-MAIL: INFO@AMRE.COM
WEB: WWW.AMRE.COM

AMERICAN REPUBLIC INSURANCE CO

NATIONAL

NATIONAL HEADQUARTERS
601 6TH AVE
DES MOINES, IA 50309-1605
PO BOX 1
DES MOINES, IA 50301

PHONE: (515) 245-2000
FAX: (515) 245-4282
TOLL FREE: (800) 247-2190
IN-STATE: (515) 247-2435

WEB: WWW.AMERICANREPUBLIC.COM

AMERICAN RESOURCES INSURANCE CO

ALABAMA
GEORGIA
INDIANA
KENTUCKY
MISSISSIPPI
SOUTH CAROLINA
TENNESSEE
VIRGINIA

1111 HILLCREST RD
MOBILE, AL 36695-3952
PO BOX 91149
MOBILE, AL 36691-1149

PHONE: (251) 639-0985
FAX: (251) 633-2388
TOLL FREE: (800) 227-6045

WEB: WWW.ARIC.COM

AMERICAN SENTINEL INSURANCE CO

PENNSYLVANIA

2407 PARK DR
HARRISBURG, PA 17110-3343
PO BOX 61140
HARRISBURG, PA 17106-1140

PHONE: (717) 540-0600
FAX: (717) 657-9499
TOLL FREE: (800) 692-7338

WEB: WWW.AMERICANSENTINEL.COM

AMERICAN SOUTHERN INSURANCE CO

NATIONAL

3715 N SIDE PKY NW BLDG 400 STE 800
ATLANTA, GA 30327-2806
PO BOX 723030
ATLANTA, GA 31139-0030

PHONE: (404) 266-9599
FAX: (404) 266-8327
TOLL FREE: (800) 241-1172

E-MAIL: INFO@AMSOU.COM
WEB: WWW.AMSOU.COM

AMERICAN SPECIALTY HEALTH INCORPORATED

NATIONAL

777 FRONT ST
SAN DIEGO, CA 92101-6002

PHONE: (619) 578-2000
FAX: (619) 237-3832
TOLL FREE: (800) 848-3555

WEB: WWW.ASHCOMPANIES.COM

AMERICAN STANDARD INSURANCE — *SEE ALSO AMERICAN FAMILY MUTUAL INSURANCE*

AMERICAN TRUST ADMINISTRATORS, INC

NATIONAL

7101 COLLEGE BLVD STE 1200
OVERLAND PARK, KS 66210
PO BOX 87
SHAWNEE MISSION, KS 66201-0087

PHONE: (913) 451-4900
FAX: (913) 451-0598
TOLL FREE: (800) 843-4121

WEB: WWW.ATAAMERICA.COM

AMERICAN UNDERWRITERS LIFE INSURANCE CO

NATIONAL

1035 S 183RD ST W
GODDARD, KS 67052
PO BOX 9510
WICHITA, KS 67277-0510

PHONE: (316) 794-2200
FAX: (316) 794-8470

WEB: WWW.IAI-ONLINE.COM

AMERICAN UNITED LIFE INSURANCE COMPANY

NATIONAL

ONE AMERICAN SQ
INDIANAPOLIS, IN 46208-0020
PO BOX 368
INDIANAPOLIS, IN 46206-0368

PHONE: (317) 285-2300
FAX: (317) 285-2594
TOLL FREE: (800) 428-2316

WEB: WWW.AUL.COM

ALABAMA
ARKANSAS
COLORADO
DELAWARE
FLORIDA
GEORGIA
ILLINOIS
INDIANA
KENTUCKY
LOUISIANA
MARYLAND
MICHIGAN
MISSISSIPPI
MISSOURI
NORTH CAROLINA
OHIO
OKLAHOMA
PENNSYLVANIA
SOUTH CAROLINA
TENNESSEE
TEXAS
VIRGINIA
WEST VIRGINIA
WISCONSIN

2960 RIVERSIDE DR
MACON, GA 31204
PO BOX 6097
MACON, GA 31208-6097

PHONE: (478) 477-0400
FAX: (478) 471-0178
TOLL FREE: (800) 849-4265

WEB: WWW.CNLF.COM

AMERICAN WHOLE HEALTH NETWORKS, INC

NATIONAL

46040 CENTER OAK PLZ STE 130
STERLING, VA 20166

PHONE: (703) 547-5100
FAX: (703) 430-9638

E-MAIL: CONTACTUSI@AWHINC.COM
WEB: WWW.ALIGNIS.COM OR WWW.AMERICANWHOLEHEALTH COM

AMERICAN YOUTH STUDENTS & SPORTS INSURANCE

NATIONAL

184 SHUMN BLVD STE 390
NAPERVILLE, IL 60563

PHONE: (630) 778-1900
FAX: (630) 778-1959 OR (630) 778-0523
TOLL FREE: (800) 338-1938

WEB: WWW.STUDENTPLANS.NET

AMERICAS CHOICE HEALTHPLANS — *SEE ALSO ACH*

AMERICAS INSURANCE CO

NATIONAL

400 POYDRAS ST STE 1990
NEW ORLEANS, LA 70130

PHONE: (504) 528-9555
FAX: (504) 523-0084

WEB: WWW.OMNIWHITTINGTON.COM

A

AMERICHOICE CLAIMS CENTER

ARIZONA	7600 N 16TH ST STE 230 PHOENIX, AZ 85020 PO BOX 41566 PHOENIX, AZ 85020	TOLL FREE: (800) 423-4421	WEB: WWW.AMERICHOICE.COM
FLORIDA *ILLINOIS* *MARYLAND* *NEBRASKA*	2725 MALL DR EAU CLAIRE, WI 54701	PHONE: (715) 858-2200 FAX: (715) 858-5501	WEB: WWW.UNITEDHEALTHGROUP.COM
NEW JERSEY	7600 N 16TH ST STE 230 PHOENIX, AZ 85020 PO BOX 41566 PHOENIX, AZ 85020	TOLL FREE: (800) 423-4421	WEB: WWW.AMERICHOICE.COM
NEW YORK	2725 MALL DR EAU CLAIRE, WI 54701	PHONE: (715) 858-2200 FAX: (715) 858-5501	WEB: WWW.UNITEDHEALTHGROUP.COM
NEW YORK *PENNSYLVANIA*	7600 N 16TH ST STE 230 PHOENIX, AZ 85020 PO BOX 41566 PHOENIX, AZ 85020	TOLL FREE: (800) 423-4421	WEB: WWW.AMERICHOICE.COM
RHODE ISLAND *WISCONSIN*	2725 MALL DR EAU CLAIRE, WI 54701	PHONE: (715) 858-2200 FAX: (715) 858-5501	WEB: WWW.UNITEDHEALTHGROUP.COM

AMERICO FINANCIAL LIFE & ANNUITY INSURANCE CO

NATIONAL	301 W 11TH ST KANSAS CITY, MO 64105 PO BOX 410288 KANSAS CITY, MO 64141-0288	PHONE: (816) 391-2000 TOLL FREE: (800) 366-6565 IN-STATE: (800) 347-2825	WEB: WWW.AMERICO.COM

ADDITIONAL COMMENTS: NATIONAL EXCEPT NEW YORK

AMERIGROUP CORPORATION

NATIONAL	CHICAGO HEALTH PLAN 211 W WACKER DR STE 1350 CHICAGO, IL 60606	PHONE: (312) 214-0400 FAX: (312) 214-0424	WEB: WWW.AMERIGROUPCORP.COM
	NEW JERSEY HEALTH PLAN 399 THORNALL ST 9TH FL EDISON, NJ 08837	PHONE: (732) 452-6000 FAX: (732) 906-5663	WEB: WWW.AMERIGROUPCORP.COM
	4425 CORPORATION LN VIRGINIA BEACH, VA 23462	PHONE: (757) 490-6900 FAX: (757) 226-7472	WEB: WWW.AMERIGROUPCORP.COM
	DC HEALTH PLAN 750 FIRST ST NE STE 1120 WASHINGTON, DC 20002	PHONE: (202) 218-4900 FAX: (202) 682-2538 TOLL FREE: (888) 576-4522	WEB: WWW.AMERIGROUPCORP.COM
	MARYLAND HEALTH PLAN 857 ELKRIDGE LANDING RD STE 300 LINTHICUM, MD 21090	PHONE: (410) 859-5800 FAX: (410) 981-4070	WEB: WWW.AMERIGROUPCORP.COM

AMERIHEALTH ADMINISTRATORS

PENNSYLVANIA	720 BLAIR MILL RD HORSHAM, PA 19044-2269	PHONE: (215) 657-8900 FAX: (215) 784-0296 TOLL FREE: (800) 492-2385	WEB: WWW.AMERIHEALTHPA.COM

AMERISURE COMPANIES

ALABAMA	1000 URBAN CTR DR STE 125 BIRMINGHAM, AL 35242-0000	PHONE: (205) 970-0799 FAX: (205) 969-3201 TOLL FREE: (800) 421-7656	WEB: WWW.AMERISURE.COM
ALABAMA *FLORIDA*	26777 HALSTED RD FARMINGTON HILLS, MI 48331-3586 PO BOX 2060 FARMINGTON HILLS, MI 48333-2060	PHONE: (248) 615-9000 FAX: (248) 615-8372 TOLL FREE: (800) 257-1900	WEB: WWW.AMERISURE.COM
FLORIDA	140 FOUNTAIN PKY STE 200 ST PETERSBURG, FL 33716-1285 PO BOX 10790 ST PETERSBURG, FL 33733-0790	PHONE: (727) 561-7100 FAX: (727) 561-7153 TOLL FREE: (800) 282-2743	WEB: WWW.AMERISURE.COM
GEORGIA *ILLINOIS*	26777 HALSTED RD FARMINGTON HILLS, MI 48331-3586 PO BOX 2060 FARMINGTON HILLS, MI 48333-2060	PHONE: (248) 615-9000 FAX: (248) 615-8372 TOLL FREE: (800) 257-1900	WEB: WWW.AMERISURE.COM
INDIANA	26777 HALSTED RD FARMINGTON HILLS, MI 48331-3586 PO BOX 2060 FARMINGTON HILLS, MI 48333-2060	PHONE: (248) 615-9000 FAX: (248) 615-8372 TOLL FREE: (800) 257-1900	WEB: WWW.AMERISURE.COM
INDIANA *KENTUCKY*	8910 PURDUE RD STE 700 INDIANAPOLIS, IN 46268 PO BOX 68876 INDIANAPOLIS, IN 46268-0876	PHONE: (317) 872-8694 FAX: (800) 528-9187 TOLL FREE: (800) 752-5929	WEB: WWW.AMERISURE.COM
KENTUCKY *MICHIGAN* *MISSISSIPPI* *MISSOURI* *NORTH CAROLINA*	26777 HALSTED RD FARMINGTON HILLS, MI 48331-3586 PO BOX 2060 FARMINGTON HILLS, MI 48333-2060	PHONE: (248) 615-9000 FAX: (248) 615-8372 TOLL FREE: (800) 257-1900	WEB: WWW.AMERISURE.COM
NORTH CAROLINA	10715 DAVID TAYLOR DR STE 500 CHARLOTTE, NC 28262-1305 PO BOX 560769 CHARLOTTE, NC 28256	PHONE: (704) 510-1135 FAX: (704) 510-8327 TOLL FREE: (800) 532-6230	WEB: WWW.AMERISURE.COM
SOUTH CAROLINA *TENNESSEE* *TEXAS*	26777 HALSTED RD FARMINGTON HILLS, MI 48331-3586 PO BOX 2060 FARMINGTON HILLS, MI 48333-2060	PHONE: (248) 615-9000 FAX: (248) 615-8372 TOLL FREE: (800) 257-1900	WEB: WWW.AMERISURE.COM
TEXAS	5221 N OCONNOR BLVD STE 400 IRVING, TX 75039 PO BOX 569680 DALLAS, TX 75356-9680	PHONE: (214) 631-6370 FAX: (214) 634-9139 TOLL FREE: (800) 441-0293	WEB: WWW.AMERISURE.COM

AMERISURE INSURANCE COMPANY

ILLINOIS *KANSAS* *MISSOURI*	701 EMERSON RD STE 320 ST LOUIS, MO 63141-6754 PO BOX 419058 ST LOUIS, MO 63141-9058	PHONE: (314) 994-3400 FAX: (314) 692-1730 TOLL FREE: (800) 325-1721	WEB: WWW.AMERISURE.COM

AMERITAS ACACIA COMPANIES — *AMERITAS LIFE INSURANCE CORP*

NATIONAL	5900 O ST LINCOLN, NE 68510 PO BOX 81889 LINCOLN, NE 68501-1889	PHONE: (402) 467-1122 TOLL FREE: (800) 745-6665	WEB: WWW.AMERITASACACIA.COM

AMICA MUTUAL INSURANCE

NATIONAL	100 AMICA WAY LINCOLN, RI 02865-1156 PO BOX 6008 PROVIDENCE, RI 02940-9986	PHONE: (401) 334-6000 FAX: (401) 334-0615 TOLL FREE: (800) 992-6422	WEB: WWW.AMICA.COM
COLORADO *NEBRASKA* *UTAH* *WYOMING*	3033 S PARKER RD STE 900 AURORA, CO 80014	TOLL FREE: (800) 572-6422	

AMTRUST SOUTH

GEORGIA	11330 LAKE FIELD DR BLDG II DULUTH, GA 30041 PO BOX 740042 ATLANTA, GA 30074-0042	PHONE: (678) 258-8000 FAX: (678) 258-8399	WEB: WWW.THECOVENANTGROUP.NET

ANTHEM BLUE CROSS AND BLUE SHIELD — *ANTHEM DENTAL*

COLORADO	13550 TRITON PK BLVD LOUISVILLE, KY 40223-3803	PHONE: (800) 880-2583 FAX: (513) 872-8174 TOLL FREE: (800) 442-1832 IN-STATE: (800) 205-5870	WEB: WWW.ANTHEM.COM OR WWW.WELLPOINT.COM
	PO BOX 5747 DENVER, CO 80217-5747	PHONE: (702) 228-2583 FAX: (303) 861-9019	WEB: WWW.ANTHEM.COM
	700 BROADWAY DENVER, CO 80217 PO BOX 5747 DENVER, CO 80217	PHONE: (303) 831-2098 FAX: (303) 863-1721 TOLL FREE: (800) 922-4770	WEB: WWW.ANTHEM.COM
CONNECTICUT	370 BASSETT RD NORTH HAVEN, CT 06473-4202 OPERATIONS CENTER AND EAST HEADQUARTERS PO BOX 533 NORTH HAVEN, CT 06473	PHONE: (203) 239-4911 FAX: (203) 985-7834 TOLL FREE: (800) 922-0948 IN-STATE: (800) 922-1742	WEB: WWW.ANTHEM.COM
	TWO GANNETT DR SOUTH PORTLAND, ME 04106-6913	PHONE: (207) 822-7000 FAX: (207) 822-7014 TOLL FREE: (800) 482-0966 IN-STATE: (800) 822-6011	WEB: WWW.ANTHEM.COM
INDIANA	HEADQUARTERS 120 MONUMENT CIR INDIANAPOLIS, IN 46204	PHONE: (317) 488-6000	WEB: WWW.ANTHEM.COM
	13550 TRITON PK BLVD LOUISVILLE, KY 40223-3803	PHONE: (800) 880-2583 FAX: (513) 872-8174 TOLL FREE: (800) 442-1832 IN-STATE: (800) 205-5870	WEB: WWW.ANTHEM.COM OR WWW.WELLPOINT.COM

INDIANA — CONTINUED	4361 IRWIN SIMPSON MASON, OH 45040	PHONE: (513) 872-8100 TOLL FREE: (800) 442-1832	WEB: WWW.ANTHEM.COM
	6740 N HIGH ST WORTHINGTON, OH 43085-7500	PHONE: (614) 438-3500 TOLL FREE: (800) 551-7265	WEB: WWW.ANTHEM.COM
	220 VIRGINIA AVE INDIANAPOLIS, IN 46204-3632	PHONE: (317) 488-6000 TOLL FREE: (800) 331-1476	WEB: WWW.ANTHEM.COM
KENTUCKY	370 BASSETT RD NORTH HAVEN, CT 06473-4202 OPERATIONS CENTER AND EAST HEADQUARTERS PO BOX 533 NORTH HAVEN, CT 06473	PHONE: (203) 239-4911 FAX: (203) 985-7834 TOLL FREE: (800) 922-0948 IN-STATE: (800) 922-1742	WEB: WWW.ANTHEM.COM
	13550 TRITON PK BLVD LOUISVILLE, KY 40223-3803	PHONE: (800) 880-2583 FAX: (513) 872-8174 TOLL FREE: (800) 442-1832 IN-STATE: (800) 205-5870	WEB: WWW.ANTHEM.COM OR WWW.WELLPOINT.COM
	4361 IRWIN SIMPSON MASON, OH 45040	PHONE: (513) 872-8100 TOLL FREE: (800) 442-1832	WEB: WWW.ANTHEM.COM
	6740 N HIGH ST WORTHINGTON, OH 43085-7500	PHONE: (614) 438-3500 TOLL FREE: (800) 551-7265	WEB: WWW.ANTHEM.COM
KENTUCKY MAINE	TWO GANNETT DR SOUTH PORTLAND, ME 04106-6913	PHONE: (207) 822-7000 FAX: (207) 822-7014 TOLL FREE: (800) 482-0966 IN-STATE: (800) 822-6011	WEB: WWW.ANTHEM.COM
MAINE NEVADA	13550 TRITON PK BLVD LOUISVILLE, KY 40223-3803	PHONE: (800) 880-2583 FAX: (513) 872-8174 TOLL FREE: (800) 442-1832 IN-STATE: (800) 205-5870	WEB: WWW.ANTHEM.COM OR WWW.WELLPOINT.COM
NEVADA	5250 S VIRGINIA ST RENO, NV 89502	PHONE: (775) 448-4000	WEB: WWW.ANTHEM.COM
	PO BOX 5747 DENVER, CO 80217-5747	PHONE: (702) 228-2583 FAX: (303) 861-9019	WEB: WWW.ANTHEM.COM
	700 BROADWAY DENVER, CO 80217 PO BOX 5747 DENVER, CO 80217	PHONE: (303) 831-2098 FAX: (303) 863-1721 TOLL FREE: (800) 922-4770	WEB: WWW.ANTHEM.COM
NEW HAMPSHIRE	TWO GANNETT DR SOUTH PORTLAND, ME 04106-6913	PHONE: (207) 822-7000 FAX: (207) 822-7014 TOLL FREE: (800) 482-0966 IN-STATE: (800) 822-6011	WEB: WWW.ANTHEM.COM

NEW HAMPSHIRE — CONTINUED	370 BASSETT RD NORTH HAVEN, CT 06473-4202 OPERATIONS CENTER AND EAST HEADQUARTERS PO BOX 533 NORTH HAVEN, CT 06473	PHONE: (203) 239-4911 FAX: (203) 985-7834 TOLL FREE: (800) 922-0948 IN-STATE: (800) 922-1742	WEB: WWW.ANTHEM.COM
	3000 GOFFS FALLS RD MANCHESTER, NH 03111-0001	PHONE: (603) 695-7000 FAX: (603) 695-7067 TOLL FREE: (800) 225-2666	WEB: WWW.ANTHEM.COM
NEW HAMPSHIRE OHIO	13550 TRITON PK BLVD LOUISVILLE, KY 40223-3803	PHONE: (800) 880-2583 FAX: (513) 872-8174 TOLL FREE: (800) 442-1832 IN-STATE: (800) 205-5870	WEB: WWW.ANTHEM.COM OR WWW.WELLPOINT.COM
OHIO	8333 ROCKSIDE RD STE 2000 CLEVELAND, OH 44125	PHONE: (614) 438-3500 FAX: (614) 433-8880 TOLL FREE: (800) 442-1832	WEB: WWW.ANTHEM.COM
	4361 IRWIN SIMPSON MASON, OH 45040	PHONE: (513) 872-8100 TOLL FREE: (800) 442-1832	WEB: WWW.ANTHEM.COM
	6740 N HIGH ST WORTHINGTON, OH 43085-7500	PHONE: (614) 438-3500 TOLL FREE: (800) 551-7265	WEB: WWW.ANTHEM.COM
VIRGINIA	13550 TRITON PK BLVD LOUISVILLE, KY 40223-3803	PHONE: (800) 880-2583 FAX: (513) 872-8174 TOLL FREE: (800) 442-1832 IN-STATE: (800) 205-5870	WEB: WWW.ANTHEM.COM OR WWW.WELLPOINT.COM
	2015 STAPLES MAIL RD RICHMOND, VA 23230-2521 PO BOX 27401 RICHMOND, VA 23279-7401	PHONE: (804) 354-7000 FAX: (804) 354-7600 TOLL FREE: (800) 451-1527	WEB: WWW.ANTHEM.COM

ANTHEM DENTAL — *SEE ALSO ANTHEM BLUE CROSS AND BLUE SHIELD*

ARAG CROUP

NATIONAL	400 LOCUST ST STE 480 DES MOINES, IA 50309 PO BOX 9171 DES MOINES, IA 50309-9171	PHONE: (515) 246-1200 FAX: (515) 246-8710 TOLL FREE: (800) 888-4184	E-MAIL: SERVICE@ARAGGROUP.COM WEB: WWW.ARAGGROUP.COM

ARCTIC ADJUSTERS, INC

ALASKA	3701 E TUDOR RD STE 206 ANCHORAGE, AK 99507-1259	PHONE: (907) 272-2595 FAX: (907) 277-2032	E-MAIL: INFO@ARCTICADJUSTERS.COM WEB: WWW.ARCTICADJUSTERS.COM

ARGONAUT CENTRAL INSURANCE COMPANY

ILLINOIS	GREAT CENTRAL REGION 3625 N SHERIDAN RD PEORIA, IL 61633-0002 PO BOX 807 PEORIA, IL 61652-0807	PHONE: (309) 688-8571 FAX: (309) 688-2738 TOLL FREE: (877) 769-5953	WEB: WWW.ARGONAUTCENTRAL.COM

ARGONAUT INSURANCE COMPANY

NATIONAL	WEST REGION PO BOX 335460 NORTH LAS VEGAS, NV 89033-5460	FAX: (702) 638-8281 TOLL FREE: (866) 766-3706	WEB: WWW.ARGONAUTINSURANCE.COM
	HOME OFFICE 250 MIDDLEFIELD RD MENLO PARK, CA 94025-3500	PHONE: (650) 326-0900 FAX: (650) 858-6631 TOLL FREE: (800) 222-7811	WEB: WWW.ARGONAUTGROUP.COM
ARIZONA	WEST REGION / WORKERS COMP OFFICE 7272 E INDIAN SCHOOL RD STE 500 SCOTTSDALE, AZ 85251	FAX: (480) 889-1881 TOLL FREE: (888) 908-3422	WEB: WWW.ARGONAUTGROUP.COM
	WEST REGION / LIABILITY OFFICE THREE HUTTON CENTRE STE 870 SANTA ANA, CA 92707	PHONE: (714) 708-4720 FAX: (714) 708-2108	WEB: WWW.ARGONAUTGROUP.COM
CALIFORNIA	WEST REGION / WORKERS COMP OFFICE 7272 E INDIAN SCHOOL RD STE 500 SCOTTSDALE, AZ 85251	FAX: (480) 889-1881 TOLL FREE: (888) 908-3422	WEB: WWW.ARGONAUTGROUP.COM
	WEST REGION 5250 N PALM AVE STE 210 FRESNO, CA 93704 PO BOX 5062 FRESNO, CA 93755	PHONE: (559) 447-7100 FAX: (559) 447-7180	WEB: WWW.ARGONAUTINSURANCE.COM
	WEST REGION / LIABILITY OFFICE THREE HUTTON CENTRE STE 870 SANTA ANA, CA 92707	PHONE: (714) 708-4720 FAX: (714) 708-2108	WEB: WWW.ARGONAUTGROUP.COM
COLORADO	WEST REGION / WORKERS COMP OFFICE 7272 E INDIAN SCHOOL RD STE 500 SCOTTSDALE, AZ 85251	FAX: (480) 889-1881 TOLL FREE: (888) 908-3422	WEB: WWW.ARGONAUTGROUP.COM
	WEST REGION / LIABILITY OFFICE THREE HUTTON CENTRE STE 870 SANTA ANA, CA 92707	PHONE: (714) 708-4720 FAX: (714) 708-2108	WEB: WWW.ARGONAUTGROUP.COM
CONNECTICUT	FINANCIAL CENTER EXECUTIVE OFFICE 695 EAST MAIN ST STAMFORD, CT 06901	PHONE: (203) 406-8787 FAX: (203) 359-4315 OR (203) 377-2044	WEB: WWW.ARGONAUTINSURANCE.COM
	EAST REGION ONE INTERNATIONAL PLZ STE 550 PHILADELPHIA, PA 19113-1546	PHONE: (610) 595-7700 FAX: (610) 595-7777 TOLL FREE: (800) 776-7668	WEB: WWW.ARGONAUTINSURANCE.COM
DELAWARE	EAST REGION ONE INTERNATIONAL PLZ STE 550 PHILADELPHIA, PA 19113-1546	PHONE: (610) 595-7700 FAX: (610) 595-7777 TOLL FREE: (800) 776-7668	WEB: WWW.ARGONAUTINSURANCE.COM
GEORGIA	ATLANTA OFFICE EAST REGION 1050 CROWN POINTE PKY STE 710 ATLANTA, GA 30338-7702 PO BOX 720293 ATLANTA, GA 30358	PHONE: (770) 668-7300 FAX: (770) 395-6426 TOLL FREE: (800) 637-5817	WEB: WWW.ARGONAUTINSURANCE.COM
IDAHO	WEST REGION / WORKERS COMP OFFICE 7272 E INDIAN SCHOOL RD STE 500 SCOTTSDALE, AZ 85251	FAX: (480) 889-1881 TOLL FREE: (888) 908-3422	WEB: WWW.ARGONAUTGROUP.COM
	WEST REGION / LIABILITY OFFICE THREE HUTTON CENTRE STE 870 SANTA ANA, CA 92707	PHONE: (714) 708-4720 FAX: (714) 708-2108	WEB: WWW.ARGONAUTGROUP.COM

ILLINOIS KANSAS	225 W WASHINGTON STE 600 CHICAGO, IL 60606	PHONE: (312) 201-7600 FAX: (312) 223-0567	WEB: WWW.ARGONAUTGROUP.COM
MAINE MARYLAND MASSACHUSETTS	EAST REGION ONE INTERNATIONAL PLZ STE 550 PHILADELPHIA, PA 19113-1546	PHONE: (610) 595-7700 FAX: (610) 595-7777 TOLL FREE: (800) 776-7668	WEB: WWW.ARGONAUTINSURANCE.COM
MICHIGAN MINNESOTA MISSOURI	225 W WASHINGTON STE 600 CHICAGO, IL 60606	PHONE: (312) 201-7600 FAX: (312) 223-0567	WEB: WWW.ARGONAUTGROUP.COM
MONTANA	WEST REGION / WORKERS COMP OFFICE 7272 E INDIAN SCHOOL RD STE 500 SCOTTSDALE, AZ 85251	FAX: (480) 889-1881 TOLL FREE: (888) 908-3422	WEB: WWW.ARGONAUTGROUP.COM
	WEST REGION / LIABILITY OFFICE THREE HUTTON CENTRE STE 870 SANTA ANA, CA 92707	PHONE: (714) 708-4720 FAX: (714) 708-2108	WEB: WWW.ARGONAUTGROUP.COM
NEBRASKA	225 W WASHINGTON STE 600 CHICAGO, IL 60606	PHONE: (312) 201-7600 FAX: (312) 223-0567	WEB: WWW.ARGONAUTGROUP.COM
NEVADA	WEST REGION / WORKERS COMP OFFICE 7272 E INDIAN SCHOOL RD STE 500 SCOTTSDALE, AZ 85251	FAX: (480) 889-1881 TOLL FREE: (888) 908-3422	WEB: WWW.ARGONAUTGROUP.COM
	WEST REGION / LIABILITY OFFICE THREE HUTTON CENTRE STE 870 SANTA ANA, CA 92707	PHONE: (714) 708-4720 FAX: (714) 708-2108	WEB: WWW.ARGONAUTGROUP.COM
NEW HAMPSHIRE NEW JERSEY	EAST REGION ONE INTERNATIONAL PLZ STE 550 PHILADELPHIA, PA 19113-1546	PHONE: (610) 595-7700 FAX: (610) 595-7777 TOLL FREE: (800) 776-7668	WEB: WWW.ARGONAUTINSURANCE.COM
NEW MEXICO	WEST REGION / WORKERS COMP OFFICE 7272 E INDIAN SCHOOL RD STE 500 SCOTTSDALE, AZ 85251	FAX: (480) 889-1881 TOLL FREE: (888) 908-3422	WEB: WWW.ARGONAUTGROUP.COM
	WEST REGION / LIABILITY OFFICE THREE HUTTON CENTRE STE 870 SANTA ANA, CA 92707	PHONE: (714) 708-4720 FAX: (714) 708-2108	WEB: WWW.ARGONAUTGROUP.COM
NEW YORK	NEW YORK REGION 500 FIFTH AVE STE 2410 NEW YORK, NY 10110	PHONE: (212) 852-4803 FAX: (212) 852-9021	WEB: WWW.ARGONAUTGROUP.COM
	EAST REGION ONE INTERNATIONAL PLZ STE 550 PHILADELPHIA, PA 19113-1546	PHONE: (610) 595-7700 FAX: (610) 595-7777 TOLL FREE: (800) 776-7668	WEB: WWW.ARGONAUTINSURANCE.COM
OREGON	WEST REGION / WORKERS COMP OFFICE 7272 E INDIAN SCHOOL RD STE 500 SCOTTSDALE, AZ 85251	FAX: (480) 889-1881 TOLL FREE: (888) 908-3422	WEB: WWW.ARGONAUTGROUP.COM
	WEST REGION / LIABILITY OFFICE THREE HUTTON CENTRE STE 870 SANTA ANA, CA 92707	PHONE: (714) 708-4720 FAX: (714) 708-2108	WEB: WWW.ARGONAUTGROUP.COM
	PO BOX 22129 PORTLAND, OR 97269	PHONE: (503) 244-0355 FAX: (503) 833-1640 TOLL FREE: (888) 875-7300	WEB: WWW.ARGONAUTINSURANCE.COM
PENNSYLVANIA	EAST REGION ONE INTERNATIONAL PLZ STE 550 PHILADELPHIA, PA 19113-1546	PHONE: (610) 595-7700 FAX: (610) 595-7777 TOLL FREE: (800) 776-7668	WEB: WWW.ARGONAUTINSURANCE.COM

RHODE ISLAND	EAST REGION ONE INTERNATIONAL PLZ STE 550 PHILADELPHIA, PA 19113-1546	PHONE: (610) 595-7700 FAX: (610) 595-7777 TOLL FREE: (800) 776-7668	WEB: WWW.ARGONAUTINSURANCE.COM
SOUTH DAKOTA	225 W WASHINGTON STE 600 CHICAGO, IL 60606	PHONE: (312) 201-7600 FAX: (312) 223-0567	WEB: WWW.ARGONAUTGROUP.COM
TEXAS	EXECUTIVE OFFICE 10101 REUNION PL STE 500 SAN ANTONIO, TX 78216	PHONE: (210) 321-8400 FAX: (210) 377-2637 TOLL FREE: (800) 470-7958	WEB: WWW.ARGONAUTGROUP.COM
	DALLAS OFFICE / SOUTH REGION 5100 N O'CONNOR RD STE 200 IRVING, TX 75039 PO BOX 152007 IRVING, TX 75015	PHONE: (800) 678-6766 FAX: (972) 506-2499 TOLL FREE: (800) 678-6766	WEB: WWW.ARGONAUTGROUP.COM
UTAH	WEST REGION / WORKERS COMP OFFICE 7272 E INDIAN SCHOOL RD STE 500 SCOTTSDALE, AZ 85251	FAX: (480) 889-1881 TOLL FREE: (888) 908-3422	WEB: WWW.ARGONAUTGROUP.COM
	WEST REGION / LIABILITY OFFICE THREE HUTTON CENTRE STE 870 SANTA ANA, CA 92707	PHONE: (714) 708-4720 FAX: (714) 708-2108	WEB: WWW.ARGONAUTGROUP.COM
VERMONT	EAST REGION ONE INTERNATIONAL PLZ STE 550 PHILADELPHIA, PA 19113-1546	PHONE: (610) 595-7700 FAX: (610) 595-7777 TOLL FREE: (800) 776-7668	WEB: WWW.ARGONAUTINSURANCE.COM
WASHINGTON	WEST REGION / WORKERS COMP OFFICE 7272 E INDIAN SCHOOL RD STE 500 SCOTTSDALE, AZ 85251	FAX: (480) 889-1881 TOLL FREE: (888) 908-3422	WEB: WWW.ARGONAUTGROUP.COM
	WEST REGION / LIABILITY OFFICE THREE HUTTON CENTRE STE 870 SANTA ANA, CA 92707	PHONE: (714) 708-4720 FAX: (714) 708-2108	WEB: WWW.ARGONAUTGROUP.COM
WISCONSIN	225 W WASHINGTON STE 600 CHICAGO, IL 60606	PHONE: (312) 201-7600 FAX: (312) 223-0567	WEB: WWW.ARGONAUTGROUP.COM
WYOMING	WEST REGION / WORKERS COMP OFFICE 7272 E INDIAN SCHOOL RD STE 500 SCOTTSDALE, AZ 85251	FAX: (480) 889-1881 TOLL FREE: (888) 908-3422	WEB: WWW.ARGONAUTGROUP.COM
	WEST REGION / LIABILITY OFFICE THREE HUTTON CENTRE STE 870 SANTA ANA, CA 92707	PHONE: (714) 708-4720 FAX: (714) 708-2108	WEB: WWW.ARGONAUTGROUP.COM

ARGUS SERVICES CORP

TEXAS	9101 LBJ FWY STE 600 DALLAS, TX 75243	PHONE: (214) 459-2000 FAX: (214) 459-2010 TOLL FREE: (800) 720-6787	E-MAIL: ARGUS1@AIRMAIL.NET WEB: WWW.ARGUSSERVICES.NET

ARISTA INSURANCE CO

NEW YORK	116 JOHN ST NEW YORK, NY 10038-3300 PO BOX 11383 NEW YORK, NY 10038-0116	PHONE: (212) 964-3449 FAX: (212) 608-4106 TOLL FREE: (800) 522-3114 IN-STATE: (800) 522-3114	

ARIZONA FOUNDATION FOR MEDICAL CARE

ARIZONA	326 E CORONADO RD PHOENIX, AZ 85004-1576	PHONE: (602) 252-4042 FAX: (602) 256-7816 TOLL FREE: (800) 624-4277	WEB: WWW.AZFIMC.COM

ARIZONA PHYSICIANS, IPA, INC

ARIZONA
3141 N 3RD AVE
PHOENIX, AZ 85013-4345
PO BOX 659421
SAN ANTONIO, TX 78265
FAX: (602) 664-5466
TOLL FREE: (800) 348-4058
WEB: WWW.MYAPIPA.COM

ARIZONA PIPE TRADES — *COMPUSYS, INC*

ARIZONA
3121 N 24TH ST
PHOENIX, AZ 85016-7396
PHONE: (602) 956-1894
FAX: (602) 956-1943
TOLL FREE: (877) 429-7473
WEB: WWW.AZPIPE.ORG

ARKANSAS BEST CORP — *CHOICE BENEFITS*

NATIONAL
3801 OLD GREENWOOD RD
FT SMITH, AR 72903-5937
PO BOX 10048
FT SMITH, AR 72917-0048
PHONE: (479) 785-6178
FAX: (479) 785-6011
WEB: WWW.CHOICEBENEFITS.COM

ARKANSAS BLUE CROSS / BLUE SHIELD

ARKANSAS

SOUTH CENTRAL REGION
100 GREENWOOD AVE STE C
HOT SPRINGS, AR 71913-4441
PHONE: (501) 620-2620
FAX: (501) 620-2650
TOLL FREE: (800) 588-5733
WEB: WWW.ARKBLUECROSS.COM

SOUTHWEST REGION
300 OLIVE ST STE 402
TEXARKANA, AR 71854-2201
PO BOX 2018
TEXARKANA, AR 75504
PHONE: (870) 773-2584
FAX: (870) 779-9138
TOLL FREE: (800) 470-9621
WEB: WWW.ARKBLUECROSS.COM

ARM LTD — *SEE ALSO ALTERNATIVE RISK MANAGEMENT LIMITED*

ARNETT HEALTH PLANS — *SEE ALSO HEALTH CARE ADMINISTRATORS, INC*

INDIANA
415 N 26TH ST STE 101
LAFAYETTE, IN 47904
PO BOX 6108
LAFAYETTE, IN 47903-5108
PHONE: (765) 448-7400
FAX: (765) 448-7700
TOLL FREE: (888) 448-7440
WEB: WWW.ARNETTPLANS.COM

ARNOT OGDEN MEDICAL CENTER

NEW YORK
600 ROE AVE
ELMIRA, NY 14905-1676
PHONE: (607) 737-4100
FAX: (607) 737-7771

ARROW MUTUAL LIABILITY INSURANCE CO

MAINE
MASSACHUSETTS
NEW HAMPSHIRE
RHODE ISLAND
23 COMMONWEALTH AVE
CHESTNUT HILL, MA 02467-1099
PHONE: (617) 244-5730
FAX: (617) 244-4106
TOLL FREE: (800) 457-9753

ARTHUR J GALLAGAR & CO

NATIONAL
2345 GRAND BLVD STE 900
KANSAS CITY, MO 64108-2671
PO BOX 419797
KANSAS CITY, MO 64141-6797
PHONE: (816) 421-7788
FAX: (816) 472-5517
TOLL FREE: (800) 934-4624
IN-STATE: (800) 934-4624
WEB: WWW.AJG.COM

ASI — *SEE ALSO ADMINISTRATIVE SERVICES, INC — SEE ALSO ASSOCIATION & SOCIETY INSURANCE CORP*

ASR CORP — *SEE ALSO ADMINISTRATION SYSTEMS RESEARCH CORP*

ASSOCIATED ADJUSTERS

NATIONAL
2909 13TH ST STE 210
GULFPORT, MS 39501
PO BOX 357
GULFPORT, MS 39502
PHONE: (228) 865-9181
FAX: (228) 868-1372
TOLL FREE: (800) 528-3629
E-MAIL: INFO@ASSOCIATED-ADJUSTERS.COM
WEB: WWW.ASSOCIATED-ADJUSTERS.COM

A

ASSOCIATED PLAN ADMINISTRATORS

CONNECTICUT
4133 WHITNEY AVE
HAMDEN, CT 06518-1432
PO BOX 1100
BEATTYVILLE, KY 41311
PHONE: (203) 287-1272
FAX: (203) 288-9428
TOLL FREE: (800) 626-3830
WEB: WWW.ASSOCIATEDPLAN.COM

ASSOCIATION & SOCIETY INSURANCE CORP — *ASI*

NATIONAL
2301 RESEARCH BLVD STE 300
ROCKVILLE, MD 20850
PO BOX 2510
ROCKVILLE, MD 20847-2510
PHONE: (301) 816-0045
FAX: (301) 816-1125
TOLL FREE: (800) 638-2610
E-MAIL: CUSTSVC@ASICORPORATION.COM
WEB: WWW.ASICORPORATION.COM

ASSUMPTION MUTUAL LIFE INSURANCE CO

ALBERTA
BRITISH COLUMBIA
MANITOBA
NEW BRUNSWICK
NEWFOUNDLAND
NOVA SCOTIA
ONTARIO
PRINCE EDWARD ISLAND
QUEBEC
SASKATCHEWAN

770 MAIN ST
MONCTON, NB E1C-8L1
PO BOX 160
MONCTON, NB E1C-8L1
PHONE: (506) 853-6040
FAX: (506) 853-5421
TOLL FREE: (800) 455-7337
WEB: WWW.ASSUMPTION.CA

ASSURANT HEALTH — *FORTIS INSURANCE*

NATIONAL
2323 GRAND BLVD
KANSAS CITY, MO 64108-6644
PHONE: (816) 474-2345
FAX: (816) 881-8996
TOLL FREE: (800) 733-7879
WEB: WWW.ASSURANTHEALTH.COM OR WWW.ASSURANTEMPLOYEEBENEFITS.COM

WISCONSIN
501 W MICHIGAN
MILWAUKEE, WI 53201
PO BOX 3050
MILWAUKEE, WI 53201-0624
PHONE: (414) 271-3011
FAX: (414) 224-0472
TOLL FREE: (800) 211-1193
WEB: WWW.HEALTH.US.FORTIS.COM

ASSURANT SOLUTIONS — *ASSURANT SOLUTIONS MIAMI*

FLORIDA
11222 QUAIL ROOST DR
MIAMI, FL 33157-6543
PO BOX 979055
MIAMI, FL 33157-9055
PHONE: (305) 253-2244
FAX: (305) 252-6987
TOLL FREE: (800) 852-2244
WEB: WWW.ASSURANTSOLUTIONS.COM

GEORGIA
260 INTERSTATE N CIR SE
ATLANTA, GA 30339-2111
PO BOX 50355
ATLANTA, GA 30302-0355
PHONE: (770) 763-1000
FAX: (770) 859-4403
WEB: WWW.ASSURANTSOLUTIONS.COM

ASSURANT SOLUTIONS MIAMI — *SEE ALSO ASSURANT SOLUTIONS*

ASSURE CARE

ILLINOIS *MICHIGAN* *MINNESOTA* *OHIO*	13700 WATERTOWER CIR STE D PLYMOUTH, MN 55441	PHONE: (763) 383-4800 FAX: (763) 383-4880 TOLL FREE: (800) 328-0927	E-MAIL: INFO@ASSURECARE.COM WEB: WWW.ASSURECARE.COM
	1742 GEORGETOWN RD STE E HUDSON, OH 44236 PO BOX 1729 STOW, OH 44224	PHONE: (330) 528-3929 FAX: (330) 342-1642 TOLL FREE: (800) 422-2026	E-MAIL: INFO@ASSURECARE.COM WEB: WWW.ASSURECARE.COM
	4050 HUNSAKER DR STE 110 EAST LANSING, MI 48823 PO BOX 1570 EAST LANSING, MI 48826	PHONE: (517) 351-6616 FAX: (517) 349-7802 TOLL FREE: (800) 968-6616	E-MAIL: INFO@ASSURECARE.COM WEB: WWW.ASSURECARE.COM
	340 QUADRANGLE DR BOLINGBROOK, IL 60440-3448	FAX: (630) 759-5219 TOLL FREE: (800) 759-7422	E-MAIL: INFO@ASSURECARE.COM WEB: WWW.ASSURECARE.COM

ASSURITY LIFE INSURANCE

NEBRASKA	1526 "K" ST LINCOLN, NE 68508 PO BOX 82533 LINCOLN, NE 68501-2533	PHONE: (402) 476-6500 FAX: (402) 437-4395 TOLL FREE: (800) 869-0355	E-MAIL: INFO@ASSURITY.COM WEB: WWW.ASSURITY.COM

ATLANTIC COAST LIFE INSURANCE CO

SOUTH CAROLINA	1565 SAMRITTENBURG BLVD CHARLESTON, SC 29407-8538 PO BOX 20010 CHARLESTON, SC 29413-0010	PHONE: (843) 763-8680 FAX: (843) 763-8687	

ATLANTIC MUTUAL

NATIONAL	1325 ELECTRIC RD ROANOKE, VA 24018 PO BOX 4657 ROANOKE, VA 24015	PHONE: (800) 444-2856 FAX: (800) 678-9847	WEB: WWW.ATLANTICMUTUAL.COM

ATLANTIC MUTUAL / CENTENNIAL INSURANCE CO

NATIONAL	SEVEN GIRALDA FARMS MADISON, NJ 07940	PHONE: (973) 408-6000 FAX: (973) 408-6120 TOLL FREE: (800) 445-9075 & (800) 945-7461 CLAIMS IN-STATE: (800) 945-7461	WEB: WWW.ATLANTICMUTUAL.COM

ATLANTIC SOUTHERN INSURANCE COMPANY

PUERTO RICO	1054 MUNOZ RIVERA AVE SAN JUAN, PR 00927-5015 PO BOX 362889 SAN JUAN, PR 00936-2889	PHONE: (787) 767-9750 FAX: (787) 764-4707 TOLL FREE: (800) 981-5564	WEB: WWW.ATLANTICSOUTHERN.COM

ATRIUM HEALTH PLAN & BLUE CROSS/BLUE SHIELD WISCONSIN — *COMPCARE BLUE*

MINNESOTA	400 SECOND ST S STE 270 HUDSON, WI 54016	PHONE: (800)249-4300 FAX: (715) 386-8326 TOLL FREE: (800) 535-4041 IN-STATE: (888)239-9514	WEB: WWW.ATRIUMHEALTHPLAN.COM

WISCONSIN	400 SECOND ST S STE 270 HUDSON, WI 54016	PHONE: (800)249-4300 FAX: (715) 386-8326 TOLL FREE: (800) 535-4041 IN-STATE: (888)239-9514	WEB: WWW.ATRIUMHEALTHPLAN.COM

ATTEMTA — *SEE ALSO COMP CAROLINA*

ATTENTA

ALABAMA	PO BOX 2408 BIRMINGHAM, AL 35201-2408	PHONE: (205) 252-9870 FAX: (205) 581-9172 TOLL FREE: (800) 277-7500	WEB: WWW.ATTENTA.COM
ALABAMA *MISSISSIPPI*	2093 LAKELAND DR JACKSON, MS 39216 PO BOX 14248 JACKSON, MS 39236-4248	PHONE: (601) 362-1973 FAX: (601) 366-3769 TOLL FREE: (800) 277-8127	WEB: WWW.ATTENTA.COM

AULTCARE

OHIO	2600 6TH ST SW CANTON, OH 44710-1799 PO BOX 6910 CANTON, OH 44706-0910	PHONE: (330) 438-6360 FAX: (330) 454-7845 TOLL FREE: (800) 344-8858	E-MAIL: AULTCARE@AULTMANS.COM WEB: WWW.AULTCARE.ORG

AUSTIN MUTUAL INSURANCE CO

ARIZONA
IOWA
MINNESOTA
MONTANA
OREGON
SOUTH DAKOTA
UTAH
WASHINGTON
WISCONSIN

	10 2ND ST NE STE 300 MINNEAPOLIS, MN 55413-2282 PO BOX 401 MINNEAPOLIS, MN 55440-0401	PHONE: (612) 378-8600 FAX: (612) 378-8696 TOLL FREE: (800) 328-4628	WEB: WWW.AUSTININSURANCEGROUP.NET

AUTO & HOME INSURANCE PLUS — *SEE ALSO CALIFORNIA CASULTY MANAGEMENT CO*

AUTOCLUB SOUTH — *SEE ALSO AAA INSURANCE CO*

AUTOMATED BENEFITS SERVICES, INC

INDIANA *KENTUCKY* *MICHIGAN* *WISCONSIN*	8220 IRVING RD STERLING HEIGHTS, MI 48312-4621 PO BOX 37504 OAK PARK, MI 48237-0504	PHONE: (586) 826-4300 FAX: (586) 693-4820 TOLL FREE: (800) 211-1536	WEB: WWW.ABS-TPA.COM

AUTOMOBILE & HOME — *SEE ALSO METROPOLITAN LIFE INSURANCE CO*

AUTOMOBILE CLUB INSURANCE CO

NATIONAL	2601 S FIGUEROA ST LOS ANGELES, CA 90007	PHONE: (213) 741-3686 FAX: (213) 741-3637	WEB: WWW.AAA-CALIF.COM

AUTOMOBILE MECHANICS LOCAL NO 701 — *WELFARE AND PENSION FUND*

ILLINOIS	500 W PLAINFIELD RD STE 100 COUNTRYSIDE, IL 60525-3582	PHONE: (708) 482-0110 FAX: (708) 482-9140 TOLL FREE: (800) 704-5270	

AV-MED HEALTH PLAN

FLORIDA	4300 NW 89TH BLVD GAINESVILLE, FL 32606-5688 PO BOX 749 GAINESVILLE, FL 32602	PHONE: (352) 372-8400 FAX: (352) 337-8726	WEB: WWW.AVMED.COM

FLORIDA — CONTINUED	9400 S DADELAND BLVD MIAMI, FL 33156-2823 PO BOX 569000 MIAMI, FL 33256-9000	PHONE: (305) 671-5437 FAX: (305) 671-6103 TOLL FREE: (800) 442-8633	E-MAIL: MEMBERS@AVMED.ORG WEB: WWW.AVMED.COM

AVALON BENEFIT SERVICES

NATIONAL	600 D ST SOUTH CHARLESTON, WV 25303 PO BOX 8130 SOUTH CHARLESTON, WV 25303	PHONE: (403) 744-7723 FAX: (304) 744-7759 TOLL FREE: (800) 310-6645	WEB: WWW.AVALONBENEFITS.COM
	6543 COMMERCE PKY STE M DUBLIN, OH 43017 PO BOX 1803 DUBLIN, OH 43017	PHONE: (800) 310-6645 FAX: (614) 796-9733	WEB: WWW.AVALONBENEFITS.COM

AXA CORPORATE SOLUTIONS REINSURANCE CO

NATIONAL	17 STATE ST FL 37 NEW YORK, NY 10004-1576	PHONE: (212) 493-9300	WEB: WWW.AXA.COM

BABB, HEIM & WOODRICH (INSURANCE BROKER FIRM) — *SEE ALSO BABB, INC*

BABB, INC — *BABB, HEIM & WOODRICH (INSURANCE BROKER FIRM)*

PENNSYLVANIA	850 RIDGE AVE PITTSBURGH, PA 15212-6095	PHONE: (412) 237-2020 FAX: (412) 322-1756 TOLL FREE: (800) 245-6102 IN-STATE: (800) 892-1015	WEB: WWW.BABBINC.COM

BADGER MUTUAL INSURANCE CO

ILLINOIS *MICHIGAN* *MINNESOTA* *WISCONSIN*	1635 W NATIONAL AVE MILWAUKEE, WI 53204-1199 PO BOX 2092 MILWAUKEE, WI 53201-2092	PHONE: (414) 383-1234 FAX: (414) 383-1535 TOLL FREE: (800) 837-7833	WEB: WWW.BADGERMUTUAL.COM

BAKERY & CONFECTIONARY UNION — *BAKERY & CONFECTIONARY HEALTH BENEFITS & PENSION FUND*

NATIONAL	10401 CONNECTICUT AVE KENSINGTON, MD 20895-3961	PHONE: (301) 468-3730 FAX: (301) 468-3789	

BALBOA INSURANCE GROUP

NATIONAL	3349 MICHELSON DR STE 200 IRVINE, CA 92612-8893 PO BOX 19702 IRVINE, CA 92623-9702	PHONE: (949) 222-8000 FAX: (949) 660-6580 TOLL FREE: (800) 854-6115	E-MAIL: INFO@BALBOAINSURANCE.COM WEB: WWW.BALBOAINSURANCE.COM

BALDWIN & LYONS, INC — *SEE ALSO PROTECTIVE INSURANCE CO*

BANKERS FIDELITY LIFE INSURANCE

ARIZONA, ARKANSAS, DELAWARE, FLORIDA, GEORGIA, IDAHO, ILLINOIS, INDIANA, IOWA, KANSAS, KENTUCKY, LOUISIANA, MARYLAND, MISSISSIPPI, MONTANA, NEBRASKA, NEVADA, NEW MEXICO, NORTH CAROLINA, NORTH DAKOTA, OHIO, OKLAHOMA, OREGON, PENNSYLVANIA, SOUTH CAROLINA, SOUTH DAKOTA, TENNESSEE, TEXAS, UTAH, VIRGINIA, WASHINGTON, WEST VIRGINIA, WYOMING

4370 PEACHTREE RD NE
ATLANTA, GA 30319-3054
PO BOX 105185
ATLANTA, GA 30348-5185

PHONE: (404) 266-5500
TOLL FREE: (800) 241-1439
IN-STATE: (800) 241-1439

WEB: WWW.BFLIC.COM

BANKERS INDEPENDENT INSURANCE CO

DISTRICT OF COLUMBIA
MARYLAND

704 QUINCE ORCHARD RD STE 310
GAITHERSBURG, MD 20878

PHONE: (301) 948-9000
FAX: (301) 948-4768
TOLL FREE: (800) 258-2396

E-MAIL: INFO@BIIC.COM
WEB: WWW.BANKERSINSURANCE.COM

BANKERS INSURANCE GROUP

ARIZONA
FLORIDA
NEVADA
SOUTH CAROLINA

360 CENTRAL AVE
ST PETERSBURG, FL 33701-3857
PO BOX 33061
ST PETERSBURG, FL 33733

PHONE: (727) 823-4000
FAX: (727) 803-4023
TOLL FREE: (800) 765-9700

E-MAIL: INFO@BANKERSINSURANCE.COM
WEB: WWW.BANKERSINSURANCE.COM

BANKERS LIFE & CASUALTY CO

NATIONAL

222 MERCHANDISE MART PLZ
CHICAGO, IL 60654-2001

PHONE: (847) 759-8100
FAX: (312) 396-7911
TOLL FREE: (800) 773-4760

WEB: WWW.BANKERSLIFE.COM

BCI INSURANCE SERVICES

CALIFORNIA

1903 O'TOOLE WAY
SAN JOSE, CA 95131

PHONE: (408) 240-4360
FAX: (408) 267-2656

E-MAIL: INFO@BCI-INS.COM
WEB: WWW.BCI-INS.COM

BCS FINANCIAL CORP/BCS INSURANCE CO — *BCS LIFE INSURANCE CO*

NATIONAL

2 MID AMERICA PLZ #200
OAKBROOK TERRACE, IL 60181

PHONE: (630) 472-7700
FAX: (630)472-7876
TOLL FREE: (800) 621-9215

WEB: WWW.BCSIGROUP.COM

BCS LIFE INSURANCE CO — *SEE ALSO BCS FINANCIAL CORP/BCS INSURANCE CO*

BEAR RIVER MUTUAL INSURANCE CO

UTAH

778 E WINCHESTER ST
MURRAY, UT 84107-7565
PO BOX 571310
MURRAY, UT 84157-1310

PHONE: (801) 267-5000
FAX: (801) 267-5033
TOLL FREE: (800) 925-5177
IN-STATE: (800) 925-5177

E-MAIL: SERVICES1@BRMUTUAL.COM
WEB: WWW.BEARRIVERMUTUAL.COM

BEECH STREET CORP

NATIONAL

25500 COMMERCENTRE DR
LAKE FOREST, CA 92630-8855

PHONE: (949) 672-1000
FAX: (949) 672-1111
TOLL FREE: (800) 877-1666

WEB: WWW.BEECHSTREET.COM

B

BEHAVIOR HEALTH SYSTEMS

NATIONAL

TWO METROPLEX DR STE 500
BIRMINGHAM, AL 35209
PO BOX 830724
BIRMINGHAM, AL 35283-0724

PHONE: (205) 879-1150
FAX: (205) 879-1178
TOLL FREE: (800) 245-1150

E-MAIL: INFO@BHS-INC.COM
WEB: WWW.BHS-INC.COM

BEHAVIORAL HEALTHCARE OPTIONS

ARIZONA

2716 N TENAYA WY 5TH FL
LAS VEGAS, NV 89128
PO BOX 14158
LAS VEGAS, NV 89114-4158

PHONE: (702) 877-5000
FAX: (702) 877-1834
TOLL FREE: (877) 393-6094

WEB: WWW.BEHAVIORALHEALTHCAREOPTIONS.COM

BELOIT MEMORIAL HOSPITAL — *(DBA) FIRST CHOICE BENEFITS MANAGEMENT*

WISCONSIN

1969 W HART RD
BELOIT, WI 53511-2298
PO BOX 658
BELOIT, WI 53512

PHONE: (608) 364-5123
FAX: (608) 362-8585
TOLL FREE: (800) 637-2641

E-MAIL: WEBMASTER@BELOITMEMORIALHOSPITAL.ORG
WEB: WWW.BELOITMEMORIALHOSPITAL.ORG

BENEFICIAL LIFE INSURANCE CO

NATIONAL

36 S STATE ST
SALT LAKE CITY, UT 84136-0001

PHONE: (801) 531-7979
FAX: (801) 531-3397
TOLL FREE: (800) 233-7979

E-MAIL: CUSTSERVE@BENFINANCIAL.COM
WEB: WWW.BENEFICIALFINANCIALGROUP.COM

BENEFIT & RISK MANAGEMENT SERVICES — *TANTARA ADMINISTRATORS*

CALIFORNIA

10860 GOLD CTR DR STE 300
RANCHO CORDOVA, CA 95670-6068
PO BOX 2650
RANCHO CORDOVA, CA 95741-2650

PHONE: (916) 858-2950
FAX: (916) 858-2970
TOLL FREE: (800) 959-4767

E-MAIL: INFO@BRMS-ONLINE.COM
WEB: WWW.BRMS-ONLINE.COM

BENEFIT ADMINISTRATIVE SYSTEMS, LTD

NATIONAL

17475 JOVANNA DR STE 1B
HOMEWOOD, IL 60430-4623

PHONE: (708) 799-7400
FAX: (708) 799-7533
TOLL FREE: (800) 523-0582
IN-STATE: (800) 843-3831

E-MAIL: ADMIN@BENADMINSYS.COM
WEB: WWW.BENADMINSYS.COM

BENEFIT ASSISTANCE CORPORATION

NATIONAL

3556 TEAYS VALLEY RD
HURRICANE, WV 25526-9163
PO BOX 950
HURRICANE, WV 25526-0950

PHONE: (304) 562-1913
FAX: (304) 562-1916
TOLL FREE: (800) 448-1131

WEB: WWW.BACWV.COM

BENEFIT CLAIMS PAYORS, INC — *DIVERSIFIED HEALTH CARE SERVICES*

ARIZONA

1717 W NORTHERN AVE STE 200
PHOENIX, AZ 85021-5478
PO BOX 37400
PHOENIX, AZ 85069-7400

PHONE: (602) 861-6868
FAX: (602) 861-6878
TOLL FREE: (800) 266-6868

WEB: WWW.DHSNYU.COM

BENEFIT CONCEPTS — *SEE ALSO BROKERAGE CONCEPTS, INC*

BENEFIT CONSULTANTS, INC

MISSOURI

13515 BARRETT PKY DR STE 265
BALLWIN, MO 63021-5870

PHONE: (314) 822-7890
FAX: (314) 822-0992
TOLL FREE: (800) 434-4620

WEB: WWW.BCI-STL.COM

BENEFIT COORDINATORS CORP — *COORDINATED GROUP OF COMPANIES*

NATIONAL

100 RYAN CT STE 200
PITTSBURGH, PA 15205-1310

PHONE: (412) 276-1111
FAX: (412) 276-6650
TOLL FREE: (800) 685-6100

BENEFIT DEPARTMENT OR CHOICE BENEFITS — *SEE ALSO ARKANSAS BEST CORP*

BENEFIT PLAN ADMINISTRATION OF WI, INC — *LEE JOST & ASSOCIATES*

WISCONSIN

11270 W PARK PL STE 950
MILWAUKEE, WI 53224-3642

PHONE: (414) 577-3700
FAX: (414) 577-3710
TOLL FREE: (800) 425-1272

BENEFIT PLAN ADMINISTRATORS, INC

NATIONAL

101 S JEFFERSON ST
ROANOKE, VA 24011-1322
PO BOX 11746
ROANOKE, VA 24022-1746

PHONE: (540) 345-2721
FAX: (540) 342-0282
TOLL FREE: (800) 277-8973

E-MAIL: BPA@BPATPA.COM
WEB: WWW.BPATPA.COM

BENEFIT PLAN SERVICES, INC

NORTH CAROLINA

1022 HUTTON LN STE 103
HIGH POINT, NC 27262
PO BOX 2793
HIGH POINT, NC 27261-2793

PHONE: (336) 889-2003
FAX: (336) 841-2556

WEB: WWW.BPSTPA.COM

BENEFIT PLANNERS, INC

NATIONAL

12668 SILICON DR
SAN ANTONIO, TX 78249-3411
PO BOX 690450
SAN ANTONIO, TX 78269-0450

PHONE: (210) 558-2100
FAX: (210) 558-2151
TOLL FREE: (866) 868-8207

E-MAIL: SERVICE@BENPLAN.COM
WEB: WWW.BENPLAN.COM

BENEFIT SUPPORT, INC

ALABAMA
ARKANSAS
FLORIDA
GEORGIA
ILLINOIS
INDIANA
KENTUCKY
MISSISSIPPI
NORTH CAROLINA
OHIO
SOUTH CAROLINA
TENNESSEE
VIRGINIA
WASHINGTON

305 GREEN ST NE
GAINESVILLE, GA 30501-3384
PO BOX 2977
GAINESVILLE, GA 30503-2977

PHONE: (770) 532-2690
FAX: (770) 532-2318
TOLL FREE: (800) 777-4782
IN-STATE: (800) 777-4782

WEB: WWW.BENEFITSUPPORT.ORG

BENEFIT SYSTEMS & SERVICES, INC

NATIONAL

760 PASQUINELLI DR STE 320
WESTMONT, IL 60559-5555

PHONE: (800) 423-1841
FAX: (630) 789-2093
TOLL FREE: (800) 423-1841

WEB: WWW.BENEFIT-SYS.COM

BENEFITSOURCE, INC

NATIONAL

23 E FRONT ST STE 201
MONROE, MI 48161-2210
PO BOX 240
MONROE, MI 48161-0240

PHONE: (734) 242-4443
FAX: (734) 242-4437
TOLL FREE: (800) 742-4441

WEB: WWW.BENEFITSOURCEINC.COM

BENESIGHT

ARIZONA
CALIFORNIA
COLORADO
IDAHO

WEST REGION
7878 N 16TH ST STE 140
PHOENIX, AZ 85020-4463
PO BOX 375
PUEBLO, CO 81002

PHONE: (602) 906-5000
FAX: (602) 395-7800
TOLL FREE: (800) 223-5228

WEB: WWW.BENESIGHT.COM

ILLINOIS *INDIANA* *IOWA* *KANSAS* *KENTUCKY* *MICHIGAN* *MINNESOTA* *MISSOURI*	CENTRAL REGION 973 FEATHER STONE RD STE 200 ROCKFORD, IL 61107 PO BOX 7046 ROCKFORD, IL 61125	PHONE: (815) 395-0080 FAX: (815) 395-0139 OR (815) 231-2445 TOLL FREE: (800) 648-4480	WEB: WWW.BENESIGHT.COM
MONTANA	WEST REGION 7878 N 16TH ST STE 140 PHOENIX, AZ 85020-4463 PO BOX 375 PUEBLO, CO 81002	PHONE: (602) 906-5000 FAX: (602) 395-7800 TOLL FREE: (800) 223-5228	WEB: WWW.BENESIGHT.COM
NEBRASKA	CENTRAL REGION 973 FEATHER STONE RD STE 200 ROCKFORD, IL 61107 PO BOX 7046 ROCKFORD, IL 61125	PHONE: (815) 395-0080 FAX: (815) 395-0139 OR (815) 231-2445 TOLL FREE: (800) 648-4480	WEB: WWW.BENESIGHT.COM
NEVADA *NEW MEXICO*	WEST REGION 7878 N 16TH ST STE 140 PHOENIX, AZ 85020-4463 PO BOX 375 PUEBLO, CO 81002	PHONE: (602) 906-5000 FAX: (602) 395-7800 TOLL FREE: (800) 223-5228	WEB: WWW.BENESIGHT.COM
NORTH DAKOTA	CENTRAL REGION 973 FEATHER STONE RD STE 200 ROCKFORD, IL 61107 PO BOX 7046 ROCKFORD, IL 61125	PHONE: (815) 395-0080 FAX: (815) 395-0139 OR (815) 231-2445 TOLL FREE: (800) 648-4480	WEB: WWW.BENESIGHT.COM
OREGON	WEST REGION 7878 N 16TH ST STE 140 PHOENIX, AZ 85020-4463 PO BOX 375 PUEBLO, CO 81002	PHONE: (602) 906-5000 FAX: (602) 395-7800 TOLL FREE: (800) 223-5228	WEB: WWW.BENESIGHT.COM
SOUTH DAKOTA	CENTRAL REGION 973 FEATHER STONE RD STE 200 ROCKFORD, IL 61107 PO BOX 7046 ROCKFORD, IL 61125	PHONE: (815) 395-0080 FAX: (815) 395-0139 OR (815) 231-2445 TOLL FREE: (800) 648-4480	WEB: WWW.BENESIGHT.COM
UTAH *WASHINGTON*	WEST REGION 7878 N 16TH ST STE 140 PHOENIX, AZ 85020-4463 PO BOX 375 PUEBLO, CO 81002	PHONE: (602) 906-5000 FAX: (602) 395-7800 TOLL FREE: (800) 223-5228	WEB: WWW.BENESIGHT.COM
WISCONSIN	CENTRAL REGION 973 FEATHER STONE RD STE 200 ROCKFORD, IL 61107 PO BOX 7046 ROCKFORD, IL 61125	PHONE: (815) 395-0080 FAX: (815) 395-0139 OR (815) 231-2445 TOLL FREE: (800) 648-4480	WEB: WWW.BENESIGHT.COM
WYOMING	WEST REGION 7878 N 16TH ST STE 140 PHOENIX, AZ 85020-4463 PO BOX 375 PUEBLO, CO 81002	PHONE: (602) 906-5000 FAX: (602) 395-7800 TOLL FREE: (800) 223-5228	WEB: WWW.BENESIGHT.COM

BENICOMP, INC

State	Address	Phone	Contact
NATIONAL	8310 CLINTON PARK DR FT WAYNE, IN 46825-3171	PHONE: (260) 482-7400 FAX: (260) 482-8991 TOLL FREE: (800) 837-7400	E-MAIL: BENICOMP@BENICOMP.COM WEB: WWW.BENICOMP.COM

BENICORP INSURANCE CO

NATIONAL	7702 WOODLAND DR STE 200 INDIANAPOLIS, IN 46278-1717 PO BOX 68917 INDIANAPOLIS, IN 46268-0917	PHONE: (317) 290-1205 FAX: (317) 216-7877 TOLL FREE: (800) 438-4002	E-MAIL: CLAIMS@BENICORP.COM WEB: WWW.BENICORP.COM

BERKLEY GROUP — *SEE ALSO BERKLEY RISK SERVICES*

BERKLEY INSURANCE CO

NATIONAL	475 STEAMBOAT RD GREENWICH, CT 06830-7144	PHONE: (203) 542-3800 FAX: (203) 542-3290 TOLL FREE: (800) 866-2308	WEB: WWW.WRBERKLEY.COM

BERKLEY RISK SERVICES

COLORADO	2000 S COLORADO BLVD ANNEX BLDG #410 DENVER, CO 80222-4356	PHONE: (303) 357-2600 FAX: (303) 357-2626 IN-STATE: (800) 502-0100	WEB: WWW.DENTALLIABILITY.COM

BERKSHIRE HATHAWAY HOMESTATE CO

CALIFORNIA	PO BOX 7008 PASADENA, CA 91109	PHONE: (626) 356-1700 FAX: (626) 356-1717 TOLL FREE: (800) 339-9809	WEB: WWW.BH-HC.COM

BERKSHIRE HATHAWAY HOMESTATE COMPANIES

NATIONAL	9290 W DODGE RD STE 300 OMAHA, NE 68114-3363	PHONE: (402) 393-7255 FAX: (402) 393-7619 TOLL FREE: (800) 488-2930	WEB: WWW.BH-HC.COM

BERKSHIRE LIFE INSURANCE CO OF AMERICA

NATIONAL	700 SOUTH ST PITTSFIELD, MA 01201-8212	PHONE: (413) 499-4321 FAX: (413) 499-4831 TOLL FREE: (800) 819-2468	E-MAIL: CUSTOMERSERVICE@BERKSHIRELIFE.COM WEB: WWW.THEBERKSHIRE.COM

BEST LIFE AND HEALTH INSURANCE CO

NATIONAL	2505 MCCABE WY IRVINE, CA 92614-6243 PO BOX 19721 IRVINE, CA 92623-9721	PHONE: (949) 253-4080 FAX: (949) 222-1005 TOLL FREE: (800) 433-3088	WEB: WWW.BESTLIFE.COM

BITUMINOUS INSURANCE CO

ALABAMA	3700 CRESTWOOD PKWY STE 650 DULUTH, GA 30096-9367 PO BOX 100067 DULUTH, GA 30096-9367	PHONE: (770) 923-7551 FAX: (770) 923-7584 TOLL FREE: (800) 822-2905	WEB: WWW.BITUMINOUSINSURANCE.COM
ARIZONA	4330 SHAWNEE MISSION PKWY STE 100 FAIRWAY, KS 66205-2522 PO BOX 718 SHAWNEE MISSION, KS 66201-0718	PHONE: (913) 262-4664 FAX: (913) 262-0997 TOLL FREE: (800) 821-5354	WEB: WWW.BITUMINOUSINSURANCE.COM
COLORADO	445 UNION BLVD STE 125 LAKEWOOD, CO 80228 PO BOX 280729 LAKEWOOD, CO 80228-0729	FAX: (303) 982-0808 TOLL FREE: (877) 746-1748	WEB: WWW.BITUMINOUSINSURANCE.COM
CONNECTICUT	FOSTER PLAZA 5 651 HOLIDAY DR PITTSBURGH, PA 15220-2757	PHONE: (412) 937-9000 FAX: (412) 937-1143 TOLL FREE: (800) 253-1232	WEB: WWW.BITUMINOUSINSURANCE.COM
DELAWARE DISTRICT OF COLUMBIA	HEAVER PLZ STE 403 1301 YORK RD LUTHERVILLE, MD 21093 PO BOX 509 LUTHERVILLE, MD 21094-0509	PHONE: (410) 321-7570 FAX: (410) 296-7413 TOLL FREE: (800) 345-5108	WEB: WWW.BITUMINOUSINSURANCE.COM

FLORIDA GEORGIA		3700 CRESTWOOD PKWY STE 650 DULUTH, GA 30096-9367 PO BOX 100067 DULUTH, GA 30096-9367	PHONE: (770) 923-7551 FAX: (770) 923-7584 TOLL FREE: (800) 822-2905	WEB: WWW.BITUMINOUSINSURANCE.COM
IDAHO		4330 SHAWNEE MISSION PKWY STE 100 FAIRWAY, KS 66205-2522 PO BOX 718 SHAWNEE MISSION, KS 66201-0718	PHONE: (913) 262-4664 FAX: (913) 262-0997 TOLL FREE: (800) 821-5354	WEB: WWW.BITUMINOUSINSURANCE.COM
		1200 VALLEY WEST DR STE 600 WEST DES MOINES, IA 50266 PO BOX 65605 WEST DES MOINES, IA 50265-0605	PHONE: (515) 223-1122 FAX: (515) 223-4315 TOLL FREE: (800) 383-1122	WEB: WWW.BITUMINOUSINSURANCE.COM
ILLINOIS		HOME OFFICE 320 18TH ST ROCK ISLAND, IL 61201-8744	PHONE: (309) 786-5401 FAX: (309) 786-7073 TOLL FREE: (800) 475-4477	WEB: WWW.BITUMINOUSINSURANCE.COM
		1600 4TH AVE 3RD FL ROCK ISLAND, IL 61201-8632	PHONE: (309) 788-9361 FAX: (309) 788-9366 TOLL FREE: (800) 592-8991	WEB: WWW.BITUMINOUSINSURANCE.COM
		10733 SUNSET OFFICE DR STE 430 ST LOUIS, MO 63127-1033	PHONE: (314) 822-4446 FAX: (314) 822-9850 TOLL FREE: (800) 723-8632	WEB: WWW.BITUMINOUSINSURANCE.COM
INDIANA		2601 FORTUNE CIR DR STE 201B INDIANAPOLIS, IN 46241 PO BOX 42608 INDIANAPOLIS, IN 46242-0608	PHONE: (317) 243-6721 FAX: (317) 241-8922 TOLL FREE: (800) 382-9991	WEB: WWW.BITUMINOUSINSURANCE.COM
IOWA		1600 4TH AVE 3RD FL ROCK ISLAND, IL 61201-8632	PHONE: (309) 788-9361 FAX: (309) 788-9366 TOLL FREE: (800) 592-8991	WEB: WWW.BITUMINOUSINSURANCE.COM
		1200 VALLEY WEST DR STE 600 WEST DES MOINES, IA 50266 PO BOX 65605 WEST DES MOINES, IA 50265-0605	PHONE: (515) 223-1122 FAX: (515) 223-4315 TOLL FREE: (800) 383-1122	WEB: WWW.BITUMINOUSINSURANCE.COM
KANSAS		4330 SHAWNEE MISSION PKWY STE 100 FAIRWAY, KS 66205-2522 PO BOX 718 SHAWNEE MISSION, KS 66201-0718	PHONE: (913) 262-4664 FAX: (913) 262-0997 TOLL FREE: (800) 821-5354	WEB: WWW.BITUMINOUSINSURANCE.COM
KENTUCKY		312 WHITTINGTON PKY STE 100A LOUISVILLE, KY 40222-4923 PO BOX 7567 LOUISVILLE, KY 40257-0567	PHONE: (502) 426-9400 FAX: (502) 426-4787 TOLL FREE: (800) 633-0607	WEB: WWW.BITUMINOUSINSURANCE.COM
LOUISIANA		111 VETERANS BLVD STE 1526 METAIRIE, LA 70005-3043 PO BOX 19994 NEW ORLEANS, LA 70179-0994	PHONE: (504) 837-5480 FAX: (504) 831-0720 TOLL FREE: (800) 605-0311	WEB: WWW.BITUMINOUSINSURANCE.COM
MAINE		FOSTER PLAZA 5 651 HOLIDAY DR PITTSBURGH, PA 15220-2757	PHONE: (412) 937-9000 FAX: (412) 937-1143 TOLL FREE: (800) 253-1232	WEB: WWW.BITUMINOUSINSURANCE.COM
MARYLAND		HEAVER PLZ STE 403 1301 YORK RD LUTHERVILLE, MD 21093 PO BOX 509 LUTHERVILLE, MD 21094-0509	PHONE: (410) 321-7670 FAX: (410) 296-7413 TOLL FREE: (800) 346-5108	WEB: WWW.BITUMINOUSINSURANCE.COM
MASSACHUSETTS		FOSTER PLAZA 5 651 HOLIDAY DR PITTSBURGH, PA 15220-2757	PHONE: (412) 937-9000 FAX: (412) 937-1143 TOLL FREE: (800) 253-1232	WEB: WWW.BITUMINOUSINSURANCE.COM

MICHIGAN	17197 N LAUREL PARK DR STE 254 LIVONIA, MI 48152-2680	PHONE: (734) 462-1120 FAX: (734) 462-1139 TOLL FREE: (800) 356-8727	WEB: WWW.BITUMINOUSINSURANCE.COM
MINNESOTA	3333 N MAYFAIR RD STE 104 MILWAUKEE, WI 53222-3226 PO BOX 1210 BROOKFIELD, WI 53085	PHONE: (262) 792-9254 FAX: (262) 792-9264 TOLL FREE: (800) 242-6258	WEB: WWW.BITUMINOUSINSURANCE.COM
MISSISSIPPI	111 VETERANS BLVD STE 1526 METAIRIE, LA 70005-3043 PO BOX 19994 NEW ORLEANS, LA 70179-0994	PHONE: (504) 837-5480 FAX: (504) 831-0720 TOLL FREE: (800) 605-0311	WEB: WWW.BITUMINOUSINSURANCE.COM
MISSOURI	4330 SHAWNEE MISSION PKWY STE 100 FAIRWAY, KS 66205-2522 PO BOX 718 SHAWNEE MISSION, KS 66201-0718	PHONE: (913) 262-4664 FAX: (913) 262-0997 TOLL FREE: (800) 821-5354	WEB: WWW.BITUMINOUSINSURANCE.COM
	10733 SUNSET OFFICE DR STE 430 ST LOUIS, MO 63127-1033	PHONE: (314) 822-4446 FAX: (314) 822-9850 TOLL FREE: (800) 723-8532	WEB: WWW.BITUMINOUSINSURANCE.COM
MONTANA *NEBRASKA*	1200 VALLEY WEST DR STE 600 WEST DES MOINES, IA 50266 PO BOX 65605 WEST DES MOINES, IA 50265-0605	PHONE: (515) 223-1122 FAX: (515) 223-4315 TOLL FREE: (800) 383-1122	WEB: WWW.BITUMINOUSINSURANCE.COM
NEVADA	4330 SHAWNEE MISSION PKWY STE 100 FAIRWAY, KS 66205-2522 PO BOX 718 SHAWNEE MISSION, KS 66201-0718	PHONE: (913) 262-4664 FAX: (913) 262-0997 TOLL FREE: (800) 821-5354	WEB: WWW.BITUMINOUSINSURANCE.COM
NEW HAMPSHIRE *NEW JERSEY*	FOSTER PLAZA 5 651 HOLIDAY DR PITTSBURGH, PA 15220-2757	PHONE: (412) 937-9000 FAX: (412) 937-1143 TOLL FREE: (800) 253-1232	WEB: WWW.BITUMINOUSINSURANCE.COM
NEW MEXICO	4330 SHAWNEE MISSION PKWY STE 100 FAIRWAY, KS 66205-2522 PO BOX 718 SHAWNEE MISSION, KS 66201-0718	PHONE: (913) 262-4664 FAX: (913) 262-0997 TOLL FREE: (800) 821-5354	WEB: WWW.BITUMINOUSINSURANCE.COM
	222 W LAS COLINAS BLVD STE 1720 IRVING, TX 75039-5426 PO BOX 167968 IRVING, TX 75016-7968	PHONE: (972) 506-9591 FAX: (972) 556-1539 TOLL FREE: (800) 683-9591	WEB: WWW.BITUMINOUSINSURANCE.COM
	1601 NW EXPRESSWAY STE 700 OKLAHOMA CITY, OK 73118 PO BOX 12936 OKLAHOMA CITY, OK 73157-2936	PHONE: (405) 947-0809 FAX: (405) 947-1006 TOLL FREE: (800) 947-0809	WEB: WWW.BITUMINOUSINSURANCE.COM
NEW YORK	FOSTER PLAZA 5 651 HOLIDAY DR PITTSBURGH, PA 15220-2757	PHONE: (412) 937-9000 FAX: (412) 937-1143 TOLL FREE: (800) 253-1232	WEB: WWW.BITUMINOUSINSURANCE.COM
NORTH CAROLINA	15720 JOHN J DELANEY DR STE 200 CHARLOTTE, NC 28277 PO BOX 474630 CHARLOTTE, NC 28247	PHONE: (704) 341-3725 FAX: (704) 341-3775 IN-STATE: (800) 642-2507	WEB: WWW.BITUMINOUSINSRUANCE.COM
NORTH DAKOTA	1200 VALLEY WEST DR STE 600 WEST DES MOINES, IA 50266 PO BOX 65605 WEST DES MOINES, IA 50265-0605	PHONE: (515) 223-1122 FAX: (515) 223-4315 TOLL FREE: (800) 383-1122	WEB: WWW.BITUMINOUSINSURANCE.COM

B

OHIO	FOSTER PLAZA 5 651 HOLIDAY DR PITTSBURGH, PA 15220-2757	PHONE: (412) 937-9000 FAX: (412) 937-1143 TOLL FREE: (800) 253-1232	WEB: WWW.BITUMINOUSINSURANCE.COM
	2601 FORTUNE CIR DR STE 201B INDIANAPOLIS, IN 46241 PO BOX 42608 INDIANAPOLIS, IN 46242-0608	PHONE: (317) 243-6721 FAX: (317) 241-8922 TOLL FREE: (800) 382-9991	WEB: WWW.BITUMINOUSINSURANCE.COM
	17197 N LAUREL PARK DR STE 254 LIVONIA, MI 48152-2680	PHONE: (734) 462-1120 FAX: (734) 462-1139 TOLL FREE: (800) 356-8727	WEB: WWW.BITUMINOUSINSURANCE.COM
OKLAHOMA	1601 NW EXPRESSWAY STE 700 OKLAHOMA CITY, OK 73118 PO BOX 12936 OKLAHOMA CITY, OK 73157-2936	PHONE: (405) 947-0809 FAX: (405) 947-1006 TOLL FREE: (800) 947-0809	WEB: WWW.BITUMINOUSINSURANCE.COM
OREGON	1200 VALLEY WEST DR STE 600 WEST DES MOINES, IA 50266 PO BOX 65605 WEST DES MOINES, IA 50265-0605	PHONE: (515) 223-1122 FAX: (515) 223-4315 TOLL FREE: (800) 383-1122	WEB: WWW.BITUMINOUSINSURANCE.COM
PENNSYLVANIA	FOSTER PLAZA 5 651 HOLIDAY DR PITTSBURGH, PA 15220-2757	PHONE: (412) 937-9000 FAX: (412) 937-1143 TOLL FREE: (800) 253-1232	WEB: WWW.BITUMINOUSINSURANCE.COM
	HEAVER PLZ STE 403 1301 YORK RD LUTHERVILLE, MD 21093 PO BOX 509 LUTHERVILLE, MD 21094-0509	PHONE: (410) 321-7670 FAX: (410) 296-7413 TOLL FREE: (800) 346-5108	WEB: WWW.BITUMINOUSINSURANCE.COM
RHODE ISLAND	FOSTER PLAZA 5 651 HOLIDAY DR PITTSBURGH, PA 15220-2757	PHONE: (412) 937-9000 FAX: (412) 937-1143 TOLL FREE: (800) 253-1232	WEB: WWW.BITUMINOUSINSURANCE.COM
SOUTH CAROLINA	15720 JOHN J DELANEY DR STE 200 CHARLOTTE, NC 28277 PO BOX 474630 CHARLOTTE, NC 28247	PHONE: (704) 341-3725 FAX: (704) 341-3775 IN-STATE: (800) 642-2507	WEB: WWW.BITUMINOUSINSRUANCE.COM
SOUTH DAKOTA	1200 VALLEY WEST DR STE 600 WEST DES MOINES, IA 50266 PO BOX 65605 WEST DES MOINES, IA 50265-0605	PHONE: (515) 223-1122 FAX: (515) 223-4315 TOLL FREE: (800) 383-1122	WEB: WWW.BITUMINOUSINSURANCE.COM
TENNESSEE	2630 ELM HILL PIKE STE 125 NASHVILLE, TN 37214-3166 PO BOX 291689 NASHVILLE, TN 37229-1689	PHONE: (615) 871-9042 FAX: (615) 871-0783 TOLL FREE: (800) 342-5786	WEB: WWW.BITUMINOUSINSURANCE.COM
TEXAS	222 W LAS COLINAS BLVD STE 1720 IRVING, TX 75039-5426 PO BOX 167968 IRVING, TX 75016-7968	PHONE: (972) 506-9591 FAX: (972) 556-1539 TOLL FREE: (800) 683-9591	WEB: WWW.BITUMINOUSINSURANCE.COM
	9830 COLONNADE BLVD STE 210 SAN ANTONIO, TX 78230-2203	PHONE: (210) 340-8199 FAX: (210) 340-8171 TOLL FREE: (888) 857-8031	WEB: WWW.BITUMINOUSINSURANCE.COM
UTAH	4330 SHAWNEE MISSION PKWY STE 100 FAIRWAY, KS 66205-2522 PO BOX 718 SHAWNEE MISSION, KS 66201-0718	PHONE: (913) 262-4664 FAX: (913) 262-0997 TOLL FREE: (800) 821-5354	WEB: WWW.BITUMINOUSINSURANCE.COM
VERMONT	FOSTER PLAZA 5 651 HOLIDAY DR PITTSBURGH, PA 15220-2757	PHONE: (412) 937-9000 FAX: (412) 937-1143 TOLL FREE: (800) 253-1232	WEB: WWW.BITUMINOUSINSURANCE.COM

VIRGINIA	HEAVER PLZ STE 403 1301 YORK RD LUTHERVILLE, MD 21093 PO BOX 509 LUTHERVILLE, MD 21094-0509	PHONE: (410) 321-7670 FAX: (410) 296-7413 TOLL FREE: (800) 346-5108	WEB: WWW.BITUMINOUSINSURANCE.COM
	7201 GLEN FOREST DR STE 200 RICHMOND, VA 23226-3759 PO BOX 26503 RICHMOND, VA 23261-6503	PHONE: (804) 282-7641 FAX: (804) 282-2433 TOLL FREE: (800) 552-0101	WEB: WWW.BITUMINOUSINSURANCE.COM
WASHINGTON	1200 VALLEY WEST DR STE 600 WEST DES MOINES, IA 50266 PO BOX 65605 WEST DES MOINES, IA 50265-0605	PHONE: (515) 223-1122 FAX: (515) 223-4315 TOLL FREE: (800) 383-1122	WEB: WWW.BITUMINOUSINSURANCE.COM
WEST VIRGINIA	FOSTER PLAZA 5 651 HOLIDAY DR PITTSBURGH, PA 15220-2757	PHONE: (412) 937-9000 FAX: (412) 937-1143 TOLL FREE: (800) 253-1232	WEB: WWW.BITUMINOUSINSURANCE.COM
	HEAVER PLZ STE 403 1301 YORK RD LUTHERVILLE, MD 21093 PO BOX 509 LUTHERVILLE, MD 21094-0509	PHONE: (410) 321-7670 FAX: (410) 296-7413 TOLL FREE: (800) 346-5108	WEB: WWW.BITUMINOUSINSURANCE.COM
WISCONSIN	3333 N MAYFAIR RD STE 104 MILWAUKEE, WI 53222-3226 PO BOX 1210 BROOKFIELD, WI 53085	PHONE: (262) 792-9254 FAX: (262) 792-9264 TOLL FREE: (800) 242-6258	WEB: WWW.BITUMINOUSINSURANCE.COM
WYOMING	445 UNION BLVD STE 125 LAKEWOOD, CO 80228 PO BOX 280729 LAKEWOOD, CO 80228-0729	FAX: (303) 982-0808 TOLL FREE: (877) 746-1748	WEB: WWW.BITUMINOUSINSURANCE.COM

BLUE CROSS AND BLUE SHIELD OF ALABAMA

ALABAMA	450 RIVERCHASE PKY E BIRMINGHAM, AL 35298-0001 PO BOX 995 BIRMINGHAM, AL 35298	PHONE: (205) 988-2100 FAX: (205) 220-6477 TOLL FREE: (800) 292-8855	E-MAIL: WEBINPUT@BCBSAL.ORG

BLUE CROSS BLUE SHIELD — *SEE ALSO FLORIDA COMBINE LIFE*

NATIONAL	636 GRAND AVE DES MOINES, IA 50309 PO BOX 9291 DES MOINES, IA 50309	PHONE: (712) 279-8500 FAX: (712) 279-8450 TOLL FREE: (800) 526-8995	WEB: WWW.WELLMARK.COM
	PO BOX 804 CUMBERLAND, MD 21117	PHONE: (301) 724-8001 FAX: (301) 724-8008 TOLL FREE: (866) 520-6099	WEB: WWW.CAREFIRST.COM
	120 FIFTH AVE PL PITTSBURGH, PA 15222-3099	PHONE: (412) 544-7000 TOLL FREE: (800) 547-3627	WEB: WWW.HIGHMARK.COM
ALABAMA	450 RIVERCHASE PKY E BIRMINGHAM, AL 35244 PO BOX 995 BIRMINGHAM, AL 35298	PHONE: (205) 988-2100 TOLL FREE: (800) 292-8868	WEB: WWW.BCBSAL.COM OR WWW.BCBSAL.ORG

B

ALASKA	7001 220TH ST SW MOUNT LAKE TERRACE, WA 98043-2124 PO BOX 327 SEATTLE, WA 98111	PHONE: (425) 918-4000 FAX: (425) 918-4900 TOLL FREE: (800) 527-6675	WEB: WWW.PREMERA.COM
ADDITIONAL COMMENTS: LIFE WISE - SERVES ARIZONA & OREGON			
ARKANSAS	SOUTHEAST REGION 1800 W 73RD ST PINE BLUFF, AR 71603-8328 PO BOX 1245 PINE BLUFF, AR 71613	PHONE: (870) 536-1223 FAX: (870) 543-2915 TOLL FREE: (800) 236-0369	WEB: WWW.ARKBLUECROSS.COM
	CENTRAL REGION 320 W CAPITOL STE 900 LITTLE ROCK, AR 72201 PO BOX 2181 LITTLE ROCK, AR 72203	FAX: (501) 379-4659 TOLL FREE: (800) 421-1112	E-MAIL: INFO@ARKBLUECROSS.COM WEB: WWW.ARKBLUECROSS.COM
	WEST CENTRAL REGION 3501 OLD GREENWOOD RD STE 5 FORT SMTIH, AR 72903	PHONE: (479) 648-1635 FAX: (479) 648-6322 TOLL FREE: (866) 254-9117	WEB: WWW.ARKBLUECROSS.COM
	NORTHWEST REGION 516 E MILLSAP RD STE 103 FAYETTEVILLE, AR 72703-6252	PHONE: (479) 527-2310 FAX: (479) 527-2323 TOLL FREE: (888) 847-1900	WEB: WWW.ARKBLUECROSS.COM
	NORTHEAST REGION 707 E MATTHEWS AVE JONESBORO, AR 72401-3127 PO BOX 1475 JONESBORO, AR 72403	PHONE: (870) 935-4871 FAX: (870) 974-5713 TOLL FREE: (800) 299-4124	E-MAIL: NEREGIONCS@ARKBLUECROSS.COM WEB: WWW.ARKBLUECROSS.COM
DISTRICT OF COLUMBIA	840 FIRST ST NE WASHINGTON, DC 20065-0001 PO BOX 96242 WASHINGTON, DC 20090-6242	PHONE: (202) 479-8000	WEB: WWW.CAREFIRST.COM
GEORGIA	CORPORATE HEADQUARTERS 3350 PEACHTREE RD NE ATLANTA, GA 30326-1048 PO BOX 9907 ATLANTA, GA 30302-4445	PHONE: (404) 842-8000 FAX: (404) 842-8010 TOLL FREE: (800) 441-2273	WEB: WWW.BCBSGA.COM
HAWAII	HMSA HAWAII MEDICAL SERVICE ASSOCIATION 818 KEEAUMOKU ST HONOLULU, HI 96814-2365 PO BOX 860 HONOLULU, HI 96808-0860	PHONE: (808) 948-6111 FAX: (808) 948-5567 TOLL FREE: (800) 648-3190 IN-STATE: (800) 790-4672	WEB: WWW.HMSA.COM
IDAHO	IDAHO CORPORATE OFFICE 1602 21ST AVE LEWISTON, ID 83501-4061 PO BOX 1106 LEWISTON, ID 83501-1106	PHONE: (208) 746-2671 FAX: (208) 798-2097 TOLL FREE: (800) 632-2022	WEB: WWW.ID.REGENCE.COM
	IDAHO CORPORATE OFFICES 3000 E PINE AVE MERIDIAN, ID 83642-5995 PO BOX 7408 BOISE, ID 83707-1408	PHONE: (208) 345-4550 FAX: (208) 331-7311 TOLL FREE: (800) 274-4018	WEB: WWW.BCIDAHO.COM
ILLINOIS	300 E RANDOLPH ST CHICAGO, IL 60601-5099 PO BOX 805107 CHICAGO, IL 60680-4112	PHONE: (312) 653-6000 FAX: (312) 856-1946 TOLL FREE: (800) 892-2803	WEB: WWW.BCBSIL.COM

IOWA	636 GRAND AVE DES MOINES, IA 50309 PO BOX 9291 DES MOINES, IA 50309	PHONE: (712) 279-8500 FAX: (712) 279-8450 TOLL FREE: (800) 526-8995	WEB: WWW.WELLMARK.COM
KANSAS	ONE PERSHING SQUARE 2301 MAIN ST KANSAS CITY, MO 64108-2442 PO BOX 419169 KANSAS CITY, MO 64141-6169	PHONE: (816) 395-2222 FAX: (816) 395-3959 TOLL FREE: (800) 892-6048	WEB: WWW.BCBSKC.COM
LOUISIANA	CORPORATE HEADQUARTERS 5525 REITZ AVE BATON ROUGE, LA 70809-3082 PO BOX 98029 BATON ROUGE, LA 70898-9029	PHONE: (225) 295-3307 FAX: (225) 295-2147 TOLL FREE: (800) 599-2583	WEB: WWW.BCBSLA.COM
MARYLAND	10455 MILL RUN CIR OWINGS MILLS, MD 21117-5559 PO BOX 804 OWINGS MILLS, MD 21117	PHONE: (410) 581-3000 FAX: (410) 998-5576 TOLL FREE: (800) 524-4555	WEB: WWW.CAREFIRST.COM
	840 FIRST ST NE WASHINGTON, DC 20065-0001 PO BOX 96242 WASHINGTON, DC 20090-6242	PHONE: (202) 479-8000	WEB: WWW.CAREFIRST.COM
MASSACHUSETTS	401 PARK DR BOSTON, MA 02215-3325 PO BOX 9196 NORTH QUINCY, MA 02171-9196	PHONE: (617) 246-5000 TOLL FREE: (800) 327-6716	WEB: WWW.BCBSMA.COM
MICHIGAN	BLUE CHOICE SERVICE CENTER 20500 CIVIC CTR DR SOUTHFIELD, MI 48076 PO BOX 5043 SOUTHFIELD, MI 48086-5043	PHONE: (248) 799-6400 FAX: (248) 799-6969 TOLL FREE: (800) 662-6667	WEB: WWW.BCBSMI.COM
	BLUE CARE NETWORK FEDERAL EMPLOYEE PROGRAM 600 LAFAYETTE E DETROIT, MI 48226 PO BOX 2599 DETROIT, MI 48231-2599	PHONE: (313) 225-9000 TOLL FREE: (800) 482-3600 IN-STATE: (800) 482-3146	WEB: WWW.BCBSMI.COM
	BLUE CARE NETWORK 616 & 269 AREA CODES 86 MONROE CENTER NW GRAND RAPIDS, MI 49518 PO BOX 894 GRAND RAPIDS, MI 49518	PHONE: (616) 957-5057 FAX: (616) 957-3476 TOLL FREE: (800) 968-2583 IN-STATE: *800) 662-6667	WEB: WWW.BCNBSMI.COM
MISSOURI	ONE PERSHING SQUARE 2301 MAIN ST KANSAS CITY, MO 64108-2442 PO BOX 419169 KANSAS CITY, MO 64141-6169	PHONE: (816) 395-2222 FAX: (816) 395-3959 TOLL FREE: (800) 892-6048	WEB: WWW.BCBSKC.COM
MONTANA	560 N PARK AVE HELENA, MT 59601-2702 PO BOX 4309 HELENA, MT 59604-4309	PHONE: (406) 444-8200 FAX: (406) 791-4119 TOLL FREE: (800) 447-7828 IN-STATE: (800) 447-7828	E-MAIL: GENERAL@BCBSMT.COM WEB: WWW.BCBSMT.COM

NEW MEXICO	PO BOX 27630 ALBUQUERQUE, NM 87125-7630	PHONE: (505) 291-3500 FAX: (505) 291-3541 TOLL FREE: (800) 835-8699	WEB: WWW.BCBSNM.COM
NEW YORK	11 W 42ND ST NEW YORK, NY 10036-8002	PHONE: (212) 476-1000 FAX: (212) 476-1281	WEB: WWW.EMPIREBLUE.COM
	UTICA BUSINESS PARK 12 RHOADS DR UTICA, NY 13502	TOLL FREE: (800) 311-3536	WEB: WWW.EXCELLUSBCBS.COM
	165 COURT ST ROCHESTER, NY 14647-0001 PO BOX 41965 ROCHESTER, NY 14604	PHONE: (585) 454-1700 FAX: (585) 238-3620 TOLL FREE: (800) 462-0116 OR (800) 724-5032 IN-STATE: (800) 847-1200	WEB: WWW.EXCELLUSBCBS.COM
	1901 MAIN ST BUFFALO, NY 14240 PO BOX 80 BUFFALO, NY 14240-0080	PHONE: (716) 884-3461 FAX: (716) 887-8981 TOLL FREE: (800) 950-0051	E-MAIL: SERVICEWNY@HEALTHNOW.COM WEB: WWW.BCBSWNY.COM
	344 S WARREN ST SYRACUSE, NY 13202 PO BOX 4809 SYRACUSE, NY 13221-4809	PHONE: (315) 671-6400	WEB: WWW.EXCELLUSBCBS.COM
NORTH CAROLINA	5901 CHAPEL HILL BLVD DURHAM, NC 27702 PO BOX 2291 DURHAM, NC 27702-2291	PHONE: (919) 489-7431 TOLL FREE: (800) 250-3630 IN-STATE: (800) 222-5028	WEB: WWW.BCBSNC.COM
OKLAHOMA	1215 S BOULDER TULSA, OK 74119 PO BOX 3283 TULSA, OK 74102-3283	PHONE: (918) 560-3500 FAX: (918) 560-7891 TOLL FREE: (800) 942-5837	WEB: WWW.BCBSOK.COM
OREGON	PORTLAND REGIONAL OFFICE 100 SW MARKET ST PORTLAND, OR 97201 PO BOX 1271 PORTLAND, OR 97207	PHONE: (503) 225-5221 TOLL FREE: (800) 452-7278	WEB: WWW.OR.REGENCE.COM
PENNSYLVANIA	19 N MAIN ST WILKES-BARRE, PA 18711-0302	PHONE: (570) 200-6515 FAX: (570) 200-6840 TOLL FREE: (800) 829-8599	WEB: WWW.BCNEPA.COM
	1901 MARKET ST PHILADELPHIA, PA 19103	PHONE: (215) 241-2400 TOLL FREE: (800) 227-3119	WEB: WWW.IBX.COM

PENNSYLVANIA — CONTINUED	120 FIFTH AVE PL PITTSBURGH, PA 15222-3099	PHONE: (412) 544-7000 TOLL FREE: (800) 547-3627	WEB: WWW.HIGHMARK.COM
PUERTO RICO	1441 FD ROOSEVELT AVE CAPARRA, PR 00920 PO BOX 71391 SAN JUAN, PR 00936	PHONE: (787) 749-4949 FAX: (787) 749-4100 TOLL FREE: (877) 715-1921	WEB: WWW.SSSPR.COM
RHODE ISLAND	444 WESTMINSTER ST PROVIDENCE, RI 02903-3279	PHONE: (401) 459-1000 FAX: (401) 351-2050 TOLL FREE: (800) 637-3718	WEB: WWW.BCBSRI.COM
SOUTH CAROLINA	I-20 E AT ALPINE RD COLUMBIA, SC 29219-0001 PO BOX 100300 COLUMBIA, SC 29202	PHONE: (803) 788-3860 TOLL FREE: (800) 868-2500	WEB: WWW.SOUTHCAROLINABLUES.COM
TENNESSEE	801 PINE ST CHATTANOOGA, TN 37402-2556 PO BOX 180150 CHATTANOOGA, TN 37401-7150	PHONE: (423) 755-5600 FAX: (423) 755-3178 TOLL FREE: (800) 565-9140	WEB: WWW.BCBST.COM
TEXAS	901 S CENTRAL EXPY RICHARDSON, TX 75080-7399 PO BOX 655730 RICHARDSON, TX 75080-5730	PHONE: (972) 766-6900 FAX: (972) 766-6060 TOLL FREE: (800) 521-2227	WEB: WWW.BCBSTX.COM
UTAH	2890 E COTTONWOOD PKY SALT LAKE CITY, UT 84121-7035 PO BOX 30270 SALT LAKE CITY, UT 84130-0270	PHONE: (801) 333-2100 FAX: (801) 333-6523 TOLL FREE: (800) 624-6519	E-MAIL: UTGENDEV@REGENCE.COM WEB: WWW.UT.REGENCE.COM
WASHINGTON	7001 220TH ST SW MOUNT LAKE TERRACE, WA 98043-2124 PO BOX 327 SEATTLE, WA 98111	PHONE: (425) 918-4000 FAX: (425) 918-4900 TOLL FREE: (800) 527-6675	WEB: WWW.PREMERA.COM
	WASHINGTON 1800 NINTH AVE SEATTLE, WA 98101-1322 PO BOX 21267 SEATTLE, WA 98111-3267	PHONE: (206) 464-3600 FAX: (206) 389-5669 TOLL FREE: (800) 458-3523	WEB: WWW.WA.REGENCE.COM
	EASTERN WASHINGTON 3900 E SPRAGUE SPOKANE, WA 99202-4847 PO BOX 3048 SPOKANE, WA 99220-3048	PHONE: (509) 536-4700 FAX: (509) 536-4771	WEB: WWW.PREMERA.COM

ADDITIONAL COMMENTS: LIFE WISE - SERVES ARIZONA & OREGON

WISCONSIN	145 S PIONEER RD FOND DU LAC, WI 54935-3871 PO BOX 2270 FOND DU LAC, WI 54936-2270	PHONE: (920) 923-7575 FAX: (920) 923-7572	WEB: WWW.BLUECROSSWISCONSIN.COM

WISCONSIN — CONTINUED	CORPORATE HEADQUARTERS 401 W MICHIGAN ST MILWAUKEE, WI 53203-2896	PHONE: (414) 226-5000 FAX: (414) 226-5040 TOLL FREE: (800) 558-1584	WEB: WWW.BLUECROSSWISCONSIN.COM

BLUE CROSS BLUE SHIELD

ARIZONA	2444 W LAS PALMARITAS DR PHOENIX, AZ 85021-4883 PO BOX 2924 PHOENIX, AZ 85062-2924	PHONE: (602) 864-4400 FAX: (602) 864-4242 TOLL FREE: (800) 232-2345	E-MAIL: WEBMASTER@BCBSAZ.COM WEB: WWW.BCBSAZ.COM
DELAWARE	PO BOX 1991 WILMINGTON, DE 19899-1991	PHONE: (302) 421-3000 FAX: (302) 421-3110 TOLL FREE: (800) 633-2563 IN-STATE: (800) 292-7865	WEB: WWW.BCBSDE.COM
FLORIDA	4800 DEERWOOD CAMPUS PKY JACKSONVILLE, FL 32246 PO BOX 1798 JACKSONVILLE, FL 32231-0014	PHONE: (904) 791-6111 TOLL FREE: (800) 727-2227	WEB: WWW.BCBSFL.COM
ILLINOIS	75 EXECUTIVE DR STE 300 AURORA, IL 60504-7947 PO BOX 2037 AURORA, IL 60507-2037	PHONE: (630) 978-7878 FAX: (630) 978-8460 TOLL FREE: (800) 538-8833	WEB: WWW.BCBSIL.COM
NEBRASKA	1233 LINCOLN MALL LINCOLN, NE 68508-2847 PO BOX 3248 OMAHA, NE 68180-3248	PHONE: (402) 458-4800 OR (402) 390-1800 FAX: (402) 477-2952 TOLL FREE: (800) 642-8516	WEB: WWW.BCBSNE.COM
NEW MEXICO	75 EXECUTIVE DR STE 300 AURORA, IL 60504-7947 PO BOX 2037 AURORA, IL 60507-2037	PHONE: (630) 978-7878 FAX: (630) 978-8460 TOLL FREE: (800) 538-8833	WEB: WWW.BCBSIL.COM
PUERTO RICO	LA CRUZ AZULDE CARR ESTATAL #1 KM.17.3 RIO PIEDRAS, PR 00927	PHONE: (787) 272-9898 FAX: (787) 272-7867	WEB: WWW.CRUZAZUL.COM
TEXAS	75 EXECUTIVE DR STE 300 AURORA, IL 60504-7947 PO BOX 2037 AURORA, IL 60507-2037	PHONE: (630) 978-7878 FAX: (630) 978-8460 TOLL FREE: (800) 538-8833	WEB: WWW.BCBSIL.COM
VERMONT	445 INDUSTRIAL LN MONTPELIER, VT 05602-0000 PO BOX 186 MONTPELIER, VT 05601-0186	PHONE: (802) 223-6131 FAX: (802) 223-1077 TOLL FREE: (800) 255-4550 IN-STATE: (800) 247-2583	WEB: WWW.BCBSVT.COM

BLUE CROSS BLUE SHIELD OF KANSAS

KANSAS	1133 SW TOPEKA BLVD TOPEKA, KS 66629-0001 PO BOX 239 TOPEKA, KS 66601	PHONE: (785) 291-4183 OR (785) 291-4180 FAX: (785) 290-0711 TOLL FREE: (800) 432-0272	E-MAIL: CSC@BCBSKS.COM WEB: WWW.BCBSKS.COM

BLUE CROSS BLUE SHIELD OF MINNESOTA

MINNESOTA	3535 BLUE CROSS RD EAGAN, MN 55122-1154 PO BOX 64560 ST PAUL, MN 55164-0560	PHONE: (651) 662-5200 FAX: (651) 662-2745 TOLL FREE: (800) 262-0820	WEB: WWW.BLUECROSSMN.COM

BLUE CROSS BLUE SHIELD OF MISSISSIPPI

LOUISIANA *MISSISSIPPI* *MISSOURI*	3545 LAKELAND DR FLOWOOD, MS 39232-9799 PO BOX 1043 JACKSON, MS 39215-1043	PHONE: (601) 932-3704 FAX: (601) 939-7035 TOLL FREE: (800) 222-8046 IN-STATE: (800) 222-8046	WEB: WWW.BCBSMS.COM

BLUE CROSS BLUE SHIELD OF TEXAS

TEXAS	4242 SUNSET DR SAN ANGELO, TX 76904-5652 PO BOX 660044 DALLAS, TX 75266-0044	PHONE: (325) 224-2170 FAX: (915) 224-2030 TOLL FREE: (877) 299-2377	WEB: WWW.BCBSTX.COM

BLUE CROSS BLUE SHIELD OF WYOMING

WYOMING	4000 HOUSE AVE CHEYENNE, WY 82001-5460 PO BOX 2266 CHEYENNE, WY 82003-2266	PHONE: (307) 634-1393 FAX: (307) 778-8582 TOLL FREE: (800) 442-2376	WEB: WWW.WYOMINGBLUE.COM

BLUE CROSS CANADA — *SEE ALSO PACIFIC BLUE CROSS*

ALBERTA	10009 108TH ST NW EDMONTON, AB T5J 3C5	PHONE: (780) 498-8000 FAX: (780) 425-4627 TOLL FREE: (800) 661-6995	WEB: WWW.AB.BLUECROSS.CA
MANITOBA	MAIN LEVEL POLO PRK SHOPPING CENTRE WINNIPEG, MB R3C-2X7 PO BOX 1046 WINNIPEG, MB R3C-2X7	PHONE: (888) 596-1032 FAX: (204) 786-5965	WEB: WWW.MB.BLUECROSS.CA
ONTARIO	185 THE WEST MALL STE 1200 ETOBICOKE, ON M9C-5P1 PO BOX 2000 ETOBICCOKE, ON M9C-5P1	PHONE: (416) 626-1447 FAX: (800) 466-1166 TOLL FREE: (800) 873-2583	WEB: WWW.USEBLUE.COM OR WWW.MEDAZIE.BLUECROSS.CA

BLUE CROSS OF CALIFORNIA

CALIFORNIA	2000 CORPORATE CENTER DR NEWBURY PARK, CA 91320	FAX: (818) 228-5104 TOLL FREE: (800) 627-8797	WEB: WWW.BLUECROSSCA.COM
	21555 OXNARD ST WOODLAND HILLS, CA 91365 PO BOX 4239 WOODLAND HILLS, CA 91365	FAX: (818) 703-2848 TOLL FREE: (800) 999-3643	WEB: WWW.BLUECROSSCA.COM

BLUE SHIELD OF CALIFORNIA

NATIONAL	NATIONAL ACCOUNTS PO BOX 1505 REDBLUFFS, CA 96080	PHONE: (415) 229-5001 TOLL FREE: (800) 535-8000	WEB: WWW.MYLIFEPATH.COM
	NATIONAL ACCOUNTS PO BOX 272570 CHICO, CA 95927-2570	TOLL FREE: (800) 241-4896	WEB: WWW.MYLIFEPATH.COM
CALIFORNIA	FEDERAL EMPLOYEE PROGRAM PO BOX 272510 CHICO, CA 95927-2510	TOLL FREE: (800) 824-8839	WEB: WWW.MYLIFEPATH.COM
	SERVICE CENTER PO BOX 272530 CHICO, CA 95927-2530	PHONE: (209) 367-2800 TOLL FREE: (800) 535-8000 IN-STATE: (800) 633-0337	WEB: WWW.MYLIFEPATH.COM
	SOUTHERN CALIFORNIA CLAIMS PO BOX 272540 CHICO, CA 95927-9540	PHONE: (415) 229-5001 TOLL FREE: (800) 535-8000	WEB: WWW.MYLIFEPATH.COM
	ALL OTHER COUNTIES PO BOX 272550 CHICO, CA 95927-2550	PHONE: (415) 229-5001 TOLL FREE: (800) 535-8000	WEB: WWW.MYLIFEPATH.COM
	CENTRAL CALIFORNIA CLAIMS PO BOX 272560 CHICO, CA 95927-2560	TOLL FREE: (800) 535-8000	WEB: WWW.MYLIFEPATH.COM
	GENERAL ELECTRIC HEALTH CARE PREFERRED PO BOX 272580 CHICO, CA 95927	TOLL FREE: (800) 688-0327	WEB: WWW.MYLIFEPATH.COM
	CORPORATE HEADQUARTERS 50 BEALE ST SAN FRANCISCO, CA 94105-1808 CORPORATE PROVIDER SERVICES PO BOX 7168 SAN FRANCISCO, CA 94120	PHONE: (415) 229-5000 FAX: (415) 229-5070 TOLL FREE: (800) 559-5905 IN-STATE: (800) 922-2099	WEB: WWW.MYLIFEPATH.COM

BLUECHOICE HEALTH PLAN

SOUTH CAROLINA	4101 PERCIVAL RD COLUMBIA, SC 29229 PO BOX 6170 COLUMBIA, SC 29260-6170	PHONE: (803) 786-8466 FAX: (803) 714-6443 TOLL FREE: (800) 327-3183	WEB: WWW.BLUECHOICESC.COM

B

BLUEGRASS FAMILY HEALTH

KENTUCKY	651 PERIMETER DR STE 300 LEXINGTON, KY 40517 PO BOX 22738 LEXINGTON, KY 40522-2738	PHONE: (800) 787-2680 TOLL FREE: (800) 787-2680	E-MAIL: WEBMASTER@BGFH.COM WEB: WWW.BGFH.COM

BMI — *SEE ALSO BUSINESS MENS INSURANCE CO*

BMI HEALTH PLANS

ARKANSAS	2425 NOWATA PL BARTLESVILLE, OK 74006 PO BOX 3767 BARTLESVILLE, OK 74006	PHONE: (918) 335-0387 FAX: (918) 335-0450 TOLL FREE: (800) 824-5034	E-MAIL: BMI@BMI-HEALTHPLANS.COM WEB: WWW.BMI-HEALTHPLANS.COM
	3116 S PICKWICK PL SPRINGFIELD, MO 65804 PO BOX 14379 SPRINGFIELD, MO 65814	FAX: (417) 886-4094 TOLL FREE: (800) 724-6332	E-MAIL: BMI@BMI-HEALTHPLANS.COM WEB: WWW.BMI-HEALTHPLANS.COM
	628 W BROADWAY ST STE 200 NORTH LITTLE ROCK, AR 72114-5545 PO BOX 9416 NORTH LITTLE ROCK, AR 72119-5989	PHONE: (501) 375-5500 FAX: (501) 375-4718 TOLL FREE: (800) 883-3895	E-MAIL: BMI@BMI-HEALTHPLANS.COM WEB: WWW.BMI-HEALTHPLANS.COM
MISSISSIPPI	3116 S PICKWICK PL SPRINGFIELD, MO 65804 PO BOX 14379 SPRINGFIELD, MO 65814	FAX: (417) 886-4094 TOLL FREE: (800) 724-6332	E-MAIL: BMI@BMI-HEALTHPLANS.COM WEB: WWW.BMI-HEALTHPLANS.COM
MISSOURI *OKLAHOMA*	2425 NOWATA PL BARTLESVILLE, OK 74006 PO BOX 3767 BARTLESVILLE, OK 74006	PHONE: (918) 335-0387 FAX: (918) 335-0450 TOLL FREE: (800) 824-5034	E-MAIL: BMI@BMI-HEALTHPLANS.COM WEB: WWW.BMI-HEALTHPLANS.COM
OKLAHOMA *TENNESSEE*	3116 S PICKWICK PL SPRINGFIELD, MO 65804 PO BOX 14379 SPRINGFIELD, MO 65814	FAX: (417) 886-4094 TOLL FREE: (800) 724-6332	E-MAIL: BMI@BMI-HEALTHPLANS.COM WEB: WWW.BMI-HEALTHPLANS.COM

BOILERMAKERS NATIONAL FUNDS

NATIONAL	754 MINNESOTA AVE KANSAS CITY, KS 66101-2766	PHONE: (913) 342-6555 TOLL FREE: (866) 342-6555	WEB: WWW.BOILERMAKERS.ORG

BOLLINGER, INC

NATIONAL	101 JFK PKY SHORT HILLS, NJ 07078-2620 PO BOX 5000 SHORT HILLS, NJ 07078-0727	PHONE: (973) 467-0444 FAX: (973) 921-2876 TOLL FREE: (800) 526-1379	WEB: WWW.BOLLINGERINSURANCE.COM

BOON-CHAPMAN BENEFIT ADMINISTRATORS — *PAID DENTAL*

NATIONAL	12301 RESEARCH BLVD BLDG 4 STE 400 AUSTIN, TX 78759 PO BOX 9150 AUSTIN, TX 78766-9150	PHONE: (512) 328-7979 FAX: (512) 459-1552 TOLL FREE: (800) 342-3279	WEB: WWW.BOONCHAPMAN.COM

ARKANSAS	4943 OLD GREENWOOD RD STE 3 FORT SMITH, AR 72903 PO BOX 6269 FORT SMITH, AR 72903	PHONE: (479) 648-9995 FAX: (479) 648-6784 TOLL FREE: (888) 860-3835	WEB: WWW.BOONCHAPMAN.COM
TEXAS	12301 RESEARCH BLVD BLDG 4 STE 400 AUSTIN, TX 78759 PO BOX 9189 AUSTIN, TX 78766-9189	PHONE: (512) 454-2681 FAX: (512) 459-1552 TOLL FREE: (800) 228-6010	WEB: WWW.BOONCHAPMAN.COM

ADDITIONAL COMMENTS: PPO NETWORK

BOSTON MUTUAL LIFE INSURANCE CO

NATIONAL	120 ROYALL ST CANTON, MA 02021-1098 PO BOX 219 CANTON, MA 02021	PHONE: (781) 828-7000 FAX: (781) 770-0490 TOLL FREE: (800) 669-2668	E-MAIL: CLIENTSERVICES@BOSTONMUTUAL.COM WEB: WWW.BOSTONMUTUAL.COM

BRADFORD FINANCIAL CENTER

ALASKA
COLORADO
ILLINOIS
INDIANA
IOWA
MINNESOTA
MISSOURI
SOUTH DAKOTA
TENNESSEE

	215 N MAIN CLARION, IA 50525-1439 PO BOX 540 CLARION, IA 50525-0540	PHONE: (515) 532-6661 FAX: (515) 532-6547 TOLL FREE: (800) 348-4419	WEB: WWW.BRADFORDFINANCIALCENTER.COM

BREMEN FARMERS MUTUAL INSURANCE CO

KANSAS	201 BREMNEKE BREMEN, KS 66412 PO BOX 98 BREMEN, KS 66412-0098	PHONE: (785) 337-2203 FAX: (785) 337-2414	

BRETHREN MUTUAL INSURANCE CO

MARYLAND *PENNSYLVANIA* *VIRGINIA*	149 N EDGEWOOD DR HAGERSTOWN, MD 21740-6599	PHONE: (301) 739-0950 FAX: (301) 739-6301 TOLL FREE: (800) 621-4264	WEB: WWW.BMICONLINE.COM

BRISTOL WEST INSURANCE GROUP — *COAST NATIONAL INSURANCE*

NATIONAL	5701 STERLING RD DAVIE, FL 33314 PO BOX 229080 HOLLYWOOD, FL 33022-9080	PHONE: (954) 316-5200 FAX: (800) 776-5632 TOLL FREE: (800) 338-2560 IN-STATE: (888) 888-0080	WEB: WWW.BRISTOLWEST.COM

BRITISH AMERICAN INSURANCE CO

TEXAS	3535 TRAVIS ST STE 300 DALLAS, TX 75204-1466 PO BOX 1590 DALLAS, TX 75221-1590	PHONE: (214) 559-4887 FAX: (214) 443-5624 TOLL FREE: (800) 964-4242	

BROADSPIRE

NATIONAL	601 SW 2ND AVE STE 2000 PORTLAND, OR 97204	PHONE: (503) 221-2440 FAX: (503) 552-6962 TOLL FREE: (800) 452-9405	WEB: WWW.CHOOSEBROADSPIRE.COM
	PO BOX 10001 VAN NUYS, CA 91410-0001	FAX: (916) 636-4801 TOLL FREE: (866) 817-4354	WEB: WWW.CHOOSEBROADSPIRE.COM
	PO BOX 15810 SACRAMENTO, CA 95852	FAX: (916) 851-7730 TOLL FREE: (800) 225-0185	WEB: WWW.CHOOSEBROADSPIRE.COM
	PO BOX 4124 CONCORD, CA 94524-4124	FAX: (925) 677-3401 TOLL FREE: (800) 874-8523	WEB: WWW.CHOOSEBROADSPIRE.COM

NATIONAL — CONTINUED	1601 SW 80TH TER PLANTATION, FL 33324 PO BOX 18944 PLANTATION, FL 33318	PHONE: (954) 452-4000 TOLL FREE: (800) 800-7885	WEB: WWW.CHOOSEBROADSPIRE.COM
ALABAMA	655 ENGINEERING DR STE 200 NORCROSS, GA 30092-3343 PO BOX 926240 NORCROSS, GA 30010-6240	PHONE: (678) 969-7337 FAX: (678) 969-7363 TOLL FREE: (800) 450-0692	WEB: WWW.CHOOSEBROADSPIRE.COM
	WESTERN REGION PO BOX 305221 NASHVILLE, TN 37230	PHONE: (615) 366-7660 FAX: (615) 366-7668 TOLL FREE: (800) 647-2039	WEB: WWW.KEMPERSERVICES.COM
ARKANSAS	WESTERN REGION PO BOX 305221 NASHVILLE, TN 37230	PHONE: (615) 366-7660 FAX: (615) 366-7668 TOLL FREE: (800) 647-2039	WEB: WWW.KEMPERSERVICES.COM
CALIFORNIA	WESTERN REGION 2920 KILGORE RD RANCHO CORDOVA, CA 95670-6157 PO BOX 15810 SACRAMENTO, CA 95852	PHONE: (916) 851-7500 FAX: (916) 851-7730 TOLL FREE: (800) 225-0185	WEB: WWW.CHOOSEBROADSPIRE.COM
	WESTERN REGION FIVE HUTTON CENTRE STE 300 SANTA ANA, CA 92707 PO BOX 66017 ANAHEIM, CA 92816-6017	PHONE: (714) 428-7100 FAX: (714) 935-5785 TOLL FREE: (800) 732-7475	WEB: WWW.CHOOSEBROADSPIRE.COM
DELAWARE	PO BOX 2036 MECHANICSBURG, PA 17055-0794	PHONE: (717) 691-7460 FAX: (717) 796-7816 OR (717)796-7816 TOLL FREE: (800) 437-3357	WEB: WWW.CHOOSEBROADSPIRE.COM
FLORIDA	TAMPA CLAIMS OFFICE 4511 N HIMES AVE STE 140 TAMPA, FL 33614 PO BOX 30539 TAMPA, FL 33607-3539	PHONE: (813) 350-7300 FAX: (813) 350-7373 TOLL FREE: (800) 258-1811	WEB: WWW.CHOOSEBROADSPIRE.COM
GEORGIA	655 ENGINEERING DR STE 200 NORCROSS, GA 30092-3343 PO BOX 926240 NORCROSS, GA 30010-6240	PHONE: (678) 969-7337 FAX: (678) 969-7363 TOLL FREE: (800) 450-0692	WEB: WWW.CHOOSEBROADSPIRE.COM
	WESTERN REGION PO BOX 305221 NASHVILLE, TN 37230	PHONE: (615) 366-7660 FAX: (615) 366-7668 TOLL FREE: (800) 647-2039	WEB: WWW.KEMPERSERVICES.COM
ILLINOIS	300 EAST CENTER DR STE 100 VERNON HILLS , IL 60061 PO BOX 8141 VERNON HILLS, IL 60061-8141	PHONE: (847) 281-3660 FAX: (847) 281-3650 TOLL FREE: (800) 239-8692	WEB: WWW.CHOOSEBROADSPIRE.COM
INDIANA	PO BOX 850 BROOKFIELD, WI 53008	PHONE: (954) 452-4000 FAX: (317) 297-0310	WEB: WWW.CHOOSEBROADSPIRE.COM
IOWA	SATELLITE OFFICE 1861 N ROCK RD STE 202 WICHITA, KS 67206	PHONE: (316) 681-2001 FAX: (316) 682-6926 TOLL FREE: (800) 345-7045	WEB: WWW.CHOOSEBROADSPIRE.COM
KANSAS	SATELLITE OFFICE 1861 N ROCK RD STE 202 WICHITA, KS 67206	PHONE: (316) 681-2001 FAX: (316) 682-6926 TOLL FREE: (800) 345-7045	WEB: WWW.CHOOSEBROADSPIRE.COM
KENTUCKY	WESTERN REGION PO BOX 305221 NASHVILLE, TN 37230	PHONE: (615) 366-7660 FAX: (615) 366-7668 TOLL FREE: (800) 647-2039	WEB: WWW.KEMPERSERVICES.COM
LOUISIANA	10700 N FWY STE 200 HOUSTON, TX 77037 PO BOX 670688 HOUSTON, TX 77267-0688	PHONE: (281) 405-6100 FAX: (281) 405-6129 TOLL FREE: (800) 352-9994	WEB: WWW.CHOOSEBROADSPIRE.COM

LOUISIANA — CONTINUED	19111 N DALLAS PKWY STE 180 DALLAS, TX 75287 PO BOX 701809 DALLAS, TX 75370-1809	PHONE: (972) 250-5000 FAX: (972) 250-5002 TOLL FREE: (800) 252-1455	WEB: WWW.CHOOSEBROADSPIRE.COM
MAINE MASSACHUSETTS	200 WHEELER RD BURLINGTON, MA 01803 PO BOX 80483 STONEHAM, MA 02180	PHONE: (781)221-8880 FAX: (781)221-8877	WEB: WWW.CHOOSEBROADSPIRE.COM
MISSISSIPPI	655 ENGINEERING DR STE 200 NORCROSS, GA 30092-3343 PO BOX 926240 NORCROSS, GA 30010-6240	PHONE: (678) 969-7337 FAX: (678) 969-7363 TOLL FREE: (800) 450-0692	WEB: WWW.CHOOSEBROADSPIRE.COM
	WESTERN REGION PO BOX 305221 NASHVILLE, TN 37230	PHONE: (615) 366-7660 FAX: (615) 366-7668 TOLL FREE: (800) 647-2039	WEB: WWW.KEMPERSERVICES.COM
MISSOURI	1600 S BRENTWOOD BLVD 7TH FL ST LOUIS, MO 63144 PO BOX 66851 ST LOUIS, MO 63166-6851	PHONE: (314) 301-7400 FAX: (314) 301-7440 TOLL FREE: (800) 232-3804	WEB: WWW.CHOOSEBROADSPIRE.COM
NEW HAMPSHIRE	200 WHEELER RD BURLINGTON, MA 01803 PO BOX 80483 STONEHAM, MA 02180	PHONE: (781)221-8880 FAX: (781)221-8877	WEB: WWW.CHOOSEBROADSPIRE.COM
NEW JERSEY	THREE CONNELL DR BERKLEY HEIGHTS, NJ 07922 PO BOX 608 BERKLEY HEIGHTS, NJ 07922-0608	PHONE: (908) 508 4800 FAX: (908) 508-4850 TOLL FREE: (866) 874-2865	WEB: WWW.CHOOSEBROADSPIRE.COM
NEW YORK	BLDG II 898 VETERANS HWY 4TH FL SMITHTOWN, NY 11788-2955 PO BOX 5000 SMITHTOWN, NY 11787-0800	PHONE: (631) 232-6700 FAX: (631) 234-3080 TOLL FREE: (888) 234-0329	WEB: WWW.CHOOSEBROADSPIRE.COM
NORTH CAROLINA	655 ENGINEERING DR STE 200 NORCROSS, GA 30092-3343 PO BOX 926240 NORCROSS, GA 30010-6240	PHONE: (678) 969-7337 FAX: (678) 969-7363 TOLL FREE: (800) 450-0692	WEB: WWW.CHOOSEBROADSPIRE.COM
	WESTERN REGION PO BOX 305221 NASHVILLE, TN 37230	PHONE: (615) 366-7660 FAX: (615) 366-7668 TOLL FREE: (800) 647-2039	WEB: WWW.KEMPERSERVICES.COM
OHIO	130 E WILSONBRIDGE RD STE 50 WORTHINGTON, OH 43085 PO BOX 231 WORTHINGTON, OH 43085-0231	PHONE: (614) 436-8990 FAX: (614) 825-1860 TOLL FREE: (800) 272-2616	WEB: WWW.CHOOSEBROADSPIRE.COM
OKLAHOMA	SATELLITE OFFICE 1861 N ROCK RD STE 202 WICHITA, KS 67206	PHONE: (316) 681-2001 FAX: (316) 682-6926 TOLL FREE: (800) 345-7045	WEB: WWW.CHOOSEBROADSPIRE.COM
PENNSYLVANIA	PO BOX 2036 MECHANICSBURG, PA 17055-0794	PHONE: (717) 691-7460 FAX: (717) 796-7816 OR (717)796-7816 TOLL FREE: (800) 437-3357	WEB: WWW.CHOOSEBROADSPIRE.COM
SOUTH CAROLINA TENNESSEE	655 ENGINEERING DR STE 200 NORCROSS, GA 30092-3343 PO BOX 926240 NORCROSS, GA 30010-6240	PHONE: (678) 969-7337 FAX: (678) 969-7363 TOLL FREE: (800) 450-0692	WEB: WWW.CHOOSEBROADSPIRE.COM
	WESTERN REGION PO BOX 305221 NASHVILLE, TN 37230	PHONE: (615) 366-7660 FAX: (615) 366-7668 TOLL FREE: (800) 647-2039	WEB: WWW.KEMPERSERVICES.COM
TEXAS	10700 N FWY STE 200 HOUSTON, TX 77037 PO BOX 670688 HOUSTON, TX 77267-0688	PHONE: (281) 405-6100 FAX: (281) 405-6129 TOLL FREE: (800) 352-9994	WEB: WWW.CHOOSEBROADSPIRE.COM

B

TEXAS — CONTINUED	19111 N DALLAS PKWY STE 180 DALLAS, TX 75287 PO BOX 701809 DALLAS, TX 75370-1809	PHONE: (972) 250-5000 FAX: (972) 250-5002 TOLL FREE: (800) 252-1455	WEB: WWW.CHOOSEBROADSPIRE.COM
VERMONT	200 WHEELER RD BURLINGTON, MA 01803 PO BOX 80483 STONEHAM, MA 02180	PHONE: (781)221-8880 FAX: (781)221-8877	WEB: WWW.CHOOSEBROADSPIRE.COM
WASHINGTON	18000 PACIFIC HWY S STE 200 SEATTLE, WA 98188-4264	PHONE: (206) 277-7600 FAX: (206) 277-7709 TOLL FREE: (877) 632-2995	WEB: WWW.CHOOSEBROADSPIRE.COM
WISCONSIN	PO BOX 850 BROOKFIELD, WI 53008	PHONE: (954) 452-4000 FAX: (317) 297-0310	WEB: WWW.CHOOSEBROADSPIRE.COM

BROKERAGE CONCEPTS, INC — *BENEFIT CONCEPTS*

NATIONAL	1021 W 8TH AVE KING OF PRUSSIA, PA 19406-1467 PO BOX 60608 KING OF PRUSSIA, PA 19406-0608	PHONE: (610) 337-2600 FAX: (610) 491-4992 TOLL FREE: (800) 220-2600	WEB: WWW.BCITPA.COM

BROOKSHIRE BROTHERS, LTD

TEXAS	1201 ELLEN TROUT DR LUFKIN, TX 75904-1233 PO BOX 1688 LUFKIN, TX 75902-1688	PHONE: (936) 634-8155 FAX: (936) 634-8646	WEB: WWW.BROOKSHIREBROTHERS.COM

BROTHERHOOD MUTUAL INSURANCE CO

INDIANA	6400 BROTHERHOOD WY FT WAYNE, IN 46825-4251 PO BOX 2227 FT WAYNE, IN 46801-2227	PHONE: (260) 482-8668 FAX: (260) 482-3589 TOLL FREE: (800) 333-3735	WEB: WWW.BROTHERHOODMUTUAL.COM

BROWN & BROWN — *LANCER CLAIM SERVICE*

NATIONAL	681 SOUTH PARKER ST STE 200 ORANGE, CA 92868-2903 PO BOX 7048 ORANGE, CA 92863	PHONE: (714) 939-0700 FAX: (714) 978-8023 TOLL FREE: (800) 821-0540 IN-STATE: (800) 645-5324	WEB: WWW.CALSURANCE.COM

BSI NORTH AMERICAN

NATIONAL	9245 N MERIDIAN ST STE 100 INDIANAPOLIS, IN 46260-1829 PO BOX 6001 INDIANAPOLIS, IN 46206-0001	PHONE: (317) 573-2004 TOLL FREE: (800) 842-3216 IN-STATE: (800) 624-8316	WEB: WWW.BSICONNECT.COM

BUFFALO DIVISION OF HEALTHNOW — *SEE ALSO HEALTHNOW NY, INC*

BUILDING LABORERS LOCAL #310 HEALTH & WELFARE

OHIO	3250 EUCLID AVE STE 150 CLEVELAND, OH 44115-2572	PHONE: (216) 431-2130 FAX: (216) 431-7707 TOLL FREE: (866) 310-2363	

BURLINGTON INSURANCE — *SEE ALSO IFG CO*

BUSINESS COUNCIL OF NEW YORK STATE, INC

NEW YORK	12 CORPORATE WOODS BLVD 4TH FL ALBANY, NY 12211-2390	PHONE: (518) 465-1571 FAX: (518) 432-7033 TOLL FREE: (800) 692-5483	WEB: WWW.BCNYS.ORG

BUSINESS MENS INSURANCE CO — *BMI*

FLORIDA	1320 S DIXIE HWY 6TH FL CORAL GABLES, FL 33146-2926	PHONE: (305) 443-2898 FAX: (305) 442-8486	E-MAIL: BMI@BMICOS.COM WEB: WWW.BMICO.COM

C AND O EMPLOYEES' HOSPITAL ASSOCIATION

NATIONAL	511 MAIN ST 2ND FL CLIFTON FORGE, VA 24422-1166	PHONE: (540) 862-5728 FAX: (540) 862-3552 TOLL FREE: (800) 679-9135	

C L FRATES AND COMPANY

NATIONAL	5005 N LINCOLN BLVD OKLAHOMA CITY, OK 73105-3336 PO BOX 26967 OKLAHOMA CITY, OK 73126-0727	PHONE: (405) 290-5600 FAX: (405) 290-5658 TOLL FREE: (800) 682-1630	WEB: WWW.CLFRATES.COM

CABINET FOR HEALTH SERVICE OF KENTUCKY

KENTUCKY	275 E MAIN ST 6 WA FRANKFORT, KY 40621 PO BOX 2110 FRANKFORT, KY 40602-2110	PHONE: (502) 564-4321 FAX: (502) 226-1898 TOLL FREE: (800) 635-2570	E-MAIL: CHS.DMSWEB@KY.GOV WEB: WWW.CHFS.KY.GOV/DMS

CAI INSURANCE AGENCY, INC — *DBA ACTUARIAL & EMPLOYEE BENEFIT SERVICES CO*

NATIONAL	3481 CENTRAL PKY STE 100 CINCINNATI, OH 45223-3397	PHONE: (513) 221-1140 FAX: (513) 872-7519 TOLL FREE: (800) 447-0220	WEB: WWW.CAIINSURANCE.COM

CAICO — *UNIVERSAL*

FLORIDA *PUERTO RICO*	MEJIZO MEHICO 16 SAN JUAN, PR 00917-0000 PO BOX 191899 SAN JUAN, PR 00919-1899	PHONE: (787) 753-8600 FAX: (787) 282-1683 IN-STATE: (800) 981-0395	WEB: WWW.CAICOPR.COM

CALCO, INC

ALASKA	445 E FIFTH AVE ANCHORAGE, AK 99501-2634 PO BOX 101422 ANCHORAGE, AK 99510-1422	PHONE: (907) 276-8177 FAX: (907) 278-7438	E-MAIL: CAL@CALCOINCTPA.COM

CALIBER ONE INDEMNITY CO

PENNSYLVANIA	ONE OXFORD VALLEY STE 505 LANGHORN, 19047 PO BOX 3006 LANGHORN, PA 19047	PHONE: (267) 306-3500 FAX: (267) 306-3803	

CALIFORNIA BENEFITS DENTAL PLAN — *GENWORTH FINANCIAL*

CALIFORNIA	3611 S HARBOR BLVD STE 150 SANTA ANA, CA 92704-7906	PHONE: (714) 540-4255 FAX: (714) 540-4754 TOLL FREE: (800) 350-3999	WEB: WWW.GEFINANCIALBENEFITS.COM

CALIFORNIA CAPITAL INSURANCE COMPANY — *CIG*

CALIFORNIA *NEVADA* *OREGON*	2300 GARDEN RD MONTEREY, CA 93940-5326 PO BOX 2093 MONTEREY, CA 93942	FAX: (831) 647-8649 TOLL FREE: (800) 682-9255	WEB: WWW.CIGINSURANCE.COM

CALIFORNIA CASUALTY INSURANCE — *A+ AUTO & HOME INSURANCE*

NATIONAL	Self-Insured	144 CENTRAL PARK SQ LOS ALAMOS, NM 87544-4107 PO BOX 418 LOS ALAMOS, NM 87544-0418	PHONE: (505) 662-4224 FAX: (888) 206-3083 TOLL FREE: (800) 841-4736	WEB: WWW.CALIFORNIACASUALTY.COM
ARIZONA	Self-Insured, Prior Authorization	PO BOX 39700 COLORADO SPRINGS, CO 80949-9700	PHONE: (602) 548-5811 FAX: (888) 206-3083 TOLL FREE: (800) 841-4736	WEB: WWW.CALIFORNIACASUALTY.COM
CALIFORNIA *COLORADO*	Self-Insured, Prior Authorization	1650 TALSTAR COLORADO SPRINGS, CO 80920-1004 PO BOX 39700 COLORADO SPRINGS, CO 80949-3970	PHONE: (719) 532-8000 FAX: (800) 840-9295 TOLL FREE: (800) 800-9410	WEB: WWW.CALIFORNIACASUALTY.COM
COLORADO *CONNECTICUT* *DELAWARE* *FLORIDA* *GEORGIA*	Self-Insured, Prior Authorization	4000 W 114TH ST STE 300 LEAWOOD, KS 66211 PO BOX 9100 MISSION, KS 66201-1700	PHONE: (913) 266-3000 FAX: (800) 230-3880 TOLL FREE: (800) 346-6840	WEB: WWW.CALCAS.COM
IDAHO	Self-Insured, Prior Authorization	PO BOX 39700 COLORADO SPRINGS, CO 80949-9700	PHONE: (602) 548-5811 FAX: (888) 206-3083 TOLL FREE: (800) 841-4736	WEB: WWW.CALIFORNIACASUALTY.COM
ILLINOIS *INDIANA*	Self-Insured, Prior Authorization	4000 W 114TH ST STE 300 LEAWOOD, KS 66211 PO BOX 9100 MISSION, KS 66201-1700	PHONE: (913) 266-3000 FAX: (800) 230-3880 TOLL FREE: (800) 346-6340	WEB: WWW.CALCAS.COM
IOWA	Self-Insured, Prior Authorization	PO BOX 39700 COLORADO SPRINGS, CO 80949-9700	PHONE: (602) 548-5811 FAX: (888) 206-3083 TOLL FREE: (800) 841-4736	WEB: WWW.CALIFORNIACASUALTY.COM
KANSAS *KENTUCKY*	Self-Insured, Prior Authorization	4000 W 114TH ST STE 300 LEAWOOD, KS 66211 PO BOX 9100 MISSION, KS 66201-1700	PHONE: (913) 266-3000 FAX: (800) 230-3880 TOLL FREE: (800) 346-6840	WEB: WWW.CALCAS.COM
LOUISIANA	Self-Insured, Prior Authorization	PO BOX 39700 COLORADO SPRINGS, CO 80949-9700	PHONE: (602) 548-5811 FAX: (888) 206-3083 TOLL FREE: (800) 841-4736	WEB: WWW.CALIFORNIACASUALTY.COM
MAINE *MARYLAND*	Self-Insured, Prior Authorization	4000 W 114TH ST STE 300 LEAWOOD, KS 66211 PO BOX 9100 MISSION, KS 66201-1700	PHONE: (913) 266-3000 FAX: (800) 230-3880 TOLL FREE: (800) 346-6840	WEB: WWW.CALCAS.COM
MINNESOTA	Self-Insured, Prior Authorization	PO BOX 39700 COLORADO SPRINGS, CO 80949-9700	PHONE: (602) 548-5811 FAX: (888) 206-3083 TOLL FREE: (800) 841-4736	WEB: WWW.CALIFORNIACASUALTY.COM
MISSOURI	Self-Insured, Prior Authorization	4000 W 114TH ST STE 300 LEAWOOD, KS 66211 PO BOX 9100 MISSION, KS 66201-1700	PHONE: (913) 266-3000 FAX: (800) 230-3880 TOLL FREE: (800) 346-6840	WEB: WWW.CALCAS.COM
MONTANA *NEBRASKA* *NEVADA*	Self-Insured, Prior Authorization	PO BOX 39700 COLORADO SPRINGS, CO 80949-9700	PHONE: (602) 548-5811 FAX: (888) 206-3083 TOLL FREE: (800) 841-4736	WEB: WWW.CALIFORNIACASUALTY.COM
NEW HAMPSHIRE	Self-Insured, Prior Authorization	4000 W 114TH ST STE 300 LEAWOOD, KS 66211 PO BOX 9100 MISSION, KS 66201-1700	PHONE: (913) 266-3000 FAX: (800) 230-3880 TOLL FREE: (800) 346-6840	WEB: WWW.CALCAS.COM
NEW MEXICO	Self-Insured, Prior Authorization	PO BOX 39700 COLORADO SPRINGS, CO 80949-9700	PHONE: (602) 548-5811 FAX: (888) 206-3083 TOLL FREE: (800) 841-4736	WEB: WWW.CALIFORNIACASUALTY.COM

OHIO	4000 W 114TH ST STE 300 LEAWOOD, KS 66211 PO BOX 9100 MISSION, KS 66201-1700	PHONE: (913) 266-3000 FAX: (800) 230-3880 TOLL FREE: (800) 346-6840	WEB: WWW.CALCAS.COM
OKLAHOMA *OREGON*	PO BOX 39700 COLORADO SPRINGS, CO 80949-9700	PHONE: (602) 548-5811 FAX: (888) 206-3083 TOLL FREE: (800) 841-4736	WEB: WWW.CALIFORNIACASUALTY.COM
PENNSYLVANIA *RHODE ISLAND* *TENNESSEE* *VERMONT* *VIRGINIA*	4000 W 114TH ST STE 300 LEAWOOD, KS 66211 PO BOX 9100 MISSION, KS 66201-1700	PHONE: (913) 266-3000 FAX: (800) 230-3880 TOLL FREE: (800) 346-6840	WEB: WWW.CALCAS.COM
WASHINGTON	PO BOX 39700 COLORADO SPRINGS, CO 80949-9700	PHONE: (602) 548-5811 FAX: (888) 206-3083 TOLL FREE: (800) 841-4736	WEB: WWW.CALIFORNIACASUALTY.COM
WEST VIRGINIA	4000 W 114TH ST STE 300 LEAWOOD, KS 66211 PO BOX 9100 MISSION, KS 66201-1700	PHONE: (913) 266-3000 FAX: (800) 230-3880 TOLL FREE: (800) 346-6840	WEB: WWW.CALCAS.COM
WYOMING	PO BOX 39700 COLORADO SPRINGS, CO 80949-9700	PHONE: (602) 548-5811 FAX: (888) 206-3083 TOLL FREE: (800) 841-4736	WEB: WWW.CALIFORNIACASUALTY.COM

CALIFORNIA CASULTY MANAGEMENT CO — *AUTO & HOME INSURANCE PLUS*

CALIFORNIA	1900 ALAMEDA DE LAST PULGAS SAN MATEO, CA 94403-1222 PO BOX M SAN MATEO, CA 94402	PHONE: (650) 574-4000 FAX: (650) 573-0659 TOLL FREE: (800) 288-7765	WEB: WWW.CALCAS.COM

CALIFORNIA FIELD IRONWORKERS TRUST FUND — *WELFARE PLAN*

ARIZONA *CALIFORNIA* *NEVADA*	131 N EL MOLINO AVE STE 330 PASADENA, CA 91101-1878	PHONE: (626) 792-7337 FAX: (626) 792-7667 TOLL FREE: (800) 527-4613	WEB: WWW.IRONWORKERBENNY.COM

CAM ADMINISTRATIVE SERVICES, INC

MICHIGAN	25800 NORTHWESTERN HWY STE 700 SOUTHFIELD, MI 48075-8410 PO BOX 5131 SOUTHFIELD, MI 48086-5131	PHONE: (248) 827-1080 FAX: (248) 827-2112 TOLL FREE: (800) 732-8906	WEB: WWW.CAMADS.COM

CAMBRIDGE INTEGRATED SERVICES GROUP, INC

NATIONAL	PO BOX 2305 MOUNT CLEMENS, MI 48046-2305	PHONE: (586) 792-6355 FAX: (586) 792-0620 TOLL FREE: (800) 482-0615	WEB: WWW.CAMBRIDGEINTEGRATED.COM
	2923 BRADLEY ST PASADENA, CA 91107-1502 PO BOX 7001 PASADENA, CA 91109	PHONE: (626) 296-4200 FAX: (626) 296-4242 TOLL FREE: (800) 542-7597	WEB: WWW.CAMBRIDGEWORLDWIDE.COM
	4B CEDAR BROOK DR CRANBURY, NJ 08512	PHONE: (609) 655-8383 FAX: (440) 914-2837 TOLL FREE: (800) 662-1170	WEB: WWW.CAMBRIDGEWORLDWIDE.COM
ARIZONA	1850 N CENTRAL AVE STE 1650 PHOENIX, AZ 85004 PO BOX 52106 PHOENIX, AZ 85072	PHONE: (602) 427-6001 FAX: (602) 427-6010 TOLL FREE: (800) 662-1170	WEB: WWW.CAMBRIDGEINTEGRATED.COM

CALIFORNIA	11030 WHITE ROCK RD STE 110 RANCHO CORDOVA, CA 95670-6055 PO BOX 15901 SACRAMENTO, CA 95852	PHONE: (916) 638-8300 FAX: (916) 635-6431 TOLL FREE: (800) 597-7677	WEB: WWW.CAMBRIDGEWORLDWIDE.COM
COLORADO	1850 N CENTRAL AVE STE 1650 PHOENIX, AZ 85004 PO BOX 52106 PHOENIX, AZ 85072	PHONE: (602) 427-6001 FAX: (602) 427-6010 TOLL FREE: (800) 662-1170	WEB: WWW.CAMBRIDGEINGETRATED.COM
CONNECTICUT	340 PEMBERWICK RD 2ND FLOOR GREENWICH, CT 06831	TOLL FREE: (800) 662-1170	WEB: WWW.CAMBRIDGEINTEGRATED.COM
HAWAII	201 MERCHANT ST STE 2400 HONOLULU, HI 96813-2982	PHONE: (808) 533-4900 FAX: (808) 540-4301 TOLL FREE: (877) 533-4900	WEB: WWW.CAMBRIDGEWORLDWIDE.COM
ILLINOIS	175 W JACKSON BLVD STE 1000 CHICAGO, IL 60604	PHONE: (312) 381-8800 FAX: (312) 381-9800 TOLL FREE: (877) 782-4101	WEB: WWW.CAMBRIDGEINTEGRATED.COM
NEVADA *NEW MEXICO*	1850 N CENTRAL AVE STE 1650 PHOENIX, AZ 85004 PO BOX 52106 PHOENIX, AZ 85072	PHONE: (602) 427-6001 FAX: (602) 427-6010 TOLL FREE: (800) 662-1170	WEB: WWW.CAMBRIDGEINGETRATED.COM
NEW YORK	340 PEMBERWICK RD 2ND FLOOR GREENWICH, CT 06831	TOLL FREE: (800) 662-1170	WEB: WWW.CAMBRIDGEINTEGRATED.COM

CAMBRIDGE MUTUAL FIRE INSURANCE CO, BAY STATE INSURANCE CO — *SEE ALSO MERRIMACK MUTUAL*

CAMERON MUTUAL INSURANCE CO

ARKANSAS	214 MCELWAIN DR CAMERON, MO 64429-1321	PHONE: (816) 632-6511 FAX: (816) 632-1022 TOLL FREE: (877) 725-2461	WEB: WWW.CAMERON-INSURANCE.COM
ARKANSAS *MISSOURI*	3851 S JEFFERSON SPRINGFIELD, MO 65807	PHONE: (417) 881-1176 FAX: (417) 881-2590 TOLL FREE: (800) 776-1[illegible]76	WEB: WWW.CAMERON-INSURANCE.COM

CANADA LIFE ASSURANCE CO — *SEE ALSO GREAT WEST LIFE*

ALBERTA	PLACE BENAVENTURE STE 5800 DELAGAUCHETIEVE W MONTREAL, PQ H5A-1B9	PHONE: (514) 874-1838 TOLL FREE: (800) 363-3520	E-MAIL: INFO@CANADALIFE.COM WEB: WWW.CANADALIFE.COM
CANADA	330 UNIVERSITY AVE TORONTO, ON M5G-1R8	PHONE: (416) 597-1440 FAX: (416) 597-6520 TOLL FREE: (800) 668-6569	E-MAIL: INFO@CANADALIFE.COM WEB: WWW.CANADALIFE.COM

CANAL GROUP — *SEE ALSO CANAL INSURANCE CO*

CANAL INSURANCE CO — *CANAL GROUP*

NATIONAL	400 E STONE AVE GREENVILLE, SC 29601-1618 PO BOX 7 GREENVILLE, SC 29602-0007	PHONE: (864) 242-5365 FAX: (864) 679-2518 TOLL FREE: (800) 452-6911	E-MAIL: INFO@CANAL-INS.COM WEB: WWW.CANAL-INS.COM

CANON COCHRAN MANAGEMENT SERVICES, INC — *CCMSI*

ALABAMA *GEORGIA*		3235 SATELLITE BLVD BLDG 400 STE 300 DULUTH, GA 30096	PHONE: (770) 984-9833 FAX: (770) 984-1415 TOLL FREE: (888) 674-2524 IN-STATE: (800)309-1251	E-MAIL: CCMSI@CCMSI.COM WEB: WWW.CCMSI.COM
IOWA *NEBRASKA*		1501 42ND ST STE 220 WEST DES MOINES, IA 50266	PHONE: (515) 223-9022 FAX: (515) 223-9387 TOLL FREE: (800) 982-2365	E-MAIL: CCMSI@CCMSI.COM WEB: WWW.CCMSI.COM
NORTH CAROLINA *SOUTH CAROLINA*		3235 SATELLITE BLVD BLDG 400 STE 300 DULUTH, GA 30096	PHONE: (770) 984-9833 FAX: (770) 984-1415 TOLL FREE: (888) 674-2524 IN-STATE: (800)309-1251	E-MAIL: CCMSI@CCMSI.COM WEB: WWW.CCMSI.COM
SOUTH DAKOTA		1501 42ND ST STE 220 WEST DES MOINES, IA 50266	PHONE: (515) 223-9022 FAX: (515) 223-9387 TOLL FREE: (800) 982-2365	E-MAIL: CCMSI@CCMSI.COM WEB: WWW.CCMSI.COM

CAPE HEALTH PLAN

MICHIGAN		26711 NORTHWESTER HWY STE 300 SOUTHFIELD, MI 48034	PHONE: (248) 386-3000 FAX: (248) 945-9498 TOLL FREE: (888) 354-2273	WEB: WWW.CAPEHEALTH.COM

CAPITAL ADVANTAGE INSURANCE CO — *SEE ALSO CAPITAL BLUE CROSS*

CAPITAL BLUE CROSS — *CAPITAL ADVANTAGE INSURANCE COMPANY*

PENNSYLVANIA		2500 ELMERTON AVE HARRISBURG, PA 17110 PO BOX 772612 HARRISBURG, PA 17177-4611	PHONE: (717) 541-7000 FAX: (717) 541-6915 TOLL FREE: (800) 962-2242	E-MAIL: WEBMASTER@CAPBLUECROSS.COM WEB: WWW.CAPBLUECROSS.COM

CAPITAL CITY INSURANCE CO, INC

ALABAMA *SOUTH CAROLINA*		3850 FERNANDINA RD COLUMBIA, SC 29210-3812 PO BOX 212157 COLUMBIA, SC 29221	FAX: (803) 731-2167 TOLL FREE: (888) 717-6827	WEB: WWW.CAPITALCITYINSURANCE.COM

CAPITAL DISTRICT PHYSICIANS' HEALTH PLAN, INC — *CDPHP*

NEW YORK	R H	500 PATROON CREEK BLVD ALBANY, NY 12206-1055	PHONE: (518) 641-3000 FAX: (518) 641-3508 TOLL FREE: (888) 258-0477	E-MAIL: INFO@CDPHP.COM WEB: WWW.CDPHP.COM

CAPITOL ADMINISTRATORS

NATIONAL	R 3H	1002 MACY DR ROSWELL, GA 30076	PHONE: (770) 650-8510 FAX: (770) 650-8508 TOLL FREE: (888) 650-6566	WEB: WWW.CAPITOL-SE.COM

CAPITOL INDEMNITY CORP — *CAPITOL TRANS AMERICA CORP*

WISCONSIN		1600 ASPEN COMMONS MIDDLETON, WI 53562 PO BOX 5900 MADISON, WI 53705-0900	PHONE: (608) 829-4200 FAX: (608) 829-7419	WEB: WWW.CAPITOLINDEMNITY.COM

CAPITOL TRANS AMERICA CORP — *SEE ALSO CAPITOL INDEMNITY CORP*

CARDAY ASSOCIATES, INC

NATIONAL	R 3 H	4600 POWDER MILL RD STE 100 BELTSVILLE, MD 20705-2675	PHONE: (301) 937-9300 FAX: (301) 902-0437 TOLL FREE: (800) 284-0042	WEB: WWW.CARDAYASSOCIATES.COM

CARE CHOICES HMO — *PREFERRED CHOICE*

MICHIGAN	34605 TWELVE MILE RD FARMINGTON HILLS, MI 48331	PHONE: (248) 489-6000 FAX: (248) 489-6109 TOLL FREE: (800) 852-9780	WEB: WWW.CARECHOICES.COM

CARE FIRST — *BLUE CROSS BLUE SHIELD*

NATIONAL	301 BAY ST STE 401 EASTON, MD 21601 PO BOX 2410 EASTON, MD 21601-2410	PHONE: (410) 822-7223 FAX: (410) 505-2371 TOLL FREE: (800) 334-3427 IN-STATE: (800) 334-3427	

CARE FIRST BLUE CHOICE — *SEE ALSO BLUE CROSS BLUE SHIELD*

CAREMARK, INC

NATIONAL	1731 GRAND STAND PKY BLDG B SAN ANTONIO, TX 78238	PHONE: (210) 706-4900 FAX: (210) 647-1602 TOLL FREE: (800) 841-5550	WEB: WWW.CAREMARK.COM
	211 COMMERCE ST STE 800 NASHVILLE, TN 37201	PHONE: (615) 743-6600 TOLL FREE: (800) 237-2767	WEB: WWW.CAREMARK.COM
	2211 SANDERS RD NORTHBROOK, IL 60062-6126	PHONE: (847) 559-4700 FAX: (847) 559-3905 TOLL FREE: (800) 323-8033	WEB: WWW.CAREMARK.COM
	9501 E SHEA BLVD SCOTTSDALE, AZ 85260-6719	PHONE: (480) 391-4600 TOLL FREE: (800) 749-6199	WEB: WWW.CAREMARK.COM
	DEPT 6175 LOS ANGELES, CA 90088	TOLL FREE: (866) 889-8208	WEB: WWW.CAREMARK.COM
	1300 E CAMPBELL RD RICHARDSON, TX 75081	PHONE: (972) 813-3600 FAX: (972) 480-5643	WEB: WWW.CAREMARK.COM

CARESOURCE

INDIANA *MICHIGAN* *OHIO*	ONE S MAIN ST DAYTON, OH 45402-2024	PHONE: (937) 224-3300 FAX: (937) 224-3388 TOLL FREE: (800) 488-0134	WEB: WWW.CSMG-ONLINE.COM

CARITEN HEALTHCARE

TENNESSEE	101 MEDTECK PKY STE 404 JOHNSON CITY, TN 37604-2192	PHONE: (423) 952-3180 FAX: (423) 952-3188 TOLL FREE: (800) 284-0042	WEB: WWW.CARITEN.COM
	1420 CENTERPOINT BLVD KNOXVILLE, TN 37932 PO BOX 22987 KNOXVILLE, TN 37933-2987	PHONE: (865) 470-7470 TOLL FREE: (800) 793-1495	WEB: WWW.CARITEN.COM

CAROLINA BENEFIT ADMINISTRATORS LLC — *CBA*

NATIONAL	333 S PINE ST SPARTANBURG, SC 29302-2626 PO BOX 3257 SPARTANBURG, SC 29304-3257	PHONE: (864) 573-6937 FAX: (864) 582-2265 TOLL FREE: (800) 476-2295	WEB: WWW.CBAOFSC.COM

CAROLINA CARE PLAN, INC

SOUTH CAROLINA	201 EXECUTIVE CENTER DR COLUMBIA, SC 29210 PO BOX 100234 COLUMBIA, SC 29202-3234	PHONE: (803) 750-7400 FAX: (803) 750-7474 TOLL FREE: (800) 868-6734	WEB: WWW.CAROLINACAREPLAN.COM

C

CAROLINA CASUALTY INSURANCE CO, INC — *CCIC*

NATIONAL

4600 TOUCHTON RD E BLDG 100
STE 400
JACKSONVILLE, FL 32256-1220
PO BOX 2575
JACKSONVILLE, FL 32203-2575

PHONE: (904) 363-0900
FAX: (904) 363-8098
TOLL FREE: (800) 874-8053

E-MAIL: INFO@CAROLINAS.COM
WEB: WWW.CAROLINACAS.COM

ADDITIONAL COMMENTS: NATIONAL EXCEPT NEW JERSEY & NEW YORK

CASUALTY UNDERWRITERS INSURANCE CO — *SEE ALSO INTER-AMERICAS INSURANCE*

CATHOLIC KNIGHTS

NATIONAL

1100 W WELLS ST
MILWAUKEE, WI 53233

FAX: (314) 351-9937
TOLL FREE: (800) 844-3728

WEB: WWW.CATHOLICKNIGHTS.ORG

CBA — *SEE ALSO CAROLINA BENEFIT ADMINISTRATORS LLC*

CBA — *SEE ALSO COMBINED BENEFITS ADMINISTRATORS*

CBA, INC — *COMPREHENSIVE BENEFITS ADMINISTRATOR, INC*

VERMONT

46 BOWDOIN ST
SOUTH BURLINGTON, VT 05403-8800
PO BOX 2365
SOUTH BURLINGTON, VT 05407-2365

PHONE: (802) 864-8321
FAX: (802) 864-8115
TOLL FREE: (800) 525-8788

E-MAIL: SERVICE@CBAVT.COM
WEB: WWW.CBAVT.COM

CBCA

NATIONAL

1720 INDIAN WOOD CIR STE C
MAUMEE, OH 43537

PHONE: (614) 635-8679
FAX: (419) 897-9648
TOLL FREE: (800) 428-8194

WEB: WWW.CBA.COM

CBCA ADMINISTRATORS, INC

NATIONAL

10 CHATHAM CTR SO
SAVANNAH, GA 31405
PO BOX 9888
SAVANNAH, GA 31412-0088

PHONE: (912) 691-1551
FAX: (912) 352-8935
TOLL FREE: (800) 631-3441

WEB: WWW.CBCA.COM

10900 HAMPSHIRE AVE S
MINNEAPOLIS, MN 55438-2306

PHONE: (952) 829-3500
FAX: (952) 946-7694
TOLL FREE: (800) 824-3882

E-MAIL: INFO@CBCA.COM
WEB: WWW.CBCA.COM

CBSA — *CORPORATE BENEFIT SERVICES OF AMERICA, INC*

NATIONAL

400 HWY 169 S STE 800
MINNEAPOLIS, MN 55426-1141
PO BOX 27267
MINNEAPOLIS, MN 55427

PHONE: (952) 546-0062
FAX: (952) 541-0193
TOLL FREE: (800) 925-2272

E-MAIL: CBSA@CBSAINC.COM
WEB: WWW.CBSAINC.COM

CCHP — *SEE ALSO CHINESE COMMUNITY HEALTH PLAN*

CCIC — *SEE ALSO CAROLINA CASUALTY INSURANCE CO, INC*

CCMSI — *SEE ALSO CANON COCHRAN MANAGEMENT SERVICES, INC*

CCMSI-MIDLAND LLC

NATIONAL

TWO E MAIN TOWN CTR BLDG STE 208
DANVILLE, IL 61832-5850
PO BOX 1430
DANVILLE, IL 61834-1430

PHONE: (217) 446-1089
FAX: (217) 443-0927
TOLL FREE: (800) 634-3506

E-MAIL: CCMSI@CCMSI.COM
WEB: WWW.CCMSI.COM

CCN — *FIRST HEALTH*

NATIONAL

HEADQUARTERS
10260 MEANLEY DR
SAN DIEGO, CA 92131

TOLL FREE: (800) 226-5116

WEB: WWW.CCNUSA.COM

3611 QUEEN PALM DR STE 200
TAMPA, FL 33619
PO BOX 5319
TAMPA, FL 33675

PHONE: (813) 663-3700
TOLL FREE: (800) 553-5044
IN-STATE: (800) 226-5116

WEB: WWW.CCNUSA.COM

CDPHP — *SEE ALSO CAPITAL DISTRICT PHYSICIANS' HEALTH PLAN, INC*

CDS ADMINISTRATORS, INC — *SEE ALSO CENTRAL DATA SERVICES, INC*

CDS GROUP HEALTH

CALIFORNIA
NEVADA

PO BOX 50190
SPARKS, NV 89435

PHONE: (800) 455-4236

WEB: WWW.CDSGROUPHEALTH.COM

NEVADA

1625 E PRATER WY C101
SPARKS, NV 89434
PO BOX 50190
SPARKS, NV 89435

PHONE: (775) 352-7252
FAX: (775) 352-7266

WEB: WWW.CDSGROUPHEALTH.COM

CEIC — *SEE ALSO CINCINNATI EQUITABLE INSURANCE CO*

CELINA INSURANCE GROUP

INDIANA
IOWA
KENTUCKY
OHIO
TENNESSEE
WEST VIRGINIA

ONE INSURANCE SQ
CELINA, OH 45822-1690

PHONE: (419) 586-5181
FAX: (419) 586-8343
TOLL FREE: (800) 552-5181
IN-STATE: (800) 552-5131

E-MAIL: HELPDESK@CELINAINSURANCE.COM
WEB: WWW.CELINAINSURANCEGROUP.COM

CELTIC INSURANCE CO — *CELTIC INDIVIDUAL HEALTH*

NATIONAL

233 S WACKER DR STE 700
CHICAGO, IL 60606
PO BOX 06410
CHICAGO, IL 60606-0410

PHONE: (312) 332-5401
FAX: (800) 600-8796
TOLL FREE: (800) 477-7870

WEB: WWW.CELTIC-NET.COM

CELTIC INDIVIDUAL HEALTH — *SEE ALSO CELTIC INSURANCE CO*

CENTRAL BENEFITS ADMINISTRATORS

NATIONAL

716 MOUNT AIRSHIRE BLVD
COLUMBUS, OH 43235
PO BOX 16526
COLUMBUS, OH 43216

PHONE: (614) 797-5200
FAX: (614) 797-5268
TOLL FREE: (800) 333-5711

WEB: WWW.CENTRALBENEFITS.COM

CENTRAL DATA SERVICES, INC — *CDS ADMINISTRATORS, INC*

NATIONAL

5 GATEWAY CTR STE 620
60 BLVD OF THE ALLIES
PITTSBURGH, PA 15222-1219

PHONE: (412) 201-2242
FAX: (412) 201-2250

CENTRAL INSURANCE CO

ARIZONA *COLORADO*	SOUTHWEST REGIONAL OFFICE 7301 N STATE HWY 161 STE 320 IRVING, TX 75039-2820 PO BOX 152010 IRVING, TX 75015-2010	PHONE: (972) 401-3400 FAX: (800) 736-7026 TOLL FREE: (800) 733-2233	E-MAIL: CLAIMS@CENTRAL-INSURANCE.COM WEB: WWW.CENTRAL-INSURANCE.COM
CONNECTICUT	NORTHEAST REGIONAL OFFICE 404 WYMAN ST STE 360 WALTHAM, MA 02451-1270 PO BOX 9124 WALTHAM, MA 02454-9124	PHONE: (781) 890-1752 FAX: (800) 877-2293 TOLL FREE: (800) 359-2233	E-MAIL: CLAIMS@CENTRAL-INSURANCE.COM WEB: WWW.CENTRAL-INSURANCE.COM
GEORGIA	SOUTHEAST REGIONAL OFFICE 11605 HAYNES BRIDGE RD STE 500 ALPHARETTA, GA 30004-8667 PO BOX 105287 ATLANTA, GA 30348-5287	PHONE: (770) 740-8000 FAX: (800) 877-2293 TOLL FREE: (800) 877-2233 IN-STATE: (800) 877-2233	E-MAIL: CLAIMS@CENTRAL-INSURANCE.COM WEB: WWW.CENTRAL-INSURANCE.COM
ILLINOIS *INDIANA*	HOME OFFICE/CENTRAL REGIONAL OFFICE 800 S WASHINGTON ST VAN WERT, OH 45891-2357 PO BOX 351 VAN WERT, OH 45891-0351	PHONE: (419) 238-1010 FAX: (800) 736-7026 TOLL FREE: (888) 263-2924	E-MAIL: CLAIMS@CENTRAL-INSURANCE.COM WEB: WWW.CENTRAL-INSURANCE.COM
MASSACHUSETTS *NEW HAMPSHIRE* *NEW JERSEY*	NORTHEAST REGIONAL OFFICE 404 WYMAN ST STE 360 WALTHAM, MA 02451-1270 PO BOX 9124 WALTHAM, MA 02454-9124	PHONE: (781) 890-1752 FAX: (800) 877-2293 TOLL FREE: (800) 359-2233	E-MAIL: CLAIMS@CENTRAL-INSURANCE.COM WEB: WWW.CENTRAL-INSURANCE.COM
NEW MEXICO	SOUTHWEST REGIONAL OFFICE 7301 N STATE HWY 161 STE 320 IRVING, TX 75039-2820 PO BOX 152010 IRVING, TX 75015-2010	PHONE: (972) 401-3400 FAX: (800) 736-7026 TOLL FREE: (800) 733-2233	E-MAIL: CLAIMS@CENTRAL-INSURANCE.COM WEB: WWW.CENTRAL-INSURANCE.COM
NEW YORK	NORTHEAST REGIONAL OFFICE 404 WYMAN ST STE 360 WALTHAM, MA 02451-1270 PO BOX 9124 WALTHAM, MA 02454-9124	PHONE: (781) 890-1752 FAX: (800) 877-2293 TOLL FREE: (800) 359-2233	E-MAIL: CLAIMS@CENTRAL-INSURANCE.COM WEB: WWW.CENTRAL-INSURANCE.COM
NORTH CAROLINA	SOUTHEAST REGIONAL OFFICE 11605 HAYNES BRIDGE RD STE 500 ALPHARETTA, GA 30004-8667 PO BOX 105287 ATLANTA, GA 30348-5287	PHONE: (770) 740-8000 FAX: (800) 877-2293 TOLL FREE: (800) 877-2233 IN-STATE: (800) 877-2233	E-MAIL: CLAIMS@CENTRAL-INSURANCE.COM WEB: WWW.CENTRAL-INSURANCE.COM
OHIO	HOME OFFICE/CENTRAL REGIONAL OFFICE 800 S WASHINGTON ST VAN WERT, OH 45891-2357 PO BOX 351 VAN WERT, OH 45891-0351	PHONE: (419) 238-1010 FAX: (800) 736-7026 TOLL FREE: (888) 263-2924	E-MAIL: CLAIMS@CENTRAL-INSURANCE.COM WEB: WWW.CENTRAL-INSURANCE.COM
OKLAHOMA	SOUTHWEST REGIONAL OFFICE 7301 N STATE HWY 161 STE 320 IRVING, TX 75039-2820 PO BOX 152010 IRVING, TX 75015-2010	PHONE: (972) 401-3400 FAX: (800) 736-7026 TOLL FREE: (800) 733-2233	E-MAIL: CLAIMS@CENTRAL-INSURANCE.COM WEB: WWW.CENTRAL-INSURANCE.COM
SOUTH CAROLINA *TENNESSEE*	SOUTHEAST REGIONAL OFFICE 11605 HAYNES BRIDGE RD STE 500 ALPHARETTA, GA 30004-8667 PO BOX 105287 ATLANTA, GA 30348-5287	PHONE: (770) 740-8000 FAX: (800) 877-2293 TOLL FREE: (800) 877-2233 IN-STATE: (800) 877-2233	E-MAIL: CLAIMS@CENTRAL-INSURANCE.COM WEB: WWW.CENTRAL-INSURANCE.COM

TEXAS	SOUTHWEST REGIONAL OFFICE 7301 N STATE HWY 161 STE 320 IRVING, TX 75039-2820 PO BOX 152010 IRVING, TX 75015-2010	PHONE: (972) 401-3400 FAX: (800) 736-7026 TOLL FREE: (800) 733-2233	E-MAIL: CLAIMS@CENTRAL-INSURANCE.COM WEB: WWW.CENTRAL-INSURANCE.COM
VIRGINIA	SOUTHEAST REGIONAL OFFICE 11605 HAYNES BRIDGE RD STE 500 ALPHARETTA, GA 30004-8667 PO BOX 105287 ATLANTA, GA 30348-5287	PHONE: (770) 740-8000 FAX: (800) 877-2293 TOLL FREE: (800) 877-2233 IN-STATE: (800) 877-2233	E-MAIL: CLAIMS@CENTRAL-INSURANCE.COM WEB: WWW.CENTRAL-INSURANCE.COM

CENTRAL PENNSYLVANIA TEAMSTERS HEALTH & WELFARE FUND

NATIONAL	1055 SPRING ST WYOMISSING, PA 19610-1747 PO BOX 15224 READING, PA 19612-5224	PHONE: (610) 320-5500 FAX: (610) 320-9209 TOLL FREE: (800) 331-0420 IN-STATE: (800) 422-8330	E-MAIL: HEALTHANDWELFARE@CENTRALPATEAMSTERS.COM WEB: WWW.CENTRALPATEAMSTERS.COM

CENTRAL RESERVE LIFE INSURANCE CO OF NORTH AMERICA — *CRL*

NATIONAL	17800 ROYALTON RD CLEVELAND, OH 44136-5197	PHONE: (440) 572-2400 FAX: (440) 572-8880 TOLL FREE: (800) 321-3997	E-MAIL: CLAIMS@CENTRALRESERVE.COM WEB: WWW.CENTRALRESERVE.COM OR WWW.CERESGP.COM

CENTRAL SECURITY LIFE INSURANCE COMPANY — *MAXCORP*

NATIONAL	2175 N GLENVILLE DR RICHARDSON, TX 75082-4329 PO BOX 833879 RICHARDSON, TX 75083-3879	PHONE: (972) 699-2770 FAX: (972) 699-2788 TOLL FREE: (866) 629-2677	WEB: WWW.CSLIC.COM

ADDITIONAL COMMENTS: NATIONAL EXCEPT - CA, CT, HI, IA, ME, MN, NH, NJ, NY, PA, RI, VT, & WI

CENTRAL STATES FUNDS

NATIONAL	DENTAL CLAIMS PO BOX 5104 DES PLAINES, IL 60017-5104	TOLL FREE: (800) 334-7591	WEB: WWW.CENTRALSTATESFUNDS.ORG
	TEAMCARE VISION PO BOX 5105 DES PLAINS, IL 60017-5105	TOLL FREE: (800) 334-7591	WEB: WWW.CENTRALSTATESFUNDS.ORG
	TEAMCARE RX PO BOX 5106 DES PLAINES, IL 60017-5106	TOLL FREE: (800) 334-7591	WEB: WWW.CENTRALSTATESFUNDS.ORG
	SOUTHEAST & SOUTHWEST AREAS 9377 W HIGGINS RD ROSEMONT, IL 60018-4938	TOLL FREE: (800) 334-7591	WEB: WWW.CENTRALSTATESFUNDS.ORG

ADDITIONAL COMMENTS: NATIONAL EXCEPT ARIZONA, CALIFORNIA, NEVADA, OREGON, WASHINGON, WYOMING

CENTRAL STATES HEALTH & LIFE INSURANCE CO OF OMAHA — *CSO*

NATIONAL	1212 N 96 ST OMAHA, NE 68114 PO BOX 34350 OMAHA, NE 68134-0350	PHONE: (402) 397-1111 FAX: (402) 399-3506	WEB: WWW.CSO.COM

ADDITIONAL COMMENTS: NATIONAL EXCEPT NEW YORK

CENTRAL VALLEY HEALTH AND WELFARE TRUST

CALIFORNIA	520 E HERNDON AVE FRESNO, CA 93720	PHONE: (559) 437-2960 FAX: (559) 437-2965 TOLL FREE: (800) 288-9870	WEB: WWW.CVTRUST.ORG

CENTRE SOLUTIONS

NATIONAL		105 E 17TH ST NEW YORK, NY 10003	PHONE: (212) 859-2600 FAX: (212) 859-2791 TOLL FREE: (800) 375-3054	WEB: WWW.CENTRESOLUTIONS.COM

CENTURION LIFE INSURANCE

NATIONAL		800 WALNUT ST DES MOINES, IA 50309-3636	PHONE: (515) 557-7307 FAX: (515) 557-7158 TOLL FREE: (800) 903-7306	WEB: WWW.WELLSFARGO.COM

CERES GROUP, INC — *SEE ALSO CONTINENTAL GENERAL INSURANCE*

CGH INSURANCE GROUP — *SEE ALSO AMERICAN MINING INSURANCE CO, INC*

CHC — *COLONIAL HEALTHCARE*

NATIONAL	R H	350 THEODORE FREMD AVE STE 300 RYE, NY 10580	PHONE: (914) 332-7528 FAX: (914) 925-3497 TOLL FREE: (800) 950-7245	WEB: WWW.COLONIALHEALTHCARE.COM
	R H	4530 WALNEY RD STE 200 CHANTILY, VA 20151	PHONE: (800) 950-7245 FAX: (301) 306-2527	E-MAIL: CHC_CLAIMS@CHC-INC.COM WEB: WWW.COLONIALHEALTHCARE.COM
	R H	500 N GULPH RD STE 520 KING OF PRUSSIA, PA 19406	PHONE: (610) 539-0300	WEB: WWW.COLONIALHEALTHCARE.COM
	R H	9901 BUSINESS PKY LANHAM, MD 20706 PO BOX 827 LANHAM, MD 20703-0827	PHONE: (301) 306-3020 TOLL FREE: (800) 950-7245	WEB: WWW.COLONIALHEALTHCARE.COM

CHC OF DELAWARE — *SEE ALSO COVENTRY HEALTH CARE*

CHC OF IOWA — *SEE ALSO COVENTRY HEALTH CARE*

CHC OF KANSAS AND PREFERRED — *SEE ALSO COVENTRY HEALTH CARE / COVENTRY ONE*

CHC OF LOUISIANA — *SEE ALSO COVENTRY HEALTH CARE*

CHEROKEE NATIONAL LIFE FINANCIAL CORP — *SEE ALSO AMERICAN UNITED LIFE INSURANCE CO*

ALABAMA, ARKANSAS, COLORADO, FLORIDA, GEORGIA, INDIANA, KANSAS, KENTUCKY, LOUISIANA, MISSISSIPPI, MISSOURI, NORTH CAROLINA, OHIO, OKLAHOMA, PENNSYLVANIA, SOUTH CAROLINA, TENNESSEE, TEXAS, VIRGINIA

		2960 RIVERSIDE DR MACON, GA 31208-6097 PO BOX 6097 MACON, GA 31208-6097	PHONE: (478) 477-0400 FAX: (478) 477-1177 TOLL FREE: (800) 849-4265	E-MAIL: CUSTOMER_SERVICE@CNLF.COM WEB: WWW.CNLF.COM

CHESTERFIELD RESOURCES, INC

NATIONAL	3520 4TH LAKE DR UNIONTOWN, OH 44685 PO BOX 1884 AKRON, OH 44309-1884	PHONE: (330) 896-2232 FAX: (330) 896-4337

CHICAGO AREA IB OF T LOCAL 703

ILLINOIS *INDIANA*	300 S ASHLAND AVE STE 502 CHICAGO, IL 60607-2746	PHONE: (312) 738-1350 FAX: (312) 738-2593

CHILDREN'S MERCY FAMILY HEALTH PARTNERS

MISSOURI	215 W PERSHING RD STE 600 KANSAS CITY, MO 64108 PO BOX 411806 KANSAS CITY, MO 64141	PHONE: (800) 347-9363 FAX: (816) 855-1890 TOLL FREE: (800) 347-9363	WEB: WWW.FHP.ORG

CHINESE COMMUNITY HEALTH PLAN — *CCHP*

CALIFORNIA	170 COLUMBUS AVE STE 210 SAN FRANCISCO, CA 94133-5160	PHONE: (415) 397-3190 FAX: (415) 397-6140	WEB: WWW.CCHPHMO.COM

CHIROPRACTIC ARIZONA NETWORK

ARIZONA *NEVADA*	3625 N 16TH ST STE 206 PHOENIX, AZ 85016-6443	PHONE: (602) 264-2606 FAX: (602) 285-0121 TOLL FREE: (888) 264-2606

CHN SOLUTIONS — *SEE ALSO CONSUMER HEALTH NETWORK*

CHP — *SEE ALSO COMMUNITY HEALTH PLAN*

CHRISTIANA CARE HEALTH PLANS

DELAWARE *MARYLAND* *PENNSYLVANIA*	11 READS WAY NEW CASTLE, DE 19720	PHONE: (302) 327-7650 FAX: (302) 327-7711 TOLL FREE: (800) 362-4214	WEB: WWW.CHRISTIANACARE.ORG

CHUBB & SON — *SEE ALSO CHUBB GROUP OF INSURANCE COMPANIES*

CHUBB GROUP OF INSURANCE COMPANIES — *CHUBB & SON*

NATIONAL	1920 L ST NW STE 700 WASHINGTON, DC 20036	PHONE: (202) 822-3200 FAX: (202) 822-3299 TOLL FREE: (800) 252-4670	WEB: WWW.CHUBB.COM
	100 S 5TH ST STE 1800 MINNEAPOLIS, MN 55402	PHONE: (612) 373-7300 FAX: (612) 373-7436 TOLL FREE: (800) 525-0614	WEB: WWW.CHUBB.COM
	WORLD HEADQUARTERS 15 MOUNTAIN VIEW RD WARREN, NJ 07059-6795 PO BOX 1615 WARREN, NJ 07059	PHONE: (908) 903-2000 FAX: (908) 903-2027 TOLL FREE: (800) 252-4670	WEB: WWW.CHUBB.COM
	4470 COX RD STE 150 GLEN ALLEN, VA 23060-3320	PHONE: (804) 935-6300 FAX: (804) 935-6333 TOLL FREE: (800) 252-4670	WEB: WWW.CHUBB.COM
	4999 LOUISE DR MECHANICSBURG, PA 17055-0000 PO BOX 2063 MECHANICSBURG, PA 17055-0797	PHONE: (717) 791-6000 FAX: (717) 791-6040 TOLL FREE: (800) 577-9992 IN-STATE: (800) 909-0900	WEB: WWW.CHUBB.COM
	82 HOP MEADOW ST SIMSBURY, CT 06070-7683	PHONE: (860) 408-2000 FAX: (860) 408-2002 TOLL FREE: (800) 252-4670	WEB: WWW.CHUBB.COM

NATIONAL — CONTINUED		5440 CORPORATE DR STE 300 TROY, MI 48098-2645 PO BOX 7078 TROY, MI 48007-7078	PHONE: (248) 641-7900 FAX: (248) 952-6080 TOLL FREE: (800) 252-4670	WEB: WWW.CHUBB.COM
ALABAMA		3445 PEACHTREE RD NE STE 900 ATLANTA, GA 30326-1276	PHONE: (404) 266-4000 FAX: (404) 264-6849 TOLL FREE: (800) 999-3669	WEB: WWW.CHUBB.COM
		1000 URBAN CTR DR STE 205 BIRMINGHAM, AL 35242	PHONE: (205) 968-5400 FAX: (205) 968-5496 TOLL FREE: (800) 252-4670	WEB: WWW.CHUBB.COM
ALASKA		WATERVIEW TWO 9155 E NICHOLS AVE STE 100 ENGLEWOOD, CO 80112 PO BOX 6520 ENGLEWOOD, CO 80155-6520	PHONE: (720) 895-5100 FAX: (720) 895-5199 TOLL FREE: (800) 333-5525	WEB: WWW.CHUBB.COM
ARIZONA		2215 WEST PINNACLE PEAK RD PHOENIX, AZ 85020	PHONE: (623) 445-2500 FAX: (623) 445-2548 TOLL FREE: (800) 252-4670	WEB: WWW.CHUBB.COM
ARKANSAS		9606 N MOPAC DR STE 925 AUSTIN, TX 78759	PHONE: (512) 634-2200 FAX: (512) 634-2222 TOLL FREE: (800) 252-4670	WEB: WWW.CHUBB.COM
		SOUTHERN ZONE OFFICE 2001 BRYAN ST STE 3400 DALLAS, TX 75201-3068	PHONE: (214) 754-0777 FAX: (214) 754-8129 IN-STATE: (800) 873-0777	WEB: WWW.CHUBB.COM
CALIFORNIA		275 BATTERY ST 12TH FL SAN FRANCISCO, CA 94111-3906	PHONE: (415) 273-6300 FAX: (800) 344-4184 TOLL FREE: (800) 252-4670	WEB: WWW.CHUBB.COM
		3090 BRISTOL ST STE 600 COSTA MESA, CA 92626 PO BOX 2620 NEWPORT BEACH, CA 92658-2620	PHONE: (714) 913-4900 FAX: (714) 913-4991 TOLL FREE: (800) 252-4670	WEB: WWW.CHUBB.COM
		5050 HOPYARD RD STE 400 PLEASANTON, CA 94588-3321	PHONE: (925) 598-6000 FAX: (925) 598-6098 TOLL FREE: (800) 252-4670	WEB: WWW.CHUBB.COM
		610 W ASH ST STE 1101 SAN DIEGO, CA 92101	PHONE: (619) 525-8000 FAX: (619) 525-8070 TOLL FREE: (800) 252-4670	WEB: WWW.CHUBB.COM
		WESTERN ZONE OFFICE 801 S FIGUEROA ST STE 2400 LOS ANGELES, CA 90017-2573 PO BOX 30850 LOS ANGELES, CA 90030-0850	PHONE: (213) 612-0880 FAX: (213) 612-5728 TOLL FREE: (800) 252-4670 IN-STATE: (800) 262-4459	WEB: WWW.CHUBB.COM
COLORADO		WATERVIEW TWO 9155 E NICHOLS AVE STE 100 ENGLEWOOD, CO 80112 PO BOX 6520 ENGLEWOOD, CO 80155-6520	PHONE: (720) 895-5100 FAX: (720) 895-5199 TOLL FREE: (800) 333-5525	WEB: WWW.CHUBB.COM
		500 PARK BLVD STE 600 ITASCA, IL 60143-2625 PO BOX 218 ITASCA, IL 60143	PHONE: (630) 875-6000 FAX: (630) 875-6060 TOLL FREE: (800) 252-4670	WEB: WWW.CHUBB.COM
CONNECTICUT		555 LONG WHARF DR NEW HAVEN, CT 06511-5941 PO BOX 1903 NEW HAVEN, CT 06509-0911	PHONE: (203) 782-4000 FAX: (203) 782-4126 TOLL FREE: (800) 252-4670	WEB: WWW.CHUBB.COM
DELAWARE		1600 JFK BLVD STE 400 PHILADELPHIA, PA 19103	PHONE: (215) 569-9660 FAX: (215) 569-9418 TOLL FREE: (800) 252-4670 CLAIMS IN-STATE: (800) 523-4738 OFFICE	WEB: WWW.CHUBB.COM

DISTRICT OF COLUMBIA	1600 JFK BLVD STE 400 PHILADELPHIA, PA 19103	PHONE: (215) 569-9660 FAX: (215) 569-9418 TOLL FREE: (800) 252-4670 CLAIMS IN-STATE: (800) 523-4738 OFFICE	WEB: WWW.CHUBB.COM
	1920 L ST NW STE 700 WASHINGTON, DC 20036	PHONE: (202) 822-3200 FAX: (202) 822-3299 TOLL FREE: (800) 252-4670	WEB: WWW.CHUBB.COM
FLORIDA	3445 PEACHTREE RD NE STE 900 ATLANTA, GA 30326-1276	PHONE: (404) 266-4000 FAX: (404) 264-6849 TOLL FREE: (800) 999-3669	WEB: WWW.CHUBB.COM
	REPUBLIC SECURITY BLDG 1301 N CONGRESS AVE STE 330 BOYNTON BEACH, FL 33426	PHONE: (561) 752-8125 FAX: (561) 752-8149 TOLL FREE: (800) 252-4670	WEB: WWW.CHUBB.COM
	3000 BAYPORT DR TAMPA, FL 33607-8410 PO BOX 31527 TAMPA, FL 33631-3527	PHONE: (813) 281-7400 FAX: (813) 281-7536 TOLL FREE: (800) 252-4670 IN-STATE: (800) 226-2482	WEB: WWW.CHUBB.COM
GEORGIA	3445 PEACHTREE RD NE STE 900 ATLANTA, GA 30326-1276	PHONE: (404) 266-4000 FAX: (404) 264-6849 TOLL FREE: (800) 999-3669	WEB: WWW.CHUBB.COM
HAWAII	WESTERN ZONE OFFICE 801 S FIGUEROA ST STE 2400 LOS ANGELES, CA 90017-2573 PO BOX 30850 LOS ANGELES, CA 90030-0850	PHONE: (213) 612-0880 FAX: (213) 612-5728 TOLL FREE: (800) 252-4670 IN-STATE: (800) 262-4459	WEB: WWW.CHUBB.COM
IDAHO *ILLINOIS*	500 PARK BLVD STE 600 ITASCA, IL 60143-2625 PO BOX 218 ITASCA, IL 60143	PHONE: (630) 875-6000 FAX: (630) 875-6060 TOLL FREE: (800) 252-4670	WEB: WWW.CHUBB.COM
ILLINOIS	NORTHERN ZONE ADMINISTRATIVE OFFICE 233 SOUTH WACKER DR STE 4700 CHICAGO, IL 60606-6303	PHONE: (312) 454-4200 FAX: (312) 454-4401 TOLL FREE: (800) 252-4670	WEB: WWW.CHUBB.COM
INDIANA	ONE INDIANA SQ STE 1350 INDIANAPOLIS, IN 46204 PO BOX 44903 INDIANAPOLIS, IN 46244-0903	PHONE: (317) 321-6000 FAX: (317) 321-6072 TOLL FREE: (800) 252-4670	WEB: WWW.CHUBB.COM
	312 WALNUT ST 18TH FL CINCINNATI, OH 45202-4066	PHONE: (513) 721-0601 FAX: (513) 721-0095 TOLL FREE: (800) 252-4670	WEB: WWW.CHUBB.COM
INDIANA *IOWA*	500 PARK BLVD STE 600 ITASCA, IL 60143-2625 PO BOX 218 ITASCA, IL 60143	PHONE: (630) 875-6000 FAX: (630) 875-6060 TOLL FREE: (800) 252-4670	WEB: WWW.CHUBB.COM
IOWA	TEN PETTICOAT LN STE 300 KANSAS CITY, MO 64106-2147 PO BOX 410038 KANSAS CITY, MO 64141	PHONE: (816) 292-4500 FAX: (816) 292-4600 TOLL FREE: (800) 252-4670 IN-STATE: (800) 821-7851	WEB: WWW.CHUBB.COM
	REGENCY 6 WEST 4600 WESTOWN PKY STE 207 WEST DES MOINES, IA 50266-1000	PHONE: (515) 440-8140 FAX: (515) 440-8160 TOLL FREE: (800) 248-7229	WEB: WWW.CHUBB.COM
KANSAS	500 PARK BLVD STE 600 ITASCA, IL 60143-2625 PO BOX 218 ITASCA, IL 60143	PHONE: (630) 875-6000 FAX: (630) 875-6060 TOLL FREE: (800) 252-4670	WEB: WWW.CHUBB.COM
	TEN PETTICOAT LN STE 300 KANSAS CITY, MO 64106-2147 PO BOX 410038 KANSAS CITY, MO 64141	PHONE: (816) 292-4500 FAX: (816) 292-4600 TOLL FREE: (800) 252-4670 IN-STATE: (800) 821-7351	WEB: WWW.CHUBB.COM

KENTUCKY	312 WALNUT ST 18TH FL CINCINNATI, OH 45202-4066	PHONE: (513) 721-0601 FAX: (513) 721-0095 TOLL FREE: (800) 252-4670	WEB: WWW.CHUBB.COM
	10350 ORMSBY PARK PL STE 201 LOUISVILLE, KY 40223	PHONE: (502) 420-0000 FAX: (502) 420-0030 TOLL FREE: (800) 252-4670	WEB: WWW.CHUBB.COM
LOUISIANA	9606 N MOPAC DR STE 925 AUSTIN, TX 78759	PHONE: (512) 634-2200 FAX: (512) 634-2222 TOLL FREE: (800) 252-4670	WEB: WWW.CHUBB.COM
	1330 POST OAK BLVD STE 2400 HOUSTON, TX 77056-3031	PHONE: (713) 297-4600 FAX: (713) 297-4750 TOLL FREE: (800) 252-4670 CLAIMS	WEB: WWW.CHUBB.COM
MAINE	555 LONG WHARF DR NEW HAVEN, CT 06511-5941 PO BOX 1903 NEW HAVEN, CT 06509-0911	PHONE: (203) 782-4000 FAX: (203) 782-4126 TOLL FREE: (800) 252-4670	WEB: WWW.CHUBB.COM
	NORTHEAST ZONE OFFICE ONE FINANCIAL CTR 8TH & 9TH FL BOSTON, MA 02111-2697	PHONE: (617) 439-4440 FAX: (617) 439-0351 TOLL FREE: (800) 252-4670	WEB: WWW.CHUBB.COM
MARYLAND	1600 JFK BLVD STE 400 PHILADELPHIA, PA 19103	PHONE: (215) 569-9660 FAX: (215) 569-9418 TOLL FREE: (800) 252-4670 CLAIMS IN-STATE: (800) 523-4738 OFFICE	WEB: WWW.CHUBB.COM
	200 SAINT PAUL PL 23RD FL BALTIMORE, MD 21202-2038	PHONE: (410) 659-6500 FAX: (410) 659-6591 TOLL FREE: (800) 252-4670	WEB: WWW.CHUBB.COM
	120 5TH AVE PITTSBURGH, PA 15222-3008	PHONE: (412) 391-6585 FAX: (412) 456-8887 TOLL FREE: (800) 252-4670 IN-STATE: (800) 248-5254	WEB: WWW.CHUBB.COM
MASSACHUSETTS	555 LONG WHARF DR NEW HAVEN, CT 06511-5941 PO BOX 1903 NEW HAVEN, CT 06509-0911	PHONE: (203) 782-4000 FAX: (203) 782-4126 TOLL FREE: (800) 252-4670	WEB: WWW.CHUBB.COM
	NORTHEAST ZONE OFFICE ONE FINANCIAL CTR 8TH & 9TH FL BOSTON, MA 02111-2697	PHONE: (617) 439-4440 FAX: (617) 439-0351 TOLL FREE: (800) 252-4670	WEB: WWW.CHUBB.COM
MICHIGAN	161 OTTOWA NW STE 214 GRAND RAPIDS, MI 49503	PHONE: (888) 900-3404 FAX: (616) 802-1987 TOLL FREE: (800) 252-4670	WEB: WWW.CHUBB.COM
	5440 CORPORATE DR STE 300 TROY, MI 48098-2645 PO BOX 7078 TROY, MI 48007-7078	PHONE: (248) 641-7900 FAX: (248) 952-6080 TOLL FREE: (800) 252-4670	WEB: WWW.CHUBB.COM
MISSISSIPPI	3445 PEACHTREE RD NE STE 900 ATLANTA, GA 30326-1276	PHONE: (404) 266-4000 FAX: (404) 264-6849 TOLL FREE: (800) 999-3669	WEB: WWW.CHUBB.COM
	1000 URBAN CTR DR STE 205 BIRMINGHAM, AL 35242	PHONE: (205) 968-5400 FAX: (205) 968-5496 TOLL FREE: (800) 252-4670	WEB: WWW.CHUBB.COM
MISSOURI	500 PARK BLVD STE 600 ITASCA, IL 60143-2625 PO BOX 218 ITASCA, IL 60143	PHONE: (630) 875-6000 FAX: (630) 875-6060 TOLL FREE: (800) 252-4670	WEB: WWW.CHUBB.COM

MISSOURI — CONTINUED	TEN PETTICOAT LN STE 300 KANSAS CITY, MO 64106-2147 PO BOX 410038 KANSAS CITY, MO 64141	PHONE: (816) 292-4500 FAX: (816) 292-4600 TOLL FREE: (800) 252-4670 IN-STATE: (800) 821-7851	WEB: WWW.CHUBB.COM
NEBRASKA	500 PARK BLVD STE 600 ITASCA, IL 60143-2625 PO BOX 218 ITASCA, IL 60143	PHONE: (630) 875-6000 FAX: (630) 875-6060 TOLL FREE: (800) 252-4670	WEB: WWW.CHUBB.COM
	TEN PETTICOAT LN STE 300 KANSAS CITY, MO 64106-2147 PO BOX 410038 KANSAS CITY, MO 64141	PHONE: (816) 292-4500 FAX: (816) 292-4600 TOLL FREE: (800) 252-4670 IN-STATE: (800) 821-7851	WEB: WWW.CHUBB.COM
	REGENCY 6 WEST 4600 WESTOWN PKY STE 207 WEST DES MOINES, IA 50266-1000	PHONE: (515) 440-8140 FAX: (515) 440-8160 TOLL FREE: (800) 248-7229	WEB: WWW.CHUBB.COM
NEW HAMPSHIRE	555 LONG WHARF DR NEW HAVEN, CT 06511-5941 PO BOX 1903 NEW HAVEN, CT 06509-0911	PHONE: (203) 782-4000 FAX: (203) 782-4126 TOLL FREE: (800) 252-4670	WEB: WWW.CHUBB.COM
	NORTHEAST ZONE OFFICE ONE FINANCIAL CTR 8TH & 9TH FL BOSTON, MA 02111-2697	PHONE: (617) 439-4440 FAX: (617) 439-0351 TOLL FREE: (800) 252-4670	WEB: WWW.CHUBB.COM
	ONE NEW HAMPSHIRE AVE STE 125 PORTSMOUTH, NH 03801	PHONE: (603) 766-0441 FAX: (603) 766-0442 TOLL FREE: (800) 252-4670	WEB: WWW.CHUBB.COM
NEW JERSEY	MID ATLANTIC ZONE OFFICE 12 VREELAND RD FLORHAM PARK, NJ 07932 PO BOX 975 FLORHAM PARK, NJ 07932	PHONE: (973) 360-6000 FAX: (973) 360-6050 TOLL FREE: (800) 252-4670	WEB: WWW.CHUBB.COM
NEW YORK	PARKER CORPORATE CENTER 1311 MAMARONECK AVE STE 370 WHITE PLAINS, NY 10605	PHONE: (914) 989-6500 FAX: (914) 989-6600 TOLL FREE: (800) 252-4670	WEB: WWW.CHUBB.COM
	333 EARLE OVINGTON BLVD STE 800 UNIONDALE, NY 11553-3644	PHONE: (516) 745-8200 FAX: (516) 745-8498 TOLL FREE: (800) 252-4670	WEB: WWW.CHUBB.COM
	EASTERN ZONE ADMINISTRATIVE OFFICE 55 WATER ST 28TH - 30TH FL NEW YORK, NY 10041-0002	PHONE: (212) 612-4000 FAX: (212) 612-4693 TOLL FREE: (800) 252-4670 IN-STATE: (800) 884-4669	WEB: WWW.CHUBB.COM
	7 SOUTHWOOD BLVD ALBANY, NY 12212-5039	PHONE: (518) 433-6200 FAX: (518) 433-6210 TOLL FREE: (800) 252-4670	WEB: WWW.CHUBB.COM
	700 CLINTON SQ ROCHESTER, NY 14604-1717	PHONE: (585) 238-8000 FAX: (716) 232-6497 TOLL FREE: (800) 252-4670	WEB: WWW.CHUBB.COM
NORTH CAROLINA	3445 PEACHTREE RD NE STE 900 ATLANTA, GA 30326-1276	PHONE: (404) 266-4000 FAX: (404) 264-6849 TOLL FREE: (800) 999-3669	WEB: WWW.CHUBB.COM
	2000 REGENCY PARKWAY STE 215 CARY, NC 27511	PHONE: (919) 278-7000 FAX: (919) 278-7017 TOLL FREE: (800) 252-4670	WEB: WWW.CHUBB.COM
	3440 TORINGDON WAY STE 307 CHARLOTTE, NC 28277	PHONE: (704) 540-6700 FAX: (704) 540-6702 TOLL FREE: (800) 252-4670	WEB: WWW.CHUBB.COM
NORTH DAKOTA	500 PARK BLVD STE 600 ITASCA, IL 60143-2625 PO BOX 218 ITASCA, IL 60143	PHONE: (630) 875-6000 FAX: (630) 875-6060 TOLL FREE: (800) 252-4670	WEB: WWW.CHUBB.COM

OHIO	312 WALNUT ST 18TH FL CINCINNATI, OH 45202-4066	PHONE: (513) 721-0601 FAX: (513) 721-0095 TOLL FREE: (800) 252-4670	WEB: WWW.CHUBB.COM
	COMMUNITY CORPORATE CENTER 445 HUTCHINSON AVE STE 570 COLUMBUS, OH 43235	PHONE: (888) 822-1514 FAX: (614) 601-3155 TOLL FREE: (800) 252-4670	WEB: WWW.CHUBB.COM
	BANK ONE CENTER 600 SUPERIOR AVE E 18TH FL CLEVELAND, OH 44114-2609	PHONE: (216) 687-1700 FAX: (216) 987-8601 TOLL FREE: (800) 252-4670	WEB: WWW.CHUBB.COM
OKLAHOMA	9606 N MOPAC DR STE 925 AUSTIN, TX 78759	PHONE: (512) 634-2200 FAX: (512) 634-2222 TOLL FREE: (800) 252-4670	WEB: WWW.CHUBB.COM
	6120 S YALE STE 450 TULSA, OK 74136-4222	PHONE: (918) 493-5600 FAX: (918) 493-5697 TOLL FREE: (800) 876-0748 IN-STATE: (800) 252-4670	WEB: WWW.CHUBB.COM
OREGON	500 PARK BLVD STE 600 ITASCA, IL 60143-2625 PO BOX 218 ITASCA, IL 60143	PHONE: (630) 875-6000 FAX: (630) 875-6060 TOLL FREE: (800) 252-4670	WEB: WWW.CHUBB.COM
	PIONEER TOWER 888 SW 5TH AVE STE 400 PORTLAND, OR 97204-2093	PHONE: (503) 221-4240 FAX: (503) 294-5425 TOLL FREE: (800) 252-4670 IN-STATE: (877) 514-9475	WEB: WWW.CHUBB.COM
PENNSYLVANIA	1600 JFK BLVD STE 400 PHILADELPHIA, PA 19103	PHONE: (215) 569-9660 FAX: (215) 569-9418 TOLL FREE: (800) 252-4670 CLAIMS IN-STATE: (800) 523-4738 OFFICE	WEB: WWW.CHUBB.COM
	120 5TH AVE PITTSBURGH, PA 15222-3008	PHONE: (412) 391-6585 FAX: (412) 456-8887 TOLL FREE: (800) 252-4670 IN-STATE: (800) 248-5254	WEB: WWW.CHUBB.COM
RHODE ISLAND	555 LONG WHARF DR NEW HAVEN, CT 06511-5941 PO BOX 1903 NEW HAVEN, CT 06509-0911	PHONE: (203) 782-4000 FAX: (203) 782-4126 TOLL FREE: (800) 252-4670	WEB: WWW.CHUBB.COM
	NORTHEAST ZONE OFFICE ONE FINANCIAL CTR 8TH & 9TH FL BOSTON, MA 02111-2697	PHONE: (617) 439-4440 FAX: (617) 439-0351 TOLL FREE: (800) 252-4670	WEB: WWW.CHUBB.COM
SOUTH CAROLINA	3445 PEACHTREE RD NE STE 900 ATLANTA, GA 30326-1276	PHONE: (404) 266-4000 FAX: (404) 264-6849 TOLL FREE: (800) 999-3669	WEB: WWW.CHUBB.COM
	3440 TORINGDON WAY STE 307 CHARLOTTE, NC 28277	PHONE: (704) 540-6700 FAX: (704) 540-6702 TOLL FREE: (800) 252-4670	WEB: WWW.CHUBB.COM
SOUTH DAKOTA	500 PARK BLVD STE 600 ITASCA, IL 60143-2625 PO BOX 218 ITASCA, IL 60143	PHONE: (630) 875-6000 FAX: (630) 875-6060 TOLL FREE: (800) 252-4670	WEB: WWW.CHUBB.COM
TENNESSEE	3445 PEACHTREE RD NE STE 900 ATLANTA, GA 30326-1276	PHONE: (404) 266-4000 FAX: (404) 264-6849 TOLL FREE: (800) 999-3669	WEB: WWW.CHUBB.COM
	840 CRESCENT CENTRE DR STE 520 FRANKLIN, TN 37067	PHONE: (615) 372-6100 FAX: (615) 372-6105 TOLL FREE: (800) 252-4670	WEB: WWW.CHUBB.COM
TEXAS	9606 N MOPAC DR STE 925 AUSTIN, TX 78759	PHONE: (512) 634-2200 FAX: (512) 634-2222 TOLL FREE: (800) 252-4670	WEB: WWW.CHUBB.COM

TEXAS — CONTINUED	SOUTHERN ZONE OFFICE 2001 BRYAN ST STE 3400 DALLAS, TX 75201-3068	PHONE: (214) 754-0777 FAX: (214) 754-8129 IN-STATE: (800) 873-0777	WEB: WWW.CHUBB.COM
	1330 POST OAK BLVD STE 2400 HOUSTON, TX 77056-3031	PHONE: (713) 297-4600 FAX: (713) 297-4750 TOLL FREE: (800) 252-4670 CLAIMS	WEB: WWW.CHUBB.COM
	613 NW LOOP 410 STE 600 SAN ANTONIO, TX 78216	PHONE: (210) 223-6600 FAX: (210) 978-8703 TOLL FREE: (800) 252-4670	WEB: WWW.CHUBB.COM
UTAH	2855 E COTTONWOOD PKY STE 340 SALT LAKE CITY, UT 84121	PHONE: (801) 944-7337 FAX: (801) 944-7338 TOLL FREE: (800) 252-4670	WEB: WWW.CHUBB.COM
VERMONT	555 LONG WHARF DR NEW HAVEN, CT 06511-5941 PO BOX 1903 NEW HAVEN, CT 06509-0911	PHONE: (203) 782-4000 FAX: (203) 782-4126 TOLL FREE: (800) 252-4670	WEB: WWW.CHUBB.COM
VIRGINIA	1600 JFK BLVD STE 400 PHILADELPHIA, PA 19103	PHONE: (215) 569-9660 FAX: (215) 569-9418 TOLL FREE: (800) 252-4670 CLAIMS IN-STATE: (800) 523-4738 OFFICE	WEB: WWW.CHUBB.COM
WISCONSIN	500 PARK BLVD STE 600 ITASCA, IL 60143-2625 PO BOX 218 ITASCA, IL 60143	PHONE: (630) 875-6000 FAX: (630) 875-6060 TOLL FREE: (800) 252-4670	WEB: WWW.CHUBB.COM
	330 E KILBOURNE AVE STE 1450 MILWAUKEE, WI 53202	PHONE: (414) 221-7600 FAX: (414) 271-8617 TOLL FREE: (800) 252-4670 IN-STATE: (800) 362-4822	WEB: WWW.CHUBB.COM

CHUBB SPECIALTY INSURANCE — *SEE ALSO CHUBB GROUP OF INSURANCE COMPANIES*

CHURCH MUTUAL INSURANCE CO

NATIONAL	3000 SCHUSTER LN MERRILL, WI 54452 PO BOX 357 MERRILL, WI 54452-0357	PHONE: (715) 536-5577 FAX: (715) 539-4651 TOLL FREE: (800) 554-2642	E-MAIL: CLAIMS@CHURCHMUTUAL.COM WEB: WWW.CHURCHMUTUAL.COM

CHURCHILL ADMINISTRATIVE PLANS, INC — *CROSSROADS HEALTHCARE MANAGEMENT/MULTIPLAN*

CONNECTICUT	CROSSROADS HEALTHCARE MANAGEMENT PO BOX 090360 STANTON, NY 10309-0360	PHONE: (866) 646-1779 FAX: (201) 871-2460	WEB: WWW.MULTIPLAN.COM

CIG — *SEE ALSO CALIFORNIA CAPITAL INSURANCE CO*

CIGNA — *SEE ALSO CONTINENTAL GENERAL INSURANCE CO*

CIGNA CORPORATION

NATIONAL	PO BOX 3310 STA DR ALBUQUERQUE, NM 87190-3310	TOLL FREE: (800) 525-5803 IN-STATE: (800) 244-6224	WEB: WWW.CIGNA.COM

CIGNA DISABILITY MANAGEMENT SOLUTIONS— *SEE ALSO CIGNA HEALTHCARE*

C

CIGNA HEALTHCARE— *SEE ALSO INTRACORE*

NATIONAL	7555 GOODWIN RD CHATTANOOGA, TN 37421	PHONE: (423)499-3100 TOLL FREE: (800) 832-3211	WEB: WWW.CIGNA.COM
	PO BOX 182223 CHATTANOOGA, TN 37422-7223	FAX: (901) 818-1265 TOLL FREE: (800) 346-6301	WEB: WWW.CIGNA.COM
	PO BOX 18223 CHATTANOOGA, TN 37422	PHONE: (903) 892-8167 FAX: (570) 496-2945 TOLL FREE: (800) 525-5803 IN-STATE: (800) 238-8801	WEB: WWW.CIGNA.COM
	PO BOX 5064 VISALIA, CA 93278	PHONE: (559) 738-2088 TOLL FREE: (800) 832-3211	WEB: WWW.CIGNA.COM
	1000 POLARIS PKY COLUMBUS, OH 43240-2005	FAX: (614) 985-4233 TOLL FREE: (800) 832-3211 IN-STATE: (800) 508-5216	WEB: WWW.CIGNA.COM
	1111 MARKET ST CHATTANOOGA, TN 37402	PHONE: (423) 321-4400 TOLL FREE: (800) 832-3211	WEB: WWW.CIGNA.COM
	12225 GREENVILLE AVE STE 1000 DALLAS, TX 75243-9382	PHONE: (972) 907-6500 FAX: (972) 907-7194 TOLL FREE: (800) 352-0611	WEB: WWW.CIGNA.COM
	1601 CHESTNUT ST PHILIDELPHIA , PA 19192	PHONE: (215) 761-1000 FAX: (404) 681-7043 TOLL FREE: (800) 244-6224	WEB: WWW.CIGNA.COM
	GLYWEED HALL 1777 SENTURY PARK BLUE BELL, PA 19422 PO BOX 3229 SCRANTON, PA 18505	PHONE: (570) 496-5000 TOLL FREE: (800) 441-7150 IN-STATE: (800) 244-6224	WEB: WWW.CIGNA.COM
	32 VALLEY ST BRISTOL, CT 06010-4991	PHONE: (860) 583-3874 FAX: (860) 585-6476 TOLL FREE: (800) 345-9458 IN-STATE: (800) 462-7486	WEB: WWW.CIGNA.COM
	ONE CIGNA DR BOURBONNAIS, IL 60914-4475	PHONE: (815) 929-6000 FAX: (860) 731-3098	WEB: WWW.CIGNA.COM

COLORADO	3900 E MEXICO AVE #1100 DENVER, CO 80210 PO BOX 182223 CHATTANOOGA, TN 37422	PHONE: (303) 782-1500 TOLL FREE: (800) 832-3211 IN-STATE: (800) 882-4462	WEB: WWW.CIGNA.COM
CONNECTICUT	900 COTTAGE GROVE RD HARTFORD, CT 06152-7314	PHONE: (860) 226-6000 FAX: (860) 226-2333 TOLL FREE: (800) 244-6224	WEB: WWW.CIGNA.COM
	TWO COLLEGE PARK DR HOOKSETT, NH 03106-1636 PO BOX 2041 CONCORD, NH 03302	PHONE: (800) 922-8380 FAX: (603) 268-7578 TOLL FREE: (800) 531-4584	WEB: WWW.CIGNA.COM
	SIX FUNDY CIRCLE STE 300 FALMOUTH, ME 04105	PHONE: (207) 781-6800 FAX: (207) 781-6836 TOLL FREE: (800) 642-5551	WEB: WWW.CIGNA.COM
FLORIDA	3101 W MARTIN LUTHER KING BLVD STE 200 TAMPA, FL 33607	PHONE: (813) 353-4400 FAX: (813) 353-4411	WEB: WWW.CIGNA.COM OR WWW.MYCIGNA.COM
	5404 CYPRESS CENTER DR STE 100 TAMPA, FL 33609 PO BOX 182223 CHATTANOOGA, TN 37422-7223	PHONE: (813) 286-4901 TOLL FREE: (800) 832-3211 IN-STATE: (800) 244-6224	WEB: WWW.CIGNA.COM
INDIANA *MAINE*	SIX FUNDY CIRCLE STE 300 FALMOUTH, ME 04105	PHONE: (207) 781-6800 FAX: (207) 781-6836 TOLL FREE: (800) 642-5551	WEB: WWW.CIGNA.COM
MAINE *MASSACHUSETTS*	TWO COLLEGE PARK DR HOOKSETT, NH 03106-1636 PO BOX 2041 CONCORD, NH 03302	PHONE: (800) 922-8380 FAX: (603) 268-7578 TOLL FREE: (800) 531-4584	WEB: WWW.CIGNA.COM
MASSACHUSETTS *NEW HAMPSHIRE* *NORTH CAROLINA*	SIX FUNDY CIRCLE STE 300 FALMOUTH, ME 04105	PHONE: (207) 781-6800 FAX: (207) 781-6836 TOLL FREE: (800) 642-5551	WEB: WWW.CIGNA.COM
NORTH CAROLINA	701 CORPORATE CTR DR RALEIGH, NC 27607 PO BOX 28087 RALEIGH, NC 27607	PHONE: (919) 854-7000 FAX: (919) 854-8135 OR (800) 558-7391 TOLL FREE: (800) 849-9000	WEB: WWW.CIGNA.COM
NORTH CAROLINA *RHODE ISLAND*	TWO COLLEGE PARK DR HOOKSETT, NH 03106-1636 PO BOX 2041 CONCORD, NH 03302	PHONE: (800) 922-8380 FAX: (603) 268-7578 TOLL FREE: (800) 531-4584	WEB: WWW.CIGNA.COM
RHODE ISLAND *SOUTH CAROLINA*	SIX FUNDY CIRCLE STE 300 FALMOUTH, ME 04105	PHONE: (207) 781-6800 FAX: (207) 781-6836 TOLL FREE: (800) 642-5551	WEB: WWW.CIGNA.COM

C

SOUTH CAROLINA	146 FAIRCHILD ST CHARLESTON, SC 29492-7506 PO BOX 190023 CHARLESTON, SC 29492	PHONE: (843) 884-4063 TOLL FREE: (800) 962-8811 IN-STATE: (800) 720-3150	WEB: WWW.CIGNA.COM
SOUTH CAROLINA *TENNESSEE*	TWO COLLEGE PARK DR HOOKSETT, NH 03106-1636 PO BOX 2041 CONCORD, NH 03302	PHONE: (800) 922-8380 FAX: (603) 268-7578 TOLL FREE: (800) 531-4584	WEB: WWW.CIGNA.COM
TENNESSEE	SIX FUNDY CIRCLE STE 300 FALMOUTH, ME 04105	PHONE: (207) 781-6800 FAX: (207) 781-6836 TOLL FREE: (800) 642-5551	WEB: WWW.CIGNA.COM
UTAH	5295 S 320 W STE 280 MURRAY, UT 84107 PO BOX 182223 CHATTANOOGA, TN 37422-7223	PHONE: (801) 261-7546 FAX: (801) 261-5349 TOLL FREE: (800) 832-3211 IN-STATE: (800) 882-4462	WEB: WWW.CIGNA.COM
VERMONT	SIX FUNDY CIRCLE STE 300 FALMOUTH, ME 04105	PHONE: (207) 781-6800 FAX: (207) 781-6836 TOLL FREE: (800) 642-5551	WEB: WWW.CIGNA.COM

CIGNA INTERNATIONAL EX PATRIOTS BENEFITS

NATIONAL	590 NAAMAN'S RD CLAYMONT, DE 19703 PO BOX 15050 WILMINGTON, DE 19850-5050	PHONE: (302) 797-3100 FAX: (302) 797-3150 OR (800) 243-6998 TOLL FREE: (800) 441-2668	WEB: WWW.CIGNA.COM

CIGNA LIFE OF CANADA

NATIONAL
ALBERTA
CANADA
ONTARIO
QUEBEC

	55 TOWN CENTER COURT STE 606 SCARBOROUGH, ON M1P-4X4	PHONE: (416) 290-6666 FAX: (416) 290-0732 TOLL FREE: (800) 668-7029	WEB: WWW.CIGNA.COM

CINCINNATI EQUITABLE INSURANCE CO — *CEIC*

INDIANA *OHIO* *PENNSYLVANIA*	525 VINE ST STE 2100 CINCINNATI, OH 45202-3166 PO BOX 3428 CINCINNATI, OH 45201-3428	PHONE: (513) 621-1826 FAX: (513) 621-4559 TOLL FREE: (800) 621-1826	WEB: WWW.CINCINNATIEQUITABLE.COM

CINCINNATI INSURANCE CO — *CINF*

NATIONAL	6200 S GILLMORE RD FAIRFIELD, OH 45014 PO BOX 145496 CINCINNATI, OH 45250-5496	PHONE: (513) 870-2000 FAX: (513) 870-2913	E-MAIL: CINCINNATI_LIFE@CINFIN.COM WEB: WWW.CINFIN.COM
ALABAMA	PO BOX 920338 NORCROSS, GA 30010-0338	PHONE: (770) 662-8753 FAX: (770) 417-4635	E-MAIL: CINCINNATI_LIFE@CINFIN.COM WEB: WWW.CINFIN.COM
FLORIDA	PO BOX 42536 ST PETERSBURG, FL 33742-4536	PHONE: (727) 576-1442 FAX: (727) 576-2958 TOLL FREE: (800) 677-1442	E-MAIL: CINCINNATI_LIFE@CINFIN.COM WEB: WWW.CINFIN.COM
GEORGIA *SOUTH CAROLINA* *TENNESSEE*	PO BOX 920338 NORCROSS, GA 30010-0338	PHONE: (770) 662-8753 FAX: (770) 417-4635	E-MAIL: CINCINNATI_LIFE@CINFIN.COM WEB: WWW.CINFIN.COM

CINF — *SEE ALSO CINCINNATI INSURANCE CO*

CITATION INSURANCE GROUP — *SEE ALSO SEQUOIA INSURANCE CO*

CITIZENS FINANCIAL CORP — *SEE ALSO CITIZENS SECURITY LIFE INSURANCE CO*

CITIZENS INSURANCE CO — *HANOVER INSURANCE*

ILLINOIS
INDIANA
OHIO

CENTRAL & EASTERN MICHIGAN REGIONAL OFFICE
645 W GRAND RIVER
HOWELL, MI 48843
PO BOX 943
HOWELL, MI 48844

FAX: (517) 540-0166
TOLL FREE: (800) 388-1300

WEB: WWW.ALLMERICA.COM

CITIZENS SECURITY LIFE INSURANCE CO — *CITIZENS FINANCIAL CORP*

ALABAMA
ARKANSAS
DELAWARE
DISTRICT OF COLUMBIA
FLORIDA
GEORGIA
INDIANA
KENTUCKY
LOUISIANA
MARYLAND
MISSISSIPPI
MISSOURI
NEW JERSEY
NORTH CAROLINA
OHIO
PENNSYLVANIA
SOUTH CAROLINA
TENNESSEE
TEXAS
VIRGINIA
WEST VIRGINIA

12910 SHELBYVILLE RD STE 300
LOUISVILLE, KY 40243-2412
PO BOX 436149
LOUISVILLE, KY 40253-6149

PHONE: (502) 244-2420
FAX: (502) 244-2439
TOLL FREE: (800) 843-7752

E-MAIL: INMILLS@CITIZENSECURITYLIFE.COM
WEB: WWW.CITIZENSFINANCIALCORP.COM

CITY OF LONG BEACH WORKERS' COMPENSATION

CALIFORNIA

333 W OCEAN BLVD 8TH FL
LONG BEACH, CA 90802-4664

PHONE: (562) 570-2245
FAX: (562) 570-2220

CITY OF LOS ANGELES WORKERS' COMPENSATION DIVISION

CALIFORNIA

700 E TEMPLE STE 210
LOS ANGELES, CA 90012-4111

PHONE: (213) 847-9405
FAX: (213) 847-9037

WEB: WWW.CITYOFLOSANGELES.ORG

CITY OF MESA EMPLOYEE BENEFITS

ARIZONA

200 S CENTER ST BLDG 3
MESA, AZ 85210-1502
PO BOX 1466
MESA, AZ 85211-1466

PHONE: (480) 644-2299
FAX: (480) 644-4548

WEB: WWW.CITYOFMESA.ORG

CIVIL SERVICE EMPLOYEES INSURANCE CO — *CSE INSURANCE GROUP*

ARIZONA
CALIFORNIA
NEVADA
OREGON
UTAH
WASHINGTON

2710 GATEWAY OAKS DR STE 150
SACRAMENTO, CA 95833-4305
PO BOX 13506
SACRAMENTO, CA 95853

PHONE: (916) 564-5126
FAX: (916) 561-7350
TOLL FREE: (800) 282-6848

WEB: WWW.CSE-INSURANCE.COM

CIVIL SERVICE EMPLOYEES INSURANCE GROUP — *CSE INSURANCE GROUP*

ARIZONA
CALIFORNIA

99 S LAKE AVE 4TH FL
PASADENA, CA 91101-4701
PO BOX 7006
PASADENA, CA 91109-7006

PHONE: (626) 793-6300
FAX: (626) 440-5828
TOLL FREE: (800) 282-6848

WEB: WWW.CSE-INSURANCE.COM

CLAIM MANAGEMENT SERVICES — *CMS*

NATIONAL

100 N 6TH AVE
WEST BEND, WI 53095
PO BOX 2790
WEST BEND, WI 53095-7970

PHONE: (262) 338-9889
FAX: (262) 338-0755
TOLL FREE: (800) 245-6142

WEB: WWW.CMSINS.COM

NATIONAL — CONTINUED	975 HANSEN RD GREEN BAY, WI 54304 PO BOX 10888 GREEN BAY, WI 54307	PHONE: (920) 497-1589 FAX: (920) 494-1483 TOLL FREE: (800) 472-7130	WEB: WWW.CMSINS.COM

CLAIMSWARE — *SEE ALSO CWI BENEFITS MANAGEMED*

CLEAR CARE CORPORATION

PENNSYLVANIA	1229 S 2ND ST CLEARFIELD, PA 16830 PO BOX 1411 CLEARFIELD, PA 16830	PHONE: (814) 765-0221 FAX: (814) 765-3011 TOLL FREE: (800) 999-0418	WEB: WWW.CLEARCARECORP.COM

CM AUTO — *SEE ALSO FIRST CHICAGO INSURANCE CO*

CMS — *SEE ALSO CLAIM MANAGEMENT SERVICES*

CMS CAP MANAGEMENT SYSTEMS

CALIFORNIA	16030 VENTURA BLVD STE 200 ENCINO, CA 91436-2754	PHONE: (714) 590-5000 FAX: (818) 461-5095 TOLL FREE: (888) 445-0062 IN-STATE: (800) 611-0111	WEB: WWW.TENETHEALTH.COM

CNA

NATIONAL	HOME OFFICE 333 S WABASH AVE CHICAGO, IL 60685-1040	PHONE: (312) 822-5000 FAX: (312) 822-6419 TOLL FREE: (800) 262-2000	WEB: WWW.CNA.COM
	27555 EXECUTIVE DR STE 350 FARMINGTON HILLS, MI 48331 PO BOX 9056 FARMINGTON HILLS, MI 48333-9056	PHONE: (248) 553-5900 FAX: (248) 553-5259 TOLL FREE: (800) 262-2710	WEB: WWW.CNA.COM
	40 WALL ST NEW YORK, NY 10005-1396 PO BOX 1046 NEW YORK, NY 10268-1046	PHONE: (212) 440-3000 FAX: (212) 440-7201 TOLL FREE: (800) 262-1145 IN-STATE: (800) 262-1145	WEB: WWW.CNA.COM
	ADDITIONAL COMMENTS: ALSO SERVICES LONDON & BERMUDA		
	5151 SAN FELIPE STE 1800 HOUSTON, TX 77056 PO BOX 27537 HOUSTON, TX 77227-9914	PHONE: (713) 513-6200 FAX: (713) 513-6298 TOLL FREE: (800) 262-3370	WEB: WWW.CNA.COM
	ONE TELERGY PKY 2ND FL EAST SYRACUSE, NY 13057-1370 PO BOX 4855 SYRACUSE, NY 13221-9944	PHONE: (315) 431-6000 FAX: (315) 431-6005 TOLL FREE: (800) 262-6344	E-MAIL: CNA_HELP@CNA.COM WEB: WWW.CNA.COM
	333 E BUTTERFIELD STE 700 LOMBARD, IL 60148 PO BOX 1562 LOMBARD, IL 60148	PHONE: (630) 719-3000 FAX: (800) 742-3619 TOLL FREE: (800) 262-4554	WEB: WWW.CNA.COM
ALBERTA	HOME OFFICE 333 S WABASH AVE CHICAGO, IL 60685-1040	PHONE: (312) 822-5000 FAX: (312) 822-6419 TOLL FREE: (800) 262-2000	WEB: WWW.CNA.COM

ARKANSAS	26 CENTURY BLVD 4TH FL STE 400 NASHVILLE, TN 37214-3439 PO BOX 305123 NASHVILLE, TN 37230	PHONE: (615) 886-3300 FAX: (615) 886-3346 TOLL FREE: (800) 251-5852	WEB: WWW.CNA.COM
BRITISH COLUMBIA *CANADA*	HOME OFFICE 333 S WABASH AVE CHICAGO, IL 60685-1040	PHONE: (312) 822-5000 FAX: (312) 822-6419 TOLL FREE: (800) 262-2000	WEB: WWW.CNA.COM
DELAWARE *DISTRICT OF COLUMBIA*	PO BOX 9167 QUINCY, MA 02269-9167	PHONE: (617) 984-4500 FAX: (617) 984-4545 TOLL FREE: (800) 972-5550	WEB: WWW.CNA.COM
INDIANA *KENTUCKY*	333 E BUTTERFIELD STE 700 LOMBARD, IL 60148 PO BOX 1562 LOMBARD, IL 60148	PHONE: (630) 719-3000 FAX: (800) 742-3619 TOLL FREE: (800) 262-4554	WEB: WWW.CNA.COM
KENTUCKY *LOUISIANA*	26 CENTURY BLVD 4TH FL STE 400 NASHVILLE, TN 37214-3439 PO BOX 305123 NASHVILLE, TN 37230	PHONE: (615) 886-3300 FAX: (615) 886-3346 TOLL FREE: (800) 251-5852	WEB: WWW.CNA.COM
MAINE	PO BOX 9167 QUINCY, MA 02269-9167	PHONE: (617) 984-4500 FAX: (617) 984-4545 TOLL FREE: (800) 972-5550	WEB: WWW.CNA.COM
MANITOBA	HOME OFFICE 333 S WABASH AVE CHICAGO, IL 60685-1040	PHONE: (312) 822-5000 FAX: (312) 822-6419 TOLL FREE: (800) 262-2000	WEB: WWW.CNA.COM
MARYLAND *MASSACHUSETTS*	PO BOX 9167 QUINCY, MA 02269-9167	PHONE: (617) 984-4500 FAX: (617) 984-4545 TOLL FREE: (800) 972-5550	WEB: WWW.CNA.COM
MEXICO	HOME OFFICE 333 S WABASH AVE CHICAGO, IL 60685-1040	PHONE: (312) 822-5000 FAX: (312) 822-6419 TOLL FREE: (800) 262-2000	WEB: WWW.CNA.COM
MICHIGAN	27555 EXECUTIVE DR STE 350 FARMINGTON HILLS, MI 48331 PO BOX 9056 FARMINGTON HILLS, MI 48333-9056	PHONE: (248) 553-5900 FAX: (248) 553-5259 TOLL FREE: (800) 262-2710	WEB: WWW.CNA.COM
	13845 BISHOPS DR STE 100 BROOKFIELD, WI 53005 PO BOX 1236 MILWAUKEE, WI 53201-1236	PHONE: (262) 821-4600 FAX: (262) 821-4601 TOLL FREE: (800) 242-9638	WEB: WWW.CNA.COM
	333 E BUTTERFIELD STE 700 LOMBARD, IL 60148 PO BOX 1562 LOMBARD, IL 60148	PHONE: (630) 719-3000 FAX: (800) 742-3619 TOLL FREE: (800) 262-4554	WEB: WWW.CNA.COM
MISSISSIPPI	26 CENTURY BLVD 4TH FL STE 400 NASHVILLE, TN 37214-3439 PO BOX 305123 NASHVILLE, TN 37230	PHONE: (615) 886-3300 FAX: (615) 886-3346 TOLL FREE: (800) 251-5852	WEB: WWW.CNA.COM

NEW BRUNSWICK	HOME OFFICE 333 S WABASH AVE CHICAGO, IL 60685-1040	PHONE: (312) 822-5000 FAX: (312) 822-6419 TOLL FREE: (800) 262-2000	WEB: WWW.CNA.COM
NEW HAMPSHIRE *NEW JERSEY*	PO BOX 9167 QUINCY, MA 02269-9167	PHONE: (617) 984-4500 FAX: (617) 984-4545 TOLL FREE: (800) 972-5550	WEB: WWW.CNA.COM
NEW JERSEY	FOUR CENTURY DR PARSIPPANY, NJ 07054	FAX: (973) 540-3602 TOLL FREE: (800) 262-3249	WEB: WWW.CNA.COM
NEW JERSEY *NEW YORK*	THREE HUNTINGTON QUAD 2ND FL MELVILLE, NY 11747 PO BOX 609 MELVILLE, NY 11747-0492	PHONE: (631) 756-7300 FAX: (631) 756-7570 OR (800) 953-7389 TOLL FREE: (800) 732-9109	WEB: WWW.CNA.COM
NEW YORK	PO BOX 9167 QUINCY, MA 02269-9167	PHONE: (617) 984-4500 FAX: (617) 984-4545 TOLL FREE: (800) 972-5550	WEB: WWW.CNA.COM
NEWFOUNDLAND *NOVA SCOTIA*	HOME OFFICE 333 S WABASH AVE CHICAGO, IL 60685-1040	PHONE: (312) 822-5000 FAX: (312) 822-6419 TOLL FREE: (800) 262-2000	WEB: WWW.CNA.COM
OKLAHOMA	26 CENTURY BLVD 4TH FL STE 400 NASHVILLE, TN 37214-3439 PO BOX 305123 NASHVILLE, TN 37230	PHONE: (615) 886-3300 FAX: (615) 886-3346 TOLL FREE: (800) 251-5852	WEB: WWW.CNA.COM
	600 N PEARL ST STE 1400 DALLAS, TX 75201-2889 PO BOX 219011 DALLAS, TX 75221	PHONE: (214) 220-1300 FAX: (214) 220-1690 TOLL FREE: (800) 262-1113	WEB: WWW.CNA.COM
ONTARIO	HOME OFFICE 333 S WABASH AVE CHICAGO, IL 60685-1040	PHONE: (312) 822-5000 FAX: (312) 822-6419 TOLL FREE: (800) 262-2000	WEB: WWW.CNA.COM
PENNSYLVANIA	PO BOX 9167 QUINCY, MA 02269-9167	PHONE: (617) 984-4500 FAX: (617) 984-4545 TOLL FREE: (800) 972-5550	WEB: WWW.CNA.COM
PRINCE EDWARD ISLAND *QUEBEC*	HOME OFFICE 333 S WABASH AVE CHICAGO, IL 60685-1040	PHONE: (312) 822-5000 FAX: (312) 822-6419 TOLL FREE: (800) 262-2000	WEB: WWW.CNA.COM
RHODE ISLAND	PO BOX 9167 QUINCY, MA 02269-9167	PHONE: (617) 984-4500 FAX: (617) 984-4545 TOLL FREE: (800) 972-5550	WEB: WWW.CNA.COM
SASKATCHEWAN	HOME OFFICE 333 S WABASH AVE CHICAGO, IL 60685-1040	PHONE: (312) 822-5000 FAX: (312) 822-6419 TOLL FREE: (800) 262-2000	WEB: WWW.CNA.COM

TENNESSEE	26 CENTURY BLVD 4TH FL STE 400 NASHVILLE, TN 37214-3439 PO BOX 305123 NASHVILLE, TN 37230	PHONE: (615) 886-3300 FAX: (615) 886-3346 TOLL FREE: (800) 251-5852	WEB: WWW.CNA.COM
TEXAS	600 N PEARL ST STE 1400 DALLAS, TX 75201-2889 PO BOX 219011 DALLAS, TX 75221	PHONE: (214) 220-1300 FAX: (214) 220-1690 TOLL FREE: (800) 262-1113	WEB: WWW.CNA.COM
UK	HOME OFFICE 333 S WABASH AVE CHICAGO, IL 60685-1040	PHONE: (312) 822-5000 FAX: (312) 822-6419 TOLL FREE: (800) 262-2000	WEB: WWW.CNA.COM
VERMONT VIRGINIA WEST VIRGINIA	PO BOX 9167 QUINCY, MA 02269-9167	PHONE: (617) 984-4500 FAX: (617) 984-4545 TOLL FREE: (800) 972-5550	WEB: WWW.CNA.COM
WISCONSIN	13845 BISHOPS DR STE 100 BROOKFIELD, WI 53005 PO BOX 1236 MILWAUKEE, WI 53201-1236	PHONE: (262) 821-4600 FAX: (262) 821-4601 TOLL FREE: (800) 242-9638	WEB: WWW.CNA.COM
	333 E BUTTERFIELD STE 700 LOMBARD, IL 60148 PO BOX 1562 LOMBARD, IL 60148	PHONE: (630) 719-3000 FAX: (800) 742-3619 TOLL FREE: (800) 262-4554	WEB: WWW.CNA.COM

CNIC HEALTH SOLUTIONS

NATIONAL	10771 EASTER AVE STE 250 CENTENNIAL, CO 80112 PO BOX 3559 ENGLEWOOD, CO 80155	PHONE: (303) 770-5710 FAX: (303) 770-2743 TOLL FREE: (800) 426-7453	E-MAIL: CUSTOMERSERVICE@CNICHS.COM WEB: WWW.CNICHS.COM
	1250 LAMOILLE HWY STE 731 ELKO, NV 89801	PHONE: (775) 777-0810 FAX: (775) 777-0811	E-MAIL: CUSTOMERSERVICE@CNICHS.COM WEB: WWW.CNICHS.COM
	740 WOOTEN RD STE 104 COLORADO SPRINGS, CO 80915 PO BOX 76149 COLORADO SPRINGS, CO 80970-6149	PHONE: (877) 321-4412 FAX: (719) 591-8817	E-MAIL: CUSTOMERSERVICE@CNICHS.COM WEB: WWW.CNICHS.COM

CNL — *SEE ALSO CHEROKEE NATIONAL LIFE FINANCIAL CORP*

CO-OP INSURANCE COOPERATIVES

NEW HAMPSHIRE VERMONT	292 COLONIAL DR MIDDLEBURY, VT 05753 PO BOX 5890 MIDDLEBURY, VT 05753	PHONE: (802) 388-7917 FAX: (802) 388-0069 TOLL FREE: (800) 639-4017 IN-STATE: (800) 388-6638	WEB: WWW.CO-OPINSURANCE.COM

COALITION AMERICA, INC

NATIONAL	4151 ASHFORD DUNWOODY RD STE 615 ATLANTA, GA 30319	PHONE: (404) 459-7201	WEB: WWW.COALITIONAMERICA.COM

C

COAST BENEFITS

NEVADA
3850 S VALLEY VIEW BLVD
LAS VEGAS, NV 89103
PO BOX 80040
LAS VEGAS, NV 89180-0040
PHONE: (702) 889-1155
FAX: (702) 889-1284

COLONIAL HEALTHCARE — *SEE ALSO CHC*

COLONIAL SUPPLEMENTAL INSURANCE — *UNUMPROVIDENT*

NATIONAL
MEXICO
PUERTO RICO
UK
1200 COLONIAL LIFE BLVD W
COLUMBIA, SC 29210
PO BOX 1365
COLUMBIA, SC 29202-1365
PHONE: (803) 798-7000
FAX: (803) 731-2618
TOLL FREE: (800) 325-4368
WEB: WWW.COLONIALLIFE.COM

COLONIAL-PENN LIFE INSURANCE

NATIONAL
399 MARKET ST DPT 1250
PHILADELPHIA, PA 19181
PHONE: (215) 928-8000
FAX: (215) 928-6042
TOLL FREE: (800) 523-4000
WEB: WWW.COLONIALPENN.COM

COLORADO PREFERRED PHYSICIAN ORGANIZATION — *WEST CARE*

COLORADO
4891 INDEPENDENCE ST STE 285
WHEAT RIDGE, CO 80033-6793
PO BOX 897
WHEAT RIDGE, CO 80034-0897
PHONE: (303) 467-3667
FAX: (303) 467-3791

COLUMBIA UNITED PROVIDERS

WASHINGTON
19120 SE 34TH ST STE 201
VANCOUVER, WA 98683-1430
PHONE: (360) 891-1520
FAX: (360) 449-8862
TOLL FREE: (800) 315-7862
WEB: WWW.CUPHEALTH.COM

COLUMBUS LIFE INSURANCE CO

OHIO
400 E 4TH ST
CINCINNATI, OH 45202-3302
PO BOX 5737
CINCINNATI, OH 45201-5737
PHONE: (513) 361-6700
FAX: (513) 361-6939
TOLL FREE: (800) 677-8383
WEB: WWW.COLUMBUSLIFE.COM

COMBINED BENEFITS ADMINISTRATORS — *CBA*

NATIONAL
4704 W JENNIFER AVE STE 104
FRESNO, CA 93722-6419
PHONE: (559) 275-3984
FAX: (559) 271-0419
TOLL FREE: (800) 709-4734
E-MAIL: CBAFRESNO@SBCGLOBAL.NET
WEB: WWW.COMBINEDBENEFITSADMINISTRATORS.COM

COMBINED INSURANCE

NATIONAL
5050 N BROADWAY ST
CHICAGO, IL 60640
PHONE: (773) 275-8000
FAX: (773) 765-1850
TOLL FREE: (800) 225-4500
WEB: WWW.COMBINED.COM

ADDITIONAL COMMENTS: NATIONAL EXCEPT ALABAMA & MISSISSIPPI

COMBINED LIFE INSURANCE CO OF NEW YORK

NEW YORK
11 BRITISH AMERICAN BLVD
LATHAM, NY 12110-1405
PHONE: (518) 220-9333
FAX: (518) 220-2921
TOLL FREE: (800) 951-6206
WEB: WWW.COMBINEDNY.COM

COMMERCE BENEFITS GROUP, THE

NATIONAL
33479 LAKE RD
AVON LAKE, OH 44012
PO BOX 900
ELYRIA, OH 44036
PHONE: (440) 930-7500
FAX: (440) 930-7501
TOLL FREE: (800) 223-9941
WEB: WWW.COMMERCEBENFITSGROUP.COM

COMMERCE INSURANCE CO, INC, THE

MASSACHUSETTS
211 MAIN ST
WEBSTER, MA 01570-2249
PHONE: (508) 943-9000
TOLL FREE: (800) 922-8276
WEB: WWW.COMMERCEINSURANCE.COM

COMMERCIAL TRAVELERS MUTUAL INSURANCE CO — *MONITOR LIFE INSURANCE CO OF NEW YORK, CT AGENCY*

NATIONAL
70 GENESEE ST
UTICA, NY 13502
PHONE: (315) 797-5200
FAX: (315) 797-3198
TOLL FREE: (800) 422-6200
E-MAIL: CUSTSVC@COMMERCIALTRAVELERS.COM
WEB: WWW.COMMERCIALTRAVELERS.COM

C

COMMONWEALTH ADMINISTRATORS

INDIANA
KENTUCKY
333 W VINE ST 500
LEXINGTON, KY 40507
PO BOX 3079
LEXINGTON, KY 40588
PHONE: (859) 226-1500
FAX: (859) 226-1599
TOLL FREE: (877) 997-7716
WEB: WWW.CATPA.COM

COMMUNITY HEALTH PLAN — *CHP*

KANSAS
MISSOURI
NEBRASKA
137 N BELT HWY
ST JOSEPH, MO 64506
PHONE: (816) 271-1247
FAX: (816) 271-1266
TOLL FREE: (800) 990-9247
WEB: WWW.MYCHP.COM

COMP CAROLINA — *ATTEMTA*

NORTH CAROLINA
603 SAINT MARY'S ST
RALEIGH, NC 27605
PO BOX 19500
RALEIGH, NC 27619
PHONE: (919) 856-2320
FAX: (919) 856-1434
TOLL FREE: (800) 258-0278
WEB: WWW.COMPCAROLINA.COM

COMPANION LIFE INSURANCE CO

NATIONAL
7909 PARKLANE RD STE 200
COLUMBIA, SC 29223
PO BOX 100102
COLUMBIA, SC 29202-3102
PHONE: (803) 735-1251
FAX: (803) 735-0736
TOLL FREE: (800) 753-0404
WEB: WWW.COMPANIONLIFE.COM

ADDITIONAL COMMENTS: NATIONAL EXCEPT FLORIDA & WEST VIRGINIA

COMPBENEFITS

ALABAMA
200 W JACKSON BLVD 9TH FL
CHICAGO, IL 60606-6910
PHONE: (312) 261-6200
FAX: (312) 427-9665
TOLL FREE: (800) 837-2341
WEB: WWW.COMPBENEFITS.COM

ALABAMA
FLORIDA
ILLINOIS
100 MANSELL CT E STE 400
ROSWELL, GA 30076-4859
PHONE: (770) 552-7101
FAX: (770) 998-6871
TOLL FREE: (800) 342-5209
WEB: WWW.COMPBENEFITS.COM

ILLINOIS
200 W JACKSON BLVD 9TH FL
CHICAGO, IL 60606-6910
PHONE: (312) 261-6200
FAX: (312) 427-9665
TOLL FREE: (800) 837-2341
WEB: WWW.COMPBENEFITS.COM

INDIANA *KANSAS* *KENTUCKY* *MISSOURI* *OHIO* *TENNESSEE* *TEXAS*

100 MANSELL CT E STE 400
ROSWELL, GA 30076-4859
PHONE: (770) 552-7101
FAX: (770) 998-6871
TOLL FREE: (800) 342-5209
WEB: WWW.COMPBENEFITS.COM

COMPREHENSIVE BENEFITS ADMINISTRATOR, INC— *SEE ALSO CBA, INC*

NATIONAL
46 BOWDOIN ST
SOUTH BURLINGTON, VT 05403-6432
PO BOX 2365
SOUTH BURLINGTON, VT 05407-2365
PHONE: (802) 864-8321
FAX: (802) 864-8115
TOLL FREE: (800) 525-8788
E-MAIL: CUSTOMERSERVICE@CBAVT.COM
WEB: WWW.CBAVT.COM

C

COMPUSYS, INC — *ARIZONA PIPE TRADES*

ARIZONA	1200 SAN PEDRO NE ALBUQUERQUE, NM 87110 PO BOX 11399 ALBUQUERQUE, NM 87192-0399	PHONE: (505) 262-1921 FAX: (505) 266-0922 TOLL FREE: (800) 926-5581	
ARIZONA *CALIFORNIA* *COLORADO*	2156 W 2200 S SALT LAKE CITY, UT 84119	PHONE: (801) 973-1001 FAX: (801) 973-1007	E-MAIL: COMPUSYS@COMPUSYSUT.COM WEB: WWW.CSERISA.COM
COLORADO	2821 S PARK RD STE 1005 AURORA, CO 80014-2602	PHONE: (303) 745-0147 FAX: (303) 745-7010 TOLL FREE: (800) 332-3807	
IDAHO	2156 W 2200 S SALT LAKE CITY, UT 84119	PHONE: (801) 973-1001 FAX: (801) 973-1007	E-MAIL: COMPUSYS@COMPUSYSUT.COM WEB: WWW.CSERISA.COM
NEW MEXICO	1200 SAN PEDRO NE ALBUQUERQUE, NM 87110 PO BOX 11399 ALBUQUERQUE, NM 87192-0399	PHONE: (505) 262-1921 FAX: (505) 266-0922 TOLL FREE: (800) 926-5581	
	1429 SECOND ST SANTA FE, NM 87505-3486 PO BOX 9054 SANTA FE, NM 87504	PHONE: (505) 988-4974 FAX: (505) 988-8943 TOLL FREE: (800) 233-3164	WEB: WWW.CSERISA.COM
OREGON	2156 W 2200 S SALT LAKE CITY, UT 84119	PHONE: (801) 973-1001 FAX: (801) 973-1007	E-MAIL: COMPUSYS@COMPUSYSUT.COM WEB: WWW.CSERISA.COM
TEXAS	1200 SAN PEDRO NE ALBUQUERQUE, NM 87110 PO BOX 11399 ALBUQUERQUE, NM 87192-0399	PHONE: (505) 262-1921 FAX: (505) 266-0922 TOLL FREE: (800) 926-5581	
	12325 HYMEADOW DR BLDG 4 STE 100 AUSTIN, TX 78750-1899	PHONE: (512) 250-9397 FAX: (512) 335-7298 TOLL FREE: (800) 933-7472	WEB: WWW.CSERISA.COM
UTAH *WASHINGTON* *WYOMING*	2156 W 2200 S SALT LAKE CITY, UT 84119	PHONE: (801) 973-1001 FAX: (801) 973-1007	E-MAIL: COMPUSYS@COMPUSYSUT.COM WEB: WWW.CSERISA.COM

CONCENTRA, INC

NATIONAL *CANADA*	5080 SPECTRUM DR STE 1200W ADDISON, TX 75001	PHONE: (972) 364-8000 FAX: (972) 387-0019 TOLL FREE: (800) 232-3550	WEB: WWW.CONCENTRA.COM

CONCORD GROUP INSURANCE CO

MAINE	27 PIPER RD MONTPELIER, VT 05602-0000 PO BOX 870 MONTPELIER, VT 05601	PHONE: (802) 229-0355 FAX: (800) 377-0426 OR (877) 620-8383 TOLL FREE: (800) 660-3838	WEB: WWW.CONCORDGROUPINSURANCE.COM
	308 CENTER ST AUBURN, ME 04210-6115 PO BOX 300 AUBURN, ME 04212-0300	PHONE: (207) 784-7337 FAX: (800) 784-3356 OR (207) 783-8189 TOLL FREE: (800) 482-7443	WEB: WWW.CONCORDGROUPINSURANCE.COM

MAINE *MASSACHUSETTS* *NEW HAMPSHIRE*	4 BOUTON ST CONCORD, NH 03301 PO BOX 2048 CONCORD, NH 03301	PHONE: (603) 225-1141 FAX: (603) 226-3096 TOLL FREE: (800) 852-3380	WEB: WWW.CONCORDGROUPINSURANCE.COM
NEW HAMPSHIRE	510 SOUTH ST CONCORD, NH 03304 PO BOX 2048 CONCORD, NH 03301	PHONE: (603) 225-1141 FAX: (603) 225-5659 TOLL FREE: (800) 888-6050	WEB: WWW.CONCORDGROUPINSURANCE.COM
NEW HAMPSHIRE *VERMONT*	27 PIPER RD MONTPELIER, VT 05602-0000 PO BOX 870 MONTPELIER, VT 05601	PHONE: (802) 229-0355 FAX: (800) 377-0426 OR (877) 620-8383 TOLL FREE: (800) 660-3338	WEB: WWW.CONCORDGROUPINSURANCE.COM
	308 CENTER ST AUBURN, ME 04210-6115 PO BOX 300 AUBURN, ME 04212-0300	PHONE: (207) 784-7337 FAX: (800) 784-3356 OR (207) 783-8189 TOLL FREE: (800) 482-7443	WEB: WWW.CONCORDGROUPINSURANCE.COM
VERMONT	4 BOUTON ST CONCORD, NH 03301 PO BOX 2048 CONCORD, NH 03301	PHONE: (603) 225-1141 FAX: (603) 226-3096 TOLL FREE: (800) 852-3380	WEB: WWW.CONCORDGROUPINSURANCE.COM

CONNECTICARE INC & AFFILIATES

CONNECTICUT *MASSACHUSETTS* *NEW YORK*	175 SCOTT SWAMP RD FARMINGTON, CT 06032 PO BOX 546 FARMINGTON, CT 06034-0546	PHONE: (860) 674-5700 FAX: (860) 674-5728 TOLL FREE: (800) 251-7722	WEB: WWW.CONNECTICARE.COM

CONSECO

NATIONAL	11825 N PENNSYLVANIA ST CARMEL, IN 46032-4603 PO BOX 1930 CARMEL, IN 46082-1930	PHONE: (317) 817-6100 IN-STATE: (800) 888-4918	WEB: WWW.CONSECO.COM

CONSOLIDATED ASSOCIATION OF RAILROAD EMPLOYEES CARE

NATIONAL	4912 MIDWAY DR TEMPLE, TX 76503-1519 PO BOX 6130 TEMPLE, TX 76503-6130	PHONE: (254) 773-1330 FAX: (254) 774-8029 TOLL FREE: (800) 334-1330	WEB: WWW.CAREHEALTHPLAN.COM

CONSOLIDATED HEALTH PLANS

NATIONAL	195 STAFFORD ST SPRINGFIELD, MA 01104	PHONE: (413) 733-4540 FAX: (413) 733-4612 TOLL FREE: (800) 633-7867	WEB: WWW.CONSOLIDATEDHEALTHPLAN.COM

CONSTITUTION LIFE INSURANCE — *SEE ALSO UNION BANKERS*

CONSTRUCTION INDUSTRY LABORERS WELFARE FUND

KANSAS *MISSOURI*	116 COMMERCE DR JEFFERSON CITY, MO 65109-1196	PHONE: (573) 893-2446 FAX: (573) 893-4369 TOLL FREE: (800) 392-8726

CONSTRUCTION INDUSTRY WELFARE FUND OF CENTRAL ILLINOIS

ILLINOIS	34 E SPRINGFIELD AVE CHAMPAIGN, IL 61820-5367	PHONE: (217) 352-5269 FAX: (217) 352-5297 TOLL FREE: (888) 445-8711

CONSUMER HEALTH NETWORK — *CHN SOLUTIONS*

CONNECTICUT *NEW JERSEY* *NEW YORK* *RHODE ISLAND*	IBIS PLAZA 3525 QUAKERBRIDGE RD HAMILTON, NJ 08619	PHONE: (609) 631-0474 FAX: (609) 631-0173 TOLL FREE: (800) 293-9795	WEB: WWW.CHN.COM

CONTINENTAL AMERICAN INSURANCE GROUP

NATIONAL	2801 DEVINE ST COLUMBIA, SC 29205-2556 PO BOX 1807 COLUMBIA, SC 29202-1807	PHONE: (803) 256-6265 FAX: (803) 779-4406 TOLL FREE: (800) 433-3036	WEB: WWW.CAIG-INS.COM

CONTINENTAL GENERAL INSURANCE — *CERES GROUP, INC*

NATIONAL	6201 JOHNSON DR SHAWNEE MISSION, KS 66202 PO BOX 29136 SHAWNEE MISSION, KS 66201-9136	PHONE: (913) 722-1110 FAX: (913) 384-3258 TOLL FREE: (800) 284-2898	WEB: WWW.CONTINENTALGENERAL.COM

CONTINENTAL GENERAL INSURANCE CO — *CIGNA*

NATIONAL	8901 INDIAN HILLS DR OMAHA, NE 68114 PO BOX 247007 OMAHA, NE 68124-7007	PHONE: (402) 397-3200 FAX: (402) 952-4771 TOLL FREE: (800) 545-8905	E-MAIL: BENEFITS@CONTINENTALGENERAL.COM WEB: WWW.CONTINENTALGENERAL.COM

CONTINENTAL LIFE INSURANCE CO OF BRENTWOOD TN

NATIONAL	101 CONTINENTAL PL BRENTWOOD, TN 37027 PO BOX 1188 BRENTWOOD, TN 37024	PHONE: (615) 377-1300	WEB: WWW.CONTLIFE.COM

ADDITIONAL COMMENTS: NATIONAL EXCEPT NEW YORK & NEW JERSEY

CONTINENTAL WESTERN GROUP

COLORADO	3641 VILLAGE DR LINCOLN, NE 68516 PO BOX 80439 LINCOLN, NE 68501	PHONE: (402) 423-7688 FAX: (402) 421-4308 TOLL FREE: (800) 456-7688	WEB: WWW.CWGINS.COM
IDAHO	ROCKY MOUNTAIN REGION 3320 E GOLDSTONE WY MERIDIAN, ID 83642	PHONE: (208) 898-5200 FAX: (208) 898-5217 TOLL FREE: (800) 480-2942	WEB: WWW.CWGINS.COM
ILLINOIS *IOWA*	11201 DOUGLAS AVE DES MOINES, IA 50322 PO BOX 1594 DES MOINES, IA 50306	PHONE: (515) 278-3000 FAX: (515) 278-3382 TOLL FREE: (800) 235-2942	WEB: WWW.CWGINS.COM
KANSAS	3641 VILLAGE DR LINCOLN, NE 68516 PO BOX 80439 LINCOLN, NE 68501	PHONE: (402) 423-7688 FAX: (402) 421-4308 TOLL FREE: (800) 456-7688	WEB: WWW.CWGINS.COM
MINNESOTA	TEN ROUNDWIND RD LUVERNE, MN 56156 PO BOX 500 LUVERNE, MN 56156-0500	PHONE: (507) 283-9561 FAX: (800) 232-9925 TOLL FREE: (800) 533-0303 IN-STATE: (800) 533-0303	WEB: WWW.CWGINS.COM
MISSOURI	11201 DOUGLAS AVE DES MOINES, IA 50322 PO BOX 1594 DES MOINES, IA 50306	PHONE: (515) 278-3000 FAX: (515) 278-3382 TOLL FREE: (800) 235-2942	WEB: WWW.CWGINS.COM
MONTANA	ROCKY MOUNTAIN REGION 3320 E GOLDSTONE WY MERIDIAN, ID 83642	PHONE: (208) 898-5200 FAX: (208) 898-5217 TOLL FREE: (800) 480-2942	WEB: WWW.CWGINS.COM

NEBRASKA	3641 VILLAGE DR LINCOLN, NE 68516 PO BOX 80439 LINCOLN, NE 68501	PHONE: (402) 423-7688 FAX: (402) 421-4308 TOLL FREE: (800) 456-7688	WEB: WWW.CWGINS.COM
NORTH DAKOTA	TEN ROUNDWIND RD LUVERNE, MN 56156 PO BOX 500 LUVERNE, MN 56156-0500	PHONE: (507) 283-9561 FAX: (800) 232-9925 TOLL FREE: (800) 533-0303 IN-STATE: (800) 533-0303	WEB: WWW.CWGINS.COM
OREGON	ROCKY MOUNTAIN REGION 3320 E GOLDSTONE WY MERIDIAN, ID 83642	PHONE: (208) 898-5200 FAX: (208) 898-5217 TOLL FREE: (800) 480-2942	WEB: WWW.CWGINS.COM
SOUTH DAKOTA	TEN ROUNDWIND RD LUVERNE, MN 56156 PO BOX 500 LUVERNE, MN 56156-0500	PHONE: (507) 283-9561 FAX: (800) 232-9925 TOLL FREE: (800) 533-0303 IN-STATE: (800) 533-0303	WEB: WWW.CWGINS.COM
UTAH WASHINGTON	ROCKY MOUNTAIN REGION 3320 E GOLDSTONE WY MERIDIAN, ID 83642	PHONE: (208) 898-5200 FAX: (208) 898-5217 TOLL FREE: (800) 480-2942	WEB: WWW.CWGINS.COM
WISCONSIN	11201 DOUGLAS AVE DES MOINES, IA 50322 PO BOX 1594 DES MOINES, IA 50306	PHONE: (515) 278-3000 FAX: (515) 278-3382 TOLL FREE: (800) 235-2942	WEB: WWW.CWGINS.COM
WYOMING	ROCKY MOUNTAIN REGION 3320 E GOLDSTONE WY MERIDIAN, ID 83642	PHONE: (208) 898-5200 FAX: (208) 898-5217 TOLL FREE: (800) 480-2942	WEB: WWW.CWGINS.COM

CONTRA COSTA HEALTH PLAN

CALIFORNIA	595 CENTER AVE STE 100 MARTINEZ, CA 94553-4629	PHONE: (925) 313-6000 FAX: (925) 313-6002 IN-STATE: (877) 661-6230	E-MAIL: CCHP@HSD.CO.CONTRA-COSTA.CA.US WEB: WWW.CONTRACOSTAHEALTHPLAN.ORG

COOK & CO, INC

MASSACHUSETTS	1025 PLAIN ST MARSHFIELD, MA 02050-2111 PO BOX 1068 MARSHFIELD, MA 02050-1068	FAX: (781) 837-5668 TOLL FREE: (800) 281-9696	WEB: WWW.COOKANDCOMPANY.COM

COOK GROUP HEALTH PLAN TRUST

NATIONAL	402 NORTH ROGERS BLOOMINGTON, IN 47404 PO BOX 489 BLOOMINGTON, IN 47402-0489	PHONE: (812) 355-2528 FAX: (812) 330-3213 TOLL FREE: (800) 593-2080	

COOPERATIVA DE SEGUROS — *DE VIDA DE PUERTO RICO*

PUERTO RICO	AMERICO MIRANDA AVE STE 400 RIO PIEDRAS, PR 00927-0000 PO BOX 363428 SAN JUAN, PR 00936	PHONE: (787) 751-5656 FAX: (787) 756-8548 TOLL FREE: (800) 986-5656	WEB: WWW.COSVI.COM

COOPERATIVE BENEFIT ADMINISTRATORS

NATIONAL	7101 A ST LINCOLN, NE 68510 PO BOX 6249 LINCOLN, NE 68506-0249	PHONE: (402) 483-9200 FAX: (402) 483-9201	

COORDINATORS GROUP OF COMPANIES— *SEE ALSO BENEFIT COORDINATORS CORP*

CORE MANAGEMENT RESOURCES

GEORGIA	515 MULBERRY ST STE 300 MACON, GA 31201 PO BOX 90 MACON, GA 31202	PHONE: (478) 741-3521 FAX: (478) 745-1843 TOLL FREE: (888) 741-2613	WEB: WWW.COREMRG.COM

C

CORESOURCE

NATIONAL	CENTRAL CLAIMS & MAILING OFFICE PO BOX 2920 CLINTON, IA 52733	PHONE: (800) 444-6965	WEB: WWW.CORESOURCE.COM
	1 SHACKLEFORD DR STE 100 LITTLE ROCK, AR 72211	TOLL FREE: (888) 604-9397	WEB: WWW.CORESOURCE.COM
	101 EISENHOWER PKY STE 300 ROSELAND, NJ 07068	PHONE: (973) 795-1220	WEB: WWW.CORESOURCE.COM
	13160 FOSTER ST STE 150 OVERLAND PARK, KS 66213 PO BOX 25946 OVERLAND PARK, KS 66225	TOLL FREE: (800) 990-9058	WEB: WWW.CORESOURCE.COM
	16225 PARK TEN PL DR STE 500 HOUSTON, TX 77084 PO BOX 2920 CLINTON, IA 52723	PHONE: (800) 832-3332 TOLL FREE: (800) 444-6965	WEB: WWW.CORESOURCE.COM
	18401 MAPLE CREEK DR TINLEY PARK, IL 60477	PHONE: (708) 342-1237 FAX: (708) 614-9895 TOLL FREE: (800) 848-3012	WEB: WWW.CORESOURCE.COM
	1902 WRIGHT PL STE 200 CARLSBAD, CA 92008	PHONE: (760) 918-5662	WEB: WWW.CORESOURCE.COM
	19125 N CREEK PKY BOTHELL, WA 98011	PHONE: (425) 488-5826	WEB: WWW.CORESOURCE.COM
	2435 N CENTRAL EXPRESSWAY STE 950 RICHARDSON, TX 75080	PHONE: (972) 335-1953	WEB: WWW.CORESOURCE.COM
	26-28 W KING ST LANCASTER, PA 17603-3809 PO BOX 83301 LANCASTER, PA 17608-3301	PHONE: (800) 223-3943 FAX: (717) 295-9368	WEB: WWW.CORESOURCE.COM

NATIONAL — CONTINUED	🏛	400 FIELD DR LAKE FOREST , IL 60045	PHONE: (847) 604-9200 FAX: (847) 615-3900 TOLL FREE: (800) 832-3332	WEB: WWW.CORESOURCE.COM
		4940 CAMPBELL BLVD STE 200 BALTIMORE, MD 21236	PHONE: (410) 931-5060 FAX: (410) 931-3653 TOLL FREE: (800) 624-7130	WEB: WWW.CORESOURCE.COM
		5200 UPPER METRO PL STE 300 DUBLIN, OH 43017-5378 PO BOX 279 SHELDON, IA 51201	PHONE: (614) 336-9604 FAX: (614) 336-8428 TOLL FREE: (800) 282-3920	WEB: WWW.CORESOURCE.COM
		700 LARKSPUR LANDING CIR STE 199 LARKSPUR, CA 94939 PO BOX 2920 CLINTON, IA 52733	TOLL FREE: (800) 444-6965	WEB: WWW.CORESOURCE.COM
		7600 N 15TH ST STE 230 PHOENIX, AZ 85020 PO BOX 2920 CLINTON, IA 52733	PHONE: (847) 283-9642 FAX: (800) 395-0384 TOLL FREE: (800) 444-6965	WEB: WWW.CORESOURCE.COM
		7830 E BROADWAY TUCSON, AZ 85710	PHONE: (520) 290-4600 TOLL FREE: (800) 888-7202	WEB: WWW.CORESOURCE.COM
		8400 E PRENTICE AVE STE 1500 GREENWOOD VILLAGE, CO 80111 PO BOX 2920 CLINTON, IA 52733	TOLL FREE: (800) 444-6965	WEB: WWW.CORESOURCE.COM
		9201 W BROADWAY AVE N STE 650 BROOKLYN PARK, MN 55445	TOLL FREE: (800) 724-2527	WEB: WWW.CORESOURCE.COM
		940 WEST VALLEY RD STE 2102 WAYNE, PA 19087-1894 PO BOX 6994 WAYNE, PA 19087-1894	PHONE: (763) 569-6400 FAX: (610) 687-1959 TOLL FREE: (800) 345-1166	WEB: WWW.CORESOURCE.COM

FLORIDA
GEORGIA
INDIANA
NORTH CAROLINA
SOUTH CAROLINA

		5200 77 CENTER DR STE 400 CHARLOTTE, NC 28217-0718	PHONE: (704) 554-4400 FAX: (704) 552-8635 TOLL FREE: (866) 433-0314 IN-STATE: (800) 821-0345	WEB: WWW.CORESOURCE.COM

CORNERSTONE BENEFITS, LLC

MICHIGAN	🏛	5435 CORPORATE DR STE 250 TROY, MI 48098	PHONE: (248) 641-2740	E-MAIL: INFO@CORNERSTONEBENEFITS.COM WEB: WWW.CORNERSTONEBENEFITS.COM

CORPORATE BENEFIT SERVICES OF AMERICA, INC— *SEE ALSO CBSA*

CORPORATE BENEFITS SERVICE, INC

NATIONAL	145 SCALEYBARK RD STE B CHARLOTTE, NC 28209-2682 PO BOX 12953 CHARLOTTE, NC 28220-2953	PHONE: (704) 373-0447 FAX: (704) 342-2777 TOLL FREE: (800) 277-9476 IN-STATE: (800) 373-4454	WEB: WWW.CORBENSER.COM

CORPORATE SYSTEMS ADMINISTRATION, INC

GEORGIA TENNESSEE	4722 LAKE PARK DR JOHNSON CITY, TN 37615-4422 PO BOX 4985 JOHNSON CITY, TN 37602-4985	PHONE: (423) 282-3420 FAX: (423) 282-2999 TOLL FREE: (800) 829-7566	WEB: WWW.CSABENEFITS.COM

CORVEL CORP

NATIONAL	N16 W23217 STONE RIDGE DR STE 110 WAUKESHA, WI 53188	PHONE: (262) 574-2001 FAX: (262) 513-2999 TOLL FREE: (800) 275-0064	WEB: WWW.CORVEL.COM
	345 RIVERVIEW ST WICHITA, KS 67203	PHONE: (316) 264-2900 FAX: (316) 264-2977 TOLL FREE: (800) 626-0149	WEB: WWW.CORVEL.COM
	1306 CONCOURSE DR STE 205 LENTHICHUM, MD 21090	PHONE: (410) 573-5120 FAX: (410) 691-1568	WEB: WWW.CORVEL.COM
	HUB PL 2ND FLOOR 1101 OPAL CT HAGERSTOWN, MD 21740	PHONE: (301) 791-0006 FAX: (301) 791-1886 TOLL FREE: (800) 427-4339	WEB: WWW.CORVEL.COM
	27 N. MERIDIAN CT STE 113 KALISPELL, MT 59901	PHONE: (406) 755-7901 FAX: (406) 755-7979 TOLL FREE: (800) 935-0660	WEB: WWW.CORVEL.COM
	11931 FOUNDATION PLACE STE 250 GOLDRIVER, CA 95670	PHONE: (916) 608-2330 FAX: (916) 608-2640 TOLL FREE: (800) 877-1440	WEB: WWW.CORVEL.COM
	1320 CENTRAL PARK BLVD STE 410 FREDERICKSBURG, VA 22401	PHONE: (540) 786-1500 FAX: (540) 548-4428 TOLL FREE: (800) 275-8463	WEB: WWW.CORVEL.COM
	1321 23RD ST S STEH2 FARGO, ND 58103	PHONE: (701) 297-0470 FAX: (701) 297-0481 TOLL FREE: (800) 297-9133	WEB: WWW.CORVEL.COM
	1910 LAKELAND DR STE A JACKSON, MS 39216	PHONE: (601) 366-1916 FAX: (601) 368-3146 TOLL FREE: (800) 929-5893	WEB: WWW.CORVEL.COM
	3001 NE BROADWAY ST STE 600 MINNEAPOLIS, MN 55413	PHONE: (612) 436-2400 FAX: (612) 436-2499 TOLL FREE: (800) 275-8893	WEB: WWW.CORVEL.COM
	3010 HIGHLAND PKY STE 600 DOWNERS GROVE, IL 60515	PHONE: (630) 874-7300 FAX: (630) 874-7500	WEB: WWW.CORVEL.COM
	3610 BUTTONWOOD DR STE 200 COLUMBIA, MO 65201	PHONE: (573) 886-8900 FAX: (573) 886-8951 TOLL FREE: (800) 281-5186	WEB: WWW.CORVEL.COM

NATIONAL — CONTINUED

4200 E SKELLY DR STE 520
TULSA, OK 74135
PHONE: (918) 497-1092
FAX: (918) 497-1099
TOLL FREE: (866) 362-3808
WEB: WWW.CORVEL.COM

4820 LAKE BROOK DR STE 150
GLEN ALLEN, VA 23058
PO BOX 2910
GLEN ALLEN, VA 23058
PHONE: (804) 273-1999
FAX: (804) 273-9817
TOLL FREE: (800) 275-8130
WEB: WWW.CORVEL.COM

5550 S 59TH STE 12
LINCOLN, NE 68516
PHONE: (402) 423-8787
FAX: (402) 423-8829
TOLL FREE: (877) 808-0005
WEB: WWW.CORVEL.COM

601 SW 2ND AVE STE 1400
PORTLAND, OR 97204-3120
PHONE: (503) 222-3144
FAX: (503) 222-0225
WEB: WWW.CORVEL.COM

ADDITIONAL COMMENTS: NO CLAIMS PROCESSED

7500 COLLEGE BLVD STE 750
OVERLAND PARK, KS 66210-4096
PHONE: (913) 498-1887
FAX: (913) 498-1885
TOLL FREE: (800) 683-1185
WEB: WWW.CORVEL.COM

810 CRESCENT CTR DR BLDG 100
FRANKLIN, TN 37067
PHONE: (615) 371-8828
FAX: (615) 371-8560
WEB: WWW.CORVEL.COM

8131 BAY MEADOW CIR W STE 203
JACKSONVILLE, FL 32256
PO BOX 24900
JACKSONVILLE, FL 32241
PHONE: (904) 737-4800
FAX: (904) 737-7678
TOLL FREE: (800) 749-2481
WEB: WWW.CORVEL.COM

14231 SEAWAY RD STE 3003
GULFPORT, MS 39503
PHONE: (228) 214-1540
FAX: (228) 214-1542
WEB: WWW.CORVEL.COM

2010 MAIN ST STE 600
IRVINE, CA 92614
PHONE: (949) 851-1473
FAX: (949) 851-1469
WEB: WWW.CORVEL.COM

ADDITIONAL COMMENTS: NATIONAL EXCEPT DISTRICT OF COLOMBIA, RHODE ISLAND & WYOMING

3550 N CENTRAL AVE STE 915
PHOENIX, AZ 85012-2117
PHONE: (602) 287-8722
FAX: (602) 287-8714
TOLL FREE: (800) 230-8288
WEB: WWW.CORVEL.COM

600 CITY PARK WAY WEST STE 700
ORANGE, CA 92868-2943
PHONE: (714) 385-8500
FAX: (714) 385-8700
WEB: WWW.CORVEL.COM

801 CHERRY ST STE 2400 UNIT #42
FORT WORTH, TX 76102
PHONE: (817) 348-0000
FAX: (817) 348-9999
WEB: WWW.CORVEL.COM

332 W SUPERIOR ST STE 505
DULUTH, MN 55802
PHONE: (218) 722-1500
FAX: (218) 733-0711
TOLL FREE: (800) 626-4509
WEB: WWW.CORVEL.COM

ALABAMA

3504 LAKE LYNDA DR STE 300
ORLANDO, FL 32817
PHONE: (407) 282-4200
FAX: (407) 282-0648
TOLL FREE: (800) 755-7501
WEB: WWW.CORVEL.COM

ALASKA

1835 S BRAGAW STE 525
ANCHORAGE, AK 99508
PHONE: (907) 274-2785
FAX: (907) 274-7583
TOLL FREE: (800) 478-6824
WEB: WWW.CORVEL.COM

NORTHWEST
4949 MEADOWS RD STE 310
LAKE OSWEGO, OR 97035
PHONE: (503) 303-1000
FAX: (503) 303-1032
TOLL FREE: (800) 275-4463
WEB: WWW.CORVEL.COM

ARKANSAS	1701 CENTERVIEW DR STE 320 LITTLE ROCK, AR 72211-4313	PHONE: (501) 255-6200 FAX: (501) 255-9332 TOLL FREE: (800) 220-9336	WEB: WWW.CORVEL.COM
CALIFORNIA	NORTHWEST 4949 MEADOWS RD STE 310 LAKE OSWEGO, OR 97035	PHONE: (503) 303-1000 FAX: (503) 303-1032 TOLL FREE: (800) 275-4463	WEB: WWW.CORVEL.COM
	30 RIVER PARK PL W STE 280 FRESNO, CA 93720	PHONE: (559) 447-0100 FAX: (559) 447-0197 TOLL FREE: (800) 683-4177	WEB: WWW.CORVEL.COM
	5030 CAMINO DE LA SIESTA STE 407 SAN DEIGO, CA 92108-3118	PHONE: (619) 278-0750 FAX: (619) 278-0755	WEB: WWW.CORVEL.COM
	625 E CARNEGIE DR STE 230 SAN BERNADINO, CA 92408	PHONE: (909) 806-2000 FAX: (909) 890-1460	WEB: WWW.CORVEL.COM
	809 BROADWAY AVE MATTOON, IL 61938 PO BOX 768 MATTOON, IL 61938-0768	PHONE: (217) 234-2006 FAX: (217) 234-2019	WEB: WWW.CORVEL.COM
	11931 FOUNDATION PL STE 250 GOLD RIVER, CA 95670-4502	PHONE: (916) 608-2630 FAX: (916) 608-2640 TOLL FREE: (800) 758-5866	WEB: WWW.CORVEL.COM
COLORADO	8610 EXPLORER DR STE 310 COLORADO SPRINGS, CO 80920	PHONE: (719) 540-0809 FAX: (719) 540-8317 TOLL FREE: (800) 473-5293	WEB: WWW.CORVEL.COM
	950 S CHERRY ST STE 1600 DENVER, CO 80246-2689	PHONE: (303) 692-9210 FAX: (303) 692-9103 TOLL FREE: (800) 929-6090	WEB: WWW.CORVEL.COM
CONNECTICUT *DELAWARE*	9030 STONEY PT PKY STE 470 RICHMOND, VA 23235	PHONE: (804) 267-2999 FAX: (804) 320-2478	WEB: WWW.CORVEL.COM
DELAWARE	20 WIGHT AVE STE 150 HUNT VALLEY, MD 21030	PHONE: (410) 403-3700 FAX: (410) 403-3725 IN-STATE: (800) 275-7005	WEB: WWW.CORVEL.COM
DISTRICT OF COLUMBIA	1306 CONCOURSE DR STE 205 LENTHICHUM, MD 21090	PHONE: (410) 573-5120 FAX: (410) 691-1568	WEB: WWW.CORVEL.COM
	11350 RANDOM HILLS RD STE 420 FAIRFAX, VA 22030	PHONE: (703) 385-5646 FAX: (703) 385-0180 TOLL FREE: (800) 496-3385	WEB: WWW.CORVEL.COM
FLORIDA	100 COLONIAL CENTER PKWY STE 110 LAKE MARY, FL 32746-2125	PHONE: (407) 321-5505 FAX: (407) 321-6660 TOLL FREE: (877) 825-1900	WEB: WWW.CORVEL.COM
	210 N UNIVERSITY DR STE 501 CORAL SPRINGS, FL 33071	PHONE: (954) 340-8990 FAX: (954) 340-9283 TOLL FREE: (800) 929-0107	WEB: WWW.CORVEL.COM
	2929 LANGLEY AVE STE 102 PENSACOLA, FL 32504	PHONE: (850) 494-6644 FAX: (850) 494-6696 TOLL FREE: (866) 494-6631	WEB: WWW.CORVEL.COM

FLORIDA — CONTINUED	325 JOHN KNOX RD BLDG F STE 240 TALLAHASSEE, FL 32303	PHONE: (850) 205-6570 FAX: (850) 205-6583 TOLL FREE: (866) 352-7915	WEB: WWW.CORVEL.COM
FLORIDA GEORGIA	3504 LAKE LYNDA DR STE 300 ORLANDO, FL 32817	PHONE: (407) 282-4200 FAX: (407) 282-0648 TOLL FREE: (800) 755-7501	WEB: WWW.CORVEL.COM
	809 BROADWAY AVE MATTOON, IL 61938 PO BOX 768 MATTOON, IL 61938-0768	PHONE: (217) 234-2006 FAX: (217) 234-2019	WEB: WWW.CORVEL.COM
GEORGIA	10700 ABBOTS BRIDGE RD STE 110 DULUTH, GA 30097	PHONE: (678) 942-7300 FAX: (678) 942-7310 TOLL FREE: (800) 275-8836	WEB: WWW.CORVEL.COM
	2421 WESTGATE DR STE D ALBANY, GA 31707 PO BOX 72121 ALBANY, GA 31708	PHONE: (229) 430-9004 FAX: (229) 639-0965	WEB: WWW.CORVEL.COM
	600 COMMERCIAL CT STE B SAVANNAH, GA 31406	PHONE: (912) 355-8841 FAX: (912) 355-8061 TOLL FREE: (888) 495-0440	WEB: WWW.CORVEL.COM
	8601 SIX FORKS THE FORUM STE 100 RALEIGH, NC 27615	PHONE: (919) 790-2260 FAX: (919) 790-1522	WEB: WWW.CORVEL.COM
	15720 JOHN J DELANEY DR STE 202 CHARLOTTE, NC 28277	PHONE: (704) 543-1382 FAX: (704) 543-1385 TOLL FREE: (800) 365-5998	WEB: WWW.CORVEL.COM
HAWAII	711 KAPIOLANI BLVD STE 150 HONOLULU, HI 96813-5249	PHONE: (808) 593-1430 FAX: (808) 593-1444 TOLL FREE: (888) 383-3803	WEB: WWW.CORVEL.COM
IDAHO	NORTHWEST 4949 MEADOWS RD STE 310 LAKE OSWEGO, OR 97035	PHONE: (503) 303-1000 FAX: (503) 303-1032 TOLL FREE: (800) 275-4463	WEB: WWW.CORVEL.COM
	200 SOUTH COLE BOISE, ID 83709	PHONE: (208) 331-7772 FAX: (208) 331-2884	WEB: WWW.CORVEL.COM
ILLINOIS	809 BROADWAY AVE MATTOON, IL 61938 PO BOX 768 MATTOON, IL 61938-0768	PHONE: (217) 234-2006 FAX: (217) 234-2019	WEB: WWW.CORVEL.COM
	3201 WEST WHITE OAKS DR STE 200 SPRINGFIELD, IL 62704-7100	PHONE: (217) 726-4550 FAX: (217) 726-4557	WEB: WWW.CORVEL.COM
	ONE N FRANKLIN STE 2400 CHICAGO, IL 60606	PHONE: (312) 456-6050 FAX: (312) 456-6090	WEB: WWW.CORVEL.COM
	123 NW 4TH ST STE 418 EVANSVILLE, IN 47708-1719	PHONE: (812) 424-9176 FAX: (812) 424-9178 TOLL FREE: (888) 959-7958	WEB: WWW.CORVEL.COM
	800 E 96TH ST STE 100 INDIANAPOLIS, IN 46240-2452	PHONE: (317) 816-6996 FAX: (317) 816-6990 TOLL FREE: (800) 959-7958	WEB: WWW.CORVEL.COM

State	Address	Contact	Web
ILLINOIS — CONTINUED	1860 E 54TH ST DAVENPORT, IA 52807-2763	PHONE: (563) 441-1599 FAX: (563) 441-1609 TOLL FREE: (877) 441-1599	WEB: WWW.CORVEL.COM
	1752 WINDSOR RD STE 101 LOVES PARK, IL 61132 PO BOX 2499 LOVES PARK, IL 61132-2499	PHONE: (815) 637-4700 FAX: (815) 637-4786	WEB: WWW.CORVEL.COM
	3668 S GEYER RD STE 360 ST LOUIS, MO 63127	PHONE: (314) 835-1100 FAX: (314) 835-1001 TOLL FREE: (888) 249-3465	WEB: WWW.CORVEL.COM
INDIANA	123 NW 4TH ST STE 418 EVANSVILLE, IN 47708-1719	PHONE: (812) 424-9176 FAX: (812) 424-9178 TOLL FREE: (888) 959-7958	WEB: WWW.CORVEL.COM
	800 E 96TH ST STE 100 INDIANAPOLIS, IN 46240-2452	PHONE: (317) 816-6996 FAX: (317) 816-6990 TOLL FREE: (800) 959-7958	WEB: WWW.CORVEL.COM
INDIANA *IOWA*	ONE N FRANKLIN STE 2400 CHICAGO, IL 60606	PHONE: (312) 456-6060 FAX: (312) 456-6090	WEB: WWW.CORVEL.COM
IOWA	1860 E 54TH ST DAVENPORT, IA 52807-2763	PHONE: (563) 441-1599 FAX: (563) 441-1609 TOLL FREE: (877) 441-1599	WEB: WWW.CORVEL.COM
	1701 48TH ST STE 275 WEST DES MOINES, IA 50266	PHONE: (515) 225-9668 FAX: (515) 225-9772 TOLL FREE: (800) 929-1160	
	270 50TH AVE SW CEDAR RAPIDS, IA 52404	PHONE: (319) 378-0606 FAX: (319) 378-0614 TOLL FREE: (800) 275-0011	WEB: WWW.CORVEL.COM
	111 N MAIN ST STE 203 AUSTIN, MN 55912	PHONE: (507) 433-7364 FAX: (507) 433-2486 TOLL FREE: (800) 275-6608	WEB: WWW.CORVEL.COM
KANSAS	809 BROADWAY AVE MATTOON, IL 61938 PO BOX 768 MATTOON, IL 61938-0768	PHONE: (217) 234-2006 FAX: (217) 234-2019	WEB: WWW.CORVEL.COM
	ONE N FRANKLIN STE 2400 CHICAGO, IL 60606	PHONE: (312) 456-6060 FAX: (312) 456-6090	WEB: WWW.CORVEL.COM
	345 RIVERVIEW ST WICHITA, KS 67203	PHONE: (316) 264-2900 FAX: (316) 264-2977 TOLL FREE: (800) 626-0149	WEB: WWW.CORVEL.COM
KENTUCKY	3504 LAKE LYNDA DR STE 300 ORLANDO, FL 32817	PHONE: (407) 282-4200 FAX: (407) 282-0648 TOLL FREE: (800) 755-7501	WEB: WWW.CORVEL.COM
	9030 STONEY PT PKY STE 470 RICHMOND, VA 23235	PHONE: (804) 267-2999 FAX: (804) 320-2478	WEB: WWW.CORVEL.COM
	ONE N FRANKLIN STE 2400 CHICAGO, IL 60606	PHONE: (312) 456-6060 FAX: (312) 456-6090	WEB: WWW.CORVEL.COM

KENTUCKY — CONTINUED	123 NW 4TH ST STE 418 EVANSVILLE, IN 47708-1719	PHONE: (812) 424-9176 FAX: (812) 424-9178 TOLL FREE: (888) 959-7958	WEB: WWW.CORVEL.COM
	12910 SHELBYVILLE RD STE 236 LOUISVILLE, KY 40243-1595	PHONE: (502) 244-5300 FAX: (502) 244-8855 TOLL FREE: (800) 834-0937	WEB: WWW.CORVEL.COM
	661 ANDERSEN DR PITTSBURGH, PA 15220	PHONE: (412) 922-4077 FAX: (412) 922-4285	WEB: WWW.CORVEL.COM
LOUISIANA	ONE GALLERIA STE 2121 METAIRIE, LA 70001	PHONE: (504) 835-5515 FAX: (504) 835-4357 TOLL FREE: (800) 503-6881	WEB: WWW.CORVEL.COM
MAINE MARYLAND	9030 STONEY PT PKY STE 470 RICHMOND, VA 23235	PHONE: (804) 267-2999 FAX: (804) 320-2478	WEB: WWW.CORVEL.COM
MARYLAND	20 WIGHT AVE STE 150 HUNT VALLEY, MD 21030	PHONE: (410) 403-3700 FAX: (410) 403-3725 IN-STATE: (800) 275-7005	WEB: WWW.CORVEL.COM
	1306 CONCOURSE DR STE 205 LENTHICHUM, MD 21090	PHONE: (410) 573-5120 FAX: (410) 691-1568	WEB: WWW.CORVEL.COM
	HUB PL 2ND FLOOR 1101 OPAL CT HAGERSTOWN, MD 21740	PHONE: (301) 791-0006 FAX: (301) 791-1886 TOLL FREE: (800) 427-4339	WEB: WWW.CORVEL.COM
MASSACHUSETTS	9030 STONEY PT PKY STE 470 RICHMOND, VA 23235	PHONE: (804) 267-2999 FAX: (804) 320-2478	WEB: WWW.CORVEL.COM
MICHIGAN	809 BROADWAY AVE MATTOON, IL 61938 PO BOX 768 MATTOON, IL 61938-0768	PHONE: (217) 234-2006 FAX: (217) 234-2019	WEB: WWW.CORVEL.COM
	800 E 96TH ST STE 100 INDIANAPOLIS, IN 46240-2452	PHONE: (317) 816-6995 FAX: (317) 816-6990 TOLL FREE: (800) 959-7958	WEB: WWW.CORVEL.COM
	39600 ORCHARD HILL PLACE STE 350 NOVINE, MI 48375	PHONE: (248) 412-2600 FAX: (248) 412-6050 TOLL FREE: (888) 426-7285	WEB: WWW.CORVEL.COM
MICHIGAN MINNESOTA	ONE N FRANKLIN STE 2400 CHICAGO, IL 60606	PHONE: (312) 456-6060 FAX: (312) 456-6090	WEB: WWW.CORVEL.COM
MINNESOTA	111 N MAIN ST STE 203 AUSTIN, MN 55912	PHONE: (507) 433-7364 FAX: (507) 433-2486 TOLL FREE: (800) 275-6608	WEB: WWW.CORVEL.COM
	14084 BAXTER DR STE 5 BAXTER, MN 56425	PHONE: (218) 829-8544 FAX: (218) 829-8551 TOLL FREE: (800) 275-0015	WEB: WWW.CORVEL.COM
MISSISSIPPI	14231 SEAWAY RD STE 3003 GULFPORT, MS 39503	PHONE: (228) 214-1540 FAX: (228) 214-1542	WEB: WWW.CORVEL.COM

MISSOURI	ONE N FRANKLIN STE 2400 CHICAGO, IL 60606	PHONE: (312) 456-6060 FAX: (312) 456-6090	WEB: WWW.CORVEL.COM
	1736 E SUNSHINE ST STE 806 SPRINGFIELD, MO 65804	PHONE: (417) 823-0322 FAX: (417) 823-0373	WEB: WWW.CORVEL.COM
	3668 S GEYER RD STE 360 ST LOUIS, MO 63127	PHONE: (314) 835-1100 FAX: (314) 835-1001 TOLL FREE: (888) 249-3465	WEB: WWW.CORVEL.COM
MONTANA	NORTHWEST 4949 MEADOWS RD STE 310 LAKE OSWEGO, OR 97035	PHONE: (503) 303-1000 FAX: (503) 303-1032 TOLL FREE: (800) 275-4463	WEB: WWW.CORVEL.COM
	200 SOUTH COLE BOISE, ID 83709	PHONE: (208) 331-7772 FAX: (208) 331-2884	WEB: WWW.CORVEL.COM
	27 N. MERIDIAN CT STE 113 KALISPELL, MT 59901	PHONE: (406) 755-7901 FAX: (406) 755-7979 TOLL FREE: (800) 935-0660	WEB: WWW.CORVEL.COM
NEBRASKA	ONE N FRANKLIN STE 2400 CHICAGO, IL 60606	PHONE: (312) 456-6060 FAX: (312) 456-6090	WEB: WWW.CORVEL.COM
	11422 MIRACLE HILLS DR STE 115 OMAHA, NE 68154	PHONE: (402) 393-0400 FAX: (402) 393-0500 TOLL FREE: (800) 711-4478	WEB: WWW.CORVEL.COM
NEVADA	11931 FOUNDATION PL STE 250 GOLD RIVER, CA 95670-4502	PHONE: (916) 608-2630 FAX: (916) 608-2640 TOLL FREE: (800) 758-5866	WEB: WWW.CORVEL.COM
	3900 PARADISE RD STE 182 LAS VEGAS, NV 89109	PHONE: (702) 699-7020 FAX: (702) 699-7005 TOLL FREE: (888) 368-4212	WEB: WWW.CORVEL.COM
NEW HAMPSHIRE	MANCHESTER (BEDFORD) OFFICE ONE BEDFORD FARMS STE 105 BEDFORD, NH 03110	PHONE: (603) 625-0184 FAX: (603) 625-0185 TOLL FREE: (800) 860-6686	WEB: WWW.CORVEL.COM
NEW JERSEY	3504 LAKE LYNDA DR STE 300 ORLANDO, FL 32817	PHONE: (407) 282-4200 FAX: (407) 282-0648 TOLL FREE: (800) 755-7501	WEB: WWW.CORVEL.COM
	9030 STONEY PT PKY STE 470 RICHMOND, VA 23235	PHONE: (804) 267-2999 FAX: (804) 320-2478	WEB: WWW.CORVEL.COM
	51 HADDONFIELD RD STE 200 CHERRY HILL, NJ 08002	PHONE: (856) 661-9670 FAX: (856) 661-9671 TOLL FREE: (800) 491-8350	WEB: WWW.CORVEL.COM
NEW MEXICO	950 S CHERRY ST STE 1600 DENVER, CO 80246-2689	PHONE: (303) 692-9210 FAX: (303) 692-9103 TOLL FREE: (800) 929-6090	WEB: WWW.CORVEL.COM
	7510 MONTGOMERY BLVD NE STE 103 ALBUQUERQUE, NM 87109-1500	PHONE: (505) 830-0222 FAX: (505) 830-0200 TOLL FREE: (888) 830-8307	WEB: WWW.CORVEL.COM

NEW YORK	3504 LAKE LYNDA DR STE 300 ORLANDO, FL 32817	PHONE: (407) 282-4200 FAX: (407) 282-0648 TOLL FREE: (800) 755-7501	WEB: WWW.CORVEL.COM
	9030 STONEY PT PKY STE 470 RICHMOND, VA 23235	PHONE: (804) 267-2999 FAX: (804) 320-2478	WEB: WWW.CORVEL.COM
	100 ELWOOD DAVIS RD N SYRACUSE, NY 13212	PHONE: (315) 451-8670 FAX: (315) 451-8675 TOLL FREE: (800) 346-6300	WEB: WWW.CORVEL.COM
	150 MOTOR PKY STE 104 HAUPPAUGE, NY 11788	PHONE: (631) 952-2200 FAX: (631) 952-2255 TOLL FREE: (866) 312-9760	WEB: WWW.CORVEL.COM
NORTH CAROLINA	8601 SIX FORKS THE FORUM STE 100 RALEIGH, NC 27615	PHONE: (919) 790-2260 FAX: (919) 790-1522	WEB: WWW.CORVEL.COM
	15720 JOHN J DELANEY DR STE 202 CHARLOTTE, NC 28277	PHONE: (704) 543-1382 FAX: (704) 543-1385 TOLL FREE: (800) 365-5998	WEB: WWW.CORVEL.COM
	860 GREENBRIAR CIR STE 405 CHESAPEAKE, VA 23320	PHONE: (757) 385-5646 FAX: (757) 385-5643	WEB: WWW.CORVEL.COM
OHIO	5555 AIRPORT HWY STE 145 TOLEDO, OH 43615	PHONE: (419) 865-6444 FAX: (419) 865-6841 TOLL FREE: (800) 665-3090	WEB: WWW.CORVEL.COM
	7530 LUCERNE DR STE 400 CLEVELAND, OH 44130 PO BOX 30306 CLEVELAND, OH 44130	PHONE: (440) 885-7377 FAX: (440) 885-2197 TOLL FREE: (800) 275-6463	WEB: WWW.CORVEL.COM
	8230 MONTEGOMERY RD STE 200 CINCINNATI, OH 45236 PO BOX 429365 CINCINNATI, OH 45242	PHONE: (513) 794-4040 FAX: (513) 794-4058 TOLL FREE: (888) 794-4040	WEB: WWW.CORVEL.COM
OKLAHOMA	1701 CENTERVIEW DR STE 320 LITTLE ROCK, AR 72211-4313	PHONE: (501) 255-6200 FAX: (501) 255-9332 TOLL FREE: (800) 220-9336	WEB: WWW.CORVEL.COM
	1900 NW EXPRESSWAY STE 1410 OKLAHOMA CITY, OK 73118-1803	PHONE: (405) 843-3532 FAX: (405) 843-3552 TOLL FREE: (800) 496-3385	WEB: WWW.CORVEL.COM
OREGON	NORTHWEST 4949 MEADOWS RD STE 310 LAKE OSWEGO, OR 97035	PHONE: (503) 303-1000 FAX: (503) 303-1032 TOLL FREE: (800) 275-4463	WEB: WWW.CORVEL.COM
	200 SOUTH COLE BOISE, ID 83709	PHONE: (208) 331-7772 FAX: (208) 331-2884	WEB: WWW.CORVEL.COM
PENNSYLVANIA	9030 STONEY PT PKY STE 470 RICHMOND, VA 23235	PHONE: (804) 267-2999 FAX: (804) 320-2478	WEB: WWW.CORVEL.COM
	661 ANDERSEN DR PITTSBURGH, PA 15220	PHONE: (412) 922-4077 FAX: (412) 922-4285	WEB: WWW.CORVEL.COM
	5010 RITTER RD STE 108 MECHANICSBURG, PA 17055	PHONE: (717) 796-0992 FAX: (717) 796-0994	WEB: WWW.CORVEL.COM

PUERTO RICO	2010 MAIN ST STE 600 IRVINE, CA 92614	PHONE: (949) 851-1473 FAX: (949) 851-1469	WEB: WWW.CORVEL.COM
	3550 N CENTRAL AVE STE 915 PHOENIX, AZ 85012-2117	PHONE: (602) 287-8722 FAX: (602) 287-8714 TOLL FREE: (800) 230-8288	WEB: WWW.CORVEL.COM
	600 CITY PARK WAY WEST STE 700 ORANGE, CA 92868-2943	PHONE: (714) 385-8500 FAX: (714) 385-8700	WEB: WWW.CORVEL.COM
	654 PLAZA 654 AVE MUNOZ RIVERA STE 704 SAN JUAN, PR 00918-4125 *ADDITIONAL COMMENTS: ALSO SERVICES BAHAMAS, BELIZE, TORTOLA, ST. THOMAS AND ALL THE SURROUNDING SMALLER ISLANDS*	PHONE: (787) 474-2187 FAX: (787) 641-2330 IN-STATE: (877) 974-2187	WEB: WWW.CORVEL.COM
	515 JUNCTION RD STE 2200 MADISON, WI 53717	PHONE: (608) 662-8220 FAX: (608) 662-8222 TOLL FREE: (888) 587-0977	WEB: WWW.CORVEL.COM
SOUTH CAROLINA	8601 SIX FORKS THE FORUM STE 100 RALEIGH, NC 27615	PHONE: (919) 790-2260 FAX: (919) 790-1522	WEB: WWW.CORVEL.COM
	15720 JOHN J DELANEY DR STE 202 CHARLOTTE, NC 28277	PHONE: (704) 543-1382 FAX: (704) 543-1385 TOLL FREE: (800) 365-5998	WEB: WWW.CORVEL.COM
	107 WESTPARK BLVD STE 150 COLUMBIA, SC 29210	PHONE: (803) 750-1518 FAX: (803) 750-1536	WEB: WWW.CORVEL.COM
SOUTH DAKOTA	ONE N FRANKLIN STE 2400 CHICAGO, IL 60606	PHONE: (312) 456-6060 FAX: (312) 456-6090	WEB: WWW.CORVEL.COM
	3900 W TECHNOLOGY CIR STE 2 SIOUX FALLS, SD 57106 PO BOX 89603 SIOUX FALLS, SD 57109-9603	PHONE: (605) 361-1360 FAX: (605) 361-1370 TOLL FREE: (800) 838-0077	WEB: WWW.CORVEL.COM
	405 NW 8TH AVE STE 310 ABERDEEN, SD 57401-2700	PHONE: (605) 229-7455 FAX: (605) 229-7465 TOLL FREE: (877) 225-1062	WEB: WWW.CORVEL.COM
TENNESSEE	3504 LAKE LYNDA DR STE 300 ORLANDO, FL 32817	PHONE: (407) 282-4200 FAX: (407) 282-0648 TOLL FREE: (800) 755-7501	WEB: WWW.CORVEL.COM
	1701 CENTERVIEW DR STE 320 LITTLE ROCK, AR 72211-4313	PHONE: (501) 255-6200 FAX: (501) 255-9332 TOLL FREE: (800) 220-9336	WEB: WWW.CORVEL.COM

TENNESSEE — CONTINUED	15720 JOHN J DELANEY DR STE 202 CHARLOTTE, NC 28277	PHONE: (704) 543-1382 FAX: (704) 543-1385 TOLL FREE: (800) 365-5998	WEB: WWW.CORVEL.COM
TEXAS	15303 DALLAS PARKWAY STE 300 ADDISON, TX 75001	PHONE: (972) 628-2840 FAX: (972) 386-5133	WEB: WWW.CORVEL.COM
	7500 VISCOUNT STE 216 EL PASO, TX 79925	PHONE: (915) 779-3666 FAX: (915) 779-9121	WEB: WWW.CORVEL.COM
	8200 NASHVILLE AVE BLDG C STE 203 LUBBOCK, TX 79423-1906	FAX: (806) 798-2655 TOLL FREE: (877) 828-9070	WEB: WWW.CORVEL.COM
	901 NE LOOP 410 STE 500 SAN ANTONIO, TX 78209	PHONE: (210) 824-5052 FAX: (210) 824-8972 TOLL FREE: (800) 215-9383 IN-STATE: (800) 215-9383	WEB: WWW.CORVEL.COM
	801 CHERRY ST STE 2400 UNIT #42 FORT WORTH, TX 76102	PHONE: (817) 348-0000 FAX: (817) 348-9999	WEB: WWW.CORVEL.COM
UTAH	950 S CHERRY ST STE 1600 DENVER, CO 80246-2689	PHONE: (303) 692-9210 FAX: (303) 692-9103 TOLL FREE: (800) 929-6090	WEB: WWW.CORVEL.COM
	200 SOUTH COLE BOISE, ID 83709	PHONE: (208) 331-7772 FAX: (208) 331-2884	WEB: WWW.CORVEL.COM
	1100 E 6600 S STE 420 SALT LAKE CITY, UT 84121	PHONE: (801) 269-8723 FAX: (801) 269-0096 TOLL FREE: (800) 275-9368	WEB: WWW.CORVEL.COM
VIRGIN ISLANDS	654 PLAZA 654 AVE MUNOZ RIVERA STE 704 SAN JUAN, PR 00918-4125	PHONE: (787) 474-2187 FAX: (787) 641-2330 IN-STATE: (877) 974-2187	WEB: WWW.CORVEL.COM

ADDITIONAL COMMENTS: ALSO SERVICES BAHAMAS, BELIZE, TORTOLA, ST. THOMAS AND ALL THE SURROUNDING SMALLER ISLANDS

VIRGINIA	9030 STONEY PT PKY STE 470 RICHMOND, VA 23235	PHONE: (804) 267-2999 FAX: (804) 320-2478	WEB: WWW.CORVEL.COM
	1306 CONCOURSE DR STE 205 LENTHICHUM, MD 21090	PHONE: (410) 573-5120 FAX: (410) 691-1568	WEB: WWW.CORVEL.COM
	15720 JOHN J DELANEY DR STE 202 CHARLOTTE, NC 28277	PHONE: (704) 543-1382 FAX: (704) 543-1385 TOLL FREE: (800) 365-5998	WEB: WWW.CORVEL.COM
	860 GREENBRIAR CIR STE 405 CHESAPEAKE, VA 23320	PHONE: (757) 385-5646 FAX: (757) 385-5643	WEB: WWW.CORVEL.COM
	11350 RANDOM HILLS RD STE 420 FAIRFAX, VA 22030	PHONE: (703) 385-5646 FAX: (703) 385-0180 TOLL FREE: (800) 496-3385	WEB: WWW.CORVEL.COM

WASHINGTON	NORTHWEST 4949 MEADOWS RD STE 310 LAKE OSWEGO, OR 97035	PHONE: (503) 303-1000 FAX: (503) 303-1032 TOLL FREE: (800) 275-4463	WEB: WWW.CORVEL.COM
	200 SOUTH COLE BOISE, ID 83709	PHONE: (208) 331-7772 FAX: (208) 331-2884	WEB: WWW.CORVEL.COM
	2101 4TH AVE STE 2300 SEATTLE, WA 98121-2345	PHONE: (206) 256-6331 FAX: (206) 441-5730 TOLL FREE: (877) 251-4522	WEB: WWW.CORVEL.COM
	325 E GEORGE HOPPER RD STE 103 BURLINGTON, WA 98233	PHONE: (877) 426-7835 FAX: (360) 757-5145	WEB: WWW.CORVEL.COM
	411 HOSPITAL WAY STE 104 BREWSTER, WA 98812 PO BOX 160 BREWSTER, WA 98812	PHONE: (509) 689-3612 FAX: (509) 689-0513 TOLL FREE: (877) 210-9369	WEB: WWW.CORVEL.COM
WEST VIRGINIA	9030 STONEY PT PKY STE 470 RICHMOND, VA 23235	PHONE: (804) 267-2999 FAX: (804) 320-2478	WEB: WWW.CORVEL.COM
	661 ANDERSEN DR PITTSBURGH, PA 15220	PHONE: (412) 922-4077 FAX: (412) 922-4285	WEB: WWW.CORVEL.COM
WISCONSIN	ONE N FRANKLIN STE 2400 CHICAGO, IL 60606	PHONE: (312) 456-6060 FAX: (312) 456-6090	WEB: WWW.CORVEL.COM
	1860 E 54TH ST DAVENPORT, IA 52807-2763	PHONE: (563) 441-1599 FAX: (563) 441-1609 TOLL FREE: (877) 441-1599	WEB: WWW.CORVEL.COM
	1752 WINDSOR RD STE 101 LOVES PARK, IL 61132 PO BOX 2499 LOVES PARK, IL 61132-2499	PHONE: (815) 637-4700 FAX: (815) 637-4786	WEB: WWW.CORVEL.COM
	111 N MAIN ST STE 203 AUSTIN, MN 55912	PHONE: (507) 433-7364 FAX: (507) 433-2486 TOLL FREE: (800) 275-6608	WEB: WWW.CORVEL.COM
	332 W SUPERIOR ST STE 505 DULUTH, MN 55802	PHONE: (218) 722-1500 FAX: (218) 733-0711 TOLL FREE: (800) 626-4509	WEB: WWW.CORVEL.COM
	515 JUNCTION RD STE 2200 MADISON, WI 53717	PHONE: (608) 662-8220 FAX: (608) 662-8222 TOLL FREE: (888) 587-0977	WEB: WWW.CORVEL.COM
WYOMING	950 S CHERRY ST STE 1600 DENVER, CO 80246-2689	PHONE: (303) 692-9210 FAX: (303) 692-9103 TOLL FREE: (800) 929-6090	WEB: WWW.CORVEL.COM

CORVEL CORP - MANAGE CARE

LOUISIANA *TEXAS*	901 NE LOOP 410 STE 500 SAN ANTONIO, TX 78254	PHONE: (210) 824-5052 FAX: (713) 977-0229 TOLL FREE: (800) 298-6993	WEB: WWW.CORVEL.COM

COTTAGE HEALTH SYSTEM

CALIFORNIA	PUEBLO AT BATH ST SANTA BARBARA, CA 93105-4351 PO BOX 689 SANTA BARBARA, CA 93102-0689	PHONE: (805) 879-8974 FAX: (805) 569-7307	WEB: WWW.SBCH.ORG

COTTON STATES INSURANCE COMPANIES

ALABAMA
FLORIDA
GEORGIA
KENTUCKY
LOUISIANA
NORTH CAROLINA
SOUTH CAROLINA
TENNESSEE
VIRGINIA

	244 PERIMETER CENTER PKY ATLANTA, GA 30346-2397 PO BOX 105303 ATLANTA, GA 30348-5303	PHONE: (770) 391-8600 FAX: (770) 391-8676 TOLL FREE: (800) 457-1658	WEB: WWW.COTTONSTATESINSURANCE.COM

COUNTRY INSURANCE AND FINANCIAL SERVICES

NATIONAL	1701 N TOWANDA AVE BLOOMINGTON, IL 61702 PO BOX 2020 BLOOMINGTON, IL 61702	PHONE: (888) 211-2555 FAX: (309) 821-8055	WEB: WWW.COUNTRYFINANCIAL.COM
ARIZONA	2449 N DIRKSEN PKY SPRINGFIELD, IL 62702-1443	PHONE: (217) 753-5220 FAX: (217) 753-3922 TOLL FREE: (800) 701-5220	WEB: WWW.COUNTRYFINANCIAL.COM
COLORADO	TWO PINE TREE DR 354E ARDEN HILLS, MN 55112-3793 PO BOX 64035 ST PAUL, MN 55164-0035	PHONE: (651) 631-7000 TOLL FREE: (800) 345-2436	WEB: WWW.COUNTRYFINANCIAL.COM
ILLINOIS	2449 N DIRKSEN PKY SPRINGFIELD, IL 62702-1443	PHONE: (217) 753-5220 FAX: (217) 753-3922 TOLL FREE: (800) 701-5220	WEB: WWW.COUNTRYFINANCIAL.COM
	3440 38TH AVE MOLINE, IL 61265-6409	PHONE: (309) 757-1650 FAX: (309) 757-0063 TOLL FREE: (800) 303-1721	WEB: WWW.COUNTRYFINANCIAL.COM
IOWA	3440 38TH AVE MOLINE, IL 61265-6409	PHONE: (309) 757-1650 FAX: (309) 757-0063 TOLL FREE: (800) 303-1721	WEB: WWW.COUNTRYFINANCIAL.COM
IOWA KANSAS	TWO PINE TREE DR 354E ARDEN HILLS, MN 55112-3793 PO BOX 64035 ST PAUL, MN 55164-0035	PHONE: (651) 631-7000 TOLL FREE: (800) 345-2436	WEB: WWW.COUNTRYFINANCIAL.COM
KANSAS	2449 N DIRKSEN PKY SPRINGFIELD, IL 62702-1443	PHONE: (217) 753-5220 FAX: (217) 753-3922 TOLL FREE: (800) 701-5220	WEB: WWW.COUNTRYFINANCIAL.COM
MINNESOTA MISSOURI	TWO PINE TREE DR 354E ARDEN HILLS, MN 55112-3793 PO BOX 64035 ST PAUL, MN 55164-0035	PHONE: (651) 631-7000 TOLL FREE: (800) 345-2436	WEB: WWW.COUNTRYFINANCIAL.COM
MISSOURI NEVADA	2449 N DIRKSEN PKY SPRINGFIELD, IL 62702-1443	PHONE: (217) 753-5220 FAX: (217) 753-3922 TOLL FREE: (800) 701-5220	WEB: WWW.COUNTRYFINANCIAL.COM
NORTH DAKOTA OKLAHOMA	TWO PINE TREE DR 354E ARDEN HILLS, MN 55112-3793 PO BOX 64035 ST PAUL, MN 55164-0035	PHONE: (651) 631-7000 TOLL FREE: (800) 345-2436	WEB: WWW.COUNTRYFINANCIAL.COM
OKLAHOMA WASHINGTON WISCONSIN	2449 N DIRKSEN PKY SPRINGFIELD, IL 62702-1443	PHONE: (217) 753-5220 FAX: (217) 753-3922 TOLL FREE: (800) 701-5220	WEB: WWW.COUNTRYFINANCIAL.COM

WISCONSIN	TWO PINE TREE DR 354E ARDEN HILLS, MN 55112-3793 PO BOX 64035 ST PAUL, MN 55164-0035	PHONE: (651) 631-7000 TOLL FREE: (800) 345-2436	WEB: WWW.COUNTRYFINANCIAL.COM

COUNTRY INSURANCE FINANCIAL SERVICES

ILLINOIS	2325 DEAN ST STE 300 ST CHARLES, IL 60175	PHONE: (630) 444-1500 FAX: (630) 444-1510	

COUNTRY PREFERRED — *SEE ALSO COUNTRY INSURANCE AND FINANCIAL SERVICES*

COUNTRY-WIDE MANAGEMENT SERVICES

NEW YORK	40 WALL ST 13TH FLOOR NEW YORK, NY 10005-1397	PHONE: (212) 344-8700 FAX: (212) 514-7291 TOLL FREE: (800) 378-5707	WEB: WWW.CWI.COM

COUNTY OF LOS ANGELES DEPT OF HUMAN RESOURCES

CALIFORNIA	333 WILSHIRE BLVD STE 1000 LOS ANGELES, CA 90010	PHONE: (213) 738-2279	WEB: DHR.LACOUNTY.INFO/

COVENANT ADMINISTRATORS

NATIONAL	PO BOX 105738 ATLANTA, GA 30348-5738	TOLL FREE: (800) 680-8728	WEB: WWW.COVENANTADMINISTRATORS.NET

COVENANT ADMINISTRATORS / MUTUAL TRUST GROUP

NATIONAL	11330 LAKEFIELD DR BLDG 2 DULUTH, GA 30097 PO BOX 105738 ATLANTA, GA 30348-5738	PHONE: (678) 258-8000 FAX: (678) 258-8299 TOLL FREE: (800) 680-8728	WEB: WWW.THECOVENANTADMINISTRATORS.NET

COVENTRY HEALTH CARE — *CHC OF DELAWARE*

DELAWARE *IOWA*	211 LAKE DR NEWARK, DE 19702	PHONE: (302) 995-6100 FAX: (302) 633-4044 TOLL FREE: (800) 727-9951 IN-STATE: (877) 227-3517	WEB: WWW.CHCDE.COM
IOWA	4320 114 ST URBANDALE, IA 50322	PHONE: (515) 225-1234 FAX: (515) 226-8954 TOLL FREE: (800) 257-4692	WEB: WWW.CHCIOWA.COM
LOUISIANA	3838 CAUSEWAY BLVD STE 3350 METAIRIE, LA 70002 PO BOX 7707 LONDON, KY 40742-7707	PHONE: (504) 834-0840 FAX: (504) 834-2694 TOLL FREE: (800) 245-8327	WEB: WWW.CHCLOUISIANA.COM
NEBRASKA	13305 BIRCH DR STE 100 OMAHA, NE 68164-5433 PO BOX 7705 LONDON, KY 40742	PHONE: (402) 498-9030 TOLL FREE: (800) 288-3343	WEB: WWW.CHCNEBRASKA.COM

NEBRASKA *VIRGINIA*	211 LAKE DR NEWARK, DE 19702	PHONE: (302) 995-6100 FAX: (302) 633-4044 TOLL FREE: (800) 727-9951 IN-STATE: (877) 227-3517	WEB: WWW.CHCDE.COM

COVENTRY HEALTH CARE / COVENTRY ONE — *CHC OF KANSAS AND PREFERRED*

KANSAS *MISSOURI*	8320 WARD PRKWY KANSAS CITY, MO 64114 PO BOX 7109 LONDON, KY 40742	PHONE: (816) 221-8400 FAX: (816) 221-7709 TOLL FREE: (800) 969-3343	WEB: WWW.CHCKANSAS.COM

COVENTRY HEALTH CARE & SOUTH CARE

DELAWARE
FLORIDA
GEORGIA
IOWA
KANSAS
LOUISIANA
MARYLAND
MISSOURI
NEBRASKA
NORTH CAROLINA
PENNSYLVANIA
SOUTH CAROLINA
TENNESSEE
WEST VIRGINIA

CHC OF GEORGIA 1100 CIRCLE 75 PKY STE 1400 ATLANTA, GA 30339 PO BOX 7711 LONDON, KY 40742	PHONE: (678) 202-2100 FAX: (866) 341-0359 TOLL FREE: (800) 470-2004	WEB: WWW.CHCGA.COM

COX INSURANCE GROUP, INC

NATIONAL	5170 COMMERCE CIR INDIANAPOLIS, IN 46237-9744 PO BOX 17008 INDIANAPOLIS, IN 46217-0080	PHONE: (317) 887-0030 FAX: (317) 888-7145	WEB: WWW.COXINSURANCEGROUP.COM

CRAWFORD & CO

NATIONAL	CLAIM OFFICE #00132 PO BOX 11506 SANTA ROSA, CA 95406	PHONE: (707) 528-1747 FAX: (707) 528-1707	WEB: WWW.CRAWFORDANDCOMPANY.COM
	CLAIM BRANCH #00765 2100 N WINERY AVE STE 101 FRESNO, CA 93703	PHONE: (559) 252-1972 FAX: (559) 252-0103	WEB: WWW.CRAWFORDANDCOMPANY.COM
	CLAIM OFFICE #00658 833 MISTLETOE LN STE 102 REDDING, CA 96002-0247	PHONE: (530) 221-6565 FAX: (530) 221-3449	E-MAIL: CA@US.CRAWCO.COM WEB: WWW.CRAWFORDANDCOMPANY.COM
	16536 BERNARDO CENTER DR STE 200 SAN DIEGO, CA 92128	PHONE: (858) 524-1515 FAX: (858) 524-1521 TOLL FREE: (888) 740-4036 IN-STATE: (800) 600-6210	WEB: WWW.CRAWFORDANDCOMPANY.COM
	1900 E GOLF RD STE 700 & 800 SCHAUMBURG, IL 60173-5053 PO BOX 681519 SCHAUMBURG, IL 60168	PHONE: (847) 517-4175 FAX: (847) 517-4181 TOLL FREE: (800) 545-2213	WEB: WWW.CRAWFORDANDCOMPANY.COM
	CLAIM BRANCH #0658 2529 W MARCH LN STE 204 STOCKTON, CA 95207-5450	PHONE: (209) 473-2944 FAX: (209) 473-0238	WEB: WWW.CRAWFORDANDCOMPANY.COM

ADDITIONAL COMMENTS: ALSO SERVICES ENGLAND & JAPAN

5620 GLENRIDGE DR NE ATLANTA, GA 30342-1399 PO BOX 5047 ATLANTA, GA 30302-5047	PHONE: (404) 256-0830 FAX: (404) 847-4025 TOLL FREE: (800) 241-2541	WEB: WWW.CRAWFORDANDCOMPANY.COM

ADDITIONAL COMMENTS: ALSO INTERNATIONAL

C

NATIONAL — CONTINUED	BRANCH 00171 FRANKLIN BUS PRK 146 S COLE RD BOISE, ID 83709-0932	PHONE: (208) 375-5021 FAX: (208) 375-4514 IN-STATE: (877) 482-8874	WEB: WWW.CRAWFORDANDCOMPANY.COM
ALASKA	1835 S BRAGAW STE 160 ANCHORAGE, AK 99508	PHONE: (907) 561-5222 FAX: (907) 561-7383 IN-STATE: (888) 549-5222	WEB: WWW.CRAWFORDANDCOMPANY.COM
ARIZONA	BRANCH 00152 7878 N 16TH ST STE 230 PHOENIX, AZ 85020-4484 PO BOX 26981 PHOENIX, AZ 85068	PHONE: (602) 216-9422 FAX: (602) 216-9478 TOLL FREE: (800) 242-1252	WEB: WWW.CRAWFORDANDCOMPANY.COM
ARKANSAS	BRANCH 00777 10801 EXECUTIVE CENTER DR STE 201 LITTLE ROCK, AR 72211-4378	PHONE: (501) 225-4494 FAX: (501) 224-9536	WEB: WWW.CRAWFORDANDCOMPANY.COM
CALIFORNIA	CLAIM OFFICE #00132 PO BOX 3116 ATASCADERO, CA 93423	PHONE: (805) 461-5865 FAX: (805) 461-5867	WEB: WWW.CRAWFORDANDCOMPANY.COM
	BRANCH 00633 1023 S PALM CANYON DR PALM SPRINGS, CA 92264	PHONE: (760) 325-8686 FAX: (760) 325-8016	WEB: WWW.CRAWFORDANDCOMPANY.COM
	CLAIM OFFICE #658 10411 OLD PLACERVILLE RD STE 200 SACRAMENTO, CA 95827-2508	PHONE: (916) 364-7487 FAX: (916) 364-0660	WEB: WWW.CRAWFORDANDCOMPANY.COM
	125 RYAN INDUSTRAIL CRT STE 105 SAN RAMON, CA 94583	PHONE: (925) 855-1322 FAX: (925) 855-1147	WEB: WWW.CRAWFORDANDCOMPANY.COM
	14477 AMARGOSA RD STE 6 VICTORVILLE, CA 92392-2340	PHONE: (760) 241-5449 FAX: (760) 241-0955	WEB: WWW.CRAWFORDANDCOMPANY.COM
	1515 W 190TH ST STE 500 GARDENA, CA 90248	PHONE: (310) 380-6000 FAX: (310) 380-6029 TOLL FREE: (800) 241-2541	WEB: WWW.CRAWFORDANDCOMPANY.COM
	CLAIM OFFICE #00283 18757 BURBANK BLVD STE 307 TARZANA , CA 91356	PHONE: (818) 757-2055 FAX: (818) 757-2072	WEB: WWW.CRAWFORDANDCOMPANY.COM
	1900 ALAMEDA DE LAS PULGAS STE 103 SAN MATEO, CA 94403-1222	PHONE: (650) 357-8980 FAX: (650) 357-8982 OR (650) 357-8983	WEB: WWW.CRAWFORDANDCOMPANY.COM
	CLAIM BRANCH #00648 3230 E IMPERIAL HWY STE 206 BREA, CA 92821-6728	PHONE: (714) 985-1200 FAX: (714) 985-1215	WEB: WWW.CRAWFORDANDCOMPANY.COM
	CLAIM OFFICE #00283 4464 MCGRATH ST STE 105 VENTURA, CA 93003-5703	PHONE: (805) 644-2271 FAX: (805) 644-2865	WEB: WWW.CRAWFORDANDCOMPANY.COM
	CLAIM BRANCH #00159 4800 STOCKDALE HWY STE 308 BAKERSFIELD, CA 93309-2636	PHONE: (661) 636-0536 FAX: (661) 636-0545	WEB: WWW.CRAWFORDANDCOMPANY.COM
	CLAIM BRANCH #00658 562 MANZANITA AVE STE 9 CHICO, CA 95926-1360	PHONE: (530) 343-8795 FAX: (530) 343-0877	E-MAIL: BR00658_CA@US.CRAWCO.COM WEB: WWW.CRAWFORDANDCOMPANY.COM
	CLAIM OFFICE #00633 900 E WASHINGTON ST STE 350 COLTON, CA 92324-8191	PHONE: (909) 825-8730 FAX: (909) 825-5349 TOLL FREE: (800) 241-2541	WEB: WWW.CRAWFORDANDCOMPANY.COM
	CLAIM OFFICE #00132 PO BOX 11506 SANTA ROSA, CA 95406	PHONE: (707) 528-1747 FAX: (707) 528-1707	WEB: WWW.CRAWFORDANDCOMPANY.COM

CALIFORNIA — CONTINUED	CLAIM BRANCH #00765 2100 N WINERY AVE STE 101 FRESNO, CA 93703	PHONE: (559) 252-1972 FAX: (559) 252-0103	WEB: WWW.CRAWFORDANDCOMPANY.COM
	CLAIM OFFICE #00658 833 MISTLETOE LN STE 102 REDDING, CA 96002-0247	PHONE: (530) 221-6565 FAX: (530) 221-3449	E-MAIL: CA@US.CRAWCO.COM WEB: WWW.CRAWFORDANDCOMPANY.COM
HAWAII	BRANCH 00295 711 KAPIOLANI BLVD STE 920 HONOLULU, HI 96813-5272	PHONE: (808) 591-2376 FAX: (808) 596-0380	WEB: WWW.CRAWFORDANDCOMPANY.COM
IDAHO	BRANCH 00171 FRANKLIN BUS PRK 146 S COLE RD BOISE, ID 83709-0932	PHONE: (208) 375-5021 FAX: (208) 375-4514 IN-STATE: (877) 482-8874	WEB: WWW.CRAWFORDANDCOMPANY.COM
MONTANA *NORTH DAKOTA*	BRANCH 00221 625 CENTRAL AVE W STE 100 GREAT FALLS, MT 59404-2874 PO BOX 3007 GREAT FALLS, MT 59403-3007	PHONE: (406) 761-7230 FAX: (406) 454-0454 IN-STATE: (888) 740-4043	WEB: WWW.CRAWFORDANDCOMPANY.COM
OREGON	12725 SW 66TH AVE STE 207 PORTLAND, OR 97223-2548	PHONE: (503) 639-2111 FAX: (503) 620-0676	WEB: WWW.CRAWFORDANDCOMPANY.COM
UTAH	BRANCH 00171 FRANKLIN BUS PRK 146 S COLE RD BOISE, ID 83709-0932	PHONE: (208) 375-5021 FAX: (208) 375-4514 IN-STATE: (877) 482-8874	WEB: WWW.CRAWFORDANDCOMPANY.COM
WYOMING	BRANCH 00221 625 CENTRAL AVE W STE 100 GREAT FALLS, MT 59404-2874 PO BOX 3007 GREAT FALLS, MT 59403-3007	PHONE: (406) 761-7230 FAX: (406) 454-0454 IN-STATE: (888) 740-4043	WEB: WWW.CRAWFORDANDCOMPANY.COM

CRL — *SEE ALSO CENTRAL RESERVE LIFE INSURANCE CO OF NORTH AMERICA*

CROSSROADS HEALTHCARE MANAGEMENT/MULTIPLAN — *SEE ALSO CHURCHILL ADMINISTRATIVE PLANS, INC*

CRUM & FORSTER INSURANCE

NATIONAL	305 MADISON AVE MORRISTOWN, NJ 07962 PO BOX 1960 MORRISTOWN, NJ 07962-1960	PHONE: (973) 490-6600 FAX: (877) 622-6191 TOLL FREE: (888) 890-1500 IN-STATE: (888) 890-1500	WEB: WWW.CFINS.COM
ALABAMA	FLORIDA REGIONAL OFFICE 901 INTERNATIONAL PKY STE 400 LAKE MARY, FL 32746-4719 PO BOX 958426 LAKE MARY, FL 32795-8426	PHONE: (407) 563-6200 TOLL FREE: (800) 423-3060	WEB: WWW.CFINS.COM
ALASKA	6404 INTERNATIONAL PKY STE 1000 PLANO, TX 75093-8227	PHONE: (972) 380-3000 FAX: (972) 380-3175 TOLL FREE: (800) 527-5531	WEB: WWW.CFINS.COM
CONNECTICUT	NORTHEAST REGION 60 STATE ST 5TH FL BOSTON, MA 02109	PHONE: (617) 406-3000 FAX: (617) 406-3019 TOLL FREE: (800) 690-5520 IN-STATE: (800) 258-5815	WEB: WWW.CFINS.COM
FLORIDA *GEORGIA*	FLORIDA REGIONAL OFFICE 901 INTERNATIONAL PKY STE 400 LAKE MARY, FL 32746-4719 PO BOX 958426 LAKE MARY, FL 32795-8426	PHONE: (407) 563-6200 TOLL FREE: (800) 423-3060	WEB: WWW.CFINS.COM
HAWAII	6404 INTERNATIONAL PKY STE 1000 PLANO, TX 75093-8227	PHONE: (972) 380-3000 FAX: (972) 380-3175 TOLL FREE: (800) 527-5531	WEB: WWW.CFINS.COM

ILLINOIS *INDIANA* *IOWA* *KANSAS*	UNITED STATES FIRE 400 N EXECUTIVE DR STE 401 BROOKFIELD, WI 53005	PHONE: (262) 784-0044 FAX: (262) 784-6257 TOLL FREE: (800) 242-4566 IN-STATE: (800) 242-4566	WEB: WWW.CFINS.COM
MASSACHUSETTS	NORTHEAST REGION 60 STATE ST 5TH FL BOSTON, MA 02109	PHONE: (617) 406-3000 FAX: (617) 406-3019 TOLL FREE: (800) 690-5520 IN-STATE: (800) 258-5815	WEB: WWW.CFINS.COM
MICHIGAN *MINNESOTA*	UNITED STATES FIRE 400 N EXECUTIVE DR STE 401 BROOKFIELD, WI 53005	PHONE: (262) 784-0044 FAX: (262) 784-6257 TOLL FREE: (800) 242-4566 IN-STATE: (800) 242-4566	WEB: WWW.CFINS.COM
MONTANA	6404 INTERNATIONAL PKY STE 1000 PLANO, TX 75093-8227	PHONE: (972) 380-3000 FAX: (972) 380-3175 TOLL FREE: (800) 527-5531	WEB: WWW.CFINS.COM
NEBRASKA	UNITED STATES FIRE 400 N EXECUTIVE DR STE 401 BROOKFIELD, WI 53005	PHONE: (262) 784-0044 FAX: (262) 784-6257 TOLL FREE: (800) 242-4566 IN-STATE: (800) 242-4566	WEB: WWW.CFINS.COM
NEVADA *NEW MEXICO*	6404 INTERNATIONAL PKY STE 1000 PLANO, TX 75093-8227	PHONE: (972) 380-3000 FAX: (972) 380-3175 TOLL FREE: (800) 527-5531	WEB: WWW.CFINS.COM
NORTH CAROLINA	FLORIDA REGIONAL OFFICE 901 INTERNATIONAL PKY STE 400 LAKE MARY, FL 32746-4719 PO BOX 958426 LAKE MARY, FL 32795-8426	PHONE: (407) 563-6200 TOLL FREE: (800) 423-3060	WEB: WWW.CFINS.COM
NORTH DAKOTA	UNITED STATES FIRE 400 N EXECUTIVE DR STE 401 BROOKFIELD, WI 53005	PHONE: (262) 784-0044 FAX: (262) 784-6257 TOLL FREE: (800) 242-4566 IN-STATE: (800) 242-4566	WEB: WWW.CFINS.COM
OHIO *OREGON*	6404 INTERNATIONAL PKY STE 1000 PLANO, TX 75093-8227	PHONE: (972) 380-3000 FAX: (972) 380-3175 TOLL FREE: (800) 527-5531	WEB: WWW.CFINS.COM
SOUTH CAROLINA	FLORIDA REGIONAL OFFICE 901 INTERNATIONAL PKY STE 400 LAKE MARY, FL 32746-4719 PO BOX 958426 LAKE MARY, FL 32795-8426	PHONE: (407) 563-6200 TOLL FREE: (800) 423-3060	WEB: WWW.CFINS.COM
SOUTH DAKOTA	UNITED STATES FIRE 400 N EXECUTIVE DR STE 401 BROOKFIELD, WI 53005	PHONE: (262) 784-0044 FAX: (262) 784-6257 TOLL FREE: (800) 242-4566 IN-STATE: (800) 242-4566	WEB: WWW.CFINS.COM
TENNESSEE	FLORIDA REGIONAL OFFICE 901 INTERNATIONAL PKY STE 400 LAKE MARY, FL 32746-4719 PO BOX 958426 LAKE MARY, FL 32795-8426	PHONE: (407) 563-6200 TOLL FREE: (800) 423-3060	WEB: WWW.CFINS.COM
WISCONSIN	UNITED STATES FIRE 400 N EXECUTIVE DR STE 401 BROOKFIELD, WI 53005	PHONE: (262) 784-0044 FAX: (262) 784-6257 TOLL FREE: (800) 242-4566 IN-STATE: (800) 242-4566	WEB: WWW.CFINS.COM

CSE INSURANCE GROUP — *SEE ALSO CIVIL SERVICE EMPLOYEES INSURANCE GROUP*

CSO — *SEE ALSO CENTRAL STATES HEALTH & LIFE INSURANCE CO OF OMAHA*

C

CT PIPE TRADES BENEFIT FUNDS ADMINISTRATORS, INC

CONNECTICUT	1155 SILAS DEANE HWY WEATHERSFIELD, CT 06109	PHONE: (860) 571-9191 FAX: (860) 571-9221 TOLL FREE: (800) 848-2129	E-MAIL: CONNECTICUTPIPETRADES@AOL.COM WEB: WWW.CONNECTICUTPIPETRADES.COM

CTI ADMINISTRATORS, INC

NATIONAL	100 CT AVE STE 306 DES MOINES, IA 50309-2295	PHONE: (515) 244-7322 FAX: (515) 244-8650 TOLL FREE: (800) 245-8813	

CUMBERLAND INSURANCE GROUP

DELAWARE *MARYLAND* *PENNSYLVANIA*	633 SHILOH PIKE BRIDGETON, NJ 08302-1479 PO BOX 556 BRIDGETON, NJ 08302-0486	PHONE: (856) 451-4050 FAX: (856) 455-8468 TOLL FREE: (800) 232-6992	WEB: WWW.CUMBERLANDGROUP.COM

CUNA MUTUAL GROUP

NATIONAL
ALBERTA
AMERICAN SAMOA
BRITISH COLUMBIA
CANADA
GUAM
MANITOBA
MEXICO
NEW BRUNSWICK
NEW ZEALAND
NEWFOUNDLAND
NOVA SCOTIA
ONTARIO
PRINCE EDWARD ISLAND
PUERTO RICO
QUEBEC
SASKATCHEWAN
VIRGIN ISLANDS

5910 MINERAL POINT RD MADISON, WI 53705-4498 PO BOX 391 MADISON, WI 53701-0391	PHONE: (608) 238-5851 FAX: (608) 238-0830 TOLL FREE: (800) 356-2644	WEB: WWW.CUNAMUTUAL.COM

CUNNINGHAM LINDSEY US, INC

NATIONAL	405 STATE HWY 121 BYP BLDG A STE 200 LEWISVILLE, TX 75067 PO BOX 703689 DALLAS, TX 75370	PHONE: (214) 488-5139 FAX: (214) 488-6570	WEB: WWW.CUNNINGHAMLINDSEY.COM
CALIFORNIA	3914 MURPHY CANYON RD STE A 207 SAN DIEGO, CA 92123	PHONE: (858) 430-1270 FAX: (858) 430-1021 TOLL FREE: (800) 235-8784	E-MAIL: PGILBERT@CL-INA.COM WEB: WWW.CUNNINGHAMLINDSEY.COM

CWI BENEFITS MANAGEMED — *CLAIMSWARE*

NATIONAL	715 CONGAREE RD GREENVILLE, SC 29607 PO BOX 6125 GREENVILLE, SC 29606-6125	PHONE: (864) 234-8200 FAX: (864) 234-8202 TOLL FREE: (800) 992-8088	WEB: WWW.CWIBENEFITS.COM

CYPRESS BENEFIT ADMINISTRATORS

WISCONSIN	PO BOX 7020 APPLETON, WI 54912	PHONE: (877) 236-0844 FAX: (920) 968-4616 TOLL FREE: (800) 437-4940	WEB: WWW.CYPRESSBENEFIT.COM

CYPRESS INSURANCE CO — *HOME STATE COMPANIES*

NATIONAL	9290 W DODGE RD STE 300 OMAHA, NE 68114	PHONE: (402) 393-7255 FAX: (402) 393-7619 TOLL FREE: (800) 488-2930	WEB: WWW.BH-HC.COM

DAIRYLAND INSURANCE CO — *SENTRY CLAIMS CENTER*

ARIZONA, CALIFORNIA, IDAHO, KANSAS, MINNESOTA, MISSOURI, MONTANA, NEBRASKA, NEVADA, NEW MEXICO, OKLAHOMA, UTAH, WASHINGTON, WYOMING

9060 E VIA LINDA
SCOTTSDALE, AZ 85258-5416
PO BOX 29460
PHOENIX, AZ 85038-9460

PHONE: (480) 860-7000
FAX: (480) 860-7702
TOLL FREE: (800) 833-2244
WEB: WWW.SENTRY.COM

DAKOTACARE

SOUTH DAKOTA

1323 S MINNESOTA AVE
SIOUX FALLS, SD 57105

PHONE: (605) 334-4000
FAX: (605) 336-0270
TOLL FREE: (800) 628-3778
IN-STATE: (800) 325-5598
WEB: WWW.DAKOTACARE.COM

DANIELSEN NATIONAL INSURANCE CO — *SEE ALSO NATIONAL AMERICAN INSURANCE CO OF CALIFORNIA*

DBA ACTUARIAL & EMPLOYEE BENEFIT SERVICES CO — *SEE ALSO CAI INSURANCE AGENCY, INC*

DBA FIRSTCARE — *SEE ALSO SOUTHWEST LIFE AND HEALTH*

(DBA) FIRST CHOICE BENEFITS MANAGEMENT — *SEE ALSO BELOIT MEMORIAL HOSPITAL*

DC CHARTERED HEALTH PLAN, INC

DISTRICT OF COLUMBIA

1025 15TH ST NW
WASHINGTON, DC 20005
PO BOX 75366 OR PO BOX 75394
WASHINGTON, DC 20013

PHONE: (202) 408-4710
FAX: (202) 408-4730
TOLL FREE: (800) 408-7511
WEB: WWW.CHARTER-HEALTH.COM

DE VIDA DE PUERTO RICO — *SEE ALSO COOPERATIVA DE SEGUROS*

DEAN HEALTH PLAN

WISCONSIN

1277 DEMING WY
MADISON, WI 53717-1971
PO BOX 56099
MADISON, WI 53705-9399

PHONE: (608) 828-1301
FAX: (608) 836-1210
TOLL FREE: (800) 279-1301
IN-STATE: (800) 356-7344
WEB: WWW.DEANCARE.COM

DEEP SOUTH SURPLUS OF TEXAS

ARIZONA, ARKANSAS, COLORADO, FLORIDA, GEORGIA, INDIANA, LOUISIANA, MICHIGAN, NEW MEXICO, NORTH CAROLINA, OHIO, SOUTH CAROLINA, TENNESSEE, TEXAS

6363 N STATE HWY 161 STE 100
IRVING, TX 75038
PO BOX 167888
IRVING, TX 75016

PHONE: (214) 493-4200
FAX: (800) 357-6884
TOLL FREE: (800) 239-6871
WEB: WWW.DEEP-SOUTH.COM

DEFINITY HEALTH

NATIONAL

CORPORATE OFFICE
1600 UTICA AVE S STE 900
ST LOUIS PARK, MN 55416

PHONE: (952) 277-5500
FAX: (952) 277-5501
WEB: WWW.DEFINITYHEALTH.COM

DEFINITY HEALTH / UNITED

NATIONAL	PO BOX 740810 ATLANTA, GA 30374-0810	PHONE: (952) 277-5687	WEB: WWW.DEFINITYHEALTH.COM

DEFINITY HEALTH / UNITED HEALTH CARE

NATIONAL	PO BOX 90613 ARLINGTON, TX 76006	PHONE: (866) 333-4648	WEB: WWW.DEFINITYHEALTH.COM

DEFINITY HEALTH & UNITED HEALTH PLAN

NATIONAL	CLAIMS OFFICE 500 COLVIN WOODS PKY TONAWANDA, NY 14150	TOLL FREE: (866) 333-4648	WEB: WWW.DEFINITYHEALTH.COM

DELTA DENTAL

NATIONAL	1513 COUNTRY CLUB RD SHERWOOD, AR 72120-6046 PO BOX 15965 NORTH LITTLE ROCK, AR 72231	PHONE: (501) 835-3400 FAX: (800) 500-8991 TOLL FREE: (800) 462-5410	WEB: WWW.DELTADENTALAR.COM
	100 FIRST ST SAN FRANCISCO, CA 94105-2634 PO BOX 997330 SACRAMENTO, CA 95899-7330	PHONE: (415) 972-8300 FAX: (415) 972-8466 TOLL FREE: (888) 335-8227	E-MAIL: CMS@DELTA.ORG WEB: WWW.DELTADENTALCA.ORG
	3560 DELTA DENTAL DR EAGAN, MN 55122-3166 PO BOX 330 MINNEAPOLIS, MN 55440-0330	PHONE: (651) 406-5916 FAX: (877) 201-6874 TOLL FREE: (800) 553-9536	WEB: WWW.DELTADENTALMN.ORG
	10 CHARLES ST STE 4 PROVIDENCE, RI 02904-2220 PO BOX 1517 PROVIDENCE, RI 02901-1517	PHONE: (401) 752-6000 FAX: (401) 752-6060 TOLL FREE: (800) 598-6684 IN-STATE: (800) 843-3582	WEB: WWW.DELTADENTALRI.COM
	4582 S ULSTER ST PKY STE 800 DENVER, CO 80237-2567 PO BOX 5468 DENVER, CO 80217-5468	PHONE: (303) 741-9300 FAX: (303) 741-9350 TOLL FREE: (800) 233-0860	WEB: WWW.DELTADENTALCO.COM
	OREGON DENTAL SERVICE 601 SW 2ND AVE PORTLAND, OR 97204-3195	PHONE: (503) 243-4494 FAX: (503) 948-5584 TOLL FREE: (800) 452-1058 IN-STATE: (877) 277-7280	WEB: WWW.ODSCOMPANIES.COM
	WASHINGTON DENTAL SERVICE 9706 4TH AVE NE SEATTLE, WA 98115-2157 PO BOX 75688 SEATTLE, WA 98175	PHONE: (206) 522-1300 FAX: (206) 523-9287 TOLL FREE: (800) 367-4104	WEB: WWW.DELTADENTALWA.COM
	1010 N MAIN ST WICHITA, KS 67201 PO BOX 49198 WICHITA, KS 67201-9198	PHONE: (316) 264-1099 FAX: (316) 462-3393 TOLL FREE: (800) 234-3375	WEB: WWW.DELTADENTALKS.COM
ALABAMA	1000 MANSELL EXCHANGE W BLDG 100 STE 100 ALPHARETTA, GA 30022-8296 PO BOX 1809 ALPHARETTA, GA 30023-1809	PHONE: (770) 645-8700 FAX: (770) 518-4757 OR (770) 518-4448 TOLL FREE: (800) 521-2651	WEB: WWW.DELTADENTALINS.COM
ARIZONA	15648 N 35TH AVE STE 111 PHOENIX, AZ 85053-3863 PO BOX 43000 PHOENIX, AZ 85080-3000	PHONE: (602) 938-3131 FAX: (602) 588-3636 TOLL FREE: (800) 352-6132	WEB: WWW.DELTADENTALAZ.COM

ARKANSAS	1513 COUNTRY CLUB RD SHERWOOD, AR 72120-6046 PO BOX 15965 NORTH LITTLE ROCK, AR 72231	PHONE: (501) 835-3400 FAX: (800) 500-8991 TOLL FREE: (800) 462-5410	WEB: WWW.DELTADENTALAR.COM
CALIFORNIA	100 FIRST ST SAN FRANCISCO, CA 94105-2634 PO BOX 997330 SACRAMENTO, CA 95899-7330	PHONE: (415) 972-8300 FAX: (415) 972-8466 TOLL FREE: (888) 335-8227	E-MAIL: CMS@DELTA.ORG WEB: WWW.DELTADENTALCA.ORG
CONNECTICUT	1639 STATE RT 10 PARSIPPANY, NJ 07054-4506 PO BOX 222 PARSIPPANY, NJ 07054-0222	PHONE: (973) 285-4000 FAX: (800) 324-7939 TOLL FREE: (800) 452-9310	WEB: WWW.DELTADENTALNJ.COM
DELAWARE DISTRICT OF COLUMBIA	ONE DELTA DR MECHANICSBURG, PA 17055-6999	PHONE: (717) 766-8500 FAX: (717) 766-8719 TOLL FREE: (800) 932-0783	WEB: WWW.MIDATLANTICDELTADENTAL.COM
FLORIDA GEORGIA	1000 MANSELL EXCHANGE W BLDG 100 STE 100 ALPHARETTA, GA 30022-8296 PO BOX 1809 ALPHARETTA, GA 30023-1809	PHONE: (770) 645-8700 FAX: (770) 518-4757 OR (770) 518-4448 TOLL FREE: (800) 521-2651	WEB: WWW.DELTADENTALINS.COM
HAWAII	HAWAII DENTAL SERVICE 700 BISHOP ST STE 700 HONOLULU, HI 96813-4196	PHONE: (808) 521-1431 FAX: (808) 529-9368 TOLL FREE: (800) 232-2533	WEB: WWW.DELTADENTALHI.ORG
IDAHO	555 E PARKCENTER BLVD BOISE, ID 83706-6503 PO BOX 2870 BOISE, ID 83701-2870	PHONE: (208) 344-4546 FAX: (208) 344-4649 TOLL FREE: (800) 388-3490 IN-STATE: (800) 356-7586	E-MAIL: BENEFITSERVICES@DELTADENTALID.COM WEB: WWW.DELTADENTALID.COM
ILLINOIS	801 OGDEN AVE LISLE, IL 60532 PO BOX 5402 LISLE, IL 60532	PHONE: (630) 964-2400 FAX: (630) 964-3068 TOLL FREE: (800) 323-1743	E-MAIL: ASKDELTA@DELTADENTALIL.COM WEB: WWW.DELTADENTALIL.COM
INDIANA	4100 OKEMOS RD OKEMOS, MI 48864 PO BOX 30416 LANSING, MI 48909-7916	PHONE: (517) 349-6000 FAX: (517) 347-5237 TOLL FREE: (800) 482-8915	WEB: WWW.DELTADENTAL.COM
IOWA	2401 SE TONES DR STE 13 ANKENY, IA 50021-8886 PO BOX 919 ANKENY, IA 50021-0919	PHONE: (515) 261 5500 FAX: (515) 261-5577 TOLL FREE: (800) 544-0718	WEB: WWW.DELTADENTALIA.COM
KENTUCKY	PO BOX 242810 LOUISVILLE, KY 40224-2810	PHONE: (502) 736-5000 FAX: (502) 736-4821 TOLL FREE: (800) 955-2030	E-MAIL: CUSTOMERSERVICE1@DDPKY.COM WEB: WWW.DELTADENTALKY.COM
LOUISIANA	1000 MANSELL EXCHANGE W BLDG 100 STE 100 ALPHARETTA, GA 30022-8296 PO BOX 1809 ALPHARETTA, GA 30023-1809	PHONE: (770) 645-8700 FAX: (770) 518-4757 OR (770) 518-4448 TOLL FREE: (800) 521-2651	WEB: WWW.DELTADENTALINS.COM
MAINE	ONE DELTA DR CONCORD, NH 03301-7426 PO BOX 2002 CONCORD, NH 03302-2002	PHONE: (603) 223-1000 FAX: (603) 223-1199 TOLL FREE: (800) 532-5700	E-MAIL: NEDELTA@NEDELTA.COM WEB: WWW.NEDELTA.COM
MARYLAND	ONE DELTA DR MECHANICSBURG, PA 17055-6999	PHONE: (717) 766-8500 FAX: (717) 766-8719 TOLL FREE: (800) 932-0783	WEB: WWW.MIDATLANTICDELTADENTAL.COM
MASSACHUSETTS	465 MEDFORD ST CHARLESTOWN, MA 02129-1454 PO BOX 9695 BOSTON, MA 02114	PHONE: (617) 886-1000 FAX: (617) 886-1199 TOLL FREE: (800) 872-0500	E-MAIL: CSSTEAM@DELTAMASS.COM WEB: WWW.DELTADENTALMASS.COM

MEXICO	1010 N MAIN ST WICHITA, KS 67201 PO BOX 49198 WICHITA, KS 67201-9198	PHONE: (316) 264-1099 FAX: (316) 462-3393 TOLL FREE: (800) 234-3375	WEB: WWW.DELTADENTALKS.COM
	240 VENTURE CIR NASHVILLE, TN 37228	PHONE: (615) 255-3175 FAX: (615) 244-8108 TOLL FREE: (800) 223-3104	WEB: WWW.DELTADENTALTN.COM
MICHIGAN	4100 OKEMOS RD OKEMOS, MI 48864 PO BOX 30416 LANSING, MI 48909-7916	PHONE: (517) 349-6000 FAX: (517) 347-5237 TOLL FREE: (800) 482-8915	WEB: WWW.DELTADENTAL.COM
MINNESOTA	3560 DELTA DENTAL DR EAGAN, MN 55122-3166 PO BOX 330 MINNEAPOLIS, MN 55440-0330	PHONE: (651) 406-5916 FAX: (877) 201-6874 TOLL FREE: (800) 553-9536	WEB: WWW.DELTADENTALMN.ORG
MISSISSIPPI	1000 MANSELL EXCHANGE W BLDG 100 STE 100 ALPHARETTA, GA 30022-8296 PO BOX 1809 ALPHARETTA, GA 30023-1809	PHONE: (770) 645-8700 FAX: (770) 518-4757 OR (770) 518-4448 TOLL FREE: (800) 521-2651	WEB: WWW.DELTADENTALINS.COM
MISSOURI	12399 GRAVOIS RD ST LOUIS, MO 63127-1702 PO BOX 8690 ST LOUIS, MO 63126-0690	PHONE: (314) 656-3000 FAX: (314) 656-2900 TOLL FREE: (800) 392-1167	WEB: WWW.DELTADENTALMO.COM
MONTANA	257 E 200 S STE 375 SALT LAKE CITY, UT 84111-2069	PHONE: (801) 575-5168 FAX: (801) 575-5171 TOLL FREE: (800) 453-5577	WEB: WWW.DELTADENTALINS.COM
MONTANA *NEVADA*	PO BOX 1809 ALPHA RETTA, GA 30023	PHONE: (800) 521-2651 TOLL FREE: (800) 893-3532	WEB: WWW.DELTADENTALINS.COM
NEW HAMPSHIRE	ONE DELTA DR CONCORD, NH 03301-7426 PO BOX 2002 CONCORD, NH 03302-2002	PHONE: (603) 223-1000 FAX: (603) 223-1199 TOLL FREE: (800) 532-5700	E-MAIL: NEDELTA@NEDELTA.COM WEB: WWW.NEDELTA.COM
NEW JERSEY	1639 STATE RT 10 PARSIPPANY, NJ 07054-4506 PO BOX 222 PARSIPPANY, NJ 07054-0222	PHONE: (973) 285-4000 FAX: (800) 324-7939 TOLL FREE: (800) 452-9310	WEB: WWW.DELTADENTALNJ.COM
NEW MEXICO	2500 LOUISIANA BLVD NE STE 600 ALBUQUERQUE, NM 87110-4302	PHONE: (505) 883-4777 FAX: (505) 883-7444 TOLL FREE: (800) 999-0963	WEB: WWW.DELTADENTALNM.COM
NEW YORK	ONE DELTA DR MECHANICSBURG, PA 17055-6999	PHONE: (717) 766-8500 FAX: (717) 766-8719 TOLL FREE: (800) 932-0783	WEB: WWW.MIDATLANTICDELTADENTAL.COM
NORTH CAROLINA	343 SIX FORKS RD STE 180 RALEIGH, NC 27609-7865	PHONE: (919) 832-6015 FAX: (919) 832-6061 TOLL FREE: (800) 662-8856	WEB: WWW.DELTADENTALNC.ORG
OHIO	4100 OKEMOS RD OKEMOS, MI 48864 PO BOX 30416 LANSING, MI 48909-7916	PHONE: (517) 349-6000 FAX: (517) 347-5237 TOLL FREE: (800) 482-8915	WEB: WWW.DELTADENTAL.COM
OKLAHOMA	16 NW 63RD ST STE 301 OKLAHOMA CITY, OK 73116-9115 PO BOX 54709 OKLAHOMA CITY, OK 73154-1709	PHONE: (405) 607-2100 FAX: (405) 607-2190 TOLL FREE: (800) 522-0188	WEB: WWW.DELTADENTALOK.ORG
PENNSYLVANIA	ONE DELTA DR MECHANICSBURG, PA 17055-6999	PHONE: (717) 766-8500 FAX: (717) 766-8719 TOLL FREE: (800) 932-0783	WEB: WWW.MIDATLANTICDELTADENTAL.COM

SOUTH CAROLINA	12399 GRAVOIS RD ST LOUIS, MO 63127-1702 PO BOX 8690 ST LOUIS, MO 63126-0690	PHONE: (314) 656-3000 FAX: (314) 656-2900 TOLL FREE: (800) 392-1167	WEB: WWW.DELTADENTALMO.COM
SOUTH DAKOTA	720 N EUCLID AVE PIERRE, SD 57501-1717 PO BOX 1157 PIERRE, SD 57501-1157	PHONE: (605) 224-7345 FAX: (605) 224-0909 TOLL FREE: (800) 627-3961	WEB: WWW.DELTADENTALSD.COM
TENNESSEE	240 VENTURE CIR NASHVILLE, TN 37228	PHONE: (615) 255-3175 FAX: (615) 244-8108 TOLL FREE: (800) 223-3104	WEB: WWW.DELTADENTALTN.COM
TEXAS	1000 MANSELL EXCHANGE W BLDG 100 STE 100 ALPHARETTA, GA 30022-8296 PO BOX 1809 ALPHARETTA, GA 30023-1809	PHONE: (770) 645-8700 FAX: (770) 518-4757 OR (770) 518-4448 TOLL FREE: (800) 521-2651	WEB: WWW.DELTADENTALINS.COM
TEXAS *UTAH*	1000 MANSELL EXCHANGE W BLDG 100 STE 100 ALPHARETTA, GA 30022-8296 PO BOX 1809 ALPHARETTA, GA 30023-1809	PHONE: (770) 645-8700 FAX: (770) 518-4757 OR (770) 518-4448 TOLL FREE: (800) 521-2651	WEB: WWW.DELTADENTALINS.COM
UTAH	257 E 200 S STE 375 SALT LAKE CITY, UT 84111-2069	PHONE: (801) 575-5168 FAX: (801) 575-5171 TOLL FREE: (800) 453-5577	WEB: WWW.DELTADENTALINS.COM
VERMONT	ONE DELTA DR CONCORD, NH 03301-7426 PO BOX 2002 CONCORD, NH 03302-2002	PHONE: (603) 223-1000 FAX: (603) 223-1199 TOLL FREE: (800) 532-5700	E-MAIL: NEDELTA@NEDELTA.COM WEB: WWW.NEDELTA.COM
VIRGINIA	4818 STARKEY RD ROANOKE, VA 24014-8512	PHONE: (540) 989-8000 FAX: (540) 725-3880 TOLL FREE: (800) 237-6060	E-MAIL: JOBS@DELTADENTALVA.COM WEB: WWW.DELTADENTALVA.COM
WEST VIRGINIA	ONE DELTA DR MECHANICSBURG, PA 17055-6999	PHONE: (717) 766-8500 FAX: (717) 766-8719 TOLL FREE: (800) 932-0783	WEB: WWW.MIDATLANTICDELTADENTAL.COM

DELTA DENTAL OF CALIFORNIA & PMI

CALIFORNIA	12898 TOWN CENTER DR CERRITOS, CA 90703	PHONE: (562) 403-4040 FAX: (562) 924-3172 TOLL FREE: (800) 801-7105 IN-STATE: (800) 422-4234	WEB: WWW.DELTADENTALCA.ORG

DELTA HEALTH SYSTEMS

NATIONAL	1234 W OAK ST STOCKTON, CA 95203-2606 PO BOX 80 STOCKTON, CA 95201	PHONE: (800) 422-6099 FAX: (209) 474-5404 TOLL FREE: (800) 422-6099	WEB: WWW.DELTAHEALTHSYSTEMS.COM

DENTAL BENEFIT PROVIDERS — *UNITED HEALTH CARE*

ALASKA
ARIZONA
CALIFORNIA
COLORADO
HAWAII
IDAHO
IOWA
MINNESOTA
MISSISSIPPI
MONTANA
NEBRASKA
NEVADA
NEW MEXICO
NORTH DAKOTA
OKLAHOMA
OREGON
SOUTH DAKOTA
TEXAS
UTAH
WASHINGTON
WISCONSIN
WYOMING

425 MARKET ST 12TH FLOOR SAN FRANCISCO, CA 94105	PHONE: (415) 778-3800 FAX: (415) 778-3833 TOLL FREE: (888) 327-7576	WEB: WWW.DBP.COM

DENTAL DEPT — *SEE ALSO FIRST ADVANTAGE DENTAL*

DENTAL HEALTH ALLIANCE

NATIONAL	2323 GRAND BLVD KANSAS CITY, MO 64108 PO BOX 41908 KANSAS CITY, MO 64608	PHONE: (800) 985-9895 TOLL FREE: (800) 522-13[illegible]3	WEB: WWW.DHA.COM

DENTAL NETWORK OF AMERICA

NATIONAL	TWO TRANSAM PLZ DR STE 500 OAKBROOK TERRACE, IL 60181-4275	PHONE: (630) 691-1133 FAX: (630) 495-0575 TOLL FREE: (800) 323-6840	WEB: WWW.DNOA.COM

DENTAL NETWORK, INC — *SEE ALSO ORAL HEALTH SERVICES*

DENTAL SOURCE OF MISSOURI AND KANSAS

KANSAS *MISSOURI*	9091 STATE LINE STE 101 KANSAS CITY, MO 64114	PHONE: (816) 523-8900 FAX: (816) 523-8988 TOLL FREE: (800) 369-3435	WEB: WWW.DENSOURCE.COM

DENTCARE DELIVERY SYSTEMS, INC / INTERNATIONAL HEALTHCARE SERVICES, INC — *SEE ALSO HEALTHPLEX, INC*

DENVER HEALTH MEDICAL PLAN — *DENVER HEALTH NURSE*

COLORADO	777 BANNOCK ST DENVER , CO 80204-4507 PO BOX 40637 DENVER, CO 80204	PHONE: (303) 436-6000	WEB: WWW.DENVERHEALTH.ORG

DEPARTMENT OF WATER & POWER CITY OF LOS ANGELES

CALIFORNIA	111 N HOPE ST LOS ANGELES, CA 90012-2607 PO BOX 51111 LOS ANGELES, CA 90051-0100	PHONE: (213) 367-4211 OR (213) 367-1942 FAX: (213) 367-2078 OR (213) 363-3666	WEB: WWW.LADWP.COM

DESERET MUTUAL — *SEE ALSO DMBA*

DESTINY HEALTH

DISTRICT OF COLUMBIA
ILLINOIS
MARYLAND
MASSACHUSETTS
VIRGINIA
WISCONSIN

	200 W MONROE STE 2100 CHICAGO, IL 60606 PO BOX 4628 OAK BROOK, IL 60523-2108	PHONE: (630) 590-4200 FAX: (630) 590-4204 TOLL FREE: (800) 247-4141	E-MAIL: CUSTOMERCARE.COM WEB: WWW.DESTINYHEALTH.COM

DETROIT & VICINITY TROWEL TRADES

MICHIGAN	700 TOWER DR STE 350 TROY, MI 48099 PO BOX 99490 TROY, MI 48098	FAX: (248) 828-6001 TOLL FREE: (800) 435-4080	WEB: WWW.DVTT.ORG

DGA — *SEE ALSO DIVERSIFIED GROUP ADMINISTRATORS*

DIAMOND STATE INSURANCE CO — *SEE ALSO UNITED NATIONAL GROUP*

DILLON COMPANIES, INC — *SEE ALSO KROGER*

DIMENSION HEALTH

D

FLORIDA	5881 NW 151ST STE 201 MIAMI LAKES, FL 33014	PHONE: (305) 821-9242 FAX: (305) 818-8814 TOLL FREE: (800) 483-4992	E-MAIL: INFO@DIMENSIONHEALTH.COM WEB: WWW.DIMENSIONHEALTH.COM

DINA DENTAL PLAN

LOUISIANA	11969 BRICKSOME AVE STE A BATON ROUGE, LA 70816-2337 PO BOX 40017 BATON ROUGE, LA 70835-0017	PHONE: (225) 291-3172 FAX: (225) 292-3075 TOLL FREE: (800) 376-3462	E-MAIL: DINAPLAN@BELLSOUTH.NET WEB: WWW.DINADENTAL.COM

DIRECTCARE AMERICA

DELAWARE
ILLINOIS
INDIANA
KENTUCKY
MARYLAND
MICHIGAN
NEW JERSEY
NEW YORK
OHIO
PENNSYLVANIA
VIRGINIA
WEST VIRGINIA
WISCONSIN

	STRATFORD PL 4301 DARROW RD STOW, OH 44224	PHONE: (330) 686-7000 FAX: (330) 686-7001 TOLL FREE: (800) 266-5896	WEB: WWW.DIRECTCAREAMERICA.COM

DISABILITY MANAGEMENT SERVICES, INC — *DMS*

NATIONAL	1350 MAIN ST STE 1600 SPRINGFIELD, MA 01103-1641	PHONE: (413) 747-0990 FAX: (413) 747-1545 TOLL FREE: (800) 804-5342	E-MAIL: DMS.INQUIRY@DI-MGMT.COM WEB: WWW.DISABILITYMANAGEMENTSERVICES.COM

DISTRICT 6 HEALTH FUND

NATIONAL	254 W 31ST 8TH FL NEW YORK, NY 10001	PHONE: (212) 696-5545 FAX: (212) 696-5556 TOLL FREE: (800) 331-1070	

DIVERSIFIED GROUP ADMINISTRATORS — *DGA*

NATIONAL	201 S JOHNSON RD BLDG 1 STE 301 HOUSTON, PA 15342-1300 PO BOX 330 CANONSBURG, PA 15317	PHONE: (724) 746-8700 FAX: (724) 746-8628 TOLL FREE: (800) 221-8490	WEB: WWW.DGATPA.COM
	2607 KINGSTON PIKE STE 190 KNOXVILLE, TN 37919 PO BOX 19804 KNOXVILLE, TN 37939	PHONE: (724) 746-8700 FAX: (865) 525-6749 TOLL FREE: (800) 762-8316	WEB: WWW.DGATPA.COM
	6345 FLANK DR STE 400 HARRISBURG, PA 17112 PO BOX 6540 HARRISBURG, PA 17112	FAX: (717) 652-8328 TOLL FREE: (800) 877-6490	WEB: WWW.DGATPA.COM

DIVERSIFIED GROUP BROKERS/DIVERSIFIED ADMINISTRATION — *EGB*

CONNECTICUT
MAINE
NEW JERSEY
NEW YORK
PENNSYLVANIA

	369 N MAIN ST MARLBOROUGH, CT 06447 PO BOX 299 MARLBOROUGH, CT 06447	PHONE: (860) 295-0238 TOLL FREE: (800) 423-5573	WEB: WWW.DGB-ONLINE.COM

DIVERSIFIED HEALTH CARE SERVICES — *SEE ALSO BENEFIT CLAIMS PAYORS, INC*

DIVISION 1181 ATU NEW YORK WELFARE

NATIONAL	101-49 WOODHAVEN BLVD OZONE PARK, NY 11416-2300	PHONE: (718) 845-5800 FAX: (718) 641-0122

DMBA — *DESERET MUTUAL*

NATIONAL	60 E SOUTH TEMPLE SALT LAKE CITY, UT 84145-1004 PO BOX 45530 SALT LAKE CITY, UT 84145-0530	PHONE: (801) 578-5600 FAX: (801) 578-5903 TOLL FREE: (800) 777-3622	WEB: WWW.DMBA.COM

DMS — *SEE ALSO DISABILITY MANAGEMENT SERVICES, INC*

DONEGAL MUTUAL INSURANCE CO

DELAWARE *MASSACHUSETTS* *PENNSYLVANIA*	1195 RIVER RD MARIETTA, PA 17547 PO BOX 302 MARIETTA, PA 17547-0302	PHONE: (717) 426-1931 FAX: (717) 426-7023 TOLL FREE: (800) 877-0600	WEB: WWW.DONEGALGROUP.COM

DUNN-EDWARDS CORP

ARIZONA *CALIFORNIA* *NEVADA* *NEW MEXICO* *TEXAS*

4885 E 52ND PL LOS ANGELES, CA 90040-2884	PHONE: (323) 771-3330 FAX: (323) 826-2830 TOLL FREE: (800) 733-3877	WEB: WWW.DUNN-EDWARDS.NET

EASTERN BENEFIT SYSTEMS — *SEE ALSO EBS*

EASTERN SHORE TEAMSTERS

DELAWARE *MARYLAND* *VIRGINIA*	1323 N SALISBURY BLVD SALISBURY, MD 21801-3674	PHONE: (410) 742-1031 FAX: (410) 742-1059

EBA&M — *EMPLOYEE BENEFITS ADMIN & MANAGEMENT CORP*

NATIONAL	699 HAMPSHIRE RD 217 WESTLAKE VILLAGE, CA 91361 PO BOX 5079 WESTLAKE VILLAGE, CA 91359-5079	PHONE: (805) 497-4581 FAX: (805) 494-7163 TOLL FREE: (800) 249-8440	WEB: WWW.EBAM.COM

EBC — *SEE ALSO EMPLOYEE BENEFIT CONSULTANTS*

EBMS — *EMPLOYEE BENEFIT MANAGEMENT SERVICES, INC*

NATIONAL	2075 OVERLAND AVE BILLINGS, MT 59102 PO BOX 21367 BILLINGS, MT 59104	PHONE: (406) 245-3575 FAX: (406) 652-5380 TOLL FREE: (800) 777-3575	WEB: WWW.EBMS.COM
UTAH	13997 S MINUTEMAN DR STE 250 DRAPER, UT 84020 PO BOX 4000 DRAPER, UT 84020	PHONE: (801) 572-0720 FAX: (801) 523-1095	WEB: WWW.EBMSTPA.COM

EBPA, INC — *EMPLOYEE BENEFIT PLAN ADMINISTRATION, INC*

NATIONAL	PO BOX 2000 EXETER, NH 03833-4593	PHONE: (603) 778-7106 FAX: (603) 773-4400 TOLL FREE: (800) 578-3272	E-MAIL: SERVICE@EBPANH.COM WEB: WWW.EBPANH.COM

EBS — *SEE ALSO EMPLOYEE BENEFIT SYSTEMS*

NATIONAL	DIVISION OF MEDICAL CLAIMS SERVICES 200 FWY DR E EAST ORANGE, NJ 07018	PHONE: (973) 676-6100 FAX: (973) 676-6794 TOLL FREE: (800) 524-0227 IN-STATE: (800) 772-3610	WEB: WWW.MCS/EBS.COM

EDS — ELECTRONIC DATA SYSTEMS — *SEE ALSO MEDI-CAL*

EDS MEDICAID AGENCY OF ALABAMA — *SEE ALSO MEDICAID OFFICE*

EDUCATORS MUTUAL INSURANCE ASSOC — *SEE ALSO EMIA*

EFG COMPANIES — *ENTERPRISE LIFE INSURANCE CO*

NATIONAL	122 W CARPENTER FWY 6TH FL IRVING, TX 75039 PO BOX 167667 IRVING, TX 75016-7667	PHONE: (972) 445-8300 FAX: (972) 445-8383 TOLL FREE: (800) 527-1984	WEB: WWW.EFGCOMPANIES.COM

EGB — *SEE ALSO DIVERSIFIED GROUP BROKERS*

ELDERPLAN

NEW YORK	745 64TH ST BROOKLYN, NY 11220	PHONE: (718) 921-7979 TOLL FREE: (800) 353-3765	

ELECTRIC INSURANCE CO

NATIONAL	75 SAM FONZO DR BEVERLY, MA 01915 PO BOX 1030 BEVERLY, MA 01915-1030	FAX: (978) 524-5512 OR (978) 236-5700 TOLL FREE: (800) 342-5342	WEB: WWW.ELECTRICINSURANCE.COM

ELI LILLY & CO

NATIONAL	LILLY CORPORATE CTR INDIANAPOLIS, IN 46285-0001	PHONE: (317) 276-2000 TOLL FREE: (800) 428-4411	WEB: WWW.LILLY.COM

EMC INSURANCE

ILLINOIS	1815 S MEYERS RD STE 500 OAK BROOK TERRACE, IL 60181 PO BOX 5001 OAK BROOK TERR, IL 60181	PHONE: (630) 620-2040 FAX: (630) 620-5195 TOLL FREE: (800) 942-7448	WEB: WWW.EMCINSURANCE.COM

EMC NATIONAL LIFE CO

NATIONAL	4095 NW URBANDALE DR URBANDALE, IA 50322-7914 PO BOX 9197 DES MOINES, IA 50306	PHONE: (515) 645-4000 FAX: (515) 645-4215 TOLL FREE: (800) 232-5818	WEB: WWW.EMCNATIONALLIFE.COM

EMI — *EMPLOYERS MUTUAL, INC*

FLORIDA	700 SE CENTRAL PARKWAY STUART, FL 34994	PHONE: (772) 287-7650 FAX: (772) 220-2887 TOLL FREE: (800) 431-2221	WEB: WWW.EMI-TPA.COM

EMIA — *EDUCATORS MUTUAL INSURANCE ASSOC*

PRINCE EDWARD ISLAND *UTAH*	852 E ARROWHEAD LN MURRAY, UT 84107-5298	PHONE: (801) 262-7476 FAX: (801) 269-9734 TOLL FREE: (800) 548-5264 IN-STATE: (800) 662-5850	E-MAIL: WEBMASTER@EDUCATORSMUTUAL.COM WEB: WWW.EDUCATORSMUTUAL.COM

EMPIRE BLUE CROSS BLUE SHIELD — *SEE ALSO BLUE CROSS BLUE SHIELD*

EMPLOYEE BENEFIT CONSULTANTS — *EBC*

NATIONAL	11200 LOMAS BLVD NE 2ND FL ALBUQUERQUE, NM 87112-5580 PO BOX 11020 ALBUQUERQUE, NM 87192-0020	PHONE: (505) 292-5533 FAX: (505) 998-1470 TOLL FREE: (800) 274-5533	E-MAIL: ALBUQUERQUE@EBCTPA.COM WEB: WWW.EBCTPA.COM
	215 STANFORD PKY FINDLAY, OH 45840-1733 PO BOX 928 FINDLAY, OH 45839-0928	PHONE: (419) 423-3823 FAX: (419) 423-0917 TOLL FREE: (800) 523-5789 IN-STATE: (800) 472-6630	E-MAIL: FINDLAY@EBCTPA.COM WEB: WWW.EBCTPA.COM
	3301 E ROYALTON RD CLEVELAND, OH 44147	PHONE: (440) 526-2730 FAX: (440) 546-2086 TOLL FREE: (800) 342-1407	E-MAIL: CLEVELAND@EBCTPA.COM WEB: WWW.EBCTPA.COM
	3301 N BALLARD RD STE B APPLETON, WI 54911 PO BOX 884 APPLETON, WI 54912	PHONE: (920) 731-5333 FAX: (920) 731-6666 TOLL FREE: (800) 342-1407	E-MAIL: APPLETON@EBCTPA.COM WEB: WWW.EBCTPA.COM
	4090 WESTOWN PKY A3 WEST DES MOINES, IA 50266	PHONE: (515) 221-2340 FAX: (515) 221-2331 TOLL FREE: (800) 342-1407	E-MAIL: DESMOINES@EBCTPA.COM WEB: WWW.EBCTPA.COM
	9200 SHELBYVILLE RD STE 500 LOUISVILLE, KY 40222	PHONE: (502) 423-0505 FAX: (502) 423-1652	E-MAIL: LOUISVILLE@EBCTPA.COM WEB: WWW.EBCTPA.COM
	9275 N 49TH ST STE 300 MILWAUKEE, WI 53223-1499	PHONE: (414) 365-4600 FAX: (414) 365-4610 TOLL FREE: (800) 558-7798	E-MAIL: MILWAUKEE@EBCTPA.COM WEB: WWW.EBCTPA.COM

ADDITIONAL COMMENTS: FLEXIBLE PLANS

EMPLOYEE BENEFIT MANAGEMENT SERVICES, INC — *SEE ALSO EBMS — SEE ALSO EBMS*

EMPLOYEE BENEFIT PLAN ADMINISTRATION, INC — *SEE ALSO EBPA, INC*

EMPLOYEE BENEFIT SERVICES

NATIONAL	AMERICAN TOWERS 401 MARKET ST STE 300 SHREVEPORT, LA 71101 PO BOX 70100 SHREVEPORT, LA 71137-0100	PHONE: (318) 424-1987 FAX: (318) 424-9702 TOLL FREE: (800) 256-2657	WEB: WWW.EBSOFLA.COM
	EAST COAST OFFICE 534 RIVER CROSSING FORT MILL, SC 29715	PHONE: (803) 396-4600 FAX: (803) 396-1800	WEB: WWW.KEYBENEFIT.COM

EMPLOYEE BENEFIT SYSTEMS — *EBS*

IOWA	214 N MAIN ST BURLINGTON, IA 52601 PO BOX 1053 BURLINGTON, IA 52601-1053	PHONE: (319) 752-3200 FAX: (319) 753-6114 TOLL FREE: (800) 373-1327	WEB: WWW.EBS-TPA.COM

EMPLOYEE BENEFITS ADMIN & MANAGEMENT CORP— *SEE ALSO EBA&M*

EMPLOYEE PLANS, LLC — *SEE ALSO INSURANCE & RISK MANAGEMENT*

EMPLOYEE SECURITY, INC — *DENTAL CHECK OF MARYLAND*

NATIONAL	7125 THOMAS EDISON DR STE 105 COLUMBIA, MD 21046	PHONE: (410) 997-3300 FAX: (410) 997-3796 TOLL FREE: (800) 638-1134	E-MAIL: BSACKS@ESIINC.NET WEB: WWW.YOURONLINEBENEFITS.COM

EMPLOYER PLAN SERVICES, INC — *EPSI BENEFITS, INC*

	2180 N LOOP W STE 400 HOUSTON, TX 77018	PHONE: (713) 932-8917 FAX: (713) 932-1162 TOLL FREE: (800) 447-6588	E-MAIL: MARKETING@EPSIBENEFITSINC.COM WEB: WWW.EPSIBENEFITSINC.COM

EMPLOYERS COMPENSATION INSURANCE

CALIFORNIA	PO BOX 9152 OXNARD, CA 93031-9152	PHONE: (805) 376-6700 FAX: (800) 499-7214 OR (800) 322-7330 TOLL FREE: (800) 520-1683	WEB: WWW.FREMONTEMPLOYERS.COM
COLORADO IDAHO MONTANA UTAH	1471 SHORELINE DR STE 200 BOISE, ID 83702-9105 PO BOX 70015 BOISE, ID 83707-0015	PHONE: (208) 336-4210 FAX: (208) 345-3719 TOLL FREE: (800) 635-5164 IN-STATE: (800) 232-3085	WEB: WWW.FREMONTEMPLOYERS.COM

EMPLOYERS COMPENSATION INSURANCE CO

CALIFORNIA	PO BOX 9057 OXNARD, CA 93031	FAX: (805) 499-7214 TOLL FREE: (800) 520-1683	WEB: WWW.EIGWC.COM

EMPLOYERS COMPENSATION INSURANCE CO.

ARIZONA CALIFORNIA	500 N BRAND BLVD STE 800 GLENDALE, CA 91203-1923 PO BOX 29074 GLENDALE, CA 91209	PHONE: (818) 549-4700 FAX: (818) 549-4770 OR (800) 323-7330	WEB: WWW.EIG.COM
CALIFORNIA COLORADO	1471 SHORELINE DR STE 200 BOISE, ID 83702 PO BOX 70015 BOISE, ID 83707	PHONE: (208) 336-4210 FAX: (208) 345-3719 TOLL FREE: (800) 635-5164 IN-STATE: (800) 232-3085	WEB: WWW.EIGWC.COM
COLORADO IDAHO	500 N BRAND BLVD STE 800 GLENDALE, CA 91203-1923 PO BOX 29074 GLENDALE, CA 91209	PHONE: (818) 549-4700 FAX: (818) 549-4770 OR (800) 323-7330	WEB: WWW.EIG.COM
IDAHO MONTANA	1471 SHORELINE DR STE 200 BOISE, ID 83702 PO BOX 70015 BOISE, ID 83707	PHONE: (208) 336-4210 FAX: (208) 345-3719 TOLL FREE: (800) 635-5164 IN-STATE: (800) 232-3085	WEB: WWW.EIGWC.COM
NEVADA	500 N BRAND BLVD STE 800 GLENDALE, CA 91203-1923 PO BOX 29074 GLENDALE, CA 91209	PHONE: (818) 549-4700 FAX: (818) 549-4770 OR (800) 323-7330	WEB: WWW.EIG.COM
UTAH	1471 SHORELINE DR STE 200 BOISE, ID 83702 PO BOX 70015 BOISE, ID 83707	PHONE: (208) 336-4210 FAX: (208) 345-3719 TOLL FREE: (800) 635-5164 IN-STATE: (800) 232-3085	WEB: WWW.EIGWC.COM

EMPLOYERS INSURANCE COMPANY OF NEVADA

CALIFORNIA
COLORADO
IDAHO
MONTANA
NEVADA
UTAH

PO BOX 35000
RENO, NV 89511

PHONE: (702) 671-7000
FAX: (702) 671-7175
TOLL FREE: (888) 900-1455

WEB: WWW.EMPLOYERSINGO.COM

EMPLOYERS INSURANCE GROUP

NEVADA

9790 GATEWAY DR STE 100
RENO, NV 89521
PO BOX 35000
RENO, NV 89511

PHONE: (888) 682-6671
FAX: (888) 527-3422
TOLL FREE: (888) 900-1455

WEB: WWW.EIGWC.COM

EMPLOYERS MUTUAL, INC — *SEE ALSO EMIA*

EMS ADMINISTRATIVE SERVICES

TEXAS

PO BOX 162528
FORT WORTH, TX 76161

PHONE: (817) 429-3768
FAX: (817) 335-9734

E-MAIL: INFO@EMSADMIN.COM
WEB: WWW.EMSADMIN.COM

ENTERPRISE GROUP PLANNING

NATIONAL

5910 HARPER RD
CLEVELAND, OH 44139-1835

PHONE: (440) 349-2210
FAX: (440) 349-4268
IN-STATE: (800) 229-2210

WEB: WWW.EGP-INC.COM

ENTERPRISE LIFE INSURANCE CO — *SEE ALSO EFG COMPANIES*

EPIC LIFE INSURANCE CO — *WPS WISCONSIN PHYSICIAN SERVICES*

ALABAMA
ALASKA
ARKANSAS
ILLINOIS
IOWA
KANSAS
LOUISIANA
MINNESOTA
MISSISSIPPI
MISSOURI
NEBRASKA
NORTH DAKOTA
OKLAHOMA
SOUTH DAKOTA
TENNESSEE
TEXAS
WISCONSIN

1765 W BROADWAY
MADISON, WI 53713
PO BOX 8430
MADISON, WI 53708-8430

PHONE: (608) 223-2100
FAX: (608) 223-2159

WEB: WWW.EPICLIFE.COM

EPOCH GROUP

NATIONAL

10795 WATSON RD
ST LOUIS, MO 63127

PHONE: (800) 365-9036
TOLL FREE: (800) 365-9036

WEB: WWW.EPOCHGRP.COM

EPSI BENEFITS, INC — *SEE ALSO EMPLOYER PLAN SERVICES, INC*

EQUITABLE LIFE & CASUALTY INSURANCE CO

NATIONAL

NUMBER 3 TRIAD CENTER STE 200
SALT LAKE CITY, UT 84180
PO BOX 2460
SALT LAKE CITY, UT 84110-2460

PHONE: (801) 579-3400
FAX: (801) 579-3790
TOLL FREE: (800) 352-5150

E-MAIL: INFO@EQUILIFE.COM
WEB: WWW.EQUILIFE.COM

ADDITIONAL COMMENTS: NATIONAL EXCEPT FLORIDA, GEORGIA, NEW JERSEY, MASSACHUSETTS, WISCONSIN, CALIFORNIA

EQUITABLE PLAN SERVICES, INC

NATIONAL	12312 ST ANDREWS DR OKLAHOMA CITY, OK 73120 PO BOX 720460 OKLAHOMA CITY, OK 73172	PHONE: (405) 755-2929 FAX: (405) 755-1185 TOLL FREE: (800) 749-2631	E-MAIL: INFO@EPSTPA.COM WEB: WWW.EPSTPA.COM

ERIE INSURANCE GROUP

DISTRICT OF COLUMBIA	12121 TECH RD SILVER SPRING, MD 20904-1992 PO BOX 4409 SILVER SPRING, MD 20914-0409	PHONE: (301) 622-5200 FAX: (301) 680-7601 TOLL FREE: (800) 492-2709	WEB: WWW.ERIEINSURANCE.COM
DISTRICT OF COLUMBIA *ILLINOIS*	4901 LOUISE DR MECHANICSBURG, PA 17055-4889 PO BOX 2013 MECHANICSBURG, PA 17055-0710	PHONE: (717) 795-8200 FAX: (717) 795-2315 TOLL FREE: (800) 382-1304	WEB: WWW.ERIEINSURANCE.COM
ILLINOIS *INDIANA*	7223 ENGLE RD STE 100 FT WAYNE, IN 46804	PHONE: (260) 432-5375 FAX: (800) 535-4684 TOLL FREE: (800) 892-5655 IN-STATE: (800) 892-5655	WEB: WWW.ERIEINSURANCE.COM
	100 ERIE INSURANCE PL ERIE, PA 16530-1699	PHONE: (814) 870-2000 FAX: (814) 870-3126 TOLL FREE: (800) 458-0811	WEB: WWW.ERIEINSURANCE.COM
INDIANA	250 E 96 ST STE 500 INDIANAPOLIS, IN 46240-3762 PO BOX 80129 INDIANAPOLIS, IN 46280-0129	PHONE: (317) 848-3420 FAX: (800) 535-4691 TOLL FREE: (800) 624-1620	WEB: WWW.ERIEINSURANCE.COM
INDIANA *MARYLAND*	4901 LOUISE DR MECHANICSBURG, PA 17055-4889 PO BOX 2013 MECHANICSBURG, PA 17055-0710	PHONE: (717) 795-8200 FAX: (717) 795-2315 TOLL FREE: (800) 382-1304	WEB: WWW.ERIEINSURANCE.COM
	ERIE BRANCH OFFICE 100 ERIR INSURANCE PL ERIE, PA 16530	PHONE: (814) 451-5000 FAX: (814) 451-5209 TOLL FREE: (877) 771-3743	WEB: WWW.ERIEINSURANCE.COM
MARYLAND	18544 BREEZE HILL DR HAGERSTOWN, MD 21741 PO BOX 4158 HAGERSTOWN, MD 21741-4158	PHONE: (301) 797-5185 FAX: (301) 714-9218 TOLL FREE: (800) 533-5602	WEB: WWW.ERIEINSURANCE.COM
	12121 TECH RD SILVER SPRING, MD 20904-1992 PO BOX 4409 SILVER SPRING, MD 20914-0409	PHONE: (301) 622-5200 FAX: (301) 680-7601 TOLL FREE: (800) 492-2709	WEB: WWW.ERIEINSURANCE.COM
	1000 MURRY RIDGE DR MURRYSVILLE, PA 15668-8517 PO BOX 605 MURRYSVILLE, PA 15668	PHONE: (724) 325-7700 FAX: (800) 553-5504 TOLL FREE: (800) 553-3367	WEB: WWW.ERIEINSURANCE.COM
MARYLAND *NEW YORK*	100 ERIE INSURANCE PL ERIE, PA 16530-1699	PHONE: (814) 870-2000 FAX: (814) 870-3126 TOLL FREE: (800) 458-0811	WEB: WWW.ERIEINSURANCE.COM
NEW YORK *NORTH CAROLINA*	4901 LOUISE DR MECHANICSBURG, PA 17055-4889 PO BOX 2013 MECHANICSBURG, PA 17055-0710	PHONE: (717) 795-8200 FAX: (717) 795-2315 TOLL FREE: (800) 382-1304	WEB: WWW.ERIEINSURANCE.COM
NORTH CAROLINA	125 EDINBURGH SOUTH DR CARY, NC 27511 PO BOX 730 CARY, NC 27512-0730	PHONE: (919) 460-4473 FAX: (919) 461-2251 TOLL FREE: (800) 533-3982	WEB: WWW.ERIEINSURANCE.COM

NORTH CAROLINA ***OHIO***	100 ERIE INSURANCE PL ERIE, PA 16530-1699	PHONE: (814) 870-2000 FAX: (814) 870-3126 TOLL FREE: (800) 458-0811	WEB: WWW.ERIEINSURANCE.COM
OHIO	4690 MUNSON CANTON, OH 44718 PO BOX 9031 CANTON, OH 44711-9031	PHONE: (330) 433-1925 FAX: (330) 433-6447 TOLL FREE: (800) 362-6541	WEB: WWW.ERIEINSURANCE.COM
	3700 POPLAR ST STE 200 PARKERSBURG, WV 26101-1062 PO BOX 598 PARKERSBURG, WV 26102-0598	PHONE: (304) 485-6900 FAX: (304) 420-2099 TOLL FREE: (800) 642-1948	WEB: WWW.ERIEINSURANCE.COM
OHIO ***PENNSYLVANIA***	4901 LOUISE DR MECHANICSBURG, PA 17055-4889 PO BOX 2013 MECHANICSBURG, PA 17055-0710	PHONE: (717) 795-8200 FAX: (717) 795-2315 TOLL FREE: (800) 382-1304	WEB: WWW.ERIEINSURANCE.COM
PENNSYLVANIA	ERIE BRANCH OFFICE 100 ERIR INSURANCE PL ERIE, PA 16530	PHONE: (814) 451-5000 FAX: (814) 451-5209 TOLL FREE: (877) 771-3743	WEB: WWW.ERIEINSURANCE.COM
	136 JAYCEE DR STE 40 JOHNSTOWN, PA 15904 PO BOX 999 JOHNSTOWN, PA 15907	PHONE: (814) 467-1888 FAX: (814) 467-1718 TOLL FREE: (800) 241-4209	WEB: WWW.ERIEINSURANCE.COM
	1400 N PROVIDENCE RD STE 216 MEDIA, PA 19063-2094	PHONE: (610) 891-6400 FAX: (610) 892-3697 TOLL FREE: (800) 821-2902	WEB: WWW.ERIEINSURANCE.COM
	2200 WEST BROAD ST BETHLEHEM, PA 18018-0286 PO BOX 4286 BETHLEHEM, PA 18018-0286	PHONE: (610) 865-1911 FAX: (610) 974-7355 TOLL FREE: (800) 322-9026	WEB: WWW.ERIEINSURANCE.COM
	301 COMMONWEALTH DR WARRENDALE, PA 15086 PO BOX 516 WARRENDALE, PA 15086-0516	PHONE: (724) 776-4000 FAX: (724) 772-7700 TOLL FREE: (800) 922-1824	WEB: WWW.ERIEINSURANCE.COM
	100 ERIE INSURANCE PL ERIE, PA 16530-1699	PHONE: (814) 870-2000 FAX: (814) 870-3126 TOLL FREE: (800) 458-0811	WEB: WWW.ERIEINSURANCE.COM
	1000 MURRY RIDGE DR MURRYSVILLE, PA 15668-8517 PO BOX 605 MURRYSVILLE, PA 15668	PHONE: (724) 325-7700 FAX: (800) 553-5504 TOLL FREE: (800) 553-3367	WEB: WWW.ERIEINSURANCE.COM
TENNESSEE ***VIRGINIA***	4901 LOUISE DR MECHANICSBURG, PA 17055-4889 PO BOX 2013 MECHANICSBURG, PA 17055-0710	PHONE: (717) 795-8200 FAX: (717) 795-2315 TOLL FREE: (800) 382-1304	WEB: WWW.ERIEINSURANCE.COM
	100 ERIE INSURANCE PL ERIE, PA 16530-1699	PHONE: (814) 870-2000 FAX: (814) 870-3126 TOLL FREE: (800) 458-0811	WEB: WWW.ERIEINSURANCE.COM
VIRGINIA	100 PELHAM DR WAYNESBORO, VA 22980 PO BOX 1207 WAYNESBORO, VA 22980-0863	PHONE: (540) 943-7000 FAX: (540) 941-2323 TOLL FREE: (800) 542-2250	WEB: WWW.ERIEINSURANCE.COM
	2820 ELECTRIC RD STE 100 ROANOKE, VA 24018-0524 PO BOX 20769 ROANOKE, VA 24018-0524	PHONE: (540) 989-8950 FAX: (540) 776-1234 TOLL FREE: (800) 533-3743	WEB: WWW.ERIEINSURANCE.COM
	2 PARGON PL 6802 PARGON PL STE 600 RICHMOND, VA 23230 PO BOX 28120 RICHMOND, VA 23228-0120	PHONE: (804) 662-5400 FAX: (804) 662-6555 TOLL FREE: (800) 322-3743	WEB: WWW.ERIEINSURANCE.COM

WEST VIRGINIA	4901 LOUISE DR MECHANICSBURG, PA 17055-4889 PO BOX 2013 MECHANICSBURG, PA 17055-0710	PHONE: (717) 795-8200 FAX: (717) 795-2315 TOLL FREE: (800) 382-1304	WEB: WWW.ERIEINSURANCE.COM
	3700 POPLAR ST STE 200 PARKERSBURG, WV 26101-1062 PO BOX 598 PARKERSBURG, WV 26102-0598	PHONE: (304) 485-6900 FAX: (304) 420-2099 TOLL FREE: (800) 642-1948	WEB: WWW.ERIEINSURANCE.COM
	100 ERIE INSURANCE PL ERIE, PA 16530-1699	PHONE: (814) 870-2000 FAX: (814) 870-3126 TOLL FREE: (800) 458-0811	WEB: WWW.ERIEINSURANCE.COM
	1000 MURRY RIDGE DR MURRYSVILLE, PA 15668-8517 PO BOX 605 MURRYSVILLE, PA 15668	PHONE: (724) 325-7700 FAX: (800) 553-5504 TOLL FREE: (800) 553-3367	WEB: WWW.ERIEINSURANCE.COM
WISCONSIN	4901 LOUISE DR MECHANICSBURG, PA 17055-4889 PO BOX 2013 MECHANICSBURG, PA 17055-0710	PHONE: (717) 795-8200 FAX: (717) 795-2315 TOLL FREE: (800) 382-1304	WEB: WWW.ERIEINSURANCE.COM
	7223 ENGLE RD STE 100 FT WAYNE, IN 46804	PHONE: (260) 432-5375 FAX: (800) 535-4684 TOLL FREE: (800) 892-5655 IN-STATE: (800) 892-5655	WEB: WWW.ERIEINSURANCE.COM
	100 ERIE INSURANCE PL ERIE, PA 16530-1699	PHONE: (814) 870-2000 FAX: (814) 870-3126 TOLL FREE: (800) 458-0811	WEB: WWW.ERIEINSURANCE.COM

ERIN GROUP ADMINISTRATORS, INC

NATIONAL	1871 SANTA BARBARA DR LANCASTER, PA 17601 PO BOX 7777 LANCASTER, PA 17604-7777	PHONE: (717) 581-1300 FAX: (717) 581-6529 TOLL FREE: (800) 433-3746	E-MAIL: MARKETING@EGA-INC.COM WEB: WWW.EGA-INC.COM

ERISA ADMINISTRATIVE SERVICES, INC — *SEE ALSO COMPUSYS, INC*

ERISA GROUP AUSTIN — *SEE ALSO COMPUSYS, INC*

ERISA GROUP INC — *SEE ALSO COMPUSYS, INC*

ESIS — *SEE ALSO ACE USA WORKERS' COMPENSATION*

NATIONAL	NW TERRITORY WORKERS COMP CLAIMS OFFICE 39300 CIVIC CTR DR STE 300 FREMONT, CA 94538-2337 PO BOX 5025 FREMONT, CA 94537-5025	PHONE: (510) 790-4600 FAX: (510) 790-4610 TOLL FREE: (800) 525-0615 IN-STATE: (866) 751-3239	WEB: WWW.ESIS.COM
INDIANA *MICHIGAN*	PO BOX 5013 SOUTHFIELD, MI 48086-5013	PHONE: (248) 455-8000 FAX: (248) 455-8060 TOLL FREE: (800) 962-3138	WEB: WWW.ESIS.COM

ESSEX INSURANCE CO

NATIONAL	4521 HIGHWOODS PKWY GLEN ALLEN, VA 23060-6148 PO BOX 2010 GLEN ALLEN, VA 23058	PHONE: (804) 273-1400 FAX: (804) 273-1435 TOLL FREE: (800) 963-7739	E-MAIL: ESSEX@MARKELINSURANCE.COM WEB: WWW.ESSEXINSURANCE.COM

EVEREADY INSURANCE CO

NEW YORK	59 MAIDEN LN NEW YORK, NY 10038-4510	PHONE: (212) 412-4700 FAX: (212) 363-1350 IN-STATE: (800) 826-8285	WEB: WWW.EVEREADYINSURANCE.COM

EVEREST HEALTHPLAN ADMINISTRATORS

NATIONAL	PO BOX 19002 PROVO, UT 84605-9002	FAX: (801) 375-2770 TOLL FREE: (800) 286-4160	WEB: WWW.EVHEALTH.COM

EVEREST REINSURANCE HOLDING

NATIONAL	477 MARTINSVILLE RD LIBERTY CORNER, NJ 07938 PO BOX 830 LIBERTY CORNER, NJ 07938-0830	PHONE: (908) 604-3000 FAX: (908) 604-3322 OR (908)604-3249 TOLL FREE: (800) 551-6501	WEB: WWW.EVERESTRE.COM

EVOLUTIONS HEALTHCARE SYSTEMS

FLORIDA	7916 EVOLUTIONS WY NEW PORT TICHEY, FL 34655 PO BOX 5001 NEW PORT RICHEY, FL 34656	PHONE: (727) 938-2222 FAX: (727) 938-2880 TOLL FREE: (800) 881-4474	WEB: WWW.EHPPO.COM

EXCELLUS BCBSRA — *SEE ALSO UNIVERA HEALTHCARE, INC.*

EXCELLUS BLUE CROSS BLUE SHIELD — *SEE ALSO BLUE CROSS BLUE SHIELD*

EXCESS REINSURANCE UNDERWRITERS AGENCY, INC

NATIONAL	307 S EVERGREEN AVE STE 101 WOODBURY, NJ 08096 PO BOX 667 WOODBURY, NJ 08096	PHONE: (856) 251-2280 FAX: (856) 251-1277	WEB: WWW.EXCESSRE.COM

EXCLUSIVE HEALTHCARE, INC

IOWA	MUTUAL OF OMAHA PLZ OMAHA, NE 68175	PHONE: (402) 342-7600 FAX: (402) 351-2775 TOLL FREE: (800) 617-2371	WEB: WWW.MUTUALOFOMAHA.COM

EYE CARE OF WISCONSIN, INC

WISCONSIN	8633 N PORT WASHINGTON RD FOX POINT, WI 53217-2213	PHONE: (414) 351-3030 FAX: (414) 351-3603 TOLL FREE: (800) 373-6370	

FAIRMONT SPECIALTY GROUP

NATIONAL	10777 WESTHEIMER STE 500 HOUSTON, TX 77042-3455 PO BOX 2807 HOUSTON, TX 77252-2807	PHONE: (713) 954-8100 FAX: (713) 954-8389 TOLL FREE: (800) 392-1970	WEB: WWW.FAIRMONTSPECIALTY.COM
HAWAII	733 BISHOP ST STE 2200 HONOLULU, HI 96813-4012 PO BOX 3937 HONOLULU, HI 96812	PHONE: (808) 537-522[illegible] FAX: (808) 523-5839 TOLL FREE: (800) 531-9966 IN-STATE: (800) 953-7999	

FALLON COMMUNITY HEALTH PLAN, INC

MASSACHUSETTS	10 CHESTNUT ST WORCESTER, MA 01608-2898 PO BOX 15121 WORCESTER, MA 01615-0121	PHONE: (508) 799-2100 FAX: (508) 797-4292 TOLL FREE: (800) 333-2535	WEB: WWW.FCHP.ORG

FAMILY HEALTH PARTNERS — *FHP*

MISSOURI	PO BOX 411806 KANSAS CITY, MO 64141-1806	PHONE: (816) 855-1813 FAX: (816) 471-1832 TOLL FREE: (800) 347-9363	WEB: WWW.FHP.ORG

FARM BUREAU FINANCIAL SERVICES

ARIZONA	5400 UNIVERSITY AVE WEST DES MOINES, IA 50266-5997	PHONE: (515) 225-5400 FAX: (515) 226-6074	WEB: WWW.FBFS.COM

ARIZONA COLORADO	Casualty/Liability	325 S HIGLEY RD HIGLEY, AZ 85236-4301 PO BOX 3000 HIGLEY, AZ 85236	PHONE: (480) 635-3600 FAX: (480) 635-3780 TOLL FREE: (800) 642-7212	WEB: WWW.FBFS.COM
INDIANA IOWA	Casualty/Liability	325 S HIGLEY RD HIGLEY, AZ 85236-4301 PO BOX 3000 HIGLEY, AZ 85236	PHONE: (480) 635-3600 FAX: (480) 635-3780 TOLL FREE: (800) 642-7212	WEB: WWW.FBFS.COM
IOWA KANSAS	Home Health, Casualty/Liability, Life	5400 UNIVERSITY AVE WEST DES MOINES, IA 50266-5997	PHONE: (515) 225-5400 FAX: (515) 226-6074	WEB: WWW.FBFS.COM
KANSAS MINNESOTA	Casualty/Liability	325 S HIGLEY RD HIGLEY, AZ 85236-4301 PO BOX 3000 HIGLEY, AZ 85236	PHONE: (480) 635-3600 FAX: (480) 635-3780 TOLL FREE: (800) 642-7212	WEB: WWW.FBFS.COM
MINNESOTA	Home Health, Casualty/Liability, Life	5400 UNIVERSITY AVE WEST DES MOINES, IA 50266-5997	PHONE: (515) 225-5400 FAX: (515) 226-6074	WEB: WWW.FBFS.COM
MISSOURI MONTANA NEBRASKA	Casualty/Liability	325 S HIGLEY RD HIGLEY, AZ 85236-4301 PO BOX 3000 HIGLEY, AZ 85236	PHONE: (480) 635-3600 FAX: (480) 635-3780 TOLL FREE: (800) 642-7212	WEB: WWW.FBFS.COM
NEBRASKA NEW MEXICO	Home Health, Casualty/Liability, Life	5400 UNIVERSITY AVE WEST DES MOINES, IA 50266-5997	PHONE: (515) 225-5400 FAX: (515) 226-6074	WEB: WWW.FBFS.COM
NEW MEXICO OKLAHOMA SOUTH DAKOTA	Casualty/Liability	325 S HIGLEY RD HIGLEY, AZ 85236-4301 PO BOX 3000 HIGLEY, AZ 85236	PHONE: (480) 635-3600 FAX: (480) 635-3780 TOLL FREE: (800) 642-7212	WEB: WWW.FBFS.COM
SOUTH DAKOTA	Home Health, Casualty/Liability, Life	5400 UNIVERSITY AVE WEST DES MOINES, IA 50266-5997	PHONE: (515) 225-5400 FAX: (515) 226-6074	WEB: WWW.FBFS.COM
TENNESSEE UTAH	Casualty/Liability	325 S HIGLEY RD HIGLEY, AZ 85236-4301 PO BOX 3000 HIGLEY, AZ 85236	PHONE: (480) 635-3600 FAX: (480) 635-3780 TOLL FREE: (800) 642-7212	WEB: WWW.FBFS.COM
UTAH	Home Health, Casualty/Liability, Life	5400 UNIVERSITY AVE WEST DES MOINES, IA 50266-5997	PHONE: (515) 225-5400 FAX: (515) 226-6074	WEB: WWW.FBFS.COM
	Casualty/Liability, Life	9865 S STATE ST SANDY, UT 84070-3205	PHONE: (801) 233-3100 FAX: (801) 233-3135 TOLL FREE: (800) 388-7752	WEB: WWW.FBFS.COM
VIRGINIA WYOMING	Casualty/Liability	325 S HIGLEY RD HIGLEY, AZ 85236-4301 PO BOX 3000 HIGLEY, AZ 85236	PHONE: (480) 635-3600 FAX: (480) 635-3780 TOLL FREE: (800) 642-7212	WEB: WWW.FBFS.COM

FARM BUREAU INSURANCE — *TEXAS FARM BUREAU CORP*

NATIONAL	Casualty/Liability, Life	SOUTHERN FARM BUREAU CASUALTY 7420 FISH POND RD WACO, TX 76710-1010 PO BOX 2689 WACO, TX 76702-2689	PHONE: (254) 772-3030 FAX: (254) 751-8732 TOLL FREE: (800) 772-6535	WEB: WWW.TXFB.ORG
ARKANSAS	Casualty/Liability, EMC, Life	10720 KANIS RD LITTLE ROCK, AR 72211-3825 PO BOX 31 LITTLE ROCK, AR 72203-0031	PHONE: (501) 224-4400 FAX: (501) 228-1458 OR (501) 228-1386 TOLL FREE: (888) 909-5949 IN-STATE: (877) 877-9287	WEB: WWW.AFBIC.COM
FLORIDA	Casualty/Liability, Life	5700 SW 34TH ST GAINESVILLE, FL 32608 PO BOX 147030 GAINESVILLE, FL 32614-7030	PHONE: (352) 378-8100 FAX: (352) 374-1551 IN-STATE: (352) 378-1321	WEB: WWW.FLORIDAFARMBUREAU.COM

GEORGIA	GEORGIA FARM BUREAU MUTUAL INSURANCE CO 1620 BASS RD MACON, GA 31210 PO BOX 7008 MACON, GA 31209-7008	PHONE: (478) 474-8411 FAX: (478) 474-4860 IN-STATE: (800) 342-1192	WEB: WWW.GFB.ORG
IDAHO	15 E WYOMING HOMEDALE, ID 83628-0000 PO BOX 1197 HOMEDALE, ID 83628-1197	PHONE: (208) 337-4041 FAX: (208) 337-4042	WEB: WWW.FBINSURANCE.COM
	275 TIERRA VISTA DR POCATELLO, ID 83205 PO BOX 4848 POCATELLO, ID 83205-4848	PHONE: (208) 232-7914 FAX: (208) 232-3608 TOLL FREE: (800) 574-1514	WEB: WWW.IDFBINS.COM
	325 E MAIN ST ANTHONY, ID 83445-1546 PO BOX 528 ST ANTHONY, ID 83445-0528	PHONE: (208) 624-3171 FAX: (208) 624-3173	WEB: WWW.FBINSURANCE.COM
	530 S ASBURY STE 3 MOSCOW, ID 83843-2243 PO BOX 8901 MOSCOW, ID 83843	PHONE: (208) 882-1531 FAX: (208) 882-9149	
	717 N MAIN STE C BELLEVUE, ID 83313-5081	PHONE: (208) 788-3529 FAX: (208) 788-3619	WEB: WWW.FBINSURANCE.COM
INDIANA	2008 N MAIN ST CROWN POINT, IN 46307 PO BOX 964 CROWN POINT, IN 46308	PHONE: (219) 663-1028 FAX: (219) 663-1868 TOLL FREE: (800) 656-9550	WEB: WWW.INFARMBUREAU.COM
KENTUCKY	PO BOX 99595 JEFFERSONTOWN, KY 40269	PHONE: (502) 266-6100 FAX: (502) 266-6104 TOLL FREE: (800) 538-8651	WEB: WWW.KYFBINS.COM
	1215 W HWY 80 SOMERSET, KY 42502 PO BOX 860 SOMERSET, KY 42502-0860	PHONE: (606) 679-4327 FAX: (606) 679-3453 TOLL FREE: (800) 538-8650	WEB: WWW.KYFBINS.COM
	1301 GARDENER LN LOUISVILLE, KY 40232 PO BOX 35009 LOUISVILLE, KY 40232-5009	PHONE: (502) 456-1664 FAX: (502) 456-1688 TOLL FREE: (800) 782-3812	WEB: WWW.KYFBINS.COM
	1382 CAMPBELL LN BOWLING GREEN, KY 42102 PO BOX 51545 BOWLING GREEN, KY 42102-5845	PHONE: (270) 782-1300 FAX: (270) 782-1397 TOLL FREE: (800) 538-8656	WEB: WWW.KYFBINS.COM
	1810 E 9TH ST HOPKINSVILLE, KY 42240 PO BOX 954 HOPKINSVILLE, KY 42241-0954	PHONE: (270) 886-8123 FAX: (270) 885-4190 TOLL FREE: (800) 538-8657	WEB: WWW.KYFBINS.COM
	230 PANBOWL RD JACKSON, KY 41339 PO BOX 1210 JACKSON, KY 41339-5210	PHONE: (606) 666-2476 FAX: (606) 666-4565 TOLL FREE: (800) 538-8647	WEB: WWW.KYFBINS.COM
	2401 MERCHANT ST LEXINGTON, KY 40510 PO BOX 11889 LEXINGTON, KY 40578	PHONE: (859) 254-8074 FAX: (859) 254-7216 TOLL FREE: (800) 782-3810	WEB: WWW.KYFBINS.COM
	2909 RING RD ELIZABETHTOWN, KY 42701 PO BOX 958 ELIZABETHTOWN, KY 42702-0958	PHONE: (270) 765-4400 FAX: (270) 765-7956 TOLL FREE: (800) 782-3811	WEB: WWW.KYFBINS.COM

KENTUCKY — CONTINUED	3036 PARRISH AVE OWENSBORO, KY 42304 PO BOX 21369 OWENSBORO, KY 42304-1369	PHONE: (270) 684-2165 FAX: (270) 684-4019 TOLL FREE: (800) 538-8655	WEB: WWW.KYFBINS.COM
	400 N 7TH ST MAYFIELD, KY 42066 PO BOX 363 MAYFIELD, KY 42066-0363	PHONE: (270) 247-4787 FAX: (270) 247-7654 TOLL FREE: (800) 538-8654	WEB: WWW.KYFBINS.COM
	506 SUNSET DR MOREHEAD, KY 40351 PO BOX 890 MOREHEAD, KY 40351	PHONE: (606) 784-7536 FAX: (606) 784-8769 TOLL FREE: (800) 538-8649	WEB: WWW.KYFBINS.COM
	9201 BUNSEN PKY LOUISVILLE, KY 40220 PO BOX 20700 LOUISVILLE, KY 40250-0700	PHONE: (502) 495-5000 FAX: (502) 495-5771	WEB: WWW.KYFBINS.COM
	957 WEAVER RD FLORENCE, KY 41042 PO BOX 337 FLORENCE, KY 41022-0337	PHONE: (859) 525-6170 FAX: (859) 525-6574 TOLL FREE: (800) 538-8653	WEB: WWW.KYFBINS.COM
LOUISIANA	9516 AIRLINE HWY BATON ROUGE, LA 70815 PO BOX 95005 BATON ROUGE, LA 70895-9005	PHONE: (225) 922-6200 FAX: (225) 922-6336	WEB: WWW.LAFBINS.COM
MICHIGAN	3355 EAGLE PARK DR NE STE 104 GRAND RAPIDS, MI 49525 PO BOX 152100 GRAND RAPIDS, MI 49515-2100	PHONE: (616) 956-1976 FAX: (616) 956-1981 TOLL FREE: (800) 332-9780	WEB: WWW.FARMBUREAUINSURANCE-MI.COM
	7373 W SAGINAW LANSING, MI 48909 PO BOX 30100 LANSING, MI 48909	PHONE: (517) 323-7000 FAX: (517) 323-6747 TOLL FREE: (800) 527-6386 IN-STATE: (800) 292-2680	WEB: WWW.FARMBUREAUINSURANCE-MI.COM
	7971 MAIN RD BIRCH RUN, MI 48415 PO BOX 169 BIRCH RUN, MI 48415-0169	PHONE: (989) 624-4777 FAX: (989) 624-4233 TOLL FREE: (800) 367-5343	WEB: WWW.FARMBUREAUINSURANCE-MI.COM
	9353 HAGGERTY RD PLYMOUTH, MI 48170 PO BOX 700980 PLYMOUTH, MI 48170	PHONE: (734) 459-1414 FAX: (734) 459-2697 TOLL FREE: (800) 322-7185	WEB: WWW.FARMBUREAUINSURANCE-MI.COM
MISSISSIPPI	6311 RIDGEWOOD RD JACKSON, MS 39211 PO BOX 1972 JACKSON, MS 39215	PHONE: (601) 957-3200 FAX: (601) 977-4880 TOLL FREE: (800) 634-2154 IN-STATE: (800) 227-8244	WEB: WWW.MSFBINS.COM
NORTH CAROLINA	5301 GLENWOOD AVE RALEIGH, NC 27612 PO BOX 27427 RALEIGH, NC 27611-7427	PHONE: (919) 782-1705 FAX: (919) 788-1044	WEB: WWW.NCFBINS.COM
OKLAHOMA	2501 N STILES AVE OKLAHOMA CITY, OK 73105 PO BOX 53332 OKLAHOMA CITY, OK 73152	PHONE: (405) 523-2300 FAX: (405) 523-2362	WEB: WWW.OKFARMINSURANCE.COM
SOUTH CAROLINA	724 KNOX ABBOTT DR WEST COLUMBIA, SC 29171-2124 PO BOX 2124 WEST COLUMBIA, SC 29171-2124	PHONE: (803) 796-6700 FAX: (803) 936-4633 TOLL FREE: (800) 799-7500	WEB: WWW.SCFBINS.COM
TEXAS	2000 S MARKET ST STE 304 BRENHAM, TX 77833-5800	PHONE: (979) 277-9039 FAX: (979) 277-9051 TOLL FREE: (866) 275-7322 CLAIMS	WEB: WWW.TXFB-INS.COM

VIRGINIA		12580 W CREEK PKY RICHMOND, VA 23238 PO BOX 27552 RICHMOND, VA 23261-7552	PHONE: (804) 290-1000 FAX: (804) 290-1089 TOLL FREE: (800) 277-8323	WEB: WWW.VAFB.COM
WYOMING		931 BOULDER DR LARAMIE, WY 82070-4324 PO BOX 1348 LARAMIE, WY 82073	PHONE: (307) 745-4835 FAX: (307) 721-7738	WEB: WWW.MWFBI.COM

FARM BUREAU INSURANCE — *MISSOURI FARM BUREAU INSURANCE SERVICES*

MISSOURI		701 S COUNTRY CLUB DR JEFFERSON CITY, MO 65109 PO BOX 658 JEFFERSON CITY, MO 65102-0658	PHONE: (573) 893-1400 FAX: (573) 893-6822 TOLL FREE: (800) 922-4632	WEB: WWW.MOFB.COM

FARM BUREAU MUTUAL INSURANCE COMPANY OF ARKANSAS INC — *SEE ALSO FARM BUREAU INSURANCE*

FARM FAMILY CASUALTY — *AMERICAN NATIONAL*

NATIONAL		344 RTE 9 W GLENMONT, NY 12077 PO BOX 656 ALBANY, NY 12201	PHONE: (518) 431-5000 FAX: (518) 431-5983 TOLL FREE: (800) 843-3276	WEB: WWW.FARMFAMILY.COM

ADDITIONAL COMMENTS: NATIONAL EXCEPT TEXAS, FLORIDA, CALIFORNIA, ALASKA, & HAWAII

FARM FAMILY LIFE & CASUALTY INSURANCE

NEW YORK		41 LIBERTY ST STE 2 BATAVIA, NY 14020	PHONE: (585) 343-5010 FAX: (585) 343-8962 TOLL FREE: (800) 876-3162 IN-STATE: (800) 948-3276	WEB: WWW.FARMFAMILY.COM

FARMERS ALLIANCE MUTUAL INSURANCE

COLORADO *IDAHO*		1122 N MAIN MCPHERSON, KS 67460 PO BOX 1401 MCPHERSON, KS 67460-1401	PHONE: (620) 241-2200 FAX: (620) 241-5482 TOLL FREE: (800) 362-1075	WEB: WWW.FAMI.COM
		1355 S COLORADO BLVD STE 113 DENVER, CO 80222-3310	PHONE: (303) 757-7883 FAX: (303) 756-0988 TOLL FREE: (800) 332-9797	WEB: WWW.FAMI.COM
KANSAS *MISSOURI* *MONTANA*		1122 N MAIN MCPHERSON, KS 67460 PO BOX 1401 MCPHERSON, KS 67460-1401	PHONE: (620) 241-2200 FAX: (620) 241-5482 TOLL FREE: (800) 362-1075	WEB: WWW.FAMI.COM
MONTANA		1355 S COLORADO BLVD STE 113 DENVER, CO 80222-3310	PHONE: (303) 757-7883 FAX: (303) 756-0988 TOLL FREE: (800) 332-9797	WEB: WWW.FAMI.COM
NEBRASKA *NORTH DAKOTA* *OKLAHOMA* *SOUTH DAKOTA*		1122 N MAIN MCPHERSON, KS 67460 PO BOX 1401 MCPHERSON, KS 67460-1401	PHONE: (620) 241-2200 FAX: (620) 241-5482 TOLL FREE: (800) 362-1075	WEB: WWW.FAMI.COM

FARMERS AUTO INSURANCE ASSOCIATION — *SEE ALSO PEKIN INSURANCE CO*

FARMERS INSURANCE

NATIONAL		4680 WILSHIRE BLVD LOS ANGELES, CA 90010-3807 PO BOX 2478 LOS ANGELES, CA 90051-0478	PHONE: (323) 932-3200 FAX: (323) 932-3101	WEB: WWW.FARMERSINSURANCE.COM
		480 N SAM HOUSTON PKY E STE 320 HOUSTON, TX 77060	PHONE: (281) 405-7100 FAX: (281) 847-2586 TOLL FREE: (800) 435-7764	WEB: WWW.FARMERSINSURANCE.COM

ALABAMA	22 INVERNESS CTR PKWY STE 560 BIRMINGHAM, AL 35242-0684 PO BOX 380397 BIRMINGHAM, AL 35238-0397	PHONE: (877) 575-4454 FAX: (205) 991-6934	WEB: WWW.FARMERSINSURANCE.COM
ARIZONA	1365 S GILBERT RD MESA, AZ 85204-6003	PHONE: (480) 926-0891 FAX: (480) 926-8951	WEB: WWW.FARMERSINSURANCE.COM
	18444 N 25TH AVE PHOENIX, AZ 85023	PHONE: (602) 863-8180 FAX: (602) 789-9477	WEB: WWW.FARMERSINSURANCE.COM
	615 W ROLLERCOASTER RD TUCSON, AZ 85704-3817	PHONE: (520) 293-6600 FAX: (520) 888-2554	WEB: WWW.FARMERSINSURANCE.COM
	1605 S PLZ WAY FLAGSTAFF, AZ 86001-7102	PHONE: (928) 774-9100 FAX: (928) 774-9285 IN-STATE: (800) 427-9107	WEB: WWW.FARMERSINSURANCE.COM
	COMMERCIAL CLAIMS 1880 S DAIRY ASHFORD STE 105 HOUSTON, TX 77077-4759 PO BOX 441788 HOUSTON, TX 77244-1788	PHONE: (281) 497-8881 FAX: (281) 497-7203 TOLL FREE: (800) 977-8881	WEB: WWW.FARMERSINSURANCE.COM
ARKANSAS	10825 FINANCIAL CTR STE 110 LITTLE ROCK, AR 72211-3587 PO BOX 268994 OKLAHOMA CITY, OK 73126-8994	PHONE: (501) 227-0553 FAX: (817) 217-1389 TOLL FREE: (800) 833-5456	WEB: WWW.FARMERSINSURANCE.COM
	4058 N COLLEGE AVE FAYETTEVILLE, AR 72703-5117 PO BOX 268994 OKLAHOMA CITY, OK 73126-8994	PHONE: (479) 575-0787 FAX: (877) 217-1389 TOLL FREE: (800) 893-3385	WEB: WWW.FARMERSINSURANCE.COM
	TEXAS SPECIAL CLAIMS CENTER 100 FARMERS CIR 2ND FL AUSTIN, TX 78728 PO BOX 149101 AUSTIN, TX 78714	PHONE: (512) 238-4750 FAX: (512) 238-4762 TOLL FREE: (800) 258-6444	WEB: WWW.FARMERSINSURANCE.COM
CALIFORNIA	PO BOX 268994 OKLAHOMA CITY, OK 73126	PHONE: (208) 239-8400	WEB: WWW.FARMERSINSURANCE.COM
	11555 DUBLIN CANYON RD PLEASANTON, CA 94588-2817 PO BOX 5040 PLEASANTON, CA 94566-5040	PHONE: (925) 847-3141 FAX: (925) 416-0948	WEB: WWW.FARMERSINSURANCE.COM
	15627 IMPERIAL HWY LA MIRADA, CA 90638	PHONE: (562) 947-2241 FAX: (562) 943-7247	WEB: WWW.FARMERSINSURANCE.COM
	1700 W CALDWELL VISALIA, CA 93277-8002	PHONE: (559) 622-8567 FAX: (559) 732-1131 TOLL FREE: (800) 435-7764	WEB: WWW.FARMERSINSURANCE.COM
	1932 W ORANGEBURG AVE MODESTO, CA 95350-3740	PHONE: (209) 521-8703 FAX: (209) 521-0238	WEB: WWW.FARMERSINSURANCE.COM
	218 W CARMEN LN STE 209 SANTA MARIA, CA 93458-7774	PHONE: (805) 922-0347 FAX: (805) 922-6030	WEB: WWW.FARMERSINSURANCE.COM
	WORKERS COMPENSATION CLAIMS 3041 COCHRAN ST SIMI VALLEY, CA 93065-2771 PO BOX 10149 VAN NUYS, CA 91410-0149	PHONE: (805) 583-7567 FAX: (805) 583-7467 TOLL FREE: (888) 486-1451	WEB: WWW.FARMERSINSURANCE.COM
	3555 WESTWIND BLVD SANTA ROSA, CA 95403-8256	PHONE: (707) 524-4500 FAX: (707) 526-7364 TOLL FREE: (866) 368-3574	WEB: WWW.FARMERSINSURANCE.COM
	3707 W GARDEN GROVE BLVD STE 100 ORANGE, CA 92868-4803	PHONE: (714) 703-3200 FAX: (714) 750-2529 TOLL FREE: (800) 435-7764	WEB: WWW.FARMERSINSURANCE.COM

CALIFORNIA — CONTINUED	SILICON VALLEY CLAIMS SERVICE CENTER 429 LEWELLYN AVE CAMPBELL, CA 95008-1948	PHONE: (408) 370-9600 FAX: (408) 370-3729 TOLL FREE: (800) 435-7764	WEB: WWW.FARMERSINSURANCE.COM
	4300 E PACIFIC COAST HWY LONG BEACH, CA 90804-2114	PHONE: (562) 986-6200 FAX: (562) 597-2443	WEB: WWW.FARMERSINSURANCE.COM
	4643 QUAIL LAKERS DR STE 101 STOCKTON, CA 95207	PHONE: (209) 957-3241 FAX: (209) 477-5124	WEB: WWW.FARMERSINSURANCE.COM
	5016 CALIFORNIA AVE STE 100 BAKERSFIELD, CA 93309-1649	PHONE: (661) 325-0144 FAX: (661) 325-6202	WEB: WWW.FARMERSINSURANCE.COM
	5280 CARROLL CANYON RD SAN DIEGO, CA 92121 PO BOX 268994 OKLAHOMA CITY, OK 73126-8994	PHONE: (858) 677-1100 FAX: (877) 217-1389	WEB: WWW.FARMERSINSURANCE.COM
	555 TECHNOLOGY CT STE 300 RIVERSIDE, CA 92507-2156	PHONE: (951) 321-6600 FAX: (877) 217-1389 TOLL FREE: (800) 435-7764	WEB: WWW.FARMERSINSURANCE.COM
	6518 ANTELOPE RD CITRUS HEIGHTS, CA 95621-8190	PHONE: (916) 727-4600 FAX: (916) 721-4609	WEB: WWW.FARMERSINSURANCE.COM
	7130 N MARKS FRESNO, CA 93711	PHONE: (559) 438-0370 FAX: (559) 438-5239	WEB: WWW.FARMERSINSURANCE.COM
	8550 BALBOA BLVD STE 295 NORTH RIDGE, CA 91325	PHONE: (818) 895-7800 FAX: (877) 217-1389	WEB: WWW.FARMERSINSURANCE.COM
	4450 WESTINGHOUSE ST VENTURA, CA 93003	PHONE: (805) 642-0291 FAX: (805) 642-0889	WEB: WWW.FARMERSINSURANCE.COM
CANADA	40 27TH ST W STE 2 BILLINGS, MT 59102	PHONE: (406) 652-3200 FAX: (406) 652-6720	WEB: WWW.FARMERSINSURANCE.COM
COLORADO	1354 E SHERWOOD DR GRAND JUNCTION, CO 81501	PHONE: (970) 241-4229 FAX: (970) 245-9580 TOLL FREE: (800) 435-7764	WEB: WWW.FARMERSINSURANCE.COM
	CLAIMS OFFICE 2301 RESEARCH BLVD STE 104 FT COLLINS, CO 80526	PHONE: (970) 225-9306 FAX: (970) 225-0553 TOLL FREE: (800) 850-4181	WEB: WWW.FARMERSINSURANCE.COM
	7535 E HAMPDEN AVE STE 200 DENVER, CO 80231-4838	PHONE: (303) 368-6400 FAX: (303) 368-6534 TOLL FREE: (800) 435-7764	WEB: WWW.FARMERSINSURANCE.COM
	855 CITADEL DR E COLORADO SPRINGS, CO 80909	PHONE: (719) 570-3000 FAX: (719) 574-1565	WEB: WWW.FARMERSINSURANCE.COM
	COMMERCIAL CLAIMS 1880 S DAIRY ASHFORD STE 105 HOUSTON, TX 77077-4759 PO BOX 441788 HOUSTON, TX 77244-1788	PHONE: (281) 497-8881 FAX: (281) 497-7203 TOLL FREE: (800) 977-8881	WEB: WWW.FARMERSINSURANCE.COM
FLORIDA	22 INVERNESS CTR PKWY STE 560 BIRMINGHAM, AL 35242-0684 PO BOX 380397 BIRMINGHAM, AL 35238-0397	PHONE: (877) 575-4454 FAX: (205) 991-6934	WEB: WWW.FARMERSINSURANCE.COM
GEORGIA	22 INVERNESS CTR PKWY STE 560 BIRMINGHAM, AL 35242-0684 PO BOX 380397 BIRMINGHAM, AL 35238-0397	PHONE: (877) 575-4454 FAX: (205) 991-6934	WEB: WWW.FARMERSINSURANCE.COM
HAWAII	4450 WESTINGHOUSE ST VENTURA, CA 93003	PHONE: (805) 642-0291 FAX: (805) 642-0889	WEB: WWW.FARMERSINSURANCE.COM
IDAHO	2520 S 5TH AVE POCATELLO, ID 83205	PHONE: (208) 232-6235 FAX: (208) 234-0383 TOLL FREE: (800) 435-7764	WEB: WWW.FARMERSINSURANCE.COM
	3071 E FRANKLIN RD STE 210 MERIDIAN, ID 83642	PHONE: (208) 893-5109 FAX: (208) 893-5352 TOLL FREE: (800) 435-7764	WEB: WWW.FARMERSINSURANCE.COM

IDAHO — CONTINUED	Casualty/Liability, EMC, (bank icon)	NORTHWEST CLAIMS DEPT E 26TH 5TH AVE SPOKANE, WA 99202	PHONE: (509) 623-4900 FAX: (509) 456-7731 TOLL FREE: (800) 376-2118 IN-STATE: (800) 255-7042	WEB: WWW.FARMERSINSURANCE.COM
ILLINOIS	EMC	3704 N BELT W BELLVILLE, IL 62226	PHONE: (618) 234-8711 FAX: (618) 234-0551 TOLL FREE: (800) 700-4111	WEB: WWW.FARMERSINSURANCE.COM
	Casualty/Liability, EMC, (bank icon)	4000 WESTBROOK DR 2ND FL AURORA, IL 60504	PHONE: (630) 851-9000 FAX: (630) 851-2880	WEB: WWW.FARMERSINSURANCE.COM
	Casualty/Liability, EMC	ILLINOIS FARMERS INS CO 925 CLOCKTOWER DR SPRINGFIELD, IL 62704	PHONE: (217) 546-1301 FAX: (217) 546-6479 IN-STATE: (800) 821-6927	WEB: WWW.FARMERSINSURANCE.COM
INDIANA	Casualty/Liability, EMC	9505 DELEGATES ROW INDIANAPOLIS, IN 46240-3807	PHONE: (317) 581-3400 FAX: (317) 580-1570 TOLL FREE: (800) 435-7764 IN-STATE: (800) 581-2111	WEB: WWW.FARMERSINSURANCE.COM
IOWA	Casualty/Liability, EMC	10985 CODY ST STE 240 OVERLAND, KS 66210	PHONE: (515) 223-1012 FAX: (913) 234-3646 TOLL FREE: (800) 833-5430	WEB: WWW.FARMERSINSURANCE.COM
KANSAS	Casualty/Liability, EMC	10985 CODY ST STE 240 OVERLAND, KS 66210	PHONE: (515) 223-1012 FAX: (913) 234-3646 TOLL FREE: (800) 833-5430	WEB: WWW.FARMERSINSURANCE.COM
	Casualty/Liability	9340 E CENTRAL STE M WICHITA, KS 67206	PHONE: (316) 630-4020 FAX: (316) 630-4050 TOLL FREE: (877) 855-3649	WEB: WWW.FARMERSINSURANCE.COM
	Casualty/Liability, EMC	INDIAN CREEK CLAIMS OFFICE 10985 CODY ST STE 240 OVERLAND PARK, KS 66210	PHONE: (913) 234-3600 FAX: (913) 234-3646 TOLL FREE: (800) 833-5443	WEB: WWW.FARMERSINSURANCE.COM
	(hard hat icon), (bank icon)	TEXAS SPECIAL CLAIMS CENTER 100 FARMERS CIR 2ND FL AUSTIN, TX 78728 PO BOX 149101 AUSTIN, TX 78714	PHONE: (512) 238-4750 FAX: (512) 238-4762 TOLL FREE: (800) 258-6444	WEB: WWW.FARMERSINSURANCE.COM
KENTUCKY	Casualty/Liability, EMC	9505 DELEGATES ROW INDIANAPOLIS, IN 46240-3807	PHONE: (317) 581-3400 FAX: (317) 580-1570 TOLL FREE: (800) 435-7764 IN-STATE: (800) 581-2111	WEB: WWW.FARMERSINSURANCE.COM
LOUISIANA	Casualty/Liability, EMC, (bank icon)	22 INVERNESS CTR PKWY STE 560 BIRMINGHAM, AL 35242-0684 PO BOX 380397 BIRMINGHAM, AL 35238-0397	PHONE: (877) 575-4454 FAX: (205) 991-6934	WEB: WWW.FARMERSINSURANCE.COM
	(hard hat icon), Casualty/Liability, EMC, (bank icon)	COMMERCIAL CLAIMS 1880 S DAIRY ASHFORD STE 105 HOUSTON, TX 77077-4759 PO BOX 441788 HOUSTON, TX 77244-1788	PHONE: (281) 497-8881 FAX: (281) 497-7203 TOLL FREE: (800) 977-8881	WEB: WWW.FARMERSINSURANCE.COM
MARYLAND	Casualty/Liability, EMC	ZURICH PERSONAL CLAIMS INSURANCE 309 INTERNATIONAL CIR STE 309 COCKEYSVILLE, MD 21030	PHONE: (410) 527-3005 FAX: (888) 859-9258 TOLL FREE: (800) 355-6458	WEB: WWW.FARMERSINSURANCE.COM
MICHIGAN	Casualty/Liability, EMC	27260 HAGGERTY RD FARMINGTON HILLS, MI 48331-3410	PHONE: (248) 488-2070 FAX: (248) 488-2191	WEB: WWW.FARMERSINSURANCE.COM
	Casualty/Liability, EMC	6011 W ST JOSEPH HWY STE 400 LANSING, MI 48917	PHONE: (800) 833-5453 FAX: (517) 886-0912 TOLL FREE: (800) 833-5453	WEB: WWW.FARMERSINSURANCE.COM
MINNESOTA	Casualty/Liability, EMC, (bank icon)	609 W TRAVELERS TRAIL BURNSVILLE, MN 55337	PHONE: (952) 890-5757 FAX: (952) 846-6270 TOLL FREE: (800) 759-1741	WEB: WWW.FARMERSINSURANCE.COM

MISSISSIPPI	22 INVERNESS CTR PKWY STE 560 BIRMINGHAM, AL 35242-0684 PO BOX 380397 BIRMINGHAM, AL 35238-0397	PHONE: (877) 575-4454 FAX: (205) 991-6934	WEB: WWW.FARMERSINSURANCE.COM
MISSOURI	10985 CODY ST STE 240 OVERLAND, KS 66210	PHONE: (515) 223-1012 FAX: (913) 234-3646 TOLL FREE: (800) 833-5430	WEB: WWW.FARMERSINSURANCE.COM
	INDIAN CREEK CLAIMS OFFICE 10985 CODY ST STE 240 OVERLAND PARK, KS 66210	PHONE: (913) 234-3600 FAX: (913) 234-3646 TOLL FREE: (800) 833-5443	WEB: WWW.FARMERSINSURANCE.COM
	721 EMERSON RD STE 600 ST LOUIS, MO 63141-0919	PHONE: (314) 995-3600 FAX: (314) 995-3697 TOLL FREE: (800) 231-2449	WEB: WWW.FARMERSINSURANCE.COM
	TEXAS SPECIAL CLAIMS CENTER 100 FARMERS CIR 2ND FL AUSTIN, TX 78728 PO BOX 149101 AUSTIN, TX 78714	PHONE: (512) 238-4750 FAX: (512) 238-4762 TOLL FREE: (800) 258-6444	WEB: WWW.FARMERSINSURANCE.COM
MONTANA	CLAIMS OFFICE 2415 CATLIN ST MISSOULA, MT 59801	PHONE: (406) 728-4220 FAX: (406) 728-8817 TOLL FREE: (888) 425-2467	WEB: WWW.FARMERSINSURANCE.COM
	40 27TH ST W STE 2 BILLINGS, MT 59102	PHONE: (406) 652-3200 FAX: (406) 652-6720	WEB: WWW.FARMERSINSURANCE.COM
NEBRASKA	4848 S 97TH ST OMAHA, NE 68127	PHONE: (402) 592-5111 FAX: (402) 592-4643 TOLL FREE: (800) 760-9299	WEB: WWW.FARMERSINSURANCE.COM
NEBRASKA *NEVADA*	COMMERCIAL CLAIMS 1880 S DAIRY ASHFORD STE 105 HOUSTON, TX 77077-4759 PO BOX 441788 HOUSTON, TX 77244-1788	PHONE: (281) 497-8881 FAX: (281) 497-7203 TOLL FREE: (800) 977-8881	WEB: WWW.FARMERSINSURANCE.COM
NEVADA	1605 S PLZ WAY FLAGSTAFF, AZ 86001-7102	PHONE: (928) 774-9100 FAX: (928) 774-9285 IN-STATE: (800) 427-9107	WEB: WWW.FARMERSINSURANCE.COM
	2030 E FLAMINGO RD STE 151 LAS VEGAS, NV 89119	PHONE: (702) 456-1122 FAX: (877) 217-1389 TOLL FREE: (800) 435-7764	WEB: WWW.FARMERSINSURANCE.COM
	480 E MOANA LN RENO, NV 89502-4675 PO BOX 268994 OKLAHOMA CITY, OK 73126-8994	PHONE: (775) 826-8665 FAX: (775) 826-3229 TOLL FREE: (800) 435-7764	WEB: WWW.FARMERSINSURANCE.COM
NEW MEXICO	COMMERCIAL CLAIMS 1880 S DAIRY ASHFORD STE 105 HOUSTON, TX 77077-4759 PO BOX 441788 HOUSTON, TX 77244-1788	PHONE: (281) 497-8881 FAX: (281) 497-7203 TOLL FREE: (800) 977-8881	WEB: WWW.FARMERSINSURANCE.COM
NORTH CAROLINA	9201 ARBORETUM PKY STE 190 RICHMOND, VA 23236	PHONE: (804) 272-8044 FAX: (804) 272-7483 TOLL FREE: (888) 726-9089	WEB: WWW.FARMERSINSURANCE.COM
NORTH DAKOTA	919 S 7TH ST STE 207 BISMARK, ND 58504	PHONE: (701) 223-0770 FAX: (701) 223-8977 TOLL FREE: (800) 531-4842	WEB: WWW.FARMERSINSURANCE.COM
	COMMERCIAL CLAIMS 1880 S DAIRY ASHFORD STE 105 HOUSTON, TX 77077-4759 PO BOX 441788 HOUSTON, TX 77244-1788	PHONE: (281) 497-8881 FAX: (281) 497-7203 TOLL FREE: (800) 977-8881	WEB: WWW.FARMERSINSURANCE.COM
OHIO	16500 SPRAGUE RD MIDDLEBURG HEIGHTS, OH 44130	PHONE: (888) 834-3237 FAX: (440) 826-1761	WEB: WWW.FARMERSINSURANCE.COM

OHIO — CONTINUED	2545 FARMER'S DR STE 440 COLUMBUS, OH 43235	PHONE: (614) 799-3200 FAX: (614) 764-9441	WEB: WWW.FARMERSINSURANCE.COM
	6125 E KEMPER RD SHARONVILLE, OH 45241	PHONE: (513) 826-0910 FAX: (440) 826-1761	WEB: WWW.FARMERSINSURANCE.COM
OKLAHOMA	CASUALTY CLAIMS 2028 E MEMORIAL RD EDMOND, OK 73013	PHONE: (405) 478-3500 FAX: (405) 478-8867 TOLL FREE: (800) 274-1644	WEB: WWW.FARMERSINSURANCE.COM
	3510 S 79TH E AVE TULSA, OK 74145	PHONE: (918) 627-4800 FAX: (918) 627-2529 IN-STATE: (800) 722-7557	WEB: WWW.FARMERSINSURANCE.COM
	TEXAS SPECIAL CLAIMS CENTER 100 FARMERS CIR 2ND FL AUSTIN, TX 78728 PO BOX 149101 AUSTIN, TX 78714	PHONE: (512) 238-4750 FAX: (512) 238-4762 TOLL FREE: (800) 258-6444	WEB: WWW.FARMERSINSURANCE.COM
OREGON	TRUCK INSURANCE EXCHANGE 13333 SW 68TH PKWY TIGARD, OR 97223 PO BOX 23306 TIGARD, OR 97281-3306	PHONE: (503) 443-6451 TOLL FREE: (800) 369-0544 IN-STATE: (800) 633-1035	WEB: WWW.FARMERSINSURANCE.COM
	TRUCK INSURANCE EXCHANGE 13333 SW 68TH PKY TIGARD, OR 97223-8304 PO BOX 372660 DENVER, CO 80237	PHONE: (503) 443-6451 FAX: (503) 443-6500 TOLL FREE: (800) 369-0544 IN-STATE: (800) 633-1035	WEB: WWW.FARMERINSURANCE.COM
	302 NE BEND RIVER MALL AVE BEND, OR 97701-7550	PHONE: (541) 383-3119 FAX: (541) 388-1695 TOLL FREE: (877) 541-3119	WEB: WWW.FARMERSINSURANCE.COM
	3025 RYAN DR SE SALEM, OR 97301-5057	PHONE: (503) 364-6801 FAX: (503) 364-6868 TOLL FREE: (800) 425-2467	WEB: WWW.FARMERSINSURANCE.COM
	CLAIMS OFFICE 450 COUNTRY CLUB RD STE 260 EUGENE, OR 97401	PHONE: (541) 465-9094 FAX: (541) 465-9056 IN-STATE: (877) 808-4301	WEB: WWW.FARMERSINSURANCE.COM
PENNSYLVANIA	ZURICH PERSONAL CLAIMS INSURANCE 309 INTERNATIONAL CIR STE 309 COCKEYSVILLE, MD 21030	PHONE: (410) 527-3005 FAX: (888) 859-9258 TOLL FREE: (800) 355-6458	WEB: WWW.FARMERSINSURANCE.COM
SOUTH DAKOTA	919 S 7TH ST STE 207 BISMARK, ND 58504	PHONE: (701) 223-0770 FAX: (701) 223-8977 TOLL FREE: (800) 531-4842	WEB: WWW.FARMERSINSURANCE.COM
	COMMERCIAL CLAIMS 1880 S DAIRY ASHFORD STE 105 HOUSTON, TX 77077-4759 PO BOX 441788 HOUSTON, TX 77244-1788	PHONE: (281) 497-8881 FAX: (281) 497-7203 TOLL FREE: (800) 977-8881	WEB: WWW.FARMERSINSURANCE.COM
TENNESSEE	1400 CTR PT BLVD STE 168 KNOXVILLE, TN 37932	PHONE: (865) 670-8707 FAX: (865) 670-7589 TOLL FREE: (866) 331-0238	WEB: WWW.FARMERSINSURANCE.COM
	CLAIMS OFFICE 5209 LINBAR DR STE 603 NASHVILLE, TN 37211	PHONE: (615) 834-4011 FAX: (615) 834-0511 TOLL FREE: (888) 428-4011	WEB: WWW.FARMERSINSURANCE.COM
	9201 ARBORETUM PKY STE 190 RICHMOND, VA 23236	PHONE: (804) 272-8044 FAX: (804) 272-7483 TOLL FREE: (888) 726-9089	WEB: WWW.FARMERSINSURANCE.COM
TEXAS	1109 NOLANA LOOP STE 104 MCALLEN, TX 78504	PHONE: (956) 631-2223 FAX: (956) 631-2388 TOLL FREE: (800) 634-5446	WEB: WWW.FARMERSINSURANCE.COM
	1250 HAWKINS BLVD EL PASO, TX 79925	PHONE: (915) 591-2409 FAX: (915) 591-4433	WEB: WWW.FARMERSINSURANCE.COM

TEXAS — CONTINUED	RIVERSIDE CLAIMS SERVICE CENTER 2505 N HWY 360 STE 500 GRAND PRAIRIE, TX 75050	PHONE: (817) 695-1155 FAX: (817) 640-7863 TOLL FREE: (888) 745-3122	WEB: WWW.FARMERSINSURANCE.COM
	317 N SPUR 63 LONGVIEW, TX 75601	PHONE: (903) 758-9772 IN-STATE: (800) 241-3136	WEB: WWW.FARMERSINSURANCE.COM
	345 OWEN LN WACO, TX 76710	PHONE: (254) 772-6162 FAX: (254) 776-3639 TOLL FREE: (800) 541-0366	WEB: WWW.FARMERSINSURANCE.COM
	3451 S WESTERN ST AMARILLO, TX 79109-4437	PHONE: (806) 355-0102 FAX: (806) 354-9799	WEB: WWW.FARMERSINSURANCE.COM
	3910 S INTERREGIONAL HWY STE 100 AUSTIN, TX 78704	PHONE: (512) 445-415[illegible] FAX: (512) 441-1338	WEB: WWW.FARMERSINSURANCE.COM
	4918 66TH ST LUBBOCK, TX 79414	PHONE: (806) 796-2300 FAX: (806) 796-2668 TOLL FREE: (800) 833-5457	WEB: WWW.FARMERSINSURANCE.COM
	5047 SHERRI ANN RD SAN ANTONIO, TX 78233	PHONE: (210) 653-0383 FAX: (210) 653-0321 TOLL FREE: (800) 435-7764	WEB: WWW.FARMERSINSURANCE.COM
	5100 ANDREWS HWY MIDLAND, TX 79703	PHONE: (432) 689-9838 FAX: (800) 592-4604 TOLL FREE: (800) 833-5461	WEB: WWW.FARMERSINSURANCE.COM
	545 INTERSTATE HWY 10 S BEAUMONT, TX 77701	PHONE: (409) 832-1036 FAX: (409) 832-9112 TOLL FREE: (800) 435-7764	WEB: WWW.FARMERSINSURANCE.COM
	COMMERCIAL CLAIMS 1880 S DAIRY ASHFORD STE 105 HOUSTON, TX 77077-4759 PO BOX 441788 HOUSTON, TX 77244-1788	PHONE: (281) 497-8881 FAX: (281) 497-7203 TOLL FREE: (800) 977-8881	WEB: WWW.FARMERSINSURANCE.COM
	TEXAS SPECIAL CLAIMS CENTER 100 FARMERS CIR 2ND FL AUSTIN, TX 78728 PO BOX 149101 AUSTIN, TX 78714	PHONE: (512) 238-4750 FAX: (512) 238-4762 TOLL FREE: (800) 258-6444	WEB: WWW.FARMERSINSURANCE.COM
UTAH	2480 S 3850 W STE 100 WEST VALLEY CITY, UT 84120	PHONE: (801) 954-2740 FAX: (801) 886-8150 TOLL FREE: (800) 988-3348	WEB: WWW.FARMERSINSURANCE.COM
	4142 RIVERDALE RD OGDEN, UT 84405-3510	PHONE: (208) 239-8400 FAX: (801) 393-8567	WEB: WWW.FARMERS.COM
VIRGINIA	9201 ARBORETUM PKY STE 190 RICHMOND, VA 23236	PHONE: (804) 272-8044 FAX: (804) 272-7483 TOLL FREE: (888) 726-9089	WEB: WWW.FARMERSINSURANCE.COM
WASHINGTON	10101 SE EVERETT MALL WY EVERETT, WA 98208	PHONE: (253) 473-4000 FAX: (253) 473-2027 TOLL FREE: (800) 992-1147	WEB: WWW.FARMERSINSURANCE.COM
	8244 122ND AVE NE KIRKLAND, WA 98033-8017 PO BOX 939 KIRKLAND, WA 98083	PHONE: (425) 889-4443 FAX: (425) 827-9350 TOLL FREE: (800) 891-3338	WEB: WWW.FARMERSINSURANCE.COM
WISCONSIN	300 N CORPORATE DR STE 310 BROOKFIELD, WI 53045	PHONE: (262) 792-2300 FAX: (262) 792-2307	WEB: WWW.FARMERSINSURANCE.COM
WYOMING	COMMERCIAL CLAIMS 1880 S DAIRY ASHFORD STE 105 HOUSTON, TX 77077-4759 PO BOX 441788 HOUSTON, TX 77244-1788	PHONE: (281) 497-8881 FAX: (281) 497-7203 TOLL FREE: (800) 977-8881	WEB: WWW.FARMERSINSURANCE.COM

WYOMING — CONTINUED		4515 E PERSHING UNIT D CHEYENNE, WY 82001	PHONE: (307) 634-0956 FAX: (307) 638-0699 TOLL FREE: (800) 833-5428	WEB: WWW.FARMERSINSURANCE.COM

FARMERS INSURANCE EXCHANGE — *TRUCK INSURANCE EXCHANGE*

ARIZONA		18444 N 25TH AVE PHOENIX, AZ 85023-1213 PO BOX 29054 PHOENIX, AZ 85038-9054	PHONE: (602) 375-6800 FAX: (602) 863-8203 TOLL FREE: (800) 419-9150	WEB: WWW.FARMERSINSURANCE.COM

FBD CONSULTING, INC

KANSAS	R3	7015 COLLEGE BLVD STE 400 OVERLAND PARK, KS 66211 PO BOX 11250 SHAWNEE MISSION, KS 66207-1250	PHONE: (913) 319-8800 FAX: (913) 319-8902 TOLL FREE: (800) 969-4015	WEB: WWW.FBDCONSULT.COM

FCE BENEFIT — *GALAXY HEALTH NETWORK*

NATIONAL	R H	631 106TH ST ARLINGTON, TX 76011 PO BOX 201425 ARLINGTON, TX 76006	PHONE: (817) 633-5822 FAX: (817) 633-5729 TOLL FREE: (800) 899-9355	E-MAIL: TXOFFICE@FCEBENEFIT.COM WEB: WWW.FCEBENEFIT.COM

FEDERAL EXPRESS FREIGHT EAST

NATIONAL		2200 FORWARD DR HARRISON, AR 72601 PO BOX 840 HARRISON, AR 72602-0840	PHONE: (870) 741-9000 FAX: (870) 365-4116 TOLL FREE: (800) 874-4723	WEB: WWW.FEDEX.COM

FEDERATED MUTUAL INSURANCE CO

NATIONAL		121 E PARK SQ OWATONNA, MN 55060 PO BOX 328 OWATONNA, MN 55060-0328	PHONE: (507) 455-5200 FAX: (507) 455-8079 TOLL FREE: (800) 533-0472	WEB: WWW.FEDERATEDINSURANCE.COM

FFG INSURANCE CO — *FIRST EXTENDED SERVICE*

NATIONAL		2001 BRYAN ST STE 200 DALLAS, TX 95201 PO BOX 130745 DALLAS, TX 75313-0745	PHONE: (214) 965-9076 FAX: (214) 965-9105 TOLL FREE: (800) 527-3448	

FHP — *SEE ALSO FAMILY HEALTH PARTNERS*

FIC INSURANCE GROUP — *FINANCIAL INDUSTRY CORP INSURANCE*

NATIONAL		6500 RIVER PL BLVD BLDG 1 AUSTIN, TX 78730 PO BOX 149138 AUSTIN, TX 78714-9138	PHONE: (512) 404-5000 FAX: (512) 404-5210 TOLL FREE: (800) 925-6000	WEB: WWW.FAMILYLIFEINS.COM

FIDELIO INSURANCE CO

DELAWARE *PENNSYLVANIA*		2826 MT CARMEL AVE GLENSIDE, PA 19038-2245	PHONE: (215) 885-2443 FAX: (215) 576-5849 TOLL FREE: (800) 262-4949 IN-STATE: (800) 262-4949	WEB: WWW.FIDELIODENTAL.COM

FIDELITY SECURITY LIFE INSURANCE CO

NATIONAL	R H	3130 BROADWAY KANSAS CITY, MO 64111-2406 PO BOX 418131 KANSAS CITY, MO 64141-9131	PHONE: (816) 756-1060 FAX: (816) 968-0580 TOLL FREE: (800) 648-8624	WEB: WWW.FSLINS.COM

FINANCIAL INDUSTRY CORP INSURANCE — *SEE ALSO FIC INSURANCE GROUP*

FIREMAN'S FUND INSURANCE CO

ALABAMA	SOUTHERN STATES REGIONAL WC CENTER 475 GREAT OAKS WAY STE 200 ALPHARETTA, GA 30022 PO BOX 740174 ATLANTA, GA 30374-0174	PHONE: (678) 393-4084 FAX: (888) 311-7748 TOLL FREE: (800) 282-6351 IN-STATE: (800) 282-6351	WEB: WWW.FIREMANSFUND.COM
ALASKA	1001 BISHOP ST STE 1900 HONOLULU, HI 96813-3649	PHONE: (808) 523-6500 FAX: (808) 523-6541 IN-STATE: (800) 272-3391	WEB: WWW.FIREMANSFUND.COM
ARIZONA	SOUTHWEST REGION 777 SAN MARIN DR BLDG 3 NOVATO, CA 94998-0002	PHONE: (415) 899-2000 FAX: (415) 899-3600 TOLL FREE: (800) 227-1700	WEB: WWW.FIREMANSFUND.COM
ARKANSAS	SOUTHERN STATES REGIONAL WC CENTER 475 GREAT OAKS WAY STE 200 ALPHARETTA, GA 30022 PO BOX 740174 ATLANTA, GA 30374-0174	PHONE: (678) 393-4084 FAX: (888) 311-7748 TOLL FREE: (800) 282-6351 IN-STATE: (800) 282-6351	WEB: WWW.FIREMANSFUND.COM
CALIFORNIA	SOUTHWEST REGION 777 SAN MARIN DR BLDG 3 NOVATO, CA 94998-0002	PHONE: (415) 899-2000 FAX: (415) 899-3600 TOLL FREE: (800) 227-1700	WEB: WWW.FIREMANSFUND.COM
COLORADO	SOUTHWEST REGION 777 SAN MARIN DR BLDG 3 NOVATO, CA 94998-0002	PHONE: (415) 899-2000 FAX: (415) 899-3600 TOLL FREE: (800) 227-1700	WEB: WWW.FIREMANSFUND.COM
CONNECTICUT *DELAWARE* *DISTRICT OF COLUMBIA*	NORTHEAST ONE HUNTINGTON QUADRANGLE STE 2N MELVILLE, NY 11747 PO BOX 9099 MELVILLE, NY 11747-9099	PHONE: (631) 756-6100 FAX: (631) 756-5819 OR (631) 756-5803 TOLL FREE: (800) 582-1998	WEB: WWW.FIREMANSFUND.COM
FLORIDA *GEORGIA*	SOUTHERN STATES REGIONAL WC CENTER 475 GREAT OAKS WAY STE 200 ALPHARETTA, GA 30022 PO BOX 740174 ATLANTA, GA 30374-0174	PHONE: (678) 393-4084 FAX: (888) 311-7748 TOLL FREE: (800) 282-6351 IN-STATE: (800) 282-6351	WEB: WWW.FIREMANSFUND.COM
HAWAII	1001 BISHOP ST STE 1900 HONOLULU, HI 96813-3649	PHONE: (808) 523-6500 FAX: (808) 523-6541 IN-STATE: (800) 272-3391	WEB: WWW.FIREMANSFUND.COM
IDAHO	NORTHWEST REGIONAL CLAIM CENTER 2995 PROSPECT PARK DR 200 RANCHO CORDOVA, CA 95670-6022 PO BOX 13340 SACRAMENTO, CA 95813	PHONE: (916) 852-4500	WEB: WWW.FIREMANSFUND.COM
ILLINOIS *INDIANA* *IOWA* *KANSAS*	33 W MONROE ST STE 1400 CHICAGO, IL 60603 PO BOX 7911 CHICAGO, IL 60680	PHONE: (312) 346-6400 FAX: (312) 441-6260 TOLL FREE: (800) 562-4221 IN-STATE: (800) 869-0934	WEB: WWW.FIREMANSFUND.COM
LOUISIANA	SOUTHERN STATES REGIONAL WC CENTER 475 GREAT OAKS WAY STE 200 ALPHARETTA, GA 30022 PO BOX 740174 ATLANTA, GA 30374-0174	PHONE: (678) 393-4084 FAX: (888) 311-7748 TOLL FREE: (800) 282-6351 IN-STATE: (800) 282-6351	WEB: WWW.FIREMANSFUND.COM

MAINE *MARYLAND* *MASSACHUSETTS*	NORTHEAST ONE HUNTINGTON QUADRANGLE STE 2N MELVILLE, NY 11747 PO BOX 9099 MELVILLE, NY 11747-9099	PHONE: (631) 756-6100 FAX: (631) 756-5819 OR (631) 756-5803 TOLL FREE: (800) 582-1998	WEB: WWW.FIREMANSFUND.COM
MICHIGAN *MINNESOTA*	33 W MONROE ST STE 1400 CHICAGO, IL 60603 PO BOX 7911 CHICAGO, IL 60680	PHONE: (312) 346-6400 FAX: (312) 441-6260 TOLL FREE: (800) 562-4221 IN-STATE: (800) 869-0934	WEB: WWW.FIREMANSFUND.COM
MISSISSIPPI	SOUTHERN STATES REGIONAL WC CENTER 475 GREAT OAKS WAY STE 200 ALPHARETTA, GA 30022 PO BOX 740174 ATLANTA, GA 30374-0174	PHONE: (678) 393-4084 FAX: (888) 311-7748 TOLL FREE: (800) 282-6351 IN-STATE: (800) 282-6351	WEB: WWW.FIREMANSFUND.COM
MONTANA	NORTHWEST REGIONAL CLAIM CENTER 2995 PROSPECT PARK DR 200 RANCHO CORDOVA, CA 95670- 6022 PO BOX 13340 SACRAMENTO, CA 95813	PHONE: (916) 852-4500	WEB: WWW.FIREMANSFUND.COM
NEBRASKA	33 W MONROE ST STE 1400 CHICAGO, IL 60603 PO BOX 7911 CHICAGO, IL 60680	PHONE: (312) 346-6400 FAX: (312) 441-6260 TOLL FREE: (800) 562-4221 IN-STATE: (800) 869-0934	WEB: WWW.FIREMANSFUND.COM
NEVADA	SOUTHWEST REGION 777 SAN MARIN DR BLDG 3 NOVATO, CA 94998-0002	PHONE: (415) 899-2000 FAX: (415) 899-3600 TOLL FREE: (800) 227-1700	WEB: WWW.FIREMANSFUND.COM
NEW HAMPSHIRE *NEW JERSEY*	NORTHEAST ONE HUNTINGTON QUADRANGLE STE 2N MELVILLE, NY 11747 PO BOX 9099 MELVILLE, NY 11747-9099	PHONE: (631) 756-6100 FAX: (631) 756-5819 OR (631) 756-5803 TOLL FREE: (800) 582-1998	WEB: WWW.FIREMANSFUND.COM
NEW MEXICO	SOUTHWEST REGION 777 SAN MARIN DR BLDG 3 NOVATO, CA 94998-0002	PHONE: (415) 899-2000 FAX: (415) 899-3600 TOLL FREE: (800) 227-1700	WEB: WWW.FIREMANSFUND.COM
NEW YORK	NORTHEAST ONE HUNTINGTON QUADRANGLE STE 2N MELVILLE, NY 11747 PO BOX 9099 MELVILLE, NY 11747-9099	PHONE: (631) 756-6100 FAX: (631) 756-5819 OR (631) 756-5803 TOLL FREE: (800) 582-1998	WEB: WWW.FIREMANSFUND.COM
NORTH CAROLINA	SOUTHERN STATES REGIONAL WC CENTER 475 GREAT OAKS WAY STE 200 ALPHARETTA, GA 30022 PO BOX 740174 ATLANTA, GA 30374-0174	PHONE: (678) 393-4084 FAX: (888) 311-7748 TOLL FREE: (800) 282-6351 IN-STATE: (800) 282-6351	WEB: WWW.FIREMANSFUND.COM
NORTH DAKOTA *OHIO*	33 W MONROE ST STE 1400 CHICAGO, IL 60603 PO BOX 7911 CHICAGO, IL 60680	PHONE: (312) 346-6400 FAX: (312) 441-6260 TOLL FREE: (800) 562-4221 IN-STATE: (800) 869-0934	WEB: WWW.FIREMANSFUND.COM
OKLAHOMA	SOUTHERN STATES REGIONAL WC CENTER 475 GREAT OAKS WAY STE 200 ALPHARETTA, GA 30022 PO BOX 740174 ATLANTA, GA 30374-0174	PHONE: (678) 393-4084 FAX: (888) 311-7748 TOLL FREE: (800) 282-6351 IN-STATE: (800) 282-6351	WEB: WWW.FIREMANSFUND.COM

OREGON		NORTHWEST REGIONAL CLAIM CENTER 2995 PROSPECT PARK DR 200 RANCHO CORDOVA, CA 95670-6022 PO BOX 13340 SACRAMENTO, CA 95813	PHONE: (916) 852-4500	WEB: WWW.FIREMANSFUND.COM
PENNSYLVANIA		NORTHEAST ONE HUNTINGTON QUADRANGLE STE 2N MELVILLE, NY 11747 PO BOX 9099 MELVILLE, NY 11747-9099	PHONE: (631) 756-6100 FAX: (631) 756-5819 OR (631) 756-5803 TOLL FREE: (800) 582-1998	WEB: WWW.FIREMANSFUND.COM
PUERTO RICO		1001 BISHOP ST STE 1900 HONOLULU, HI 96813-3649	PHONE: (808) 523-6500 FAX: (808) 523-6541 IN-STATE: (800) 272-3391	WEB: WWW.FIREMANSFUND.COM
RHODE ISLAND		NORTHEAST ONE HUNTINGTON QUADRANGLE STE 2N MELVILLE, NY 11747 PO BOX 9099 MELVILLE, NY 11747-9099	PHONE: (631) 756-6100 FAX: (631) 756-5819 OR (631) 756-5803 TOLL FREE: (800) 582-1998	WEB: WWW.FIREMANSFUND.COM
SOUTH CAROLINA		SOUTHERN STATES REGIONAL WC CENTER 475 GREAT OAKS WAY STE 200 ALPHARETTA, GA 30022 PO BOX 740174 ATLANTA, GA 30374-0174	PHONE: (678) 393-4084 FAX: (888) 311-7748 TOLL FREE: (800) 282-6351 IN-STATE: (800) 282-6351	WEB: WWW.FIREMANSFUND.COM
SOUTH DAKOTA		33 W MONROE ST STE 1400 CHICAGO, IL 60603 PO BOX 7911 CHICAGO, IL 60680	PHONE: (312) 346-6400 FAX: (312) 441-6260 TOLL FREE: (800) 562-4221 IN-STATE: (800) 869-0934	WEB: WWW.FIREMANSFUND.COM
TENNESSEE *TEXAS*		SOUTHERN STATES REGIONAL WC CENTER 475 GREAT OAKS WAY STE 200 ALPHARETTA, GA 30022 PO BOX 740174 ATLANTA, GA 30374-0174	PHONE: (678) 393-4084 FAX: (888) 311-7748 TOLL FREE: (800) 282-6351 IN-STATE: (800) 282-6351	WEB: WWW.FIREMANSFUND.COM
UTAH		SOUTHWEST REGION 777 SAN MARIN DR BLDG 3 NOVATO, CA 94998-0002	PHONE: (415) 899-2000 FAX: (415) 899-3600 TOLL FREE: (800) 227-1700	WEB: WWW.FIREMANSFUND.COM
VERMONT		NORTHEAST ONE HUNTINGTON QUADRANGLE STE 2N MELVILLE, NY 11747 PO BOX 9099 MELVILLE, NY 11747-9099	PHONE: (631) 756-6100 FAX: (631) 756-5819 OR (631) 756-5803 TOLL FREE: (800) 582-1998	WEB: WWW.FIREMANSFUND.COM
VIRGINIA		SOUTHERN STATES REGIONAL WC CENTER 475 GREAT OAKS WAY STE 200 ALPHARETTA, GA 30022 PO BOX 740174 ATLANTA, GA 30374-0174	PHONE: (678) 393-4084 FAX: (888) 311-7748 TOLL FREE: (800) 282-6351 IN-STATE: (800) 282-6351	WEB: WWW.FIREMANSFUND.COM
WASHINGTON		NORTHWEST REGIONAL CLAIM CENTER 2995 PROSPECT PARK DR 200 RANCHO CORDOVA, CA 95670-6022 PO BOX 13340 SACRAMENTO, CA 95813	PHONE: (916) 852-4500	WEB: WWW.FIREMANSFUND.COM

WISCONSIN	33 W MONROE ST STE 1400 CHICAGO, IL 60603 PO BOX 7911 CHICAGO, IL 60680	PHONE: (312) 346-6400 FAX: (312) 441-6260 TOLL FREE: (800) 562-4221 IN-STATE: (800) 869-0934	WEB: WWW.FIREMANSFUND.COM
WYOMING	NORTHWEST REGIONAL CLAIM CENTER 2995 PROSPECT PARK DR 200 RANCHO CORDOVA, CA 95670-6022 PO BOX 13340 SACRAMENTO, CA 95813	PHONE: (916) 852-4500	WEB: WWW.FIREMANSFUND.COM

FIRST ADMINISTRATORS, INC

NATIONAL	604 LOCUST ST STE 1600 DES MOINES, IA 50309 PO BOX 9380 DES MOINES, IA 50306-9120	PHONE: (515) 323-7604 FAX: (515) 323-7701 TOLL FREE: (800) 622-3339	WEB: WWW.FIRSTADMINISTRATORS.COM
ILLINOIS *IOWA* *SOUTH DAKOTA*	512 MAIN ST STE 200 RAPID CITY, SD 57701 PO BOX 8150 RAPID CITY, SD 57709-8150	PHONE: (605) 343-2509 FAX: (605) 343-8887	WEB: WWW.FIRSTADMINISTRATORS.COM

F

FIRST ADVANTAGE DENTAL — *DENTAL DEPT*

MASSACHUSETTS	31 B HALL DR AMHERST, MA 01002-2751	PHONE: (413) 253-9505 FAX: (413) 256-3188 TOLL FREE: (800) 998-1011	WEB: WWW.FIRSTADVANTAGEDENTAL.COM

FIRST CHICAGO INSURANCE CO — *CM AUTO*

ILLINOIS	300 S WACKER DR STE 1250 CHICAGO, IL 60606-6601	PHONE: (312) 347-1200 FAX: (312) 347-1205 TOLL FREE: (888) 262-8864	WEB: WWW.FIRSTCHICAGOINSURANCE.COM

FIRST CHOICE HEALTH NETWORK

ALASKA
IDAHO
MONTANA
OREGON
WASHINGTON

	PO BOX 2289 SEATTLE, WA 98111	TOLL FREE: (800) 231-6935	WEB: WWW.FCHN.COM

FIRST COMMUNITY HEALTH PLAN INC — *MEDICARE SUPPLEMENT*

ALABAMA	699-A GALLATIN ST STE A2 HUNTSVILLE, AL 35801-4912	PHONE: (256) 532-2780 FAX: (256) 532-2790 TOLL FREE: (800) 734-7826	WEB: WWW.FIRSTCOMM.ORG

FIRST EXTENDED SERVICE — *SEE ALSO FFG INSURANCE CO*

FIRST HEALTH

NATIONAL	3200 HIGHLAND AVE DOWNERS GROVE, IL 60515	PHONE: (630) 737-7900	WEB: WWW.FIRSTHEALTH.COM

FIRST HEALTH CCN — *COVENTRY HEALTHCARE*

NATIONAL	4141 SCOTTSDALE RD SCOTTSDALE, AZ 85251 PO BOX 3000 SCOTTSDALE, AZ 85271-3000	TOLL FREE: (800) 937-6824	WEB: WWW.FIRSTHEALTH.COM

FIRST HEALTH SERVICES CORP

ALASKA	1835 S BRAGAW STE 200 ANCHORAGE, AK 99508 PO BOX 240808 ANCHORAGE, AK 99524	PHONE: (907) 644-6800 FAX: (907) 644-8126 IN-STATE: (800) 780-9972	WEB: WWW.ALASKA.FHSC.COM

FIRST INSURANCE CO OF HAWAII

HAWAII	1100 WARD AVE HONOLULU, HI 96814-1600 PO BOX 2866 HONOLULU, HI 96803-2866	PHONE: (808) 527-7777 FAX: (808) 545-3120 TOLL FREE: (800) 272-5202	WEB: WWW.FICOH.COM

FIRST LINE NATIONAL INSURANCE CO — *SEE ALSO HARTFORD MUTUAL INSURANCE CO*

FIRST STATE MANAGEMENT GROUP

MASSACHUSETTS	150 FEDERAL ST BOSTON, MA 02110-1753	PHONE: (617) 526-7600 FAX: (617) 526-0600

FIRST UNITED AMERICAN LIFE INSURANCE CO

NEW YORK	1020 7TH N ST LIVERPOOL, NY 13088 PO BOX 3125 SYRACUSE, NY 13220-3125	PHONE: (315) 451-2544 FAX: (315) 451-7679	WEB: WWW.UNITEDAMERICAN.COM

FIRSTCARE

TEXAS	12940 N HWY 183 AUSTIN, TX 78750	PHONE: (806) 356-5151 FAX: (512) 257-6018 TOLL FREE: (800) 461-3742	WEB: WWW.FIRSTCARE.COM

FISERV / BPI RISK MANAGEMENT

NATIONAL	12668 SILICON DR SAN ANTONIO, TX 78249 PO BOX 690450 SAN ANTONIO, TX 78269-0450	PHONE: (210) 558-2100 FAX: (210) 558-2151 TOLL FREE: (800) 460-5778	WEB: WWW.BENPLAN.COM

FISERV HEALTH BENESIGHT

NATIONAL	SOUTHEAST REGION 600 COLONIAL CENTER PKWY LAKE MARY, FL 32746-4764	PHONE: (407) 708-5000 FAX: (407) 708-1365 TOLL FREE: (800) 551-9988	WEB: WWW.BENESIGHT.COM

FISERV HEALTH-KANSAS

NATIONAL	300 W DOUGLAS STE 800 WICHITA, KS 67202 PO BOX 2697 WICHITA, KS 67201-2697	PHONE: (316) 264-5311 FAX: (316) 264-8077 TOLL FREE: (800) 235-7160	WEB: WWW.FISERVHEALTH.COM

FISERVE HEALTH HARRINGTON — *SEE ALSO HARRINGTON BENEFIT SERVICES, INC*

FLEX CORP — *HAND & ASSOC*

NATIONAL	5700 NW CENTRAL DR STE 320 HOUSTON, TX 77092-2092	PHONE: (713) 460-4850 FAX: (713) 460-0361 IN-STATE: (800) 856-3539	WEB: WWW.FLEXCORP125.COM

FLORIDA COMBINE LIFE — *BLUE CROSS BLUE SHIELD*

FLORIDA	PO BOX 100135 COLUMBIA, SC 29202-3135	PHONE: (877) 203-9921 TOLL FREE: (877) 203-9921	WEB: WWW.BCBSFL.COM

FLORIDA HEALTH CARE PLAN, INC

FLORIDA
1340 RIDGEWOOD AVE
HOLLY HILL, FL 32117
PO BOX 9910
DAYTONA BEACH, FL 32120-9910
PHONE: (386) 676-7100
FAX: (386) 676-7119
TOLL FREE: (800) 352-9824
WEB: WWW.FHCP.COM

FLORISTS MUTUAL INSURANCE — *HORTICA*

ILLINOIS
1 HORTICULTURAL LN
EDWARDSVILLE, IL 62025
PO BOX 428
EDWARDSVILLE, IL 62025
PHONE: (618) 656-4240
FAX: (800) 233-3642
TOLL FREE: (800) 851-7740
WEB: WWW.HORTICA-INSURANCE.COM

FMH BENEFITS

NATIONAL
13160 FOSTER ST STE 150
OVERLAND PARK, KS 66213
PO BOX 25946
OVERLAND PARK, KS 66225
FAX: (913) 681-0886
TOLL FREE: (800) 990-9058
WEB: WWW.F-M-H.COM

FOREIGN SERVICE BENEFIT PLAN / MUTUAL OF OMAHA — *AMERICAN FOREIGN SERVICE PROTECTIVE ASSOCIATION*

NATIONAL
1716 N ST NW
WASHINGTON, DC 20036-2907
PHONE: (202) 833-4910
FAX: (202) 833-4918
E-MAIL: AFSPA@AFSPA.ORG
WEB: WWW.AFSPA.ORG

FORTIS INSURANCE — *SEE ALSO ASSURANT HEALTH*

FOX-EVERETT, INC

NATIONAL
3780 I-55 N FRONTAGE RD STE 200
JACKSON, MS 39211
PO BOX 23096
JACKSON, MS 39225-3096
PHONE: (601) 981-6000
FAX: (601) 718-5399
TOLL FREE: (877) 476-6327
WEB: WWW.FOXEVERETT.COM

FRANK M. VACCARO & ASSOCIATES, INC

NEW JERSEY
PENNSYLVANIA
27 ROLAND AVE
MOUNT LAUREL, NJ 08054
PHONE: (856) 793-2501
FAX: (856) 793-3111
TOLL FREE: (800) 883-3682

FREEDOM LIFE INSURANCE — *SEE ALSO NATIONAL FOUNDATION LIFE INSURANCE CO*

FREMONT INSURANCE CO

MICHIGAN
933 E MAIN ST
FREMONT, MI 49412-9751
PHONE: (231) 924-0300
FAX: (231) 924-0880
TOLL FREE: (888) 968-3664
WEB: WWW.FMIC.COM

FRINGE BENEFIT COORDINATORS

FLORIDA
1239 NW 10TH AVE
GAINESVILLE, FL 32601-4154
PHONE: (352) 372-2028
FAX: (352) 372-9805
TOLL FREE: (800) 367-5826
IN-STATE: (888) 876-3332
E-MAIL: INFO@FBC-INC.COM
WEB: WWW.FBC-INC.COM

GAB BUSINESS SERVICE — *SEE ALSO GAB ROBINS NORTH AMERICA*

GAB ROBINS NORTH AMERICA

NATIONAL
NINE CAMPUS DR STE 7
PARSIPANNY, NJ 07054-4513
PO BOX 316
PARSIPPANY, NJ 07054-0316
PHONE: (973) 993-3400
FAX: (973) 993-9379
TOLL FREE: (800) 621-5410
WEB: WWW.GABROBINSNA.COM

ARIZONA	1661 E CAMELBACK RD STE 260 PHOENIX, AZ 85016-3922	PHONE: (602) 248-4130 FAX: (602) 248-4139 TOLL FREE: (800) 621-5410	WEB: WWW.GABROBINSNA.COM
CALIFORNIA	10989 TRADE CTR DR STE 150 RANCHO CORDOVA, CA 95670-6130 PO BOX 269037 SACRAMENTO, CA 95827-9037	PHONE: (916) 853-6600 FAX: (916) 853-8183 TOLL FREE: (800) 621-5410	E-MAIL: ANSWERS@GABROBINS.COM WEB: WWW.GABROBINSNA.COM
	3230 E IMPERIAL HWY STE 209 BREA, CA 92821-6746	PHONE: (714) 577-4700 FAX: (714) 577-5872 TOLL FREE: (800) 621-5410	E-MAIL: ANSWERS@GABROBINS.COM WEB: WWW.GABROBINSNA.COM
COLORADO	7600 E EASTMAN AVE STE 350 DENVER, CO 80231-7162 PO BOX 370750 DENVER, CO 80237-0750	PHONE: (303) 831-7222 FAX: (303) 861-2947 TOLL FREE: (800) 621-5410	WEB: WWW.GABROBINS.COM
ILLINOIS *INDIANA*	*IOWA* *KENTUCKY*	*MINNESOTA* *MISSOURI*	
	9196 W EMERALD STE 140 BOISE, ID 83704	PHONE: (208) 322-2822 FAX: (208) 375-3078 TOLL FREE: (800) 621-5410	E-MAIL: ANSWERS@GABROBINS.COM WEB: WWW.GABROBINS.COM
MONTANA	PO BOX 4107 MISSOULA, MT 59806	PHONE: (406) 549-4187 FAX: (406) 721-2735 TOLL FREE: (800) 621-5410	E-MAIL: ANSWERS@GABROBINS.COM WEB: WWW.GABROBINS.COM
NEVADA *NEW MEXICO*	1661 E CAMELBACK RD STE 260 PHOENIX, AZ 85016-3922	PHONE: (602) 248-4130 FAX: (602) 248-4139 TOLL FREE: (800) 621-5410	WEB: WWW.GABROBINSNA.COM
NORTH DAKOTA *SOUTH DAKOTA*	401 E 8TH ST STE 216 SIOUX FALLS, SD 57103	PHONE: (605) 362-8991 FAX: (605) 362-8879 TOLL FREE: (800) 621-5410	E-MAIL: ANSWERS@GABROBINS.COM WEB: WWW.GABROBINS.COM
TENNESSEE	965 RDG LK BLVD STE 208 MEMPHIS, TN 38120-0416	PHONE: (901) 761-7830 FAX: (901) 767-6403 TOLL FREE: (800) 621-5410	E-MAIL: ANSWER@GABROBINS.COM WEB: WWW.GABROBINS.COM
TEXAS	1341 W MOCKINGBIRD LN STE 900 W DALLAS, TX 75247-6907	PHONE: (214) 631-4455 FAX: (214) 631-4261 TOLL FREE: (800) 621-5410	E-MAIL: ANSWERS@GABROBINS.COM WEB: WWW.GABROBINSNA.COM
	8700 COMMERCE PARK STE 235 HOUSTON, TX 77036-7497	PHONE: (713) 988-6700 FAX: (713) 270-3800 TOLL FREE: (800) 621-5410	E-MAIL: ANSWERS@GABROBINS.COM WEB: WWW.GABROBINSNA.COM
UTAH	7600 E EASTMAN AVE STE 350 DENVER, CO 80231-7162 PO BOX 370750 DENVER, CO 80237-0750	PHONE: (303) 831-7222 FAX: (303) 861-2947 TOLL FREE: (800) 621-5410 IN-STATE: (800) 747-7222	WEB: WWW.GABROBINS.COM
WISCONSIN	9196 W EMERALD STE 140 BOISE, ID 83704	PHONE: (208) 322-2822 FAX: (208) 375-3078 TOLL FREE: (800) 621-5410	E-MAIL: ANSWERS@GABROBINS.COM WEB: WWW.GABROBINS.COM
WYOMING	7600 E EASTMAN AVE STE 350 DENVER, CO 80231-7162 PO BOX 370750 DENVER, CO 80237-0750	PHONE: (303) 831-7222 FAX: (303) 861-2947 TOLL FREE: (800) 621-5410	WEB: WWW.GABROBINS.COM
	400 2ND ST STE A ROCK SPRINGS, WY 82901-6260 PO BOX 1373 ROCK SPRINGS, WY 82902-1373	PHONE: (307) 382-2650 FAX: (307) 382-8147 TOLL FREE: (800) 621-5410 IN-STATE: (800) 621-5410	WEB: WWW.GABROBINS.COM

GAINSCO

NATIONAL	5400 COMMERCE AIRPORT FREE STE A FT WORTH, TX 76117 PO BOX 199023 DALLAS, TX 75219	PHONE: (817) 336-2500 FAX: (800) 523-3522 TOLL FREE: (800) 699-1561	E-MAIL: CLAIMS@GAINSCO.COM WEB: WWW.GAINSCO.COM

GALLAGHER BENEFIT ADMINISTRATORS, INC — *GBA*

NATIONAL	750 WARRENVILLE RD STE 200 LISLE, IL 60532-1297 PO BOX 5227 LISLE, IL 60532	PHONE: (630) 493-9570 FAX: (630) 493-3800 TOLL FREE: (800) 323-1726 IN-STATE: (800) 345-0109	WEB: WWW.GALLAGHERBENEFITS.COM

GARMI, INC — *GREAT AMERICAN INSURANCE CO*

ARIZONA	750 CITY DR S ORANGE, CA 92868 PO BOX 14180 ORANGE, CA 92868	PHONE: (714) 740-3150 IN-STATE: (800) 531-9010	WEB: WWW.GARMI.COM

GATES MCDONALD HEALTH PLUS

NATIONAL	215 N FRONT ST COLUMBUS, OH 43215 PO BOX 182720 COLUMBUS, OH 43218-2720	PHONE: (614) 677-3700 FAX: (888) 329-6261 TOLL FREE: (800) 642-7587	WEB: WWW.GMCDHEALTHPLUS.COM

GATEWAY HEALTH PLAN

PENNSYLVANIA	US STEEL TOWER FL 41 600 GRANT ST PITTSBURG, PA 15219	PHONE: (412) 255-4640 FAX: (412) 255-4670 TOLL FREE: (800) 392-1147	WEB: WWW.GATEWAYHEALTHPLAN.COM

GBA — *SEE ALSO GALLAGHER BENEFIT ADMINISTRATORS, INC*

GBSIO — *SEE ALSO GROUP BENEFIT SERVICES, INC*

GCAN INSURANCE CO

CANADA	480 UNIVERSITY AVE STE 1700 TORONTO, ON M5G-1V6	PHONE: (416) 598-4651 FAX: (416) 598-5478	WEB: WWW.GCAN.COM

GE FINANCIAL ASSURANCE — *SEE ALSO UNION FIDELITY INSURANCE CO*

GE FINANCIAL SERVICE — *SEE ALSO AMERICAN MAYFLOWER*

GE INSURANCE SOLUTIONS — *SEE ALSO INDUSTRIAL RISK INSURERS*

NATIONAL	5200 METCALF AVE OVERLAND PARK, KS 66202-1265 PO BOX 2991 SHAWNEE MISSION, KS 66201	PHONE: (913) 676-5200 FAX: (913) 676-5221 TOLL FREE: (800) 255-6931	WEB: WWW.GEINSURANCESOLUTIONS.COM
CALIFORNIA	111 SUTTER ST STE 400 SAN FRANCISCO, CA 94104	PHONE: (415) 834-2200 FAX: (415) 834-2202 TOLL FREE: (800) 227-0813	WEB: WWW.ERCGROUP.COM
	865 S FIGUEROA ST STE 1320 LOS ANGELES, CA 90017	PHONE: (213) 439-5670 FAX: (213) 439-5680 TOLL FREE: (800) 243-4120	WEB: WWW.ERCGROUP.COM
KANSAS	5200 METCALF AVE OVERLAND PARK, KS 66202-1265 PO BOX 2991 SHAWNEE MISSION, KS 66201	PHONE: (913) 676-5200 FAX: (913) 676-5221 TOLL FREE: (800) 255-6931	WEB: WWW.GEINSURANCESOLUTIONS.COM

GEHA — GOVERNMENT EMPLOYEES HOSPITAL ASSOCIATION

NATIONAL	℞	17306 E 24 HWY INDEPENDENCE, MO 64056 PO BOX 4665 INDEPENDENCE, MO 64051-4665	PHONE: (816) 257-5500 TOLL FREE: (800) 821-6136	WEB: WWW.GEHA.COM

GEICO DIRECT

NATIONAL		ONE GEICO BLVD FREDERICKSBURG, VA 22412-0004	PHONE: (301) 986-2500 FAX: (561) 244-0791 TOLL FREE: (800) 824-5404	WEB: WWW.GEICO.COM
ALABAMA		1 GEICO CTR MACON, GA 31210	PHONE: (478) 744-5000 FAX: (478) 744-5915 TOLL FREE: (800) 841-3000 IN-STATE: (800) 841-9160	WEB: WWW.GEICO.COM
ALASKA ARIZONA		PO BOX 509119 SAN DIEGO, CA 95120	PHONE: (858) 513-5500 FAX: (858) 513-5905 TOLL FREE: (800) 841-3000	E-MAIL: R4NETSERVE@GEICO.COM WEB: WWW.GEICO.COM
ARKANSAS		1 GEICO CTR MACON, GA 31210	PHONE: (478) 744-5000 FAX: (478) 744-5915 TOLL FREE: (800) 841-3000 IN-STATE: (800) 841-9160	WEB: WWW.GEICO.COM
CALIFORNIA		PO BOX 509119 SAN DIEGO, CA 95120	PHONE: (858) 513-5500 FAX: (858) 513-5905 TOLL FREE: (800) 841-3000	E-MAIL: R4NETSERVE@GEICO.COM WEB: WWW.GEICO.COM
COLORADO		4201 SPRING VALLEY RD DALLAS, TX 75244-3631	PHONE: (972) 701-8700 FAX: (972) 701-1614 TOLL FREE: (800) 841-3000	WEB: WWW.GEICO.COM
CONNECTICUT		750 WOODBURY RD WOODBURY, NY 11797-2519	PHONE: (516 496-5764 FAX: (516) 213-8425 TOLL FREE: (800) 841-3000 IN-STATE: (800) 645-7550	WEB: WWW.GEICO.COM
GEORGIA		1 GEICO CTR MACON, GA 31210	PHONE: (478) 744-5000 FAX: (478) 744-5915 TOLL FREE: (800) 841-3000 IN-STATE: (800) 841-9160	WEB: WWW.GEICO.COM
HAWAII IDAHO		PO BOX 509119 SAN DIEGO, CA 95120	PHONE: (858) 513-5500 FAX: (858) 513-5905 TOLL FREE: (800) 841-3000	E-MAIL: R4NETSERVE@GEICO.COM WEB: WWW.GEICO.COM
ILLINOIS INDIANA		1 GEICO CTR MACON, GA 31210	PHONE: (478) 744-5000 FAX: (478) 744-5915 TOLL FREE: (800) 841-3000 IN-STATE: (800) 841-9160	WEB: WWW.GEICO.COM
IOWA KANSAS		4201 SPRING VALLEY RD DALLAS, TX 75244-3631	PHONE: (972) 701-8700 FAX: (972) 701-1614 TOLL FREE: (800) 841-3000	WEB: WWW.GEICO.COM
KENTUCKY LOUISIANA		1 GEICO CTR MACON, GA 31210	PHONE: (478) 744-5000 FAX: (478) 744-5915 TOLL FREE: (800) 841-3000 IN-STATE: (800) 841-9160	WEB: WWW.GEICO.COM
MAINE		750 WOODBURY RD WOODBURY, NY 11797-2519	PHONE: (516 496-5764 FAX: (516) 213-8425 TOLL FREE: (800) 841-3000 IN-STATE: (800) 645-7550	WEB: WWW.GEICO.COM
MICHIGAN MINNESOTA MISSISSIPPI MISSOURI		1 GEICO CTR MACON, GA 31210	PHONE: (478) 744-5000 FAX: (478) 744-5915 TOLL FREE: (800) 841-3000 IN-STATE: (800) 841-9160	WEB: WWW.GEICO.COM
MONTANA		PO BOX 509119 SAN DIEGO, CA 95120	PHONE: (858) 513-5500 FAX: (858) 513-5905 TOLL FREE: (800) 841-3000	E-MAIL: R4NETSERVE@GEICO.COM WEB: WWW.GEICO.COM

NEBRASKA	Casualty/Liability, EMC	4201 SPRING VALLEY RD DALLAS, TX 75244-3631	PHONE: (972) 701-8700 FAX: (972) 701-1614 TOLL FREE: (800) 841-3000	WEB: WWW.GEICO.COM
NEVADA	Casualty/Liability, EMC, Medicare	PO BOX 509119 SAN DIEGO, CA 95120	PHONE: (858) 513-5500 FAX: (858) 513-5905 TOLL FREE: (800) 841-3000	E-MAIL: R4NETSERVE@GEICO.COM WEB: WWW.GEICO.COM
NEW HAMPSHIRE NEW JERSEY	Casualty/Liability, EMC	750 WOODBURY RD WOODBURY, NY 11797-2519	PHONE: (516 496-5764 FAX: (516) 213-8425 TOLL FREE: (800) 841-3000 IN-STATE: (800) 645-7550	WEB: WWW.GEICO.COM
NEW MEXICO	Casualty/Liability, EMC	4201 SPRING VALLEY RD DALLAS, TX 75244-3631	PHONE: (972) 701-8700 FAX: (972) 701-1614 TOLL FREE: (800) 841-3000	WEB: WWW.GEICO.COM
NEW YORK	Casualty/Liability, EMC	750 WOODBURY RD WOODBURY, NY 11797-2519	PHONE: (516 496-5764 FAX: (516) 213-8425 TOLL FREE: (800) 841-3000 IN-STATE: (800) 645-7550	WEB: WWW.GEICO.COM
NORTH CAROLINA	Casualty/Liability, EMC	ONE GEICO BLVD FREDERICKSBURG, VA 22412-0004	PHONE: (540) 286-2500 FAX: (561) 244-0791 TOLL FREE: (800) 841-3000	WEB: WWW.GEICO.COM
NORTH DAKOTA	Casualty/Liability, EMC	4201 SPRING VALLEY RD DALLAS, TX 75244-3631	PHONE: (972) 701-8700 FAX: (972) 701-1614 TOLL FREE: (800) 841-3000	WEB: WWW.GEICO.COM
OHIO OKLAHOMA	Casualty/Liability, EMC	1 GEICO CTR MACON, GA 31210	PHONE: (478) 744-5000 FAX: (478) 744-5915 TOLL FREE: (800) 841-3000 IN-STATE: (800) 841-9160	WEB: WWW.GEICO.COM
OREGON	Casualty/Liability, EMC, Medicare	PO BOX 509119 SAN DIEGO, CA 95120	PHONE: (858) 513-5500 FAX: (858) 513-5905 TOLL FREE: (800) 841-3000	E-MAIL: R4NETSERVE@GEICO.COM WEB: WWW.GEICO.COM
RHODE ISLAND	Casualty/Liability, EMC	750 WOODBURY RD WOODBURY, NY 11797-2519	PHONE: (516 496-5764 FAX: (516) 213-8425 TOLL FREE: (800) 841-3000 IN-STATE: (800) 645-7550	WEB: WWW.GEICO.COM
SOUTH CAROLINA	Casualty/Liability, EMC	1 GEICO CTR MACON, GA 31210	PHONE: (478) 744-5000 FAX: (478) 744-5915 TOLL FREE: (800) 841-3000 IN-STATE: (800) 841-9160	WEB: WWW.GEICO.COM
SOUTH DAKOTA TEXAS	Casualty/Liability, EMC	4201 SPRING VALLEY RD DALLAS, TX 75244-3631	PHONE: (972) 701-8700 FAX: (972) 701-1614 TOLL FREE: (800) 841-3000	WEB: WWW.GEICO.COM
UTAH	Casualty/Liability, EMC, Medicare	PO BOX 509119 SAN DIEGO, CA 95120	PHONE: (858) 513-5500 FAX: (858) 513-5905 TOLL FREE: (800) 841-3000	E-MAIL: R4NETSERVE@GEICO.COM WEB: WWW.GEICO.COM
VERMONT	Casualty/Liability, EMC	750 WOODBURY RD WOODBURY, NY 11797-2519	PHONE: (516 496-5764 FAX: (516) 213-8425 TOLL FREE: (800) 841-3000 IN-STATE: (800) 645-7550	WEB: WWW.GEICO.COM
VIRGINIA	Casualty/Liability, EMC	ONE GEICO BLVD FREDERICKSBURG, VA 22412-0004	PHONE: (540) 286-2500 FAX: (561) 244-0791 TOLL FREE: (800) 841-3000	WEB: WWW.GEICO.COM
WASHINGTON	Casualty/Liability, EMC, Medicare	PO BOX 509119 SAN DIEGO, CA 95120	PHONE: (858) 513-5500 FAX: (858) 513-5905 TOLL FREE: (800) 841-3000	E-MAIL: R4NETSERVE@GEICO.COM WEB: WWW.GEICO.COM
WYOMING	Casualty/Liability, EMC	4201 SPRING VALLEY RD DALLAS, TX 75244-3631	PHONE: (972) 701-8700 FAX: (972) 701-1614 TOLL FREE: (800) 841-3000	WEB: WWW.GEICO.COM

GENERAL CASUALTY

NATIONAL	2545 TAYLOR RD MONTGOMERY, AL 36117-4706 PO BOX 235004 MONTGOMERY, AL 36123-5004	PHONE: (334) 270-6000 FAX: (334) 270-6115 TOLL FREE: (800) 633-5606	WEB: WWW.GENERAL CASUALTY.COM
CONNECTICUT	82 HOP MEADOW ST SIMSBURY, CT 06070 PO BOX 519 SIMSBURY, CT 06070	PHONE: (800) 362-5448 FAX: (860) 408-3267 TOLL FREE: (888) 865-7756 IN-STATE: (800) 961-1121	WEB: WWW.GENERALCASUALTY.COM
	ONE GENERAL DR SUN PRAIRE , WI 53596 PO BOX 519 SIMSBURY, CT 06070-0519	PHONE: (860) 651-1065 FAX: (860) 408-3268 TOLL FREE: (800) 961-1121	WEB: WWW.GENERALCASUALTY.COM
GEORGIA	1922 N LAKE PKY TUCKER, GA 30084 PO BOX 450409 ATLANTA, GA 31145-0409	PHONE: (770) 493-1931 FAX: (770) 493-1220	WEB: WWW.GENERALCASUALTY.COM
ILLINOIS *IOWA* *KANSAS* *MARYLAND* *MASSACHUSETTS* *NEBRASKA*	82 HOP MEADOW ST SIMSBURY, CT 06070 PO BOX 519 SIMSBURY, CT 06070	PHONE: (800) 362-5448 FAX: (860) 408-3267 TOLL FREE: (888) 865-7756 IN-STATE: (800) 961-1121	WEB: WWW.GENERALCASUALTY.COM
NEW YORK	ONE GENERAL DR SUN PRAIRE , WI 53596 PO BOX 519 SIMSBURY, CT 06070-0519	PHONE: (860) 651-1065 FAX: (860) 408-3268 TOLL FREE: (800) 961-1121	WEB: WWW.GENERALCASUALTY.COM
NORTH DAKOTA *OHIO* *PENNSYLVANIA*	82 HOP MEADOW ST SIMSBURY, CT 06070 PO BOX 519 SIMSBURY, CT 06070	PHONE: (800) 362-5448 FAX: (860) 408-3267 TOLL FREE: (888) 865-7756 IN-STATE: (800) 961-1121	WEB: WWW.GENERALCASUALTY.COM
PENNSYLVANIA	ONE GENERAL DR SUN PRAIRE , WI 53596 PO BOX 519 SIMSBURY, CT 06070-0519	PHONE: (860) 651-1065 FAX: (860) 408-3268 TOLL FREE: (800) 961-1121	WEB: WWW.GENERALCASUALTY.COM
SOUTH DAKOTA *VIRGINIA* *WISCONSIN*	82 HOP MEADOW ST SIMSBURY, CT 06070 PO BOX 519 SIMSBURY, CT 06070	PHONE: (800) 362-5448 FAX: (860) 408-3267 TOLL FREE: (888) 865-7756 IN-STATE: (800) 961-1121	WEB: WWW.GENERALCASUALTY.COM

GENERAL CASUALTY COMPANY OF WISCONSIN

WISCONSIN	ONE GENERAL DR SUN PRAIRIE, WI 53596	PHONE: (608) 278-5375 FAX: (608) 837-0788 TOLL FREE: (800) 362-5448	WEB: WWW.GENERALCASUALTY.COM

GENESIS HEALTHCARE

	101 E STATE ST KENNETT SQUARE, PA 19348	PHONE: (610) 444-6350 FAX: (610) 925-4000	E-MAIL: INFO@GENESISHCC.COM WEB: WWW.GENESISHCC.COM

GENWORTH FINANCIAL — *SEE ALSO CALIFORNIA BENEFITS DENTAL PLAN*

GERBER LIFE INSURANCE CO

NATIONAL	PO BOX 477199 BROADVIEW HEIGHTS, OH 44147-7916	FAX: (231) 928-2475 TOLL FREE: (800) 628-0011 IN-STATE: (800) 628-0011	E-MAIL: INFO@GERBERLIFE.COM WEB: WWW.GERBERLIFE.COM

G

GERLING GLOBAL REINSURANCE CORPORATION OF AMERICA

NATIONAL	717 5TH AVE NEW YORK, NY 10022-8101	PHONE: (212) 225-1000 FAX: (212) 754-3260	WEB: WWW.GERLING.COM

GHI

NATIONAL	441 NINTH AVE NEW YORK, NY 10001-1681 PO BOX 2832 NEW YORK, NY 10116-2832	PHONE: (212) 501-4444 TOLL FREE: (800) 624-2414	WEB: WWW.GHI.COM

GHP — *SEE ALSO GROUP HEALTH PLAN*

GILSBAR, INC

ALABAMA
ARKANSAS
KENTUCKY
LOUISIANA
MISSISSIPPI
TENNESSEE
TEXAS

	2100 COVINGTON CTR COVINGTON, LA 70433 PO BOX 998 COVINGTON, LA 70434-0998	PHONE: (985) 892-3520 FAX: (985) 898-1666 TOLL FREE: (800) 445-7227	E-MAIL: GILSBAR@GILSBAR.COM WEB: WWW.GILSBAR.COM

GLOBAL RISK INSURANCE CO — *SEE ALSO ALLIANZ INSURANCE CO*

GLOBE LIFE & ACCIDENT INSURANCE CO

NATIONAL	204 N ROBINSON OKLAHOMA CITY, OK 73102	PHONE: (405) 270-1400 FAX: (405) 270-1496 TOLL FREE: (800) 654-5433 IN-STATE: (800) 654-5433	WEB: WWW.GLOBEONTHEWEB.COM

GMAC INSURANCE

NATIONAL	PO BOX 1623 WINSTON SALEM, NC 27102	PHONE: (336) 770-2000 FAX: (336) 435-2300 TOLL FREE: (800) 847-6442	WEB: WWW.GMACINSURANCE.COM

GMP EMPLOYERS RETIREE TRUST

NATIONAL	5245 BIG PINE WY SE FT MYERS, FL 33907-5998	PHONE: (239) 936-6242 FAX: (239) 936-3438	WEB: WWW.GMPTRUST.COM

GO AMERICAN AUTO INSURANCE — *SEE ALSO AMERICAN AMBASSADOR CASUALTY CO*

GOLDEN EAGLE INSURANCE

CALIFORNIA	1340 TREAT BLVD STE 400 WALNUT CREEK, CA 94597 PO BOX 8096 WALNUT CREEK, CA 94596	PHONE: (925) 938-1141 FAX: (925) 942-6198 TOLL FREE: (800) 457-7007 IN-STATE: (800) 537-8855	WEB: WWW.GOLDENEAGLE-INS.COM
	525 B ST SAN DIEGO, CA 92101 PO BOX 85826 SAN DIEGO, CA 92186-5826	PHONE: (619) 744-6000 FAX: (619) 744-6112 TOLL FREE: (800) 688-8661	WEB: WWW.GOLDENEAGLECORP.COM

GOLDEN RULE INSURANCE CO

NATIONAL	712 11TH ST LAWRENCEVILLE, IL 62439-2395	PHONE: (618) 943-8000 FAX: (618) 943-8031	WEB: WWW.GOLDENRULE.COM
	7440 WOODLAND DR INDIANAPOLIS, IN 46278-1719	PHONE: (317) 297-4123 FAX: (317) 290-8927 IN-STATE: (800) 265-7791	E-MAIL: FS@GOLDENRULE.COM WEB: WWW.GOLDENRULE.COM

ADDITIONAL COMMENTS: NATIONAL EXCEPT NEW YORK

GOODVILLE MUTUAL CASUALTY, INC

DELAWARE
ILLINOIS
INDIANA
KANSAS
MARYLAND
OHIO
OKLAHOMA
PENNSYLVANIA

625 W MAIN
NEW HOLLAND, PA 17557
PO BOX 489
NEW HOLLAND, PA 17557-0489
PHONE: (717) 354-4921
FAX: (717) 354-5158
WEB: WWW.GOODVILLE.COM

GOTHAM INSURANCE CO — *MUTUAL MARINE*

NATIONAL

919 3RD AVE 10TH FL
NEW YORK, NY 10022
PHONE: (212) 551-0600
FAX: (212) 986-1310
TOLL FREE: (800) 367-0224
WEB: WWW.NYMAGIC.COM

GOVERNMENT EMPLOYEES HOSPITAL ASSOCIATION — *SEE ALSO GEHA*

GRAIN DEALERS MUTUAL INSURANCE CO

NATIONAL

6201 CORPORATE DR
INDIANAPOLIS, IN 46278
PO BOX 1747
INDIANAPOLIS, IN 46206-1747
PHONE: (317) 388-4500
FAX: (800) 828-4124
TOLL FREE: (800) 428-7081
WEB: WWW.GRAINDEALERS.COM

NORTH CAROLINA

2301 W MEADOWVIEW RD STE 101
GREENSBORO, NC 27407
PO BOX 26716
GREENSBORO, NC 27417-6716
PHONE: (336) 547-6796
FAX: (800) 732-8925
TOLL FREE: (800) 932-0301
WEB: WWW.GRAINDEALERS.COM

GRAMERCY INSURANCE CO

GEORGIA
LOUISIANA
OKLAHOMA

5000 QUORUM DR STE 111
DALLAS, TX 75254-7583
PHONE: (888) 202-0422
FAX: (972) 233-6252
WEB: WWW.GRAMERCYINSURANCE.COM

GRAND VALLEY HEALTH PLAN

MICHIGAN

829 FOREST HILLS AVE SE
GRAND RAPIDS, MI 49546-2325
PHONE: (616) 949-2410
FAX: (616) 949-4978
WEB: WWW.GVHP.COM

GRANGE INSURANCE — *SEE ALSO GRANGE MUTUAL CASUALTY CO*

GRANGE INSURANCE ASSOCIATION

CALIFORNIA
COLORADO
IDAHO
OREGON
WASHINGTON
WYOMING

1410 N MULLAN RD STE 110
SPOKANE, WA 99206-4045
PHONE: (509) 924-7039
FAX: (509) 926-0988
TOLL FREE: (800) 824-2702
WEB: WWW.GRANGE.COM

GRANGE INSURANCE GROUP

CALIFORNIA
COLORADO
IDAHO
OREGON
WASHINGTON
WYOMING

200 CEDAR ST
SEATTLE, WA 98121
PHONE: (303) 382-3315
FAX: (206) 448-2687
TOLL FREE: (800) 546-8850
WEB: WWW.GRANGE.COM

GRANGE MUTUAL CASUALTY CO — *GRANGE INSURANCE*

GEORGIA
KENTUCKY
MICHIGAN
OHIO
SOUTH CAROLINA
TENNESSEE

650 S FRONT ST
COLUMBUS, OH 43206
PO BOX 182657
COLUMBUS, OH 43218

PHONE: (614) 337-4400
FAX: (800) 686-4689
TOLL FREE: (800) 422-0550
IN-STATE: (800) 686-0025

WEB: WWW.GRANGEINSURANCE.COM

GRANGE MUTUAL INSURANCE CO

GEORGIA

512 S HOUSTON LK RD
WARNER ROBINS, GA 31088
PO BOX 182758
COLUMBUS, OH 43272-5583

PHONE: (478) 971-2000
FAX: (800) 342-8089
TOLL FREE: (800) 342-3785

WEB: WWW.GRANGEINSURANCE.COM

INDIANA

6415 MUTUAL DR
FT WAYNE, IN 46825
PO BOX 182326
COLUMBUS, OH 43218-2326

PHONE: (260) 483-1636
FAX: (800) 589-8762
TOLL FREE: (800) 589-5590
IN-STATE: (800) 589-5590

WEB: WWW.GRANGEINSURANCE.COM

KENTUCKY

2444 HARRODSBURG RD
LEXINGTON, KY 40503
PO BOX 8035
LEXINGTON, KY 40533-8035

PHONE: (859) 278-5481
FAX: (800) 837-0802
TOLL FREE: (800) 837-0801

WEB: WWW.GRANGEINSURANCE.COM

GRAY INSURANCE CO

ARIZONA
COLORADO
NEVADA
UTAH
VIRGINIA
WYOMING

3601 N I-10 SERVICE RD W
METAIRIE, LA 70002
PO BOX 6202
METAIRIE, LA 70009

PHONE: (504) 888-7790
FAX: (504) 887-5658

WEB: WWW.GRAYINSCO.COM

GREAT AMERICAN INSURANCE CO

NATIONAL

580 WALNUT ST
CINCINNATI, OH 45202
PO BOX 2575
CINCINNATI, OH 45201-2575

PHONE: (513) 369-5013
FAX: (513) 369-3655
TOLL FREE: (800) 972-3008

WEB: WWW.GREATAMERICANINSURANCE.COM

GREAT DIVIDE INSURANCE CO — *NAUTILUS INSURANCE GROUP*

NATIONAL

7233 E BUTHERUS DR
SCOTTSDALE, AZ 85260-2410

PHONE: (480) 951-0905
FAX: (480) 951-9730
TOLL FREE: (800) 842-8972

E-MAIL: NICMARKETING@NAUTILUS-INS.COM
WEB: WWW.NAUTILUSINSGROUP.COM

GREAT LAKES HEALTH PLAN

MICHIGAN

17117 W NINE MILE RD STE 1600
SOUTHFIELD, MI 48075

PHONE: (248) 559-5656
FAX: (248) 559-4640
TOLL FREE: (800) 903-5253

WEB: WWW.GLHP.COM

GREAT REPUBLIC LIFE INSURANCE CO

ALASKA
IDAHO
NEVADA
OREGON
UTAH
WASHINGTON

1900 W NICKERSON ST STE 200
SEATTLE, WA 98119-1650

PHONE: (206) 285-1422
FAX: (206) 282-5865
TOLL FREE: (800) 388-7330

GREAT WEST CASUALTY CO

ALABAMA	Workers Comp, Self-Insured, Prior Authorization	SOUTHEASTERN REGION 2030 FALLING WATER RD STE 300 KNOXVILLE, TN 37922 PO BOX 31289 KNOXVILLE, TN 37930-1289	PHONE: (865) 670-8850 FAX: (865) 670-6300 TOLL FREE: (800) 998-9288	WEB: WWW.GWCCNET.COM
ARIZONA	Workers Comp, Self-Insured, Prior Authorization	WESTERN REGION 2950 E GOLDSTONE DR MERIDIAN, ID 83642 PO BOX 8007 BOISE, ID 83707	FAX: (208) 898-3905 TOLL FREE: (800) 628-4415	WEB: WWW.GWCCNET.COM
ARKANSAS	Workers Comp, Self-Insured, Prior Authorization	SOUTHERN REGION 624 SIX FLAGS DR STE 240 ARLINGTON, TX 76005 PO BOX 5408 ARLINGTON, TX 76011	FAX: (817) 385-2770 TOLL FREE: (800) 257-8757	WEB: WWW.GWCCNET.COM
CALIFORNIA COLORADO	Workers Comp, Self-Insured, Prior Authorization	WESTERN REGION 2950 E GOLDSTONE DR MERIDIAN, ID 83642 PO BOX 8007 BOISE, ID 83707	FAX: (208) 898-3905 TOLL FREE: (800) 628-4415	WEB: WWW.GWCCNET.COM
GEORGIA	Workers Comp, Self-Insured, Prior Authorization	SOUTHEASTERN REGION 2030 FALLING WATER RD STE 300 KNOXVILLE, TN 37922 PO BOX 31289 KNOXVILLE, TN 37930-1289	PHONE: (865) 670-8850 FAX: (865) 670-6300 TOLL FREE: (800) 998-9288	WEB: WWW.GWCCNET.COM
IDAHO	Workers Comp, Self-Insured, Prior Authorization	WESTERN REGION 2950 E GOLDSTONE DR MERIDIAN, ID 83642 PO BOX 8007 BOISE, ID 83707	FAX: (208) 898-3905 TOLL FREE: (800) 628-4415	WEB: WWW.GWCCNET.COM
IOWA KANSAS MINNESOTA	Self-Insured, Workers Comp, Self-Insured, Prior Authorization, Main Office	CORPORATE OFFICE MIDWESTERN REGION 1100 W 29TH ST SOUTH SIOUX CITY, NE 68776 PO BOX 277 SOUTH SIOUX CITY, NE 68776-0277	PHONE: (402) 494-2411 FAX: (402) 494-7450 TOLL FREE: (800) 228-8602	E-MAIL: Z.MARKETING@GWCCNET.COM WEB: WWW.GWCCNET.COM
MISSISSIPPI	Workers Comp, Self-Insured, Prior Authorization	SOUTHEASTERN REGION 2030 FALLING WATER RD STE 300 KNOXVILLE, TN 37922 PO BOX 31289 KNOXVILLE, TN 37930-1289	PHONE: (865) 670-8850 FAX: (865) 670-6300 TOLL FREE: (800) 998-9288	WEB: WWW.GWCCNET.COM
MISSOURI	Self-Insured, Workers Comp, Self-Insured, Prior Authorization, Main Office	CORPORATE OFFICE MIDWESTERN REGION 1100 W 29TH ST SOUTH SIOUX CITY, NE 68776 PO BOX 277 SOUTH SIOUX CITY, NE 68776-0277	PHONE: (402) 494-2411 FAX: (402) 494-7450 TOLL FREE: (800) 228-8602	E-MAIL: Z.MARKETING@GWCCNET.COM WEB: WWW.GWCCNET.COM
MONTANA	Workers Comp, Self-Insured, Prior Authorization	WESTERN REGION 2950 E GOLDSTONE DR MERIDIAN, ID 83642 PO BOX 8007 BOISE, ID 83707	FAX: (208) 898-3905 TOLL FREE: (800) 628-4415	WEB: WWW.GWCCNET.COM
NEBRASKA	Self-Insured, Workers Comp, Self-Insured, Prior Authorization, Main Office	CORPORATE OFFICE MIDWESTERN REGION 1100 W 29TH ST SOUTH SIOUX CITY, NE 68776 PO BOX 277 SOUTH SIOUX CITY, NE 68776-0277	PHONE: (402) 494-2411 FAX: (402) 494-7450 TOLL FREE: (800) 228-8602	E-MAIL: Z.MARKETING@GWCCNET.COM WEB: WWW.GWCCNET.COM

NEW MEXICO	WESTERN REGION 2950 E GOLDSTONE DR MERIDIAN, ID 83642 PO BOX 8007 BOISE, ID 83707	FAX: (208) 898-3905 TOLL FREE: (800) 628-4415	WEB: WWW.GWCCNET.COM
NORTH CAROLINA	SOUTHEASTERN REGION 2030 FALLING WATER RD STE 300 KNOXVILLE, TN 37922 PO BOX 31289 KNOXVILLE, TN 37930-1289	PHONE: (865) 670-8850 FAX: (865) 670-6300 TOLL FREE: (800) 998-9288	WEB: WWW.GWCCNET.COM
NORTH DAKOTA	CORPORATE OFFICE MIDWESTERN REGION 1100 W 29TH ST SOUTH SIOUX CITY, NE 68776 PO BOX 277 SOUTH SIOUX CITY, NE 68776-0277	PHONE: (402) 494-2411 FAX: (402) 494-7450 TOLL FREE: (800) 228-8602	E-MAIL: Z.MARKETING@GWCCNET.COM WEB: WWW.GWCCNET.COM
OKLAHOMA	SOUTHERN REGION 624 SIX FLAGS DR STE 240 ARLINGTON, TX 76005 PO BOX 5408 ARLINGTON, TX 76011	FAX: (817) 385-2770 TOLL FREE: (800) 257-8757	WEB: WWW.GWCCNET.COM
OREGON	WESTERN REGION 2950 E GOLDSTONE DR MERIDIAN, ID 83642 PO BOX 8007 BOISE, ID 83707	FAX: (208) 898-3905 TOLL FREE: (800) 628-4415	WEB: WWW.GWCCNET.COM
SOUTH CAROLINA	SOUTHEASTERN REGION 2030 FALLING WATER RD STE 300 KNOXVILLE, TN 37922 PO BOX 31289 KNOXVILLE, TN 37930-1289	PHONE: (865) 670-8850 FAX: (865) 670-6300 TOLL FREE: (800) 998-9288	WEB: WWW.GWCCNET.COM
SOUTH DAKOTA	CORPORATE OFFICE MIDWESTERN REGION 1100 W 29TH ST SOUTH SIOUX CITY, NE 68776 PO BOX 277 SOUTH SIOUX CITY, NE 68776-0277	PHONE: (402) 494-2411 FAX: (402) 494-7450 TOLL FREE: (800) 228-8602	E-MAIL: Z.MARKETING@GWCCNET.COM WEB: WWW.GWCCNET.COM
TENNESSEE	SOUTHEASTERN REGION 2030 FALLING WATER RD STE 300 KNOXVILLE, TN 37922 PO BOX 31289 KNOXVILLE, TN 37930-1289	PHONE: (865) 670-8850 FAX: (865) 670-6300 TOLL FREE: (800) 998-9288	WEB: WWW.GWCCNET.COM
TEXAS	SOUTHERN REGION 624 SIX FLAGS DR STE 240 ARLINGTON, TX 76005 PO BOX 5408 ARLINGTON, TX 76011	FAX: (817) 385-2770 TOLL FREE: (800) 257-8757	WEB: WWW.GWCCNET.COM
UTAH	WESTERN REGION 2950 E GOLDSTONE DR MERIDIAN, ID 83642 PO BOX 8007 BOISE, ID 83707	FAX: (208) 898-3905 TOLL FREE: (800) 628-4415	WEB: WWW.GWCCNET.COM
VIRGINIA	SOUTHEASTERN REGION 2030 FALLING WATER RD STE 300 KNOXVILLE, TN 37922 PO BOX 31289 KNOXVILLE, TN 37930-1289	PHONE: (865) 670-8850 FAX: (865) 670-6300 TOLL FREE: (800) 998-9288	WEB: WWW.GWCCNET.COM
WASHINGTON	WESTERN REGION 2950 E GOLDSTONE DR MERIDIAN, ID 83642 PO BOX 8007 BOISE, ID 83707	FAX: (208) 898-3905 TOLL FREE: (800) 628-4415	WEB: WWW.GWCCNET.COM

WISCONSIN	CORPORATE OFFICE MIDWESTERN REGION 1100 W 29TH ST SOUTH SIOUX CITY, NE 68776 PO BOX 277 SOUTH SIOUX CITY, NE 68776-0277	PHONE: (402) 494-2411 FAX: (402) 494-7450 TOLL FREE: (800) 228-8602	E-MAIL: Z.MARKETING@GWCCNET.COM WEB: WWW.GWCCNET.COM
WYOMING	WESTERN REGION 2950 E GOLDSTONE DR MERIDIAN, ID 83642 PO BOX 8007 BOISE, ID 83707	FAX: (208) 898-3905 TOLL FREE: (800) 628-4415	WEB: WWW.GWCCNET.COM

GREAT WEST HEALTHCARE

NATIONAL	1000 GREAT WEST DR KENNETT, MO 63857-3749	TOLL FREE: (800) 325-5079	WEB: WWW.GREATWESTHEALTHCARE.COM OR WWW.MYGRESTWESTHEALTHCARE.COM
	6909 E GREENWAY PKY STE 180 SCOTTSDALE, AZ 85254	FAX: (602) 508-8972 TOLL FREE: (800) 233-5402	WEB: WWW.GREATWEST.COM
	8350 N CENTRAL EXPY STE M1000 DALLAS, TX 75206-1607	PHONE: (972) 813-6630 TOLL FREE: (800) 663-8081	WEB: WWW.MYGREATWEST.COM
	8515 E ORCHARD RD GREENWOOD VILLAGE, CO 80111-5037 PO BOX 1700 DENVER, CO 80201-1700	TOLL FREE: (800) 537-2033	WEB: WWW.MYGREATWEST.COM
	CLAIMS OFFICE 1000 GREAT WEST DR KENNETT, MO 63857	PHONE: (620) 224-5100 TOLL FREE: (800) 722-0087	WEB: WWW.GREATWESTHEALTHCARE.COM OR WWW. MYGREATWESTHEALTHCARE.COM
ALABAMA	PROVIDER RELATIONS SOUTHEAST REGION 1000 GREAT WEST DR KENNETT, MO 63857	PHONE: (888) 663-8081 FAX: (303) 801-5574 TOLL FREE: (800) 663-8081	WEB: WWW.GREATWESTHEALTHCARE.COM
ALASKA	PROVIDER RELATIONS PACIFIC REGION 655 N CENTRAL AVE 19TH FL GLENDALE, CA 91203	PHONE: (888) 663-8081 FAX: (866) 817-9344 TOLL FREE: (800) 663-8081	WEB: WWW.GREATWESTHEALTHCARE.COM
ARKANSAS	PROVIDER RELATIONS SOUTHWEST REGION 1000 GREATWEST DR KENNETT, MO 63857	PHONE: (888) 663-8081 FAX: (800) 663-8081	WEB: WWW.GREATWESTHEALTHCARE.COM OR WWW.MYGREATWESTHEALTHCARE.COM
CALIFORNIA	PROVIDER RELATIONS PACIFIC REGION 655 N CENTRAL AVE 19TH FL GLENDALE, CA 91203	PHONE: (888) 663-8081 FAX: (866) 817-9344 TOLL FREE: (800) 663-8081	WEB: WWW.GREATWESTHEALTHCARE.COM
CANADA	60 OSBOURNE ST N WINNIPEG, MB R3C 1V3 PO BOX 6000 WINNIPEG, MB R3C 3A5	PHONE: (204) 946-1190 TOLL FREE: (800) 665-0551 IN-STATE: (800) 957-9777	WEB: WWW.GREATWEST.COM
CONNECTICUT	PROVIDER RELATIONS EAST REGION ONE CENTENNIAL AVE PISCATAWAY, NJ 08855	PHONE: (732) 357-2900 FAX: (732) 357-2901 TOLL FREE: (888) 604-2200	WEB: WWW.GREATWESTHEALTHCARE.COM

DELAWARE *DISTRICT OF COLUMBIA*	PROVIDER RELATIONS EAST REGION ONE CENTENNIAL AVE PISCATAWAY, NJ 08855	PHONE: (732) 357-2900 FAX: (732) 357-2901 TOLL FREE: (888) 604-2200	WEB: WWW.GREATWESTHEALTHCARE.COM
FLORIDA *GEORGIA*	PROVIDER RELATIONS SOUTHEAST REGION 1000 GREAT WEST DR KENNETT, MO 63857	PHONE: (888) 663-8081 FAX: (303) 801-5574 TOLL FREE: (800) 663-8081	WEB: WWW.GREATWESTHEALTHCARE.COM
HAWAII *IDAHO*	PROVIDER RELATIONS PACIFIC REGION 655 N CENTRAL AVE 19TH FL GLENDALE, CA 91203	PHONE: (888) 663-8081 FAX: (866) 817-9344 TOLL FREE: (800) 663-8081	WEB: WWW.GREATWESTHEALTHCARE.COM
ILLINOIS *INDIANA* *IOWA* *KANSAS* *KENTUCKY*	PROVIDER RELATIONS MIDWEST REGION 1000 GREAT WEST DR KENNETT, MO 63857	PHONE: (888) 663-8081 FAX: (303) 801-5364 TOLL FREE: (800) 663-8081	WEB: WWW.GREATWESTHEALTHCARE.COM OR WWW.MYGREATWESTHEALTHCARE.COM
LOUISIANA	PROVIDER RELATIONS SOUTHWEST REGION 1000 GREATWEST DR KENNETT, MO 63857	PHONE: (888) 663-8081 FAX: (800) 663-8081	WEB: WWW.GREATWESTHEALTHCARE.COM OR WWW.MYGREATWESTHEALTHCARE.COM
MAINE *MARYLAND* *MASSACHUSETTS*	PROVIDER RELATIONS EAST REGION ONE CENTENNIAL AVE PISCATAWAY, NJ 08855	PHONE: (732) 357-2900 FAX: (732) 357-2901 TOLL FREE: (888) 604-2200	WEB: WWW.GREATWESTHEALTHCARE.COM
MICHIGAN *MINNESOTA*	PROVIDER RELATIONS MIDWEST REGION 1000 GREAT WEST DR KENNETT, MO 63857	PHONE: (888) 663-8081 FAX: (303) 801-5364 TOLL FREE: (800) 663-8081	WEB: WWW.GREATWESTHEALTHCARE.COM OR WWW.MYGREATWESTHEALTHCARE.COM
MISSISSIPPI	PROVIDER RELATIONS SOUTHWEST REGION 1000 GREATWEST DR KENNETT, MO 63857	PHONE: (888) 663-8081 FAX: (800) 663-8081	WEB: WWW.GREATWESTHEALTHCARE.COM OR WWW.MYGREATWESTHEALTHCARE.COM
MISSOURI	PROVIDER RELATIONS MIDWEST REGION 1000 GREAT WEST DR KENNETT, MO 63857	PHONE: (888) 663-8081 FAX: (303) 801-5364 TOLL FREE: (800) 663-8081	WEB: WWW.GREATWESTHEALTHCARE.COM OR WWW.MYGREATWESTHEALTHCARE.COM
NEW HAMPSHIRE *NEW JERSEY* *NEW MEXICO*	PROVIDER RELATIONS EAST REGION ONE CENTENNIAL AVE PISCATAWAY, NJ 08855	PHONE: (732) 357-2900 FAX: (732) 357-2901 TOLL FREE: (888) 604-2200	WEB: WWW.GREATWESTHEALTHCARE.COM
NORTH CAROLINA	PROVIDER RELATIONS SOUTHEAST REGION 1000 GREAT WEST DR KENNETT, MO 63857	PHONE: (888) 663-8081 FAX: (303) 801-5574 TOLL FREE: (800) 663-8081	WEB: WWW.GREATWESTHEALTHCARE.COM
OHIO	PROVIDER RELATIONS MIDWEST REGION 1000 GREAT WEST DR KENNETT, MO 63857	PHONE: (888) 663-8081 FAX: (303) 801-5364 TOLL FREE: (800) 663-8081	WEB: WWW.GREATWESTHEALTHCARE.COM OR WWW.MYGREATWESTHEALTHCARE.COM
	1000 GREST WEST DR KENNETT, MO 63857	PHONE: (440) 716-1777 FAX: (572) 559-6000 TOLL FREE: (800) 663-8081	WEB: WWW.GREATWEST.COM/PROVIDERS OR WWW.MYGREATWEST.COM
OKLAHOMA	PROVIDER RELATIONS SOUTHWEST REGION 1000 GREATWEST DR KENNETT, MO 63857	PHONE: (888) 663-8081 FAX: (800) 663-8081	WEB: WWW.GREATWESTHEALTHCARE.COM OR WWW.MYGREATWESTHEALTHCARE.COM

OREGON	PROVIDER RELATIONS PACIFIC REGION 655 N CENTRAL AVE 19TH FL GLENDALE, CA 91203	PHONE: (888) 663-8081 FAX: (866) 817-9344 TOLL FREE: (800) 663-8081	WEB: WWW.GREATWESTHEALTHCARE.COM
	CLAIMS OFFICE 1000 GREAT WEST DR KENNETT, MO 63857	PHONE: (620) 224-5100 TOLL FREE: (800) 722-0037	WEB: WWW.GREATWESTHEALTHCARE.COM OR WWW. MYGREATWESTHEALTHCARE.COM
PENNSYLVANIA *RHODE ISLAND*	PROVIDER RELATIONS EAST REGION ONE CENTENNIAL AVE PISCATAWAY, NJ 08855	PHONE: (732) 357-2900 FAX: (732) 357-2901 TOLL FREE: (888) 604-2200	WEB: WWW.GREATWESTHEALTHCARE.COM
SOUTH CAROLINA *TENNESSEE*	PROVIDER RELATIONS SOUTHEAST REGION 1000 GREAT WEST DR KENNETT, MO 63857	PHONE: (888) 663-8081 FAX: (303) 801-5574 TOLL FREE: (800) 663-8081	WEB: WWW.GREATWESTHEALTHCARE.COM
TEXAS	PROVIDER RELATIONS SOUTHWEST REGION 1000 GREATWEST DR KENNETT, MO 63857	PHONE: (888) 663-8081 FAX: (800) 663-8081	WEB: WWW.GREATWESTHEALTHCARE.COM OR WWW.MYGREATWESTHEALTHCARE.COM
VERMONT *VIRGINIA*	PROVIDER RELATIONS EAST REGION ONE CENTENNIAL AVE PISCATAWAY, NJ 08855	PHONE: (732) 357-2900 FAX: (732) 357-2901 TOLL FREE: (888) 604-2200	WEB: WWW.GREATWESTHEALTHCARE.COM
WASHINGTON	PROVIDER RELATIONS PACIFIC REGION 655 N CENTRAL AVE 19TH FL GLENDALE, CA 91203	PHONE: (888) 663-8081 FAX: (866) 817-9344 TOLL FREE: (800) 663-8081	WEB: WWW.GREATWESTHEALTHCARE.COM
WEST VIRGINIA	PROVIDER RELATIONS EAST REGION ONE CENTENNIAL AVE PISCATAWAY, NJ 08855	PHONE: (732) 357-2900 FAX: (732) 357-2901 TOLL FREE: (888) 604-2200	WEB: WWW.GREATWESTHEALTHCARE.COM
WISCONSIN	PROVIDER RELATIONS MIDWEST REGION 1000 GREAT WEST DR KENNETT, MO 63857	PHONE: (888) 663-8081 FAX: (303) 801-5364 TOLL FREE: (800) 663-8081	WEB: WWW.GREATWESTHEALTHCARE.COM OR WWW.MYGREATWESTHEALTHCARE.COM
WYOMING	6101 YELLOWSTONE RD STE 259 D CHEYENNE, WY 82009 PO BOX 12018 CHEYENNE, WY 82003	PHONE: (307) 637-8128 TOLL FREE: (800) 685-1060	WEB: WWW.MYGREATWEST.COM

GREAT WEST LIFE — *CANADA LIFE ASSURANCE CO*

ALBERTA	1901 SCARTH ST REGINA, SK S4P-4L4 PO BOX 4408 REGINA, SK S4P-3W7	PHONE: (306) 751-6020	WEB: WWW.GWL.CA

GREATER NEW YORK MUTUAL INSURANCE CO

CONNECTICUT	200 MADISON AVE NEW YORK, NY 10016-6023	PHONE: (212) 683-9700 FAX: (212) 779-6871 TOLL FREE: (800) 522-5504	WEB: WWW.GNY.COM
	95 GLASTONBURY BLVD 2ND FL GLASTONBURY, CT 06033-4438	PHONE: (860) 652-7090 FAX: (860) 652-7095 TOLL FREE: (800) 842-8354	WEB: WWW.GNY.COM

GREENTREE ADMINISTRATORS

NATIONAL	87 INTERSTATE 10 N 102 BEAUMONT, TX 77726 PO BOX 7306 BEAUMONT, TX 77726	PHONE: (409) 832-2335 TOLL FREE: (800) 470-8363	E-MAIL: PROVIDER@GREENTREEADMIN.COM WEB: WWW.GREENTREEADMIN.COM

GROCERS INSURANCE

NATIONAL	6400 SE LAKE RD PORTLAND, OR 97222 PO BOX 22146 PORTLAND, OR 97269	PHONE: (503) 833-1600 FAX: (503) 833-1699 TOLL FREE: (800) 777-3602	WEB: WWW.GROCINS.COM

GROUP & PENSION ADMINISTRATORS

NATIONAL	1500 N GREENVILLE AVE 4TH FL RICHARDSON, TX 75080-3541 PO BOX 834150 RICHARDSON, TX 75081	PHONE: (972) 238-7900 FAX: (972) 669-8155 TOLL FREE: (800) 827-7223 IN-STATE: (888) 611-7427	WEB: WWW.GPATPA.COM

GROUP BENEFIT ADMINISTRATORS — *WESTERN TEAMSTERS*

IDAHO *UTAH*	2621 S 3270 W SALT LAKE CITY, UT 84119 PO BOX 30749 SALT LAKE CITY, UT 84130	PHONE: (801) 972-1177 FAX: (801) 972-3364	

GROUP BENEFIT SERVICES, INC — *GBSIO*

NATIONAL	SIX N PARK DR STE 300 HUNT VALLEY, MD 21030	PHONE: (410) 832-1300 FAX: (410) 832-1315 TOLL FREE: (800) 638-6085	WEB: WWW.GBSIO.NET

GROUP DEKKO LLC

NATIONAL	6928 N 400 E KENDALLVILLE, IN 46755 PO BOX 2000 KENDALLVILLE, IN 46755	PHONE: (260) 347-0700 FAX: (260) 347-9537 TOLL FREE: (800) 829-9449	WEB: WWW.DEKKO.COM

GROUP HEALTH COOPERATIVE

IDAHO	521 WALL ST SEATTLE, WA 98121-1524	PHONE: (206) 448-5600 FAX: (206) 901-4612	E-MAIL: INFO@GHC.ORG WEB: WWW.GHC.ORG
	5615 W SUNSET HWY SPOKANE, WA 99224-9454 PO BOX 204 SPOKANE, WA 99210-0204	PHONE: (509) 838-9100 FAX: (509) 458-0368 TOLL FREE: (888) 742-3542	E-MAIL: INFO@GHC.ORG WEB: WWW.GHC.ORG

GROUP HEALTH COOPERATIVE

WISCONSIN	PO BOX 44971 MADISON, WI 53744-4971	PHONE: (608) 251-4156 FAX: (608) 257-3842 TOLL FREE: (800) 605-4327	WEB: WWW.GHC-HMO.COM
	2503 N HILLCREST PKY ALTOONA, WI 54720-2569 PO BOX 3217 EAU CLAIRE, WI 54702-3217	PHONE: (715) 552-4300 FAX: (715) 836-7683 TOLL FREE: (888) 203-7770	WEB: WWW.GROUP-HEALTH.COM

GROUP HEALTH MANAGERS

MICHIGAN	26205 FIVE MILE RD REDFORD, MI 48239-3154	PHONE: (313) 535-7100 FAX: (313) 535-7434 TOLL FREE: (800) 992-2508	WEB: WWW.IHGHM.COM

GROUP HEALTH PLAN — *GHP*

ILLINOIS *MISSOURI*	111 CORP OFFICE DR STE 400 EARTH CITY, MO 63045	TOLL FREE: (800) 755-3901	E-MAIL: INFO-GHP@CVTV.COM WEB: WWW.GHP.COM

GROUP INSURANCE SERVICE CENTER

NATIONAL	20 WINTER ST PEMBROOK, MA 02359-1987 PO BOX 9120 MARSHFIELD, MA 02050-9120	PHONE: (781) 829-8400 FAX: (781) 829-8723 TOLL FREE: (800) 242-4472 IN-STATE: (800) 242-3834	WEB: WWW.GISCINC.COM

GROUP SERVICES & ADMINISTRATION, INC

KANSAS *OKLAHOMA*	3113 CLASSEN BLVD OKLAHOMA CITY, OK 73118-3818	PHONE: (405) 528-4400 FAX: (405) 528-5558 TOLL FREE: (800) 475-4445	E-MAIL: GSAOKC@EARTHLINK.NET

GROUP SERVICES, INC

NATIONAL	3066 VICTORIA ST BETTENDORF, IA 52722-2793	PHONE: (563) 332-5552 FAX: (563) 332-7826 TOLL FREE: (800) 925-8846	

GUARANTEE TRUST LIFE

NATIONAL	1275 MILWAUKEE AVE GLENVIEW, IL 60025 PO BOX 1144 GLENVIEW, IL 60025	PHONE: (847) 699-0600 FAX: (847) 699-3227 OR (847) 699-6309 TOLL FREE: (800) 338-7452	WEB: WWW.GTLIC.COM

GUARDIAN LIFE INSURANCE CO OF AMERICA

NATIONAL	HOME OFFICE PO BOX 26100 LEHIGH VALEY, PA 18002-6100	PHONE: (212) 598-8400 FAX: (212) 598-8344 TOLL FREE: (800) 441-6455	WEB: WWW.GUARDIANLIFE.COM
	2300 E CAPITAL DR APPLETON, WI 54911 PO BOX 8007 OR PO BOX 8024 APPLETON, WI 54912	PHONE: (920) 749-9200 FAX: (920) 749-7119 OR 7120 TOLL FREE: (800) 873-4542	WEB: WWW.GLIC.COM
	3900 BURGESS PL BETHLEHEM, PA 18017 PO BOX 26020 LEHIGH VALLEY, PA 18002	PHONE: (610) 861-0733 FAX: (610) 807-8419 TOLL FREE: (888) 482-7342	WEB: WWW.GUARDIANLIFE.COM OR WWW.GLIC.COM
	WESTERN REGIONAL HOME OFFICE 777 E MAGNESIUM SPOKANE, WA 99208-5800	PHONE: (509) 468-6000 FAX: (509) 468-6320 TOLL FREE: (800) 873-4542	WEB: WWW.GUARDIANLIFE.COM
	BOSTON GROUP CLAIMS OFFICE ONE LAKESHORE DR BRIDGEWATER, MA 02324-1057 PO BOX 8024 APPLETON, WI 54912	FAX: (781) 982-3975 TOLL FREE: (800) 685-4542	WEB: WWW.GUARDIANLIFE.COM

GUIDEONE INSURANCE

NATIONAL	1111 ASHWORTH RD WEST DES MOINES, IA 50265-3538	PHONE: (515) 267-5500 FAX: (515) 267-5653 TOLL FREE: (877) 448-4331	WEB: WWW.GUIDEONE.COM
ALABAMA	2305 W PARK PL STE A STONE MOUNTAIN, GA 30087	PHONE: (770) 469-6006 FAX: (770) 879-2773 TOLL FREE: (800) 659-1232	WEB: WWW.GUIDEONE.COM

ALASKA *ARIZONA*	PMB 305 2351 SUNSET BLVD STE 170 ROCKLIN, CA 95765-4306	PHONE: (916) 624-3288 FAX: (916) 624-3378 TOLL FREE: (800) 647-9324	WEB: WWW.GUIDEONE.COM
ARKANSAS	300 W ARBROOK BLVD STE A ARLINGTON, TX 76014 PO BOX 99618 ARLINGTON, TX 76096-9618	PHONE: (817) 465-1441 FAX: (817) 465-2925 TOLL FREE: (800) 441-1554	E-MAIL: ARLINGTONBRANCH@GUIDONE.COM WEB: WWW.GUIDEONE.COM
CALIFORNIA	PMB 305 2351 SUNSET BLVD STE 170 ROCKLIN, CA 95765-4306	PHONE: (916) 624-3288 FAX: (916) 624-3378 TOLL FREE: (800) 647-9324	WEB: WWW.GUIDEONE.COM
CONNECTICUT *DELAWARE*	7702 WOODLAND DR STE 100 INDIANAPOLIS, IN 46278-2709	PHONE: (317) 802-0998 FAX: (317) 802-9249 TOLL FREE: (800) 678-2143	WEB: WWW.GUIDEONE.COM
FLORIDA	PO BOX 390 PERRY, FL 32348	PHONE: (850) 584-9535 FAX: (850) 584-9536 TOLL FREE: (800) 359-5127	WEB: WWW.GUIDEONE.COM
IDAHO	PMB 305 2351 SUNSET BLVD STE 170 ROCKLIN, CA 95765-4306	PHONE: (916) 624-3288 FAX: (916) 624-3378 TOLL FREE: (800) 647-9324	WEB: WWW.GUIDEONE.COM
ILLINOIS *INDIANA* *MAINE* *MARYLAND* *MASSACHUSETTS* *MICHIGAN*	7702 WOODLAND DR STE 100 INDIANAPOLIS, IN 46278-2709	PHONE: (317) 802-0998 FAX: (317) 802-9249 TOLL FREE: (800) 678-2143	WEB: WWW.GUIDEONE.COM
MISSOURI *NEVADA*	PMB 305 2351 SUNSET BLVD STE 170 ROCKLIN, CA 95765-4306	PHONE: (916) 624-3288 FAX: (916) 624-3378 TOLL FREE: (800) 647-9324	WEB: WWW.GUIDEONE.COM
NEW HAMPSHIRE *NEW JERSEY*	7702 WOODLAND DR STE 100 INDIANAPOLIS, IN 46278-2709	PHONE: (317) 802-0998 FAX: (317) 802-9249 TOLL FREE: (800) 678-2143	WEB: WWW.GUIDEONE.COM
NEW MEXICO	PMB 305 2351 SUNSET BLVD STE 170 ROCKLIN, CA 95765-4306	PHONE: (916) 624-3288 FAX: (916) 624-3378 TOLL FREE: (800) 647-9324	WEB: WWW.GUIDEONE.COM
NEW YORK *OHIO*	7702 WOODLAND DR STE 100 INDIANAPOLIS, IN 46278-2709	PHONE: (317) 802-0998 FAX: (317) 802-9249 TOLL FREE: (800) 678-2143	WEB: WWW.GUIDEONE.COM
OREGON	PMB 305 2351 SUNSET BLVD STE 170 ROCKLIN, CA 95765-4306	PHONE: (916) 624-3288 FAX: (916) 624-3378 TOLL FREE: (800) 647-9324	WEB: WWW.GUIDEONE.COM
PENNSYLVANIA *RHODE ISLAND*	7702 WOODLAND DR STE 100 INDIANAPOLIS, IN 46278-2709	PHONE: (317) 802-0998 FAX: (317) 802-9249 TOLL FREE: (800) 678-2143	WEB: WWW.GUIDEONE.COM
UTAH	PMB 305 2351 SUNSET BLVD STE 170 ROCKLIN, CA 95765-4306	PHONE: (916) 624-3288 FAX: (916) 624-3378 TOLL FREE: (800) 647-9324	WEB: WWW.GUIDEONE.COM
VERMONT	7702 WOODLAND DR STE 100 INDIANAPOLIS, IN 46278-2709	PHONE: (317) 802-0998 FAX: (317) 802-9249 TOLL FREE: (800) 678-2143	WEB: WWW.GUIDEONE.COM
WASHINGTON	PMB 305 2351 SUNSET BLVD STE 170 ROCKLIN, CA 95765-4306	PHONE: (916) 624-3288 FAX: (916) 624-3378 TOLL FREE: (800) 647-9324	WEB: WWW.GUIDEONE.COM
WEST VIRGINIA	7702 WOODLAND DR STE 100 INDIANAPOLIS, IN 46278-2709	PHONE: (317) 802-0998 FAX: (317) 802-9249 TOLL FREE: (800) 678-2143	WEB: WWW.GUIDEONE.COM
WYOMING	PMB 305 2351 SUNSET BLVD STE 170 ROCKLIN, CA 95765-4306	PHONE: (916) 624-3288 FAX: (916) 624-3378 TOLL FREE: (800) 647-9324	WEB: WWW.GUIDEONE.COM

GULF GUARANTY EMPLOYEE BENEFIT SERVICES, INC

ALABAMA *LOUISIANA* *MISSISSIPPI* *TEXAS*	4785 I-55 N STE 210 JACKSON, MS 39206 PO BOX 14977 JACKSON, MS 39236-4977	PHONE: (601) 981-9505 FAX: (601) 981-6805 TOLL FREE: (800) 890-7337	WEB: WWW.GGEBS.COM

GULFCO LIFE INSURANCE CO

LOUISIANA	660 N MAIN MARKSVILLE, LA 71351 PO BOX 157 MARKSVILLE, LA 71351-0157	PHONE: (318) 253-7564 FAX: (318) 253-4903	WEB: WWW.GULFCOLIFE.COM

GUY CARPENTER

NATIONAL	CORPORATE OFFICE ONE MADISON AVE NEW YORK, NY 10010	PHONE: (917) 937-3000 FAX: (917) 937-3500	WEB: WWW.GUYCARP.COM
PENNSYLVANIA	EXCESS REINSURANCE TWO LOGAN SQ 10TH FL PHILADELPHIA, PA 19103-2772	PHONE: (215) 864-3600 FAX: (215) 636-9929	WEB: WWW.GUYCARP.COM

HALLMARK SERVICES CORP — *SEE ALSO BLUE CROSS BLUE SHIELD*

HALLMARK SERVICES CORP HEADQUARTERS — *SEE ALSO BLUE CROSS BLUE SHIELD*

HAND & ASSOC — *SEE ALSO FLEX CORP*

HANOVER INSURANCE — *SEE ALSO CITIZENS INSURANCE CO*

HANOVER INSURANCE CO — *ALLMERICA FINANCIAL*

ARIZONA *ARKANSAS*	2200 PROFESSIONAL DR STE 200 ROSEVILLE, CA 95661-9971	PHONE: (916) 773-8077 FAX: (916) 773-8853 IN-STATE: (800) 955-8850	WEB: WWW.ALLMERICA.COM
ARKANSAS	10816 EXECUTIVE CTR DR STE 113 LITTLE ROCK, AR 72211-4381 PO BOX 24868 LITTLE ROCK, AR 72221-4868	PHONE: (501) 223-8249 FAX: (501) 223-8766 TOLL FREE: (800) 332-5513 IN-STATE: (800) 332-5513	WEB: WWW.ALLMERICA.COM
	OKLAHOMA REGIONAL OFFICE 5110 S YALE AVE STE 500 TULSA, OK 74135	PHONE: (918) 488-8700 TOLL FREE: (800) 256-9038	WEB: WWW.HANOVER.COM
CALIFORNIA *COLORADO*	2200 PROFESSIONAL DR STE 200 ROSEVILLE, CA 95661-9971	PHONE: (916) 773-8077 FAX: (916) 773-8853 IN-STATE: (800) 955-8850	WEB: WWW.ALLMERICA.COM
CONNECTICUT	CONNECTICUT REGIONAL OFFICE 95 GLASTON BLVD GLASTONBURY, CT 06033	PHONE: (860) 368-5030 FAX: (860) 368-5067 TOLL FREE: (800) 373-7822	WEB: WWW.ALLMERICA.COM
GEORGIA	GEORGIA REGIONAL OFFICE 6600 PEACHTREE DUNWOODY RD 600 EMBASSY ROW STE 500 ATLANTA, GA 30328 PO BOX 10319 ATLANTA, GA 30348	PHONE: (770) 353-6200 FAX: (770) 353-6169 TOLL FREE: (800) 343-4801	WEB: WWW.ALLMERICA.COM
IDAHO	2200 PROFESSIONAL DR STE 200 ROSEVILLE, CA 95661-9971	PHONE: (916) 773-8077 FAX: (916) 773-8853 IN-STATE: (800) 955-8850	WEB: WWW.ALLMERICA.COM
ILLINOIS	ILLINOIS REGIONAL OFFICE 333 W PIERCE RD STE 300 ITASCA, IL 60143 PO BOX 478 ITASCA, IL 60143-0478	PHONE: (630) 773-4266 FAX: (630) 773-3638 TOLL FREE: (800) 685-5669	WEB: WWW.ALLMERICA.COM
IOWA	2200 PROFESSIONAL DR STE 200 ROSEVILLE, CA 95661-9971	PHONE: (916) 773-8077 FAX: (916) 773-8853 IN-STATE: (800) 955-8850	WEB: WWW.ALLMERICA.COM

IOWA		ILLINOIS REGIONAL OFFICE 333 W PIERCE RD STE 300 ITASCA, IL 60143 PO BOX 478 ITASCA, IL 60143-0478	PHONE: (630) 773-4266 FAX: (630) 773-3638 TOLL FREE: (800) 685-5669	WEB: WWW.ALLMERICA.COM
KANSAS *LOUISIANA*		2200 PROFESSIONAL DR STE 200 ROSEVILLE, CA 95661-9971	PHONE: (916) 773-8077 FAX: (916) 773-8853 IN-STATE: (800) 955-8850	WEB: WWW.ALLMERICA.COM
LOUISIANA		LOUISIANA REGIONAL OFFICE 2400 VETERANS BLVD STE 400 KENNER, LA 70063 PO BOX 1758 KENNER, LA 70063-1758	PHONE: (504) 464-6012 FAX: (504) 461-4454 TOLL FREE: (800) 628-0250 IN-STATE: (800) 477-7661	WEB: WWW.ALLMERICA.COM
MAINE		MAINE REGIONAL OFFICE 27 PEARL ST PORTLAND, ME 04101 PO BOX 9801 PORTLAND, ME 04104	PHONE: (207) 771-5000 FAX: (207) 771-5100 TOLL FREE: (800) 492-0532	WEB: WWW.HANOVER.COM
MASSACHUSETTS		CORPORATE HEAD QUARTERS 440 LINCOLN ST WORCESTER, MA 01653 PO BOX 15145 WORCESTER, MA 01615-0145	PHONE: (508) 855-8000 OR (508) 855-1000 FAX: (800) 399-4734 TOLL FREE: (800) 628-0250 IN-STATE: (800) 922-8427	WEB: WWW.ALLMERICA.COM
MINNESOTA *MISSOURI*		2200 PROFESSIONAL DR STE 200 ROSEVILLE, CA 95661-9971	PHONE: (916) 773-8077 FAX: (916) 773-8853 IN-STATE: (800) 955-8850	WEB: WWW.ALLMERICA.COM
MISSOURI		OKLAHOMA REGIONAL OFFICE 5110 S YALE AVE STE 500 TULSA, OK 74135	PHONE: (918) 488-8700 TOLL FREE: (800) 256-9038	WEB: WWW.HANOVER.COM
MONTANA *NEBRASKA* *NEVADA*		2200 PROFESSIONAL DR STE 200 ROSEVILLE, CA 95661-9971	PHONE: (916) 773-8077 FAX: (916) 773-8853 IN-STATE: (800) 955-8850	WEB: WWW.ALLMERICA.COM
NEW HAMPSHIRE		TEN CORPORATE DR STE 201 BEDFORD, NH 03110	PHONE: (603) 472-9990 FAX: (603) 472-5588 TOLL FREE: (800) 628-0250 IN-STATE: (800) 421-9990	WEB: WWW.ALLMERICA.COM
NEW JERSEY		NEW JERSEY REGIONAL OFFICE 860 CENTENNIAL AVE PISCATAWAY, NJ 08854 PO BOX 1090 PISCATAWAY, NJ 08855	PHONE: (732) 457-0577 FAX: (732) 457-0282 TOLL FREE: (800) 628-0250 IN-STATE: (800) 257-5720	WEB: WWW.ALLMERICA.COM
NEW MEXICO		2200 PROFESSIONAL DR STE 200 ROSEVILLE, CA 95661-9971	PHONE: (916) 773-8077 FAX: (916) 773-8853 IN-STATE: (800) 955-8850	WEB: WWW.ALLMERICA.COM
NEW YORK		NEW JERSEY REGIONAL OFFICE 860 CENTENNIAL AVE PISCATAWAY, NJ 08854 PO BOX 1090 PISCATAWAY, NJ 08855	PHONE: (732) 457-0577 FAX: (732) 457-0282 TOLL FREE: (800) 628-0250 IN-STATE: (800) 257-5720	WEB: WWW.ALLMERICA.COM
		100 JERICHO QUADRANGLE JERICHO, NY 11753	PHONE: (516) 932-8150 FAX: (516) 932-8170	WEB: WWW.ALLMERICA.COM OR HANOVER.COM
		NEW YORK UPSTATE REGIONAL OFFICE 103 COMMERCE BLVD LIVERPOOL, NY 13088 PO BOX 4898 SYRACUSE, NY 13221-4898	PHONE: (315) 451-3970 FAX: (800) 955-7668 TOLL FREE: (800) 888-4925 IN-STATE: (800) 628-0250	WEB: WWW.HANOVER.COM
NORTH DAKOTA		2200 PROFESSIONAL DR STE 200 ROSEVILLE, CA 95661-9971	PHONE: (916) 773-8077 FAX: (916) 773-8853 IN-STATE: (800) 955-8850	WEB: WWW.ALLMERICA.COM

OKLAHOMA		10816 EXECUTIVE CTR DR STE 113 LITTLE ROCK, AR 72211-4381 PO BOX 24868 LITTLE ROCK, AR 72221-4868	PHONE: (501) 223-8249 FAX: (501) 223-8766 TOLL FREE: (800) 332-5513 IN-STATE: (800) 332-5513	WEB: WWW.ALLMERICA.COM
		OKLAHOMA REGIONAL OFFICE 5110 S YALE AVE STE 500 TULSA, OK 74135	PHONE: (918) 488-8700 TOLL FREE: (800) 256-9038	WEB: WWW.HANOVER.COM
OREGON		2200 PROFESSIONAL DR STE 200 ROSEVILLE, CA 95661-9971	PHONE: (916) 773-8077 FAX: (916) 773-8853 IN-STATE: (800) 955-8850	WEB: WWW.ALLMERICA.COM
RHODE ISLAND		CONNECTICUT REGIONAL OFFICE 95 GLASTON BLVD GLASTONBURY, CT 06033	PHONE: (860) 368-5030 FAX: (860) 368-5067 TOLL FREE: (800) 373-7822	WEB: WWW.ALLMERICA.COM
SOUTH DAKOTA *TEXAS*		2200 PROFESSIONAL DR STE 200 ROSEVILLE, CA 95661-9971	PHONE: (916) 773-8077 FAX: (916) 773-8853 IN-STATE: (800) 955-8850	WEB: WWW.ALLMERICA.COM
TEXAS		7557 RAMBLER RD DALLAS, TX 75231	PHONE: (214) 615-1510 FAX: (214) 750-3996 TOLL FREE: (800) 608-8141	WEB: WWW.HANOVER.COM
UTAH		2200 PROFESSIONAL DR STE 200 ROSEVILLE, CA 95661-9971	PHONE: (916) 773-8077 FAX: (916) 773-8853 IN-STATE: (800) 955-8850	WEB: WWW.ALLMERICA.COM
VIRGINIA		VIRGINIA REGIONAL OFFICE 7130 GLEN FOREST DR STE 400 RICHMOND, VA 23226 PO BOX 85612 RICHMOND, VA 23285-5612	PHONE: (804) 288-3113 FAX: (804) 288-9340 OR (804) 288-6946 TOLL FREE: (800) 552-3950 IN-STATE: (800) 552-3960	WEB: WWW.ALLMERICA.COM
WASHINGTON		2200 PROFESSIONAL DR STE 200 ROSEVILLE, CA 95661-9971	PHONE: (916) 773-8077 FAX: (916) 773-8853 IN-STATE: (800) 955-8850	WEB: WWW.ALLMERICA.COM
WISCONSIN		ILLINOIS REGIONAL OFFICE 333 W PIERCE RD STE 300 ITASCA, IL 60143 PO BOX 478 ITASCA, IL 60143-0478	PHONE: (630) 773-4266 FAX: (630) 773-3638 TOLL FREE: (800) 685-5669	WEB: WWW.ALLMERICA.COM

HANOVER INSURANCE GROUP

INDIANA		INDIANAPOLIS REGIONAL OFFICE 3950 PRIORITY WY S DR STE 200 INDIANAPOLIS, IN 46240 PO BOX 80812 INDIANAPOLIS, IN 46280	PHONE: (317) 580-9980 FAX: (317) 580-9981 TOLL FREE: (800) 289-2422	WEB: WWW.HANOVER.COM
MICHIGAN		MICHIGANS GREAT LAKES REGIONAL OFFICE 4100 EMBASSY DR SE GRAND RAPIDS, MI 49501 PO BOS 1928 GRAND RAPIDS, MI 49501	PHONE: (616) 942-2425 FAX: (616) 940-0769 OR (800) 270-8590 TOLL FREE: (800) 999-9621	WEB: WWW.HANOVER.COM
OHIO		INDIANAPOLIS REGIONAL OFFICE 3950 PRIORITY WY S DR STE 200 INDIANAPOLIS, IN 46240 PO BOX 80812 INDIANAPOLIS, IN 46280	PHONE: (317) 580-9980 FAX: (317) 580-9981 TOLL FREE: (800) 289-2422	WEB: WWW.HANOVER.COM

HAP — *SEE ALSO HEALTH ALLIANCE PLAN OF MICHIGAN*

HARLEYSVILLE INSURANCE

NATIONAL		355 MAPLE AVE HARLEYSVILLE, PA 19438-2297	PHONE: (215) 256-5000 FAX: (215) 256-5799 TOLL FREE: (800) 523-6344	WEB: WWW.HARLEYSVILLEGROUP.COM

HARRINGTON BENEFIT SERVICES, INC — *FISERV HEALTH*

NATIONAL	130 W 2ND ST STE 400 DAYTON, OH 45402 PO BOX 1391 DAYTON, OH 45401-1391	PHONE: (937) 226-8610 FAX: (937) 226-8640 TOLL FREE: (800) 222-2733 IN-STATE: (800) 523-9398	WEB: WWW.FISERVHEALTH-HARRINGTON.COM
	1302 N HWY 81 DUNCAN, OK 73533	PHONE: (580) 252-9355 FAX: (580) 252-2510 TOLL FREE: (800) 852-0914	WEB: WWW.HARRINGTONBENEFITS.COM
	55 E JACKSON BLVD CHICAGO, IL 60604-4103 PO BOX 74207 CHICAGO, IL 60690	PHONE: (312) 346-2626 FAX: (312) 663-9902 TOLL FREE: (800) 858-8563	WEB: WWW.HARRINGTONBENEFITS.COM
	675 BROOKSEDGE BLVD WESTERVILLE, OH 43081 PO BOX 16789 COLUMBUS, OH 43216	PHONE: (614) 212-7000 FAX: (614) 212-7080 TOLL FREE: (800) 848-4623	WEB: WWW.HARRINGTONBENEFITS.COM

HARTFORD FINANCIAL SERVICES GROUP — *SEE ALSO HARTFORD INSURANCE CO*

HARTFORD INSURANCE CO — *SE WORKERS COMPENSATION CLAIM CENTER*

NATIONAL	200 COLONIAL CENTER PKWY STE 500 LAKE MARY, FL 32746 PO BOX 14170 LEXINGTON, KY 40512	PHONE: (877) 673-9222 FAX: (860) 757-5984	WEB: WWW.THEHARTFORD.COM
ALABAMA	101 SOUTHHALL LN MAITLAND, FL 32751 PO BOX 940669 MAITLAND, FL 32794	FAX: (407) 875-8188 TOLL FREE: (800) 824-1732	WEB: WWW.THEHARTFORD.COM
	2502 ROCKY PT DR STE 400 TAMPA, FL 33607 PO BOX 30773 TAMPA, FL 33630-3733	PHONE: (813) 286-8243 FAX: (813) 286-8997 TOLL FREE: (800) 243-5860	WEB: WWW.THEHARTFORD.COM
ARIZONA	SOUTHWEST WORKERS COMP CLAIMS CENTER 785 GREENS PKWY HOUSTON, TX 77067 PO BOX 4626 HOUSTON, TX 77210	PHONE: (877) 889-9222 FAX: (877) 538-8966	WEB: WWW.THEHARTFORD.COM
ARKANSAS *COLORADO*	SOUTHWEST WORKERS COMP CLAIMS CENTER 785 GREENS PKWY HOUSTON, TX 77067 PO BOX 4626 HOUSTON, TX 77210	PHONE: (877) 889-9222 FAX: (877) 538-8966	WEB: WWW.THEHARTFORD.COM
CONNECTICUT	55 FARMINGTON AVE 1ST FL HARTFORD, CT 06105-3711 PO BOX 2923 HARTFORD, CT 06104-2923	PHONE: (860) 520-1600 FAX: (860) 520-2288 TOLL FREE: (866) 542-3330	WEB: WWW.THEHARTFORD.COM
CONNECTICUT *DELAWARE*	TWO ARMSTRONG RD SHELTON, CT 06484-4735 PO BOX 1000 SHELTON, CT 06484-1000	PHONE: (888) 625-2652 FAX: (860) 757-6747 TOLL FREE: (800) 766-9119	WEB: WWW.THEHARTFORD.COM
DISTRICT OF COLUMBIA *FLORIDA* *GEORGIA*	2502 ROCKY PT DR STE 400 TAMPA, FL 33607 PO BOX 30773 TAMPA, FL 33630-3733	PHONE: (813) 286-8243 FAX: (813) 286-8997 TOLL FREE: (800) 243-5860	WEB: WWW.THEHARTFORD.COM

IDAHO	Workers Comp, Vision	SOUTHWEST WORKERS COMP CLAIMS CENTER 785 GREENS PKWY HOUSTON, TX 77067 PO BOX 4626 HOUSTON, TX 77210	PHONE: (877) 889-9222 FAX: (877) 538-8966	WEB: WWW.THEHARTFORD.COM
ILLINOIS *INDIANA*		*IOWA* *KANSAS*	*KENTUCKY*	
	Workers Comp, Vision, Prior Authorization	7300 W 110TH ST OVERLAND PARK, KS 66210 PO BOX 2927 SHAWNEE MISSION, KS 66201	PHONE: (913) 693-8500 FAX: (877) 905-3340 OR (913) 693-8567 TOLL FREE: (877) 952-9222	WEB: WWW.THEHARTFORD.COM
LOUISIANA	Workers Comp, Vision	SOUTHWEST WORKERS COMP CLAIMS CENTER 785 GREENS PKWY HOUSTON, TX 77067 PO BOX 4626 HOUSTON, TX 77210	PHONE: (877) 889-9222 FAX: (877) 538-8966	WEB: WWW.THEHARTFORD.COM
MAINE	Self-Insured, Vision	TWO ARMSTRONG RD SHELTON, CT 06484-4735 PO BOX 1000 SHELTON, CT 06484-1000	PHONE: (888) 625-2652 FAX: (860) 757-6747 TOLL FREE: (800) 766-9119	WEB: WWW.THEHARTFORD.COM
MARYLAND	Self-Insured, Vision, Main Office	2502 ROCKY PT DR STE 400 TAMPA, FL 33607 PO BOX 30773 TAMPA, FL 33630-3733	PHONE: (813) 286-8243 FAX: (813) 286-8997 TOLL FREE: (800) 243-5860	WEB: WWW.THEHARTFORD.COM
MASSACHUSETTS	Self-Insured, Vision	TWO ARMSTRONG RD SHELTON, CT 06484-4735 PO BOX 1000 SHELTON, CT 06484-1000	PHONE: (888) 625-2652 FAX: (860) 757-6747 TOLL FREE: (800) 766-9119	WEB: WWW.THEHARTFORD.COM
MICHIGAN *MINNESOTA*	Workers Comp, Vision, Prior Authorization	7300 W 110TH ST OVERLAND PARK, KS 66210 PO BOX 2927 SHAWNEE MISSION, KS 66201	PHONE: (913) 693-8500 FAX: (877) 905-3340 OR (913) 693-8567 TOLL FREE: (877) 952-9222	WEB: WWW.THEHARTFORD.COM
MISSISSIPPI	Self-Insured, Vision, Main Office	2502 ROCKY PT DR STE 400 TAMPA, FL 33607 PO BOX 30773 TAMPA, FL 33630-3733	PHONE: (813) 286-8243 FAX: (813) 286-8997 TOLL FREE: (800) 243-5860	WEB: WWW.THEHARTFORD.COM
MISSOURI	Workers Comp, Vision, Prior Authorization	7300 W 110TH ST OVERLAND PARK, KS 66210 PO BOX 2927 SHAWNEE MISSION, KS 66201	PHONE: (913) 693-8500 FAX: (877) 905-3340 OR (913) 693-8567 TOLL FREE: (877) 952-9222	WEB: WWW.THEHARTFORD.COM
MONTANA	Workers Comp, Vision	SOUTHWEST WORKERS COMP CLAIMS CENTER 785 GREENS PKWY HOUSTON, TX 77067 PO BOX 4626 HOUSTON, TX 77210	PHONE: (877) 889-9222 FAX: (877) 538-8966	WEB: WWW.THEHARTFORD.COM
NEBRASKA	Workers Comp, Vision, Prior Authorization	7300 W 110TH ST OVERLAND PARK, KS 66210 PO BOX 2927 SHAWNEE MISSION, KS 66201	PHONE: (913) 693-8500 FAX: (877) 905-3340 OR (913) 693-8567 TOLL FREE: (877) 952-9222	WEB: WWW.THEHARTFORD.COM
NEW HAMPSHIRE *NEW JERSEY*	Self-Insured, Vision	TWO ARMSTRONG RD SHELTON, CT 06484-4735 PO BOX 1000 SHELTON, CT 06484-1000	PHONE: (888) 625-2652 FAX: (860) 757-6747 TOLL FREE: (800) 766-9119	WEB: WWW.THEHARTFORD.COM
NEW JERSEY	Workers Comp, Vision, Main Office	300 S STATE 7TH FL SYRACUSE, NY 13202 PO BOX 4771 SYRACUSE, NY 13221	PHONE: (877) 469-9222 FAX: (877) 536-3201	WEB: WWW.THEHARTFORD.COM

H

NEW MEXICO	Disability, EMC	SOUTHWEST WORKERS COMP CLAIMS CENTER 785 GREENS PKWY HOUSTON, TX 77067 PO BOX 4626 HOUSTON, TX 77210	PHONE: (877) 889-9222 FAX: (877) 538-8966	WEB: WWW.THEHARTFORD.COM
NEW YORK	Casualty/Liability, EMC	TWO ARMSTRONG RD SHELTON, CT 06484-4735 PO BOX 1000 SHELTON, CT 06484-1000	PHONE: (888) 625-2652 FAX: (860) 757-6747 TOLL FREE: (800) 766-9119	WEB: WWW.THEHARTFORD.COM
	Disability, EMC, 🏛	300 S STATE 7TH FL SYRACUSE, NY 13202 PO BOX 4771 SYRACUSE, NY 13221	PHONE: (877) 469-9222 FAX: (877) 536-3201	WEB: WWW.THEHARTFORD.COM
NORTH CAROLINA	Casualty/Liability, EMC, 🏛	2502 ROCKY PT DR STE 400 TAMPA, FL 33607 PO BOX 30773 TAMPA, FL 33630-3733	PHONE: (813) 286-8243 FAX: (813) 286-8997 TOLL FREE: (800) 243-5860	WEB: WWW.THEHARTFORD.COM
OKLAHOMA	Disability, EMC	SOUTHWEST WORKERS COMP CLAIMS CENTER 785 GREENS PKWY HOUSTON, TX 77067 PO BOX 4626 HOUSTON, TX 77210	PHONE: (877) 889-9222 FAX: (877) 538-8966	WEB: WWW.THEHARTFORD.COM
RHODE ISLAND	Casualty/Liability, EMC	TWO ARMSTRONG RD SHELTON, CT 06484-4735 PO BOX 1000 SHELTON, CT 06484-1000	PHONE: (888) 625-2652 FAX: (860) 757-6747 TOLL FREE: (800) 766-9119	WEB: WWW.THEHARTFORD.COM
SOUTH CAROLINA	Casualty/Liability, EMC, 🏛	2502 ROCKY PT DR STE 400 TAMPA, FL 33607 PO BOX 30773 TAMPA, FL 33630-3733	PHONE: (813) 286-8243 FAX: (813) 286-8997 TOLL FREE: (800) 243-5860	WEB: WWW.THEHARTFORD.COM
SOUTH DAKOTA	Disability, EMC, ☎	7300 W 110TH ST OVERLAND PARK, KS 66210 PO BOX 2927 SHAWNEE MISSION, KS 66201	PHONE: (913) 693-8500 FAX: (877) 905-3340 OR (913) 693-8567 TOLL FREE: (877) 952-9222	WEB: WWW.THEHARTFORD.COM
TEXAS	Disability, EMC	SOUTHWEST WORKERS COMP CLAIMS CENTER 785 GREENS PKWY HOUSTON, TX 77067 PO BOX 4626 HOUSTON, TX 77210	PHONE: (877) 889-9222 FAX: (877) 538-8966	WEB: WWW.THEHARTFORD.COM
	Casualty/Liability	MIDWEST COMMERCIAL AUTO & GENERAL LIABILITY CLAIMS SERVICE CENTER PO BOX 3118 NAPERVILLE, IL 60566-7118	PHONE: (877) 625-2652 FAX: (860) 757-5707	WEB: WWW.THEHARTFORD.COM
UTAH	Disability, EMC	SOUTHWEST WORKERS COMP CLAIMS CENTER 785 GREENS PKWY HOUSTON, TX 77067 PO BOX 4626 HOUSTON, TX 77210	PHONE: (877) 889-9222 FAX: (877) 538-8966	WEB: WWW.THEHARTFORD.COM
VIRGINIA	Casualty/Liability, EMC, 🏛	2502 ROCKY PT DR STE 400 TAMPA, FL 33607 PO BOX 30773 TAMPA, FL 33630-3733	PHONE: (813) 286-8243 FAX: (813) 286-8997 TOLL FREE: (800) 243-5860	WEB: WWW.THEHARTFORD.COM
WISCONSIN	Disability, EMC, ☎	7300 W 110TH ST OVERLAND PARK, KS 66210 PO BOX 2927 SHAWNEE MISSION, KS 66201	PHONE: (913) 693-8500 FAX: (877) 905-3340 OR (913) 693-8567 TOLL FREE: (877) 952-9222	WEB: WWW.THEHARTFORD.COM

H

WYOMING		SOUTHWEST WORKERS COMP CLAIMS CENTER 785 GREENS PKWY HOUSTON, TX 77067 PO BOX 4626 HOUSTON, TX 77210	PHONE: (877) 889-9222 FAX: (877) 538-8966	WEB: WWW.THEHARTFORD.COM

HARTFORD LIFE — *SEE ALSO HARTFORD INSURANCE CO*

HARTFORD MUTUAL INSURANCE CO — *FIRST LINE NATIONAL INSURANCE CO*

DELAWARE
DISTRICT OF COLUMBIA
MARYLAND
NEW JERSEY
NORTH CAROLINA
TENNESSEE
VIRGINIA

		200 N MAIN ST BEL AIR, MD 21014-3544	PHONE: (410) 838-4000 FAX: (410) 838-8675 TOLL FREE: (800) 638-3659	WEB: WWW.HARTFORDMUTUAL.COM

HARTFORD, THE

ILLINOIS *IOWA*		4245 MERIDIAN PKY AURORA, IL 60504 PO BOX 400 SHAWNEE MISSION, KS 66201	PHONE: (630) 692-8000 FAX: (630) 692-6601 TOLL FREE: (800) 843-7006	WEB: WWW.THEHARTFORD.COM

HARVARD COMMUNITY HEALTH PLAN — *SEE ALSO HARVARD PILGRIM HEALTH CARE, INC*

HARVARD PILGRIM HEALTH CARE, INC

NATIONAL		1600 CROWN COLONY DR QUINCY, MA 02169-0913	PHONE: (617) 509-1000 FAX: (617) 509-1050 TOLL FREE: (888) 888-4742	WEB: WWW.HPHC.ORG
MASSACHUSETTS		93 WORCHESTER ST WELLESLEY, MA 02481-0000 PO BOX 699183 QUINCY, MA 02269-9183	PHONE: (888) 333-4742 FAX: (617) 509-1983 TOLL FREE: (800) 338-4247	E-MAIL: PROVIDER_CALLCENTER@HPHC.ORG WEB: WWW.HARVARDPILGRIM.ORG

HARVARD UNIVERSITY GROUP HEALTH PROGRAM — *UNIVERSITY HEALTH SERVICES*

MASSACHUSETTS	℞	75 MT AUBURN ST CAMBRIDGE, MA 02138-4960	PHONE: (617) 495-2008 FAX: (617) 496-6125	E-MAIL: MSERVICE@UHS.HARDVARD.EDU WEB: WWW.UHS.HARVARD.EDU

HAWKEYE SECURITY INSURANCE

IOWA *KANSAS* *MISSOURI*		1245 JORDAN CREEK PKY WEST DES MOINES, IA 50266 PO BOX 1848 DES MOINES, IA 50306-1848	PHONE: (515) 471-3600 FAX: (515) 284-0391 TOLL FREE: (800) 747-7833 OR (800) 558-1396	WEB: WWW.HAWKEYESECURITY-INS.COM
MISSOURI		10825 WATSON RD STE 230 ST LOUIS, MO 63127	PHONE: (314) 957-4100 FAX: (314) 957-4283 IN-STATE: (800) 558-1396	WEB: WWW.HAWKEYESECURITY-INS.COM
NEBRASKA		1245 JORDAN CREEK PKY WEST DES MOINES, IA 50266 PO BOX 1848 DES MOINES, IA 50306-1848	PHONE: (515) 471-3600 FAX: (515) 284-0391 TOLL FREE: (800) 747-7833 OR (800) 558-1396	WEB: WWW.HAWKEYESECURITY-INS.COM

HCA — *SEE ALSO WESLEY MEDICAL CENTER*

HCC BENEFITS CORPORATION

NATIONAL	3	225 TOWN PARK DR STE 145 KENNESAW, GA 30144	PHONE: (800) 447-0460	WEB: WWW.HCCLIFE.COM

HCH ADMINISTRATORS, INC

NATIONAL	209 W RB GARRETT AVE PEORIA, IL 61605 PO BOX 285 PEORIA, IL 61650-0285	PHONE: (309) 673-7330 TOLL FREE: (800) 322-1516	WEB: WWW.HCHADMIN.COM

HEALTH ADVANTAGE HMO PARTNERS

ARKANSAS	320 W CAPITAL DR LITTLE ROCK, AR 72203 PO BOX 8069 LITTLE ROCK, AR 72203	PHONE: (800) 843-1329 FAX: (501) 212-8513 TOLL FREE: (800) 354-9904	WEB: WWW.HEALTHADVANTAGE-HMO.COM

HEALTH AGENCIES OF THE WEST, INC

CALIFORNIA	500 N STATE COLLEGE BLVD STE 880 ORANGE, CA 92868-1646	PHONE: (714) 769-3000 FAX: (714) 769-3010 TOLL FREE: (800) 556-0800	E-MAIL: INFO@HEALTHAGENCIES.COM WEB: WWW.HEALTHAGENCIES.COM

HEALTH ALLIANCE

ILLINOIS *IOWA*	301 S VINE ST URBANA, IL 61801 PO BOX 6003 URBANA, IL 61803	PHONE: (217) 337-8100 FAX: (217) 337-8008 TOLL FREE: (800) 851-3379	WEB: WWW.HEALTHALLIANCE.ORG

H

HEALTH ALLIANCE PLAN OF MICHIGAN — *HAP*

MICHIGAN	2850 W GRAND BLVD DETROIT, MI 48202-2692	PHONE: (313) 872-8100 TOLL FREE: (800) 422-4641 IN-STATE: (800) 367-3292	WEB: WWW.HAP.ORG

HEALTH AMERICA — *HEALTH ASSURANCE*

PENNSYLVANIA	3721 TECHPORT DR HARRISBURG, PA 17111 PO BOX 67103 HARRISBURG, PA 17106-7103	PHONE: (717) 540-4260 FAX: (717) 541-5921 TOLL FREE: (800) 788-6445

HEALTH ASSURANCE — *SEE ALSO HEALTH AMERICA*

HEALTH BENEFIT TRUST FUND LOCAL 94

NEW YORK	331-337 W 44TH ST NEW YORK, NY 10036-5402	PHONE: (212) 541-9880 FAX: (212) 245-7886	WEB: WWW.LOCAL94.COM

HEALTH BENEFIT, INC

PENNSYLVANIA	375 HORSHAM RD STE 206 HORSHAM, PA 19044 PO BOX 1040 WILLOW GROVE, PA 19090	PHONE: (215) 957-1700 FAX: (215) 957-1717

HEALTH CARE ADMINISTRATORS, INC — *ARNETT HEALTH PLANS*

INDIANA	415 N 26TH ST STE 101 LAFAYETTE, IN 47904-6108 PO BOX 6108 LAFAYETTE, IN 47903-6108	PHONE: (765) 448-7400 FAX: (765) 448-7700 TOLL FREE: (888) 448-7447	WEB: WWW.ARNETTPLAN.COM

HEALTH ECONOMICS GROUP, INC

NATIONAL	1050 UNIVERSITY AVE STE A ROCHESTER, NY 14607	PHONE: (585) 241-9500 FAX: (585) 241-9518 TOLL FREE: (800) 666-6690	E-MAIL: MEDICAL@HEGINC.COM WEB: WWW.HEGINC.COM

HEALTH FIRST

FLORIDA	6450 US HWY 1 ROCKLEDGE, FL 32955	PHONE: (321) 434-4300	WEB: WWW.HEALTH-FIRST.ORG

HEALTH FUTURE, LLC

OREGON	825 E MAIN ST STE D MEDFORD, OR 97504-7156	PHONE: (541) 772-3062 FAX: (541) 772-3181 TOLL FREE: (800) 452-2558	WEB: WWW.HEALTHFUTURE.ORG

HEALTH GROUP LLC, THE

ILLINOIS INDIANA OHIO	8802 N MERIDIAN ST STE 100 INDIANAPOLIS, IN 46260-5371	PHONE: (317) 571-5300 FAX: (317) 571-5342 TOLL FREE: (800) 878-8802	WEB: WWW.THCG.ORG

HEALTH INSURANCE PLAN OF GREATER NEW YORK

CONNECTICUT MASSACHUSETTS NEW YORK	55 WATER ST NEW YORK, NY 10041-8190	PHONE: (646) 447-5000 TOLL FREE: (800) 447-8255	WEB: WWW.HIPUSA.COM

HEALTH NET — *SEE ALSO PHYSICIANS HEALTH SERVICES OF NEW YORK, INC*

CALIFORNIA	21281 BURBANK BLVD WOODLAND HILLS, CA 91367-6607 PO BOX 9103 VAN NUYS, CA 91409-9103	PHONE: (818) 676-5000 TOLL FREE: (800) 641-7761 IN-STATE: (800) 929-9224	WEB: WWW.HEALTHNET.COM
OREGON	13221 SW 68TH PWY TIGARD, OR 97223	PHONE: (888) 802-7001 TOLL FREE: (888) 802-7001	E-MAIL: SERVICE@HEALTHNET.COM WEB: WWW.HEALTHNET.COM
SOUTH CAROLINA	TRI NORTH REGION PO BOX 870140 SURFSIDE BEACH, SC 29587-9740	PHONE: (877) 874-2273	WEB: WWW.HEALTHNETFEDERALSERVICES.COM
WASHINGTON	13221 SW 68TH PWY TIGARD, OR 97223	PHONE: (888) 802-7001 TOLL FREE: (888) 802-7001	E-MAIL: SERVICE@HEALTHNET.COM WEB: WWW.HEALTHNET.COM

HEALTH NET

ARIZONA	1230 W WSHINGTON ST. STE 401 TEMPE, AZ 85281	PHONE: (602) 794-1515 FAX: (602) 794-1803 TOLL FREE: (800) 289-3818	WEB: WWW.HEALTHNET.COM
CONNECTICUT NEW JERSEY NEW YORK PENNSYLVANIA	NORTHEAST REGION ONE FAR MILL CROSSING SHELTON, CT 06484-6121 PO BOX 904 SHELTON, CT 06484-0944	PHONE: (203) 402-4700 OR (203) 402-6003 FAX: (203) 225-4000 TOLL FREE: (800) 848-4747	WEB: WWW.HEALTHNET.COM

HEALTH NETWORK AMERICA, INC

NATIONAL	246 INDUSTRIAL WY W EATONTOWN, NJ 07724	PHONE: (732) 676-2630 FAX: (732) 676-2656 TOLL FREE: (800) 332-7772	WEB: WWW.HEALTHNETWORKAMERICA.COM

HEALTH NEW ENGLAND

CONNECTICUT MASSACHUSETTS	ONE MONARCH PL STE 1500 SPRINGFIELD, MA 01144-1500	PHONE: (413) 787-4000 FAX: (413) 731-7498 TOLL FREE: (800) 842-4464	WEB: WWW.HNE.COM

HEALTH PARTNERS

MINNESOTA *NORTH DAKOTA*	8100 34TH AVE S BLOOMINGTON, MN 55425 PO BOX 1309 MINNEAPOLIS, MN 55440-1309	PHONE: (952) 883-6000 FAX: (952) 883-5666 TOLL FREE: (800) 883-2177	WEB: WWW.HEALTHPARTNERS.COM
PENNSYLVANIA	901 MARKET ST PHILADELPHIA, PA 19107	PHONE: (215) 849-9606 FAX: (215) 849-7097 OR (215) 849-7097 TOLL FREE: (888) 991-9023	WEB: WWW.HEALTHPART.COM
SOUTH DAKOTA	8100 34TH AVE S BLOOMINGTON, MN 55425 PO BOX 1309 MINNEAPOLIS, MN 55440-1309	PHONE: (952) 883-6000 FAX: (952) 883-5666 TOLL FREE: (800) 883-2177	WEB: WWW.HEALTHPARTNERS.COM

HEALTH PARTNERS CENTRAL MINNESOTA CLINICS/PHARMACY

MINNESOTA	1245 15TH ST N ST CLOUD, MN 56303-1821	PHONE: (320) 259-7321 FAX: (320) 203-2105 TOLL FREE: (800) 284-3142	WEB: WWW.HEALTHPARTNERS.COM

HEALTH PLAN — *SEE ALSO HEALTHFIRST TPA, INC*

HEALTH PLAN ADMINISTRATORS, INC

NATIONAL	523 COLEMAN CENTER DR ROCKFORD, IL 61108 PO BOX 15250 ROCKFORD, IL 61132	PHONE: (815) 633-5800 FAX: (815) 633-0277 TOLL FREE: (800) 397-5800	E-MAIL: AGENTSUPPORT@HPA-INC.COM WEB: WWW.HPA-INC.COM

HEALTH PLAN OF NEVADA, INC — *SIERRA HEALTH SERVICES*

NEVADA	2716 N. TENAYA WAY LAS VEGAS, NV 89114 PO BOX 15645 LAS VEGAS, NV 89114-5645	PHONE: (702) 242-7300 FAX: (702) 242-9038 TOLL FREE: (800) 777-1840	WEB: WWW.SIERRAHEALTH.COM OR WWW.HEALTHPLANOFNEVADA,COM

HEALTH PLAN SERVICES

NATIONAL	3501 E FRONTAGE RD TAMPA, FL 33607 PO BOX 30098 TAMPA, FL 33630-3098	PHONE: (813) 289-1000 FAX: (813) 289-7937 TOLL FREE: (800) 237-7767	WEB: WWW.HEALTHPLAN.COM

HEALTH PLAN, THE

OHIO *WEST VIRGINIA*	52160 NATIONAL RD E ST CLAIRSVILLE, OH 43950 PO BOX 10 ST CLAIRSVILLE, OH 43950	PHONE: (740) 695-3585 FAX: (740) 695-5297 TOLL FREE: (800) 624-6961	WEB: WWW.HEALTHPLAN.ORG

HEALTH PLUS OF MICHIGAN

MICHIGAN	2050 S LINDEN RD FLINT, MI 48501-1700 PO BOX 1700 FLINT, MI 48501-1700	PHONE: (810) 230-2000 FAX: (810) 230-2208 TOLL FREE: (800) 332-9161 IN-STATE: (800) 345-9956	WEB: WWW.HEALTHPLUS.COM

HEALTH SERVICES BENEFITS ADMINISTRATORS — *HEALTH SERVICES FOUNDATION*

CALIFORNIA	160 AIRWAY BLVD LIVERMORE, CA 94551	PHONE: (925) 449-7070 FAX: (925) 443-2035 IN-STATE: (800) 528-4357	E-MAIL: WEBMASTER@HSBA.COM WEB: WWW.HSBA.COM

HEALTH SERVICES FOUNDATION — *SEE ALSO HEALTH SERVICES BENEFITS ADMINISTRATORS*

HEALTH SPECIAL RISK, INC

NATIONAL	4001 N JOSEY LN CARROLLTON, TX 75007-1520	PHONE: (972) 492-6474 FAX: (972) 492-4946 TOLL FREE: (800) 328-1174	WEB: WWW.HEALTHSPECIALRISK.COM

HEALTH SYSTEMS INTERNATIONAL

NATIONAL	5975 CASTLE CREEK PKY STE 100 INDIANAPOLIS, IN 46250	PHONE: (317) 806-2000 FAX: (317) 806-2032 TOLL FREE: (800) 962-6831	WEB: WWW.US-HSI.COM

HEALTHCARE PARTNERS MEDICAL GROUP, INC

CALIFORNIA	19191 S VERMONT AVE 7TH FL TORRANCE, CA 90505 PO BOX 6099 TORRANCE, CA 90504	PHONE: (310) 214-0811 FAX: (310) 352-6219 TOLL FREE: (800) 403-4160	WEB: WWW.HEALTHCAREPARTNERS.COM

HEALTHCARE SOLUTIONS GROUP, INC

NATIONAL	2401 CHANDLER RD STE 300 MUSKOGEE, OK 74403 PO BOX 1309 MUSKOGEE, OK 74402	PHONE: (918) 687-1261 FAX: (918) 781-4981 TOLL FREE: (800) 749-1422	WEB: WWW.HSG.COM

HEALTHCARE USA OF MISSOURI LLC

MISSOURI	10 S BROADWAY STE 1200 ST LOUIS, MO 63102 PO BOX 7629 LONDON, KY 40742	PHONE: (314) 241-5300 FAX: (314) 241-8010 TOLL FREE: (800) 566-6444	WEB: WWW.CHCHCUSA.COM

HEALTHCOMP

NATIONAL	1818 WESTLAKE AVE N STE 314 SEATTLE, WA 98109	PHONE: (206) 378-1686 TOLL FREE: (800) 647-7247	WEB: WWW.HEALTHCOMP.COM
	621 SANTA FE FRESNO, CA 93721 PO BOX 45018 FRESNO, CA 93718-5018	PHONE: (559) 499-2450 FAX: (559) 499-2464 TOLL FREE: (800) 442-7247	WEB: WWW.HEALTHCOMP.COM

HEALTHFIRST 65 PLUS — *SEE ALSO MANAGED HEALTH, INC*

HEALTHFIRST TPA, INC — *HEALTH PLAN*

NATIONAL	821 E SE LOOP 323 STE 200 TYLER, TX 75701-1908 PO BOX 130217 TYLER, TX 75713	PHONE: (903) 581-2600 FAX: (903) 509-5725 TOLL FREE: (800) 477-2287 IN-STATE: (800) 477-2287	WEB: WWW.HFTPA.COM

HEALTHLINK, INC

NATIONAL	12443 OLIVE BLVD ST LOUIS, MO 63141	PHONE: (314) 989-6000 FAX: (314) 989-6635 TOLL FREE: (877) 284-0101	WEB: WWW.HEALTHLINK.COM

HEALTHNET OREGON

KENTUCKY *OREGON* *WASHINGTON*	PO BOX 14130 LEXINGTON, KY 40512	TOLL FREE: (888) 802-7001	WEB: WWW.HEALTHNET.COM

HEALTHNOW NY, INC — *BUFFALO DIVISION OF HEALTHNOW*

NEW YORK	1901 MAIN ST BUFFALO, NY 14208-0080 PO BOX 80 BUFFALO, NY 14240-1199	PHONE: (716) 887-6900 FAX: (716) 887-8981 TOLL FREE: (800) 888-0757	WEB: WWW.HEALTHNOWNY.COM

HEALTHPLAN MANAGEMENT, INC — *AMERICAN CHOICE HEALTH PLAN*

NATIONAL	101 WAUKEGAN RD STE 700 LAKE BLUFF, IL 60044	PHONE: (847) 234-8870 FAX: (847) 234-9244	

HEALTHPLEX, INC — *DENTCARE DELIVERY SYSTEMS, INC / INTERNATIONAL HEALTHCARE SERVICES, INC*

NEW JERSEY *NEW YORK*	333 EARL OVINGTON BLVD UNIONDALE, NY 11553	PHONE: (516) 542-2200 FAX: (516) 794-3186 TOLL FREE: (800) 468-0608 IN-STATE: (8000 468-0600	E-MAIL: INFO@HEALTHPLEX.COM WEB: WWW.HEALTHPLEX.COM

HEALTHSPRING

ALABAMA	TWO PERIMETER PARK S STE 300 W BIRMINGHAM, AL 35243-2329	PHONE: (205) 968-1000 FAX: (205) 968-1092 TOLL FREE: (800) 888-7647	WEB: WWW.HEALTHSPINGOFALABAMA.COM
TENNESSEE	44 VANTAGE WY STE 300 NASHVILLE, TN 37228 PO BOX 2000 NASHVILLE, TN 37202	PHONE: (615) 291-7000 FAX: (615) 401-4647 OR (615) 401-4662 TOLL FREE: (800) 881-9466 IN-STATE: (800) 230-6138	WEB: WWW.MYHEALTHSPRING.COM

HEART OF AMERICA HEALTH PLAN

NORTH DAKOTA	810 S MAIN AVE RUGBY, ND 58368	PHONE: (701) 776-5848 FAX: (701) 776-5425 TOLL FREE: (800) 525-5661	WEB: WWW.HOAHP.COM

HELLER ASSOCIATES

NATIONAL	2755 BRISTOL ST STE 250 COSTA MESA, CA 92626-5985	PHONE: (714) 549-7052 FAX: (714) 549-4816 TOLL FREE: (800) 552-2929	E-MAIL: CLAIMS@HELLERTPA.COM WEB: WWW.HELLERTPA.COM
	8228 MAYFIELD RD STE 5B CHESTERLAND, OH 44026	PHONE: (440) 729-1999 FAX: (440) 729-2566 TOLL FREE: (800) 552-2929	E-MAIL: CLAIMS@HELLERTPA.COM WEB: WWW.HELLERTPA.COM

HELMSMAN MANAGEMENT SERVICES, INC — *LIBERTY MUTUAL INSURANCE*

NATIONAL	225 W BROADWAY STE 500 GLENDALE, CA 91204 PO BOX 29073 GLENDALE, CA 91209	PHONE: (818) 240-1234 FAX: (603) 334-0221 TOLL FREE: (800) 281-1120	WEB: WWW.LIBERTYMUTUAL.COM/HELMSMAN

HERITAGE INSURANCE MANAGERS, INC — *INSURANCE ASSOCIATES*

ARKANSAS *TEXAS*	919 ISOM RD STE A SAN ANTONIO, TX 78216-4136 PO BOX 659570 SAN ANTONIO, TX 78265-9570	PHONE: (210) 829-7467 FAX: (210) 822-4113 TOLL FREE: (800) 456-7480	E-MAIL: INFO@HERITAGE-INS.COM WEB: WWW.HERITAGE-INS.COM

HIGHMARK — *SEE ALSO BLUE CROSS BLUE SHIELD*

HILB ROGAL & HOBBS COMPANY / HRH

OHIO

2245 N BANK DR
COLUMBUS, OH 43220-5438
PO BOX 20945
COLUMBUS, OH 43220-0945

PHONE: (614) 457-7000
FAX: (614) 457-1507
TOLL FREE: (800) 837-0503
IN-STATE: (800) 837-0503

WEB: WWW.HRH COM

HIP HEALTH PLAN OF NEW YORK

NATIONAL

55 WATER ST
NEW YORK, NY 10041
PO BOX 2845
NEW YORK, NY 10016

PHONE: (212) 630-5000
FAX: (646)447-3165
TOLL FREE: (800) 447-8255

WEB: WWW.HIPUSA.COM

HMA, INC

NATIONAL

1600 W BROADWAY RD STE 300
TEMPE, AZ 85282-1137

PHONE: (480) 921-8944
FAX: (480) 894-5230
TOLL FREE: (800) 448-3535

WEB: WWW.HMA-INC.COM

HOLYOKE MUTUAL INSURANCE CO

CONNECTICUT
MASSACHUSETTS

39 NORMAN ST
SALEM, MA 01970-3357
PO BOX 2006
SALEM, MA 01970

PHONE: (978) 744-6123
FAX: (978) 744-5677
TOLL FREE: (800) 225-2533

E-MAIL: INFO@HOLYOKEMUTUAL.COM
WEB: WWW.HOLYOKEMUTUAL.COM

HOMETOWN HEALTH PLAN

NEVADA

830 HARVARD WY
RENO, NV 89502-1823

PHONE: (775) 982-3000
FAX: (775) 982-3171
TOLL FREE: (800) 336-0123

WEB: WWW.HOMETOWNHEALTH.COM

HOMETOWN INSURANCE GROUP, INC. — *SEE ALSO THE HEALTH PLAN*

HORACE MANN COMPANIES

NATIONAL

ONE HORACE MANN PLZ
SPRINGFIELD, IL 62715

PHONE: (217) 789-2500
FAX: (217) 788-5161
TOLL FREE: (800) 999-1030

WEB: WWW.HORACEMANN.COM

HORIZON BLUE CROSS BLUE SHIELD OF NEW JERSEY

NEW JERSEY

THREE PENN PLZ E
NEWARK, NJ 07105-2200
PO BOX 820
NEWARK, NJ 07101-0820

PHONE: (973) 466-4000
TOLL FREE: (800) 355-2583

E-MAIL: HORIZONBLUE.COM
WEB: WWW.HORIZON-BCBSNJ.COM

HOSPITAL BENEFITS, INC

NATIONAL

765 DOUGLAS AVE
ALTAMONTE SPRINGS, FL 32714-2566
PO BOX 162148
ALTAMONTE SPRINGS, FL 32716

PHONE: (407) 862-0311
FAX: (407) 862-0201
TOLL FREE: (800) 883-0311

WEB: WWW.HBIFLM.COM

HOTEL & RESTAURANT EMPLOYEES INT'L UNION WELFARE PENSION FUNDS

NATIONAL

711 N COMMONS DR
AURORA, IL 60504
PO BOX 6020
AURORA, IL 60598

PHONE: (630) 236-5100
FAX: (630) 236-4394

WEB: WWW.HEREIUFUND.COM

H

HOUSING AUTHORITY INSURANCE GROUP

NATIONAL
189 COMMERCE CT
CHESHIRE, CT 06410-1253
PO BOX 189
CHESHIRE, CT 06410-0189
PHONE: (203) 272-8220
FAX: (203) 250-8377
WEB: WWW.HOUSINGCENTER.COM

HOUSTON CASULTY COMPANY

NATIONAL
13403 NORTHWEST FWY
HOUSTON, TX 77040-6094
PHONE: (713) 462-1000
FAX: (713) 744-9675
WEB: WWW.HCCH.COM

HUMAN RESOURCE BENEFIT ADMINISTRATORS

NATIONAL
9000 E NICHOLS AVE
CENTENNIAL, CO 80112
PHONE: (303) 792-3311
FAX: (303) 790-0599
TOLL FREE: (800) 742-4722
WEB: WWW.HRBENEFITS.NET

HUMANA DENTAL SERVICES

NATIONAL
325 REID ST
GREEN BAY, WI 54115
PO BOX 19049
GREEN BAY, WI 54307-9049
PHONE: (920) 337-3977
FAX: (920) 337-7331
TOLL FREE: (800) 955-0783
WEB: WWW.HUMANADENTAL.COM

HUMANA, INC

NATIONAL
PO BOX 14601
LEXINGTON, KY 40512-4512
TOLL FREE: (800) 457-4708
IN-STATE: (800) 448-6262
WEB: WWW.HUMANA.COM

300 N MADISON ST STE 100
GREEN BAY, WI 54301
PHONE: (920) 617-1705
FAX: (920) 617-1744
TOLL FREE: (800) 558-4444
WEB: WWW.HUMANA.COM

500 W MAIN ST
LOUISVILLE, KY 40202
PHONE: (502) 580-1000
FAX: (502) 580-2799
TOLL FREE: (800) 486-2620
WEB: WWW.HUMANA.COM

CONNECTICUT
FLORIDA
GEORGIA
OHIO
655 EDEN PARK DR STE 100
CINCINNATI, OH 45202-6056
PO BOX 14610
LEXINGTON, KY 40512-4610
PHONE: (513) 784-5200
FAX: (513) 784-5310
TOLL FREE: (800) 543-7158
WEB: WWW.HUMANA.COM

IAC — *SEE ALSO INDIVIDUAL ASSURANCE CO*

IBA HEALTH PLANS / IBA PHP

MICHIGAN
106 FARMERS ALLEY STE 300
KALAMAZOO, MI 49005
PHONE: (269) 341-8000
FAX: (269) 341-6832
TOLL FREE: (800) 548-6574
IN-STATE: (800) 722-3644
WEB: WWW.IBAHEALTHPLANS.COM

IBEW

NATIONAL
900 SEVENTH ST NW
WASHINGTON, DC 20001
PHONE: (202) 833-7000
FAX: (202) 728-7676
WEB: WWW.IBEW.ORG

ALASKA
NINTH DISTRICT
2500 VENTURE OAKS WY STE 250
SACRAMENTO, CA 95833-4221
PHONE: (916) 567-0381
FAX: (916) 567-0385
WEB: WWW.IBEWNINTHDISTRICT.ORG

ADDITIONAL COMMENTS: ALSO SERVICES PACIFIC ISLANDS

ARKANSAS		10TH DISTRICT 5726 MARLIN RD STE 500 CHATTANOOGA, TN 37411-4043	PHONE: (423) 894-9095 FAX: (423) 892-4513	WEB: WWW.IBEW10TH.ORG
CALIFORNIA	No Info Given	NINTH DISTRICT 2500 VENTURE OAKS WY STE 250 SACRAMENTO, CA 95833-4221	PHONE: (916) 567-0381 FAX: (916) 567-0385	WEB: WWW.IBEWNINTHDISTRICT.ORG
ADDITIONAL COMMENTS: ALSO SERVICES PACIFIC ISLANDS				
COLORADO		8TH DISTRICT 2225 W BROADWAY STE H IDAHO FALLS, ID 83402	PHONE: (208) 529-6555 FAX: (208) 529-3632	E-MAIL: IVPD_08@IBEW.ORG WEB: WWW.IBEW8TH.ORG
DISTRICT OF COLUMBIA	Main Office	4TH DISTRICT 8260 N CREEK RD STE 140 CINCINATTI, OH 45236	PHONE: (513) 821-5480 FAX: (513) 821-3560	WEB: WWW.4IBEW.COM
HAWAII	No Info Given	NINTH DISTRICT 2500 VENTURE OAKS WY STE 250 SACRAMENTO, CA 95833-4221	PHONE: (916) 567-0381 FAX: (916) 567-0385	WEB: WWW.IBEWNINTHDISTRICT.ORG
ADDITIONAL COMMENTS: ALSO SERVICES PACIFIC ISLANDS				
IDAHO		8TH DISTRICT 2225 W BROADWAY STE H IDAHO FALLS, ID 83402	PHONE: (208) 529-6555 FAX: (208) 529-3632	E-MAIL: IVPD_08@IBEW.ORG WEB: WWW.IBEW8TH.ORG
ILLINOIS *INDIANA*	No Info Given	6TH DISTRICT 8174 CASS AVE DARIAN, IL 60561	PHONE: (630) 434-1683 FAX: (630) 434-0508	E-MAIL: IVPD_06@IBEW.ORG WEB: WWW.IBEW6TH.ORG
IOWA		11TH DISTRICT 300 S JEFFERSON STE 300 SPRINGFIELD, MO 65806	PHONE: (417) 831-1507 FAX: (417) 831-1509	WEB: WWW.IBEW11TH.ORG
KENTUCKY *MARYLAND*	Main Office	4TH DISTRICT 8260 N CREEK RD STE 140 CINCINATTI, OH 45236	PHONE: (513) 821-5480 FAX: (513) 821-3560	WEB: WWW.4IBEW.COM
MICHIGAN *MINNESOTA*	No Info Given	6TH DISTRICT 8174 CASS AVE DARIAN, IL 60561	PHONE: (630) 434-1683 FAX: (630) 434-0508	E-MAIL: IVPD_06@IBEW.ORG WEB: WWW.IBEW6TH.ORG
MISSOURI		11TH DISTRICT 300 S JEFFERSON STE 300 SPRINGFIELD, MO 65806	PHONE: (417) 831-1507 FAX: (417) 831-1509	WEB: WWW.IBEW11TH.ORG
MONTANA		8TH DISTRICT 2225 W BROADWAY STE H IDAHO FALLS, ID 83402	PHONE: (208) 529-6555 FAX: (208) 529-3632	E-MAIL: IVPD_08@IBEW.ORG WEB: WWW.IBEW8TH.ORG
NEBRASKA		11TH DISTRICT 300 S JEFFERSON STE 300 SPRINGFIELD, MO 65806	PHONE: (417) 831-1507 FAX: (417) 831-1509	WEB: WWW.IBEW11TH.ORG

NORTH CAROLINA	10TH DISTRICT 5726 MARLIN RD STE 500 CHATTANOOGA, TN 37411-4043	PHONE: (423) 894-9095 FAX: (423) 892-4513	WEB: WWW.IBEW10TH.ORG
NORTH DAKOTA	11TH DISTRICT 300 S JEFFERSON STE 300 SPRINGFIELD, MO 65806	PHONE: (417) 831-1507 FAX: (417) 831-1509	WEB: WWW.IBEW11TH.ORG
OHIO	4TH DISTRICT 8260 N CREEK RD STE 140 CINCINATTI, OH 45236	PHONE: (513) 821-5480 FAX: (513) 821-3560	WEB: WWW.4IBEW.COM
OREGON	NINTH DISTRICT 2500 VENTURE OAKS WY STE 250 SACRAMENTO, CA 95833-4221	PHONE: (916) 567-0381 FAX: (916) 567-0385	WEB: WWW.IBEWNINTHDISTRICT.ORG
ADDITIONAL COMMENTS: ALSO SERVICES PACIFIC ISLANDS			
SOUTH CAROLINA	10TH DISTRICT 5726 MARLIN RD STE 500 CHATTANOOGA, TN 37411-4043	PHONE: (423) 894-9095 FAX: (423) 892-4513	WEB: WWW.IBEW10TH.ORG
SOUTH DAKOTA	11TH DISTRICT 300 S JEFFERSON STE 300 SPRINGFIELD, MO 65806	PHONE: (417) 831-1507 FAX: (417) 831-1509	WEB: WWW.IBEW11TH.ORG
TENNESSEE	10TH DISTRICT 5726 MARLIN RD STE 500 CHATTANOOGA, TN 37411-4043	PHONE: (423) 894-9095 FAX: (423) 892-4513	WEB: WWW.IBEW10TH.ORG
UTAH	8TH DISTRICT 2225 W BROADWAY STE H IDAHO FALLS, ID 83402	PHONE: (208) 529-6555 FAX: (208) 529-3632	E-MAIL: IVPD_08@IBEW.ORG WEB: WWW.IBEW8TH.ORG
VIRGINIA	4TH DISTRICT 8260 N CREEK RD STE 140 CINCINATTI, OH 45236	PHONE: (513) 821-5480 FAX: (513) 821-3560	WEB: WWW.4IBEW.COM
WASHINGTON	NINTH DISTRICT 2500 VENTURE OAKS WY STE 250 SACRAMENTO, CA 95833-4221	PHONE: (916) 567-0381 FAX: (916) 567-0385	WEB: WWW.IBEWNINTHDISTRICT.ORG
ADDITIONAL COMMENTS: ALSO SERVICES PACIFIC ISLANDS			
WASHINGTON WEST VIRGINIA	4TH DISTRICT 8260 N CREEK RD STE 140 CINCINATTI, OH 45236	PHONE: (513) 821-5480 FAX: (513) 821-3560	WEB: WWW.4IBEW.COM
WISCONSIN	6TH DISTRICT 8174 CASS AVE DARIAN, IL 60561	PHONE: (630) 434-1683 FAX: (630) 434-0508	E-MAIL: IVPD_06@IBEW.ORG WEB: WWW.IBEW6TH.ORG
WYOMING	8TH DISTRICT 2225 W BROADWAY STE H IDAHO FALLS, ID 83402	PHONE: (208) 529-6555 FAX: (208) 529-3632	E-MAIL: IVPD_08@IBEW.ORG WEB: WWW.IBEW8TH.ORG

ICW GROUP — *INSURANCE COMPANY OF THE WEST*

NATIONAL	11455 EL CAMNIO REAL SAN DIEGO, CA 92130-2045 PO BOX 85563 SAN DIEGO, CA 92186-5563	PHONE: (858) 350-2400 FAX: (858) 350-2755 TOLL FREE: (800) 877-1111	WEB: WWW.ICWGROUP.COM

IDAHO FARM BUREAU MUTUAL INSURANCE CO — *SEE ALSO FARM BUREAU INSURANCE*

IDS LIFE OF NEW YORK

NEW YORK	20 MADISON AVE EXT 122203 ALBANY, NY 12203-5326 PO BOX 5144 ALBANY, NY 12205-5144	PHONE: (518) 869-8613 FAX: (518) 869-8753 TOLL FREE: (800) 797-9000	WEB: WWW.AMERIPRISEINTERNATIONAL.COM

IFG CO — *BURLINGTON INSURANCE*

NATIONAL	238 INTERNATIONAL RD BURLINGTON, NC 27215-5177	PHONE: (336) 586-2500 FAX: (336) 586-2867 TOLL FREE: (877) 434-2567	WEB: WWW.BURLINGTONINSURANCE.COM

ILLINOIS MUTUAL LIFE INSURANCE CO

NATIONAL	300 SW ADAMS ST PEORIA, IL 61634-0002	PHONE: (309) 674-8255 FAX: (309) 673-8137 TOLL FREE: (800) 437-7355	E-MAIL: INFO@ILLINOISMUTUAL.COM WEB: WWW.ILLINOISMUTUAL.COM

ILWU/PMA COASTWISE CLAIMS OFFICE

CALIFORNIA OREGON WASHINGTON	814 MISSION ST STE 300 SAN FRANCISCO, CA 94103-3030	PHONE: (415) 543-0114 FAX: (415) 495-0511 TOLL FREE: (800) 955-7376	WEB: WWW.ILW.ORG

IMA OF KANSAS

NATIONAL	8200 E 32ND ST N WICHITA, KS 67226 PO BOX 2992 WICHITA, KS 67201-2992	PHONE: (316) 267-9221 FAX: (316) 266-6254 TOLL FREE: (800) 288-6732 IN-STATE: (800) 288-6732	WEB: WWW.IMACORP.COM

IMA, INC — *SEE ALSO INSURANCE MANAGEMENT ADMINISTRATORS OF LOUISIANA*

IMT INSURANCE CO

ILLINOIS IOWA	1108 PIERCE ST SIOUX CITY, IA 51105 PO BOX 723 SIOUX CITY, IA 51102	PHONE: (712) 255-5335 FAX: (712) 255-4935 TOLL FREE: (800) 365-5519 IN-STATE: (800) 274-3531	WEB: WWW.IMTINS.COM
	4445 CORPORATE DR WEST DES MOINES, IA 50266 PO BOX 9208 WEST DES MOINES, IA 50306	PHONE: (515) 327-2777 FAX: (515) 327-2889 TOLL FREE: (800) 274-3531	WEB: WWW.IMTINS.COM
NEBRASKA SOUTH DAKOTA	1108 PIERCE ST SIOUX CITY, IA 51105 PO BOX 723 SIOUX CITY, IA 51102	PHONE: (712) 255-5336 FAX: (712) 255-4935 TOLL FREE: (800) 365-5519 IN-STATE: (800) 274-3531	WEB: WWW.IMTINS.COM
SOUTH DAKOTA WISCONSIN	4445 CORPORATE DR WEST DES MOINES, IA 50266 PO BOX 9208 WEST DES MOINES, IA 50306	PHONE: (515) 327-2777 FAX: (515) 327-2889 TOLL FREE: (800) 274-3531	WEB: WWW.IMTINS.COM

INDEPENDENCE BLUE CROSS

DELAWARE PENNSYLVANIA	OPERATIONS SUPPORT C3 1901 MARKET ST PHILADELPHIA, PA 19103-1480 PO BOX 898815 CAMP HILL, PA 17089-8815	PHONE: (215) 567-3590 FAX: (215) 238-7912 TOLL FREE: (800) 227-3119	WEB: WWW.IBX.COM

INDEPENDENT EMPLOYEE BENEFITS CORP — *IEBC*

ILLINOIS	28 N 1ST ST GENEVA, IL 60134 PO BOX 470 GENEVA, IL 60134-0470	PHONE: (630) 232-7166 FAX: (630) 232-7186 TOLL FREE: (800) 448-5825	

INDEPENDENT HEALTH

NEW YORK	511 FARBER LAKES DR BUFFALO, NY 14221	PHONE: (716) 631-3001 FAX: (716) 635-3785 TOLL FREE: (800) 247-1466	WEB: WWW.INDEPENDENTHEALTH.COM

INDIANA FARM BUREAU INSURANCE — *SEE ALSO FARM BUREAU INSURANCE*

INDIANA INSURANCE

ILLINOIS	3333 WARRENVILLE RD 4TH FL LISLE, IL 60532 PO BOX 5211 LISLE, IL 60532-5211	PHONE: (630) 505-1442 FAX: (877) 642-3611 TOLL FREE: (800) 331-9974	WEB: WWW.INDIANA-INS.COM
INDIANA	350 E 96TH ST INDIANAPOLIS, IN 46240-3702 PO BOX 6063 INDIANAPOLIS, IN 46206-6063	PHONE: (317) 581-6400 FAX: (800) 598-4999	WEB: WWW.INDIANA-INS.COM
KENTUCKY	THREE LAKEVIEW PLACE 22 CENTURY BLVD STE 250 NASHVILLE, TN 37214 PO BOX 292489 NASHVILLE, TN 37229	PHONE: (615) 231-7000 OR (615) 889-3052 FAX: (866) 564-2055 TOLL FREE: (800) 613-4170	WEB: WWW.LIBERTYRAM.COM OR INDIANA-INS.COM
MICHIGAN	3333 WARRENVILLE RD 4TH FL LISLE, IL 60532 PO BOX 5211 LISLE, IL 60532-5211	PHONE: (630) 505-1442 FAX: (877) 642-3611 TOLL FREE: (800) 331-9974	WEB: WWW.INDIANA-INS.COM
TENNESSEE	THREE LAKEVIEW PLACE 22 CENTURY BLVD STE 250 NASHVILLE, TN 37214 PO BOX 292489 NASHVILLE, TN 37229	PHONE: (615) 231-7000 OR (615) 889-3052 FAX: (866) 564-2055 TOLL FREE: (800) 613-4170	WEB: WWW.LIBERTYRAM.COM OR INDIANA-INS.COM

INDIANA INSURANCE / REGIONAL AGENCY MARKET

OHIO	6281 TRI RIDGE BLVD LOVELAND, OH 45140-8318	PHONE: (513) 576-3200 FAX: (800) 436-9611 TOLL FREE: (800) 436-9600	WEB: WWW.INDIANA-INS.COM

INDIANA TEAMSTERS HEALTH BENEFIT & FUND

INDIANA	1233 SHELBY ST INDIANAPOLIS, IN 46203-1942	PHONE: (317) 639-3573 FAX: (317) 639-3548	WEB: WWW.LOCAL135.COM

INDIANAPOLIS LIFE

INDIANA	611 6TH AVE DES MOINES, IA 50309	PHONE: (800) 800-9882 TOLL FREE: (800) 428-7031	E-MAIL: CORPCOM@INDINANAPOLIS.COM WEB: WWW.INDIANAPOLISLIFE.COM
	9200 KEYSTONE CROSSING STE 800 INDIANAPOLIS, IN 46240	PHONE: (317) 927-6500 FAX: (317) 927-3326 TOLL FREE: (800) 428-7031 IN-STATE: (800) 800-9882	E-MAIL: CORPCOM@INDIANAPOLISLIFE.COM WEB: WWW.INDIANAPOLISLIFE.COM

INDIVIDUAL ASSURANCE COMPANY — *IAC*

NATIONAL		2400 W 75TH ST PRAIRIE VILLAGE, KS 66208-3509 PO BOX 8357 PRAIRIE VILLAGE, KS 66208-0357	PHONE: (800) 821-5434 FAX: (913) 432-1585 TOLL FREE: (800) 821-5434	WEB: WWW.IAC-GROUP.COM

INDUSTRIAL ALLIANCE PACIFIC INSURANCE AND FINANCIAL SERVICES

NATIONAL *CANADA*		2165 W BROADWAY VANCOUVER, BC V6K-4N5 PO BOX 5900 VANCOUVER, BC V6B-5H6	PHONE: (604) 734-1667 FAX: (604) 734-8221	WEB: WWW.IAPLIFE.COM

INDUSTRIAL RISK INSURERS — *GE INSURANCE SOLUTIONS*

NATIONAL		5200 METCALF AVE OVERLAND, KS 66020 PO BOX 2991 OVERLAND, KS 66021	PHONE: (860) 507-1300 FAX: (888) 964-7348 TOLL FREE: (800) 243-8308	WEB: WWW.INDUSTRIALRISK.COM

INFINITY INSURANCE COMPANIES

NATIONAL	3	PO BOX 105044 ATLANTA, GA 30348-5046	PHONE: (205) 870-4000 FAX: (225) 295-9258 OR (800) 214-5727 TOLL FREE: (800) 782-2020	WEB: WWW.INFINITY-GROUP.COM OR WWW.INFINITYAUTO.COM
		11700 GREATOAKS WAY ALPHARETTA, GA 30022 PO BOX 105091 ATLANTA, GA 30348-5091	PHONE: (678) 627-6000 TOLL FREE: (800) 852-8888	WEB: WWW.INFINITY-INSURANCE.COM
		3700 COLONNIAD PKWY BIRMINGHAM, AL 35243 PO BOX 830693 BIRMINGHAM, AL 35283-0695	PHONE: (205) 803-8100 FAX: (205) 803-8106 TOLL FREE: (800) 782-2020	WEB: WWW.INFINITY-INSURANCE.COM
CALIFORNIA		10820 183RD ST STE 209 CERRITOS, CA 90703	PHONE: (562) 402-7713 FAX: (562) 653-2268 TOLL FREE: (800) 782-2040	WEB: WWW.INFINITY-INSURANCE.COM
		10969 TRADE CTR DR STE 106 RANCHO CORDOVA, CA 95670-6140	PHONE: (916) 853-1245 FAX: (916) 853-4629 TOLL FREE: (800) 243-1245	WEB: WWW.INFINITY-INSURANCE.COM
		1991 W 190TH ST STE 202 TORRANCE, CA 90504-6254	PHONE: (310) 225-4760 FAX: (310) 225-4768	WEB: WWW.INFINITY-INSURANCE.COM
		5850 CANOGA AVE STE 210 WOODLAND HILLS, CA 91364	PHONE: (818) 715-0735 FAX: (818) 715-9758	WEB: WWW.INFINITY-INSURANCE.COM
OHIO		4807 ROCKSIDE RD CLEVELAND, OH 44131	FAX: (216) 520-1026 TOLL FREE: (800) 782-1020	WEB: WWW.INFINITYAUTO.COM
PENNSYLVANIA		PARK WEST OFFICE CENTER ONE CLIFF MINE RD STE 330 PITTSBURGH, PA 15275 PO BOX 105046 ATLANTA, GA 30348-5046	PHONE: (412) 788-8430 FAX: (800) 214-5727 TOLL FREE: (800) 334-1661	WEB: WWW.INFINITY-INSURANCE.COM

ING

NATIONAL		5780 POWERS FERRY RD NW ATLANTA, GA 30327-4390 PO BOX 105006 ATLANTA, GA 30348-5006	PHONE: (770) 980-5100 FAX: (770) 980-5112 TOLL FREE: (800) 872-7542	WEB: WWW.ING.COM

INSURANCE & RISK MANAGEMENT — *EMPLOYEE PLANS, LLC*

NATIONAL	℞ 3 H	1111 CHESTNUT HILLS PKY FT WAYNE, IN 46814 PO BOX 2362 FT WAYNE, IN 46801-2362	PHONE: (260) 625-7500 FAX: (260) 625-7525 OR (260) 625-7530 TOLL FREE: (800) 395-8601	WEB: WWW.EMPLOYEEPLANSLLC.COM

INSURANCE COMPANY OF THE WEST — *SEE ALSO ICW GROUP*

INSURANCE HEALTH

NATIONAL	PO BOX 42034 HAZELWOOD, MS 63042	PHONE: (208) 368-7770 FAX: (208) 336-1050 TOLL FREE: (800) 800-1212 IN-STATE: (800) 328-4316

INSURANCE MANAGEMENT ADMINISTRATORS OF LOUISIANA — *IMA, INC*

NATIONAL	1325 BARKSDALE BLVD STE 300 BOSSIER CITY, LA 71111-1120 PO BOX 71120 BOSSIER CITY, LA 71171	PHONE: (318) 747-0577 FAX: (318) 747-5074	WEB: WWW.IMALA.COM

INSURANCE SERVICING GROUP — *BANK OF AMERICA*

NATIONAL	4161 PIEDMONT PKWY GREENSBORO, NC 27420 PO BOX 21848 GREENSBORO, NC 27420-1848	PHONE: (800) 879-1703 FAX: (336) 805-2026 TOLL FREE: (888) 356-4892	WEB: WWW.BANKAMERICA.COM

INSURERS ADMINISTRATIVE CORP / IAC — *DENTAL CLAIMS*

NATIONAL	PO BOX 39119 PHOENIX, AZ 85069-9119	PHONE: (602) 870-1400 FAX: (602) 395-0496 TOLL FREE: (800) 843-3106	WEB: WWW.IACUSA.COM

INTEGRITY BENEFIT NETWORK

NATIONAL	PO BOX 4537 MARIETTA, GA 30061-4537	PHONE: (770) 428-1604 FAX: (770) 426-0290	WEB: WWW.IBNTPA.COM

INTEGRITY MUTUAL INSURANCE CO — *MEMBER OF THE GRANGE MUTUAL CASUALTY GROUP*

IOWA *MINNESOTA* *WISCONSIN*	2121 E CAPITOL DR APPLETON, WI 54911 PO BOX 539 APPLETON, WI 54912-0539	PHONE: (920) 734-4511 FAX: (920) 730-5712 TOLL FREE: (800) 452-3421	E-MAIL: ISALES@IMICO.COM WEB: WWW.INTEGRITYINSURANCEOM.COM

INTER VALLEY HEALTH PLAN

CALIFORNIA	300 S PARK AVE STE 300 POMONA, CA 91766-1501 PO BOX 6002 POMONA, CA 91769-6002	PHONE: (909) 623-6333 FAX: (909) 622-2907 TOLL FREE: (800) 251-8191	WEB: WWW.IVHP.COM

INTER-AMERICAS INSURANCE — *CASUALTY UNDERWRITERS INSURANCE COMPANY*

NATIONAL	1035 S 183 W GODDARD, KS 67052 PO BOX 9510 WICHITA, KS 67277	PHONE: (800) 333-2525 FAX: (316) 794-8470 TOLL FREE: (800) 333-2525	WEB: WWW.IAI-ONLINE.COM

INTERNATIONAL AMERICAN MANAGEMENT CO — *SEE ALSO AMERICAN CENTENNIAL INSURANCE CO*

INTERNATIONAL BROTHERHOOD OF TEAMSTERS — *SEE ALSO TEAMSTERS*

INTERSTATE BANKERS INSURANCE

ILLINOIS	8501 W HIGGINS RD STE 710 CHICAGO, IL 60631-2801	PHONE: (773) 693-3930 FAX: (773) 693-3278

INTRACORP — *CIGNA HEALTHCARE*

NATIONAL

PO BOX 5200
FRANTON, PA 18503
PHONE: (412) 747-7477
TOLL FREE: (800) 882-4462
WEB: WWW.CIGNA.COM

1110 MARKET ST
CHATTANOOGA, TN 37402
PO BOX 182223
CHATTANOOGA, TN 37422-7223
PHONE: (423) 499-3642 OR (423) 321-4400
TOLL FREE: (800) 244-6224
WEB: WWW.INTRACORP.COM

1601 CHESTNUT ST
PITTSBURGH, PA 19192
PHONE: (215) 610-6000
WEB: WWW.INTRACORP.COM

1601 CHESTNUT ST TWO LIBERTY PL
PHILADELPHIA, PA 19192
PHONE: (856) 346-5000
TOLL FREE: (800) 258-8834
WEB: WWW.CIGNA.COM

1601 CHESTNUT ST 17DFL
PITTSBURGH, PA 19192
PHONE: (412) 747-4410
FAX: (646) 356-7711
TOLL FREE: (800) 882-4462
IN-STATE: (800) 551-3539
E-MAIL: YOURCIGNALIFESERVICECENTER@CIGNA.COM
WEB: WWW.CIGNA.COM

400 N BRAND BLVD
GLENDALE , CA 91203
PHONE: (818) 500-6262 OR (818) 500-6901
TOLL FREE: (800) 606-6343
WEB: WWW.CIGNA.COM

4100 INTERNATIONAL PKY STE 1010
CARROLLTON, TX 75007
PHONE: (972) 307-2700
TOLL FREE: (800) 237-3777
WEB: WWW.CIGNA.COM

7942 W BELL RD C5-PMB609
GLENDALE, AZ 85308
PHONE: (602) 516-3000
FAX: (602) 825-8530
TOLL FREE: (800) 288-3907
WEB: WWW.INTRACORP.COM

INVESTORS HERITAGE LIFE INSURANCE CO

ALABAMA
KENTUCKY

200 CAPITOL AVE
FRANKFORT, KY 40601
PO BOX 717
FRANKFORT, KY 40602
PHONE: (502) 223-2361
FAX: (502) 875-7084
TOLL FREE: (800) 422-2011
WEB: WWW.INVESTORSHERITAGE.COM

IOWA MUTUAL INSURANCE GROUP

ILLINOIS
IOWA
NEBRASKA

509 9TH ST
DEWITT, IA 52742-0060
PO BOX 290
DEWITT, IA 52742-0290
PHONE: (563) 659-3231
TOLL FREE: (800) 456-5259
E-MAIL: CLAIM@IOWAMUTUAL.COM
WEB: WWW.IOWAMUTUAL.COM

ISLAND INSURANCE CO, LTD

HAWAII

1165 BETHEL ST
HONOLULU, HI 96813-2203
PO BOX 1520
HONOLULU, HI 96806-1520
PHONE: (808) 564-8222
FAX: (808) 539-9738
TOLL FREE: (888) 312-2525
WEB: WWW.ISLANDINSURANCE.COM

ISLAND PEER REVIEW ORGANIZATION, INC— *SEE ALSO PEER REVIEW ORGANIZATIONS*

ITT HARTFORD INSURANCE GROUP — *SEE ALSO SPECIALTY RISK SERVICES*

J P FARLEY CORPORATION

NATIONAL

465 JACK KRAMER DR
MEMPHIS, TN 38117
PO BOX 41779
MEMPHIS, TN 38174-1779

PHONE: (901) 725-6435
FAX: (901) 725-6437

WEB: WWW.JPFARLEY.COM

JAS, INC

ARIZONA
UTAH

4885 S 900 E STE 202
SALT LAKE CITY, UT 84117-5725

PHONE: (801) 266-3256
FAX: (801) 266-4383
TOLL FREE: (800) 345-3248

E-MAIL: JAS@JASBENEFITS.COM
WEB: WWW.JASBENEFITS.COM

JEFFERSON LIFE INSURANCE

LOUISIANA
TEXAS

14160 DALLAS PKWY STE 500
DALLAS, TX 75254-4319
PO BOX 800409
DALLAS, TX 75380

PHONE: (972) 404-0295
FAX: (972) 503-9388
TOLL FREE: (800) 840-8137
IN-STATE: (800) 840-8137

JEFFERSON PILOT FINANCIAL — *LINCOLN FINANCIAL GROUP*

NATIONAL

ONE GRANITE PL
CONCORD, NH 03301-3253
PO BOX 515
CONCORD, NH 03302-0515

PHONE: (603) 226-5000
FAX: (603) 226-5985
TOLL FREE: (800) 258-3648

WEB: WWW.JPFINANCIAL.COM

JEFFERSON PILOT FINANCIAL — *LINCOLN FINANCIAL GROUP*

NATIONAL

8801 INDIAN HILLS DR
OMAHA, NE 68114-4066
PO BOX 2640
OMAHA, NE 68103-2640

PHONE: (402) 361-7300
FAX: (402) 361-2941
TOLL FREE: (800) 423-2765

WEB: WWW.JPFINANCIAL.COM

JELD-WEN HEALTH BENEFIT PLAN — *SEE ALSO SHASTA ADMINISTRATIVE SERVICES*

JEWELERS MUTUAL INSURANCE CO

NATIONAL

24 JEWELERS PARK DR
NEENAH, WI 54956
PO BOX 468
NEENAH, WI 54957-0468

PHONE: (920) 725-4326
FAX: (920) 725-9401
TOLL FREE: (800) 558-6411

WEB: WWW.JEWELERSMUTUAL.COM

JFP BENEFIT MANAGEMENT

MICHIGAN

100 S JACKSON ST STE 200
JACKSON, MI 49201
PO BOX 189
JACKSON, MI 49204-0189

PHONE: (517) 784-0535
FAX: (517) 784-0821
IN-STATE: (800) 589-7660

WEB: WWW.JFPBENEFITMANAGEMENT.COM

JLT SERVICES CORP

NATIONAL

PO BOX 1511
LATHAM, NY 12110

PHONE: (518) 782-3000
FAX: (518) 782-3157
TOLL FREE: (800) 366-5273

WEB: WWW.JLTSERVICES.COM

300 S WACKER DR 7TH FL
CHICAGO, IL 60606

PHONE: (312) 922-9350
FAX: (312) 922-2849
TOLL FREE: (800) 222-9958

WEB: WWW.JLTSERVICES.COM

92 BROOKSIDE RD
WATERBURY, CT 06708-1402
PO BOX 1471
WATERBURY, CT 06721-1471

PHONE: (203) 756-8061
FAX: (203) 754-3941

WEB: WWW.JLTSERVICES.COM

ADDITIONAL COMMENTS: COMPANY IS INTERNATIONAL - HEADQUARTERS OUT OF LONDON, ENGLAND

JM FAMILY ENTERPRISES

NATIONAL	8019 BAYBERRY RD JACKSONVILLE, FL 32256-7411	PHONE: (904) 443-6655 FAX: (904) 443-6670 TOLL FREE: (800) 736-3936	WEB: WWW.JMFAMILY.COM

JMH HEALTH PLAN

FLORIDA	HIGHLAND PROFESSIONAL BLDG 1801 NW 9TH AVE STE 100 MIAMI, FL 33136	PHONE: (305) 575-3700 FAX: (305) 545-5212 TOLL FREE: (800) 721-2993	E-MAIL: PROVIDERSERVICES@JMHHP.COM WEB: WWW.JMHHP.COM

JOHN DEERE HEALTH

ILLINOIS *IOWA* *TENNESSEE*	408 N CEDAR BLUFF RD STE 400 KNOXVILLE, TN 39723	PHONE: (865) 690-5572 FAX: (865) 690-2741 TOLL FREE: (800) 224-6602	WEB: WWW.JOHNDEEREHEALTH.COM
	7213 NOAH REID RD STE 102 CHATTANOOGA, TN 37404	PHONE: (423) 499-0673 FAX: (423) 954-9907 TOLL FREE: (800) 224-6602	WEB: WWW.JOHNDEEREHEALTH.COM
TENNESSEE	2033 MEADOW VIEW LN STE 300 KINGSPORT, TN 37660	PHONE: (423) 378-5122 FAX: (423) 378-4752 TOLL FREE: (800) 224-6602	WEB: WWW.JOHNDEEREHEALTH.COM
VIRGINIA	408 N CEDAR BLUFF RD STE 400 KNOXVILLE, TN 39723	PHONE: (865) 690-5572 FAX: (865) 690-2741 TOLL FREE: (800) 224-6602	WEB: WWW.JOHNDEEREHEALTH.COM
	7213 NOAH REID RD STE 102 CHATTANOOGA, TN 37404	PHONE: (423) 499-0673 FAX: (423) 954-9907 TOLL FREE: (800) 224-6602	WEB: WWW.JOHNDEEREHEALTH.COM

JOHN DEERE HEALTH / UNITED HEALTH

ILLINOIS	7210 N VILLA LAKE DR STE A PEORIA, IL 61614	PHONE: (309) 692-2160 FAX: (309) 692-3165 TOLL FREE: (800) 747-1446	WEB: WWW.JOHNDEEREHEALTH.COM
IOWA	1195 E POST RD STE 1 MARION, IA 52302	FAX: (319) 373-7195 TOLL FREE: (800) 747-1446	WEB: WWW.JOHNDEEREHEALTH.COM
	1660 EMBASSY W DR STE 150 DUBUQUE, IA 52002	PHONE: (563) 588-2831 FAX: (563) 588-2920 TOLL FREE: (800) 747-1446	WEB: WWW.JOHNDEEREHEALTH.COM
	3022 AIRPORT BLVD WATERLOO, IA 50704 PO BOX 9000 WATERLOO, IA 50704-9000	PHONE: (319) 291-3291 FAX: (319) 291-7838 TOLL FREE: (800) 747-1446 IN-STATE: (800) 224-5596	WEB: WWW.JOHNDEEREHEALTH.COM
	3740 UTICA RDG RD STE A BETTENDORF, IA 52722-1624	PHONE: (563) 344-7400 FAX: (319) 359-1665 TOLL FREE: (800) 747-1446	WEB: WWW.JOHNDEEREHEALTH.COM

JOHN DEERE HEALTH/UNITED HEALTH

ILLINOIS	1300 RIVER DR STE 200 MOLINE, IL 61265	PHONE: (309) 765-1200 FAX: (309) 748-1022 TOLL FREE: (800) 747-1446	WEB: WWW.JOHNDEEREHEALTH.COM

JOHN HANCOCK — *SEE ALSO MANULIFE FINANCIAL*

JOHN MUIR MEDICAL CENTER

CALIFORNIA	1601 YGNACIO VLY RD WALNUT CREEK, CA 94598-3122	PHONE: (925) 939-3000 FAX: (925) 947-5318	WEB: WWW.JOHNMUIRHEALTH.COM

JOHNSON INSURANCE

SOUTH CAROLINA	176 MCSWAIN DR COLUMBIA, SC 29169 PO BOX 21308 COLUMBIA, SC 29221-1308	PHONE: (803) 739-0001 FAX: (803) 739-2200 TOLL FREE: (877) 840-0936	

JP FARLEY CORP

NATIONAL	29055 CLEMENS RD WESTLAKE, OH 44145-1135 PO BOX 458022 WESTLAKE, OH 44145-8022	PHONE: (440) 250-4300 FAX: (440) 250-4301 TOLL FREE: (800) 634-0173	E-MAIL: BENEFITS@JPFARLEY.COM WEB: WWW.JPFARLEY.COM

K & K INSURANCE GROUP

NATIONAL	1712 MAGNAVOX WY FT WAYNE, IN 46804-1538 PO BOX 2338 FT WAYNE, IN 46801-2338	PHONE: (260) 459-5000 FAX: (260) 459-5910	WEB: WWW.KANDKINSURANCE.COM

KAISER PERMANENTE

CALIFORNIA	425 MARKET ST STE 925 SAN FRANCISCO, CA 94105-2463	PHONE: (510) 987-3135 FAX: (415) 512-6030 IN-STATE: (800) 464-4000	WEB: WWW.KAISERPERMANENTE.ORG OR WWW.KP.ORG
	450 N LAKE AVE PASADENA, CA 91101-1216	PHONE: (800) 464-4000 TOLL FREE: (800) 954-8000	WEB: WWW.KAISERPERMANENTE.ORG OR WWW.KP.ORG
COLORADO	PO BOX 5316 CLEVELAND, OH 44101-9774	PHONE: (303) 344-7932 TOLL FREE: (800) 686-7100 IN-STATE: (800) 441-9742	WEB: WWW.KAISERPERMANENTE.ORG
DISTRICT OF COLUMBIA	REGIONAL OFFICE 2101 E JEFFERSON ST ROCKVILLE, MD 20849 PO BOX 6233 ROCKVILLE, MD 20849-6233	PHONE: (301) 816-6264 TOLL FREE: (800) 368-5784 IN-STATE: (800) 777-7902	WEB: WWW.KAISERPERMANENTE.ORG
GEORGIA	3495 PIEDMONT RD NE ATLANTA, GA 30305 PO BOX 149489 ATLANTA, GA 31150	PHONE: (404) 233-0555 FAX: (404) 364-4998 TOLL FREE: (800) 611-1811	WEB: WWW.KAISERPERMANENTE.ORG OR WWW.KP.ORG
HAWAII	1441 KAPIOLANI BLVD 17TH FLOOR HONOLULU, HI 96814	PHONE: (808) 432-4983 FAX: (808) 432-4989	WEB: WWW.KP.ORG
MARYLAND	REGIONAL OFFICE 2101 E JEFFERSON ST ROCKVILLE, MD 20849 PO BOX 6233 ROCKVILLE, MD 20849-6233	PHONE: (301) 816-6264 TOLL FREE: (800) 368-5784 IN-STATE: (800) 777-7902	WEB: WWW.KAISERPERMANENTE.ORG
OHIO	ADMINISTRATIVE OFFICE NORTH POINT TOWER STE 1200 CLEVELAND, OH 44114	PHONE: (216) 479-5243 TOLL FREE: (800) 686-7100	WEB: WWW.KAISERPERMANENTE.ORG

OREGON	500 NE MULTNOMAH STE 100 PORTLAND, OR 97232-2031	PHONE: (503) 813-4827 FAX: (503) 813-2710 TOLL FREE: (800) 813-2000	WEB: WWW.KAISERPERMANENTE.ORG OR WWW.KP.ORG
VIRGINIA	REGIONAL OFFICE 2101 E JEFFERSON ST ROCKVILLE, MD 20849 PO BOX 6233 ROCKVILLE, MD 20849-6233	PHONE: (301) 816-6264 TOLL FREE: (800) 368-5784 IN-STATE: (800) 777-7902	WEB: WWW.KAISERPERMANENTE.CRG
WASHINGTON	500 NE MULTNOMAH STE 100 PORTLAND, OR 97232-2031	PHONE: (503) 813-4827 FAX: (503) 813-2710 TOLL FREE: (800) 813-2000	WEB: WWW.KAISERPERMANENTE.ORG OR WWW.KP.ORG

KANAWHA INSURANCE CO — *KMG AMERICA*

MASSACHUSETTS *SOUTH CAROLINA*	210 S WHITE ST LANCASTER, SC 29720 PO BOX 610 LANCASTER, SC 29721	PHONE: (800) 635-4252 TOLL FREE: (800) 635-4252	WEB: WWW.KMGAMERICA.COM

KANSAS CITY LIFE INSURANCE CO

MISSOURI	PO BOX 219325 KANSAS CITY, MO 64121-9325	PHONE: (816) 753-7299 FAX: (816) 931-4006 TOLL FREE: (800) 874-5254	WEB: WWW.KCLGROUPBENEFITS.COM

KEENAN & ASSOCIATES

CALIFORNIA	2355 CRENSHAW BLVD STE 200 TORRANCE, CA 90501-3329 PO BOX 42035 HAZELWOOD, MO 63402	PHONE: (310) 212-3344 FAX: (310) 212-3381 IN-STATE: (800) 653-3626	WEB: WWW.KEENANASSOC.COM
	3550 VINE ST STE 260 RIVERSIDE, CA 92507 PO BOX 42035 HAZELWOOD, MO 63402	PHONE: (951) 788-0330 FAX: (909) 788-8013	WEB: WWW.KEENANASSOC.COM

KEMPER AUTO AND HOME — *UNITRIN*

NATIONAL	80 BLUE RAVINE RD STE 200 FOLSOM, CA 95630-4702 PO BOX 6660 FOLSOM, CA 95763-6660	PHONE: (916) 294-2500 FAX: (916) 294-2600 TOLL FREE: (800) 679-1839	WEB: WWW.KEMPERINSURANCE.COM OR WWW.KEMPERAUTOANDHOME.COM
ALABAMA *FLORIDA* *GEORGIA* *INDIANA*	2430 WHITEHALL PARK DR STE 100 CHARLOTTE, NC 28273 PO BOX 7768 CHARLOTTE, NC 28241-7768	PHONE: (704) 423-6000 FAX: (704) 423-6001 OR (800) 428-7690 TOLL FREE: (800) 464-5108	WEB: WWW.KEMPERAUTOANDHOME.COM
ILLINOIS	400 S EXECUTIVE DR STE 200 BROOKFIELD, WI 53008 PO BOX 1237 BROOKFIELD, WI 53005	PHONE: (262) 207-8525 FAX: (262) 754-9867 TOLL FREE: (800) 773-7366 IN-STATE: (800) 233-5667	WEB: WWW.UNITRIN.COM
INDIANA	250 N PATRICK BLVD STE 100 BROOKFIELD, WI 53008 PO BOX 770 BROOKFIELD, WI 53008-0770	PHONE: (262) 792-9380 FAX: (262) 792-9818 TOLL FREE: (800) 242-8808	WEB: WWW.KEMPERAUTOANDHOME.COM

KENTUCKY	NEW HAMPSHIRE	PENNSYLVANIA	VIRGINIA
MAINE	NEW JERSEY	SOUTH CAROLINA	WEST VIRGINIA
MARYLAND	NEW YORK	TENNESSEE	
MICHIGAN	OHIO	VERMONT	

2430 WHITEHALL PARK DR STE 100
CHARLOTTE, NC 28273
PO BOX 7768
CHARLOTTE, NC 28241-7768

PHONE: (704) 423-6000
FAX: (704) 423-6001 OR (800) 428-7690
TOLL FREE: (800) 464-5108

WEB: WWW.KEMPERAUTOANDHOME.COM

KEMPER INSURANCE COMPANIES

CANADA

36 KING ST E STE 500
TORONTO, ON M5C-135

PHONE: (416) 260-8444
FAX: (416) 361-6113
TOLL FREE: (866) 566-6602

WEB: WWW.KEMPERINSURANCE.COM

KEMPTON GROUP

OKLAHOMA

525 CENTRAL PARK DR STE 300
OKLAHOMA CITY, OK 73105
PO BOX 54889
OKLAHOMA CITY, OK 73154-1889

PHONE: (405) 521-1711
FAX: (405) 521-9804
TOLL FREE: (800) 521-1711

E-MAIL: SERVICE@KEMPTONGROUP.COM
WEB: WWW.KEMPTONGROUP.COM

KENTUCKY FARM BUREAU MUTUAL INSURANCE CO — *SEE ALSO FARM BUREAU INSURANCE*

KEYSTONE HEALTH PLAN CENTRAL

PENNSYLVANIA

2500 ELMERTON AVE
HARRISBURG, PA 17177

TOLL FREE: (800) 669-7075

WEB: WWW.CAPBLUECROSS.COM

KEYSTONE INSURANCE CO — *SEE ALSO AAA MID-ATLANTIC INSURANCE GROUP*

KEYSTONE MERCY HEALTH PLAN

PENNSYLVANIA

200 STEVENS DR STE 350
PHILADELPHIA, PA 19113
PO BOX 7115
LONDON, KY 40742

PHONE: (215) 937-8000
FAX: (215) 937-5363
TOLL FREE: (800) 521-6860
IN-STATE: (800) 521-6007

WEB: WWW.KMHP.COM

KHS — *KMG AMERICA*

NATIONAL

545 N PLEASANTBURG DR STE 202
GREENVILLE, SC 29607
PO BOX 5150
GREENVILLE, SC 29606

FAX: (864) 240-3170
TOLL FREE: (800) 476-5150

WEB: WWW.KHSONLINE.COM

KIPP & COMPANY

OREGON

1208 SW 13TH AVE STE 200
PORTLAND, OR 97205-1705
PO BOX 1400
PORTLAND, OR 97207

PHONE: (503) 279-9943
FAX: (503) 279-8196
TOLL FREE: (800) 824-9789

WEB: WWW.KIPPCO.COM

KITSAP PHYSICIANS SERVICE — *KPS*

ALASKA
WASHINGTON

400 WARREN AVE
BREMERTON, WA 98337-1487
PO BOX 339
BREMERTON, WA 98337

PHONE: (360) 377-5576
FAX: (360) 415-6514
TOLL FREE: (800) 552-7114

WEB: WWW.KPSHEALTHPLANS.COM

KLAIS & CO

NATIONAL
1867 W MARKET ST
AKRON, OH 44313-6977
PHONE: (330) 867-8443
FAX: (330) 867-0827
TOLL FREE: (800) 331-1096
WEB: WWW.KLAIS.COM

KMG AMERICA — *SEE ALSO KHS*

KOHLER CO

NATIONAL
444 HIGHLAND DR
KOHLER, WI 53044
PHONE: (920) 457-4441
FAX: (920) 457-0669
TOLL FREE: (800) 456-’675

KPS — *SEE ALSO KITSAP PHYSICIANS SERVICE*

KPS HEALTH PLAN

WASHINGTON
400 WARREN AVE
BREMERTON, WA 98337-0039
PO BOX 339
BREMERTON, WA 97337
PHONE: (360) 478-6796
TOLL FREE: (800) 552-7114
WEB: WWW.KPSHEALTHPLANS.COM

KROGER — *DILLON COMPANIES, INC*

KANSAS
2700 E 4TH ST
HUTCHINSON, KS 67501-1972
PO BOX 1608
HUTCHINSON, KS 67504-1608
PHONE: (620) 665-5511
FAX: (620) 669-3169
TOLL FREE: (800) 362-2183
WEB: WWW.KROGER.COM

LABORERS HEALTH AND WELFARE TRUST FUNDS — *TRUST FUND OFFICE*

NATIONAL
4399 SANTA ANITA AVE STE 200
EL MONTE, CA 91731-1648
PO BOX 8024
EL MONTE, CA 91734-2324
PHONE: (626) 279-3000
FAX: (626) 350-6330
TOLL FREE: (800) 887-5679

LANCER CLAIM SERVICE — *SEE ALSO BROWN & BROWN*

LANCER CORP

NATIONAL
PO BOX 200224
SAN ANTONIO, TX 78220
PHONE: (210) 310-7000
FAX: (210) 310-7305
TOLL FREE: (800) 729-1500
WEB: WWW.LANCERCORP.COM

LANDCAR CASUALTY COMPANY

UTAH
9350 S 150 E STE 1000
SANDY, UT 84070
PHONE: (801) 262-9739
FAX: (801) 563-4199
TOLL FREE: (800) 733-7339

LANDMARK HEALTH CARE INC

CALIFORNIA
1750 HOWE AVE STE 300
SACRAMENTO, CA 95825-3369
PHONE: (916) 929-7806
FAX: (916) 929-8350
TOLL FREE: (800) 638-4557
E-MAIL: INFO@LMHEALTHCARE.COM
WEB: WWW.LANDMARKHEALTHCARE.COM

LAWRENCE E. SMITH & ASSOCIATES, INC

NATIONAL
1819 CLARKSON RD STE 300
ST LOUIS, MO 63017
PO BOX 411216
ST LOUIS, MO 63141-1216
PHONE: (636) 532-1660
FAX: (636) 532-1737
TOLL FREE: (800) 325-1350
WEB: WWW.LESMITH.NET

LBA HEALTH PLANS

MARYLAND
9475 DEERE CO RD STE 408
TIMONIUM, MD 21093
PO BOX 17098
OWINGS MILLS, MD 21117
PHONE: (410) 453-6135
TOLL FREE: (800) 858-4468
E-MAIL: CUSTOMERCARE@LBAX.COM
WEB: WWW.DOCFIRST.COM

LEE JOST & ASSOCIATES — *SEE ALSO BENEFIT PLAN ADMINISTRATION OF WI, INC*

LEMARS MUTUAL INSURANCE CO OF IOWA

IOWA	ONE PARK LN LE MARS, IA 51031 PO BOX 1608 LE MARS, IA 51031-1608	PHONE: (712) 546-7847 FAX: (712) 546-9648 TOLL FREE: (800) 545-6480 IN-STATE: (800) 352-4945	WEB: WWW.LEMM.COM
NEBRASKA	ONE PARK LN LE MARS, IA 51031 PO BOX 1608 LE MARS, IA 51031-1608	PHONE: (712) 546-7847 FAX: (712) 546-9648 TOLL FREE: (800) 545-6480 IN-STATE: (800) 352-4945	WEB: WWW.LEMM.COM
OKLAHOMA	ONE PARK LN LE MARS, IA 51031 PO BOX 1608 LE MARS, IA 51031-1608	PHONE: (712) 546-7847 FAX: (712) 546-9648 TOLL FREE: (800) 545-6480 IN-STATE: (800) 352-4945	WEB: WWW.LEMM.COM
SOUTH DAKOTA	ONE PARK LN LE MARS, IA 51031 PO BOX 1608 LE MARS, IA 51031-1608	PHONE: (712) 546-7847 FAX: (712) 546-9648 TOLL FREE: (800) 545-6480 IN-STATE: (800) 352-4945	WEB: WWW.LEMM.COM

LEWER AGENCY, INC

NATIONAL	4534 WORNALL RD KANSAS CITY, MO 64111	PHONE: (816) 753-4390 FAX: (816) 561-6840 TOLL FREE: (800) 821-7715	E-MAIL: CLAIMS@LEWER.COM WEB: WWW.LEWER.COM

LEXINGTON INSURANCE CO

NATIONAL	100 SUMMER ST BOSTON, MA 02110	PHONE: (617) 330-1100 FAX: (617) 439-9793 TOLL FREE: (800) 355-4891	E-MAIL: LEXINGTONINS@AIG.COM WEB: WWW.LEXINGTONINSURANCE.COM

LIBERTY INTERNATIONAL UNDERWRITERS

NATIONAL, AMERICAN SAMOA, BRITISH COLUMBIA, CANADA, GUAM, MANITOBA, MEXICO, NEW BRUNSWICK, NEWFOUNDLAND, NOVA SCOTIA, ONTARIO, PRINCE EDWARD ISLAND, PUERTO RICO, QUEBEC, SASKATCHEWAN, VIRGIN ISLANDS

55 WATER ST 18TH FL NEW YORK, NY 10041-0034	PHONE: (212) 208-4100 FAX: (212) 208-2864 TOLL FREE: (800) 677-9163	WEB: WWW.LIBERTYIU.COM

LIBERTY LIFE INSURANCE CO

LOUISIANA *SOUTH CAROLINA*	2000 WADE HAMPTON BLVD GREENVILLE, SC 29615 PO BOX 789 GREENVILLE, SC 29602	PHONE: (864) 609-8111 FAX: (864) 609-8084	WEB: WWW.LIBERTYLIFE.COM

LIBERTY MUTUAL

INDIANA *KENTUCKY*	STE 302 ORMSBY TWO 10350 ORMSBY PARK PL LOUISVILLE, KY 40223	PHONE: (502) 425-3450 FAX: (502) 426-2332 TOLL FREE: (800) 430-2482	WEB: WWW.LIBERTYMUTUAL.COM

LIBERTY MUTUAL GROUP — *SEE ALSO INDIANA INSURANCE*

LIBERTY MUTUAL INSURANCE — *SEE ALSO HELMSMAN MANAGEMENT SERVICES, INC*

LIBERTY NORTHWEST

ALASKA
IDAHO
MONTANA
OREGON
WASHINGTON

650 NE HOLLADAY ST
PORTLAND, OR 97208
PO BOX 4555
PORTLAND, OR 97207

PHONE: (503) 239-5800
TOLL FREE: (800) 275-5600

WEB: WWW.LIBERTYNORTHWEST.COM

LIFE AT THE SOUTH

NATIONAL

100 W BAY ST
JACKSONVILLE, FL 32202-3838
PO BOX 44130
JACKSONVILLE, FL 32231-4130

PHONE: (904) 350-9660
FAX: (904) 353-5878
TOLL FREE: (800) 888-2738

WEB: WWW.LIFE-SOUTH.COM

LIFE INSURANCE CO OF ALABAMA

ALABAMA
ARKANSAS
GEORGIA
KENTUCKY
LOUISIANA
MISSISSIPPI
NORTH CAROLINA
SOUTH CAROLINA
TENNESSEE

310 BROAD ST
GADSDEN, AL 35901-3716
PO BOX 349
GADSDEN, AL 35902-0349

PHONE: (256) 543-2022
FAX: (256) 549-0070
TOLL FREE: (800) 226-2371

WEB: WWW.LICOA.COM

LIFE OF THE SOUTH SERVICE CO

NATIONAL

100 W BAY ST
JACKSONVILLE, FL 32202
PO BOX 44130
JACKSONVILLE, FL 32231-4130

PHONE: (904) 350-9660
FAX: (904) 355-5878
TOLL FREE: (800) 888-2738

WEB: WWW.LIFE-SOUTH.COM

LIFEWELL HEALTH PLANS

GEORGIA

1701 BARRETT LAKE BLVD STE 290
KENNESAW, GA 30144

PHONE: (770) 420-1500
FAX: (770) 420-1502

WEB: WWW.LWHP.COM

LIFEWISE HEALTH PLAN OF OREGON — *PREMIERE BLUE CROSS*

OREGON

815 SW BOND ST.
BEND, OR 97201

PHONE: (503) 295-6707
FAX: (503) 279-5295
TOLL FREE: (800) 777-1502
IN-STATE: (800) 722-2103

WEB: WWW.LIFEWISEOR.COM

LINECO

NATIONAL

2000 SPRINGER DR
LOMBARD, IL 60148

FAX: (630) 916-0298
TOLL FREE: (800) 323-7268

WEB: WWW.LINECO.ORG

LITITZ MUTUAL INSURANCE COMPANY

DELAWARE
PENNSYLVANIA

TWO N BROAD ST
LITITZ, PA 17543-7007
PO BOX 900
LITITZ, PA 17543

PHONE: (717) 626-4751
FAX: (717) 626-0971
TOLL FREE: (800) 626-4751

WEB: WWW.LITITZMUTUAL.COM

LOCAL 1014 HEALTH AND WELFARE

NATIONAL

3460 FLETCHER AVE
EL MONTE, CA 91731-3099

PHONE: (310) 639-1014
FAX: (310) 631-8139
IN-STATE: (800) 660-1014

WEB: WWW.LOCAL1014.ORG OR
WWW.LOCAL1014MEDICAL.ORG

LOCAL 1245 HEALTH FUND

NEW JERSEY *NEW YORK*	390 MAIN RD MONTVILLE, NJ 07045 PO BOX 426 MONTVILLE, NJ 07045	PHONE: (973) 299-6700 FAX: (973) 299-2838 TOLL FREE: (800) 451-8391

LOCAL 338 HEALTH & WELFARE FUND

NEW JERSEY *NEW YORK*	97-45 QUEENS BLVD REGO PARK, NY 11374	PHONE: (718) 997-7400 FAX: (718) 997-0821	WEB: WWW.LOCAL338.COM

LOCAL 365 UAW WELFARE FUND

NEW JERSEY *NEW YORK*	30-07 39TH AVE LONG ISLAND CITY, NY 11101	PHONE: (718) 392-3600 FAX: (718) 361-9381 TOLL FREE: (800) 453-4091	WEB: WWW.COMPREHENSIVE-BENEFIT.COM

LOCAL 802 MUSICIANS HEALTH BENEFIT

NEW JERSEY *NEW YORK*	322 W 48TH ST NEW YORK, NY 10036-1308	PHONE: (212) 245-4802 FAX: (212) 245-2304	WEB: WWW.LOCAL802AFM.ORG

LOCAL UNION 164 IBEW JOINT WELFARE

NATIONAL	205 ROBIN RD STE 330 PARAMUS, NJ 07652 PO BOX 25 NEWARK, NJ 07101-0025	PHONE: (201) 225-1641 FAX: (201) 225-0694 OR (201) 225-0628

LOCAL UNION NO 682 HEALTH & WELFARE

ILLINOIS *MISSOURI*	4260 SHORELINE DR EARTH CITY, MO 63045	PHONE: (314) 344-8899 FAX: (314) 344-4407 TOLL FREE: (800) 556-1742

LOMA LINDA UNIVERSITY ADVENTIST HEALTH SCIENCES CENTER

CALIFORNIA	RISK MANAGEMENT 11161 ANDERSON ST STE 200 LOMA LINDA, CA 92354-2825 PO BOX 1770 LOMA LINDA, CA 92354-0570	PHONE: (909) 558-4386 FAX: (909) 558-4775	WEB: WWW.LLUMC.EDU

LOOMIS CO

NATIONAL	680 PILOT STE D LAS VEGAS, NV 89119	PHONE: (702) 770-2654 FAX: (702) 737-5913	E-MAIL: LASVEGAS@LOOMISCO.COM WEB: WWW.LOOMISCO.COM
	LOOMIS BENEFITS WEST 111 SW COLUMBIA STE 1075 PORTLAND, OR 97201-5814 PO BOX 1020 PORTLAND, OR 97207-1020	PHONE: (503) 221-6700 FAX: (503) 228-1433 TOLL FREE: (800) 367-3721	WEB: WWW.LOOMISCO.COM
	175 ADMIRAL COCHRANE DR STE 112 ANNAPOLIS, MD 21401	PHONE: (410) 224-2995 FAX: (410) 224-2006	WEB: WWW.LOOMISCO.COM
	23 LAUQUE DR MONTVILLE, NJ 07045	PHONE: (973) 334-2900 FAX: (973) 334-3910	E-MAIL: RGITLAN@LOOMISCO.COM WEB: WWW.LOOMISCO.COM

NATIONAL — CONTINUED	850 N PARK RD WYOMISSING, PA 19610-1340 PO BOX 7011 WYOMISSING, PA 19610-7011	PHONE: (610) 374-4040 FAX: (610) 374-6578 TOLL FREE: (800) 782-0392	E-MAIL: INFO@LOOMISCO.COM WEB: WWW.LOOMISCO.COM
FLORIDA	2929 E COMMERCIAL BLVD #705 FT LAUDERDALE, FL 33308	PHONE: (954) 772-0448 FAX: (954) 772-0447	WEB: WWW.LOOMISCO.COM

LOUISIANA FARM BUREAU MUTUAL INSURANCE CO — *SEE ALSO FARM BUREAU INSURANCE*

LOVELACE HEALTH PLAN, INC

NEW MEXICO	4101 INDIAN SCHOOL RD NE STE 110 ALBUQUERQUE, NM 87110-0000 PO BOX 760 PUEBLO, CO 81002	PHONE: (505) 262-7363 FAX: (505) 262-7719 TOLL FREE: (800) 808-7363	WEB: WWW.LOVELACEHEALTHPLAN.COM

LWP CLAIMS SOLUTIONS, INC

ARIZONA *CALIFORNIA* *COLORADO* *UTAH*	2180 S 1300 E STE 508 SALT LAKE CITY, UT 84106-7805	PHONE: (801) 972-7540 FAX: (801) 972-7546 TOLL FREE: (800) 807-7540 IN-STATE: (800) 807-7540	WEB: WWW.LWPCLAIMS.COM

M-CARE ADMINISTRATION

MICHIGAN	2301 COMMONWEALTH BLVD ANN ARBOR, MI 48105-2945 PO BOX 130799 ANN ARBOR, MI 48113-0799	PHONE: (734) 747-8700 FAX: (734) 747-7152 TOLL FREE: (800) 658-3878 IN-STATE: (800) 527-5549	E-MAIL: CUSTSERV@MCARE.ORG WEB: WWW.MCARE.ORG

M-PLAN

NATIONAL	8802 N MERIDIAN ST STE 100 INDIANAPOLIS, IN 46260-5371 PO BOX 357 LINTHICUM, MD 21090-0357	PHONE: (317) 571-5300 FAX: (317) 571-5306 TOLL FREE: (800) 878-8802	WEB: WWW.MPLAN.COM

MACHIGONNE BENEFIT ADMINISTRATORS

MAINE	2 GANNETT DR SOUTH PORTLAND, ME 04106 PO BOX 3859 PORTLAND, ME 04104-3859	PHONE: (207) 822-4650 FAX: (207) 822-5888 OR (207) 822-4610 TOLL FREE: (800) 245-3529 IN-STATE: (800) 585-6150	

MADISON NATIONAL LIFE INSURANCE CO, INC

NATIONAL *GUAM* *PUERTO RICO* *VIRGIN ISLANDS*	6120 UNIVERSITY AVE MIDDLETON, WI 53562 PO BOX 5008 MADISON, WI 53705	PHONE: (608) 238-2691 FAX: (608) 238-7028 TOLL FREE: (800) 356-9601	WEB: WWW.MADISONLIFE.COM

MAGNA CARTA — *SOUTHERN CALIFORNIA BRANCH*

ARIZONA *CALIFORNIA* *NEW YORK* *UK*	11755 WILSHIRE BLVD STE 1850 LOS ANGELES, CA 90025-1569	PHONE: (310) 445-8000 FAX: (310) 445-8001 TOLL FREE: (888) 239-7523	WEB: WWW.MCARTA.COM

MAGNA CARTA CO — *SEE ALSO PUBLIC SERVICE MUTUAL INSURANCE CO*

MAGNA CARTA COMPANIES

NATIONAL	121 SW MORRISON ST STE 1800 PORTLAND, OR 97204-3148	PHONE: (503) 553-3700 FAX: (503) 553-3701 TOLL FREE: (800) 317-6775	WEB: WWW.MCARTA.COM

NATIONAL — CONTINUED	ONE PARK AVE NEW YORK, NY 10016-5802	PHONE: (212) 591-9500 FAX: (212) 591-9600 TOLL FREE: (800) 223-5213 IN-STATE: (888) 663-7275	WEB: WWW.MCARTA.COM
ARIZONA	SOUTHWESTERN BRANCH 2425 E CAMELBACK RD STE 660 PHOENIX, AZ 85016-9266	PHONE: (602) 954-6612 FAX: (602) 954-7518 TOLL FREE: (800) 309-5829	WEB: WWW.MCARTA.COM
COLORADO	6400 S FIDDLER'S GREEN CIRLCLE STE 1900 ENGLEWOOD, CO 80111	PHONE: (303) 796-8102 FAX: (303) 796-8221 TOLL FREE: (800) 807-8639	WEB: WWW.MCARTA.COM

ADDITIONAL COMMENTS: OFFICE IS MOVING - CALL TO UPDATE NEW ADDRESS

MAILHANDLERS BENEFIT PLAN

NATIONAL *PUERTO RICO*	PO BOX 8402 LONDON, KY 40742	PHONE: (301) 738-1216 FAX: (301) 517-2126 TOLL FREE: (800) 410-7778	WEB: WWW.MHBP.COM

MAINE GENERAL HEALTH

MAINE	30 CHASE AVE WATERVILLE, ME 04901	PHONE: (207) 626-1000 FAX: (207) 872-4003 OR (207) 621-9380	

MAKSIN MANAGEMENT CORP

NATIONAL	2500 MCCLELLAN AVE STE 160 PENNSAUKEN, NJ 08109-4613	PHONE: (856) 486-7400 FAX: (856) 486-7228 TOLL FREE: (800) 547-9646	WEB: WWW.MAKSIN.COM

MANAGED BENEFITS ADMINISTRATOR — *SEE ALSO MBA*

MANAGED CARE CONSULTANTS, INC (MCC) — *MCC HEALTH CARE SYSTEMS*

NEVADA	311 N PECOS RD STE 100 HENDERSON, NV 89074-1354 PO BOX 98998 LAS VEGAS, NV 89193	PHONE: (702) 792-2994 FAX: (702) 451-7307 TOLL FREE: (800) 748-6842 IN-STATE: (800) 545-1715	E-MAIL: CUSTOMER_SERVICE@MCCNEVADA.COM WEB: WWW.MCCNEVADA.COM

MANAGED HEALTH, INC — *HEALTHFIRST 65 PLUS*

NEW YORK	25 BROADWAY STE 900 NEW YORK, NY 10004-1010	PHONE: (212) 801-6000 FAX: (212) 801-1799 TOLL FREE: (888) 260-1010	WEB: WWW.HEALTHNY.COM

M

MANHATTAN INSURANCE GROUP

NATIONAL	10700 NW FREEWAY 3RD FLOOR HOUSTON, TX 77092-7323 PO BOX 925309 HOUSTON, TX 77292-5309	PHONE: (713) 529-0045 FAX: (713) 529-5863 TOLL FREE: (800) 669-9030	E-MAIL: CS@MANHATTANLIFE.COM WEB: WWW.MANHATTANLIFE.COM

MANHATTEN INSURANCE GROUP & COMPANIES

NATIONAL	ADMINISTRATIVE OFFICES 10700 NW FREEWAY 3RD FL HOUSTON, TX 77092 PO BOX 8119 FT WASHINGTON, PA 19034-8119	FAX: (713) 529-5863 TOLL FREE: (800) 877-7756	E-MAIL: CS@MANHATTENLIFE.COM WEB: WWW.MANHATTENLIFE.COM
TEXAS	10700 NW FREEWAY 3RD FLOOR HOUSTON, TX 77092	PHONE: (713) 529-0045 FAX: (713) 529-5863 TOLL FREE: (800) 669-9030	E-MAIL: CS@MANHATENLIFE.COM WEB: WWW.MANHATTENLIFE.COM

MANHATTEN LIFE INSURANCE COMPANY

CONNECTICUT	FIVE WATERSIDE CROSSING 3RD FL WINDSOR, CT 06095	PHONE: (860)298-9343 FAX: (860)298-9538 TOLL FREE: (888) 222-0843	WEB: WWW.MANHATTENLIFE.COM

MANITOBA BLUE CROSS — *SEE ALSO BLUE CROSS CANADA*

MANPOWER, INC

WISCONSIN	5301 N IRONWOOD RD MILWAUKEE, WI 53217 PO BOX 2053 MILWAUKEE, WI 53201-2053	PHONE: (414) 961-1000 FAX: (414) 906-7847	WEB: WWW.MANPOWER.COM OR WWW.USMANPOWER.COM OR WWW.MANPOWERPROFESSIONAL.COM

MANULIFE FINANCIAL — *JOHN HANCOCK*

NATIONAL	2000 MANSFIELD RM 1310 MONTREAL, QC H3A-3A1	PHONE: (514) 287-4243 FAX: (514) 288-8062 TOLL FREE: (800) 268-6195	E-MAIL: GCSC@MARITIMELIFE.CA WEB: WWW.MANULIFE.COM
	500 KING ST N WATERLOO, ON N2J-4C6 PO BOX 1602 WATERLOO, ON N2J-4C6	PHONE: (519) 747-7000 FAX: (519) 747-6116 TOLL FREE: (888) 626-3543	WEB: WWW.MANULIFE.COM
	STE 1200 550 6TH AVE SW CALGARY, AB T2P-0S2 PO BOX 2592 STATION M CALGARY, AB T2P-5P4	PHONE: (403) 750-7300 FAX: (403) 265-1284 OR (403) 750-7320 TOLL FREE: (800) 667-5165 IN-STATE: (800) 268-6195	WEB: WWW.MANULIFE.COM

ADDITIONAL COMMENTS: ALSO SERVICES ASIA & JAPAN

BRITISH COLUMBIA *CANADA* *NOVA SCOTIA*	PO BOX 1030 HALIFAX, NS B3J-2X5	PHONE: (902) 453-7300 FAX: (604) 688-2140 OR (902) 429-7292	WEB: WWW.MANULIFE.COM

MARICOPA INTEGRATED SYSTEM HEALTHCARE — *MIRACLE BY HEALTHCARE*

ARIZONA	575 E RIVER RD TUCSON, AZ 85704	PHONE: (602) 344-8700	WEB: WWW.UPH.ORG

MARKEL WEST

NATIONAL	21820 BURBANK BLVD STE 330 WOODLAND HILLS, CA 91367-6485	PHONE: (818) 595-0600 FAX: (818) 316-0380 TOLL FREE: (800) 969-5999	WEB: WWW.MARKELCORP.COM

MARRIOTT INTERNATIONAL, INC

NATIONAL	MARRIOTT DR WASHINGTON, DC 20058-0001	PHONE: (301) 380-9000 FAX: (301) 380-4814 TOLL FREE: (800) 638-8108	WEB: WWW.MARRIOTT.COM

MARSH

NATIONAL	1166 AVE OF THE AMERICAS NEW YORK, NY 10036	PHONE: (212) 345-5000 FAX: (212) 345-5197	WEB: WWW.MARSH.COM
	1440 RENAISSANCE DR PARK RIDGE, IL 60068-1400	PHONE: (847) 803-3100 FAX: (847) 375-9223 TOLL FREE: (800) 323-2106	WEB: WWW.MARSH.COM

M

Medigap · Pharmacy · Prior Authorization · Self-Insured · TPA · Vision · Workers Comp · Main Office · No Info Given

NATIONAL — CONTINUED	ONE CALIFORNIA ST SAN FRANCISCO, CA 94111 PO BOX 193880 SAN FRANCISCO, CA 94119	PHONE: (415) 983-5100 FAX: (415) 983-8080 IN-STATE: (800) 253-2233	WEB: WWW.MARSH.COM

MARSH RISK & INS SERVICES — *SEE ALSO MARSH*

MARTIN'S POINT HEALTH CARE

MAINE NEW HAMPSHIRE NEW YORK VERMONT	331 VERANDA ST PORTLAND, ME 04104-5040 PO BOX 9746 PORTLAND, ME 04104-5040	PHONE: (207) 828-2402 TOLL FREE: (800) 897-1957	WEB: WWW.MARTINSPOINT.ORG

MASS HEALTH — *MEDICAID OF MASSACHUSETTS*

MASSACHUSETTS	55 SUMMER ST BOSTON, MA 02110 PO BOX 9118 BOSTON, MA 02112	PHONE: (617) 210-5000 TOLL FREE: (800) 841-2900	E-MAIL: MAINQUIRIES@UNISYS.COM WEB: WWW.MASS.GOV/DMA

MASS MUTUAL FINANCIAL GROUP

NATIONAL	1295 STATE ST SPRINGFIELD, MA 01111-0001	PHONE: (413) 788-8411 FAX: (413) 744-6005 TOLL FREE: (800) 272-2216	E-MAIL: MCYBULSKI@MASSMUTUAL.COM WEB: WWW.MASSMUTUAL.COM
MINNESOTA	801 NICOLLET MALL STE 2050 MINNEAPOLIS, MN 55402	PHONE: (612) 333-1413 FAX: (612) 333-9041 OR (413) 744-8545 TOLL FREE: (800) 272-2216 OR (800) 487-7844 IN-STATE: (888) 492-6038	WEB: WWW.MASSMUTUAL.COM

MAXCORP — *SEE ALSO CENTRAL SECURITY LIFE INSURANCE CO*

MBA — *MANAGED BENEFITS ADMINISTRATOR*

ARIZONA CALIFORNIA	3625 S WEST TEMPLE STE 200 SALT LAKE CITY, UT 84115-4539 PO BOX 651109 SALT LAKE CITY, UT 84165-1109	PHONE: (801) 268-3334 FAX: (801) 268-3335 TOLL FREE: (800) 877-3727 IN-STATE: (800) 877-3727	E-MAIL: CLAIMS@MBA.TO WEB: WWW.MBA.TO
CALIFORNIA	2868 PROSPECT PARK DR STE 600 RANCHO CORDOVA, CA 95670 PO BOX 873 SACRAMENTO, CA 95812	PHONE: (916) 631-1225 FAX: (916) 636-9705 TOLL FREE: (800) 888-1801	WEB: WWW.CMI-MBA.COM
IDAHO	3625 S WEST TEMPLE STE 200 SALT LAKE CITY, UT 84115-4539 PO BOX 651109 SALT LAKE CITY, UT 84165-1109	PHONE: (801) 268-3334 FAX: (801) 268-3335 TOLL FREE: (800) 877-3727 IN-STATE: (800) 877-3727	E-MAIL: CLAIMS@MBA.TO WEB: WWW.MBA.TO
MONTANA	809 S RAILWAY WORLAND, WY 82401 PO BOX 98 WORLAND, WY 82401	FAX: (307) 347-6227 TOLL FREE: (800) 246-4622	E-MAIL: CLAIMS@MBA.TO WEB: WWW.MBA.TO
NEVADA NEW MEXICO	3625 S WEST TEMPLE STE 200 SALT LAKE CITY, UT 84115-4539 PO BOX 651109 SALT LAKE CITY, UT 84165-1109	PHONE: (801) 268-3334 FAX: (801) 268-3335 TOLL FREE: (800) 877-3727 IN-STATE: (800) 877-3727	E-MAIL: CLAIMS@MBA.TO WEB: WWW.MBA.TO

SOUTH DAKOTA	809 S RAILWAY WORLAND, WY 82401 PO BOX 98 WORLAND, WY 82401	FAX: (307) 347-6227 TOLL FREE: (800) 246-4622	E-MAIL: CLAIMS@MBA.TO WEB: WWW.MBA.TO
UTAH	3625 S WEST TEMPLE STE 200 SALT LAKE CITY, UT 84115-4539 PO BOX 651109 SALT LAKE CITY, UT 84165-1109	PHONE: (801) 268-3334 FAX: (801) 268-3335 TOLL FREE: (800) 877-3727 IN-STATE: (800) 877-3727	E-MAIL: CLAIMS@MBA.TO WEB: WWW.MBA.TO

MCC HEALTH CARE SYSTEMS — *SEE ALSO MANAGED CARE CONSULTANTS, INC (MCC)*

MDA — *SEE ALSO ROBERT PLAN CORP*

MDX HAWAII — *MEDICAL DATA EXCHANGE*

HAWAII	500 ALA MOANA BLVD STE 2-200 HONOLULU, HI 96813-4614	PHONE: (808) 522-7500 FAX: (808) 522-7561 TOLL FREE: (800) 688-6060	

MEADOWBROOK INSURANCE GROUP

NATIONAL	26255 AMERICAN DR SOUTHFIELD, MI 48034-6112 PO BOX 2054 SOUTHFIELD, MI 48034	PHONE: (248) 358-1100 FAX: (248) 358-1614 OR (248) 358-3251 TOLL FREE: (800) 482-2726	WEB: WWW.MEADOWBROOK.COM

MED-PAY, INC

MISSOURI	1650 E BATTLEFIELD STE 300 SPRINGFIELD, MO 65804 PO BOX 10909 SPRINGFIELD, MO 65808	PHONE: (417) 886-6886 FAX: (417) 890-0741 TOLL FREE: (800) 777-9087	WEB: WWW.MED-PAY.COM

MEDAVANT HEALTHARE SOLUTIONS

NATIONAL	4515 GEORGE RD STE 370 TAMPA, FL 33634	PHONE: (813) 251-3135 FAX: (813) 882-7001	WEB: WWW.MEDAVANT.COM

MEDCORP SOUTHWEST, INC — *SEE ALSO BOON-CHAPMAN BENEFIT ADMINISTRATORS*

MEDEX GLOBAL GROUP, INC

NATIONAL	8501 LASALLE RD STE 200 TOWSON, MD 21286 PO BOX 19056 BALTIMORE, MD 21284	PHONE: (410) 453-6300 FAX: (410) 453-6301 TOLL FREE: (800) 537-2029	E-MAIL: INFO@MEDEXASSIST.COM WEB: WWW.MEDEXASSIST.COM

MEDI-CAL — *EDS - ELECTRONIC DATA SYSTEMS*

NATIONAL	3215 PROSPECT PARK DR RANCHO CORDOVA, CA 95670-6017 PO BOX 13029 SACRAMENTO, CA 95813-4029	PHONE: (916) 636-1200 FAX: (916) 638-8971 IN-STATE: (800) 541-5555	WEB: WWW.MEDI-CAL.CA.GOV

MEDICAID OFFICE

NATIONAL	312 HURRICANE LN WILLISTON, VT 05495	PHONE: (802) 879-5901	WEB: WWW.OVHA.STATE.VT.US

M

NATIONAL — CONTINUED		ALASKA DEPARTMENT OF HEALTH AND SOCIAL SERVICES 350 MAIN ST RM 404 JUNEAU, AK 99811 PO BOX 110601 JUNEAU, AK 99811	PHONE: (907) 465-3030 FAX: (800) 780-9982	E-MAIL: WEBMASTER@HEALTHSTATE.AK.US WEB: WWW.HSS.STATE.AK.US
ALABAMA		501 DEXTER AVE MONTGOMERY, AL 36104 PO BOX 5624 MONTGOMERY, AL 36103-5624	PHONE: (334) 242-5000 TOLL FREE: (800) 362-1504	E-MAIL: PROVREP@ALXIX.SLG.EDS.COM WEB: WWW.MEDICAID.STATE.AL.US
ALASKA		ALASKA DEPARTMENT OF HEALTH AND SOCIAL SERVICES 350 MAIN ST RM 404 JUNEAU, AK 99811 PO BOX 110601 JUNEAU, AK 99811	PHONE: (907) 465-3030 FAX: (800) 780-9982	E-MAIL: WEBMASTER@HEALTHSTATE.AK.US WEB: WWW.HSS.STATE.AK.US
AMERICAN SAMOA		DEPARTMENT OF HUMAN SERVICES OF HAWAII PO BOX 1220 HONOLULU, HI 96807-1220	PHONE: (808) 524-3370 TOLL FREE: (800) 882-4608 IN-STATE: (800) 235-4378	WEB: WWW.MED-QUEST.US
ARIZONA		ARIZONA HEALTH CARE COST CONTAINMENT OF ARIZONA 801 E JEFFERSON PHOENIX, AZ 85034	PHONE: (602) 417-4000 FAX: (602) 252-2136 TOLL FREE: (800) 962-6690 IN-STATE: (800) 554-8713	WEB: WWW.AHCCCS.STATE.AZ.US
ARKANSAS		DEPARTMENT OF HUMAN SERVICES OF ARKANSAS DONAGHEY PLZ SOUTH LITTLE ROCK, AR 72203 PO BOX 1437 LITTLE ROCK, AR 72203-1437	PHONE: (501) 682-8650 OR (501) 682-9556 FAX: (501) 682-1197 TOLL FREE: (800) 482-5431 IN-STATE: (800) 457-4454	WEB: WWW.MEDICAID.STATE.AR.US
CALIFORNIA		CALIFORNIA DEPARTMENT OF HEALTH SERVICES 714 P ST STE 1253 SACRAMENTO, CA 95814 MS 4000 PO BOX 997413 SACRAMENTO, CA 95899-7413	PHONE: (916) 636-1200 FAX: (916) 636-8971 TOLL FREE: (877) 267-2323	E-MAIL: INFO@DHS.CAHWNET.GOV WEB: WWW.MEDI-CAL.CA.GOV
COLORADO		DEPARTMENT OF HEALTHCARE POLICY AND FINANCING OF COLORADO 1570 GRANT ST DENVER, CO 80203	PHONE: (303) 866-2993 FAX: (303) 866-4411 TOLL FREE: (800) 221-3943	WEB: WWW.CHCPF.STATE.CO.US
CONNECTICUT		DEPARTMENT OF SOCIAL SERVICES OF CONNECTICUT 25 SIGOURNEY ST HARTFORD, CT 06106-5033	PHONE: (860) 424-4908 FAX: (860) 951-9544	E-MAIL: PGE.DSS@PO.STATE.CT.US WEB: WWW.DSS.STATE.CT.US
DELAWARE		DELAWARE HEALTH AND SOCIAL SERVICES 1901 N DUPONT HWY NEW CASTLE, DE 19720 PO BOX 906 NEW CASTLE, DE 19720	PHONE: (302) 255-9040 FAX: (302) 255-4429 TOLL FREE: (800) 390-6093	E-MAIL: DHSSINFO@STATE.DE.US WEB: WWW.ASSIST.DHHS.DELAWARE.GOV

M

DISTRICT OF COLUMBIA	DC DEPARTMENT OF HEALTH 825 N CAPITAL ST NE 5TH FL WASHINGTON DC, DC 20002	PHONE: (202) 442-5999 FAX: (202) 442-4788	WEB: WWW.DCHEALTH.DC.GOV
FLORIDA	AGENCY FOR HEALTHCARE ADMINISTRATION OF FLORIDA 2727 MAHAN DR TALLAHASSEE, FL 32308	TOLL FREE: (888) 419-3456	WEB: WWW.FLORIDAHEALTHSTAT.COM
GEORGIA	GEORGIA DEPARTMENT OF COMMUNITY HEALTH TWO PEACHTREE ST NW ATLANTA, GA 30303	PHONE: (770) 570-3300 FAX: (270) 804-7442 TOLL FREE: (866) 322-4260 IN-STATE: (800) 766-4456	WEB: WWW.COMMUNITYHEALTH.STATE.GA.US
IDAHO	IDAHO DEPARTMENT OF HEALTH AND WELFARE 450 W STATE ST BOISE, ID 83720-0036	PHONE: (208) 334-5500 FAX: (208) 334-6558 TOLL FREE: (800) 685-3757	E-MAIL: FELLERG@IDHW.STATE.ID.US WEB: WWW.HEALTHANDWELFARE.IDAHO.GOV
ILLINOIS	DEPARTMENT OF PUBLIC AID OF ILLINOIS 201 S GRAND AVE E SPRINGFIELD, IL 62763	PHONE: (217) 782-1200 FAX: (217) 785-1306 TOLL FREE: (800) 226-0768	WEB: WWW.HFS.ILLINOIS.GOV\
INDIANA	FAMILY AND SOCIAL SERVICES ADMINISTRATION OF INDIANA 402 W WASHINGTON ST INDIANAPOLIS, IN 46207-7083 PO BOX 7083 INDIANAPOLIS, IN 46207-7083	PHONE: (317) 233-4455 FAX: (317) 233-4693 TOLL FREE: (800) 889-9949	WEB: WWW.IN.GOV/FSSA/HEALTHCARE/
IOWA	DEPARTMENT OF HUMAN SERVICES OF IOWA 1200 UNIVERSITY AVE CITY VIEW PLAZA DES MOINES, IA 50314-2330	PHONE: (515) 283-9238 FAX: (515) 283-9040 TOLL FREE: (800) 338-8366	WEB: WWW.DHS.STATE.IA.US
KANSAS	DEPARTMENT OF SOCIAL AND REHAB SERVICES OF KANSAS 915 SW HARRISON ST TOPEKA, KS 66612	PHONE: (785) 274-4200 FAX: (785) 296-2173 TOLL FREE: (800) 766-1491	WEB: WWW.SRSKANSAS.ORG
LOUISIANA	LOUISIANA DEPARTMENT OF HEALTH AND WELFARE 1201 CAPITAL ACCESS RD BATON ROUGE, LA 70821-0629 PO BOX 629 BATON ROUGE, LA 70821-0629	PHONE: (225) 342-9500 FAX: (225) 342-5568	WEB: WWW.DHH.STATE.LA.US
MAINE	MAINE DEPARTMENT OF HEALTH AND HUMAN SERVICES 11 STATE HOUSE STATION AUGUSTA, ME 04333-0011	PHONE: (207) 624-7539 FAX: (207) 287-9229 TOLL FREE: (800) 977-6740 IN-STATE: (800) 321-5557	WEB: WWW.STATE.ME.US OR WWW.STATE.MAINE.GOV/DHHS/BMS
MARYLAND	DEPARTMENT OF HUMAN RESOURCES OF MARYLAND PO BOX 1935 BALTIMORE, MD 21203-7259	PHONE: (410) 767-5800 FAX: (410) 333-7141 TOLL FREE: (800) 322-6737	E-MAIL: DHRHELP@DHR.STATE.MD.US WEB: WWW.DHR.STATE.ME.US

MASSACHUSETTS	OFFICE OF HEALTH AND HUMAN SERVICES OF MASSACHUSETTES 600 WASHINGTON ST BOSTON, MA 02111	PHONE: (617) 210-5000 FAX: (617) 210-5820 TOLL FREE: (800) 841-2900 IN-STATE: (877) 382-8890	E-MAIL: MAINQUIRIES@UNISYS.COM WEB: WWW.MASS.GOV/MASSHEALTH
MICHIGAN	MICHIGAN DEPARTMENT OF COMMUNITY HEALTH 320 S WALNUT ST LANSING, MI 48913	PHONE: (517) 373-3500	WEB: WWW.MICHIGAN.GOV/MDCH
MINNESOTA	DEPARTMENT OF HUMAN SERVICES OF MINNESOTA 160 E KELLOGG BLVD ST PAUL, MN 55101-1494	PHONE: (651) 266-4444 FAX: (651) 266-4439	WEB: WWW.CO.RAMSEY.MN.US
MISSISSIPPI	OFFICE OF THE GOVERNOR OF MISSISSIPPI 239 N LAMAR ST STE 801 JACKSON, MS 39201-1399	PHONE: (601) 359-1399 FAX: (601) 359-6048 TOLL FREE: (800) 421-2408	WEB: WWW.DOM.STATE.MS.US
MISSOURI	DEPARTMENT OF SOCIAL SERVICES OF MISSOURI 615 HOWETON COURT JEFFERSON CITY, MO 65102 PO BOX 1527 JEFFERSON CITY, MO 65102-1527	PHONE: (573) 751-4815 FAX: (531) 751-3203 IN-STATE: (800) 392-2161	WEB: WWW.EMOMED.COM
MONTANA	PO BOX 4936 HELENA, MT 59604-4936	PHONE: (406) 449-7693 FAX: (406) 442-4402 IN-STATE: (800) 624-3958	WEB: WWW.DPHHS.MT.GOV
NEBRASKA	NEBRASKA DEPARTMENT OF HEALTH AND HUMAN SERVICES SYSTEM PO BOX 95044 LINCOLN, NE 68509-5044	PHONE: (402) 471-2306 TOLL FREE: (800) 430-3244	WEB: WWW.HHS.STATE.NE.US
NEVADA	NEVADA DEPARTMENT OF HUMAN RESOURCES 3416 GONI RD BUILDING D CARSON CITY, NV 89706	PHONE: (775) 687-4210 FAX: (775) 687-4264	WEB: WWW.NVAGING.NET
NEW HAMPSHIRE	NEW HAMPSHIRE DEPARTMENT OF HEALTH AND HUMAN SERVICES 129 PLEASANT ST CONCORD, NH 03301	PHONE: (603) 271-5254 FAX: (603) 271-8113 OR (603) 271-8431 IN-STATE: (800) 423-8303	WEB: WWW.DHHS.STATE.NH.US
NEW MEXICO	DEPARTMENT OF HUMAN SERVICES OF NEW MEXICO PO BOX 2348 SANTE FE, NM 87504-2348	PHONE: (505) 827-3100 FAX: (505) 827-3185 TOLL FREE: (888) 997-2583 IN-STATE: (800) 282-4477	WEB: WWW.STATE.NM.US/HSD/MAD
NEW YORK	NEW YORK STATE DEPARTMENT OF HEALTH EMPIRE STATE PLZ CORNING TOWER BLDG ALBANY, NY 12237	PHONE: (518) 486-9057 FAX: (518) 486-6852 TOLL FREE: (800) 541-2831	E-MAIL: MEDICAID@HEALTH.STATE.NY.US WEB: WWW.HEATLH.STATE.NY.US

M

NORTH CAROLINA	NORTH CAROLINA DEPARTMENT OF HEALTH AND HUMAN SERVICES 2001 MAIL SERVIE ENTER RALEIGH, NC 27699-2001	PHONE: (919) 855-4400 FAX: (919) 733-6608 TOLL FREE: (800) 688-6696	E-MAIL: CARE.LINE@NCMAIL.NET WEB: WWW.DHHS.STATE.NC.US/DMA
NORTH DAKOTA	DEPARTMENT OF HUMAN SERVICES OF NORTH DAKOTA 600 E BLVD AVE DEPT 325 BISMARCK, ND 58505-0250	PHONE: (701) 328-2321 FAX: (701) 328-1544 IN-STATE: (800) 755-2604	E-MAIL: DHSMED@STATE.ND.US WEB: WWW.STATE.ND.US/HUMANSERVICES
OHIO	OHIO HEALTH PLANS 80 E FULTON ST COLUMBUS, OH 43215	PHONE: (614) 728-3288 FAX: (614) 752-3986 TOLL FREE: (800) 324-8630 IN-STATE: (800) 686-1516	WEB: WWW.JFS.OHIO.GOV/OHP
OKLAHOMA	HEALTH CARE AUTHORITY OF OKLAHOMA 4545 N LINCOLN BLVD STE 124 OKLAHOMA CITY, OK 73105	PHONE: (405) 522-7300 FAX: (405) 522-7100 TOLL FREE: (800) 522-0310 IN-STATE: (800) 522-0114	WEB: WWW.OHCA.STATE.OK.US
OREGON	OREGON DEPARTMENT OF HUMAN SERVICES 500 SUMMER ST NE 3RD FL SALEM, OR 97301	PHONE: (503) 945-5772 FAX: (503) 373-7689 IN-STATE: (800) 336-6016	WEB: WWW.OREGON.GOV
PENNSYLVANIA	DEPARTMENT OF PUBLIC WELFARE OF PENNSYLVANIA PO BOX 2675 HARRISBURG, PA 17105-2675	PHONE: (717) 787-1870 FAX: (717) 787-4639 TOLL FREE: (800) 692-7462	WEB: WWW.DPW.STATE.PA.US
PUERTO RICO	MEDICAID OFFICE OF PUERTO RICO AND VIRGIN ISLANDS GPO BOX 70184 SAN JUAN, PR 00936	PHONE: (877) 725-4300 OR (212) 616-2205 (NY) FAX: (787) 759-8179	
RHODE ISLAND	DEPARTMENT OF HUMAN SERVICES OF RHODE ISLAND 600 NEW LONDON AVE CRANSTON, RI 02920	PHONE: (401) 462-5300 FAX: (401) 521-4875	WEB: WWW.DHS.STATE.RI.US
SOUTH CAROLINA	SOUTH CAROLINA DEPARTMENT OF HEALTH AND HUMAN SERVICES 1801 MAIN ST COLUMBIA, SC 29201 PO BOX 8206 COLUMBIA, SC 29202-8206	PHONE: (803) 898-2500 TOLL FREE: (888) 549-0820	E-MAIL: INFO@DHHS.STATE.SC.US WEB: WWW.DHHS.STATE.SC.US OR WWW.SCDHHS.GOV
SOUTH DAKOTA	DEPARTMENT OF SOCIAL SERVICES OF SOUTH DAKOTA 700 GOVERNERS DR, RICHARD KNEIP BLDG PIERRE, SD 57501	PHONE: (605) 773-3495 FAX: (605) 773-5246	WEB: HTTP://WWW.STATE.SD.US/SOCIAL/MEDICAL/INDEX.HTM
TENNESSEE	DEPARTMENT OF FINANCE AND ADMINISTRATION OF TENNESSEE 312 8TH AVE N 13 FL NASHVILLE, TN 37243	PHONE: (615) 741-0320 FAX: (800) 772-7647	E-MAIL: GAYLE@STATE.TN.US/TENNCARE/ WEB: WWW.STATE.TN.US/TENNCARE/

TEXAS	Home Health, Rx, Medical, Dental, Vision, Disability, HMO, EMC, HCPCS, (M), Phone	HEALTH AND HUMAN SERVICES COMMISSION OF TEXAS 4900 N LAMAR BLVD 4TH FL AUSTIN, TX 78751 PO BOX 13247 AUSTIN, TX 78711-3247	PHONE: (512) 424-6500 TOLL FREE: (800) 252-8263	E-MAIL: CONTACT@HHSC.STATE.TX.US WEB: WWW.HHSC.STATE.TX.US
UTAH	Home Health, Rx, Medical, Dental, Vision, Disability, HMO, EMC, HCPCS, Phone, Government	UTAH DEPARTMENT OF HEALTH 288 N 1460 W SALT LAKE CITY, UT 84116 PO BOX 143106 SALT LAKE CITY, UT 84114-3106	PHONE: (801) 538-6155 FAX: (801) 538-6805 TOLL FREE: (800) 662-9651	WEB: HTTP://HEALTH.UTAH.GOV/MEDICAID/
VIRGIN ISLANDS	Home Health, Rx, Medical, Dental, Vision, Disability, HMO, EMC, HCPCS, Phone	MEDICAID OFFICE OF PUERTO RICO AND VIRGIN ISLANDS GPO BOX 70184 SAN JUAN, PR 00936	PHONE: (877) 725-4300 OR (212) 616-2205 (NY) FAX: (787) 759-8179	
VIRGINIA	Home Health, Rx, Medical, Dental, Vision, Disability, HMO, EMC, HCPCS, (M), Phone	VIRGINIA DEPARTMENT OF MEDICAL ASSISTANCE SERVICES 600 E BROAD ST STE 1300 RICHMOND, VA 23219	PHONE: (804) 786-6273 FAX: (804) 225-4512 TOLL FREE: (800) 772-9996 IN-STATE: (800) 884-9730	E-MAIL: COMM@DSS.STATE.VA.US WEB: WWW.DMAS.VIRGINIA.GOV
WASHINGTON	Home Health, Rx, Medical, Dental, Vision, Disability, HMO, EMC, HCPCS, (M), Phone	DEPARTMENT OF SOCIAL AND HEALTH SERVICES OF WASHINGTON PO BOX 45505 OLYMPIA, WA 98504-5505	TOLL FREE: (800) 562-3022	WEB: WWW.ADSA.DSHS.WA.GOV
WEST VIRGINIA	Home Health, Rx, Medical, Dental, Vision, Disability, HMO, EMC, (M), Phone	WEST VIRGINIA DEPARTMENT OF HEALTH AND HUMAN RESOURCES 350 CAPITOL ST RM 251 CHARLESTON, WV 25301-3709	PHONE: (304) 558-1700 FAX: (304) 558-2515 TOLL FREE: (800) 688-5810 IN-STATE: (800) 433-3019	E-MAIL: MEDMAN@WVHHR.ORG WEB: WWW.WVDHHR.ORG
WISCONSIN	Rx, Medical, Vision	WISCONSIN DEPARTMENT OF HEALTH AND FAMILY SERVICES PO BOX 6678 MADISON, WI 53716-0678	PHONE: (608) 221-5720 FAX: (608) 250-6563 TOLL FREE: (800) 362-3002	E-MAIL: WEBMASTER@DHFS.STATE.WI.US WEB: WWW.DHFS.STATE
WYOMING	Government	WYOMING DEPARTMENT OF HEATLH 6101 YELLOWSTONE RD STE 210 CHEYENNE, WY 82002 PO BOX 547 CHEYENNE, WY 82003-0547	PHONE: (307) 777-7531 FAX: (307) 777-6974 TOLL FREE: (800) 251-1268	WEB: WWW.DFSWEB.STATE.WY.US

M

MEDICAID OFFICE / UNISYS

NEW JERSEY	Medical, Disability	DEPARTMENT OF HUMAN SERVICES OF NEW JERSEY QUACKERBRIDGE PLZ BLDG 7 TRENTON, NJ 08625 PO BOX 716 TRENTON, NJ 08625	PHONE: (609) 588-2600 FAX: (609) 588-3583	E-MAIL: ANN.CKOHLER@DHS.STATE.NJ.US WEB: WWW.STATE.NJ.US/HUMANSERVICES/DMAHS

MEDICAL ASSOCIATES HEALTH PLANS AND HEALTH CHOICES

ILLINOIS *IOWA* *WISCONSIN*	Casualty/Liability, Home Health, Rx, Medical, Vision, HMO, EMC, HCPCS, Phone, Government	1605 ASSOCIATES DR STE 101 DUBUQUE, IA 52004 PO BOX 5002 DUBUQUE, IA 52004	PHONE: (563) 556-8070 FAX: (563) 556-5134 TOLL FREE: (800) 747-8900	WEB: WWW.MAHEALTHCARE.COM

MEDICAL DATA EXCHANGE — *SEE ALSO MDX HAWAII*

MEDICAL NETWORK OF COLORADO SPRINGS — *MEMORIAL HOSPITAL MEDICAL NETWORK*

COLORADO	2420 E PIKES PEAK AVE STE 144 COLORADO SPRINGS, CO 80909 PO BOX 828 COLORADO SPRINGS, CO 80901	PHONE: (719) 365-5025 FAX: (719) 365-5004 TOLL FREE: (800) 207-1018	WEB: WWW.MYMEDNET.COM

MEDICAL PROTECTIVE COMPANY, THE

NATIONAL	5814 REED RD FORT WAYNE, IN 46835	FAX: (800) 398-6726 TOLL FREE: (800) 463-3776	WEB: WWW.GEMEDICALPROTECTIVE.COM
CALIFORNIA	1925 PALOMAR OAKS WAY STE 215 CARLSBAD, CA 92008-6526 PO BOX 3757 LA MESA, CA 91944	FAX: (866) 231-5897 TOLL FREE: (800) 463-3776	WEB: WWW.MEDPRO.COM
KANSAS	PO BOX 80637 SHAWNEE MISSION, KS 66286	PHONE: (913) 789-6600 FAX: (913) 789-6481 TOLL FREE: (800) 344-1899	WEB: WWW.GEMEDICALPROTECTIVE COM

MEDICARE — DMERC CARRIERS

ALABAMA	PALMETTO GBA BLUE CROSS BLUE SHIELD OF SOUTH CAROLINA REGION C PO BOX 100141 COLUMBIA, SC 29202-3141	PHONE: (866) 238-9650	WEB: WWW.PALMETTOGBA.COM
ALASKA *AMERICAN SAMOA*	CIGNA MEDICARE REGION D PO BOX 690 NASHVILLE, TN 37202	PHONE: (866) 243-7272 TOLL FREE: (877) 320-0390	WEB: WWW.CIGNAGOVERMENTSERVICES.COM
ADDITIONAL COMMENTS: ALSO SERVICES MARIANA ISLANDS			
ARKANSAS	PALMETTO GBA BLUE CROSS BLUE SHIELD OF SOUTH CAROLINA REGION C PO BOX 100141 COLUMBIA, SC 29202-3141	PHONE: (866) 238-9650	WEB: WWW.PALMETTOGBA.COM
ARKANSAS *CALIFORNIA*	CIGNA MEDICARE REGION D PO BOX 690 NASHVILLE, TN 37202	PHONE: (866) 243-7272 TOLL FREE: (877) 320-0390	WEB: WWW.CIGNAGOVERMENTSERVICES.COM
ADDITIONAL COMMENTS: ALSO SERVICES MARIANA ISLANDS			
COLORADO	PALMETTO GBA BLUE CROSS BLUE SHIELD OF SOUTH CAROLINA REGION C PO BOX 100141 COLUMBIA, SC 29202-3141	PHONE: (866) 238-9650	WEB: WWW.PALMETTOGBA.COM
CONNECTICUT *DELAWARE*	HEALTHNOW NEW YORK, INC REGION A PO BOX 6800 WILKES - BARRE, PA 18773-6800	PHONE: (866) 419-9458	WEB: WWW.UMD.NYCPIC.COM
DISTRICT OF COLUMBIA	ADMINASTAR FEDERAL, INC REGION B PO BOX 7027 INDIANAPOLIS, IN 46207-7027	TOLL FREE: (877) 299-7900	WEB: WWW.ADMINASTAR.COM
FLORIDA *GEORGIA*	PALMETTO GBA BLUE CROSS BLUE SHIELD OF SOUTH CAROLINA REGION C PO BOX 100141 COLUMBIA, SC 29202-3141	PHONE: (866) 238-9650	WEB: WWW.PALMETTOGBA.COM

M

GUAM *HAWAII* *IDAHO*	CIGNA MEDICARE REGION D PO BOX 690 NASHVILLE, TN 37202	PHONE: (866) 243-7272 TOLL FREE: (877) 320-0390	WEB: WWW.CIGNAGOVERMENTSERVICES.COM
ADDITIONAL COMMENTS: ALSO SERVICES MARIANA ISLANDS			
ILLINOIS *INDIANA*	ADMINASTAR FEDERAL, INC REGION B PO BOX 7027 INDIANAPOLIS, IN 46207-7027	TOLL FREE: (877) 299-7900	WEB: WWW.ADMINASTAR.COM
IOWA *KANSAS*	CIGNA MEDICARE REGION D PO BOX 690 NASHVILLE, TN 37202	PHONE: (866) 243-7272 TOLL FREE: (877) 320-0390	WEB: WWW.CIGNAGOVERMENTSERVICES.COM
ADDITIONAL COMMENTS: ALSO SERVICES MARIANA ISLANDS			
KENTUCKY *LOUISIANA*	PALMETTO GBA BLUE CROSS BLUE SHIELD OF SOUTH CAROLINA REGION C PO BOX 100141 COLUMBIA, SC 29202-3141	PHONE: (866) 238-9650	WEB: WWW.PALMETTOGBA.COM
MAINE	HEALTHNOW NEW YORK, INC REGION A PO BOX 6800 WILKES - BARRE, PA 18773-6800	PHONE: (866) 419-9458	WEB: WWW.UMD.NYCPIC.COM
MARYLAND	ADMINASTAR FEDERAL, INC REGION B PO BOX 7027 INDIANAPOLIS, IN 46207-7027	TOLL FREE: (877) 299-7900	WEB: WWW.ADMINASTAR.COM
MASSACHUSETTS	HEALTHNOW NEW YORK, INC REGION A PO BOX 6800 WILKES - BARRE, PA 18773-6800	PHONE: (866) 419-9458	WEB: WWW.UMD.NYCPIC.COM
MICHIGAN *MINNESOTA*	ADMINASTAR FEDERAL, INC REGION B PO BOX 7027 INDIANAPOLIS, IN 46207-7027	TOLL FREE: (877) 299-7900	WEB: WWW.ADMINASTAR.COM
MISSISSIPPI	PALMETTO GBA BLUE CROSS BLUE SHIELD OF SOUTH CAROLINA REGION C PO BOX 100141 COLUMBIA, SC 29202-3141	PHONE: (866) 238-9650	WEB: WWW.PALMETTOGBA.COM
MISSOURI *MONTANA* *NEBRASKA*	CIGNA MEDICARE REGION D PO BOX 690 NASHVILLE, TN 37202	PHONE: (866) 243-7272 TOLL FREE: (877) 320-0390	WEB: WWW.CIGNAGOVERMENTSERVICES.COM
ADDITIONAL COMMENTS: ALSO SERVICES MARIANA ISLANDS			
NEW HAMPSHIRE *NEW JERSEY*	HEALTHNOW NEW YORK, INC REGION A PO BOX 6800 WILKES - BARRE, PA 18773-6800	PHONE: (866) 419-9458	WEB: WWW.UMD.NYCPIC.COM
NEW MEXICO	PALMETTO GBA BLUE CROSS BLUE SHIELD OF SOUTH CAROLINA REGION C PO BOX 100141 COLUMBIA, SC 29202-3141	PHONE: (866) 238-9650	WEB: WWW.PALMETTOGBA.COM
NEW YORK	HEALTHNOW NEW YORK, INC REGION A PO BOX 6800 WILKES - BARRE, PA 18773-6800	PHONE: (866) 419-9458	WEB: WWW.UMD.NYCPIC.COM

M

NORTH CAROLINA	PALMETTO GBA BLUE CROSS BLUE SHIELD OF SOUTH CAROLINA REGION C PO BOX 100141 COLUMBIA, SC 29202-3141	PHONE: (866) 238-9650	WEB: WWW.PALMETTOGBA.COM
NORTH DAKOTA	CIGNA MEDICARE REGION D PO BOX 690 NASHVILLE, TN 37202	PHONE: (866) 243-7272 TOLL FREE: (877) 320-0390	WEB: WWW.CIGNAGOVERMENTSERVICES.COM
ADDITIONAL COMMENTS: ALSO SERVICES MARIANA ISLANDS			
OHIO	ADMINASTAR FEDERAL, INC REGION B PO BOX 7027 INDIANAPOLIS, IN 46207-7027	TOLL FREE: (877) 299-7900	WEB: WWW.ADMINASTAR.COM
OKLAHOMA	PALMETTO GBA BLUE CROSS BLUE SHIELD OF SOUTH CAROLINA REGION C PO BOX 100141 COLUMBIA, SC 29202-3141	PHONE: (866) 238-9650	WEB: WWW.PALMETTOGBA.COM
OREGON	CIGNA MEDICARE REGION D PO BOX 690 NASHVILLE, TN 37202	PHONE: (866) 243-7272 TOLL FREE: (877) 320-0390	WEB: WWW.CIGNAGOVERMENTSERVICES.COM
ADDITIONAL COMMENTS: ALSO SERVICES MARIANA ISLANDS			
PENNSYLVANIA	HEALTHNOW NEW YORK, INC REGION A PO BOX 6800 WILKES - BARRE, PA 18773-6800	PHONE: (866) 419-9458	WEB: WWW.UMD.NYCPIC.COM
PUERTO RICO	PALMETTO GBA BLUE CROSS BLUE SHIELD OF SOUTH CAROLINA REGION C PO BOX 100141 COLUMBIA, SC 29202-3141	PHONE: (866) 238-9650	WEB: WWW.PALMETTOGBA.COM
RHODE ISLAND	HEALTHNOW NEW YORK, INC REGION A PO BOX 6800 WILKES - BARRE, PA 18773-6800	PHONE: (866) 419-9458	WEB: WWW.UMD.NYCPIC.COM
SOUTH CAROLINA	PALMETTO GBA BLUE CROSS BLUE SHIELD OF SOUTH CAROLINA REGION C PO BOX 100141 COLUMBIA, SC 29202-3141	PHONE: (866) 238-9650	WEB: WWW.PALMETTOGBA.COM
SOUTH DAKOTA	CIGNA MEDICARE REGION D PO BOX 690 NASHVILLE, TN 37202	PHONE: (866) 243-7272 TOLL FREE: (877) 320-0390	WEB: WWW.CIGNAGOVERMENTSERVICES.COM
ADDITIONAL COMMENTS: ALSO SERVICES MARIANA ISLANDS			
TENNESSEE	PALMETTO GBA BLUE CROSS BLUE SHIELD OF SOUTH CAROLINA REGION C PO BOX 100141 COLUMBIA, SC 29202-3141	PHONE: (866) 238-9650	WEB: WWW.PALMETTOGBA.COM
UTAH	CIGNA MEDICARE REGION D PO BOX 690 NASHVILLE, TN 37202	PHONE: (866) 243-7272 TOLL FREE: (877) 320-0390	WEB: WWW.CIGNAGOVERMENTSERVICES.COM
ADDITIONAL COMMENTS ALSO SERVICES MARIANA ISLANDS			

M

VERMONT	HEALTHNOW NEW YORK, INC REGION A PO BOX 6800 WILKES - BARRE, PA 18773-6800	PHONE: (866) 419-9458	WEB: WWW.UMD.NYCPIC.COM
VIRGIN ISLANDS	PALMETTO GBA BLUE CROSS BLUE SHIELD OF SOUTH CAROLINA REGION C PO BOX 100141 COLUMBIA, SC 29202-3141	PHONE: (866) 238-9650	WEB: WWW.PALMETTOGBA.COM
VIRGINIA	ADMINASTAR FEDERAL, INC REGION B PO BOX 7027 INDIANAPOLIS, IN 46207-7027	TOLL FREE: (877) 299-7900	WEB: WWW.ADMINASTAR.COM
WASHINGTON	CIGNA MEDICARE REGION D PO BOX 690 NASHVILLE, TN 37202	PHONE: (866) 243-7272 TOLL FREE: (877) 320-0390	WEB: WWW.CIGNAGOVERMENTSERVICES.COM
ADDITIONAL COMMENTS: ALSO SERVICES MARIANA ISLANDS			
WEST VIRGINIA *WISCONSIN*	ADMINASTAR FEDERAL, INC REGION B PO BOX 7027 INDIANAPOLIS, IN 46207-7027	TOLL FREE: (877) 299-7900	WEB: WWW.ADMINASTAR.COM
WYOMING	CIGNA MEDICARE REGION D PO BOX 690 NASHVILLE, TN 37202	PHONE: (866) 243-7272 TOLL FREE: (877) 320-0390	WEB: WWW.CIGNAGOVERMENTSERVICES.COM
ADDITIONAL COMMENTS: ALSO SERVICES MARIANA ISLANDS			

MEDICARE — PART A INTERMEDIARIES

ALABAMA	CAHABA BLUE CROSS BLUE SHIELD OF ALABAMA 450 RIVERCHASE PKY E BIRMINGHAM, AL 35244-2858 PO BOX 831039 BIRMINGHAM, AL 35283-1039	PHONE: (205) 220-2100 FAX: (205) 220-4841 TOLL FREE: (866) 539-5598	WEB: WWW.BCBSAL.COM
ALASKA	NORIDIAN MUTUAL INSURANCE CO 901 40TH ST S STE 1 FARGO, ND 58103 PO BOX 6709 FARGO, ND 58108-6709	PHONE: (701) 282-1100 FAX: (701) 282-1002 TOLL FREE: (866) 380-4741	WEB: WWW.NORIDIANMEDICARE.COM
ARIZONA	BLUE CROSS BLUE SHIELD OF ARIZONA PO BOX 37700 PHOENIX, AZ 85069-7700	PHONE: (602) 864-4400 TOLL FREE: (877) 567-3128	WEB: WWW.MEDICAREAZ.COM
ARKANSAS	ARKANSAS BLUE CROSS BLUE SHIELD 601 S GAINES ST LITTLE ROCK, AR 72203 PO BOX 1418 LITTLE ROCK, AR 72217	PHONE: (501) 378-2000 FAX: (501) 210-9137 TOLL FREE: (866) 548-0527	WEB: WWW.ARKMEDICARE.COM
CALIFORNIA	UNITED GOVERNMENT SERVICES 5151 B CAMINO CAMARILLO, CA 93012 PO BOX 9150 OXNARD, CA 93031	PHONE: (805) 367-0731 OR (805) 367-0596 TOLL FREE: (800) MEDICARE	WEB: WWW.UGSMEDICARE.COM
ADDITIONAL COMMENTS: ALSO SERVICES NORTHERN MARIANA ISLANDS			

COLORADO	TRAILBLAZER HEALTH ENTERPRISES 8330 LBJ FREEWAY EXECUTIVE CENTER 3 DALLAS, TX 75243 PO BOX 660030 DALLAS, TX 75266-0030	PHONE: (469) 372-1816 FAX: (469) 372-1765 TOLL FREE: (888) 763-9836	WEB: WWW.TRAILBLAZERHEALTH.COM
CONNECTICUT *DELAWARE*	EMPIRE HEALTHCOICE ASSURANCE, INC PO BOX 4846 SYRACUSE, NY 13221-4846	TOLL FREE: (800) MEDICARE	WEB: WWW.EMPIREMEDICARE.COM
DISTRICT OF COLUMBIA	CAREFIRST OF MARYLAND BLUE CROSS BLUE SHIELD 1946 GREENSPRING DR TIMONIUM , MD 21093	PHONE: (866) 488-0545 TOLL FREE: (800) 633-4227	WEB: WWW.HIGHMARKMEDICARESERVICES.COM
FLORIDA	FIRST COAST SERVICE OPTIONS PO BOX 2711 JACKSONVILLE, FL 32231	PHONE: (877) 602-8816 FAX: (904) 791-8316 TOLL FREE: (800) 633-4227	WEB: WWW.FLORIDAMEDICARE.COM
GEORGIA	BLUE CROSS BLUE SHIELD OF GEORGIA 3350 PEACHTREE RD NE ATLANTA, GA 30326 PO BOX 9048 COLUMBUS, GA 31908-9048	PHONE: (706) 571-5371 FAX: (706) 571-5431 TOLL FREE: (577) 567-3095	WEB: WWW.GEORGIAMEDICARE.COM
GUAM	UNITED GOVERNMENT SERVICES 5151 B CAMINO CAMARILLO, CA 93012 PO BOX 9150 OXNARD, CA 93031	PHONE: (805) 367-0731 OR (805) 367-0596 TOLL FREE: (800) MEDICARE	WEB: WWW.UGSMEDICARE.COM
ADDITIONAL COMMENTS: ALSO SERVICES NORTHERN MARIANA ISLANDS			
IDAHO	BLUE CROSS BLUE SHIELD OF OREGON 200 SW MARKET ST PORTLAND, OR 97201 PO BOX 6702 FARGO, ND 58108-6782	PHONE: (866) 497-7857 FAX: (503) 228-5304 TOLL FREE: (800) 933-0614	WEB: WWW.NORIDIAN.COM
ILLINOIS *INDIANA*	ADMINISTAR FEDERAL, INC ANTHEM INSURANCE COMPANIES, INC 8115 KNUE RD INDIANAPOLIS, IN 46250-1936 PO BOX 6130 INDIANAPOLIS, IN 46250	PHONE: (800) 633-4227 FAX: (317) 841-4691 TOLL FREE: (800) 622-4792	WEB: WWW.MEDICARE.GOV
IOWA	CAHABA BLUE CROSS BLUE SHIELD OF ALABAMA 450 RIVERCHASE PKY E BIRMINGHAM, AL 35244-2858 PO BOX 831039 BIRMINGHAM, AL 35283-1039	PHONE: (205) 220-2100 FAX: (205) 220-4841 TOLL FREE: (866) 539-5598	WEB: WWW.BCBSAL.COM
KANSAS	BLUE CROSS BLUE SHIELD OF KANSAS PO BOX 3543 TOPEKA, KS 66601-3543	PHONE: (785) 291-7000 FAX: (785) 291-7098 TOLL FREE: (877) 567-7270	E-MAIL: MEDICARE@BCBSKS.COM WEB: WWW.KANSASMEDICARE.COM
KENTUCKY	ADMINISTAR FEDERAL, INC ANTHEM INSURANCE COMPANIES, INC 8115 KNUE RD INDIANAPOLIS, IN 46250-1936 PO BOX 6130 INDIANAPOLIS, IN 46250	PHONE: (800) 633-4227 FAX: (317) 841-4691 TOLL FREE: (800) 622-4792	WEB: WWW.MEDICARE.GOV

LOUISIANA	Medical, Disability, EMC, HCPCS	BLUE CROSS BLUE SHIELD OF MISSISSIPPI 1064 FLYNT DR FLOWOOD, MS 39232-9570 PO BOX 23046 JACKSON, MS 39225-3046	PHONE: (877) 567-3097 FAX: (601) 664-4214 OR (601) 939-5362	WEB: WWW.TRISPAN.COM
MAINE	Medical, Disability, EMC, HCPCS	ANTHEM PLANS OF MAINE ASSOC HOSPITAL SERVICE TWO GANNETT DR SOUTH PORTLAND, ME 04106-6911	PHONE: (207) 253-3348 FAX: (207) 822-7926 TOLL FREE: (800) 633-4227	WEB: WWW.ANTHEM.COM
MARYLAND	Rx, Medical, Disability, EMC, HCPCS, Telephone	CARE FIRST OF MARYLAND BLUE CROSS BLUE SHIELD OF MARYLAND 10455 MILL RUN CIR OWINGS MILLS, MD 21117	PHONE: (866) 488-0545 FAX: (410) 561-7951 TOLL FREE: (800) 633-4227	E-MAIL: MEDICARE_A@CAREFIRST.COM WEB: WWW.MEDICARE.GOV
MASSACHUSETTS	Medical, Disability, EMC, HCPCS	ANTHEM PLANS OF MAINE ASSOC HOSPITAL SERVICE TWO GANNETT DR SOUTH PORTLAND, ME 04106-6911	PHONE: (207) 253-3348 FAX: (207) 822-7926 TOLL FREE: (800) 633-4227	WEB: WWW.ANTHEM.COM
MICHIGAN	Medical, Disability, EMC, HCPCS	UNITED GOVERNMENT SERVICES 5151 B CAMINO CAMARILLO, CA 93012 PO BOX 9150 OXNARD, CA 93031	PHONE: (805) 367-0731 OR (805) 367-0596 TOLL FREE: (800) MEDICARE	WEB: WWW.UGSMEDICARE.COM
ADDITIONAL COMMENTS: ALSO SERVICES NORTHERN MARIANA ISLANDS				
MINNESOTA	Medical, Disability, EMC, HCPCS	NORIDIAN MUTUAL INSURANCE CO 901 40TH ST S STE 1 FARGO, ND 58103 PO BOX 6709 FARGO, ND 58108-6709	PHONE: (701) 282-1100 FAX: (701) 282-1002 TOLL FREE: (866) 380-4741	WEB: WWW.NORIDIANMEDICARE.COM
MISSISSIPPI *MISSOURI*	Medical, Disability, EMC, HCPCS	BLUE CROSS BLUE SHIELD OF MISSISSIPPI 1064 FLYNT DR FLOWOOD, MS 39232-9570 PO BOX 23046 JACKSON, MS 39225-3046	PHONE: (877) 567-3097 FAX: (601) 664-4214 OR (601) 939-5362	WEB: WWW.TRISPAN.COM
MONTANA	EMC	BLUE CROSS BLUE SHIELD OF MONTANA 3360 10TH AVE S GREAT FALLS, MT 59403 PO BOX 5017 GREAT FALLS, MT 59403-5017	PHONE: (406) 791-4000 FAX: (406) 791-9355 TOLL FREE: (866) 737-8928	WEB: WWW.MEDICARE.BCBSMT.COM
NEBRASKA	Medical, Disability, EMC, HCPCS	BLUE CROSS BLUE SHIELD OF NEBRASKA 7261 MERCY RD OMAHA, NE 68180-0001 PO BOX 3248 OMAHA, NE 68180-0001	PHONE: (402) 390-1820 FAX: (402) 343-3525 OR (402) 343-3407 TOLL FREE: (800) MEDICARE OR (800) 642-8980	WEB: WWW.BCBSNE.COM
NEVADA	Medical, Disability, EMC, HCPCS	UNITED GOVERNMENT SERVICES 5151 B CAMINO CAMARILLO, CA 93012 PO BOX 9150 OXNARD, CA 93031	PHONE: (805) 367-0731 OR (805) 367-0596 TOLL FREE: (800) MEDICARE	WEB: WWW.UGSMEDICARE.COM
ADDITIONAL COMMENTS: ALSO SERVICES NORTHERN MARIANA ISLANDS				
NEW HAMPSHIRE	Medical, Disability, EMC, HCPCS	ANTHEM HEALTH PLANS OF NEW HAMPSHIRE 3000 GOFFS FALLS RD MANCHESTER, NH 03111-0001	PHONE: (603) 395-7000 FAX: (603) 695-7741 TOLL FREE: (866) 680-0749	WEB: WWW.ANTHEMBCBSNH.COM

M

NEW JERSEY	RIVER BEND GOVERNMENT ADMINISTRATORS BLUE CROSS BLUE SHIELD OF TN 730 CHESTNUT ST CHATTANOOGA, TN 37402-1790	PHONE: (866) 641-2007 FAX: (423) 535-6518 TOLL FREE: (877) 296-6189	E-MAIL: RIVERBENDGBA@BCBST.COM WEB: WWW.RIVERBENDGBA.COM
NEW MEXICO	TRAILBLAZER HEALTH ENTERPRISES 8330 LBJ FREEWAY EXECUTIVE CENTER 3 DALLAS, TX 75243 PO BOX 660030 DALLAS, TX 75266-0030	PHONE: (469) 372-1816 FAX: (469) 372-1765 TOLL FREE: (888) 763-9836	WEB: WWW.TRAILBLAZERHEALTH.COM
NEW YORK	EMPIRE HEALTHCOICE ASSURANCE, INC PO BOX 4846 SYRACUSE, NY 13221-4846	TOLL FREE: (800) MEDICARE	WEB: WWW.EMPIREMEDICARE.COM
NORTH DAKOTA	NORIDIAN MUTUAL INSURANCE CO 901 40TH ST S STE 1 FARGO, ND 58103 PO BOX 6709 FARGO, ND 58108-6709	PHONE: (701) 282-1100 FAX: (701) 282-1002 TOLL FREE: (866) 380-4741	WEB: WWW.NORIDIANMEDICARE.COM
OHIO	ADMINISTAR FEDERAL, INC ANTHEM INSURANCE COMPANIES, INC 8115 KNUE RD INDIANAPOLIS, IN 46250-1936 PO BOX 6130 INDIANAPOLIS, IN 46250	PHONE: (800) 633-4227 FAX: (317) 841-4691 TOLL FREE: (800) 622-4792	WEB: WWW.MEDICARE.GOV
OKLAHOMA	BLUE CROSS BLUE SHIELD OF OKLAHOMA 1215 S BOULDER AVE TULSA, OK 74119 PO BOX 3283 TULSA, OK 74102-3283	PHONE: (918) 560-3500 FAX: (918) 560-3506 TOLL FREE: (877) 567-3094	WEB: WWW.BCBSOK.COM
PENNSYLVANIA	VERITUS MEDICARE SERVICES PO BOX 890385 PITTSBURGH, PA 17089	FAX: (412) 544-8054 TOLL FREE: (800) 633-4227	E-MAIL: VERITUSMEDICARE@HIGHMARK.COM WEB: WWW.VERITUSMEDICARE.COM
PUERTO RICO	COOPERATIVE DE SEGUROS DEVIDA DE PUERTO RICO 400 AMERICO MIRANDA AVE SAN JUAN , PR 00927 PO BOX 70391 SAN JUAN , PR 00936-3428	PHONE: (800) 638-4227 FAX: (787) 756-8199	WEB: WWW.TRIPLES-MED.ORG
SOUTH CAROLINA	PALMETTO GBA BLUE CROSS BLUE SHIELD OF SOUTH CAROLINA 17 TECHNOLOGY CIR COLUMBIA, SC 29203-9511 PO BOX 100190 COLUMBIA, SC 29202-3190	PHONE: (866) 238-9654 FAX: (803) 935-0595 TOLL FREE: (866) 238-9654	WEB: WWW.PALMETTOGBA.COM
TENNESSEE	RIVER BEND GOVERNMENT ADMINISTRATORS BLUE CROSS BLUE SHIELD OF TN 730 CHESTNUT ST CHATTANOOGA, TN 37402-1790	PHONE: (866) 641-2007 FAX: (423) 535-6518 TOLL FREE: (877) 296-6189	E-MAIL: RIVERBENDGBA@BCBST.COM WEB: WWW.RIVERBENDGBA.COM
TEXAS	TRAILBLAZER HEALTH ENTERPRISES 8330 LBJ FREEWAY EXECUTIVE CENTER 3 DALLAS, TX 75243 PO BOX 660030 DALLAS, TX 75266-0030	PHONE: (469) 372-1816 FAX: (469) 372-1765 TOLL FREE: (888) 763-9836	WEB: WWW.TRAILBLAZERHEALTH.COM

M

UTAH	BLUE CROSS BLUE SHIELD OF OREGON 200 SW MARKET ST PORTLAND, OR 97201 PO BOX 6702 FARGO, ND 58108-6782	PHONE: (866) 497-7857 FAX: (503) 228-5304 TOLL FREE: (800) 933-0614	WEB: WWW.NORIDIAN.COM
VERMONT	ANTHEM HEALTH PLANS OF NEW HAMPSHIRE 3000 GOFFS FALLS RD MANCHESTER, NH 03111-0001	PHONE: (603) 395-7000 FAX: (603) 695-7741 TOLL FREE: (866) 680-0749	WEB: WWW.ANTHEMBCBSNH.COM
VIRGIN ISLANDS	COOPERATIVE DE SEGUROS DEVIDA DE PUERTO RICO 400 AMERICO MIRANDA AVE SAN JUAN , PR 00927 PO BOX 70391 SAN JUAN , PR 00936-3428	PHONE: (800) 638-4227 FAX: (787) 756-8199	WEB: WWW.TRIPLES-MED.ORG
VIRGINIA	UNITED GOVERNMENT SERVICES 5151 B CAMINO CAMARILLO, CA 93012 PO BOX 9150 OXNARD, CA 93031	PHONE: (805) 367-0731 OR (805) 367-0596 TOLL FREE: (800) MEDICARE	WEB: WWW.UGSMEDICARE.COM
ADDITIONAL COMMENTS: ALSO SERVICES NORTHERN MARIANA ISLANDS			
WASHINGTON	NORIDIAN MUTUAL INSURANCE CO 901 40TH ST S STE 1 FARGO, ND 58103 PO BOX 6709 FARGO, ND 58108-6709	PHONE: (701) 282-1100 FAX: (701) 282-1002 TOLL FREE: (866) 380-4741	WEB: WWW.NORIDIANMEDICARE.COM
WISCONSIN	UNITED GOVERNMENT SERVICES 5151 B CAMINO CAMARILLO, CA 93012 PO BOX 9150 OXNARD, CA 93031	PHONE: (805) 367-0731 OR (805) 367-0596 TOLL FREE: (800) MEDICARE	WEB: WWW.UGSMEDICARE.COM
ADDITIONAL COMMENTS: ALSO SERVICES NORTHERN MARIANA ISLANDS			
WYOMING	BLUE CROSS BLUE SHIELD OF WYOMING 4000 HOUSE AVE CHEYENNE, WY 82001-1446 PO BOX 908 CHEYENNE, WY 82003-0908	PHONE: (307) 432-2860 FAX: (307) 432-2901 TOLL FREE: (877) 567-3093	WEB: WWW.MEDICAREWY.COM

M

MEDICARE — PART B CARRIERS

ALABAMA	CAHABA BLUE CROSS BLUE SHIELD OF ALABAMA 450 RIVERCHASE PKY E BIRMINGHAM, AL 35244-2858 PO BOX 830139 BIRMINGHAM, AL 35283-1039	PHONE: (205) 220-2100 FAX: (205) 220-4841 TOLL FREE: (866) 539-5598	E-MAIL: ALMEDICARE@BCBSAL.ORG WEB: WWW.CAHABAGBA.COM
ALASKA	NORIDIAN MUTUAL INSURANCE CO 4305 13TH AVE SW FARGO, ND 58103-3309 PO BOX 6706 FARGO, ND 58108-6706	PHONE: (701) 282-1100 FAX: (701) 282-1002 TOLL FREE: (877) 908-8431 IN-STATE: (800) 933-0614	WEB: WWW.NORIDIANMEDICARE.COM
AMERICAN SAMOA	NORIDIAN MUTUAL INSURANCE CO 4305 13TH AVE SW FARGO, ND 58103-3309 PO BOX 6706 FARGO, ND 58108-6706	PHONE: (701) 282-1100 FAX: (701) 282-1002 TOLL FREE: (877) 908-8431 IN-STATE: (800) 933-0614	WEB: WWW.NORIDIANMEDICARE.COM
ADDITIONAL COMMENTS: ALSO SERVICES NORTHERN MARIANA ISLANDS			

ARKANSAS	ARKANSAS BLUE CROSS BLUE SHIELD 515 W PERSHING BLVD NORTH LITTLE ROCK, AR 72114 PO BOX 8150 LITTLE ROCK, AR 72203	PHONE: (501) 378-2000 FAX: (501) 210-9153 TOLL FREE: (866) 345-0274	E-MAIL: TLWHITE@ARKBLUECROSS.COM WEB: WWW.ARKMEDICARE.COM
CALIFORNIA	NATIONAL HERITAGE INSURANCE CO 402 OTTERSON DR CHICO, CA 95928-8206 PO BOX 2800 CHICO, CA 95976	PHONE: (877) 527-6613 TOLL FREE: (877) 591-1587 IN-STATE: (866) 502-9054	E-MAIL: NHICMEDICARE@EDS.COM WEB: WWW.MEDICARENHIC.COM
COLORADO	NORIDIAN MUTUAL INSURANCE CO 4305 13TH AVE SW FARGO, ND 58103-3309 PO BOX 6706 FARGO, ND 58108-6706	PHONE: (701) 282-1100 FAX: (701) 282-1002 TOLL FREE: (877) 908-8431 IN-STATE: (800) 933-0614	WEB: WWW.NORIDIANMEDICARE.COM
ADDITIONAL COMMENTS: ALSO SERVICES NORTHERN MARIANA ISLANDS			
CONNECTICUT	FIRST COAST SERVICE OPTIONS PO BOX 2525 JACKSONVILLE, FL 32219	PHONE: (904) 791-6111 OR (866) 454-9007 TOLL FREE: (877) 847-4992	WEB: WWW.FLORIDAMEDICARE.COM
DISTRICT OF COLUMBIA	TRAILBLAZER HEALTH ENTERPRISES 8330 LBJ FREEWAY DALLAS, TX 75243 PO BOX 660156 DALLAS, TX 75266-0156	PHONE: (469) 372-1816 FAX: (469) 372-1765 TOLL FREE: (877) 391-2610	WEB: WWW.TRAILBLAZERHEALTH.COM
FLORIDA	FIRST COAST SERVICE OPTIONS PO BOX 2525 JACKSONVILLE, FL 32219	PHONE: (904) 791-6111 OR (866) 454-9007 TOLL FREE: (877) 847-4992	WEB: WWW.FLORIDAMEDICARE.COM
GEORGIA	CAHABA BLUE CROSS BLUE SHIELD OF ALABAMA 450 RIVERCHASE PKY E BIRMINGHAM, AL 35244-2858 PO BOX 830139 BIRMINGHAM, AL 35283-1039	PHONE: (205) 220-2100 FAX: (205) 220-4841 TOLL FREE: (866) 539-5598	E-MAIL: ALMEDICARE@BCBSAL.ORG WEB: WWW.CAHABAGBA.COM
HAWAII	NORIDIAN MUTUAL INSURANCE CO 4305 13TH AVE SW FARGO, ND 58103-3309 PO BOX 6706 FARGO, ND 58108-6706	PHONE: (701) 282-1100 FAX: (701) 282-1002 TOLL FREE: (877) 908-8431 IN-STATE: (800) 933-0614	WEB: WWW.NORIDIANMEDICARE.COM
ADDITIONAL COMMENTS: ALSO SERVICES NORTHERN MARIANA ISLANDS			
IDAHO	GOVERMENT SERVICES TWO VANTAGE WY NASHVILLE, TN 37228-1504 PO BOX 1465 NASHVILLE, TN 37202-1465	PHONE: (615) 244-5680 FAX: (615) 782-4651 TOLL FREE: (800) 342-8900 IN-STATE: (800) 627-2782	WEB: WWW.CIGNAGOVERMENTSEVICES.COM
ILLINOIS	WISCONSIN PHYSICIANS SERVICE INSURANCE CORP 1717 W BROADWAY MADISON, WI 53713 PO BOX 8190 MADISON, WI 53713	PHONE: (608) 221-4711 FAX: (608) 301-2625 TOLL FREE: (877) 908-8475	WEB: WWW.WPSIC.COM
INDIANA	8115 KNUE RD INDIANAPOLIS, IN 46250-1936 PO BOX 6130 INDIANAPOLIS, IN 46250	PHONE: (800) 633-4227 FAX: (317) 841-4691 TOLL FREE: (800) 622-4792	WEB: WWW.MEDICARE.GOV

M

IOWA		NORIDIAN MUTUAL INSURANCE CO 4305 13TH AVE SW FARGO, ND 58103-3309 PO BOX 6706 FARGO, ND 58108-6706	PHONE: (701) 282-1100 FAX: (701) 282-1002 TOLL FREE: (877) 908-8431 IN-STATE: (800) 933-0614	WEB: WWW.NORIDIANMEDICARE.COM
ADDITIONAL COMMENTS: ALSO SERVICES NORTHERN MARIANA ISLANDS				
KANSAS		BLUE CROSS BLUE SHIELD OF KANSAS PO BOX 3543 TOPEKA, KS 66601-3543	PHONE: (785) 291-7000 FAX: (785) 291-7098 TOLL FREE: (877) 567-7270	E-MAIL: MEDICARE@BCBSKS.COM WEB: WWW.KANSASMEDICARE.COM
KENTUCKY		8115 KNUE RD INDIANAPOLIS, IN 46250-1936 PO BOX 6130 INDIANAPOLIS, IN 46250	PHONE: (800) 633-4227 FAX: (317) 841-4691 TOLL FREE: (800) 622-4792	WEB: WWW.MEDICARE.GOV
LOUISIANA		ARKANSAS BLUE CROSS BLUE SHIELD 515 W PERSHING BLVD NORTH LITTLE ROCK, AR 72114 PO BOX 8150 LITTLE ROCK, AR 72203	PHONE: (501) 378-2000 FAX: (501) 210-9153 TOLL FREE: (866) 345-0274	E-MAIL: TLWHITE@ARKBLUECROSS.COM WEB: WWW.ARKMEDICARE.COM
MAINE *MASSACHUSETTS*		NATIONAL HERITAGE INSURANCE CO 402 OTTERSON DR CHICO, CA 95928-8206 PO BOX 2800 CHICO, CA 95976	PHONE: (877) 527-6613 TOLL FREE: (877) 591-1587 IN-STATE: (866) 502-9054	E-MAIL: NHICMEDICARE@EDS.COM WEB: WWW.MEDICARENHIC.COM
MICHIGAN *MINNESOTA*		WISCONSIN PHYSICIANS SERVICE INSURANCE CORP 1717 W BROADWAY MADISON, WI 53713 PO BOX 8190 MADISON, WI 53713	PHONE: (608) 221-4711 FAX: (608) 301-2625 TOLL FREE: (877) 908-8475	WEB: WWW.WPSIC.COM
MISSISSIPPI		CAHABA BLUE CROSS BLUE SHIELD OF ALABAMA 450 RIVERCHASE PKY E BIRMINGHAM, AL 35244-2858 PO BOX 830139 BIRMINGHAM, AL 35283-1039	PHONE: (205) 220-2100 FAX: (205) 220-4841 TOLL FREE: (866) 539-5598	E-MAIL: ALMEDICARE@BCBSAL.ORG WEB: WWW.CAHABAGBA.COM
MISSOURI		ARKANSAS BLUE CROSS BLUE SHIELD 515 W PERSHING BLVD NORTH LITTLE ROCK, AR 72114 PO BOX 8150 LITTLE ROCK, AR 72203	PHONE: (501) 378-2000 FAX: (501) 210-9153 TOLL FREE: (866) 345-0274	E-MAIL: TLWHITE@ARKBLUECROSS.COM WEB: WWW.ARKMEDICARE.COM
		BLUE CROSS BLUE SHIELD OF KANSAS PO BOX 3543 TOPEKA, KS 66601-3543	PHONE: (785) 291-7000 FAX: (785) 291-7098 TOLL FREE: (877) 567-7270	E-MAIL: MEDICARE@BCBSKS.COM WEB: WWW.KANSASMEDICARE.COM
MONTANA		BLUE CROSS BLUE SHIELD OF MONTANA 2501 BELTVIEW HELENA, MT 59604 PO BOX 4310 HELENA, MT 59604	FAX: (406) 442-9968 TOLL FREE: (800) 633-4227	WEB: WWW.MEDICARE.BCBSMT.COM
NEBRASKA		BLUE CROSS BLUE SHIELD OF KANSAS PO BOX 3543 TOPEKA, KS 66601-3543	PHONE: (785) 291-7000 FAX: (785) 291-7098 TOLL FREE: (877) 567-7270	E-MAIL: MEDICARE@BCBSKS.COM WEB: WWW.KANSASMEDICARE.COM

M

NEVADA	NORIDIAN MUTUAL INSURANCE CO 4305 13TH AVE SW FARGO, ND 58103-3309 PO BOX 6706 FARGO, ND 58108-6706	PHONE: (701) 282-1100 FAX: (701) 282-1002 TOLL FREE: (877) 908-8431 IN-STATE: (800) 933-0614	WEB: WWW.NORIDIANMEDICARE.COM
ADDITIONAL COMMENTS: ALSO SERVICES NORTHERN MARIANA ISLANDS			
NEW HAMPSHIRE	NATIONAL HERITAGE INSURANCE CO 402 OTTERSON DR CHICO, CA 95928-8206 PO BOX 2800 CHICO, CA 95976	PHONE: (877) 527-6613 TOLL FREE: (877) 591-1587 IN-STATE: (866) 502-9054	E-MAIL: NHICMEDICARE@EDS.COM WEB: WWW.MEDICARENHIC.COM
NEW JERSEY	EMPIRE HEALTHCHOICE ASSURANCE, INC PO BOX 5202 BINGHAMTON, NY 13902-5202	PHONE: (914) 248-2865 FAX: (716) 887-8548 TOLL FREE: (877) 567-7173	WEB: WWW.UMD.NYCPIC.COM
NEW MEXICO	ARKANSAS BLUE CROSS BLUE SHIELD 515 W PERSHING BLVD NORTH LITTLE ROCK, AR 72114 PO BOX 8150 LITTLE ROCK, AR 72203	PHONE: (501) 378-2000 FAX: (501) 210-9153 TOLL FREE: (866) 345-0274	E-MAIL: TLWHITE@ARKBLUECROSS.COM WEB: WWW.ARKMEDICARE.COM
NEW YORK	HEALTH NOW NEW YORK, INC 1901 MAIN ST BUFFALO, NY 14208 PO BOX 5202 BINGHAMTON, NY 13902-5202	PHONE: (716) 887-6900 FAX: (716) 887-8548 TOLL FREE: (877) 567-7173	WEB: WWW.UMD.NYCPIC.COM
	EMPIRE HEALTHCHOICE ASSURANCE, INC PO BOX 5202 BINGHAMTON, NY 13902-5202	PHONE: (914) 248-2865 FAX: (716) 887-8548 TOLL FREE: (877) 567-7173	WEB: WWW.UMD.NYCPIC.COM
NORTH CAROLINA	GOVERMENT SERVICES TWO VANTAGE WY NASHVILLE, TN 37228-1504 PO BOX 1465 NASHVILLE, TN 37202-1465	PHONE: (615) 244-5680 FAX: (615) 782-4651 TOLL FREE: (800) 342-8900 IN-STATE: (800) 627-2782	WEB: WWW.CIGNAGOVERMENTSEVICES.COM
NORTH DAKOTA	NORIDIAN MUTUAL INSURANCE CO 4305 13TH AVE SW FARGO, ND 58103-3309 PO BOX 6706 FARGO, ND 58108-6706	PHONE: (701) 282-1100 FAX: (701) 282-1002 TOLL FREE: (877) 908-8431 IN-STATE: (800) 933-0614	WEB: WWW.NORIDIANMEDICARE.COM
ADDITIONAL COMMENTS: ALSO SERVICES NORTHERN MARIANA ISLANDS			
OKLAHOMA	ARKANSAS BLUE CROSS BLUE SHIELD 515 W PERSHING BLVD NORTH LITTLE ROCK, AR 72114 PO BOX 8150 LITTLE ROCK, AR 72203	PHONE: (501) 378-2000 FAX: (501) 210-9153 TOLL FREE: (866) 345-0274	E-MAIL: TLWHITE@ARKBLUECROSS.CCM WEB: WWW.ARKMEDICARE.COM
PENNSYLVANIA	VERITUS MEDICARE SERVICES PO BOX 890157 CAMP HILL, PA 17089-0157	PHONE: (412) 544-7000 FAX: (412) 544-8054 TOLL FREE: (800) 633-4227	E-MAIL: VERITUSMEDICARE@HIGHMARK.COM WEB: WWW.VERITUSMEDICARE.COM
PUERTO RICO	TRIPLE-S INC / MEDICARE 1441 ROOSEVELT AVE CAPARRA HEIGHTS, PR 00920 PO BOX 71391 SAN JUAN, PR 00936-1391	FAX: (787) 277-6688 TOLL FREE: (877) 715-1921	WEB: WWW.TRIPLES-MED.ORG

M

RHODE ISLAND	ARKANSAS BLUE CROSS BLUE SHIELD 515 W PERSHING BLVD NORTH LITTLE ROCK, AR 72114 PO BOX 8150 LITTLE ROCK, AR 72203	PHONE: (501) 378-2000 FAX: (501) 210-9153 TOLL FREE: (866) 345-0274	E-MAIL: TLWHITE@ARKBLUECROSS.COM WEB: WWW.ARKMEDICARE.COM
SOUTH CAROLINA	PALMETTO GBA BLUE CROSS BLUE SHIELD OF SOUTH CAROLINA 17 TECHNOLOGY CIR COLUMBIA, SC 29203-9511 PO BOX 100190 COLUMBIA, SC 29202-3190	PHONE: (866) 238-9654 FAX: (803) 935-0595 TOLL FREE: (866) 238-9654	WEB: WWW.PALMETTOGBA.COM
SOUTH DAKOTA	NORIDIAN MUTUAL INSURANCE CO 4305 13TH AVE SW FARGO, ND 58103-3309 PO BOX 6706 FARGO, ND 58108-6706	PHONE: (701) 282-1100 FAX: (701) 282-1002 TOLL FREE: (877) 908-8431 IN-STATE: (800) 933-0614	WEB: WWW.NORIDIANMEDICARE.COM
ADDITIONAL COMMENTS: ALSO SERVICES NORTHERN MARIANA ISLANDS			
TENNESSEE	GOVERMENT SERVICES TWO VANTAGE WY NASHVILLE, TN 37228-1504 PO BOX 1465 NASHVILLE, TN 37202-1465	PHONE: (615) 244-5680 FAX: (615) 782-4651 TOLL FREE: (800) 342-8900 IN-STATE: (800) 627-2782	WEB: WWW.CIGNAGOVERMENTSEVICES.COM
TEXAS	TRAILBLAZER HEALTH ENTERPRISES 8330 LBJ FREEWAY DALLAS, TX 75243 PO BOX 660156 DALLAS, TX 75266-0156	PHONE: (469) 372-1816 FAX: (469) 372-1765 TOLL FREE: (877) 391-2610	WEB: WWW.TRAILBLAZERHEALTH.COM
UTAH	BLUE CROSS BLUE SHIELD OF UTAH 2890 E COTTONWOOD PKY SALT LAKE CITY, UT 84121 PO BOX 30270 SALT LAKE CITY, UT 84130-0270	PHONE: (801) 333-2100 FAX: (801) 333-6505 TOLL FREE: (800) 624-6519	E-MAIL: UT.MEDICAREGENERAL@REGENCE.COM WEB: WWW.REGENCE.COM
VERMONT	NATIONAL HERITAGE INSURANCE CO 402 OTTERSON DR CHICO, CA 95928-8206 PO BOX 2800 CHICO, CA 95976	PHONE: (877) 527-6613 TOLL FREE: (877) 591-1587 IN-STATE: (866) 502-9054	E-MAIL: NHICMEDICARE@EDS.COM WEB: WWW.MEDICARENHIC.COM
VIRGIN ISLANDS	TRIPLE-S INC / MEDICARE 1441 ROOSEVELT AVE CAPARRA HEIGHTS, PR 00920 PO BOX 71391 SAN JUAN, PR 00936-1391	FAX: (787) 277-6688 TOLL FREE: (877) 715-1921	WEB: WWW.TRIPLES-MED.ORG
VIRGINIA	TRAILBLAZER HEALTH ENTERPRISES 8330 LBJ FREEWAY DALLAS, TX 75243 PO BOX 660156 DALLAS, TX 75266-0156	PHONE: (469) 372-1816 FAX: (469) 372-1765 TOLL FREE: (877) 391-2610	WEB: WWW.TRAILBLAZERHEALTH.COM
WASHINGTON	NORIDIAN MUTUAL INSURANCE CO 4305 13TH AVE SW FARGO, ND 58103-3309 PO BOX 6706 FARGO, ND 58108-6706	PHONE: (701) 282-1100 FAX: (701) 282-1002 TOLL FREE: (877) 908-8431 IN-STATE: (800) 933-0614	WEB: WWW.NORIDIANMEDICARE.COM
ADDITIONAL COMMENTS: ALSO SERVICES NORTHERN MARIANA ISLANDS			

M

WISCONSIN	WISCONSIN PHYSICIANS SERVICE INSURANCE CORP 1717 W BROADWAY MADISON, WI 53713 PO BOX 8190 MADISON, WI 53713	PHONE: (608) 221-4711 FAX: (608) 301-2625 TOLL FREE: (877) 908-8475	WEB: WWW.WPSIC.COM

MEDICARE REGIONAL HOME HEALTH INTERMEDIARIES

ALABAMA	PALMETTO GBA BLUE CROSS BLUE SHIELD OF SOUTH CAROLINA REGION IV I 20 E AT ALPINE RD COLUMBIA, SC 29219	PHONE: (803) 788-3860 TOLL FREE: (800) MEDICARE IN-STATE: (800) 288-2227	WEB: WWW.PALMETTOGBA.COM
ALASKA *AMERICAN SAMOA* *ARIZONA*	UNITED GOVERNMENT SERVICES REGION V PO BOX 9150 OXNARD, CA 93031	PHONE: (805) 367-0731 TOLL FREE: (866) 380-4745	WEB: WWW.UGSMEDICARE.COM
ADDITIONAL COMMENTS: ALSO SERVICES NORTHERN MARIANA ISLANDS			
ARKANSAS	PALMETTO GBA BLUE CROSS BLUE SHIELD OF SOUTH CAROLINA REGION IV I 20 E AT ALPINE RD COLUMBIA, SC 29219	PHONE: (803) 788-3860 TOLL FREE: (800) MEDICARE IN-STATE: (800) 288-2227	WEB: WWW.PALMETTOGBA.COM
CALIFORNIA	UNITED GOVERNMENT SERVICES REGION V PO BOX 9150 OXNARD, CA 93031	PHONE: (805) 367-0731 TOLL FREE: (866) 380-4745	WEB: WWW.UGSMEDICARE.COM
ADDITIONAL COMMENTS: ALSO SERVICES NORTHERN MARIANA ISLANDS			
COLORADO	BLUE CROSS BLUE SHIELD OF ALABAMA REGION VII PO BOX 830139 BIRMINGHAM, AL 35283-0139	PHONE: (205) 988-2100 TOLL FREE: (800) 517-6425	E-MAIL: ALMEDICARE@BCBSAL.ORG WEB: WWW.CAHABAGBA.COM
CONNECTICUT	ANTHEM HEALTH PLANS OF MAINE REGION I TWO GANNETT DR SOUTH PORTLAND, ME 04106-6911	PHONE: (207) 822-7000 TOLL FREE: (877) 567-9250	WEB: WWW.ANTHEM.COM
DELAWARE *DISTRICT OF COLUMBIA*	BLUE CROSS BLUE SHIELD OF ALABAMA REGION VII PO BOX 830139 BIRMINGHAM, AL 35283-0139	PHONE: (205) 988-2100 TOLL FREE: (800) 517-6425	E-MAIL: ALMEDICARE@BCBSAL.ORG WEB: WWW.CAHABAGBA.COM
FLORIDA *GEORGIA*	PALMETTO GBA BLUE CROSS BLUE SHIELD OF SOUTH CAROLINA REGION IV I 20 E AT ALPINE RD COLUMBIA, SC 29219	PHONE: (803) 788-3860 TOLL FREE: (800) MEDICARE IN-STATE: (800) 288-2227	WEB: WWW.PALMETTOGBA.COM
GUAM *HAWAII* *IDAHO*	UNITED GOVERNMENT SERVICES REGION V PO BOX 9150 OXNARD, CA 93031	PHONE: (805) 367-0731 TOLL FREE: (866) 380-4745	WEB: WWW.UGSMEDICARE.COM
ADDITIONAL COMMENTS: ALSO SERVICES NORTHERN MARIANA ISLANDS			
ILLINOIS	PALMETTO GBA BLUE CROSS BLUE SHIELD OF SOUTH CAROLINA REGION IV I 20 E AT ALPINE RD COLUMBIA, SC 29219	PHONE: (803) 788-3860 TOLL FREE: (800) MEDICARE IN-STATE: (800) 288-2227	WEB: WWW.PALMETTOGBA.COM
IOWA *KANSAS*	BLUE CROSS BLUE SHIELD OF ALABAMA REGION VII PO BOX 830139 BIRMINGHAM, AL 35283-0139	PHONE: (205) 988-2100 TOLL FREE: (800) 517-6425	E-MAIL: ALMEDICARE@BCBSAL.ORG WEB: WWW.CAHABAGBA.COM

M

KENTUCKY *LOUISIANA*	PALMETTO GBA BLUE CROSS BLUE SHIELD OF SOUTH CAROLINA REGION IV I 20 E AT ALPINE RD COLUMBIA, SC 29219	PHONE: (803) 788-3860 TOLL FREE: (800) MEDICARE IN-STATE: (800) 288-2227	WEB: WWW.PALMETTOGBA.COM
MAINE	ANTHEM HEALTH PLANS OF MAINE REGION I TWO GANNETT DR SOUTH PORTLAND, ME 04106-6911	PHONE: (207) 822-7000 TOLL FREE: (877) 567-9250	WEB: WWW.ANTHEM.COM
MARYLAND	BLUE CROSS BLUE SHIELD OF ALABAMA REGION VII PO BOX 830139 BIRMINGHAM, AL 35283-0139	PHONE: (205) 988-2100 TOLL FREE: (800) 517-6425	E-MAIL: ALMEDICARE@BCBSAL.ORG WEB: WWW.CAHABAGBA.COM
MASSACHUSETTS	ANTHEM HEALTH PLANS OF MAINE REGION I TWO GANNETT DR SOUTH PORTLAND, ME 04106-6911	PHONE: (207) 822-7000 TOLL FREE: (877) 567-9250	WEB: WWW.ANTHEM.COM
MICHIGAN *MINNESOTA*	UNITED GOVERNMENT SERVICES REGION V 675 W WASHINGTON ST MILWAUKEE, WI 53124	PHONE: (414) 226-6203 TOLL FREE: (866) 419-9462	WEB: WWW.UGSMEDICARE.COM
MISSISSIPPI	PALMETTO GBA BLUE CROSS BLUE SHIELD OF SOUTH CAROLINA REGION IV I 20 E AT ALPINE RD COLUMBIA, SC 29219	PHONE: (803) 788-3860 TOLL FREE: (800) MEDICARE IN-STATE: (800) 288-2227	WEB: WWW.PALMETTOGBA.COM
MISSOURI *MONTANA* *NEBRASKA*	BLUE CROSS BLUE SHIELD OF ALABAMA REGION VII PO BOX 830139 BIRMINGHAM, AL 35283-0139	PHONE: (205) 988-2100 TOLL FREE: (800) 517-6425	E-MAIL: ALMEDICARE@BCBSAL.ORG WEB: WWW.CAHABAGBA.COM
NEW HAMPSHIRE	ANTHEM HEALTH PLANS OF MAINE REGION I TWO GANNETT DR SOUTH PORTLAND, ME 04106-6911	PHONE: (207) 822-7000 TOLL FREE: (877) 567-9250	WEB: WWW.ANTHEM.COM
NEW JERSEY	UNITED GOVERNMENT SERVICES REGION V 675 W WASHINGTON ST MILWAUKEE, WI 53124	PHONE: (414) 226-6203 TOLL FREE: (866) 419-9462	WEB: WWW.UGSMEDICARE.COM
NEW MEXICO	PALMETTO GBA BLUE CROSS BLUE SHIELD OF SOUTH CAROLINA REGION IV I 20 E AT ALPINE RD COLUMBIA, SC 29219	PHONE: (803) 788-3860 TOLL FREE: (800) MEDICARE IN-STATE: (800) 288-2227	WEB: WWW.PALMETTOGBA.COM
	UNITED GOVERNMENT SERVICES REGION V 675 W WASHINGTON ST MILWAUKEE, WI 53124	PHONE: (414) 226-6203 TOLL FREE: (866) 419-9462	WEB: WWW.UGSMEDICARE.COM
NORTH CAROLINA	PALMETTO GBA BLUE CROSS BLUE SHIELD OF SOUTH CAROLINA REGION IV I 20 E AT ALPINE RD COLUMBIA, SC 29219	PHONE: (803) 788-3860 TOLL FREE: (800) MEDICARE IN-STATE: (800) 288-2227	WEB: WWW.PALMETTOGBA.COM
NORTH DAKOTA	BLUE CROSS BLUE SHIELD OF ALABAMA REGION VII PO BOX 830139 BIRMINGHAM, AL 35283-0139	PHONE: (205) 988-2100 TOLL FREE: (800) 517-6425	E-MAIL: ALMEDICARE@BCBSAL.ORG WEB: WWW.CAHABAGBA.COM

OHIO *OKLAHOMA*	PALMETTO GBA BLUE CROSS BLUE SHIELD OF SOUTH CAROLINA REGION IV I 20 E AT ALPINE RD COLUMBIA, SC 29219	PHONE: (803) 788-3860 TOLL FREE: (800) MEDICARE IN-STATE: (800) 288-2227	WEB: WWW.PALMETTOGBA.COM
PENNSYLVANIA	BLUE CROSS BLUE SHIELD OF ALABAMA REGION VII PO BOX 830139 BIRMINGHAM, AL 35283-0139	PHONE: (205) 988-2100 TOLL FREE: (800) 517-6425	E-MAIL: ALMEDICARE@BCBSAL.ORG WEB: WWW.CAHABAGBA.COM
PUERTO RICO	UNITED GOVERNMENT SERVICES REGION V 675 W WASHINGTON ST MILWAUKEE, WI 53124	PHONE: (414) 226-6203 TOLL FREE: (866) 419-9462	WEB: WWW.UGSMEDICARE.COM
RHODE ISLAND	ANTHEM HEALTH PLANS OF MAINE REGION I TWO GANNETT DR SOUTH PORTLAND, ME 04106-6911	PHONE: (207) 822-7000 TOLL FREE: (877) 567-9250	WEB: WWW.ANTHEM.COM
SOUTH CAROLINA	PALMETTO GBA BLUE CROSS BLUE SHIELD OF SOUTH CAROLINA REGION IV I 20 E AT ALPINE RD COLUMBIA, SC 29219	PHONE: (803) 788-3860 TOLL FREE: (800) MEDICARE IN-STATE: (800) 288-2227	WEB: WWW.PALMETTOGBA.COM
SOUTH DAKOTA	BLUE CROSS BLUE SHIELD OF ALABAMA REGION VII PO BOX 830139 BIRMINGHAM, AL 35283-0139	PHONE: (205) 988-2100 TOLL FREE: (800) 517-6425	E-MAIL: ALMEDICARE@BCBSAL.ORG WEB: WWW.CAHABAGBA.COM
TENNESSEE *TEXAS*	PALMETTO GBA BLUE CROSS BLUE SHIELD OF SOUTH CAROLINA REGION IV I 20 E AT ALPINE RD COLUMBIA, SC 29219	PHONE: (803) 788-3860 TOLL FREE: (800) MEDICARE IN-STATE: (800) 288-2227	WEB: WWW.PALMETTOGBA.COM
UTAH	BLUE CROSS BLUE SHIELD OF ALABAMA REGION VII PO BOX 830139 BIRMINGHAM, AL 35283-0139	PHONE: (205) 988-2100 TOLL FREE: (800) 517-6425	E-MAIL: ALMEDICARE@BCBSAL.ORG WEB: WWW.CAHABAGBA.COM
VERMONT	ANTHEM HEALTH PLANS OF MAINE REGION I TWO GANNETT DR SOUTH PORTLAND, ME 04106-6911	PHONE: (207) 822-7000 TOLL FREE: (877) 567-9250	WEB: WWW.ANTHEM.COM
VIRGIN ISLANDS	UNITED GOVERNMENT SERVICES REGION V 675 W WASHINGTON ST MILWAUKEE, WI 53124	PHONE: (414) 226-6203 TOLL FREE: (866) 419-9462	WEB: WWW.UGSMEDICARE.COM
VIRGINIA	BLUE CROSS BLUE SHIELD OF ALABAMA REGION VII PO BOX 830139 BIRMINGHAM, AL 35283-0139	PHONE: (205) 988-2100 TOLL FREE: (800) 517-6425	E-MAIL: ALMEDICARE@BCBSAL.ORG WEB: WWW.CAHABAGBA.COM
WASHINGTON	UNITED GOVERNMENT SERVICES REGION V PO BOX 9150 OXNARD, CA 93031	PHONE: (805) 367-0731 TOLL FREE: (866) 380-4745	WEB: WWW.UGSMEDICARE.COM
ADDITIONAL COMMENTS: ALSO SERVICES NORTHERN MARIANA ISLANDS			
WEST VIRGINIA	BLUE CROSS BLUE SHIELD OF ALABAMA REGION VII PO BOX 830139 BIRMINGHAM, AL 35283-0139	PHONE: (205) 988-2100 TOLL FREE: (800) 517-6425	E-MAIL: ALMEDICARE@BCBSAL.ORG WEB: WWW.CAHABAGBA.COM

M

WISCONSIN		UNITED GOVERNMENT SERVICES REGION V 675 W WASHINGTON ST MILWAUKEE, WI 53124	PHONE: (414) 226-6203 TOLL FREE: (866) 419-9462	WEB: WWW.UGSMEDICARE.COM
WYOMING		BLUE CROSS BLUE SHIELD OF ALABAMA REGION VII PO BOX 830139 BIRMINGHAM, AL 35283-0139	PHONE: (205) 988-2100 TOLL FREE: (800) 517-6425	E-MAIL: ALMEDICARE@BCBSAL.ORG WEB: WWW.CAHABAGBA.COM

MEDICARE SUPPLEMENT — *SEE ALSO FIRSTCOMMUNITY HEALTH PLAN INC*

MEDICO INSURANCE COMPANY

NATIONAL		1515 S 75TH ST OMAHA, NE 68124 PO BOX 3477 OMAHA, NE 68103	PHONE: (402) 391-6900 FAX: (402) 398-0898 TOLL FREE: (800) 228-6080	WEB: WWW.GOMEDICO.COM

MEDIVERSAL, INC

ILLINOIS *INDIANA* *LOUISIANA* *MISSISSIPPI*		CENTRAL REGION 2906 N STATE ST STE 205 JACKSON, MS 39216	PHONE: (601) 362-3193 FAX: (601) 362-3194 TOLL FREE: (800) 318-1963	WEB: WWW.MEDIVERSAL.COM
NEVADA		ADMINISTRATIVE OFFICES WESTERN REGION 6166 W SAHARA AVE LAS VEGAS, NV 89146	PHONE: (702) 248-2542 FAX: (702) 248-2622 TOLL FREE: (800) 318-1963	WEB: WWW.MEDIVERSAL.COM
TEXAS		CENTRAL REGION 2906 N STATE ST STE 205 JACKSON, MS 39216	PHONE: (601) 362-3193 FAX: (601) 362-3194 TOLL FREE: (800) 318-1963	WEB: WWW.MEDIVERSAL.COM

MEDMARC INSURANCE GROUP

NATIONAL		14280 PARK MEADOW DR STE 300 CHANTILLY, VA 20151-2219 PO BOX 10809 CHANTILLY, VA 20153-0809	PHONE: (703) 652-1300 FAX: (703) 652-1389 TOLL FREE: (800) 356-6886	WEB: WWW.MEDMARC.COM

MEDSAVE USA

NATIONAL		1400 OLD COUNTRY RD STE 109 WESTBURY, NY 11590	PHONE: (516) 622-1700 FAX: (516) 622-1733	E-MAIL: INFO@MEDSAVEUSA.COM WEB: WWW.MEDSAVEUSA.COM

MEGA LIFE & HEALTH — *UICI*

OKLAHOMA		1331 W MEMORIAL RD STE 112 OKLAHOMA CITY, OK 73114 PO BOX 548801 OKLAHOMA CITY, OK 73154-8801	PHONE: (405) 848-0179 FAX: (405) 302-1486 TOLL FREE: (800) 725-7887	

MEIJER, INC

ILLINOIS
INDIANA
KENTUCKY
MICHIGAN
OHIO

		2929 WALKER AVE NW BLDG 985 GRAND RAPIDS, MI 49501	PHONE: (616) 453-6711 FAX: (616) 365-5755 TOLL FREE: (800) 346-8281	WEB: WWW.MEIJER.COM

MEMBER OF THE GRANGE MUTUAL CASUALTY GROUP — *SEE ALSO INTEGRITY MUTUAL INSURANCE CO*

M

MEMORIAL HOSPITAL MEDICAL NETWORK — *SEE ALSO MEDICAL NETWORK OF COLORADO SPRINGS*

MENNONITE MUTUAL AID — *MMA*

NATIONAL	1110 N MAIN ST GOSHEN, IN 46528 PO BOX 483 GOSHEN, IN 46527	PHONE: (574) 533-9511 FAX: (574) 537-6643 TOLL FREE: (800) 348-7468	WEB: WWW.MMA-ONLINE.ORG

MERCER ADMINISTRATION

NATIONAL	2610 NORTHGATE DR IOWA CITY, IA 52244 PO BOX 4542 IOWA CITY, IA 52244-1520	PHONE: (319) 887-4000 FAX: (319) 351-0603	WEB: WWW.ONLINEBENEFITSACCESS.COM

MERCHANTS INSURANCE GROUP

MASSACHUSETTS	FIVE BEDFORD FARMS STE 101 BEDFORD, NH 03110 PO BOX 4981 MANCHESTER, NH 03108-4981	PHONE: (603) 622-9966 FAX: (603) 622-0606 TOLL FREE: (800) 258-3574 IN-STATE: (800) 562-1130	WEB: WWW.MERCHANTSGROUP.COM
MICHIGAN	250 MAIN ST BUFFALO, NY 14202 PO BOX 78 BUFFALO, NY 14240	PHONE: (716) 849-3333 FAX: (716) 849-3105 TOLL FREE: (800) 462-1077	WEB: WWW.MERCHANTSGROUP.COM
NEW HAMPSHIRE	FIVE BEDFORD FARMS STE 101 BEDFORD, NH 03110 PO BOX 4981 MANCHESTER, NH 03108-4981	PHONE: (603) 622-9966 FAX: (603) 622-0606 TOLL FREE: (800) 258-3574 IN-STATE: (800) 562-1130	WEB: WWW.MERCHANTSGROUP.COM
	250 MAIN ST BUFFALO, NY 14202 PO BOX 78 BUFFALO, NY 14240	PHONE: (716) 849-3333 FAX: (716) 849-3105 TOLL FREE: (800) 462-1077	WEB: WWW.MERCHANTSGROUP.COM
NEW JERSEY	309 FELLOWSHIP RD STE 300 MT LAUREL, NJ 08054 PO BOX 868 MOORESTOWN, NJ 08057	PHONE: (856) 235-8890 FAX: (856) 273-8342 TOLL FREE: (800) 322-8608	WEB: WWW.MERCHANTSGROUP.COM
NEW YORK	250 MAIN ST BUFFALO, NY 14202 PO BOX 78 BUFFALO, NY 14240	PHONE: (716) 849-3333 FAX: (716) 849-3105 TOLL FREE: (800) 462-1077	WEB: WWW.MERCHANTSGROUP.COM
	309 FELLOWSHIP RD STE 300 MT LAUREL, NJ 08054 PO BOX 868 MOORESTOWN, NJ 08057	PHONE: (856) 235-8890 FAX: (856) 273-8342 TOLL FREE: (800) 322-8608	WEB: WWW.MERCHANTSGROUP.COM
OHIO	250 MAIN ST BUFFALO, NY 14202 PO BOX 78 BUFFALO, NY 14240	PHONE: (716) 849-3333 FAX: (716) 849-3105 TOLL FREE: (800) 462-1077	WEB: WWW.MERCHANTSGROUP.COM
PENNSYLVANIA	250 MAIN ST BUFFALO, NY 14202 PO BOX 78 BUFFALO, NY 14240	PHONE: (716) 849-3333 FAX: (716) 849-3105 TOLL FREE: (800) 462-1077	WEB: WWW.MERCHANTSGROUP.COM
	309 FELLOWSHIP RD STE 300 MT LAUREL, NJ 08054 PO BOX 868 MOORESTOWN, NJ 08057	PHONE: (856) 235-8890 FAX: (856) 273-8342 TOLL FREE: (800) 322-8608	WEB: WWW.MERCHANTSGROUP.COM
RHODE ISLAND *VERMONT*	FIVE BEDFORD FARMS STE 101 BEDFORD, NH 03110 PO BOX 4981 MANCHESTER, NH 03108-4981	PHONE: (603) 622-9966 FAX: (603) 622-0606 TOLL FREE: (800) 258-3574 IN-STATE: (800) 562-1130	WEB: WWW.MERCHANTSGROUP.COM

M

MERCURY CASUALTY CO

CALIFORNIA	9635 GRANITE RIDGE DR STE 200 SAN DIEGO, CA 92123 PO BOX 82167 SAN DIEGO, CA 92138-2167	PHONE: (858) 694-4100 FAX: (858) 694-4161	WEB: WWW.MERCURYINSURANCE.COM

MERCURY INSURANCE GROUP

CALIFORNIA	11150 INTERNATIONAL DR STE 100 RANCHO CORDOVA, CA 95670-6072 PO BOX 997195 SACRAMENTO, CA 95899	PHONE: (916) 636-1500 FAX: (916) 636-1598 TOLL FREE: (800) 521-9693	WEB: WWW.MERCURYINSURANCE.COM
	1700 GREENBRIAR LN BREA, CA 92821-5968	PHONE: (714) 255-5000 TOLL FREE: (800) 824-6194	WEB: WWW.MERCURYINSURANCE.COM
	4484 WILSHIRE BLVD LOS ANGELES, CA 90010-3710 PO BOX 54600 LOS ANGELES, CA 90054-0600	PHONE: (323) 937-1060 FAX: (323) 857-7185 TOLL FREE: (800) 824-6194 IN-STATE: (800) 431-6654	WEB: WWW.MERCURYINSURANCEGROUP.COM
	555 W IMPERIAL HWY BREA, CA 92822 PO BOX 1150 BREA, CA 92822-1150	PHONE: (714) 671-6700 FAX: (714) 672-4826 TOLL FREE: (888) 313-6372 IN-STATE: (800) 824-6194	WEB: WWW.MERCURYINSURANCE.COM

MERCY HEALTH PLANS OF MISSOURI

ARKANSAS *KANSAS* *MISSOURI* *OKLAHOMA*	14528 S OUTER 40 STE 300 CHESTERFIELD, MO 63017 PO BOX 4568 SPRINGFIELD, MO 65808-4568	PHONE: (314) 214-8100 FAX: (314) 214-8101 TOLL FREE: (800) 830-1918 IN-STATE: (800) 596-4315	WEB: WWW.MERCYHEALTHPLANS.COM

MERCYCARE INSURANCE CO

ILLINOIS *WISCONSIN*	3430 PALMER DR JANESVILLE, WI 53546 PO BOX 2770 JANESVILLE, WI 53547	PHONE: (608) 752-3431 FAX: (608) 752-3751 TOLL FREE: (800) 752-3431	WEB: WWW.MERCYHEALTHSYSTEM.ORG

MERIT LIFE — *SEE ALSO AMERICAN GENERAL FINANCE*

MERITAIN HEALTH

NATIONAL	300 CORPORATE PKY AMHERST, NY 14226-1207 PO BOX 9501 AMHERST, NY 14226	PHONE: (716) 446-5500 FAX: (716) 319-5725 TOLL FREE: (800) 828-6922	E-MAIL: INFO@MERITAIN.COM WEB: WWW.MERITAIN.COM
	515 OLIVE ST STE 300 ST LOUIS, MO 63101-1876	PHONE: (314) 588-0826 FAX: (314) 588-7372 TOLL FREE: (800) 828-6922 IN-STATE: (800) 828-6922	E-MAIL: INFO@NAHP.COM WEB: WWW.NAHP.COM

MERRIMACK MUTUAL — *CAMBRIDGE MUTUAL FIRE INSURANCE CO, BAY STATE INSURANCE CO*

CONNECTICUT, *ILLINOIS*, *MAINE*, *MASSACHUSETTS*, *NEW HAMPSHIRE*, *NEW JERSEY*, *NEW YORK*, *RHODE ISLAND*

95 OLD RIVER RD ANDOVER, MA 01810-1078 PO BOX 9009 ANDOVER, MA 01810-9009	PHONE: (978) 475-3300 FAX: (800) 323-5112 TOLL FREE: (800) 225-0770	

M

METLIFE AUTO & HOME

ILLINOIS *OREGON* *WASHINGTON*	9001 WESLEYAN RD STE 400 INDIANAPOLIS, ID 46268	PHONE: (815) 233-2000 FAX: (317) 874-4001 TOLL FREE: (800) 854-6011	WEB: WWW.METLIFE.COM

METLIFE DENTAL

NATIONAL	PO BOX 14093 LEXINGTON, KY 40512	TOLL FREE: (800) 942-0854	WEB: WWW.METLIFE.COM/DENTAL
	SIX FOUNDER S BLVD STE E EL PASO, TX 79906 PO BOX 981282 EL PASO, TX 79998	FAX: (859) 389-6505 TOLL FREE: (800) 942-0854	WEB: WWW.METLIFE.COM/DENTAL

METROPOLITAN LIFE INSURANCE CO

NATIONAL	27-01 QUEENS PLZ N LONG ISLAND CITY, NY 11101	PHONE: (212) 578-2211	WEB: WWW.METLIFE.COM
	5950 AIRPORT RD ORISKANY, NY 13424 PO BOX 6132 UTICA, NY 13504	PHONE: (315) 797-6000 FAX: (315) 792-2514 TOLL FREE: (800) 638-5433 IN-STATE: (800) 300-4296	WEB: WWW.METLIFE.COM
	700 QUAKER LN STE 100 WARWICK, RI 02887 PO BOX 495 WARWICK, RI 02884	PHONE: (401) 827-2000 OR (401) 828-2000 FAX: (401) 273-9902	WEB: WWW.METLIFE.COM
	9797 SPRINGBORO PIKE DAYTON, OH 45448 PO BOX 410300 CHARLOTTE, NC 28241	PHONE: (937) 859-2400 FAX: (800) 854-6011	WEB: WWW.METLIFE.COM
ILLINOIS	177 S COMMONS DR AURORA, IL 60504	PHONE: (630) 820-7500	WEB: WWW.METLIFE.COM

MGIS COMPANIES — *MGIS P & C*

UTAH	1849 W NORTH TEMPLE STE D SALT LAKE CITY, UT 84116-3067 PO BOX 16110 SALT LAKE CITY, UT 84116-0110	PHONE: (801) 990-2400 FAX: (801) 990-2401 TOLL FREE: (800) 969-6447	E-MAIL: INFO@MGIS.COM WEB: WWW.MGIS.COM

MGIS P & C — *SEE ALSO MGIS COMPANIES*

MHNET

NATIONAL	4006 BELTLINE RD STE 205 ADDISON, TX 75001-5831	PHONE: (972) 588-2400 FAX: (972) 931-1938 TOLL FREE: (800) 866-7242	WEB: WWW.MHNET.COM

MICHIGAN EMPLOYEE BENEFIT SERVICES

MICHIGAN	3809 LAKE EASTBROOK BLVD GRAND RAPIDS, MI 49546	PHONE: (616) 458-6327 FAX: (616) 458-3495 TOLL FREE: (800) 968-9682	E-MAIL: CUSTSERV@MEBS.COM WEB: WWW.MEBS.COM

MICHIGAN FARM BUREAU MUTUAL INSURANCE CO— *SEE ALSO FARM BUREAU INSURANCE*

M

MICHIGAN MILLERS MUTUAL INSURANCE

ILLINOIS
INDIANA
IOWA
KANSAS
KENTUCKY
NEW YORK
SOUTH DAKOTA
WISCONSIN

2425 E GRAND RIVER
LANSING, MI 48912
PO BOX 30060
LANSING, MI 48909-0060

PHONE: (517) 482-6211
FAX: (517) 482-6245
TOLL FREE: (800) 888-1914

WEB: WWW.MIMILLERS.COM

MID-AMERICAN BENEFITS, INC

NEBRASKA

5310 N 99TH ST STE 1
OMAHA, NE 68134

PHONE: (402) 571-6224
FAX: (402) 573-8058
TOLL FREE: (800) 364-9505

E-MAIL: CLAIMS@MID-AMERICANBENEFITS.COM
WEB: WWW.MID-AMERICANBENEFITS.COM

MID-CONTINENT GROUP — *AMERICAN FINANCIAL GROUP*

OKLAHOMA

1437 S BOULDER STE 200
TULSA, OK 74119
PO BOX 1409
TULSA, OK 74101-9974

PHONE: (918) 587-7221
FAX: (918) 588-1293
TOLL FREE: (800) 722-4994

WEB: WWW.MCG-INS.COM

MIDDLESEX INSURANCE — *SENTRY CLAIMS CENTER*

CONNECTICUT
MAINE
MASSACHUSETTS
NEW HAMPSHIRE

THREE CARLISLE RD
WESTFORD, MA 01886-3601
PO BOX 584
WESTFORD, MA 01886-0584

PHONE: (978) 392-7000
FAX: (978) 392-7033
TOLL FREE: (800) 225-1390

WEB: WWW.DAIRYLAND-INSURANCE.COM

MIDDLESEX MUTUAL ASSURANCE CO

CONNECTICUT

213 COURT ST
MIDDLETOWN, CT 06457-3346
PO BOX 891
MIDDLETOWN, CT 06457

PHONE: (860) 347-4621
FAX: (877) 449-8299
TOLL FREE: (800) 899-0032
IN-STATE: (800) 622-3780

WEB: WWW.MIDDLESEXMUTUAL.COM

MIDLAND CO — *AMERICAN MODERN INSURANCE GROUP*

NATIONAL

7000 MIDLAND BLVD
AMELIA, OH 45102-2607
PO BOX 5323
CINCINNATI, OH 45201

PHONE: (513) 943-7200
FAX: (800) 217-5150
TOLL FREE: (800) 759-9008

E-MAIL: SERVICECENTER@AMIG.COM
WEB: WWW.AMIG.COM

MIDLAND NATIONAL LIFE INSURANCE CO

NATIONAL
GUAM
PUERTO RICO
VIRGIN ISLANDS

ONE MIDLAND PLAZA
SIOUX FALLS, SD 57193

TOLL FREE: (800) 283-5433

WEB: WWW.MIDLANDNATIONAL.COM

ADDITIONAL COMMENTS: EXCEPT NEW YORK

MIDWEST LIFE INSURANCE COMPANY OF TENNESSEE — *SEE ALSO UICI*

MIDWEST SECURITY ADMINISTRATORS — *MIDWEST SECURITY INSURANCE*

ILLINOIS
INDIANA
IOWA
MICHIGAN
OHIO
WISCONSIN

1150 SPRINGHURST DR STE 140
GREEN BAY, WI 54304-9035

PHONE: (920) 496-2500
FAX: (920) 496-2515
TOLL FREE: (800) 236-2515

WEB: WWW.MIDWESTSECURITY.COM

MIDWEST SECURITY INSURANCE — *SEE ALSO MIDWEST SECURITY ADMINISTRATORS*

M

MIDWEST SECURITY INSURANCE CO

ILLINOIS
INDIANA
IOWA
MICHIGAN
NEBRASKA
OHIO
WISCONSIN

2700 MIDWEST DR
ONALASKA, WI 54650

FAX: (608) 783-8581
TOLL FREE: (800) 542-6640

WEB: WWW.MIDWESTSECURITY.COM

MILLERS CAPITAL INSURANCE CO

DELAWARE
MARYLAND
PENNSYLVANIA
VIRGINIA

805 N FRONT ST
HARRISBURG, PA 17102-3400
;PO BOX 1246
HARRISBURG, PA 17108-1246

PHONE: (717) 232-3211
FAX: (717) 232-3973 OR
(717) 233-2519

WEB: WWW.MILLERSINSURANCE.COM

MINNESOTA LIFE INSURANCE CO — *SEE ALSO SECURIAN*

MISSOURI FARM BUREAU INSURANCE SERVICES — *SEE ALSO FARM BUREAU INSURANCE*

MMA — *SEE ALSO MENNONITE MUTUAL AID*

MOLINA HEALTHCARE

CALIFORNIA

CORPORATE OFFICE
ONE GOLDEN SHORE
LONG BEACH, CA 90802
PO BOX 22693
LONG BEACH, CA 90801

PHONE: (562) 435-3666
FAX: (562) 901-2775
TOLL FREE: (800) 526-8196

WEB: WWW.MOLINAHEALTHCARE.COM

BOTHELL OFFICES
21540 30TH DR SE STE 400
BOTHELL, WA 98021-7015
PO BOX 1469
BOTHELL, WA 98041-1469

PHONE: (425) 424-1100
FAX: (425) 487-8987
TOLL FREE: (800) 869-7175

WEB: WWW.MOLINAHEALTHCARE.COM

INDIANA

8001 BROADWAY STE 400
MERILLVILLE, IN 46410
PO BOX 22717
LONG BEACH, CA 90801

PHONE: (219) 795-3200
TOLL FREE: (800) 642-4509

WEB: WWW.MOLINAHEALTHCARE.COM

MICHIGAN

CORPORATE OFFICE
ONE GOLDEN SHORE
LONG BEACH, CA 90802
PO BOX 22693
LONG BEACH, CA 90801

PHONE: (562) 435-3666
FAX: (562) 901-2775
TOLL FREE: (800) 526-8196

WEB: WWW.MOLINAHEALTHCARE.COM

100 W BIG BEAVER STE 600
TROY, MI 48084-5209
PO BOX 22668
LONG BEACH, CA 90801

PHONE: (248) 925-1700
FAX: (248) 925-1709
TOLL FREE: (888) 898-7969

WEB: WWW.MOLINAHEALTHCARE.COM

UTAH

7050 S UNION PARK CENTER STE 200
MIDVALE, UT 84047

PHONE: (801) 858-0400
TOLL FREE: (877) 603-7722

WEB: WWW.MOLINAHEALTHCARE.COM

UTAH
WASHINGTON

CORPORATE OFFICE
ONE GOLDEN SHORE
LONG BEACH, CA 90802
PO BOX 22693
LONG BEACH, CA 90801

PHONE: (562) 435-3666
FAX: (562) 901-2775
TOLL FREE: (800) 526-8196

WEB: WWW.MOLINAHEALTHCARE.COM

WASHINGTON	BOTHELL OFFICES 21540 30TH DR SE STE 400 BOTHELL, WA 98021-7015 PO BOX 1469 BOTHELL, WA 98041-1469	PHONE: (425) 424-1100 FAX: (425) 487-8987 TOLL FREE: (800) 869-7175	WEB: WWW.MOLINAHEALTHCARE.COM
	SPOKANE OFFICES 5709 W SUNSET HWY STE 200 SPOKANE, WA 99224 PO BOX 2470 SPOKANE, WA 99210	PHONE: (509) 459-6690 FAX: (800) 816-3778 TOLL FREE: (800) 423-9899	WEB: WWW.MOLINAHEALTHCARE.COM

MONITOR LIFE INSURANCE CO OF NEW YORK, CT AGENCY — *SEE ALSO COMMERCIAL TRAVELERS MUTUAL INSURANCE CO*

MONTGOMERY INSURANCE

ALABAMA *FLORIDA* *GEORGIA* *MISSISSIPPI*	3555 KOGER BLVD STE 200 ATLANTA, GA 30328	PHONE: (678) 380-8734 FAX: (678) 380-7595 TOLL FREE: (800) 762-5573 IN-STATE: (800) 222-6003	WEB: WWW.MONLIFE.COM

MONTGOMERY MUTUAL INSURANCE CO

DELAWARE *MARYLAND*	17810 MEETINGHOUSE RD SANDY SPRING, MD 20860 PO BOX 8 SANDY SPRING, MD 20860	PHONE: (301) 924-4700 FAX: (301) 924-6006 TOLL FREE: (800) 638-8933 IN-STATE: (800) 638-8933	WEB: WWW.MONTGOMERY-INS.COM
NORTH CAROLINA *SOUTH CAROLINA* *VIRGINIA*	PO BOX 11350 CHARLOTTE, NC 28220-1350	PHONE: (704) 523-2731 FAX: (800) 432-4297 TOLL FREE: (800) 334-0078	WEB: WWW.MONTGOMERY-INS.COM
VIRGINIA *WASHINGTON* *WEST VIRGINIA*	17810 MEETINGHOUSE RD SANDY SPRING, MD 20860 PO BOX 8 SANDY SPRING, MD 20860	PHONE: (301) 924-4700 FAX: (301) 924-6006 TOLL FREE: (800) 638-8933 IN-STATE: (800) 638-8933	WEB: WWW.MONTGOMERY-INS.COM

MONUMENTAL LIFE INSURANCE CO

NATIONAL	300 W MORGAN ST DURHAM, NC 27701 PO BOX 61 DURHAM, NC 27702	PHONE: (919) 687-8200 FAX: (919) 687-8359 TOLL FREE: (800) 638-3080	WEB: WWW.MONLIFE.COM
	TWO E CHASE ST BALTIMORE, MD 21202	PHONE: (410) 685-2900 FAX: (410) 385-6970 TOLL FREE: (800) 638-3080	WEB: WWW.MONLIFE.COM
GEORGIA	1090 WASHINGTON AVE STE 108 MACON, GA 31201 PO BOX 4585 MACON, GA 31208-4585	PHONE: (478) 741-9905 FAX: (478) 741-9925 TOLL FREE: (800) 638-3080	WEB: WWW.MONLIFE.COM

MONY LIFE INSURANCE COMPANY — *MONY LIFE INSURANCE COMPANY OF AMERICA*

NATIONAL	ONE MONY PLZ SYRACUSE, NY 13202 PO BOX 4720 SYRACUSE, NY 13221	PHONE: (315) 477-3000 FAX: (315) 477-3185 TOLL FREE: (800) 487-6669	WEB: WWW.MONY.COM

MONY LIFE INSURANCE COMPANY OF AMERICA — *SEE ALSO MONY LIFE INSURANCE CO*

MOTORISTS INSURANCE GROUP — *SEE ALSO AMERICAN HARDWARE MUTUAL INSURANCE CO*

MOUNTAIN STATE BLUE CROSS BLUE SHIELD

WEST VIRGINIA	700 MARKET SQ PARKERSBURG, WV 26101-4629 PO BOX 7026 WHEELING, WV 26003	PHONE: (304) 424-7700 FAX: (304) 424-0326 TOLL FREE: (800) 543-7822	WEB: WWW.MSBCBS.COM

MOUNTAIN STATES ADMINISTRATIVE SERVICES

NATIONAL	7202 E ROSEWOOD TUCSON, AZ 85710 PO BOX 32702 TUCSON, AZ 85751	PHONE: (520) 722-0811 FAX: (520) 722-7127 TOLL FREE: (800) 866-4731	WEB: WWW.MYMSAS.COM

MS ADMINISTRATORS

NATIONAL	3451 E COPPERPOINT DR STE 201 MERIDIAN, ID 83642 PO BOX 45073 BOISE, ID 83711	PHONE: (208) 343-2964 FAX: (208) 363-0257	WEB: WWW.MSADMIN.COM

MULTI LINES INSURANCE

WISCONSIN	400 S EXECUTIVE DR STE 200 BROOKFIELD, WI 53005 PO BOX 1237 BROOKFIELD, WI 63008-1237	PHONE: (262) 207-8500 FAX: (262) 207-8510 TOLL FREE: (800) 733-7366	WEB: WWW.UNITRINMLI.COM

MUTUAL ASSURANCE ADMINISTRATORS

NATIONAL	3121 QUAIL SPRINGS PKY OKLAHOMA CITY, OK 73134 PO BOX 42096 OKLAHOMA CITY, OK 73123-2096	PHONE: (405) 848-1975 FAX: (405) 607-2694 TOLL FREE: (800) 825-3540	E-MAIL: CLAIMS@MAA-TPA.COM WEB: WWW.MAA-TPA.COM

MUTUAL OF AMERICA

NATIONAL	EMPLOYEE BENEFITS 320 PARK AVE NEW YORK, NY 10022-6815	PHONE: (212) 224-1010 FAX: (212) 224-2502 TOLL FREE: (800) 872-6732	WEB: WWW.MUTUALOFAMERICA.COM

MUTUAL OF ENUMCLAW INSURANCE CO

IDAHO *OREGON* *UTAH* *WASHINGTON*	1460 WELLS ST ENUMCLAW, WA 98022-3003	PHONE: (360) 825-2591 FAX: (360) 825-6885 TOLL FREE: (800) 366-5551	WEB: WWW.MUTUALOFENUMCLAW.COM

MUTUAL OF OMAHA

NATIONAL	2700 X-RAY DR GASTONIA, NC 28054	PHONE: (704) 853-7900 FAX: (704) 853-7911 TOLL FREE: (800) 638-8432	WEB: WWW.MUTUALOFOMAHA.COM
	WOODWARD CLAIMS PROCESSING CENTER 3200 OKLAHOMA AVE WOODWARD, OK 73802-4000 PO BOX 9 WOODWARD, OK 73802	PHONE: (580) 256-1717 FAX: (580) 256-2324 TOLL FREE: (800) 462-2877	WEB: WWW.MUTUALOFOMAHACOMPANY.COM
	OMAHA GROUP PROCESSING CTR MUTUAL OF OMAHA PLZ OMAHA, NE 68175	PHONE: (402) 342-7600 FAX: (402) 351-5783 TOLL FREE: (800) 775-1000 IN-STATE: (800) 335-5883	E-MAIL: INDIVIDUALSERVICE@MUTUALOFOMAHA.COM WEB: WWW.MUTUALOFOMAHA.COM

M

MUTUAL SAVINGS LIFE INSURANCE CO

ALABAMA	Medical, Telephone, Bank	2801 HWY 31 S DECATUR, AL 35603-1509 PO BOX 2222 DECATUR, AL 35609-2222	PHONE: (256) 552-7353 FAX: (256) 552-7354 TOLL FREE: (800) 239-7654	E-MAIL: INFO@MSLDEC.COM WEB: WWW.MSLDEC.COM

MYERS STEVENS

ALASKA *CALIFORNIA* *OREGON* *WASHINGTON*	Medical, Bank	26101 MARGUERITE PKWY MISSION VIEJO, CA 92692-3203	PHONE: (949) 348-0656 FAX: (949) 348-2630 TOLL FREE: (800) 827-4695	E-MAIL: INFO@MYERS-STEVENS.COM WEB: WWW.MYERS-STEVENS.COM

NALC HEALTH BENEFIT PLAN — *NATIONAL ASSOCIATION OF LETTER CARRIERS*

NATIONAL	Umbrella, Medical, EMC, HCPCS, Telephone, Bank	20547 WAVERLY CT ASHBURN, VA 20149-0001	PHONE: (703) 729-4677 FAX: (703) 729-0076 TOLL FREE: (888) 636-6252	WEB: WWW.NALC.ORG/DEPART/HBP

NAMIC — *NATIONAL ASSOCIATION OF MUTUAL INSURANCE COMPANIES*

NATIONAL	Casualty/Liability, Bank	3601 VINCENNES RD INDIANAPOLIS, IN 46268-1154 PO BOX 68700 INDIANAPOLIS, IN 46268-1104	PHONE: (317) 875-5250 FAX: (317) 879-8408 TOLL FREE: (800) 336-2642	WEB: WWW.NAMIC.ORG

NARRAGANSETT BAY INSURANCE CO — *SEE ALSO PAWTUCKET MUTUAL INSURANCE CO*

NASHVILLE BRANCH — *SEE ALSO INDIANA INSURANCE*

NATIONAL AMERICAN INSURANCE CO OF CALIFORNIA — *DANIELSEN NATIONAL INSURANCE CO*

CALIFORNIA	Casualty/Liability, Bank	PO BOX 32039 LONG BEACH, CA 90832	PHONE: (562) 279-1300 FAX: (562) 628-2440 TOLL FREE: (800) 928-8601	E-MAIL: WEBMASTER@NAICC.COM WEB: WWW.NAICC.COM

NATIONAL AMERICAN INSURANCE CO.

NATIONAL	Auto, Casualty/Liability, Telephone, Bank	1010 MANVEL AVE CHANDLER, OK 74834 PO BOX 38 CHANDLER, OK 74834	PHONE: (405) 258-0804 FAX: (405) 258-1329 TOLL FREE: (800) 332-2210	WEB: WWW.NAICO.COM

NATIONAL ASSOCIATION OF LETTER CARRIERS — *SEE ALSO NALC HEALTH BENEFIT PLAN*

NATIONAL ASSOCIATION OF MUTUAL INSURANCE COMPANIES — *SEE ALSO NAMIC*

NATIONAL BENEFIT LIFE INSURANCE CO

NATIONAL	Medical, Disability, Medicare, Bank	333 W 34TH ST 10TH FL NEW YORK, NY 10001-2402 PO BOX 2366 NEW YORK, NY 10116	PHONE: (212) 615-7500 FAX: (212) 615-7345 TOLL FREE: (800) 221-2554	

NATIONAL CLAIMS ADMINISTRATIVE SOURCES — *NCAS*

NATIONAL	Medical, Dental, Vision, Disability, Workers' Comp, HMO, EMC, HCPCS, Bank	10715 RED RUN BLVD STE 125 OWINGS MILLS, MD 21117 PO BOX 1196 OWINGS MILLS, MD 21117-1196	PHONE: (443) 471-4000 FAX: (443) 471-1924 TOLL FREE: (800) 423-9791	WEB: WWW.NCAS.COM

NATIONAL CONTINENTAL PROGRESSIVE CASUALTY INSURANCE CO

NEW JERSEY	Casualty/Liability, EMC	100 CANAL POINTE BLVD STE 117 PRINCETON, NJ 08543 PO BOX 7637 PRINCETON, NJ 08543	FAX: (609) 452-8812 TOLL FREE: (800) 444-0013	WEB: WWW.PROGRESSIVE.COM

N

NATIONAL FAMILY CARE LIFE INSURANCE CO

ARKANSAS *LOUISIANA* *OKLAHOMA* *TEXAS*	13530 INWOOD RD DALLAS, TX 75244-5305 PO BOX 809043 DALLAS, TX 75380-9043	PHONE: (972) 387-8553 FAX: (972) 788-1156 TOLL FREE: (800) 527-0996	

NATIONAL FARMERS UNION PROPERTY & CASUALTY CO

NATIONAL	5619 DTC PARKWAY STE 300 GREENWOOD VILLAGE, CO 80111-3136	PHONE: (303) 337-5500 FAX: (303)695-4518 TOLL FREE: (800) 347-1961	WEB: WWW.NFUIC.COM

NATIONAL FOUNDATION LIFE INSURANCE CO — *FREEDOM LIFE INSURANCE*

TEXAS	801 CHERRY ST UNIT 33 FT WORTH, TX 76102-6883	PHONE: (817) 878-3300 FAX: (817) 878-3480 TOLL FREE: (800) 221-9039	WEB: WWW.USHEALTHGROUP.COM

NATIONAL GRANGE MUTUAL INSURANCE CO — *MAIN STREET AMERICAN GROUP*

CONNECTICUT *DELAWARE*	220 SALINA MEADOWS PKY STE 200 SYRACUSE, NY 13212 PO BOX 4828 SYRACUSE, NY 13221-4828	PHONE: (315) 434-1400 FAX: (315) 434-1429 TOLL FREE: (800) 962-5515	WEB: WWW.MSAGROUP.COM
DELAWARE	27 B MIDSTATE DR AUBURN, MA 01501-1839	PHONE: (508) 832-7171 FAX: (800) 606-7992 TOLL FREE: (800) 343-0562 IN-STATE: (877) 425-2467	WEB: WWW.MSAGROUP.COM
DELAWARE *FLORIDA*	5101 COX RD STE 100 GLEN ALLEN, VA 23060 PO BOX 6419 GLEN ALLEN, VA 23058	PHONE: (804) 270-6611 FAX: (888) 646-1004 TOLL FREE: (800) 446-7649	WEB: WWW.MSAGROUP.COM
	55 WEST ST KEENE, NH 03431-3374 PO BOX 2300 KEENE, NH 03431	PHONE: (603) 352-4000 TOLL FREE: (800) 258-5310	WEB: WWW.MSAGROUP.COM
FLORIDA	27 B MIDSTATE DR AUBURN, MA 01501-1839	PHONE: (508) 832-7171 FAX: (800) 606-7992 TOLL FREE: (800) 343-0562 IN-STATE: (877) 425-2467	WEB: WWW.MSAGROUP.COM
FLORIDA *INDIANA* *MAINE*	220 SALINA MEADOWS PKY STE 200 SYRACUSE, NY 13212 PO BOX 4828 SYRACUSE, NY 13221-4828	PHONE: (315) 434-1400 FAX: (315) 434-1429 TOLL FREE: (800) 962-5515	WEB: WWW.MSAGROUP.COM
MAINE *MARYLAND*	27 B MIDSTATE DR AUBURN, MA 01501-1839	PHONE: (508) 832-7171 FAX: (800) 606-7992 TOLL FREE: (800) 343-0562 IN-STATE: (877) 425-2467	WEB: WWW.MSAGROUP.COM
	5101 COX RD STE 100 GLEN ALLEN, VA 23060 PO BOX 6419 GLEN ALLEN, VA 23058	PHONE: (804) 270-6611 FAX: (888) 646-1004 TOLL FREE: (800) 446-7649	WEB: WWW.MSAGROUP.COM
	55 WEST ST KEENE, NH 03431-3374 PO BOX 2300 KEENE, NH 03431	PHONE: (603) 352-4000 TOLL FREE: (800) 258-5310	WEB: WWW.MSAGROUP.COM
MARYLAND *MASSACHUSETTS*	220 SALINA MEADOWS PKY STE 200 SYRACUSE, NY 13212 PO BOX 4828 SYRACUSE, NY 13221-4828	PHONE: (315) 434-1400 FAX: (315) 434-1429 TOLL FREE: (800) 962-5515	WEB: WWW.MSAGROUP.COM

N

MASSACHUSETTS	27 B MIDSTATE DR AUBURN, MA 01501-1839	PHONE: (508) 832-7171 FAX: (800) 606-7992 TOLL FREE: (800) 343-0562 IN-STATE: (877) 425-2467	WEB: WWW.MSAGROUP.COM
	5101 COX RD STE 100 GLEN ALLEN, VA 23060 PO BOX 6419 GLEN ALLEN, VA 23058	PHONE: (804) 270-6611 FAX: (888) 646-1004 TOLL FREE: (800) 446-7649	WEB: WWW.MSAGROUP.COM
	55 WEST ST KEENE, NH 03431-3374 PO BOX 2300 KEENE, NH 03431	PHONE: (603) 352-4000 TOLL FREE: (800) 258-5310	WEB: WWW.MSAGROUP.COM
MISSOURI *NEW HAMPSHIRE*	220 SALINA MEADOWS PKY STE 200 SYRACUSE, NY 13212 PO BOX 4828 SYRACUSE, NY 13221-4828	PHONE: (315) 434-1400 FAX: (315) 434-1429 TOLL FREE: (800) 962-5515	WEB: WWW.MSAGROUP.COM
NEW HAMPSHIRE *NEW JERSEY*	27 B MIDSTATE DR AUBURN, MA 01501-1839	PHONE: (508) 832-7171 FAX: (800) 606-7992 TOLL FREE: (800) 343-0562 IN-STATE: (877) 425-2467	WEB: WWW.MSAGROUP.COM
	5101 COX RD STE 100 GLEN ALLEN, VA 23060 PO BOX 6419 GLEN ALLEN, VA 23058	PHONE: (804) 270-6611 FAX: (888) 646-1004 TOLL FREE: (800) 446-7649	WEB: WWW.MSAGROUP.COM
	55 WEST ST KEENE, NH 03431-3374 PO BOX 2300 KEENE, NH 03431	PHONE: (603) 352-4000 TOLL FREE: (800) 258-5310	WEB: WWW.MSAGROUP.COM
NEW JERSEY *NEW YORK*	220 SALINA MEADOWS PKY STE 200 SYRACUSE, NY 13212 PO BOX 4828 SYRACUSE, NY 13221-4828	PHONE: (315) 434-1400 FAX: (315) 434-1429 TOLL FREE: (800) 962-5515	WEB: WWW.MSAGROUP.COM
NEW YORK *NORTH CAROLINA*	27 B MIDSTATE DR AUBURN, MA 01501-1839	PHONE: (508) 832-7171 FAX: (800) 606-7992 TOLL FREE: (800) 343-0562 IN-STATE: (877) 425-2467	WEB: WWW.MSAGROUP.COM
	5101 COX RD STE 100 GLEN ALLEN, VA 23060 PO BOX 6419 GLEN ALLEN, VA 23058	PHONE: (804) 270-6611 FAX: (888) 646-1004 TOLL FREE: (800) 446-7649	WEB: WWW.MSAGROUP.COM
	55 WEST ST KEENE, NH 03431-3374 PO BOX 2300 KEENE, NH 03431	PHONE: (603) 352-4000 TOLL FREE: (800) 258-5310	WEB: WWW.MSAGROUP.COM
NORTH CAROLINA *OHIO* *PENNSYLVANIA* *SOUTH CAROLINA*	220 SALINA MEADOWS PKY STE 200 SYRACUSE, NY 13212 PO BOX 4828 SYRACUSE, NY 13221-4828	PHONE: (315) 434-1400 FAX: (315) 434-1429 TOLL FREE: (800) 962-5515	WEB: WWW.MSAGROUP.COM

SOUTH CAROLINA *TENNESSEE*		27 B MIDSTATE DR AUBURN, MA 01501-1839	PHONE: (508) 832-7171 FAX: (800) 606-7992 TOLL FREE: (800) 343-0562 IN-STATE: (877) 425-2457	WEB: WWW.MSAGROUP.COM
		5101 COX RD STE 100 GLEN ALLEN, VA 23060 PO BOX 6419 GLEN ALLEN, VA 23058	PHONE: (804) 270-6611 FAX: (888) 646-1004 TOLL FREE: (800) 446-7549	WEB: WWW.MSAGROUP.COM
		55 WEST ST KEENE, NH 03431-3374 PO BOX 2300 KEENE, NH 03431	PHONE: (603) 352-4000 TOLL FREE: (800) 258-5310	WEB: WWW.MSAGROUP.COM
TENNESSEE *VERMONT* *VIRGINIA*		220 SALINA MEADOWS PKY STE 200 SYRACUSE, NY 13212 PO BOX 4828 SYRACUSE, NY 13221-4828	PHONE: (315) 434-1400 FAX: (315) 434-1429 TOLL FREE: (800) 962-5515	WEB: WWW.MSAGROUP.COM
VIRGINIA		27 B MIDSTATE DR AUBURN, MA 01501-1839	PHONE: (508) 832-7171 FAX: (800) 606-7992 TOLL FREE: (800) 343-0562 IN-STATE: (877) 425-2467	WEB: WWW.MSAGROUP.COM
		5101 COX RD STE 100 GLEN ALLEN, VA 23060 PO BOX 6419 GLEN ALLEN, VA 23058	PHONE: (804) 270-6611 FAX: (888) 646-1004 TOLL FREE: (800) 446-7649	WEB: WWW.MSAGROUP.COM
		55 WEST ST KEENE, NH 03431-3374 PO BOX 2300 KEENE, NH 03431	PHONE: (603) 352-4000 TOLL FREE: (800) 258-5310	WEB: WWW.MSAGROUP.COM
WEST VIRGINIA		220 SALINA MEADOWS PKY STE 200 SYRACUSE, NY 13212 PO BOX 4828 SYRACUSE, NY 13221-4828	PHONE: (315) 434-1400 FAX: (315) 434-1429 TOLL FREE: (800) 962-5515	WEB: WWW.MSAGROUP.COM

NATIONAL GUARDIAN LIFE INSURANCE CO

NATIONAL		TWO E GILMAN ST MADISON, WI 53703 PO BOX 1191 MADISON, WI 53701-1191	PHONE: (608) 257-5611 FAX: (608) 257-4308 TOLL FREE: (800) 548-2962	WEB: WWW.NATIONALGUARDIAN.COM

NATIONAL GUARDIAN LIFE INSURANCE GROUP

NATIONAL		TWO E GILMAN ST MADISON, WI 53703 PO BOX 1191 MADISON, WI 53701	FAX: (608) 257-3940 TOLL FREE: (800) 548-2962 IN-STATE: (800) 762-9383	E-MAIL: NGL@NGLIC.COM WEB: WWW.NGLIC.COM

NATIONAL HEALTH INSURANCE CO

NATIONAL		1901 N STATE HWY 360 GRAND PRAIRIE, TX 75050-1412 PO BOX 619999 DALLAS, TX 75261-6199	PHONE: (817) 640-1900 FAX: (817) 640-3437 TOLL FREE: (800) 237-1900	

NATIONAL HOSPITAL NETWORK SYSTEM — *ROBINSON HEALTH CARE COMPANIES, INC*

NATIONAL	3	475 HANDY RD HARRODSBURG, KY 40330	PHONE: (859) 734-7346 FAX: (859) 734-0898 TOLL FREE: (800) 532-1941	

N

NATIONAL INDEMNITY CO

NATIONAL

4016 FARNAM ST
OMAHA, NE 68131-3016
3024 HARNEY
OMAHA, NE 68131

PHONE: (402) 536-3000
FAX: (402) 536-3031
TOLL FREE: (800) 356-5750

E-MAIL: CLAIMS@NATIONALINDEMNITY.COM
WEB: WWW.NATIONALINDEMNITY.COM

NATIONAL MERIT INSURANCE — *SEE ALSO UNIGARD INSURANCE CO*

NATIONAL MUTUAL BENEFIT

COLORADO
ILLINOIS
IOWA
MICHIGAN
MINNESOTA
NORTH DAKOTA
SOUTH DAKOTA
WISCONSIN
WYOMING

6522 GRAND TETON PLZ
MADISON, WI 53719
PO BOX 1527
MADISON, WI 53701

PHONE: (608) 833-1936
FAX: (608) 833-8714
TOLL FREE: (800) 779-1936

WEB: WWW.NMBLIFE.COM

NATIONAL RURAL LETTER CARRIERS' ASSOCIATION — *UNION OF POSTAL WORKERS*

NATIONAL

2050 REMOUNT RD
GASTONIA, NC 28054

PHONE: (704) 853-7900
FAX: (704) 853-7911
TOLL FREE: (800) 638-8432

WEB: WWW.MUTUALOFOMAHA.COM

NATIONAL SECURITY INSURANCE CO

ALABAMA
ARKANSAS
FLORIDA
GEORGIA
KENTUCKY
MISSISSIPPI
MISSOURI
OKLAHOMA
SOUTH CAROLINA
TENNESSEE
TEXAS

661 E DAVIS ST
ELBA, AL 36323-9478
PO BOX 703
ELBA, AL 36323

PHONE: (334) 897-2273
FAX: (334) 897-5694
TOLL FREE: (800) 239-2358

WEB: WWW.NATIONALSECURITYINSURANCE.COM

NATIONAL STATES INSURANCE CO

NATIONAL

1830 CRAIG PARK CT
ST LOUIS, MO 63146

PHONE: (314) 878-0101
FAX: (314) 878-8118
TOLL FREE: (800) 868-6788

NATIONWIDE AGRA BUSINESS

NATIONAL

1100 LOCUST ST DEPT 3010
DES MOINES, IA 50391-3010

FAX: (620) 669-0252
TOLL FREE: (800) 228-6700

WEB: WWW.NATIONWIDEAGRABUSINESS.COM

NATIONWIDE HEALTH PLANS — *SEE ALSO ALLIED INSURANCE CO*

CALIFORNIA
OHIO

5525 PARK CTR CIR
DUBLIN, OH 43017-3584
PO BOX 182690
COLUMBUS, OH 43218-2690

PHONE: (614) 854-2184
FAX: (614) 858-3401
TOLL FREE: (800) 626-2904

WEB: WWW.NATIONWIDEHEALTHPLANS.COM

NATIONWIDE INSURANCE

NATIONAL

ONE NATIONWIDE PLZ
COLUMBUS, OH 43215

PHONE: (614) 249-7111
FAX: (614) 249-7705
TOLL FREE: (800) 882-2822

WEB: WWW.NATIONWIDE.COM

NATIONWIDE MUTUAL INSURANCE CO

ALABAMA

3300 WILLISTON RD
GAINESVILLE, FL 32608
PO BOX 147081
GAINESVILLE, FL 32614-7081

PHONE: (352) 377-8500
FAX: (352) 338-4815
TOLL FREE: (800) 421-3535
IN-STATE: (800) 438-2936

WEB: WWW.NATIONWIDE.COM

4500 N PT PKY
ALPHARETTA, GA 30022-2409
PO BOX 1612
ALPHARETTA, GA 30009

PHONE: (770) 667-6600
FAX: (888) 839-6141
TOLL FREE: (800) 421-3535
IN-STATE: (888) 839-6140

WEB: WWW.NATIONWIDE.COM

NORTH CAROLINA	4401 CREEDMOOR RD RALEIGH, NC 27612 PO BOX 30000 RALEIGH, NC 27622-3000	PHONE: (919) 781-3322 FAX: (919) 881-3335 TOLL FREE: (800) 421-3535	WEB: WWW.NATIONWIDE.COM
VIRGINIA	116 NATIONWIDE DR LYNCHBURG, VA 24502	PHONE: (434) 238-1100 FAX: (434) 238-1116 TOLL FREE: (800) 421-3535 IN-STATE: (888) 866-9961	WEB: WWW.NATIONWIDE.COM

NAUTILUS INSURANCE GROUP — *SEE ALSO GREAT DIVIDE INSURANCE CO*

NCAS — *SEE ALSO NATIONAL CLAIMS ADMINISTRATIVE SOURCES*

NEIGHBORHOOD HEALTH PARTNERSHIP

FLORIDA	7600 CORPORATE CTR DR MIAMI, FL 33126 PO BOX 025680 MIAMI, FL 33102-5680	PHONE: (305) 715-2200 FAX: (305) 715-2220 TOLL FREE: (800) 354-0222	WEB: WWW.MYNHP.COM

NEIGHBORHOOD HEALTH PLAN

MASSACHUSETTS	253 SUMMER ST BOSTON, MA 02210-1120	PHONE: (617) 772-5500 FAX: (617) 772-5513 TOLL FREE: (800) 433-5556	WEB: WWW.NHP.ORG

NEW ERA LIFE INSURANCE CO

NATIONAL	200 WESTLAKE PARK BLVD STE 1200 HOUSTON, TX 77079 PO BOX 4884 HOUSTON, TX 77210-4884	PHONE: (281) 368-7200 FAX: (281) 368-7286 TOLL FREE: (800) 552-7879	WEB: WWW.NEWERALIFE.COM

NEW JERSEY MANUFACTURERS INSURANCE CO

NEW JERSEY	301 SULLIVAN WY WEST TRENTON, NJ 08628	PHONE: (609) 883-1300 FAX: (609) 883-4835 TOLL FREE: (800) 232-6600	WEB: WWW.NJM.COM

NEW LONDON COUNTY MUTUAL INSURANCE CO — *NLC INSURANCE COMPANIES*

CONNECTICUT *MASSACHUSETTS* *RHODE ISLAND*	101 HIGH ST NORWICH, CT 06360-5605 PO BOX 40 NORWICH, CT 06360	PHONE: (860) 887-3553 FAX: (860) 887-2898 TOLL FREE: (800) 243-4080 IN-STATE: (800) 962-0800	WEB: WWW.NLCINSURANCE.COM

NGS AMERICAN, INC

NATIONAL	27575 HARPER AVE ST CLAIR SHORES, MI 48081 PO BOX 7676 ST CLAIR SHORES, MI 48080-7676	PHONE: (586) 779-7676 FAX: (586) 779-0117 TOLL FREE: (800) 521-1555	WEB: WWW.NGS-AMERICAN.COM

NLC — *SUMMIT INSURANCE CAMPANY*

RHODE ISLAND	101 HIGH ST NORWIH, CT 06360	FAX: (860) 887-2898 TOLL FREE: (866) 287-5098	WEB: WWW.SUMMITINSURANCE.COM

NLC INSURANCE COMPANIES — *SEE ALSO NEW LONDON COUNTY MUTUAL INSURANCE CO*

NOITU INSURANCE TRUST FUND

NATIONAL	148-06 HILLSIDE AVE JAMAICA, NY 11435	PHONE: (718) 291-3434 FAX: (718) 291-0531	WEB: WWW.NOITU.ORG

NORTH AMERICA ADMINISTRATORS, LP

NATIONAL		1212 8TH AVE SOUTH NASHVILLE, TN 37203 PO BOX 1984 NASHVILLE, TN 37202-1984	PHONE: (615) 256-3561 FAX: (615) 255-6654 TOLL FREE: (800) 411-3650	WEB: WWW.NAA-LP.COM

NORTH CAROLINA MUTUAL LIFE INSURANCE CO

NATIONAL		411 W CHAPEL HILL ST DURHAM, NC 27701	PHONE: (919) 682-9201 FAX: (919) 683-1694 TOLL FREE: (800) 626-1899	E-MAIL: INFO@NCMUTUALLIFE.COM WEB: WWW.NCMUTUALLIFE.COM

NORTH POINTE INSURANCE CO

FLORIDA, ILLINOIS, INDIANA, MICHIGAN, NEW JERSEY, NEW YORK, OHIO, PENNSYLVANIA

		28819 FRANKLIN RD SOUTHFIELD, MI 48034 PO BOX 2223 SOUTHFIELD, MI 48037	PHONE: (248) 358-1171 FAX: (248) 357-3895 TOLL FREE: (800) 229-6742	E-MAIL: CLAIMS@HPIC.COM WEB: WWW.NPIC.COM

NORTHEAST INSURANCE CO

MAINE		482 PAYNE RD 4TH FL SCARBOROUGH, ME 04074-8929 PO BOX 1418 SCARBOROUGH, ME 04070-1418	PHONE: (207) 883-2232 FAX: (207) 883-1564 TOLL FREE: (800) 456-1819	WEB: WWW,PRESERVER.COM

NORTHERN ADJUSTERS, INC

ALASKA		1401 RUDAKOF CIR STE 100 ANCHORAGE, AK 99508-3108	PHONE: (907) 338-7484 FAX: (907) 338-6364	E-MAIL: NEWCLAIM@NADJ.COM WEB: WWW.NADJ.COM
		3517 REWAK DR FAIRBANKS, AK 99709-4913	PHONE: (907) 479-2294 FAX: (907) 479-2571	E-MAIL: NEWCLAIM@NADJ.COM WEB: WWW.NADJ.COM

NORTHLAND INSURANCE CO — *TRAVELERS INSURANCE COMPANIES*

NATIONAL		MAILCODE 103N 385 WASHINGTON ST ST PAUL, MN 55102-1309 PO BOX 64805 ST PAUL, MN 55164-0805	PHONE: (651) 310-4100 FAX: (651) 310-4093 TOLL FREE: (800) 328-5972	WEB: WWW.NORTHLANDINS.COM

NORTHWEST ADMINISTRATORS — *WESTERN TEAMSTERS*

CALIFORNIA IDAHO NEVADA		2323 E LAKE AVE SEATTLE, WA 98102-3305 PO BOX 32403 SEATTLE, WA 98124-1203	FAX: (206) 726-3209 TOLL FREE: (800) 872-5439	E-MAIL: SEATTLE.PERSONNEL@NWADMIN.COM WEB: WWW.NWADMIN.COM
OREGON		LLOYD FIVE HUNDRED BLDG 500 NE MULTNOMAH STE 720 PORTLAND, OR 97323	PHONE: (503) 238-6961	WEB: WWW.NWADMIN.COM
WASHINGTON		2323 E LAKE AVE SEATTLE, WA 98102-3305 PO BOX 32403 SEATTLE, WA 98124-1203	FAX: (206) 726-3209 TOLL FREE: (800) 872-5439	E-MAIL: SEATTLE.PERSONNEL@NWADMIN.COM WEB: WWW.NWADMIN.COM

N

NORTHWEST TEXAS HEALTHCARE SYSTEM

COLORADO
KANSAS
NEW MEXICO
OKLAHOMA
TEXAS

1501 S COULTER DR
AMARILLO, TX 79106-1770
PO BOX 1110
AMARILLO, TX 79175
PHONE: (806) 354-1000
FAX: (806) 354-1122
WEB: WWW.NWTEXASHEALTHCARE.COM

NOVA HEALTHCARE ADMINISTRATORS — *INDEPENDANT HEALTH*

NEW YORK

PO BOX 9010
BUFFALO, NY 14321
PHONE: (716) 773-1143
FAX: (716) 773-1276
TOLL FREE: (800) 333-3195
IN-STATE: (800) 999-5703
WEB: WWW.INDEPENDANTHEALTH.COM

NY LIFE ADMINISTRATION CORP — *NY LIFE LONG TERM CARE*

NATIONAL

6200 BRIDGE POINT PKWY STE 400
AUSTIN, TX 78730
PO BOX 559005
AUSTIN, TX 78755-9005
PHONE: (512) 703-5555
FAX: (512) 703-5566
TOLL FREE: (800) 723-5555
WEB: WWW.NEWYORKLIFELTC.COM

NY LIFE LONG TERM CARE — *SEE ALSO NY LIFE ADMINISTRATION CORP*

OAK AGENCY

ARIZONA
ILLINOIS
INDIANA
IOWA
KANSAS
MICHIGAN
MINNESOTA
NEBRASKA
NORTH DAKOTA
OHIO
SOUTH DAKOTA
WISCONSIN

340 W BUTTERFIELD RD
ELMHURST, IL 60126-5024
PHONE: (630) 833-9770
FAX: (630) 833-4484
TOLL FREE: (800) 441-4228
WEB: WWW.CALLOAK.COM

OCCIDENTAL FIRE & CASUALTY CO OF NORTH CAROLINA — *WHILSHIRE AND COMPANY*

NATIONAL

702 OBERLIN RD
RALEIGH, NC 27605
PO BOX 10800
RALEIGH, NC 27605-0800
PHONE: (919) 833-1600
FAX: (919) 834-0855
TOLL FREE: (800) 525-7486

ODS COMPANIES

OREGON

601 SW 2ND AVE
PORTLAND, OR 97204-3154
PHONE: (503) 228-6554
FAX: (503) 243-3895
TOLL FREE: (800) 852-5195
IN-STATE: (800) 452-1058
WEB: WWW.ODSCOMPANIES.COM

OHIO BUREAU OF WORKERS' COMPENSATION

OHIO

1005 FOURTH ST
PORTSMOUTH, OH 45662-4195
PO BOX 1307
PORTSMOUTH, OH 45662-1307
PHONE: (740) 353-2187
FAX: (866) 236-8353
TOLL FREE: (800) 644-6292
WEB: WWW.OHIOBWC.COM

1225 W HUNTER ST
LOGAN, OH 43138
PO BOX 630
LOGAN, OH 43138-0630
PHONE: (740) 385-5608
FAX: (866) 366-8348
TOLL FREE: (800) 644-6292
WEB: WWW.OHIOBWC.COM

125 E COURT ST 8TH 9TH AND 10TH FL
CINCINNATI, OH 45202-1276
PHONE: (513) 852-3341
FAX: (866) 281-9353
TOLL FREE: (800) 644-6292
WEB: WWW.OHIOBWC.COM

2025 E FOURTH ST
LIMA, OH 45804-4101
PHONE: (419) 227-3127
FAX: (419) 225-5399 OR (866) 336-8346
TOLL FREE: (800) 644-6292
WEB: WWW.OHIOBWC.COM

OHIO — CONTINUED		240 TAPPAN DR N MANSFIELD, OH 44906 PO BOX 8051 MANSFIELD, OH 44906-8051	PHONE: (419) 747-4090 FAX: (866) 336-8350 TOLL FREE: (800) 644-6292	WEB: WWW.OHIOBWC.COM
		30 W SPRING ST 11TH FL COLUMBUS, OH 43215-2256 PO BOX 15518 COLUMBUS, OH 43215-0518	PHONE: (614) 728-5550 FAX: (866) 336-8352 TOLL FREE: (800) 644-6292	WEB: WWW.OHIOBWC.COM
		3401 PARK CTR DR STE 100 DAYTON, OH 45414 PO BOX 13910 DAYTON, OH 45413	PHONE: (937) 264-5000 FAX: (866) 281-9543 TOLL FREE: (800) 644-6292	WEB: WWW.OHIOBWC.COM
		345 HIGH ST HAMILTON, OH 45011	PHONE: (513) 785-4500 FAX: (866) 336-8343 TOLL FREE: (800) 644-6292	WEB: WWW.OHIOBWC.COM
		400 THIRD ST SE CANTON, OH 44702	PHONE: (330) 438-0638 FAX: (330) 438-0596 TOLL FREE: (800) 644-6292	WEB: WWW.OHIOBWC.COM
		4800 E 100 31ST ST GARFIELD HEIGHTS, OH 44105	PHONE: (216) 584-0100 FAX: (866) 457-0590 TOLL FREE: (800) 644-6292	WEB: WWW.OHIOBWC.COM
		615 W SUPERIOR AVE 6TH FL CLEVELAND, OH 44113-1889	PHONE: (216) 787-3050 FAX: (866) 336-8345 TOLL FREE: (800) 644-6292	WEB: WWW.OHIOBWC.COM
		61501 SOUTH GATE RD CAMBRIDGE, OH 43725	PHONE: (740) 435-4200 FAX: (866) 457-0597 TOLL FREE: (800) 898-6446	WEB: WWW.OHIOBWC.COM
		8650 GOVERNOR S HILL DR CINCINNATI, OH 45249	PHONE: (513) 583-4400 FAX: (513) 583-4531 TOLL FREE: (800) 644-6292	WEB: WWW.OHIOBWC.COM
		ONE GOVERNMENT CTR STE 1236 TOLEDO, OH 43604 PO BOX 794 TOLEDO, OH 43697-0794	PHONE: (419) 245-2609 FAX: (866) 452-0594 TOLL FREE: (800) 644-2692	WEB: WWW.OHIOBWC.COM
		ONE S LIMESTONE ST 5TH FL` SPRINGFIELD, OH 45501 PO BOX 1467 SPRINGFIELD, OH 45501-1467	PHONE: (937) 327-1425 FAX: (866) 457-0593 TOLL FREE: (800) 644-6292	WEB: WWW.OHIOBWC.COM

OHIO CASUALTY GROUP

NATIONAL		9450 SEWARD RD FAIRFIELD, OH 45014 PO BOX 188060 FAIRFIELD, OH 45018	PHONE: (513) 603-2400 FAX: (513) 867-3215 TOLL FREE: (800) 843-6446	WEB: WWW.OCAS.COM
ALABAMA		3101 BEAUMONT CENTER CIR LEXINGTON, KY 40513 PO BOX 119001 LEXINGTON, KY 40591	PHONE: (859) 219-3800 FAX: (513) 881-1387 TOLL FREE: (888) 572-6184	E-MAIL: LEXINGTON.CLAIMS@OCAS.COM WEB: WWW.OCAS.COM
ARIZONA		PO BOX 5620 DENVER, CO 80217	PHONE: (303) 221-1152 FAX: (888) 329-3730 TOLL FREE: (800) 326-6446	WEB: WWW.OCAS.COM
ARKANSAS		3101 BEAUMONT CENTER CIR LEXINGTON, KY 40513 PO BOX 119001 LEXINGTON, KY 40591	PHONE: (859) 219-3800 FAX: (513) 881-1387 TOLL FREE: (888) 572-6184	E-MAIL: LEXINGTON.CLAIMS@OCAS.COM WEB: WWW.OCAS.COM
COLORADO		PO BOX 5620 DENVER, CO 80217	PHONE: (303) 221-1152 FAX: (888) 329-3730 TOLL FREE: (800) 326-6446	WEB: WWW.OCAS.COM

O

FLORIDA *GEORGIA*	3101 BEAUMONT CENTER CIR LEXINGTON, KY 40513 PO BOX 119001 LEXINGTON, KY 40591	PHONE: (859) 219-3800 FAX: (513) 881-1387 TOLL FREE: (888) 572-6184	E-MAIL: LEXINGTON.CLAIMS@OCAS.COM WEB: WWW.OCAS.COM
IOWA *KANSAS*	PO BOX 5620 DENVER, CO 80217	PHONE: (303) 221-1152 FAX: (888) 329-3730 TOLL FREE: (800) 326-6446	WEB: WWW.OCAS.COM
KENTUCKY *LOUISIANA* *MISSISSIPPI*	3101 BEAUMONT CENTER CIR LEXINGTON, KY 40513 PO BOX 119001 LEXINGTON, KY 40591	PHONE: (859) 219-3800 FAX: (513) 881-1387 TOLL FREE: (888) 572-6184	E-MAIL: LEXINGTON.CLAIMS@OCAS.COM WEB: WWW.OCAS.COM
MISSOURI *MONTANA* *NEW MEXICO*	PO BOX 5620 DENVER, CO 80217	PHONE: (303) 221-1152 FAX: (888) 329-3730 TOLL FREE: (800) 326-6446	WEB: WWW.OCAS.COM
OKLAHOMA	3101 BEAUMONT CENTER CIR LEXINGTON, KY 40513 PO BOX 119001 LEXINGTON, KY 40591	PHONE: (859) 219-3800 FAX: (513) 881-1387 TOLL FREE: (888) 572-6184	E-MAIL: LEXINGTON.CLAIMS@OCAS.COM WEB: WWW.OCAS.COM
OREGON	PO BOX 5620 DENVER, CO 80217	PHONE: (303) 221-1152 FAX: (888) 329-3730 TOLL FREE: (800) 326-6446	WEB: WWW.OCAS.COM
TENNESSEE *TEXAS*	3101 BEAUMONT CENTER CIR LEXINGTON, KY 40513 PO BOX 119001 LEXINGTON, KY 40591	PHONE: (859) 219-3800 FAX: (513) 881-1387 TOLL FREE: (888) 572-6184	E-MAIL: LEXINGTON.CLAIMS@OCAS.COM WEB: WWW.OCAS.COM
UTAH *WASHINGTON* *WYOMING*	PO BOX 5620 DENVER, CO 80217	PHONE: (303) 221-1152 FAX: (888) 329-3730 TOLL FREE: (800) 326-6446	WEB: WWW.OCAS.COM

OHIO MUTUAL INSURANCE GROUP

OHIO	1725 HOPLEY AVE BUCYRUS, OH 44820-3569 PO BOX 111 BUCYRUS, OH 44820	PHONE: (419) 562-3011 FAX: (419) 562-0995	WEB: WWW.OMIG.COM

OHIO NATIONAL FINANCIAL SERVICE

NATIONAL	ONE FINANCIAL WY CINCINNATI, OH 45242 PO BOX 237 CINCINNATI, OH 45201	PHONE: (513) 794-6100 FAX: (513) 794-4521 TOLL FREE: (800) 366-6654	WEB: WWW.OHIONATIONAL.COM

OLD AMERICAN INSURANCE CO

NATIONAL	3520 BROADWAY KANSAS CITY, MO 64111 PO BOX 218573 KANSAS CITY, MO 64121	PHONE: (816) 753-4900 FAX: (816) 753-1198 TOLL FREE: (800) 733-6242	WEB: WWW.OAIC.COM

OLD GUARD-WESTFIELD INSURANCE

DELAWARE	410 N CASS ST MIDDLETOWN, DE 19709-1038 PO BOX 918 MIDDLETOWN, DE 19709	PHONE: (302) 449-0306 FAX: (302) 449-0318	WEB: WWW.WESTFIELDGRP.COM

OLD REPUBLIC INSURANCE CO

PENNSYLVANIA	133 OAKLAND AVE GREENSBURG, PA 15601 PO BOX 2200 GREENSBURG, PA 15601-9937	PHONE: (724) 834-5000 FAX: (724) 838-5404	WEB: WWW.OLDREPUBLIC.COM

OLD REPUBLIC INTERNATIONAL

NATIONAL	307 N MICHIGAN AVE CHICAGO, IL 60601	PHONE: (312) 346-8100 FAX: (312) 346-2050 TOLL FREE: (800) 621-0365	WEB: WWW.OLDREPUBLIC.COM

OLD SURETY LIFE INSURANCE CO

NATIONAL	5235 N LINCOLN BLVD OKLAHOMA CITY, OK 73105 PO BOX 54407 OKLAHOMA CITY, OK 73154-1407	PHONE: (405) 523-2112 FAX: (405) 524-4011 TOLL FREE: (800) 272-5466	

OLD UNITED LIFE INSURANCE CO

NATIONAL	8500 SHAWNEE MISSION PKY STE 200 MERRIAM, KS 66202 PO BOX 795 SHAWNEE MISSION, KS 66201	PHONE: (913) 236-6090 FAX: (808) 777-2628 TOLL FREE: (800) 866-6090	WEB: WWW.OLDUNITED.COM

OMNICARE HEALTH PLAN

MICHIGAN	PO BOX 7150 LONDON, KY 40742	PHONE: (866) 316-3784 FAX: (313) 465-1600 TOLL FREE: (866) 314-3784	WEB: WWW.OMNICAREHEALTHPLAN.COM

ONE BEACON INSURANCE

NATIONAL	6400 SHERIDIAN DR WILLIAMSVILLE, NY 14221 PO BOX 302 BUFFALO, NY 14240	FAX: (716) 932-9290 TOLL FREE: (800) 828-7212 IN-STATE: (800) 462-7267	E-MAIL: INFO@ONEBEACON.COM WEB: WWW.ONEBEACON.COM
MAINE	707 SABLE OAKS DR SOUTH PORTLAND, ME 04106-3279 PO BOX 527 PORTLAND, ME 04112-0527	PHONE: (207) 791-1790 FAX: (207) 871-0393 TOLL FREE: (800) 343-2601 IN-STATE: (800) 343-2601	E-MAIL: INFO@ONEBEACON.COM WEB: WWW.ONEBEACON.COM
MAINE *MASSACHUSETTS*	ONE BEACON ST BOSTON, MA 02108-3100	PHONE: (617) 725-6000 FAX: (617) 725-6702	E-MAIL: INFO@ONEBEACON.COM WEB: WWW.ONEBEACON.COM
MASSACHUSETTS	EIGHT ESSEX CTR DR PEABODY, MA 01960-2959 PO BOX 6029 PEABODY, MA 01961-6029	PHONE: (978) 532-6880 FAX: (978) 977-9018 IN-STATE: (800) 332-3995	E-MAIL: INFO@ONEBEACON.COM WEB: WWW.ONEBEACON.COM
MASSACHUSETTS *NEW HAMPSHIRE*	ONE BEACON ST BOSTON, MA 02108-3100	PHONE: (617) 725-6000 FAX: (617) 725-6702	E-MAIL: INFO@ONEBEACON.COM WEB: WWW.ONEBEACON.COM
NEW HAMPSHIRE	JEFFERSON MILL 630 N COMMERCIAL ST STE 207 MANCHESTER, NH 03101 PO BOX 712 FOXBORO, MA 02035	PHONE: (603) 669-3830 FAX: (603) 624-9542 OR (888) 416-1165 IN-STATE: (800) 542-3830	E-MAIL: INFO@ONEBEACON.COM WEB: WWW.ONEBEACON.COM
NEW JERSEY	44 WHIPPANY RD MORRISTOWN, NJ 07960	PHONE: (973) 630-6600 FAX: (973) 630-6640 TOLL FREE: (800) 624-1274	E-MAIL: INFO@ONEBEACON.COM WEB: WWW.ONEBEACON.COM
NEW YORK	201 N SERVICE RD MELVILLE, NY 11747-3126 PO BOX 9070 MELVILLE, NY 11747-9070	PHONE: (631) 423-4400 FAX: (631) 547-4666 TOLL FREE: (800) 258-0418	E-MAIL: INFO@ONEBEACON.COM WEB: WWW.ONEBEACON.COM
NEW YORK *RHODE ISLAND* *VERMONT*	ONE BEACON ST BOSTON, MA 02108-3100	PHONE: (617) 725-6000 FAX: (617) 725-6702	E-MAIL: INFO@ONEBEACON.COM WEB: WWW.ONEBEACON.COM

OPTICARE OF UTAH, INC

UTAH	1901 W PKWY BLVD SALT LAKE CITY, UT 84119	PHONE: (801) 886-2020 FAX: (801) 954-0054 TOLL FREE: (800) 363-0950	WEB: WWW.OPTICAREOFUTAH.COM

OPTIMA HEALTH PLAN — *SENTARA HEALTH MANAGEMENT*

VIRGINIA	4417 CORPORATION LN VIRGINIA BEACH, VA 23462-3162	PHONE: (800) 508-0528 FAX: (757) 552-7199 TOLL FREE: (800) 736-8272	E-MAIL: MEMBERS@OPTIMAHEALTH.COM WEB: WWW.OPTIMAHEALTH.COM

OPTIMUM REINSURANCE CO

NATIONAL	3434 FAIRMOUNT DALLAS, TX 75219-4701 PO BOX 660010 DALLAS, TX 75266-0010	PHONE: (214) 528-2020 FAX: (214) 528-2777	WEB: WWW.OPTIMUMRE.COM

ORAL HEALTH SERVICES — *DENTAL NETWORK, INC*

ALABAMA	5775 BLUE LAGOON DR STE 400 MIAMI, FL 33126-2034 PO BOX 025779 MIAMI, FL 33102-5779	PHONE: (305) 262-1333 FAX: (305) 262-6119 TOLL FREE: (800) 432-3376 IN-STATE: (800) 223-5447	WEB: WWW.COMPBENEFITS.COM

OREGON CASUALITIES MCO — *SEE ALSO ALLSTATE INSURANCE CO*

OSF HEALTH PLANS

ILLINOIS	7915 N HALE AVE STE D PEORIA, IL 61615 PO BOX 5128 PEORIA, IL 61601-5128	PHONE: (309) 677-8200 FAX: (309) 677-8259 TOLL FREE: (800) 673-4699	E-MAIL: MEMBER@OSFHEALTHCARE.ORG WEB: WWW OSFHEALTHPLANS.COM

OXFORD HEALTH PLANS

CONNECTICUT *DELAWARE* *NEW JERSEY* *NEW YORK* *PENNSYLVANIA*	PO BOX 7081 BRIDGEPORT, CT 06601-7081	PHONE: (800) 666-1353	WEB: WWW.OXFORDHEALTH.COM
	48 MONROE TPKE TRUMBULL, CT 06611-1341 PO BOX 7082 BRIDGEPORT, CT 06601-7082	PHONE: (203) 459-6000 TOLL FREE: (800) 444-6222 IN-STATE: (800) 201-7004	WEB: WWW.UNITEDHEALTHGROUP.COM

OXFORD LIFE INSURANCE CO — *U-HAUL EMPLOYEES*

NATIONAL	2721 N CENTRAL AVE PHOENIX, AZ 85004-1121	PHONE: (602) 263-6666 FAX: (602) 264-2369 TOLL FREE: (888) 757-3732	E-MAIL: INFO@OXFORDLIFE.COM WEB: WWW.OXFORDLIFE.COM

P5 HEALTH SERVICES

NATIONAL	2455 E PARLEYS WAY SALT LAKE CITY, UT 84109-1217 PO BOX 9554 SALT LAKE CITY, UT 84109	PHONE: (801) 474-2555 FAX: (801) 474-2522 TOLL FREE: (800) 551-4049	WEB: WWW.P5HEALTH.COM

PACIFIC BLUE CROSS — *BLUE CROSS CANADA*

BRITISH COLUMBIA	4250 CANADA WY BURNABY, BC V6B 4E1 PO BOX 7000 VANCOUVER, BC V6B 4E1	PHONE: (604) 419-2000 FAX: (604) 419-2990 TOLL FREE: (800) 487-3228 IN-STATE: (888) 275-4672	WEB: WWW.PAC.BLUECROSS.CA

PACIFIC GAS & ELECTRIC CO

CALIFORNIA	77 BEALE ST MAIL CODE B23H SAN FRANCISCO, CA 94105-1814 PO BOX 7779 SAN FRANCISCO, CA 94120-7779	PHONE: (415) 973-8700 FAX: (415) 973-7828	

P

PACIFIC SOURCE HEALTH PLANS

IDAHO *OREGON* *WASHINGTON*	110 INTERNATIONAL WAY SPRINGFIELD, OR 97477 PO BOX 7068 EUGENE, OR 97401-0068	PHONE: (541) 686-1242 FAX: (541) 684-5559 TOLL FREE: (800) 624-6052	WEB: WWW.PACIFICSOURCE.COM

PACIFICARE HEALTH SYSTEMS, INC — *PACIFICARE IOF CALIFORNIA*

NATIONAL	5995 PLZ DR CYPRESS, CA 90630-5028 PO BOX 6006 CYPRESS, CA 90630-0006	PHONE: (714) 952-1121 FAX: (714) 226-3914 TOLL FREE: (800) 624-8822	WEB: WWW.PACIFICARE.COM
ARIZONA	410 N 44TH ST PHOENIX, AZ 85008 PO BOX 52078 PHOENIX, AZ 85072-2078	PHONE: (602) 244-8200 FAX: (480) 350-9500 TOLL FREE: (800) 347-8600	WEB: WWW.PACIFICARE.COM
ARIZONA *CALIFORNIA*	5001 LBJ FWY STE 600 TWR II BLDG DALLAS, TX 75244-6130 PO BOX 400046 SAN ANTONIO, TX 78229	PHONE: (972) 866-1693 TOLL FREE: (800) 825-9355	WEB: WWW.PACIFICARE.COM
COLORADO	6455 S YOSEMITE ST GREENWOOD VILLAGE, CO 80155 PO BOX 6699 ENGLEWOOD, CO 80155-6770	PHONE: (303) 220-5800 FAX: (303) 714 3736 TOLL FREE: (800) 255-1180	WEB: WWW.PACIFICARE.COM
COLORADO *NEVADA*	410 N 44TH ST PHOENIX, AZ 85008 PO BOX 52078 PHOENIX, AZ 85072-2078	PHONE: (602) 244-8200 FAX: (480) 350-9500 TOLL FREE: (800) 347-8600	WEB: WWW.PACIFICARE.COM
NEVADA	700 E WARM SPRINGS RD LAS VEGAS, NV 89119	PHONE: (702) 269-7500	WEB: WWW.PACIFICARE.COM
OKLAHOMA	7666 E 61ST ST STE 500 TULSA, OK 74133	PHONE: (918) 459-1100	WEB: WWW.PACIFICARE.COM
OREGON	FIVE CENTER POINTE DR STE 600 LAKE OSWEGO, OR 97035	PHONE: (503) 603-7355 FAX: (503) 603-7393 TOLL FREE: (800) 922-1444	WEB: WWW.PACIFICARE.COM
TEXAS	7666 E 61ST ST STE 500 TULSA, OK 74133	PHONE: (918) 459-1100	WEB: WWW.PACIFICARE.COM
WASHINGTON	FIVE CENTER POINTE DR STE 600 LAKE OSWEGO, OR 97035	PHONE: (503) 603-7355 FAX: (503) 603-7393 TOLL FREE: (800) 922-1444	WEB: WWW.PACIFICARE.COM
WASHINGTON	7525 SE 24TH MERCER ISLAND, WA 98040	TOLL FREE: (800) 829-2925	WEB: WWW.PACIFICARE.COM

PAID DENTAL — *SEE ALSO BOON-CHAPMAN BENEFIT ADMINISTRATORS*

PAN AMERICAN LIFE INSURANCE CO

NATIONAL	601 POYDRAS ST NEW ORLEANS, LA 70130 PO BOX 60219 NEW ORLEANS, LA 70160-0219	PHONE: (504) 566-1300 FAX: (504) 566-3109 TOLL FREE: (877) 939-4500	WEB: WWW.PANAMERICANLIFE.COM

PARAGON BENEFITS, INC

NATIONAL	6065 BUSINESS PARK DR COLUMBUS, GA 31909 PO BOX 12288 COLUMBUS, GA 31917	PHONE: (706) 327-9218 FAX: (706) 571-9955 TOLL FREE: (800) 277-9218	WEB: WWW.PARAGONBENEFITS.COM

PARAMOUNT HEALTH CARE

OHIO
1901 INDIAN WOOD CIR
MAUMEE, OH 43537
PO BOX 928
TOLEDO, OH 43697-0928
PHONE: (419) 887-2500
FAX: (419) 887-2029
TOLL FREE: (800) 462-3589
WEB: WWW.PARAMOUNTHEALTHCARE.COM

PARTNER REINSURANCE COMPANY OF THE U.S.

CONNECTICUT
ONE GREENWICH PLZ
GREENWICH, CT 06830-6352
PHONE: (203) 485-4200
FAX: (203) 485-4300
WEB: WWW.PARTNERRE.COM

PARTNERS MUTUAL INSURANCE CO

IOWA
MICHIGAN
WISCONSIN
20935 SWENSON DR STE 200
WAUKESHA, WI 53186-2057
PO BOX 2003
MILWAUKEE, WI 53201-2003
PHONE: (262) 798-5050
FAX: (262) 798-5040
TOLL FREE: (800) 551-5151
WEB: WWW.PARTNERSMUTUAL.COM

PARTNERS NATIONAL HEALTH PLANS

NORTH CAROLINA
5640 HANES MILL RD
WINSTON SALEM, NC 27105-1322
PO BOX 17509
WINSTON SALEM, NC 27116-7509
PHONE: (336) 760-4822
FAX: (336) 659-2963
TOLL FREE: (800) 942-5695
WEB: WWW.PARTNERSHEALTH.COM

PATH MARK STORES, INC

NEW JERSEY
200 MILIK ST
CARTERET, NJ 07008-1194
PHONE: (732) 499-3000
FAX: (732) 499-4285
TOLL FREE: (800) 221-0507
WEB: WWW.PATHMARK.COM

PAWTUCKET MUTUAL INSURANCE COMPANY — *NARRAGANSETT BAY INSURANCE COMPANY*

RHODE ISLAND
25 MAPLE ST
PAWTUCKET, RI 02860-2104
PHONE: (401) 725-5600
FAX: (401) 721-9899
WEB: WWW.PAWMUT.COM

PBP HEALTH PLAN — *SEE ALSO PEOPLE BEFORE PROFITS*

PEARL & ASSOCIATES

NATIONAL
1200 E GLEN AVE
PEORIA HEIGHTS, IL 61616
PHONE: (309) 688-9000
FAX: (309) 688-5444
TOLL FREE: (800) 447-4982
IN-STATE: (800) 322-2488
WEB: WWW.PEARLINS.COM

PEER REVIEW ORGANIZATIONS

NATIONAL
IOWA FOUNDATION FOR MEDICAL CARE
6000 WESTOWN PKY
WEST DES MOINES, IA 50266-7771
PHONE: (515) 223-2900
FAX: (515) 223-3131 OR (515) 223-2131
TOLL FREE: (800) 383-2856
E-MAIL: RPOCHTER@IFMC.ORG
WEB: WWW.IFMC.ORG

GEORGIA
GEORGIA MEDICAL CARE FOUNDATION
1455 LINCOLN PARKWY STE 800
ATLANTA, GA 30346-2289
PHONE: (404) 982-0411
FAX: (404) 982-7591
IN-STATE: (800) 982-0411
WEB: WWW.GMCF.ORG

KENTUCKY
HEALTH CARE EXCEL
1951 BISHOP LAND STE 300
LOUISVILLE, KY 40218
PO BOX 35035
LOUISVILLE, KY 40232-5035
PHONE: (502) 454-5112
FAX: (502) 454-5113
WEB: WWW.HCE.ORG

MASSACHUSETTS
MASSACHUSETTS PEER REVIEW ORGANIZATION (MASSPRO)
245 WINTER ST
WALTHAM, MA 02451
PHONE: (781) 890-0011
FAX: (781) 487-0083
TOLL FREE: (800) 252-5533
WEB: WWW.MASSPRO.ORG

P

NEW YORK		1979 MARCUS AVE STE 105 LAKE SUCCESS, NY 11042-1002	PHONE: (516) 326-7767 FAX: (516) 328-2310 TOLL FREE: (800) 852-3685	WEB: WWW.IPRO.ORG

PEERLESS INSURANCE

PENNSYLVANIA		275 GRANDVIEW AVE STE 300 CAMP HILL, PA 17001 PO BOX 8851 CAMP HILL, PA 17001	PHONE: (717) 763-7331 FAX: (717) 975-4832 TOLL FREE: (800) 732-3700	WEB: WWW.PEERLESS-INS.COM

PEERLESS INSURANCE CO

NEW HAMPSHIRE		NETHERLANDS 62 MAPLE AVE KEENE, NH 03431-1625 PO BOX 2053 KEENE, NH 03431-2053	PHONE: (603) 352-3221 FAX: (603) 352-4363 TOLL FREE: (800) 542-5385	WEB: WWW.PEERLESS-INS.COM
NEW JERSEY NEW YORK VERMONT		5062 BRITTONFIELD PKY EAST SYRACUSE, NY 13057 PO BOX 4858 SYRACUSE, NY 13221	PHONE: (315) 431-6100 FAX: (800) 526-0681 TOLL FREE: (800) 443-4000	WEB: WWW.PEERLESS-INS.COM

PEHP — *PUBLIC EMPLOYEES HEALTH PROGRAM*

UTAH		560 E 200 S SALT LAKE CITY, UT 84102-2004	PHONE: (801) 366-7555 FAX: (801) 366-7596 TOLL FREE: (800) 765-7347	WEB: WWW.PEHP.ORG

PEKIN INSURANCE CO — *FARMERS AUTO INSURANCE ASSOCIATION*

ILLINOIS		2505 COURT ST PEKIN, IL 61558 PO BOX 129 PEKIN, IL 61558-0129	PHONE: (309) 346-1161 FAX: (309) 346-9466 TOLL FREE: (800) 322-0160	WEB: WWW.PEKININSURANCE.COM

PEMCO INSURANCE CO

WASHINGTON		325 EASTLAKE AVE E SEATTLE, WA 98109-5466 PO BOX 778 SEATTLE, WA 98111-0778	PHONE: (206) 628-4000 FAX: (206) 628-5976 TOLL FREE: (800) 552-7440	WEB: WWW.PEMCO.COM

PENINSULA INSURANCE CO

DELAWARE
MARYLAND
PENNSYLVANIA
TENNESSEE
VIRGINIA
WEST VIRGINIA

		112 E MARKET ST SALISBURY, MD 21803 PO BOX 108 SALISBURY, MD 21803-0108	PHONE: (410) 742-5132 FAX: (410) 546-1273 TOLL FREE: (800) 492-1205	WEB: WWW.PENINSULAINSURANCE.COM

PENN CORPORATION FINANCIAL COMPANIES — *SEE ALSO PENNSYLVANIA LIFE INSURANCE CO*

PENN NATIONAL INSURANCE — *SEE ALSO PENNSYLVANIA NATIONAL MUTUAL CASUALTY INSURANCE CO*

PENN TREATY AMERICAN COMPANIES

NATIONAL		3440 LEHIGH ST ALLENTOWN, PA 18103-7001	PHONE: (610) 965-2222 FAX: (610) 967-4616 TOLL FREE: (800) 222-3469	WEB: WWW.PENNTREATY.COM

PENN WESTERN BENEFITS, INC

NATIONAL

7701 THORNDIKE RD
GREENSBORO, NC 27409
PO BOX 7834
GREENSBORO, NC 27417-0834

PHONE: (336) 665-9400
FAX: (336) 664-1300
TOLL FREE: (888) 792-7828

WEB: WWW.PENNWESTERN.COM

PENN-AMERICA INSURANCE CO

NATIONAL

420 S YORK RD
HATBORO, PA 19040-3949

PHONE: (215) 443-3600
FAX: (215) 443-3604
TOLL FREE: (800) 788-4780

WEB: WWW.PENN-AMERICA.COM

PENNSYLVANIA LIFE INSURANCE CO — *PENN CORPORATION FINANCIAL COMPANIES*

NATIONAL

1001 HEATHROW PARK LN STE 5001
LAKE MARY, FL 32746
PO BOX 958465
LAKE MARY, FL 32795-8465

PHONE: (407) 628-1776
TOLL FREE: (800) 275-6667

E-MAIL: ASKPENN@PENNLIFE.COM
WEB: WWW.PENNLIFE.COM

PENNSYLVANIA LUMBERMEN'S MUTUAL INSURANCE CO

NATIONAL

THE CURTIS CENTER
INDEPENDENCE W 2ND FL
PHILADELPHIA, PA 19106

PHONE: (215) 625-9233
FAX: (215) 625-9097
TOLL FREE: (800) 752-1895

E-MAIL: INFO@PALUMBERMENS.COM
WEB: WWW.PALUMBERMENS.COM

PENNSYLVANIA MILLERS INSURANCE CO

PENNSYLVANIA

72 N FRANKLIN ST
WILKES-BARRE, PA 18773-0016

PHONE: (570) 822-8111
FAX: (570) 829-2060
TOLL FREE: (800) 233-3347

WEB: WWW.PENNMILLERS.COM

PENNSYLVANIA NATIONAL MUTUAL CASUALTY INSURANCE CO — *PENN NATIONAL INSURANCE*

ALABAMA
DELAWARE
MARYLAND
NEW JERSEY
NORTH CAROLINA
PENNSYLVANIA
SOUTH CAROLINA
TENNESSEE
VIRGINIA

TWO N 2ND ST
HARRISBURG, PA 17101
PO BOX 2361
HARRISBURG, PA 17105-2361

PHONE: (717) 234-4941
FAX: (717) 255-6852
TOLL FREE: (800) 388-4764

E-MAIL: COMMUNICATIONS@PNAT.COM
WEB: WWW.PENNNATIONALINSURANCE.COM

PEOPLE BEFORE PROFITS — *PBP HEALTH PLAN*

NATIONAL

1023 N ROYAL ST
ALEXANDRIA, VA 22314-1596

FAX: (703) 836-8937
TOLL FREE: (800) 544-7111

E-MAIL: INFO@PBP.ORG
WEB: WWW.POSTMASTERS.ORG/PBP.ASP

PERSONAL INSURANCE ADMINISTRATORS — *SEE ALSO PIA*

PERSONALCARE HEALTH MANAGEMENT

ILLINOIS

2110 FOX DR
CHAMPAIGN, IL 61820

PHONE: (217) 366-1226
FAX: (217) 366-5410
TOLL FREE: (888) 366-6730

WEB: WWW.PERSONALCAREHMO.ORG

PHARMACIST MUTUAL

NATIONAL

808 U.S. HWY 18 W
ALGONA, IA 50511-7234
PO BOX 370
ALGONA, IA 50511-0370

PHONE: (515) 295-2461
FAX: (515) 295-9306
TOLL FREE: (800) 247-5930

E-MAIL: INFO@PHMIC.COM
WEB: WWW.PHMIC.COM

P

PHCO — *PHYSICIANS HOSPITAL COMMUNITY ORGANIZAION*

IDAHO
WASHINGTON

400 S JEFFERSON
SPOKANE, WA 99204
PO BOX 490
SPOKANE, WA 99210

PHONE: (509) 473-4927
FAX: (509) 473-4805
TOLL FREE: (888) 298-1574

WEB: WWW.PHCO.ORG

PHILADELPHIA AMERICAN LIFE

NATIONAL

200 W LAKE PARK BLVD STE 1200
HOUSTON, TX 77079-2612
PO BOX 4884
HOUSTON, TX 77210-4884

PHONE: (281) 368-7200
FAX: (281) 368-7282
TOLL FREE: (800) 552-7879

WEB: WWW.NEWERALIFE.COM

PHILADELPHIA BENEFITS CORP

NEW JERSEY

1000 ATRIUM WY ATRIUM 1 STE 203
MOUNT LAUREL, NJ 08054

FAX: (888) 722-4735
TOLL FREE: (888) 722-4748

WEB: WWW.PHILABENEFITS.COM

PHILADELPHIA CONTRIBUTIONSHIP COMPANIES

PENNSYLVANIA

212 S FOURTH ST
PHILADELPHIA, PA 19106-3787

PHONE: (215) 627-1752
FAX: (215) 627-8303
TOLL FREE: (888) 627-1752
OR (800) 269-1409
IN-STATE: (800) 346-9229

E-MAIL: INFO@CONTRIBUTIONSHIP.COM
WEB: WWW.CONTRIBUTIONSHIP.COM

PHILLIPS ADMINISTRATIVE SERVICES

NATIONAL

411 2ND AVE SW
ALBANY, OR 97321
PO BOX 218
ALBANY, OR 97321

PHONE: (541) 928-1717
FAX: (541) 928-6039
TOLL FREE: (800) 356-9822

WEB: WWW.PAS-BENEFITS.COM

PHOENIX LIFE INSURANCE CO

NATIONAL

31 TECH VALLEY DR
EAST GREENBUSH, NY 12061

PHONE: (518) 479-8000
FAX: (518) 479-8057
TOLL FREE: (800) 628-1936

WEB: WWW.PHOENIXWM.COM

PHYSICIANS BENEFITS TRUST

NATIONAL

1440 RENAISSANCE DR
PARK RIDGE, IL 60068-1400

PHONE: (847) 803-3100
FAX: (847) 493-4600
TOLL FREE: (800) 621-0748

PHYSICIANS HEALTH PLAN OF MID MICHIGAN

MICHIGAN

1400 E MICHIGAN
LANSING, MI 48912
PO BOX 30377
LANSING, MI 48909-7877

PHONE: (517) 364-8400
FAX: (517) 364-8460
TOLL FREE: (800) 832-9186

WEB: WWW.PHPMM.ORG

PHYSICIANS HEALTH PLAN OF NORTHERN INDIANA, INC

INDIANA

8101 W JEFFERSON BLVD
FT WAYNE, IN 46804-4163
PO BOX 2359
FT WAYNE, IN 46801-2359

PHONE: (260) 432-6690
FAX: (260) 432-0493
TOLL FREE: (800) 982-6257

E-MAIL: CUSTSVC@PHPNI.COM
WEB: WWW.PHPIN.COM

PHYSICIANS HEALTH PLAN OF SOUTHWEST MICHIGAN — *UNITED HEALTHCARE/ BRONSON HEALTH PLANS/ABA PHP*

MICHIGAN

106 FARMER'S ALLEY STE 300
KALAMAZOO, MI 49005
PO BOX 51100
KALAMAZOO, MI 49005-1100

TOLL FREE: (800) 548-6574
IN-STATE: (800) 722-3644

WEB: WWW.PHPIBA.COM

PHYSICIANS HEALTH SERVICES OF NEW YORK, INC — *HEALTH NET*

CONNECTICUT *DELAWARE* *DISTRICT OF COLUMBIA* *MAINE* *MARYLAND* *MASSACHUSETTS* *NEW HAMPSHIRE* *NEW JERSEY*

	H	399 KNOLLWOOD RD STE 212 WHITE PLAINS, NY 10603-1900	PHONE: (914) 682-8006 FAX: (914) 682-5692 TOLL FREE: (800) 848-4747	WEB: WWW.HEALTH.NET
NEW JERSEY *NEW YORK*	H	405 LEXINGTON AVE NEW YORK, NY 10174-0002	PHONE: (212) 856-4500 FAX: (212) 661-8184 TOLL FREE: (800) 848-4747	WEB: WWW.PHSHMO.COM
NEW YORK *PENNSYLVANIA* *RHODE ISLAND* *VERMONT*	H	399 KNOLLWOOD RD STE 212 WHITE PLAINS, NY 10603-1900	PHONE: (914) 682-8006 FAX: (914) 682-5692 TOLL FREE: (800) 848-4747	WEB: WWW.HEALTH.NET

PHYSICIANS HOSPITAL COMMUNITY ORGANIZAION — *SEE ALSO PHCO*

PHYSICIANS PLUS INSURANCE CORP

WISCONSIN		22 E MIFFLIN ST STE 200 MADISON, WI 53703-2700 PO BOX 2078 MADISON, WI 53701-2078	PHONE: (608) 282-8900 FAX: (608) 258-1912 TOLL FREE: (800) 545-5015	WEB: WWW.PPLUSIC.COM

PIA — *PERSONAL INSURANCE ADMINISTRATORS*

NATIONAL	℞ 3	PO BOX 6040 AGOURA HILLS, CA 91376-6040	FAX: (818) 735-3567 TOLL FREE: (800) 468-4343	E-MAIL: INFO@PIA-INC.COM WEB: WWW.PIA.CLAIMS.COM

PICA GROUP SERVICES, INC

NATIONAL		110 WESTWOOD PL BRENTWOOD, TN 37027	PHONE: (615) 371-8776 FAX: (615) 371-9108 TOLL FREE: (888) 949-2762	WEB: WWW.PICAGROUP.COM

PIMA HEALTH SYSTEM

ARIZONA	H	5055 E BROADWAY A200 TUCSON, AZ 85711-3644	FAX: (520) 745-6386 TOLL FREE: (800) 423-3801	WEB: WWW.PIMAHEALTHSYSTEM.ORG

PINNACLE RISK MANAGEMENT SERVICES

ARIZONA *OREGON* *WASHINGTON*	3	PO BOX 19990 PORTLAND, OR 97280-0990	PHONE: (503) 245-9756 FAX: (503) 246-1581	WEB: WWW.FINNACLERISK.COM

PINNACLE WEST CAPITOL CORP

NATIONAL		400 N 5TH PHOENIX, AZ 85004-3902 PO BOX 53999 PHOENIX, AZ 85072-3999	PHONE: (602) 250-1000 FAX: (602) 250-2453 TOLL FREE: (800) 547-2983	WEB: WWW.PINNACLEWEST.COM

PITNEY BOWES, INC

NATIONAL		ONE ELMCROFT RD STAMFORD, CT 06926-0700	PHONE: (203) 356-5000 TOLL FREE: (800) 672-6937	WEB: WWW.PITNEYBOWES.COM

PPOM/FLORA MIDWEST

INDIANA
KENTUCKY
MICHIGAN
OHIO
PENNSYLVANIA
WEST VIRGINIA

28588 N WESTERN HIGHWAY
SOUTHFIELD, MI 48034
PHONE: (800) 831-1166
TOLL FREE: (800) 966-0200
WEB: WWW.PPOM.COM

PREFERRED CARE

NEW HAMPSHIRE
NEW YORK
VERMONT

259 MONROE AVE
ROCHESTER, NY 14607-3693
PHONE: (585) 325-3920
FAX: (585) 325-3122
TOLL FREE: (800) 933-3920
IN-STATE: (800) 933-3920
WEB: WWW.PREFERREDCARE.ORG

PREFERRED CHOICE — *SEE ALSO CARE CHOICES HMO*

PREFERRED HEALTH SYSTEMS INSURANCE CO

KANSAS

8535 E 21ST ST N
WICHITA, KS 67206
PHONE: (316) 609-2345
FAX: (316) 609-2481
TOLL FREE: (800) 990-0345
WEB: WWW.PHSYSTEMS.COM

PREFERRED MUTUAL INSURANCE CO

MASSACHUSETTS
NEW HAMPSHIRE
NEW JERSEY
NEW YORK

ONE PREFERRED WY
NEW BERLIN, NY 13411
PO BOX 88
NORWICH, NY 13815
PHONE: (607) 847-6161
FAX: (607) 847-8046
TOLL FREE: (800) 333-7642
E-MAIL: INFO@PMINSCO.COM
WEB: WWW.PMINSCO.COM

PREFERRED ONE

MICHIGAN
MINNESOTA
MONTANA
NORTH DAKOTA
SOUTH DAKOTA
WISCONSIN

3
6105 GOLDEN HILLS
GOLDEN VALLEY, MN 55416
PHONE: (763) 847-4000
FAX: (763) 847-4010
TOLL FREE: (800) 940-5049
WEB: WWW.PREFERREDONE.COM

PREMERA BLUE CROSS — *SEE ALSO BLUE CROSS BLUE SHIELD*

PRESBYTERIAN HEALTH PLAN

NEW MEXICO

2501 BUENA VISTA SE
ALBUQUERQUE, NM 87106-4261
PO BOX 26666
ALBUQUERQUE, NM 87125-6666
PHONE: (505) 841-1234
FAX: (505) 923-8163
TOLL FREE: (800) 356-2219
E-MAIL: INFO@PHS.ORG
WEB: WWW.PHS.ORG

PRESERVER GROUP, THE

NEW JERSEY

95 RT 17 S
PARAMUS, NJ 07653-0931
PHONE: (201) 291-2000
FAX: (201) 291-9827
IN-STATE: (800) 242-0332
WEB: WWW.PRESERVER.COM

PRIMARY HEALTH NETWORK, INC

IDAHO

800 PARK BLVD STE 760
BOISE, ID 83712
PO BOX 5679
BOISE, ID 83705
PHONE: (208) 344-1811
FAX: (208) 433-4600
TOLL FREE: (800) 688-5008
E-MAIL: SERVICE@PRIMARYHEALTH.COM
WEB: WWW.PRIMARYHEALTH.COM

PRINCIPAL FINANCIAL GROUP

NATIONAL

SPRINGFIELD SERVICE CENTER
PO BOX 39710
COLORADO SPRINGS, CO 80949-3910
PHONE: (417) 877-0085
FAX: (866) 446-5658
TOLL FREE: (800) 422-5002
WEB: WWW.PRINCIPAL.COM

NATIONAL — CONTINUED	PO BOX 5319 TAMPA, FL 33675	TOLL FREE: (800) 533-5044	WEB: WWW.PRINCIPAL.COM
	1245 CORPORATE BLVD STE 200 AURORA, IL 60504-9955	PHONE: (630) 978-4669 FAX: (630) 978-5117 IN-STATE: (800) 247-4695	WEB: WWW.PRINCIPAL.COM
	AMES SERVICE CENTER 414 S 17TH ST AMES, IA 50010-8106	PHONE: (515) 232-0127 FAX: (515) 663-8900 TOLL FREE: (800) 443-9456	WEB: WWW.PRINCIPAL.COM
	711 HIGH ST DES MOINES, IA 50392-0001	PHONE: (515) 247-5111 TOLL FREE: (800) 247-4695	WEB: WWW.PRINCIPAL.COM
	7330 SAN PEDRO STE 700 SAN ANTONIO, TX 78216	PHONE: (800) 986-3343 TOLL FREE: (800) 247-4695	WEB: WWW.PRINCIPAL.COM
	ONE INTERNATIONAL PLZ STE 100 PHILADELPHIA, PA 19113 PO BOX 39710 COLORADO SPRINGS, CO 80949-3910	PHONE: (610) 362-0920 FAX: (610) 362-0930 TOLL FREE: (800) 522-1279	WEB: WWW.PRINCIPAL.COM

PRINCIPLE FINANCIAL GROUP

NATIONAL	8909 PURDUE RD INDIANAPOLIS, IN 46268 PO BOX 39170 COLORADO SPRINGS, CO 80949-3910	FAX: (866) 317-3113 TOLL FREE: (800) 331-3287	WEB: WWW.PRINCIPLE.COM

PRODUCER'S EXCHANGE BENEFIT SERVICES, INC

TEXAS	4004 BELTLINE RD STE 160 ADDISON, TX 75001-5846	PHONE: (972) 774-1100 FAX: (972) 774-1220 TOLL FREE: (800) 443-2595	WEB: WWW.PEBSI.COM

PROFESSIONAL ADMINISTRATORS, INC

NATIONAL	3751 MAGUIRE BLVD STE 100 ORLANDO, FL 32803 PO BOX 140415 ORLANDO, FL 32814-0415	PHONE: (407) 896-0521 FAX: (407) 897-6976 TOLL FREE: (800) 282-2460	WEB: WWW.PROFADMIN.COM

PROFESSIONAL BENEFIT ADMINISTRATORS, INC

NATIONAL	15 SPINNING WHEEL RD STE 210 HINSDALE, IL 60521 PO BOX 4687 OAK BROOK, IL 60522-4687	PHONE: (630) 655-3755 FAX: (630) 655-3781	WEB: WWW.PBACLAIMS.COM

PROGRESSIVE CASUALTY INSURANCE CO

NATIONAL	PO BOX 31260 TAMPA, FL 33631	FAX: (877) 280-5587 TOLL FREE: (800) 776-4737	WEB: WWW.PROGRESSIVE.COM
	1 POSTON RD STE 300 CHARLESTON, SC 29407 PO BOX 31260 TAMPA, FL 33631	FAX: (877) 280-5587 TOLL FREE: (800) 776-4737	WEB: WWW.PROGRESSIVE.COM

NATIONAL — CONTINUED	1001 BALTIMORE PIKE STE 201 SPRINGSFIELD, PA 19064	PHONE: (610) 604-7600 FAX: (610) 604-9826 TOLL FREE: (800) 274-4499	WEB: WWW.PROGRESSIVE.COM
	PINE CENTER PROFESSIONAL BLDG 11279 PERRY HWY STE 201 WEXFORD, PA 15090	PHONE: (724) 742-5000 FAX: (724) 776-1204 TOLL FREE: (800) 274-4499	WEB: WWW.PROGRESSIVE.COM
	1500 W 51ST ST STE 106 SIOUX FALLS, SD 57105	PHONE: (605) 575-3640 FAX: (605) 334-9374 TOLL FREE: (800) 274-4499 OR (800) PROGRESSIVE	WEB: WWW.PROGRESSIVE.COM
	15957 CONNEAUT LAKE RD STE 1 MEADEVILLE, PA 16335-4761	TOLL FREE: (800) 274-4499	WEB: WWW.PROGRESSIVE.COM
	1789 INDIANWOOD CIR STE 150 MAUMEE, OH 43537 PO BOX 31260 TAMPA, FL 33631	PHONE: (800) 274-4499	WEB: WWW.PROGRESSIVE.COM
	2041 ANDERSON FERRY RD CINCINNATI, OH 45238-3325	FAX: (513) 347-4835 TOLL FREE: (800) 274-4499	WEB: WWW.PROGRESSIVE.COM
	5000 TILGHMAN ST STE 300 ALLENTOWN, PA 18104	PHONE: (610) 336-6980 FAX: (610) 336-6870 TOLL FREE: (800) 274-4499	WEB: WWW.PROGRESSIVE.COM
	6300 WILSON MILLS RD MAYFIELD VILLAGE, OH 44143	PHONE: (440) 461-5000 TOLL FREE: (800) 776-4737 IN-STATE: (800) 321-9843	WEB: WWW.PROGRESSIVE.COM
	6450 POE AVE STE 500 DAYTON, OH 45414	PHONE: (937) 264-5600 FAX: (937) 454-0099 TOLL FREE: (800) 274-4499	WEB: WWW.PROGRESSIVE.COM
	PINE CENTER PROFESSIONAL BLDG 780 E MARKET ST STE 105 WESTCHESTER, PA 19382	PHONE: (610) 719-2910 FAX: (610) 430-7443 TOLL FREE: (800) 274-4499	WEB: WWW.PROGRESSIVE.COM
	9211 LAKE HEFFNER PKY STE 200 OKLAHOMA CITY, OK 73120	PHONE: (405) 302-1800 FAX: (405) 749-0572 TOLL FREE: (800) PROGRESSIVE	WEB: WWW.PROGRESSIVE.COM
	WAYCROSS N OFFICE CTR 431 OHIO PIKE STE 302 CINCINNATI, OH 45255-3375	TOLL FREE: (800) 776-4737	WEB: WWW.PROGRESSIVE.COM
OHIO	1300 BRANDYWINE BLVD ZANESVILLE, OH 43701	PHONE: (740) 450-5400 FAX: (740) 452-9736 TOLL FREE: (800) 274-4499	WEB: WWW.PROGRESSIVE.COM
	190 MONTROSE WEST AVE STE 150 COPLEY , OH 44321	PHONE: (330) 665-7100 FAX: (330) 668-3804 TOLL FREE: (800) 274-4499	WEB: WWW.PROGRESSIVE.COM
	2610 HUBBARD RD MADISON, OH 44057	PHONE: (440) 417-1200 FAX: (440) 417-1858 TOLL FREE: (800) 274-4499	WEB: WWW.PROGRESSIVE.COM
	2722 E KEMPER RD CINCINNATI, OH 45241	PHONE: (513) 588-2700 FAX: (513) 771-1211 TOLL FREE: (800) 274-4499	WEB: WWW.PROGRESSIVE.COM
	3660 STUTZ DR STE LL101 CANFIELD, OH 44406	PHONE: (330) 702-5000 FAX: (330) 533-8969 TOLL FREE: (800) 274-4499	WEB: WWW.PROGRESSIVE.COM
	5340 MEADOW LN CT ELYRIA, OH 44035	PHONE: (440) 934-9700 FAX: (440) 934-3503 TOLL FREE: (800) 274-4499	WEB: WWW.PROGRESSIVE.COM

OHIO — CONTINUED	5500 FRANTZ RD STE 114 DUBLIN, OH 43017	PHONE: (614) 764-5260 FAX: (614) 798-0701 TOLL FREE: (800) 274-4499	WEB: WWW.PROGRESSIVE.COM
	7580 N CLIFF AVE STE 1000 BROOKLYN, OH 44144	PHONE: (216) 778-6700 FAX: (216) 661-0531 TOLL FREE: (800) 274-4499	WEB: WWW.PROGRESSIVE.COM
OKLAHOMA	1315 NW SHERITON RD LAWTON, OK 73505	PHONE: (580) 355-1578 FAX: (580) 355-1676 TOLL FREE: (800) 274-4499	WEB: WWW.PROGRESSIVE.COM
OREGON	3512 EXCEL DR STE 101 MEDFORD, OR 97504-4169	PHONE: (800) 776-4737 FAX: (541) 282-0330 TOLL FREE: (800) 274-4499	WEB: WWW.PROGRESSIVE.COM
	7150 SW SANDBURG RD TIGARD, OR 97223-8069	PHONE: (503) 403-3600 FAX: (503) 403-3608 TOLL FREE: (800) 274-4499	WEB: WWW.PROGRESSIVE.COM
PENNSYLVANIA	100 SCENERY DR STE B STATE COLLEGE, PA 16801	PHONE: (814) 861-2380 FAX: (814) 235-1821 TOLL FREE: (800) 274-4499	WEB: WWW.PROGRESSIVE.COM
	102 STATE RD 611 STE 1 BARTONSVILLE, PA 18321	PHONE: (570) 619-6700 OR (570) 776-4737 FAX: (570) 629-8754 OR (570) 992-1407 TOLL FREE: (800) 274-4499 IN-STATE: (800) 776-4737	WEB: WWW.PROGRESSIVE.COM
	1370 WASHINGTON PIKE STE 401 BRIDGEVILLE, PA 15017	PHONE: (412) 220-5800 FAX: (412) 257-8999 TOLL FREE: (800) 274-4499	WEB: WWW.PROGRESSIVE.COM
	2200 STAFFORD AVE STE 300 SCRANTON, PA 18505	PHONE: (570) 496-3000 FAX: (570) 969-1008 TOLL FREE: (800) 274-4499	WEB: WWW.PROGRESSIVE.COM
	300 OXFORD DR STE 400 MONROEVILLE, PA 15146-2121	PHONE: (412) 858-7800 FAX: (412) 373-6933 OR (412) 858-7911 TOLL FREE: (800) 274-4499	WEB: WWW.PROGRESSIVE.COM
	3421 CONCORD RD YORK, PA 17402	PHONE: (717) 840-3600 FAX: (717) 751-0911 TOLL FREE: (800) 274-4499	WEB: WWW.PROGRESSIVE.COM
	5165 CAMPUS DR STE 100 PLYMOUTH MEETING, PA 19462	PHONE: (610) 567-3600 FAX: (610) 397-0840 TOLL FREE: (800) 274-4499	WEB: WWW.PROGRESSIVE.COM
	FIVE HEARTHSTONE CT STE 203 READING, PA 19606	PHONE: (610) 370-4890 FAX: (610) 779-8949 TOLL FREE: (800) 274-4499	WEB: WWW.PROGRESSIVE.COM
SOUTH DAKOTA	1018 B 14TH ST SE WATERTOWN, SD 57201	PHONE: (605) 882-3910 FAX: (605) 882-3419 TOLL FREE: (800) 274-4499	WEB: WWW.PROGRESSIVE.COM
TENNESSEE	555 MARRIOTT DR STE 500 NASHVILLE, TN 37214	PHONE: (615) 391-7400 FAX: (615) 884-1066 TOLL FREE: (800) 274-4499	WEB: WWW.PROGRESSIVE.COM

PROGRESSIVE DIVERSIFIED INSURANCE CO

NATIONAL	6300 WILSON MILLS RD PS MAYFIELD VILLAGE, OH 44143-2109	PHONE: (440) 473-3600 FAX: (800) 229-1590 TOLL FREE: (800) 274-4499	WEB: WWW.PROGRESSIVE.COM

PRONATIONAL INSURANCE CO

NATIONAL	2600 PROFESSIONAL DR OKEMOS, MI 48864 PO BOX 150 OKEMOS, MI 48805-0150	PHONE: (517) 349-6500 FAX: (517) 349-8978 TOLL FREE: (800) 292-1036	WEB: WWW.PROINSURANCE.COM

PROTECTIVE INSURANCE CO — *BALDWIN & LYONS, INC*

NATIONAL	1099 N MERIDIAN ST STE 700 INDIANAPOLIS, IN 46204-1036	PHONE: (317) 636-9800 FAX: (317) 972-4735 TOLL FREE: (800) 231-6024 IN-STATE: (800) 845-2931	WEB: WWW.BALDWINANDLYONS.COM

PROTECTIVE LIFE CO — *SEE ALSO WISCONSIN NATIONAL LIFE INSURANCE CO*

PROVIDENCE HEALTH PLANS

NATIONAL	3601 SW MURRAY BLVD STE 10 BEAVERTON, OR 97005 PO BOX 3125 PORTLAND, OR 97208	PHONE: (503) 574-7500 FAX: (503) 574-8600 TOLL FREE: (888) 244-6643 IN-STATE: (800) 793-9338	WEB: WWW.PROVIDENCE.ORG/HEALTHPLANS

PROVIDENCE MUTUAL FIRE INSURANCE CO

RHODE ISLAND	340 E AVE WARRICK, RI 02886-1802 PO BOX 6066 PROVIDENCE, RI 02940	PHONE: (401) 827-1800 FAX: (401) 822-1921 TOLL FREE: (877) 763-1800	WEB: WWW.PROVIDENCEMUTUAL.COM

PROVIDENT AMERICAN INSURANCE CO

LOUISIANA	10501 N CENTRAL EXPY STE 200 DALLAS, TX 75231-4177 PO BOX 679005 DALLAS, TX 75367-9005	PHONE: (214) 696-9091 FAX: (214) 696-4756 TOLL FREE: (800) 933-9456	WEB: WWW.PROVIDENTAMERICAN.COM

PROVIDENT NATION WIDE

NATIONAL	300 CONTINENTAL DR NEWARK, DE 19713-4322 PO BOX 15750 WILMINGTON, DE 19850	PHONE: (302) 452-4000 FAX: (302) 452-4255 TOLL FREE: (800) 523-4681	WEB: WWW.NATIONWIDEPROVIDENT.COM

PUBLIC EMPLOYEES HEALTH PROGRAM — *SEE ALSO PEHP*

PUBLIC EMPLOYEES RETIREMENT SYSTEM — *PUBLIC RETIREMENT SYSTEM*

OHIO	1628 J P ROGERS DR VALEDOSTA, GA 31601	PHONE: (614) 466-2085 FAX: (229) 247-4405 TOLL FREE: (800) 227-7377	WEB: WWW.OPERS.ORG

PUBLIC RETIREMENT SYSTEM — *SEE ALSO PUBLIC EMPLOYEES RETIREMENT SYSTEM*

PUBLIC SERVICE MUTUAL INSURANCE CO — *MAGNA CARTA CO*

CONNECTICUT	25 BRAINTREE DR STE 306 BOSTON, MA 02184-2705	PHONE: (781) 848-9200 FAX: (781) 848-1085 TOLL FREE: (800) 225-5196 IN-STATE: (800) 972-5045	WEB: WWW.MCARTA.COM
DELAWARE	TWO MERIDIAN BLVD WYOMISSING, PA 19610-3202	TOLL FREE: (800) 988-6879	WEB: WWW.MCARTA.COM

PYRAMID LIFE

ALABAMA, ARIZONA, ARKANSAS, COLORADO, FLORIDA, GEORGIA, IDAHO, ILLINOIS, INDIANA, IOWA, KANSAS, KENTUCKY, LOUISIANA, MICHIGAN, MISSISSIPPI, MISSOURI, MONTANA, NEBRASKA, NEVADA, NORTH CAROLINA, NORTH DAKOTA, OHIO, OKLAHOMA, OREGON, PENNSYLVANIA, SOUTH CAROLINA, SOUTH DAKOTA, TENNESSEE, TEXAS, UTAH, VERMONT, WISCONSIN

PO BOX 12922
PENSACOLA, FL 32591
FAX: (850) 432-7733
TOLL FREE: (800) 777-1126
WEB: WWW.PYRAMIDLIFE.COM

QBE REINSURANCE CO

NEW YORK
88 PINE ST 16TH FL
NEW YORK, NY 10005-1819
PHONE: (212) 422-1212
FAX: (212) 422-1313
E-MAIL: CLAIMS@QBEUSA.COM
WEB: WWW.QBE.COM

QUALCARE, INC

NEW JERSEY
PO BOX 249
PISCATAWAY, NJ 08855
PHONE: (732) 562-0833
FAX: (732) 562-1120
TOLL FREE: (800) 992-6613
WEB: WWW.QUALCARE-USA.COM

QUALCHOICE HMO

OHIO
6000 PARKLAND BLVD
CLEVELAND, OH 44124
PHONE: (440) 460-0093
FAX: (440) 460-4004
TOLL FREE: (888) 460-9090
WEB: WWW.QCPE.COM

QUALITY IMPROVEMENT ORGANIZATION — *SOUTH DAKOTA FOUNDATION FOR MEDICAL CARE*

SOUTH DAKOTA
1323 S MINNESOTA AVE
SIOUX FALLS, SD 57105
PHONE: (605) 336-3505
FAX: (605) 373-0580
TOLL FREE: (800) 658-2285
WEB: WWW.SDFMC.ORG

REGENCE BLUE CROSS BLUE SHIELD — *SEE ALSO BLUE CROSS BLUE SHIELD*

REGENCY EMPLOYEE BENEFITS — *ROBINS GROUP*

NATIONAL
330 SUPERIOR MALL
PORT HURON, MI 48060
PO BOX 610609
PORT HURON, MI 48061-0609
PHONE: (810) 987-7711
FAX: (810) 987-7603
TOLL FREE: (800) 369-3718

REGIONAL MEDICAL ADMINISTRATORS, INC — *WELLPATH*

GEORGIA
1851 N PARK AVE
GLEN RAVEN, NC 27217
PO BOX 4128
GLEN RAVEN, NC 27215-0901
PHONE: (336) 226-7950
FAX: (336) 570-0599
TOLL FREE: (800) 711-1507
IN-STATE: (866) 208-3610
WEB: WWW.REGIONALMEDICALADMINISTRATOR.COM

RELIABLE LIFE INSURANCE CO

NATIONAL
12115 LACKLAND RD
ST LOUIS, MO 63146
PHONE: (314) 819-4300
FAX: (314) 819-4789
TOLL FREE: (800) 630-8645
WEB: WWW.UNITRIN.COM

RELIANCE STANDARD LIFE INSURANCE CO

NATIONAL
2001 MARKET ST STE 1500
PHILADELPHIA, PA 19103
PHONE: (267) 256-3500
FAX: (267) 256-3548 OR (267) 256-3543
TOLL FREE: (800) 644-1103
WEB: WWW.RSLI.COM

NATIONAL — CONTINUED	590 MADISON AVE 29TH FL NEW YORK, NY 10022-4635	PHONE: (212) 303-8400 FAX: (212) 303-8435 TOLL FREE: (800) 353-3986	WEB: WWW.RSLI.COM
ARIZONA *CALIFORNIA* *NEW MEXICO*	11221 N 28TH DR STE E111 PHOENIX, AZ 85029	PHONE: (602) 954-6516 FAX: (602) 954-9282 TOLL FREE: (800) 992-4775 IN-STATE: (800) 351-7100	WEB: WWW.RSLI.COM

REPUBLIC AMERICAN LIFE INSURANCE CO

ARIZONA	8200 BROOKRIVER DR STE 600N DALLAS, TX 75247-4069	PHONE: (214) 631-6310 OR (800) 753-4243 FAX: (214) 638-6431 TOLL FREE: (800) 876-8776	

REPUBLIC GROUP, THE

TEXAS	5525 LBJ FREEWAY DALLAS, TX 75240-6241 PO BOX 809056 DALLAS, TX 75380-9056	PHONE: (972) 788-6001 FAX: (972) 788-6709 TOLL FREE: (800) 344-2275	WEB: WWW.REPUBLICGROUP.COM

REPUBLIC INDEMNITY CO OF AMERICA

ARIZONA	100 PINE ST STE 1400 SAN FRANCISCO, CA 94111-5867 PO BOX 7878 SAN FRANCISCO, CA 94210-7878	PHONE: (415) 954-1000 FAX: (415) 954-1178 TOLL FREE: (800) 662-1485	WEB: WWW.REPUBLICINDEMNITY.COM
	15821 VENTURA BLVD STE 370 ENCINO, CA 91436-2915 PO BOX 20036 ENCINO, CA 91436-2915	PHONE: (818) 990-9860 FAX: (818) 986-6559 TOLL FREE: (800) 821-4520	WEB: WWW.REPUBLICINDEMNITY.COM
CALIFORNIA	100 PINE ST STE 1400 SAN FRANCISCO, CA 94111-5867 PO BOX 7878 SAN FRANCISCO, CA 94210-7878	PHONE: (415) 954-1000 FAX: (415) 954-1178 TOLL FREE: (800) 662-1485	WEB: WWW.REPUBLICINDEMNITY.COM
	15821 VENTURA BLVD STE 370 ENCINO, CA 91436-2915 PO BOX 20036 ENCINO, CA 91436-2915	PHONE: (818) 990-9860 FAX: (818) 986-6559 TOLL FREE: (800) 821-4520	WEB: WWW.REPUBLICINDEMNITY.COM

REPUBLIC WESTERN INSURANCE CO

NATIONAL	2721 N CENTRAL AVE PHOENIX, AZ 85004-1127 PO BOX 21748 PHOENIX, AZ 85036	PHONE: (602) 263-6755 FAX: (602) 745-6436 TOLL FREE: (800) 528-7134	WEB: WWW.REPWEST.COM

RESERVE NATIONAL INSURANCE CO

NATIONAL	6100 NW GRAND BLVD OKLAHOMA CITY, OK 73118 PO BOX 26620 OKLAHOMA CITY, OK 73126	PHONE: (405) 848-7931 FAX: (405) 842-0499 TOLL FREE: (800) 654-9106	E-MAIL: CUSTOMERSERVICE@RESERVENATIONAL.COM WEB: WWW.RESERVENATIONAL.COM

RESOURCE LIFE INSURANCE COMPANY

NATIONAL	1345 RIVER BEND DR DALLAS, TX 75247-4915 PO BOX 191248 DALLAS, TX 75219	PHONE: (214) 634-7014 FAX: (214) 637-7494	

R

RISK MANAGEMENT — *SEE ALSO LOMA LINDA UNIVERSITY ADVENTIST HEALTH SCIENCES CENTER*

RITE AID CORP

NATIONAL	30 HUNTER LN CAMP HILL, PA 17011-2400 PO BOX 3165 HARRISBURG, PA 17105	PHONE: (717) 761-2633 FAX: (717) 975-3761 TOLL FREE: (800) 748-3243	WEB: WWW.RITEAID.COM

RIVERBEND GOVERNMENT BENEFITS ADMINISTRATOR

NATIONAL	730 CHESTNUT ST CHATTANOOGA, TN 37402	FAX: (423) 752-6518 TOLL FREE: (877) 296-6189	E-MAIL: RIVERBENDGBA@BCBST.COM WEB: WWW.RIVERBENDGBA.COM

RLI CORP

ILLINOIS	9025 N LINDBERGH DR PEORIA, IL 61615-1431	PHONE: (309) 692-1000 FAX: (309) 692-1068 TOLL FREE: (800) 331-4929	WEB: WWW.RLICORP.COM

RMSCO, INC

NATIONAL	115 CONTNUUM LIVERPOOL, NY 13088 PO BOX 6309 SYRACUSE, NY 13217	PHONE: (315) 474-8200 FAX: (315) 448-9132	WEB: WWW.RMSCOINC.COM

ROBERT F MAY COMPANY — *WESTERN TEAMSTERS*

COLORADO *WYOMING*	1010 ACOMA ST DENVER, CO 80204	PHONE: (303) 629-0931	WEB: WWW.WESTERNTEAMSTERS.COM

ROBERT PLAN CORP — *MDA*

CONNECTICUT	999 STEWART AVE BETHPAGE, NY 11714 PO BOX 14000 NEW BRUNSWICK, NJ 08906-4000	FAX: (516) 393-6249 OR (516) 393-6248 TOLL FREE: (888) 398-3500	WEB: WWW.RPC.COM
NEW YORK	999 STEWART AVE BETHPAGE, NY 11714 PO BOX 9048 BETHPAGE, NY 11714	PHONE: (516) 576-3400 FAX: (516) 393-6592OR (516) 393-6224 OR (516) 393-4541 TOLL FREE: (800) 327-3000	E-MAIL: DRIVEIN@RPC.COM WEB: WWW.RPC.COM

ROBERT, BOUCK & ASSOCIATES

ILLINOIS
INDIANA
IOWA
KANSAS
MISSOURI
NEBRASKA
OKLAHOMA

126 N 30TH ST STE 205 QUINCY, IL 62301	PHONE: (217) 223-8354 FAX: (217) 223-8621	

ROBINS GROUP — *SEE ALSO REGENCY EMPLOYEE BENEFITS*

ROBINSON HEALTH CARE COMPANIES, INC — *SEE ALSO NATIONAL HOSPITAL NETWORK SYSTEM*

ROCKWOOD CASUALTY INSURANCE CO

DELAWARE *MARYLAND*	654 MAIN ST ROCKWOOD, PA 15557	PHONE: (814) 926-4661 FAX: (814) 926-4070 TOLL FREE: (800) 837-9062	WEB: WWW.ROCKWOODCASUALTY.COM

R

ROCKY MOUNTAIN HEALTH PLANS

COLORADO		2775 CROSSROADS BLVD GRAND JUNCTION, CO 81506 PO BOX 10600 GRAND JUNCTION, CO 81502	PHONE: (970) 244-7760 FAX: (970) 244-7880 TOLL FREE: (800) 843-0719	WEB: WWW.RMHP.ORG

ROYAL & SUNALLIANCE

NATIONAL		PO BOX 8194 WALNUT CREEK, CA 94596-8194	PHONE: (925) 934-9660 FAX: (925) 932-8952 TOLL FREE: (800) 523-6269	WEB: WWW.RSAUSA.COM
	3	200 OLD COUNTRY RD STE 375 MINIOLA, NY 11701	PHONE: (516) 939-0600 FAX: (516) 640-3380 TOLL FREE: (800) 523-6273 IN-STATE: (800) 298-6127	WEB: WWW.ROYALSUNALLIANCE-USA.COM
		9000 ARROWPOINT BLVD CHARLOTTE, NC 28273 PO BOX 1000 CHARLOTTE, NC 28201	PHONE: (704) 522-2000 OR (704) 602-4500 FAX: (704) 522-3200 TOLL FREE: (800) 621-2297 OR (800) 236-7750	WEB: WWW.ROYALSUNALLIANCE-USA.COM
		NINE FARM SPRINGS RD FARMINGTON, CT 06032-2576 PO BOX 420 HARTFORD, CT 06141-0420	PHONE: (860) 674-6600 FAX: (860) 674-6797 OR (860) 674-6659 TOLL FREE: (800) 243-7060	WEB: WWW.RSAUSA.COM
NEW JERSEY		210 LAKE DR E STE 301 CHERRY HILL, NJ 08002	PHONE: (856) 755-4500 FAX: (856) 755-0070	WEB: WWW.ROYALSUNALLIANCE-USA.COM
NEW YORK		301 PLAINFIELD RD STE 300 SYRACUSE, NY 13212 PO BOX 4701 SYRACUSE, NY 13221	PHONE: (315) 426-4000 FAX: (315) 426-4088 TOLL FREE: (800) 524-4504 IN-STATE: (888) 314-5035	WEB: WWW.ROYALSUNALLIANCE-USA.COM
PENNSYLVANIA		210 LAKE DR E STE 301 CHERRY HILL, NJ 08002	PHONE: (856) 755-4500 FAX: (856) 755-0070	WEB: WWW.ROYALSUNALLIANCE-USA.COM
TEXAS		16633 DALLAS PKY STE 210 ADDISON, TX 75001-6822 PO BOX 9008 ADDISON, TX 75001-9008	PHONE: (972) 735-9941 FAX: (972) 713-5264 TOLL FREE: (800) 523-6244	WEB: WWW.RSAUSA.COM
WEST VIRGINIA		210 LAKE DR E STE 301 CHERRY HILL, NJ 08002	PHONE: (856) 755-4500 FAX: (856) 755-0070	WEB: WWW.ROYALSUNALLIANCE-USA.COM

ROYAL NEIGHBORS OF AMERICA

NATIONAL		230 16TH ST ROCK ISLAND, IL 61201	PHONE: (309) 788-4561 FAX: (309) 788-4936	WEB: WWW.ROYALNEIGHBORS.ORG

ADDITIONAL COMMENTS: NATIONAL EXCEPT ALABAMA, ALASKA, LOUISIANA, MASSACHUSETTS, NEW HAMPSHIRE, NEW YORK, NORTH CAROLINA, SOUTH CAROLINA

ROYAL STATE GROUP

HAWAII	R 6d H	819 S BERETANIA ST STE 100 HONOLULU, HI 96813-2501	PHONE: (808) 539-1600 FAX: (808) 538-1458	WEB: WWW.ROYALSTATE.COM

RURAL MUTUAL INSURANCE CO

WISCONSIN		1212 DEMING WY MADISON, WI 53717 PO BOX 5555 MADISON, WI 53705-0555	PHONE: (608) 836-5525 FAX: (608) 828-5483 TOLL FREE: (800) 362-7881	WEB: WWW.RURALINS.COM
		2417 SILVERNAIL RD PEWAUKEE, WI 53072	PHONE: (262) 544-4991 FAX: (262) 544-4335 TOLL FREE: (800) 801-9560	WEB: WWW.RURALINS.COM

R

WISCONSIN — CONTINUED		W 11109 ROGERS ST BLACK RIVER FALLS, WI 54615-0000	PHONE: (715) 284-9416 FAX: (866) 828-6616 TOLL FREE: (800) 301-0490	WEB: WWW.RURALINS.COM

S & S HEALTHCARE STRATEGIES

NATIONAL		PO BOX 46511 CINCINNATTI, OH 45250-0511	PHONE: (866) 266-1110 FAX: (513) 772-9174 TOLL FREE: (800) 596-6622	WEB: WWW.S&SHEALTHCARE.COM

SAFECO INSURANCE

WASHINGTON		4333 BROOKLYN AVE NE SEATTLE, WA 98185	PHONE: (206) 545-5000 FAX: (206) 545-6090 TOLL FREE: (800) 332-3226	WEB: WWW.SAFECO.COM

SAFECO INSURANCE CO OF AMERCIA

NATIONAL		PO BOX 34700 SEATTLE, WA 98124	PHONE: (701) 232-3717 FAX: (888) 268-8840 TOLL FREE: (800) 332-3226	WEB: WWW.SAFECO.COM
		14123 DENVER W PKWY GOLDEN, CO 80401-3116	TOLL FREE: (800) 332-3226	WEB: WWW.SAFECO.COM
		2055 SUGARLOAF CIR DULUTH, GA 30097-9432 PO BOX 100027 DULUTH, GA 30096-9427	PHONE: (678) 417--3251 FAX: (678) 417-3333 TOLL FREE: (800) 332-3226	WEB: WWW.SAFECO.COM
		2300 MAITLAND CENTER PKY STE 220 MAITLAND, FL 32751 PO BOX 461 ST LOUIS, MO 63166	FAX: (888) 268-8840 TOLL FREE: (800) 332-3226	WEB: WWW.SAFECO.COM
		330 N BRAND BLVD 10TH FL GLENDALE, CA 91203-2340 PO BOX 29082 GLENDALE, CA 91029-9082	PHONE: (818) 956-4200 FAX: (818) 956-4202 TOLL FREE: (800) 332-3226	WEB: WWW.SAFECO.COM
		810 ROYAL PKWY STE 200 NASHVILLE, TN 37217 PO BOX 461 ST LOUIS, MS 63166	PHONE: (615) 360-1122 FAX: (888) 268-8840 TOLL FREE: (800) 332-3226	WEB: WWW.SAFECO.COM
CONNECTICUT		PO BOX 461 ST LOUIS, MO 63166	PHONE: (800) 245-5355 FAX: (888) 268-8840 TOLL FREE: (800) 332-3226	WEB: WWW.SAFECO.COM
TEXAS		1600 N COLLINS BLVD RICHARDSON, TX 75080-3591 PO BOX 833960 RICHARDSON, TX 75083-3960	PHONE: (972) 808-4000 FAX: (972) 808-4755 TOLL FREE: (800) 332-3226	WEB: WWW.SAFECO.COM
WASHINGTON		PO BOX 2726 SPOKANE, WA 99220-2726	PHONE: (509) 928-6800 FAX: (888) 268-8840 TOLL FREE: (800) 332-3226	WEB: WWW.SAFECO.COM

SAFECO INSURANCE CO OF AMERICA

NATIONAL		4101 SW KRUSE WY LAKE OSWEGO, OR 97035-2542 PO BOX 1900 LAKE OSWEGO, OR 97035-0900	PHONE: (503) 635-9111 TOLL FREE: (800) 332-3226	WEB: WWW.SAFECO.COM
		SAFECO PLZ 4333 BROOKLYN AVE NE SEATTLE, WA 98185	PHONE: (206) 545-5000 FAX: (206) 545-0165 TOLL FREE: (800) 332-3226	WEB: WWW.SAFECO.COM

S

ARIZONA	120 VANTIS ST STE 130 ALISO VIEJO, CA 92656-0000 PO BOX 25150 SANTA ANA, CA 92799-5150	PHONE: (949) 860-6000 FAX: (949) 860-6600 TOLL FREE: (800) 332-3226	WEB: WWW.SAFECO.COM
CALIFORNIA	400 TAYLOR BLVD PLEASANT HILL, CA 94523-2147 PO BOX 4030 CONCORD, CA 94524	PHONE: (925) 969-2000 FAX: (925) 969-2034 TOLL FREE: (800) 332-3226	WEB: WWW.SAFECO.COM

SAFEGUARD HEALTH ENTERPRISES, INC — *SAFEGUARD HEALTH PLAN*

CALIFORNIA	95 ENTERPRISE STE 100 ALISO VIEJO, CA 92656 PO BOX 30930 LAGUNA HILLS, CA 92654-0930	PHONE: (949) 425-4300 FAX: (949) 425-4586 TOLL FREE: (800) 880-1800	WEB: WWW.SAFEGUARD.NET

SAFEGUARD HEALTH PLAN — *SEE ALSO SAFEGUARD HEALTH ENTERPRISES, INC*

SAFETY NATIONAL CASUALTY CORP

NATIONAL	2043 WOODLAND PKY ST LOUIS, MO 63146	PHONE: (314) 995-5300 FAX: (314) 995-3897 TOLL FREE: (888) 995-5300	WEB: WWW.SNCC.COM

SAGAMORE HEALTH NETWORK

INDIANA	11555 N MERIDIAN ST STE 400 CARMEL, IN 46032-6910	PHONE: (317) 573-2900 FAX: (317) 580-8488 TOLL FREE: (800) 435-4095	WEB: WWW.SAGAMOREHN.COM

SAIF CORP — *STATE ACCIDENT INSURANCE FUND CORP*

OREGON	400 HIGH ST SE SALEM, OR 97312-1000	PHONE: (503) 373-8000 TOLL FREE: (800) 285-8525	WEB: WWW.SAIF.COM

SAMBA — *SPECIAL AGENTS MUTUAL BENEFIT ASSOCIATION*

NATIONAL	11301 OLD GEORGETOWN RD ROCKVILLE, MD 20852-2800	PHONE: (301) 984-1440 TOLL FREE: (800) 638-6589	WEB: WWW.SAMBAPLANS.COM

SAN DIEGO ELECTRICAL HEALTH & WELFARE TRUST

CALIFORNIA	4747 VIEWRIDGE AVE STE 100 SAN DIEGO, CA 92123-1644 PO BOX 231219 SAN DIEGO, CA 92194-1219	PHONE: (858) 569-6322 FAX: (858) 565-2951 TOLL FREE: (800) 632-2569	

SCAN HEALTH PLAN

CALIFORNIA	3800 KILROY AIRPORT WAY STE 100 LONG BEACH, CA 90806 PO BOX 22616 LONG BEACH, CA 90801	PHONE: (562) 989-5100 FAX: (562) 989-5200 TOLL FREE: (877) 247-5091	WEB: WWW.SCANHEALTHPLAN.COM

SCOTT & WHITE HEALTH PLAN

TEXAS	2401 S 31ST ST TEMPLE, TX 76508-0001	PHONE: (254) 298-3000 FAX: (254) 298-3018 TOLL FREE: (800) 321-7947	WEB: WWW.SW.ORG

SEABRIGHT INSURANCE

ALABAMA	14550 TORREY CHASE BLVD STE 605 HOUSTON, TX 77014-1019	PHONE: (832) 204-3000 FAX: (832) 204-3070 TOLL FREE: (877) 878-2940	WEB: WWW.SBIC.COM
ALASKA *ARIZONA*	2101 4TH AVE STE 1600 SEATTLE, WA 98121-2377 PO BOX 91107 SEATTLE, WA 98111	PHONE: (206) 770-8300 FAX: (206) 269-8903 TOLL FREE: (888) 636-1580	WEB: WWW.SEABRIGHT.COM

ARKANSAS		14550 TORREY CHASE BLVD STE 605 HOUSTON, TX 77014-1019	PHONE: (832) 204-3000 FAX: (832) 204-3070 TOLL FREE: (877) 878-2940	WEB: WWW.SBIC.COM
CALIFORNIA		2101 4TH AVE STE 1600 SEATTLE, WA 98121-2377 PO BOX 91107 SEATTLE, WA 98111	PHONE: (206) 770-8300 FAX: (206) 269-8903 TOLL FREE: (888) 636-1580	WEB: WWW.SEABRIGHT.COM
		681 S PARKER ST STE 220 ORANGE, CA 92868 PO BOX 11027 ORANGE, CA 92856	PHONE: (714) 480-6200 FAX: (714) 918-5971 TOLL FREE: (800) 597-2755	WEB: WWW.SEABRIGHT.COM
COLORADO *FLORIDA*		2101 4TH AVE STE 1600 SEATTLE, WA 98121-2377 PO BOX 91107 SEATTLE, WA 98111	PHONE: (206) 770-8300 FAX: (206) 269-8903 TOLL FREE: (888) 636-1580	WEB: WWW.SEABRIGHT.COM
FLORIDA *GEORGIA*		14550 TORREY CHASE BLVD STE 605 HOUSTON, TX 77014-1019	PHONE: (832) 204-3000 FAX: (832) 204-3070 TOLL FREE: (877) 878-2940	WEB: WWW.SBIC.COM
GEORGIA *HAWAII*		2101 4TH AVE STE 1600 SEATTLE, WA 98121-2377 PO BOX 91107 SEATTLE, WA 98111	PHONE: (206) 770-8300 FAX: (206) 269-8903 TOLL FREE: (888) 636-1580	WEB: WWW.SEABRIGHT.COM
HAWAII		841 BISHOP ST STE 1060 HONOLULU, HI 96813	PHONE: (808) 545-4553 FAX: (808) 748-7370 IN-STATE: (800) 499-2493	WEB: WWW.SEABRIGHT.COM
ILLINOIS *LOUISIANA*		2101 4TH AVE STE 1600 SEATTLE, WA 98121-2377 PO BOX 91107 SEATTLE, WA 98111	PHONE: (206) 770-8300 FAX: (206) 269-8903 TOLL FREE: (888) 636-1580	WEB: WWW.SEABRIGHT.COM
LOUISIANA *MISSISSIPPI*		14550 TORREY CHASE BLVD STE 605 HOUSTON, TX 77014-1019	PHONE: (832) 204-3000 FAX: (832) 204-3070 TOLL FREE: (877) 878-2940	WEB: WWW.SBIC.COM
NEVADA *NEW MEXICO*		2101 4TH AVE STE 1600 SEATTLE, WA 98121-2377 PO BOX 91107 SEATTLE, WA 98111	PHONE: (206) 770-8300 FAX: (206) 269-8903 TOLL FREE: (888) 636-1580	WEB: WWW.SEABRIGHT.COM
OKLAHOMA		14550 TORREY CHASE BLVD STE 605 HOUSTON, TX 77014-1019	PHONE: (832) 204-3000 FAX: (832) 204-3070 TOLL FREE: (877) 878-2940	WEB: WWW.SBIC.COM
OREGON *TEXAS*		2101 4TH AVE STE 1600 SEATTLE, WA 98121-2377 PO BOX 91107 SEATTLE, WA 98111	PHONE: (206) 770-8300 FAX: (206) 269-8903 TOLL FREE: (888) 636-1580	WEB: WWW.SEABRIGHT.COM
TEXAS		14550 TORREY CHASE BLVD STE 605 HOUSTON, TX 77014-1019	PHONE: (832) 204-3000 FAX: (832) 204-3070 TOLL FREE: (877) 878-2940	WEB: WWW.SBIC.COM
UTAH *WASHINGTON*		2101 4TH AVE STE 1600 SEATTLE, WA 98121-2377 PO BOX 91107 SEATTLE, WA 98111	PHONE: (206) 770-8300 FAX: (206) 269-8903 TOLL FREE: (888) 636-1580	WEB: WWW.SEABRIGHT.COM

SEABRIGHT INSURANCE

NATIONAL		4300 B ST STE 304 ANCHORAGE, AK 99503-5929	PHONE: (907) 563-6303 FAX: (907) 273-3370 TOLL FREE: (800) 770-6303	WEB: WWW.SBIC.COM

SECURE DENTAL — *SOUTHWEST DENTAL*

ARIZONA		3625 N 16TH ST STE 206 PHOENIX, AZ 85016-6447 PO BOX 29697 PHOENIX, AZ 85038-9697	PHONE: (602) 234-3266 FAX: (602) 285-0121	E-MAIL: CLAIMS@SECUREDENTAL.COM WEB: WWW.SECURECAREDENTAL.COM

SECURE HEALTH PLANS

GEORGIA	3920 ARKWRIGHT RD STE 405 MACON, GA 31210	PHONE: (478) 314-2400 FAX: (478) 314-2523	WEB: WWW.SHPG.COM

SECURIAN — *MINNESOTA LIFE INSURANCE CO*

NATIONAL	400 ROBERT ST N ST PAUL, MN 55101	PHONE: (651) 665-3500 FAX: (651) 665-4488	WEB: WWW.SECURIAN.COM

SECURITY ADMINISTRATIVE SERVICES — *SEE ALSO SECURITY HEALTH PLAN OF WISCONSIN, INC*

SECURITY AMERICAN FINANCIAL ENTERPRISES — *SEE ALSO SECURITY LIFE INSURANCE CO OF AMERICA*

SECURITY HEALTH PLAN OF WISCONSIN, INC — *SECURITY ADMINISTRATIVE SERVICES*

NATIONAL	1515 SAINT JOSEPH AVE MARSHFIELD, WI 54449 PO BOX 8000 MARSHFIELD, WI 54449-8000	PHONE: (715) 221-9555 FAX: (715) 221-9500 TOLL FREE: (800) 472-2363	E-MAIL: SHPCSWEB@MFIDCLIN.EDU WEB: WWW.SECURITYHEALTH.ORG

SECURITY LIFE INSURANCE CO OF AMERICA — *SECURITY AMERICAN FINANCIAL ENTERPRISES*

NATIONAL	10901 RED CIRCLE DR MINNETONKA, MN 55343-9137	PHONE: (952) 544-2121 FAX: (952) 945-3409 TOLL FREE: (800) 328-4667	WEB: WWW.SECURITYLIFE.COM

SECURITY NATIONAL LIFE INSURANCE CO — *AMERICAN HOME SECURITY LIFE*

ARIZONA *IDAHO* *KANSAS*	*KENTUCKY* *LOUISIANA* *MISSISSIPPI*	*NEVADA* *NEW MEXICO* *OKLAHOMA*	*TEXAS* *UTAH* *WYOMING*
	5300 S 360 W STE 250 SALT LAKE CITY, UT 84123-2709 PO BOX 57220 SALT LAKE CITY, UT 84157	PHONE: (801) 264-1060 FAX: (801) 265-9882 TOLL FREE: (800) 574-7117	E-MAIL: CONTACT@SECURITYNATIONAL.COM WEB: WWW.SECURITYNATIONAL.COM

SEIBELS BRUCE GROUP

SOUTH CAROLINA	1501 LADY ST COLUMBIA, SC 29201 PO BOX 1 COLUMBIA, SC 29202	PHONE: (803) 748-2865 FAX: (803) 748-8392 TOLL FREE: (800) 525-8835	WEB: WWW.SEIBELS.COM

SEIU LOCAL 36 BENEFIT FUNDS

PENNSYLVANIA	1500 ROBINSON 425 15TH ST STE 1500 PHILADELPHIA, PA 19102	PHONE: (215) 568-3262 FAX: (215) 561-2362 TOLL FREE: (800) 338-9025	WEB: WWW.SEIU36.COM

SELECT HEALTH

UTAH	4646 W LAKE PARK BLVD SALT LAKE CITY, UT 84130 PO BOX 30192 SALT LAKE CITY, UT 84130-0192	PHONE: (801) 442-5000 FAX: (801) 442-5003 TOLL FREE: (800) 538-5038 IN-STATE: (800) 442-5038	E-MAIL: WEBMASTER@IHC.COM WEB: WWW.IHC.COM

SELECTIVE INSURANCE CO

NATIONAL	7401 BEAUFONT SPRINGS DR STE 400 RICHMOND, VA 23225 PO BOX 13325 RICHMOND, VA 23225-0325	PHONE: (804) 272-7568 FAX: (877) 378-3033 TOLL FREE: (800) 568-9656	WEB: WWW.SELECTIVEINSURANCE.COM
	1275 GLENLIVET DR ALLENTOWN, PA 18106-3106 PO BOX 25333 LEHIGH VALLEY, PA 18002-5333	FAX: (610) 530-2612 TOLL FREE: (800) 374-9656 IN-STATE: (866) 455-9969	WEB: WWW.SELECTIVEINSURANCE.COM
MARYLAND	SIX N PARK DR STE 200 HUNT VALLEY, MD 21030-1842	PHONE: (410) 771-6500 FAX: (410) 771-0889 TOLL FREE: (800) 685-9656	WEB: WWW.SELECTIVEINSURANCE.COM
NEW JERSEY	1395 YARDVILLE HAMILTON SQ RD TRENTON, NJ 08619 PO BOX 7950 TRENTON, NJ 08650-7950	PHONE: (609) 890-2200 FAX: (609) 586-3748 TOLL FREE: (800) 365-9556	WEB: WWW.SELECTIVEINSURANCE.COM

SELECTIVE INSURANCE COMPANY OF AMERICA

NATIONAL	40 WANTAGE AVE BRANCHVILLE, NJ 07890 PO BOX 13325 RICHMOND, VA 23225	PHONE: (973) 948-3000 FAX: (973) 948-2089 TOLL FREE: (800) 777-9656	WEB: WWW.SELECTIVEINSURANCE.COM

SELF FUNDING ADMINISTRATORS

NATIONAL	339 BUSCHS FRONTAGE RD STE 207 ANNAPOLIS, MD 21401 PO BOX 6596 ANNAPOLIS, MD 21401-0596	PHONE: (410) 757-4200 FAX: (410) 349-9724 TOLL FREE: (800) 424-8611	WEB: WWW.SELF-FUNDING-ADMIN.COM

SELF INSURED BENEFIT ADMINISTRATORS

NATIONAL	101 STARCREST DR CLEARWATER, FL 33765 PO BOX 6090 CLEARWATER, FL 33758	PHONE: (727) 532-0400 FAX: (727) 530-0882 TOLL FREE: (800) 683-7422	WEB: WWW.SIBATPA.COM OR WWW.BOUCHARDINSURANCE.COM

SELF INSURED SERVICES CO — *SISCO*

NATIONAL	151 W 8TH ST 300 SECURITY BLDG DUBUQUE, IA 52001 PO BOX 28 DUBUQUE, IA 52004	PHONE: (563) 583-7301 FAX: (563) 587-5500 TOLL FREE: (800) 793-5235	WEB: WWW.CB-SISCO.COM

SELMAN & CO

NATIONAL	6110 PARKLAND BLVD STE 200 CLEVELAND, OH 44124-4187 PO BOX 248108 CLEVELAND, OH 44124-4187	PHONE: (440) 646-9336 FAX: (440) 646-9339 TOLL FREE: (800) 735-5262	E-MAIL: CUSTOMERSERVICE@SELMAN.CC WEB: WWW.SELMAN.CC

SENECA

NATIONAL	160 WATER ST 16TH FL NEW YORK, NY 10028	PHONE: (212) 344-3000 FAX: (212) 422-7541	WEB: WWW.SENECAINSURANCE.COM

SENTARA HEALTH MANAGEMENT — *SEE ALSO OPTIMA HEALTH PLAN*

SENTINEL SECURITY LIFE INSURANCE COMPANY

UTAH	2121 S STATE ST SALT LAKE CITY, UT 84115 PO BOX 65478 SALT LAKE CITY, UT 84115	PHONE: (801) 484-8514	

S

SENTRY CLAIMS CENTER — *SEE ALSO DAIRYLAND INSURANCE CO — SEE ALSO MIDDLESEX INSURANCE*

SENTRY DAIRYLAND

ALABAMA	1025 BOULDERS PKY STE 100 RICHMOND, VA 23260-6363 PO BOX 26363 RICHMOND, VA 23260-6363	PHONE: (715) 346-6000 FAX: (804) 323-4883 OR (804) 323-4860 TOLL FREE: (800) 338-2487	WEB: WWW.SENTRY.COM

SENTRY INSURANCE MUTUAL CO

NATIONAL	1421 STRONGS AVE STEVENS POINT, WI 54481 PO BOX 8026 STEVENS POINT, WI 54481-8026	PHONE: (715) 346-6000 FAX: (715) 346-6161 TOLL FREE: (800) 638-8763	WEB: WWW.SENTRYINSURANCE.COM
ARIZONA	9060 E VIALINDA BLVD SCOTTSDALE, AZ 85258-5417 PO BOX 29460 PHOENIX, AZ 85038	PHONE: (480) 860-7000 FAX: (480) 860-7987 TOLL FREE: (800) 833-2244	WEB: WWW.SENTRYINSURANCE.COM

SENTRY SELECT INSURANCE CO

NATIONAL	4400 E 53RD ST DAVENPORT, IA 52807 PO BOX 8023 DAVENPORT, IA 52808	PHONE: (800) 447-0633 FAX: (888) 533-7827 TOLL FREE: (800) 635-3377	WEB: WWW.SENTRYINSURANCE.COM

SEQUOIA INSURANCE CO — *CITATION INSURANCE GROUP*

CALIFORNIA	PO BOX 14206 ORANGE, CA 92863-1206	PHONE: (714) 456-1900 FAX: (714) 456-1950 TOLL FREE: (888) 704-1384	
	2125 WYLIE DR STE B2 MODESTO, CA 95355-3800 PO BOX 576409 MODESTO, CA 95357-6409	PHONE: (209) 529-5155 FAX: (209) 529-5144	
	SAN RAMON CLAIMS OFFICE 2333 SAN RAMON VALLEY BLVD STE 370 SAN RAMON, CA 94583-4444 PO BOX 3648 WALNUT CREEK, CA 94598	PHONE: (925) 952-9596 FAX: (925) 952-9668 TOLL FREE: (800) 227-8642	E-MAIL: KENK@SEQUOIAINS.COM WEB: WWW.SEQUOIAINS.COM
	4600 NORTHGATE BLVD STE 115 SACRAMENTO, CA 95834	PHONE: (916) 925-1779 FAX: (916) 925-5199 TOLL FREE: (800) 799-8119	
	5595 WINFIELD BLVD STE 200 SAN JOSE, CA 95153-1220 PO BOX 53123 SAN JOSE, CA 95153-0123	PHONE: (408) 360-1350 FAX: (408) 360-1356 TOLL FREE: (800) 794-3794	

SERVCO LIFE INSURANCE CO — *ADMINISTRATION & CLAIMS SERVICE CENTER*

ARKANSAS
LOUISIANA
MISSISSIPPI
OKLAHOMA
TEXAS

	13201 NW FWY STE 801 HOUSTON, TX 77040-6025 PO BOX 41194 HOUSTON, TX 77241-1194	TOLL FREE: (800) 444-2490

SERVICE INSURANCE CO

FLORIDA	4730 STATE RD 64 E BRADENTON, FL 34208 PO BOX 9729 BRADENTON, FL 34206-9729	PHONE: (941) 746-4107 FAX: (941) 748-5463 TOLL FREE: (800) 780-8423	WEB: WWW.SERVICEINSURANCECO.COM

SERVICE LIFE & CASUALTY

ARIZONA *TEXAS*	6907 CAPITOL OF TX HWY STE 370 AUSTIN, TX 78731 PO BOX 26800 AUSTIN, TX 78755-0800	PHONE: (512) 343-0600 FAX: (512) 343-8673 TOLL FREE: (800) 299-6977	WEB: WWW.SERVICE-INS-GROUP.COM

SF ADMINISTRATORS

CALIFORNIA	642 HARRISON ST SAN FRANCISCO, CA 94107	PHONE: (415) 777-3707	

SHASTA ADMINISTRATIVE SERVICES — *SEE ALSO JELD-WEN HEALTH BENEFIT PLAN*

NATIONAL	2751 SW AIRPORT WY REDMOND, OR 97756 PO BOX 1747 REDMOND, OR 97756	PHONE: (541) 504-2777 FAX: (541) 504-2710 TOLL FREE: (800) 441-4518	WEB: WWW.SHASTAADMIN.COM

SHEFFIELD OLSON & MCQUEEN, INC

NATIONAL	2145 FORD PKY STE 300 ST PAUL, MN 55116-1914	FAX: (651) 695-1646 TOLL FREE: (800) 486-7664 IN-STATE: (888) 330-3408	E-MAIL: CUSTOMERSERVICE@SOMI.COM WEB: WWW.SOMI.COM

SHELBY INSURANCE CO

ALABAMA *FLORIDA*	3760 RIVER RUN DR BIRMINGHAM, AL 35243-4718 PO BOX 43360 BIRMINGHAM, AL 35243	PHONE: (205) 970-7000 FAX: (888) 286-9458 TOLL FREE: (800) 444-2955	WEB: WWW.VESTA.COM

SHELTER INSURANCE COMPANIES

ARKANSAS, COLORADO, ILLINOIS, INDIANA, IOWA, KANSAS, KENTUCKY, LOUISIANA, MISSISSIPPI, MISSOURI, NEBRASKA, OKLAHOMA, TENNESSEE

	1817 W BROADWAY COLUMBIA, MO 65218-0001 PO BOX 6006 COLUMBIA, MO 65205-6006	PHONE: (573) 445-8441 TOLL FREE: (800) 743-5837	WEB: WWW.SHELTERINSURANCE.COM

SHENANDOAH LIFE INSURANCE CO

VIRGINIA	2301 BRAMBLETON AVE SW ROANOKE, VA 24015 PO BOX 12847 ROANOKE, VA 24029-2847	PHONE: (540) 985-4400 FAX: (540) 985-4444 TOLL FREE: (800) 848-5433	WEB: WWW.SHENLIFE.COM

SIERRA HEALTH & LIFE INSURANCE CO, INC — *SIERRA HEALTH CARE OPTIONS*

NEVADA	2720 N TENAYA WY LAS VEGAS, NV 89128-0424 PO BOX 15645 LAS VEGAS, NV 89114	PHONE: (702) 242-7000 FAX: (702) 242-9038 TOLL FREE: (800) 888-2264	WEB: WWW.SIERRAHEALTH.COM

S

SIERRA HEALTH CARE

NATIONAL	2700 TENAYA LAS VEGAS, NV 89114	PHONE: (702) 242-7840 TOLL FREE: (800) 698-4828	

SIERRA HEALTH CARE OPTIONS — *SEE ALSO SIERRA HEALTH & LIFE INSURANCE CO, INC*

SIERRA HEALTH SERVICES — *SEE ALSO HEALTH PLAN OF NEVADA, INC*

SIERRA PROVIDENCE HEALTH NETWORK

TEXAS	1625 MEDICAL CENTER DR EL PASO, TX 79902	PHONE: (915) 577-6540 FAX: (915) 577-8398	WEB: WWW.SPHN.COM

SIGNET STAR REINSURANCE CO

CONNECTICUT	475 STEAMBOAT RD GREENWICH, CT 06830-0000	PHONE: (203) 542-3200 FAX: (203) 542-3290 TOLL FREE: (800) 866-2308	WEB: WWW.WRBERKLEY.COM

SIHO — *SEE ALSO SOUTHEASTERN INDIANA HEALTH ORGANIZATION*

SISCO — *SEE ALSO SELF INSURED SERVICES CO*

SMITH ADMINISTRATORS

TEXAS	3800 SANDSHELL DR 260 FORT WORTH, TX 76137 PO BOX 161125 FORT WORTH, TX 76161-1125	PHONE: (817) 335-2582 FAX: (817) 335-9734 TOLL FREE: (800) 867-2582	WEB: WWW.SMITHADMIN.COM
UTAH	PO BOX 522428 SALT LAKE CITY, UT 84152-2428	PHONE: (801) 261-5511 FAX: (801) 263-0279 TOLL FREE: (800) 261-5511	WEB: WWW.SMITHADMIN.COM

SOCIETY INSURANCE — *SOCIETY INSURANCE: A MUTUAL CO*

ILLINOIS *INDIANA* *IOWA* *WISCONSIN*	150 CAMELOT DR FOND DU LAC, WI 54935 PO BOX 1029 FOND DU LAC, WI 54936	PHONE: (920) 922-1220 FAX: (920) 922-0747 TOLL FREE: (800) 242-9703 IN-STATE: (888) 576-2438	WEB: WWW.SOCIETYINSURANCE.COM

SOCIETY INSURANCE: A MUTUAL CO — *SEE ALSO SOCIETY INSURANCE*

SOMPO JAPAN INSURANCE COMPANY OF AMERICA

NATIONAL	225 LIBERTY ST 43RD FL NEW YORK, NY 10281-1008	PHONE: (212) 416-1200 FAX: (212) 416-1280	WEB: WWW.SOMPO-JAPAN-US.COM

SONS OF NORWAY

NATIONAL	1455 W LAKE ST MINNEAPOLIS, MN 55408-2666	PHONE: (612) 827-3611 FAX: (612) 827-0658 TOLL FREE: (800) 945-8851	E-MAIL: CBS@SOFN.COM WEB: WWW.SONSOFNORWAY.COM

SOUTHEASTERN INDIANA HEALTH ORGANIZATION — *SIHO*

INDIANA *KENTUCKY*	417 WASHINGTON ST COLUMBUS, IN 47201 PO BOX 1787 COLUMBUS, IN 47202-1787	PHONE: (812) 378-7000 FAX: (812) 378-7048 TOLL FREE: (800) 443-2980	WEB: WWW.SIHO.ORG

SOUTHERN BENEFIT ADMINISTRATORS, INC

NATIONAL	2001 CALDWELL DR GOODLETTSVILLE, TN 37072 PO BOX 1449 GOODLETTSVILLE, TN 37070-1449	PHONE: (615) 859-0131 FAX: (615) 859-0818 TOLL FREE: (800) 831-4914	

SOUTHERN CALIFORNIA — *SEE ALSO UNITED FOOD & COMMERCIAL WORKERS' TRUST FUND*

SOUTHERN CALIFORNIA BRANCH — *SEE ALSO MAGNA CARTA*

SOUTHERN CALIFORNIA EDISON CO

CALIFORNIA	8631 RUSH ST ROSEMEAD, CA 91770-3738 PO BOX 5038 ROSEMEAD, CA 91770-5038	PHONE: (626) 302-6890 FAX: (626) 302-4790 TOLL FREE: (800) 655-6444	

SOUTHERN CALIFORNIA PIPE TRADES TRUST FUND

CALIFORNIA	501 SHATTO PL 5TH FL LOS ANGELES, CA 90020-1713	PHONE: (213) 385-6161 FAX: (213) 487-3640 IN-STATE: (800) 595-7473	

SOUTHERN GROUP ADMINISTRATORS, INC

NORTH CAROLINA	200 S MARSHALL ST WINSTON-SALEM, NC 27101-5251	PHONE: (336) 723-7111 FAX: (336) 722-4748 TOLL FREE: (800) 334-8159	WEB: WWW.SOGROUP.COM

SOUTHERN TRUST INSURANCE CO

ALABAMA *GEORGIA* *TENNESSEE*	5444 RIVERSIDE DR MACON, GA 31210 PO BOX 250 MACON, GA 31202-0250	PHONE: (478) 474-0555 FAX: (478) 757-0906 TOLL FREE: (800) 476-5566	WEB: WWW.STINS.COM

SOUTHLAND NATIONAL INSURANCE CORP

ALABAMA	1812 UNIVERSITY BLVD TUSCALOOSA, AL 35401-1518 PO BOX 1520 TUSCALOOSA, AL 35403-1520	PHONE: (205) 345-7410 FAX: (205) 343-1239 TOLL FREE: (800) 277-8762	

SOUTHWEST — *SEE ALSO AMERICAN GUARANTY LIFE INSURANCE CO*

SOUTHWEST ADMINISTRATORS — *WESTERN TEAMSTERS*

CALIFORNIA *NEVADA*	1000 S FREEMONT AVE BLDG A9 WEST ALHAMBRA, CA 91803-8800 PO BOX 1121 ALHAMBRA, CA 91802-1121	PHONE: (626) 284-4792 TOLL FREE: (877) 350-4792	WEB: WWW.SWADMIN.COM
NEVADA	2910 EL CAMINO AVE STE 206 LAS VEGAS, NV 89102	PHONE: (702) 252-7001 FAX: (702) 220-3297	WEB: WWW.SWADMIN.COM

S

SOUTHWEST BUSINESS CORP

TEXAS	9311 SAN PEDRO STE 600 SAN ANTONIO, TX 78216 PO BOX 795027 SAN ANTONIO, TX 78279-5027	PHONE: (210) 525-1241 FAX: (210) 525-1240 TOLL FREE: (800) 527-0066	WEB: WWW.SWBC.COM

SOUTHWEST CARPENTERS HEALTH & WELFARE TRUST

CALIFORNIA	533 S FREEMONT AVE LOS ANGELES, CA 90071 PO BOX 17973 LOS ANGELES, CA 90071	PHONE: (213) 386-8590 FAX: (213) 739-9329 TOLL FREE: (800) 252-9255	

SOUTHWEST LIFE AND HEALTH — *DBA FIRSTCARE*

TEXAS	1901 W LOOP 289 STE 9 LUBBOCK, TX 79407	TOLL FREE: (800) 240-3270	WEB: WWW.FIRSTCARE.COM

SOUTHWEST SERVICE ADMINISTRATORS, INC

ARIZONA *HAWAII* *NEW MEXICO*	4775 INDIAN SCHOOL RD NE STE 105 ALBUQUERQUE, NM 87110-3927	PHONE: (505) 265-8422 FAX: (505) 266-9358 TOLL FREE: (800) 432-6636	

SPECIAL AGENTS MUTUAL BENEFIT ASSOCIATION — *SEE ALSO SAMBA*

SPECIALTY RISK SERVICES — *ITT HARTFORD INSURANCE GROUP*

NATIONAL	828 ROYAL PKY STE 200 NASHVILLE, TN 37214 PO BOX 305104 NASHVILLE, TN 37230	PHONE: (615) 883-4324 FAX: (615) 874-0636 TOLL FREE: (800) 293-1265	

SPECTERA

NATIONAL	2811 LORD BALTIMORE DR BALTIMORE, MD 21244-2644	PHONE: (410) 265-6033 FAX: (410) 265-5872 TOLL FREE: (800) 638-6265 IN-STATE: (800) 638-3120	WEB: WWW.SPECTERA.COM

SRC SERVICES, INC

NATIONAL	221 DAWSON RD COLUMBIA, SC 29223 PO BOX 23759 COLUMBIA, SC 29224-3759	PHONE: (803) 736-1999 FAX: (803) 736-9952 TOLL FREE: (800) 869-0808	WEB: WWW.SRC-WEB.COM

SRC, AN AETNA COMPANY — *SEE ALSO STRATEGIC RESOURCE CO*

STANDARD INSURANCE CO

NATIONAL	1100 SW 6TH AVE PORTLAND, OR 97204-1020 PO BOX 711 PORTLAND, OR 97204	PHONE: (971) 248-2755 FAX: (971) 321-6776 TOLL FREE: (800) 348-3226	WEB: WWW.STANDARD.COM

STANDARD LIFE & ACCIDENT INSURANCE CO

NATIONAL *MEXICO* *PUERTO RICO*	ONE MOODY PLZ GALVESTON, TX 77550-7947 PO BOX 1850 GALVESTON, TX 77553-1850	PHONE: (409) 763-4661 FAX: (409) 621-3094 TOLL FREE: (888) 350-1488	WEB: WWW.SLAICO.COM

STANDARD LIFE & CASUALTY INSURANCE COMPANY

ALABAMA
FLORIDA
GEORGIA
NORTH CAROLINA
SOUTH CAROLINA
TENNESSEE
TEXAS
UTAH

PO BOX 510690
SALT LAKE CITY, UT 84151
PHONE: (801) 538-0376
TOLL FREE: (800) 377-0695

STANDARD MUTUAL INSURANCE CO

ILLINOIS *INDIANA*	1028 S GRAND AVE W SPRINGFIELD, IL 62704 PO BOX 19267 SPRINGFIELD, IL 62794-9267	PHONE: (217) 546-2894 FAX: (217) 793-1216 TOLL FREE: (877) 816-3652	WEB: WWW.STANDARDMUTUAL.COM

STANTON GROUP

NATIONAL	3405 ANNAPOLIS LN N STE 100 PLYMOUTH, MN 55447	PHONE: (763) 278-4000 FAX: (763) 278-4601 TOLL FREE: (800) 284-4464	WEB: WWW.STANTON-GROUP.COM

STATE ACCIDENT INSURANCE FUND CORP — *SEE ALSO SAIF CORP*

STATE AUTO INSURANCE

ILLINOIS *INDIANA*	2955 N MERIDIAN ST INDIANAPOLIS, IN 46208-4714	PHONE: (317) 931-7000 TOLL FREE: (800) 777-7324	

STATE AUTO INSURANCE COMPANIES — *SEE ALSO STATE AUTOMOBILE MUTUAL INSURANCE CO*

STATE AUTOMOBILE MUTUAL INSURANCE CO — *STATE AUTO INSURANCE COMPANIES*

ALABAMA	112 S MAIN ST GREER, SC 29650-2017 PO BOX 199 GREER, SC 29652-0199	PHONE: (864) 877-3311 FAX: (864) 879-4025 TOLL FREE: (800) 234-1878	WEB: WWW.STATEAUTO.COM
ALABAMA *ARIZONA* *ARKANSAS*	518 E BROAD ST COLUMBUS, OH 43215-3976 PO BOX 182822 COLUMBUS, OH 43218-2822	PHONE: (614) 464-5000 FAX: (614) 464-4868 TOLL FREE: (800) 444-9950	WEB: WWW.STATEAUTO.COM
FLORIDA *GEORGIA*	112 S MAIN ST GREER, SC 29650-2017 PO BOX 199 GREER, SC 29652-0199	PHONE: (864) 877-3311 FAX: (864) 879-4025 TOLL FREE: (800) 234-1878	WEB: WWW.STATEAUTO.COM
FLORIDA *GEORGIA* *ILLINOIS* *INDIANA* *KANSAS* *KENTUCKY* *MARYLAND*	518 E BROAD ST COLUMBUS, OH 43215-3976 PO BOX 182822 COLUMBUS, OH 43218-2822	PHONE: (614) 464-5000 FAX: (614) 464-4868 TOLL FREE: (800) 444-9950	WEB: WWW.STATEAUTO.COM
MARYLAND	4900 RITTER RD MECHANICSBURG, PA 17055-4893 PO BOX 2006 MECHANICSBURG, PA 17055-0733	PHONE: (717) 697-1121 FAX: (717) 697-2803 TOLL FREE: (800) 288-1872	WEB: WWW.STATEAUTO.COM
MICHIGAN	17197 N LAUREL PARK DR STE 167 LIVONIA, MI 48152-2686	PHONE: (734) 462-6100 FAX: (734) 462-6105 TOLL FREE: (800) 888-5469	WEB: WWW.STATEAUTO.COM
MICHIGAN *MINNESOTA* *MISSOURI* *NORTH CAROLINA*	518 E BROAD ST COLUMBUS, OH 43215-3976 PO BOX 182822 COLUMBUS, OH 43218-2822	PHONE: (614) 464-5000 FAX: (614) 464-4868 TOLL FREE: (800) 444-9950	WEB: WWW.STATEAUTO.COM

S

NORTH CAROLINA	112 S MAIN ST GREER, SC 29650-2017 PO BOX 199 GREER, SC 29652-0199	PHONE: (864) 877-3311 FAX: (864) 879-4025 TOLL FREE: (800) 234-1878	WEB: WWW.STATEAUTO.COM
NORTH DAKOTA *OHIO*	518 E BROAD ST COLUMBUS, OH 43215-3976 PO BOX 182822 COLUMBUS, OH 43218-2822	PHONE: (614) 464-5000 FAX: (614) 464-4868 TOLL FREE: (800) 444-9950	WEB: WWW.STATEAUTO.COM
PENNSYLVANIA	4900 RITTER RD MECHANICSBURG, PA 17055-4893 PO BOX 2006 MECHANICSBURG, PA 17055-0733	PHONE: (717) 697-1121 FAX: (717) 697-2803 TOLL FREE: (800) 288-1872	WEB: WWW.STATEAUTO.COM
SOUTH CAROLINA	518 E BROAD ST COLUMBUS, OH 43215-3976 PO BOX 182822 COLUMBUS, OH 43218-2822	PHONE: (614) 464-5000 FAX: (614) 464-4868 TOLL FREE: (800) 444-9950	WEB: WWW.STATEAUTO.COM
SOUTH CAROLINA *TENNESSEE* *VIRGINIA*	112 S MAIN ST GREER, SC 29650-2017 PO BOX 199 GREER, SC 29652-0199	PHONE: (864) 877-3311 FAX: (864) 879-4025 TOLL FREE: (800) 234-1878	WEB: WWW.STATEAUTO.COM
VIRGINIA	518 E BROAD ST COLUMBUS, OH 43215-3976 PO BOX 182822 COLUMBUS, OH 43218-2822	PHONE: (614) 464-5000 FAX: (614) 464-4868 TOLL FREE: (800) 444-9950	WEB: WWW.STATEAUTO.COM
WEST VIRGINIA	4900 RITTER RD MECHANICSBURG, PA 17055-4893 PO BOX 2006 MECHANICSBURG, PA 17055-0733	PHONE: (717) 697-1121 FAX: (717) 697-2803 TOLL FREE: (800) 288-1872	WEB: WWW.STATEAUTO.COM

STATE COMPENSATION INSURANCE FUND

CALIFORNIA	10 RIVERPARK PL E FRESNO, CA 93755 PO BOX 65005 PINEDALE, CA 93650	PHONE: (559) 433-2700 FAX: (559) 433-2751	WEB: WWW.SCIF.COM
	10105 PACIFIC HEIGHTS BLVD SAN DIEGO, CA 92121-2939 PO BOX 85488 SAN DIEGO, CA 92186-5488	PHONE: (858) 552-7100 TOLL FREE: (888) 222-3211	WEB: WWW.SCIF.COM
	HOME OFFICE 1275 MARKET ST STE 1250 SAN FRANCISCO, CA 94103-1410	PHONE: (415) 565-1234 FAX: (415) 565-4985 TOLL FREE: (888) 222-3211	WEB: WWW.SCIF.COM
	1450 NEOTOMAS AVE SANTA ROSA, CA 95405-7575 PO BOX 65005 PINEDALE, CA 93650-5005	PHONE: (707) 573-6500 TOLL FREE: (888) 222-3211	WEB: WWW.SCIF.COM
	1750 E 4TH ST 8TH FL SANTA ANA, CA 92705-3909 PO BOX 419 SANTA ANA, CA 92702	PHONE: (714) 565-5000 FAX: (714) 565-5958 TOLL FREE: (888) 222-3211	WEB: WWW.SCIF.COM
	2275 GATEWAY OAKS DR SACRAMENTO, CA 95833-3224 PO BOX 3171 SUISUN CITY, CA 94585-6171	PHONE: (916) 924-5100 TOLL FREE: (888) 222-3211	WEB: WWW.SCIF.COM
	2440 SIX ST EUREKA, CA 95501-1115 PO BOX 4973 EUREKA, CA 95502-4973	PHONE: (707) 443-9721 FAX: (707) 443-0644 TOLL FREE: (888) 222-3211	WEB: WWW.SCIF.COM
	2901 N VENTURA RD OXNARD, CA 93036 PO BOX 9045 OXNARD, CA 93031-9045	PHONE: (805) 988-5300 FAX: (805) 988-5528 TOLL FREE: (888) 222-3211	WEB: WWW.SCIF.COM

CALIFORNIA — CONTINUED		2955 PERALTA OAKS CT OAKLAND, CA 94605-5319 PO BOX 3171 SUISUN CITY, CA 94585-6171	PHONE: (510) 577-3000 TOLL FREE: (888) 222-3211	WEB: WWW.SCIF.COM
		303 2ND ST STE 600 S SAN FRANCISCO, CA 94107-6311 PO BOX 7455 SAN FRANCISCO, CA 94120-7455	PHONE: (415) 974-8200 FAX: (415) 974-8091 TOLL FREE: (888) 222-3211	WEB: WWW.SCIF.COM
		3247 W MARCH LANE STOCKTON, CA 95219-2351 PO BOX 8000 STOCKTON, CA 95208	PHONE: (209) 476-2600 TOLL FREE: (888) 222-3211	WEB: WWW.SCIF.COM
		364 KNOLLCREST DR REDDING, CA 96002-0104 PO BOX 3171 SUISUN CITY, CA 94585-6171	PHONE: (530) 223-7000 TOLL FREE: (888) 222-3211	WEB: WWW.SCIF.COM
		375 W HOSPITALITY LN SAN BERNARDINO, CA 92408-3203 PO BOX 1316 SAN BERNARDINO, CA 92402-1316	PHONE: (909) 384-4500 TOLL FREE: (888) 222-3211 IN-STATE: (800) 342-7214	WEB: WWW.SCIF.COM
		STATE CONTRACT SERVICES 400 CITADEL DR STE 100 COMMERCE, CA 90040-1558 PO BOX 910932 COMMERCE, CA 90091-0932	PHONE: (323) 727-5600 FAX: (323) 727-5710 TOLL FREE: (888) 222-3211	WEB: WWW.SCIF.COM
		STATE CONTRACT SERVICES 5900 STATE FARM DR STE 200 ROHNERT PARK, CA 94927-1609 PO BOX 1609 ROHNERT PARK, CA 94927-1609	PHONE: (707) 586-5000 TOLL FREE: (888) 222-3211	WEB: WWW.SCIF.COM
		6203 SAN IGNACIO AVE SAN JOSE, CA 95119-1371 PO BOX 530957 SAN JOSE, CA 95153-5357	PHONE: (408) 363-7600 FAX: (408) 363-7866 OR (408) 363-7471 IN-STATE: (800) 499-8668	WEB: WWW.SCIF.COM
		6301 DAY ST RIVERSIDE, CA 92507-0902 PO BOX 5025 RIVERSIDE, CA 92517-5025	PHONE: (951) 656-8300 FAX: (909) 697-8567 TOLL FREE: (888) 222-3211	WEB: WWW.SCIF.COM
		S CA AREA GROUP INSURANCE PROGRAMS 900 CORPORATE CENTER DR MONTEREY PARK, CA 91754-7618 PO BOX 92503 LOS ANGELES, CA 90009	PHONE: (323) 981-6620 TOLL FREE: (888) 222-3211	WEB: WWW.SCIF.COM
		9801 CAMINO MEDIA BAKERSFIELD, CA 93311-1311 PO BOX 21810 BAKERSFIELD, CA 93390-1810	PHONE: (661) 664-4000 FAX: (661) 664-4101 TOLL FREE: (888) 394-6252	WEB: WWW.SCIF.COM

STATE FARM INSURANCE CO

ALABAMA		5400 NEW ALBANY RD E NEW ALBANY, OH 13054-8861 PO BOX 3040 NEWARK, OH 43058-3040	FAX: (740) 364-3040 TOLL FREE: (877) 543-3619 IN-STATE: (888) 620-5212	WEB: WWW.STATEFARM.COM
ALASKA *ARIZONA*		2702 IRELAND GROVE RD BLOOMINGTON, IL 61702	PHONE: (309) 763-0009 FAX: (888) 309-8608 TOLL FREE: (800) 472-2364	WEB: WWW.STATEFARM.COM
ARKANSAS		5400 NEW ALBANY RD E NEW ALBANY, OH 13054-8861 PO BOX 3040 NEWARK, OH 43058-3040	FAX: (740) 364-3040 TOLL FREE: (877) 543-3619 IN-STATE: (888) 620-5212	WEB: WWW.STATEFARM.COM

S

CALIFORNIA *COLORADO*	2702 IRELAND GROVE RD BLOOMINGTON, IL 61702	PHONE: (309) 763-0009 FAX: (888) 309-8608 TOLL FREE: (800) 472-2364	WEB: WWW.STATEFARM.COM
CONNECTICUT *DELAWARE* *DISTRICT OF COLUMBIA*	5400 NEW ALBANY RD E NEW ALBANY, OH 13054-8861 PO BOX 3040 NEWARK, OH 43058-3040	FAX: (740) 364-3040 TOLL FREE: (877) 543-3619 IN-STATE: (888) 620-5212	WEB: WWW.STATEFARM.COM
FLORIDA	2702 IRELAND GROVE RD BLOOMINGTON, IL 61702	PHONE: (309) 763-0009 FAX: (888) 309-8608 TOLL FREE: (800) 472-2364	WEB: WWW.STATEFARM.COM
GEORGIA	5400 NEW ALBANY RD E NEW ALBANY, OH 13054-8861 PO BOX 3040 NEWARK, OH 43058-3040	FAX: (740) 364-3040 TOLL FREE: (877) 543-3619 IN-STATE: (888) 620-5212	WEB: WWW.STATEFARM.COM
HAWAII	2702 IRELAND GROVE RD BLOOMINGTON, IL 61702	PHONE: (309) 763-0009 FAX: (888) 309-8608 TOLL FREE: (800) 472-2364	WEB: WWW.STATEFARM.COM
IDAHO *ILLINOIS* *INDIANA* *IOWA*	2702 IRELAND GROVE RD BLOOMINGTON, IL 61702	PHONE: (309) 763-0009 FAX: (888) 309-8608 TOLL FREE: (800) 472-2364	WEB: WWW.STATEFARM.COM
KANSAS *KENTUCKY* *LOUISIANA* *MAINE* *MARYLAND* *MASSACHUSETTS*	5400 NEW ALBANY RD E NEW ALBANY, OH 13054-8861 PO BOX 3040 NEWARK, OH 43058-3040	FAX: (740) 364-3040 TOLL FREE: (877) 543-3619 IN-STATE: (888) 620-5212	WEB: WWW.STATEFARM.COM
MICHIGAN *MINNESOTA*	2702 IRELAND GROVE RD BLOOMINGTON, IL 61702	PHONE: (309) 763-0009 FAX: (888) 309-8608 TOLL FREE: (800) 472-2364	WEB: WWW.STATEFARM.COM
MONTANA *NEBRASKA* *NEVADA*	2702 IRELAND GROVE RD BLOOMINGTON, IL 61702	PHONE: (309) 763-0009 FAX: (888) 309-8608 TOLL FREE: (800) 472-2364	WEB: WWW.STATEFARM.COM
NEW HAMPSHIRE *NEW JERSEY*	5400 NEW ALBANY RD E NEW ALBANY, OH 13054-8861 PO BOX 3040 NEWARK, OH 43058-3040	FAX: (740) 364-3040 TOLL FREE: (877) 543-3619 IN-STATE: (888) 620-5212	WEB: WWW.STATEFARM.COM
NEW MEXICO	2702 IRELAND GROVE RD BLOOMINGTON, IL 61702	PHONE: (309) 763-0009 FAX: (888) 309-8608 TOLL FREE: (800) 472-2364	WEB: WWW.STATEFARM.COM
NEW YORK *NORTH CAROLINA*	5400 NEW ALBANY RD E NEW ALBANY, OH 13054-8861 PO BOX 3040 NEWARK, OH 43058-3040	FAX: (740) 364-3040 TOLL FREE: (877) 543-3619 IN-STATE: (888) 620-5212	WEB: WWW.STATEFARM.COM
NORTH DAKOTA	2702 IRELAND GROVE RD BLOOMINGTON, IL 61702	PHONE: (309) 763-0009 FAX: (888) 309-8608 TOLL FREE: (800) 472-2364	WEB: WWW.STATEFARM.COM
OHIO *OKLAHOMA*	5400 NEW ALBANY RD E NEW ALBANY, OH 13054-8861 PO BOX 3040 NEWARK, OH 43058-3040	FAX: (740) 364-3040 TOLL FREE: (877) 543-3619 IN-STATE: (888) 620-5212	WEB: WWW.STATEFARM.COM
OREGON	2702 IRELAND GROVE RD BLOOMINGTON, IL 61702	PHONE: (309) 763-0009 FAX: (888) 309-8608 TOLL FREE: (800) 472-2364	WEB: WWW.STATEFARM.COM
PENNSYLVANIA *RHODE ISLAND* *SOUTH CAROLINA*	5400 NEW ALBANY RD E NEW ALBANY, OH 13054-8861 PO BOX 3040 NEWARK, OH 43058-3040	FAX: (740) 364-3040 TOLL FREE: (877) 543-3619 IN-STATE: (888) 620-5212	WEB: WWW.STATEFARM.COM

SOUTH DAKOTA	2702 IRELAND GROVE RD BLOOMINGTON, IL 61702	PHONE: (309) 763-0009 FAX: (888) 309-8608 TOLL FREE: (800) 472-2364	WEB: WWW.STATEFARM.COM
TENNESSEE *TEXAS*	5400 NEW ALBANY RD E NEW ALBANY, OH 13054-8861 PO BOX 3040 NEWARK, OH 43058-3040	FAX: (740) 364-3040 TOLL FREE: (877) 543-3619 IN-STATE: (888) 620-5212	WEB: WWW.STATEFARM.COM
UTAH	2702 IRELAND GROVE RD BLOOMINGTON, IL 61702	PHONE: (309) 763-0009 FAX: (888) 309-8608 TOLL FREE: (800) 472-2364	WEB: WWW.STATEFARM.COM
VERMONT *VIRGINIA*	5400 NEW ALBANY RD E NEW ALBANY, OH 13054-8861 PO BOX 3040 NEWARK, OH 43058-3040	FAX: (740) 364-3040 TOLL FREE: (877) 543-3619 IN-STATE: (888) 620-5212	WEB: WWW.STATEFARM.COM
WASHINGTON	2702 IRELAND GROVE RD BLOOMINGTON, IL 61702	PHONE: (309) 763-0009 FAX: (888) 309-8608 TOLL FREE: (800) 472-2364	WEB: WWW.STATEFARM.COM
WEST VIRGINIA	5400 NEW ALBANY RD E NEW ALBANY, OH 13054-8861 PO BOX 3040 NEWARK, OH 43058-3040	FAX: (740) 364-3040 TOLL FREE: (877) 543-3619 IN-STATE: (888) 620-5212	WEB: WWW.STATEFARM.COM
WISCONSIN *WYOMING*	2702 IRELAND GROVE RD BLOOMINGTON, IL 61702	PHONE: (309) 763-0009 FAX: (888) 309-8608 TOLL FREE: (800) 472-2364	WEB: WWW.STATEFARM.COM

STATE MUTUAL — *SEE ALSO WAKELY & ASSOCIATES*

STATE NATIONAL INSURANCE CO, INC

NATIONAL	8200 ANDERSON BLVD FORT WORTH, TX 76120 PO BOX 24622 FORT WORTH, TX 76124	PHONE: (817) 265-2000 FAX: (817) 548-0596 TOLL FREE: (800) 877-4567	WEB: WWW.STATENATIONAL.COM

STATE OF ALASKA WORKERS' COMP DIVISION

ALASKA	3301 EAGLE ST STE 304 ANCHORAGE, AK 99503 PO BOX 107019 ANCHORAGE, AK 99510-7019	PHONE: (907) 269-4980 FAX: (907) 269-4975	WEB: WWW.LABOR.STATE.AK.US

STATE OF NEW YORK INSURANCE DEPT LIQUIDATION BUREAU

NEW YORK	123 WILLIAM ST NEW YORK, NY 10038-3804	PHONE: (212) 341-6400 FAX: (212) 341-6104	WEB: WWW.NYLB.ORG

STATEWIDE INSURANCE CO

NEW YORK	20 MAIN ST HEMPSTEAD, NY 11551-9001	PHONE: (516) 564-8000 FAX: (516) 564-8017 TOLL FREE: (800) 499-5646

STAY WELL— *SEE ALSO WELL CARE HEALTH PLANS*

STERLING

ALABAMA, ALASKA, ARIZONA, ARKANSAS, DELAWARE, HAWAII, IDAHO, ILLINOIS, INDIANA, IOWA, KANSAS, KENTUCKY, LOUISIANA, MICHIGAN, MINNESOTA, MISSISSIPPI, MISSOURI, MONTANA, NEBRASKA, NEVADA, NEW MEXICO, NORTH CAROLINA, NORTH DAKOTA, OHIO, OKLAHOMA, OREGON, PENNSYLVANIA, SOUTH CAROLINA, SOUTH DAKOTA, TENNESSEE, TEXAS, UTAH, VIRGINIA, WASHINGTON, WEST VIRGINIA, WYOMING

PO BOX 5348 OR PO BOX 1917
BELLINGHAM, WA 98227

FAX: (360) 392-9100
TOLL FREE: (888) 858-8572
OR (888) 858-8551

WEB: WWW.STERLINGPLANS.COM

STERLING BENEFIT SOLUTIONS

ALASKA, ARKANSAS, COLORADO, DELAWARE, DISTRICT OF COLUMBIA, GEORGIA, ILLINOIS, IOWA, KANSAS, KENTUCKY, LOUISIANA, MAINE, MICHIGAN, MISSISSIPPI, MONTANA, NEBRASKA, NEVADA, NEW HAMPSHIRE, NEW MEXICO, NORTH CAROLINA, OKLAHOMA, OREGON, PENNSYLVANIA, RHODE ISLAND, SOUTH CAROLINA, SOUTH DAKOTA, TENNESSEE, TEXAS, VERMONT, WEST VIRGINIA, WISCONSIN, WYOMING

10975 GRANDVIEW DR BLDG 27
STE 100
OVERLAND PARK, KS 66210

FAX: (913) 498-9096
TOLL FREE: (877) 937-1137

E-MAIL: BENEFITS@AMERICANSTERLING.COM
WEB: WWW.STERLINGBENEFITSOLUTIONS.COM

STONE BRIDGE LIFE INS — *SEE ALSO AEGON MARKETING*

STONEBRIDGE INSURANCE CO

TEXAS

2700 W PLANO PKWY
PLANO, TX 75075
PO BOX 869092
PLANO, TX 75086-9092

PHONE: (800) 692-5246
FAX: (972) 881-4527 OR
(972) 881-4532
TOLL FREE: (800) 622-2923

WEB: WWW.PLANPLUS.COM

STRATEGIC RESOURCE COMPANY — *SRC, AN AETNA COMPANY*

NATIONAL

PO BOX 23759
COLUMBIA, SC 29224-3759

PHONE: (803) 736-6463
FAX: (803) 865-3204
TOLL FREE: (800) 736-1999

E-MAIL: SRCMOREINFO@STRATEGIC-RESOURCE.COM
WEB: WWW.SRC-WEB.COM

SUMMA CARE HEALTH PLAN

OHIO

10 N MAIN ST
AKRON, OH 44308-1920
PO BOX 3620
AKRON, OH 44308

PHONE: (330) 996-8410
FAX: (330) 996-8746
TOLL FREE: (800) 996-8411

WEB: WWW.SUMMACARE.COM

SUN LIFE ASSURANCE CO OF CANADA

CANADA

FINANCIAL (MAIN OFFICE FOR CANADA)
150 KING ST W
TORONTO, ON M5V-1J9
PO BOX 4023 STA A
TORONTO, ON M5W-2P7

PHONE: (416) 753-4300
FAX: (416) 408-0653
TOLL FREE: (800) 361-6212

WEB: WWW.SUNLIFE.CA

S

SUN LIFE FINANCIAL

NATIONAL
US HOME OFFICE
ONE SUN LIFE EXECUTIVE PARK
WELLESLEY HILLS, MA 02481-0000
PO BOX 9133
WELLESLEY HILLS, MA 02481-9133
PHONE: (781) 237-6030
FAX: (781) 431-7472
TOLL FREE: (800) 786-5433
WEB: WWW.SUNLIFE-USA.COM

SUPERIOR INSURANCE SERVICE

WASHINGTON
817 HARVEY RD
AUBURN, WA 98002
PHONE: (253) 939-090[illegible]
FAX: (253) 939-0947
TOLL FREE: (800) 488-7257
WEB: WWW.SUPERIORINSURANCESERVICE.COM

SWISS RE LIFE & HEALTH AMERICA, INC

NATIONAL
175 KING ST
ARMONK, NY 10504
PHONE: (914) 828-8000
FAX: (914) 828-7000
TOLL FREE: (877) 794-7773
IN-STATE: (888) 794-7773
WEB: WWW.SWISSRE.COM

SWISS REASSURANCE

CANADA
1010 SHERBROOKE ST W STE 930
MONTREAL, PQ H3A-2R7
PHONE: (514) 288-3134
FAX: (514) 288-8588
TOLL FREE: (800) 361-6391
WEB: WWW.SWISSRE.COM

T & M FINANCIAL

KANSAS
3706 S TOPEKA BLVD STE 400
TOPEKA, KS 66609-1292
PHONE: (785) 266-8333
FAX: (785) 266-7819

T I G SPECIALTY INSURANCE

NATIONAL
PO BOX 4131
CONCORD, CA 94524-9700
PHONE: (925) 335-5000
FAX: (925) 957-1830
TOLL FREE: (800) 548-8475
WEB: WWW.TIGSPECIALTY.COM

CORPORATE OFFICE
5205 N O'CONNOR BLVD
IRVING, TX 75039-3707
PHONE: (972) 831-5000
FAX: (800) 785-8721
TOLL FREE: (888) 844-0016
WEB: WWW.TIGSPECIALTY.COM

TEXAS
5205 N O'CONNOR BLVD
IRVING, TX 75039
PO BOX 152870
IRVING, TX 75015
PHONE: (972) 831-5000
FAX: (800) 785-8721
TOLL FREE: (800) 472-7583
WEB: WWW.TIGSPECIALTY.COM

TANTARA ADMINISTRATORS — *SEE ALSO BENEFIT & RISK MANAGEMENT SERVICES*

TARRANT HEALTH SERVICES — *TEXAS HEALTH CARE*

TEXAS
2821 LACKLAND RD STE 300
FORT WORTH, TX 76116
PHONE: (817) 740-8400
FAX: (817) 740-8570
WEB: WWW.TXHEALTHCARE.COM

TBG ADMINISTRATIVE SERVICES

ARIZONA
GEORGIA
NEVADA
TEXAS
PO BOX 1725
WAUSAU, WI 54402
PHONE: (715) 845-6088
FAX: (715) 842-0413
TOLL FREE: (800) 826-0012
E-MAIL: WEBSITE@TBGASI.COM
WEB: WWW.TBGASI.COM

TEACHERS PROTECTIVE MUTUAL LIFE INSURANCE CO

INDIANA
MARYLAND
NEW JERSEY
OHIO
PENNSYLVANIA
VIRGINIA

116-118 N PRINCE ST
LANCASTER, PA 17608
PO BOX 597
LANCASTER, PA 17608-0597
PHONE: (717) 394-7156
FAX: (717) 394-7024
TOLL FREE: (800) 555-3122
E-MAIL: TPM@TPMINS.COM
WEB: WWW.TPMINS.COM

T

TEAMSTER LOCAL 731

ILLINOIS		1000 BURR RIDGE PKY BURR RIDGE, IL 60527	PHONE: (630) 887-4100	E-MAIL: IBTLU731@AOL.COM

TEAMSTERS — INTERNATIONAL BROTHERHOOD OF TEAMSTERS

NATIONAL		25 LOUISIANA AVE NW WASHINGTON, DC 20001	PHONE: (202) 624-6800	WEB: WWW.TEAMSTER.ORG

TEAMSTERS ALLIED BENEFIT — SEE ALSO WESTCHESTER TEAMSTERS HEALTH & WELFARE

TEAMSTERS BENEFIT TRUST

CALIFORNIA WYOMING		39420 LIBERTY ST STE 260 FREMONT, CA 94538 PO BOX 5820 FREMONT, CA 94537-5820	PHONE: (510) 796-4676 FAX: (510) 795-0680 TOLL FREE: (800) 533-0119	WEB: WWW.TBTFUND.ORG

TEAMSTERS LOCAL 145 HEALTH SERVICES

CONNECTICUT		3272 MAIN ST STE 202 STRATFORD, CT 06614	PHONE: (203) 375-6088 FAX: (203) 375-6106 TOLL FREE: (800) 291-6795 IN-STATE: (800) 291-6795	

TENCO SERVICES, INC

NATIONAL		620 OLD HICKORY BLVD STE 206 JACKSON, TN 38305	PHONE: (731) 668-4639 FAX: (731) 664-6960	E-MAIL: CLAIMS@TENCO.COM WEB: WWW.TENCO.COM
GEORGIA		8735 DUNWOODY PL STE 3 ATLANTA, GA 30350	PHONE: (770) 518-1935 FAX: (770) 518-7817	E-MAIL: CLAIMS@TENCO.COM WEB: WWW.TENCO.COM
KENTUCKY		10001 TAYLORSVILLE RD STE 200 LOUISVILLE, KY 40299 PO BOX 24283 LOUISVILLE, KY 40224	PHONE: (502) 267-1259 FAX: (502) 267-4535	E-MAIL: CLAIMS@TENCO.COM WEB: WWW.TENCO.COM
		1106 LOVERS LN STE C1 BOWLING GREEN, KY 42103	PHONE: (270) 842-3222 FAX: (270) 842-3205	E-MAIL: CLAIMS@TENCO.COM WEB: WWW.TENCO.COM
KENTUCKY OHIO		3027 DIXIE HWY STE 117 EDGEWOOD, KY 41017 PO BOX 18878 COVINGTON, KY 41018	PHONE: (859) 426-9100 FAX: (859) 426-9101	E-MAIL: CLAIMS@TENCO.COM WEB: WWW.TENCO.COM
TENNESSEE		PO BOX 1313 CLEVELAND, TN 37311-1313	PHONE: (423) 472-3251 FAX: (423) 875-5535	E-MAIL: CLAIMS@TENCO.COM WEB: WWW.TENCO.COM
		PO BOX 38 TULLAHOMA, TN 37388-0038	PHONE: (423) 875-5522 FAX: (423) 875-5535 TOLL FREE: (800) 228-3620	E-MAIL: CLAIMS@TENCO.COM WEB: WWW.TENCO.COM
		244 E CTR ST STE 1 KINGSPORT, TN 37660	PHONE: (423) 246-2496 FAX: (423) 246-9612	E-MAIL: CLAIMS@TENCO.COM WEB: WWW.TENCO.COM
		3310 WEST END AVE STE 465 NASHVILLE, TN 37203 PO BOX 129003 NASHVILLE, TN 37212	PHONE: (615) 292-0098 FAX: (615) 292-0061 TOLL FREE: (800) 621-1313	E-MAIL: CLAIMS@TENCO.COM WEB: WWW.TENCO.COM
		3501 DAYTON BLVD CHATTANOOGA, TN 37415 PO BOX 15598 CHATTANOOGA, TN 37415-5598	PHONE: (423) 875-5522 FAX: (423) 875-5535	E-MAIL: CLAIMS@TENCO.COM WEB: WWW.TENCO.COM
		5401 KINGSTON PIKE STE 190 KNOXVILLE, TN 37919-1483 PO BOX 11483 KNOXVILLE, TN 37919	PHONE: (865) 588-0237 FAX: (865) 588-4163	E-MAIL: CLAIMS@TENCO.COM WEB: WWW.TENCO.COM

TENNESSEE — CONTINUED	675B S JEFFERSON AVE COOKEVILLE, TN 38501 PO BOX 2246 COOKEVILLE, TN 38502-2246	PHONE: (931) 526-2246 FAX: (931) 528-6523	E-MAIL: CLAIMS@TENCO.COM WEB: WWW.TENCO.COM
	8245 TOURNAMENT DR STE 250 MEMPHIS, TN 38125	PHONE: (901) 748-0090 FAX: (901) 748-0092	E-MAIL: CLAIMS@TENCO.COM WEB: WWW.TENCO.COM
	PO BOX 31313 CLARKSVILLE, TN 37040	PHONE: (931) 647-3593	E-MAIL: CLAIMS@TENCO.COM WEB: WWW.TENCO.COM

TENNESSEE FARM BUREAU — *SEE ALSO TENNESSEE FARMERS INSURANCE CO*

TENNESSEE FARMERS INSURANCE CO — *TENNESSEE FARM BUREAU*

TENNESSEE	147 BEARCREEK PIKE COLUMBIA, TN 38401-2266 PO BOX 307 COLUMBIA, TN 38402	PHONE: (931) 388-7872 FAX: (931) 381-7571	WEB: WWW.TENNESSEEFARMERS.COM

TEXAS HEALTH CARE — *SEE ALSO TARRANT HEALTH SERVICES*

TEXAS SPECIAL CLAIMS CENTER — *SEE ALSO FARMERS INSURANCE*

TEXAS WORKERS' COMPENSATION COMMISSION

TEXAS	3001 N CAMERON ST VICTORIA, TX 77901-3931	PHONE: (512) 804-4000 FAX: (512) 804-4101 IN-STATE: (800) 252-7031	E-MAIL: CUSTOM.RELATIONS@TWCC.STATE.TX.US WEB: WWW.TDI.STATE.TX.US

THE HARTFORD INSURANCE CO

NATIONAL	NORTHERN CALIFORNIA REGIONAL OFFICE 12009 FOUNDATION PL RANCHO CORDOVA, CA 95670-4533 PO BOX 15277 SACRAMENTO, CA 95851	PHONE: (916) 294-1000 FAX: (916) 294-1200	WEB: WWW.THEHARTFORD.COM

THE HEALTH PLAN — *HOMETOWN INSURANCE GROUP, INC.*

OHIO	100 LILLIAN GISH BLVD MASSILLON, OH 44647 PO BOX 4816 MASILLON, OH 44648	PHONE: (330) 834-2200 FAX: (330) 837-6869 IN-STATE: (877) 236-2289	WEB: WWW.HEALTHPLAN.ORG

THOMAS M. MURPHY & ASSOCIATES, INC — *MANAGING AGENCY GROUP*

NATIONAL	1 ENTERPRISE DR STE 210 SHELTON, CT 06484	PHONE: (203) 924-2994 FAX: (203) 924-2644 TOLL FREE: (800) 243-2534	WEB: WWW.TMMANDA.COM

THREE RIVERS BENEFIT CORP

NATIONAL	518 8TH ST SIOUX CITY, IA 51104 PO BOX 3440 SIOUX CITY, IA 51102-3440	PHONE: (712) 258-1525 FAX: (712) 255-3521 TOLL FREE: (800) 798-8115	E-MAIL: TRBCLAIMS@CABLEONE.NET WEB: WWW.THREERIVERSBENEFIT.COM

THRIVENT FINANCIAL FOR LUTHERANS

NATIONAL	4321 N BALLARD RD APPLETON, WI 54919-0001	PHONE: (920) 628-5721 FAX: (920) 628-4757 TOLL FREE: (800) 847-4336	E-MAIL: MAIL@THRIVENT.COM WEB: WWW.THRIVENT.COM
	625 4TH AVE S MINNEAPOLIS, MN 55415-1624	PHONE: (800) 847-4836 FAX: (920) 628-2806 TOLL FREE: (800) 847-4836 IN-STATE: (800) 847-4836	E-MAIL: MAIL@THRIVENT.COM WEB: WWW.THRIVENT.COM

TIAA CREF

NATIONAL	730 3RD AVE 26TH FL NEW YORK, NY 10017-3206	PHONE: (212) 916-5800 FAX: (800) 914-8922 TOLL FREE: (800) 223-1200	WEB: WWW.TIAA-CREF.ORG

TIC INTERNATIONAL CORP

ILLINOIS *INDIANA* *MICHIGAN*	6525 CENTURION DR LANSING, MI 48917	PHONE: (517) 321-7502 FAX: (517) 321-7508	WEB: WWW.TICI.COM
	11590 N MERIDIAN STE 600 CARMEL, IN 46032-4529	PHONE: (317) 580-8656 FAX: (317) 580-8678 IN-STATE: (800) 321-3856	E-MAIL: TIC@TICI.COM WEB: WWW.TICI.COM

TITAN INSURANCE CO

ARIZONA
INDIANA
MICHIGAN
NEW MEXICO
TEXAS

	901 WILSHIRE DR STE 550 TROY, MI 48004 PO BOX 7027 TROY, MI 48007-7024	PHONE: (248) 244-9770 FAX: (248) 244-6103 TOLL FREE: (800) 347-7930	

TOA REINSURANCE COMPANY OF AMERICA

NATIONAL	177 MADISON AVE MORRISTOWN, NJ 07962-1930 PO BOX 1930 MORRISTOWN, NJ 07962-1930	PHONE: (973) 898-9480 FAX: (973) 898-9495	E-MAIL: INFO@TOARE.COM WEB: WWW.TOARE.COM

TOPA INSURANCE CO

NATIONAL	1800 AVE OF THE STARS STE 1200 LOS ANGELES, CA 90067-0810 PO BOX 67810 LOS ANGELES, CA 90067-0810	PHONE: (310) 201-0451 FAX: (310) 286-7495 TOLL FREE: (877) 353-8672 IN-STATE: (800) 949-6505	WEB: WWW.TOPAINS.COM

TOTAL BENEFIT SERVICES

NATIONAL	2809 CENTRAL ST EVANSTON, IL 60201	PHONE: (847) 853-8800 FAX: (847) 853-8209	E-MAIL: TBS@TOTALBENEFITSERVICES.COM WEB: WWW.TOTALBENEFITSERVICES.COM

TOTAL DENTAL ADMINISTRATOR OF UTAH

CALIFORNIA	969 E MURRAY HOLLADAY RD #4E SALT LAKE CITY, UT 84117	PHONE: (801) 268-9740 FAX: (801) 268-9873 TOLL FREE: (800) 880-3536	WEB: WWW.TOTALDENTALADMIN.COM

TOTAL HEALTH CARE, INC

MICHIGAN	3011 W GRAND BLVD STE 1600 DETROIT, MI 48202	PHONE: (313) 871-2000 FAX: (313) 871-6400 IN-STATE: (800) 826-2862	E-MAIL: THE@THC-ONLINE.COM WEB: WWW.TOTALHEALTHCAREONLINE.COM

TOTAL HEALTH CHOICE

FLORIDA	8701 SW 137TH AVE STE 200 MIAMI, FL 33183 PO BOX 11626 ALBANY, NY 12211-9998	PHONE: (305) 408-5700 FAX: (305) 408-5861 TOLL FREE: (800) 887-6888	WEB: WWW.THC-ONLINE.COM

TOWER LIFE INSURANCE CO

NATIONAL	TOWER LIFE BLDG 310 S ST MARY ST STE 500 SAN ANTONIO, TX 78205-3164	PHONE: (210) 554-4400 FAX: (210) 554-4401 TOLL FREE: (800) 880-4576	WEB: WWW.TOWERLIFE.COM

TR PAUL, INC

NATIONAL	14 COMMERCE RD NEWTOWN, CT 06470-1607 PO BOX 5508 NEWTOWN, CT 06470-5508	PHONE: (203) 426-8161 FAX: (203) 270-0927 TOLL FREE: (800) 678-8161	E-MAIL: CUSTSER@TRPAUL.COM WEB: WWW.TRPAUL.COM

TRANS AMERICA WORKSITE MARKETING

NATIONAL	1400 CENTERVILLE DR LITTLE ROCK, AR 72211 PO BOX 8063 LITTLE ROCK, AR 72203-8063	PHONE: (501) 372-5550 FAX: (501) 227-1651 TOLL FREE: (800) 322-0426	

TRANS HEALTH — *FUNDAMENTAL HEALTH*

NATIONAL	910 RIDGEBROOK RD SPARKS, MD 21152	FAX: (505) 242-7114 TOLL FREE: (800) 454-5909	WEB: WWW.THICARE.COM

TRANS-NATIONAL LIFE INSURANCE CO

TEXAS	1535 W LOOP S STE 405 HOUSTON, TX 77027-9087	PHONE: (713) 622-1080 FAX: (713) 622-4060	

TRANSAMERICA ASSURANCE CO — *AEGON*

NATIONAL	PO BOX 512101 LOS ANGELES, CA 90099-4008	PHONE: (213) 742-3558 FAX: (213) 741-6623	WEB: WWW.TRRANSAMERICA.COM
	1100 WALNUT ST KANSAS CITY, MO 64106	PHONE: (816) 855-5000 TOLL FREE: (800) 852-4678	WEB: WWW.TRANSAMERICA.COM OR WWW.MYTRANSAMERICA.COM

TRAVELERS INSURANCE — *ST PAUL TRAVELERS*

ALABAMA	CALLER SERVICE #1818 ALPHARETTA, GA 30023-1818	FAX: (866) 680-3951 TOLL FREE: (800) 238-6214	WEB: WWW.TRAVELERS.COM OR WWW.STPAULTRAVELERS.COM
AMERICAN SAMOA	PO BOX 6890 PORTLAND, OR 97228-6890	FAX: (866) 291-4268 TOLL FREE: (800) 898-6883	WEB: WWW.TRAVELERS.COM
ARIZONA	PO BOX 29047 PHOENIX, AZ 85038-9047	FAX: (602) 861-8682 TOLL FREE: (800) 447-0618	WEB: WWW.TRAVELERS.COM
ARKANSAS	PO BOX 660456 DALLAS, TX 75266-0456	PHONE: (210) 527-2700 FAX: (877) 786-5577 TOLL FREE: (800) 238-6208	WEB: WWW.TRAVELERS.COM OR WWW.STPAULTRAVELERS.COM
CALIFORNIA	PO BOX 13089 SACRAMENTO, CA 95813-4089	FAX: (877) 749-0077 TOLL FREE: (800) 727-3995	WEB: WWW.TRAVELERS.COM
	205 LENNON LN WALNUT CREEK, CA 94596 PO BOX 8112 WALNUT CREEK, CA 94596-8112	PHONE: (925) 945-4000 FAX: (877) 801-9679 TOLL FREE: (800) 842-7354	WEB: WWW.TRAVELERS.COM
	21688 GATEWAY CENTER DR DIAMOND BAR, CA 91765-8511 PO BOX 6510 DIAMOND BAR, CA 91765-8510	PHONE: (909) 612-3000 FAX: (877) 801-9677 TOLL FREE: (800) 258-3710	WEB: WWW.TRAVELERS.COM

CANADA		60 LAKEFRONT BLVD 2ND FL BUFFALO, NY 14202-4396 PO BOX 4614 BUFFALO, NY 14240-4614	PHONE: (716) 855-5055 FAX: (716) 855-5196 TOLL FREE: (800) 662-2310 IN-STATE: (800) 753-0381	WEB: WWW.TRAVELERS.COM OR WWW.STPAULTRAVELERS.COM
COLORADO		7600 E ORCHARD RD STE 200 N GREENWOOD VILLAGE, CO 80111 PO BOX 173762 DENVER, CO 80217-3762	PHONE: (800) 227-1538 FAX: (877) 801-9674 TOLL FREE: (800) 227-1538	WEB: WWW.TRAVELERS.COM
CONNECTICUT *DELAWARE*		PO BOX 5008 HARTFORD, CT 06102-5008	PHONE: (860) 954-6936 FAX: (877) 786-5573 TOLL FREE: (877) 828-4110	WEB: WWW.STPAULTRAVELERS.COM
DISTRICT OF COLUMBIA		14048 PARK EAST CIR CHANTILLY, VA 20151-2225 PO BOX 10892 CHANTILLY, VA 20153-0892	PHONE: (703) 818-6124 FAX: (703) 222-3374 TOLL FREE: (800) 368-3562	WEB: WWW.TRAVELERS.COM OR WWW.STPAULTRAVELERS.COM
FLORIDA		2420 LAKEMONT AVE 100 ORLANDO, FL 32804 PO BOX 715 ORLANDO, FL 32802-0715	FAX: (877) 266-1419 TOLL FREE: (800) 842-6771	WEB: WWW.TRAVELERS.COM OR WWW.STPAULTRAVELERS.COM
GEORGIA		CALLER SERVICE #1818 ALPHARETTA, GA 30023-1818	FAX: (866) 680-3951 TOLL FREE: (800) 238-6214	WEB: WWW.TRAVELERS.COM OR WWW.STPAULTRAVELERS.COM
GUAM		PO BOX 6890 PORTLAND, OR 97228-6890	FAX: (866) 291-4268 TOLL FREE: (800) 898-6883	WEB: WWW.TRAVELERS.COM
HAWAII		220 S KINGS ST STE 1100 HONOLULU, HI 96813-4542 PO BOX 1059 HONOLULU, HI 96808-1059	PHONE: (808) 540-3816 FAX: (808) 540-3892 TOLL FREE: (888) 819-8728	WEB: WWW.TRAVELERS.COM
IDAHO		PO BOX 7427 BOISE, ID 83707-1427	PHONE: (208) 388-0277 FAX: (208) 388-1905	WEB: WWW.TRAVELERS.COM
ILLINOIS		215 SHUMAN BLVD NAPERVILLE, IL 60563-8458 PO BOX 3204 NAPERVILLE, IL 60566-3204	FAX: (877) 795-9975 TOLL FREE: (800) 842-6172 IN-STATE: (800) 626-3548	WEB: WWW.TRAVELERS.COM
IOWA		7101 VISTA DR WEST DES MOINES, IA 50266-9313 PO BOX 9191 DES MOINES, IA 50306-9191	PHONE: (515) 221-3600 FAX: (877) 749-0078 TOLL FREE: (800) 448-2249	WEB: WWW.TRAVELERS.COM
KANSAS		7600 COLLEGE BLVD OVERLAND PARK, KS 66210-1853 PO BOX 3928 OVERLAND PARK, KS 66201-1328	FAX: (877) 389-4686 TOLL FREE: (800) 255-5072	WEB: WWW.TRAVELERS.COM
LOUISIANA		PO BOX 61124 NEW ORLEANS, LA 70161-1124	PHONE: (504) 832-7300 FAX: (877) 801-9685 TOLL FREE: (800) 842-6440	WEB: WWW.STPAULTRAVELERS.COM
MAINE		PO BOX 9511 MANCHESTER, NH 03108-9923	FAX: (603) 471-6545 TOLL FREE: (800) 842-1495	WEB: WWW.TRAVELERS.COM OR WWW.STPAULTRAVELERS.COM
MARYLAND		PO BOX 17158 BALTIMORE, MD 21297-1158	FAX: (443) 353-1116 TOLL FREE: (800) 842-0091	WEB: WWW.TRAVELERS.COM
MASSACHUSETTS		44 BEDFORD ST MIDDLEBORO, MA 02346-1046 PO BOX 1450 MIDDLEBORO, MA 02344-1450	PHONE: (800) 422-3340 FAX: (877) 786-5584	WEB: WWW.TRAVELERS.COM OR WWW.STPAULTRAVELERS.COM
MICHIGAN		26555 EVERGREEN RD STE 1410 SOUTHFIELD, MI 48076-4206	FAX: (877) 749-9980 TOLL FREE: (800) 932-7149	WEB: WWW.STPAULTRAVELERS.COM
MINNESOTA		385 WASHINGTON ST ST PAUL, MN 55102 PO BOX 64907 MINNEAPOLIS, MN 55164	FAX: (877) 389-4682 OR (877) 288-2793 TOLL FREE: (800) 842-3073	WEB: WWW.TRAVELERS.COM

T

MISSISSIPPI	PO BOX 61124 NEW ORLEANS, LA 70161-1124	PHONE: (504) 832-7300 FAX: (877) 801-9685 TOLL FREE: (800) 842-6440	WEB: WWW.STPAULTRAVELERS.COM
	9020 OVERLOOK BLVD STE 140 BRENTWOOD, TN 37024 PO BOX 792 BRENTWOOD, TN 37024-0792	PHONE: (615) 372-7700 FAX: (615) 372-7800 OR (877) 786-5582 TOLL FREE: (800) 342-4064	WEB: WWW.STPAULTRAVELERS.COM
MISSOURI	PO BOX 66852 ST LOUIS, MO 63166-6852	FAX: (866) 538-6708 OR (866) 538-6707 TOLL FREE: (800) 932-7147	WEB: WWW.TRAVELERS.COM
	7600 COLLEGE BLVD OVERLAND PARK, KS 66210-1853 PO BOX 3928 OVERLAND PARK, KS 66201-1328	FAX: (877) 389-4686 TOLL FREE: (800) 255-5072	WEB: WWW.TRAVELERS.COM
MONTANA	PO BOX 389 GREAT FALLS, MT 59403	FAX: (406) 452-9694 TOLL FREE: (866) 703-0547	WEB: WWW.TRAVELERS.COM
NEBRASKA	7101 VISTA DR WEST DES MOINES, IA 50266-9313 PO BOX 9191 DES MOINES, IA 50306-9191	PHONE: (515) 221-3600 FAX: (877) 749-0078 TOLL FREE: (800) 448-2249	WEB: WWW.TRAVELERS.COM
	7600 COLLEGE BLVD OVERLAND PARK, KS 66210-1853 PO BOX 3928 OVERLAND PARK, KS 66201-1328	FAX: (877) 389-4686 TOLL FREE: (800) 255-5072	WEB: WWW.TRAVELERS.COM
NEVADA	1850 E FLAMINGO RD STE 202 LAS VEGAS, NV 89119-5111	FAX: (702) 862-4858 TOLL FREE: (877) 250-1683	WEB: WWW.TRAVELERS.COM
NEW HAMPSHIRE	PO BOX 9511 MANCHESTER, NH 03108-9923	FAX: (603) 471-6545 TOLL FREE: (800) 842-1495	WEB: WWW.TRAVELERS.COM OR WWW.STPAULTRAVELERS.COM
NEW JERSEY	PO BOX 9093 MELVILLE, NY 11747	PHONE: (631) 577-7265 FAX: (866) 889-8376 TOLL FREE: (800) 987-4735	WEB: WWW.TRAVELERS.COM
NEW MEXICO	PO BOX 29047 PHOENIX, AZ 85038-9047	FAX: (602) 861-8682 TOLL FREE: (800) 447-0618	WEB: WWW.TRAVELERS.COM
	PO BOX 20819 ALBUQUERQUE, NM 87154-0819	PHONE: (505) 889-5200 FAX: (505) 889-5209 TOLL FREE: (800) 990-7718	WEB: WWW.TRAVELERS.COM
NEW YORK	60 LAKEFRONT BLVD 2ND FL BUFFALO, NY 14202-4396 PO BOX 4614 BUFFALO, NY 14240-4614	PHONE: (716) 855-5055 FAX: (716) 855-5196 TOLL FREE: (800) 662-2310 IN-STATE: (800) 753-0381	WEB: WWW.TRAVELERS.COM OR WWW.STPAULTRAVELERS.COM
	80 WOLF RD ALBANY, NY 12205-2688 PO BOX 466 ALBANY, NY 12201-0466	PHONE: (800) 832-5329 FAX: (877) 784-5329 TOLL FREE: (800) 223-4820	WEB: WWW.TRAVELERS.COM OR WWW.STPAULTRAVELERS.COM
	PO BOX 9093 MELVILLE, NY 11747	PHONE: (631) 577-7265 FAX: (866) 889-8376 TOLL FREE: (800) 987-4735	WEB: WWW.TRAVELERS.COM
NORTH CAROLINA	11440 CARMEL COMMONS BLVD 3RD FL CHARLOTTE, NC 28226-5303 PO BOX 473502 CHARLOTTE, NC 28247-3502	PHONE: (704) 544-3500 FAX: (877) 389-4687 TOLL FREE: (800) 759-5194	WEB: WWW.TRAVELERS.COM OR WWW.STPAULTRAVELERS.COM
NORTH DAKOTA	385 WASHINGTON ST ST PAUL, MN 55102 PO BOX 64907 MINNEAPOLIS, MN 55164	FAX: (877) 389-4682 OR (877) 288-2793 TOLL FREE: (800) 842-3073	WEB: WWW.TRAVELERS.COM
OHIO	PO BOX 8014 NORTH OLMSTED, OH 44070-8014	FAX: (440) 716-2946 TOLL FREE: (800) 321-6833	WEB: WWW.TRAVELERS.COM

OKLAHOMA		PO BOX 660456 DALLAS, TX 75266-0456	PHONE: (210) 527-2700 FAX: (877) 786-5577 TOLL FREE: (800) 238-6208	WEB: WWW.TRAVELERS.COM OR WWW.STPAULTRAVELERS.COM
OREGON		PO BOX 6890 PORTLAND, OR 97228-6890	FAX: (866) 291-4268 TOLL FREE: (800) 898-6883	WEB: WWW.TRAVELERS.COM
PENNSYLVANIA		PO BOX 13933 READING, PA 19612-3933	PHONE: (610) 371-3800 FAX: (610) 371-3860 TOLL FREE: (800) 842-9897	WEB: WWW.TRAVELERS.COM
		112 WASHINGTON PLACE 700 TWO CHATHAM CTR PITTSBURGH, PA 15219-3498 PO BOX 1507 PITTSBURGH, PA 15230-1507	PHONE: (800) 238-6285 FAX: (412) 471-0329	WEB: WWW.TRAVELERS.COM
PUERTO RICO		2420 LAKEMONT AVE 100 ORLANDO, FL 32804 PO BOX 715 ORLANDO, FL 32802-0715	FAX: (877) 266-1419 TOLL FREE: (800) 842-6771	WEB: WWW.TRAVELERS.COM OR WWW.STPAULTRAVELERS.COM
RHODE ISLAND		44 BEDFORD ST MIDDLEBORO, MA 02346-1046 PO BOX 1450 MIDDLEBORO, MA 02344-1450	PHONE: (800) 422-3340 FAX: (877) 786-5584	WEB: WWW.TRAVELERS.COM OR WWW.STPAULTRAVELERS.COM
SOUTH CAROLINA		11440 CARMEL COMMONS BLVD 3RD FL CHARLOTTE, NC 28226-5303 PO BOX 473502 CHARLOTTE, NC 28247-3502	PHONE: (704) 544-3500 FAX: (877) 389-4687 TOLL FREE: (800) 759-6194	WEB: WWW.TRAVELERS.COM OR WWW.STPAULTRAVELERS.COM
SOUTH DAKOTA		385 WASHINGTON ST ST PAUL, MN 55102 PO BOX 64907 MINNEAPOLIS, MN 55164	FAX: (877) 389-4682 OR (877) 288-2793 TOLL FREE: (800) 842-3073	WEB: WWW.TRAVELERS.COM
TENNESSEE		9020 OVERLOOK BLVD STE 140 BRENTWOOD, TN 37024 PO BOX 792 BRENTWOOD, TN 37024-0792	PHONE: (615) 372-7700 FAX: (615) 372-7800 OR (877) 786-5582 TOLL FREE: (800) 342-4064	WEB: WWW.STPAULTRAVELERS.COM
TEXAS		PO BOX 660456 DALLAS, TX 75266-0456	PHONE: (210) 527-2700 FAX: (877) 786-5577 TOLL FREE: (800) 238-6208	WEB: WWW.TRAVELERS.COM OR WWW.STPAULTRAVELERS.COM
		10800 RICHMOND AVE HOUSTON, TX 77042-4794 PO BOX 42927 HOUSTON, TX 77242-2927	PHONE: (713) 787-4000 FAX: (877) 749-0075 TOLL FREE: (800) 235-3610	WEB: WWW.TRAVELERS.COM
UTAH		7600 E ORCHARD RD STE 200 N GREENWOOD VILLAGE, CO 80111 PO BOX 173762 DENVER, CO 80217-3762	PHONE: (800) 227-1538 FAX: (877) 801-9674 TOLL FREE: (800) 227-1538	WEB: WWW.TRAVELERS.COM
VERMONT		PO BOX 9511 MANCHESTER, NH 03108-9923	FAX: (603) 471-6545 TOLL FREE: (800) 842-1495	WEB: WWW.TRAVELERS.COM OR WWW.STPAULTRAVELERS.COM
VIRGIN ISLANDS		2420 LAKEMONT AVE 100 ORLANDO, FL 32804 PO BOX 715 ORLANDO, FL 32802-0715	FAX: (877) 266-1419 TOLL FREE: (800) 842-6771	WEB: WWW.TRAVELERS.COM OR WWW.STPAULTRAVELERS.COM
VIRGINIA		14048 PARK EAST CIR CHANTILLY, VA 20151-2225 PO BOX 10892 CHANTILLY, VA 20153-0892	PHONE: (703) 818-6124 FAX: (703) 222-3374 TOLL FREE: (800) 368-3562	WEB: WWW.TRAVELERS.COM OR WWW.STPAULTRAVELERS.COM
		300 ARBORETUM PL RICHMOND, VA 23236-3480 PO BOX 85554 RICHMOND, VA 23285-5554	PHONE: (804) 330-6360 FAX: (800) 842-7944 TOLL FREE: (800) 635-4543	WEB: WWW.TRAVELERS.COM OR WWW.STPAULTRAVELERS.COM

T

WASHINGTON	PO BOX 6890 PORTLAND, OR 97228-6890	FAX: (866) 291-4268 TOLL FREE: (800) 898-6883	WEB: WWW.TRAVELERS.COM
WEST VIRGINIA	112 WASHINGTON PLACE 700 TWO CHATHAM CTR PITTSBURGH, PA 15219-3498 PO BOX 1507 PITTSBURGH, PA 15230-1507	PHONE: (800) 238-6285 FAX: (412) 471-0329	WEB: WWW.TRAVELERS.COM
WISCONSIN	BROOKFIELD CLAIMS SERVICE CENTER 445 S MOORELAND RD BROOKFIELD, WI 53005-4254 PO BOX 2940 MILWAUKEE, WI 53201-2940	PHONE: (262) 797-3104 FAX: (877) 389-4688 TOLL FREE: (800) 225-4144	WEB: WWW.STPAULTRAVELERS.COM
WYOMING	PO BOX 6890 PORTLAND, OR 97228-6890	FAX: (866) 291-4268 TOLL FREE: (800) 898-6883	WEB: WWW.TRAVELERS.COM

TRAVELERS INSURANCE COMPANIES — *SEE ALSO NORTHLAND INSURANCE CO*

TRAVELERS PROTECTIVE ASSOCIATION OF AMERICA

NATIONAL	3755 LINDELL BLVD ST LOUIS, MO 63108-3411	PHONE: (314) 371-0533 FAX: (314) 371-0537	E-MAIL: SUPPORT@TPAHQ.ORG WEB: WWW.TPAHQ.ORG

TRI STAR RISK MANAGEMENT

CALIFORNIA	125 TECHNOLOGY RD IRVINE, CA 92618-2402 PO BOX 19775 IRVINE, CA 92623-9775	PHONE: (949) 753-5900 FAX: (949) 753-5934 TOLL FREE: (800) 782-5888	

TRI-STATE INSURANCE CO OF MINNESOTA — *SEE ALSO CONTINENTAL WESTERN GROUP*

TRI-TEC EMPLOYEE BENEFITS, INC

NATIONAL	2184 COMMONS PKY OKEMOS, MI 48864 PO BOX 804 OKEMOS, MI 48805-0804	PHONE: (517) 349-8980 FAX: (517) 349-7615 TOLL FREE: (800) 782-0947	E-MAIL: TRI-TEC@TRI-TECEMP.COM WEB: WWW.TRI-TECEMP.COM

TRICARE

NATIONAL	CORPORATE OFFICE SKYLINE 5 STE 810 5111 LEESBURG PIKE FALLS CHURCH , VA 22041-3206	TOLL FREE: (877) 874-2273	E-MAIL: QUESTIONS@TMA.OSD.MIL WEB: WWW.TRICARE.OSD.MIL
ALABAMA	SOUTH REGION PO BOX 7031 CAMDEN, SC 29020-7031	TOLL FREE: (800) 444-5445	WEB: WWW.TRICARE.OSD.MIL
ALASKA *ARIZONA*	WEST REGION PO BOX 77028 MADISON, WI 53707-7028	PHONE: (888) 874-9378	WEB: WWW.TRIWEST.COM
ARKANSAS	SOUTH REGION PO BOX 7031 CAMDEN, SC 29020-7031	TOLL FREE: (800) 444-5445	WEB: WWW.TRICARE.OSD.MIL

T

CALIFORNIA *COLORADO*	WEST REGION PO BOX 77028 MADISON, WI 53707-7028	PHONE: (888) 874-9378	WEB: WWW.TRIWEST.COM
CONNECTICUT *DELAWARE* *DISTRICT OF COLUMBIA*	NORTH REGION PO BOX 870140 SURFSIDE BEACH, SC 29587-9740	PHONE: (843) 665-7822 TOLL FREE: (877) 874-2273	WEB: WWW.HEALTHNETFEDERALSERVICES.COM
FLORIDA *GEORGIA*	SOUTH REGION PO BOX 7031 CAMDEN, SC 29020-7031	TOLL FREE: (800) 444-5445	WEB: WWW.TRICARE.OSD.MIL
HAWAII *IDAHO*	WEST REGION PO BOX 77028 MADISON, WI 53707-7028	PHONE: (888) 874-9378	WEB: WWW.TRIWEST.COM
ILLINOIS *INDIANA*	NORTH REGION PO BOX 870140 SURFSIDE BEACH, SC 29587-9740	PHONE: (843) 665-7822 TOLL FREE: (877) 874-2273	WEB: WWW.HEALTHNETFEDERALSERVICES.COM
IOWA	WEST REGION PO BOX 77028 MADISON, WI 53707-7028	PHONE: (888) 874-9378	WEB: WWW.TRIWEST.COM
	NORTH REGION PO BOX 870140 SURFSIDE BEACH, SC 29587-9740	PHONE: (843) 665-7822 TOLL FREE: (877) 874-2273	WEB: WWW.HEALTHNETFEDERALSERVICES.COM
KANSAS	WEST REGION PO BOX 77028 MADISON, WI 53707-7028	PHONE: (888) 874-9378	WEB: WWW.TRIWEST.COM
KENTUCKY	NORTH REGION PO BOX 870140 SURFSIDE BEACH, SC 29587-9740	PHONE: (843) 665-7822 TOLL FREE: (877) 874-2273	WEB: WWW.HEALTHNETFEDERALSERVICES.COM
LOUISIANA	SOUTH REGION PO BOX 7031 CAMDEN, SC 29020-7031	TOLL FREE: (800) 444-5445	WEB: WWW.TRICARE.OSD.MIL
MAINE *MARYLAND* *MASSACHUSETTS* *MICHIGAN*	NORTH REGION PO BOX 870140 SURFSIDE BEACH, SC 29587-9740	PHONE: (843) 665-7822 TOLL FREE: (877) 874-2273	WEB: WWW.HEALTHNETFEDERALSERVICES.COM

MINNESOTA	WEST REGION PO BOX 77028 MADISON, WI 53707-7028	PHONE: (888) 874-9378	WEB: WWW.TRIWEST.COM
MISSISSIPPI	SOUTH REGION PO BOX 7031 CAMDEN, SC 29020-7031	TOLL FREE: (800) 444-5445	WEB: WWW.TRICARE.OSD.MIL
MISSOURI	WEST REGION PO BOX 77028 MADISON, WI 53707-7028	PHONE: (888) 874-9378	WEB: WWW.TRIWEST.COM
	NORTH REGION PO BOX 870140 SURFSIDE BEACH, SC 29587-9740	PHONE: (843) 665-7822 TOLL FREE: (877) 874-2273	WEB: WWW.HEALTHNETFEDERALSERVICES.COM
MONTANA *NEBRASKA* *NEVADA*	WEST REGION PO BOX 77028 MADISON, WI 53707-7028	PHONE: (888) 874-9378	WEB: WWW.TRIWEST.COM
NEW HAMPSHIRE *NEW JERSEY*	NORTH REGION PO BOX 870140 SURFSIDE BEACH, SC 29587-9740	PHONE: (843) 665-7822 TOLL FREE: (877) 874-2273	WEB: WWW.HEALTHNETFEDERALSERVICES.COM
NEW MEXICO	WEST REGION PO BOX 77028 MADISON, WI 53707-7028	PHONE: (888) 874-9378	WEB: WWW.TRIWEST.COM
NEW YORK *NORTH CAROLINA*	NORTH REGION PO BOX 870140 SURFSIDE BEACH, SC 29587-9740	PHONE: (843) 665-7822 TOLL FREE: (877) 874-2273	WEB: WWW.HEALTHNETFEDERALSERVICES.COM
NORTH DAKOTA	WEST REGION PO BOX 77028 MADISON, WI 53707-7028	PHONE: (888) 874-9378	WEB: WWW.TRIWEST.COM
OHIO	NORTH REGION PO BOX 870140 SURFSIDE BEACH, SC 29587-9740	PHONE: (843) 665-7822 TOLL FREE: (877) 874-2273	WEB: WWW.HEALTHNETFEDERALSERVICES.COM
OKLAHOMA	SOUTH REGION PO BOX 7031 CAMDEN, SC 29020-7031	TOLL FREE: (800) 444-5445	WEB: WWW.TRICARE.OSD.MIL

T

OREGON	WEST REGION PO BOX 77028 MADISON, WI 53707-7028	PHONE: (888) 874-9378	WEB: WWW.TRIWEST.COM
PENNSYLVANIA *RHODE ISLAND*	NORTH REGION PO BOX 870140 SURFSIDE BEACH, SC 29587-9740	PHONE: (843) 665-7822 TOLL FREE: (877) 874-2273	WEB: WWW.HEALTHNETFEDERALSERVICES.COM
SOUTH CAROLINA	SOUTH REGION PO BOX 7031 CAMDEN, SC 29020-7031	TOLL FREE: (800) 444-5445	WEB: WWW.TRICARE.OSD.MIL
SOUTH DAKOTA	WEST REGION PO BOX 77028 MADISON, WI 53707-7028	PHONE: (888) 874-9378	WEB: WWW.TRIWEST.COM
TENNESSEE	SOUTH REGION PO BOX 7031 CAMDEN, SC 29020-7031	TOLL FREE: (800) 444-5445	WEB: WWW.TRICARE.OSD.MIL
	NORTH REGION PO BOX 870140 SURFSIDE BEACH, SC 29587-9740	PHONE: (843) 665-7822 TOLL FREE: (877) 874-2273	WEB: WWW.HEALTHNETFEDERALSERVICES.COM
TEXAS	SOUTH REGION PO BOX 7031 CAMDEN, SC 29020-7031	TOLL FREE: (800) 444-5445	WEB: WWW.TRICARE.OSD.MIL
TEXAS *UTAH*	WEST REGION PO BOX 77028 MADISON, WI 53707-7028	PHONE: (888) 874-9378	WEB: WWW.TRIWEST.COM
VERMONT *VIRGINIA*	NORTH REGION PO BOX 870140 SURFSIDE BEACH, SC 29587-9740	PHONE: (843) 665-7822 TOLL FREE: (877) 874-2273	WEB: WWW.HEALTHNETFEDERALSERVICES.COM
WASHINGTON	WEST REGION PO BOX 77028 MADISON, WI 53707-7028	PHONE: (888) 874-9378	WEB: WWW.TRIWEST.COM
WEST VIRGINIA *WISCONSIN*	NORTH REGION PO BOX 870140 SURFSIDE BEACH, SC 29587-9740	PHONE: (843) 665-7822 TOLL FREE: (877) 874-2273	WEB: WWW.HEALTHNETFEDERALSERVICES.COM

WYOMING	WEST REGION PO BOX 77028 MADISON, WI 53707-7028	PHONE: (888) 874-9378	WEB: WWW.TRIWEST.COM

TRICARE FOR LIFE

NATIONAL	TRICARE FOR LIFE PO BOX 7890 MADISON, WI 53707-7890	PHONE: (866) 773-0404	WEB: WWW.TRICARE4U.COM

TRIPLE-S, INC — *SEE ALSO BLUE CROSS BLUE SHIELD*

TRIUMPHE CASUALTY CO — *VFS INSURANCE GROUP*

NATIONAL	7025 ALBERT PICK RD STE 105 GREENSBORO, NC 27409 PO BOX 26131 GREENSBORO, NC 27402	PHONE: (336) 931-3774 FAX: (336) 931-3773 TOLL FREE: (888) 601-3871	WEB: WWW.TRIUMPHECASUALTY.COM

TRUCK INSURANCE EXCHANGE — *SEE ALSO FARMERS INSURANCE EXCHANGE*

TRUSTEED PLANS SERVICE CORP

NATIONAL	6901 6TH AVE TACOMA, WA 98406-1705 PO BOX 1894 TACOMA, WA 98401-1894	PHONE: (253) 564-5850 FAX: (253) 564-5881 TOLL FREE: (800) 426-9786	

TRUSTMARK INSURANCE

NATIONAL	400 FIELD DR LAKE FOREST, IL 60045-2586	PHONE: (847) 615-1500 FAX: (847) 615-3910 TOLL FREE: (800) 877-9077 IN-STATE: (800) 877-9077	WEB: WWW.TRUSTMARKINS.COM
	8324 S AVE BOARDMAN, OH 44512	PHONE: (330) 758-9526 FAX: (330) 758-3242 TOLL FREE: (800) 544-7312	WEB: WWW.TRUSTMARKINS.COM

TUCKER ADMINISTRATORS, INC — *TUCKER COMPANIES*

NATIONAL	3800 ARCO CORPORATE DR STE 450 CHARLOTTE, NC 28273-0001	PHONE: (704) 525-9666 FAX: (704) 525-9534	E-MAIL: TUCKER@TUCKERADMINISTRATORS.COM WEB: WWW.TUCKERADMINISTRATORS.COM

TUFTS HEALTH PLAN

MASSACHUSETTS	333 WYMAN ST WALTHAM, MA 02451-1209 PO BOX 9112 WALTHAM, MA 02454-9112	FAX: (617) 466-8583 TOLL FREE: (800) 442-0422	WEB: WWW.TUFTSHEALTHPLAN.COM

U-HAUL EMPLOYEES — *SEE ALSO OXFORD LIFE INSURANCE CO*

UA LOCAL 180 PLUMBERS, PIPEFITTERS, & SERVICE TECHNICIANS

MICHIGAN	33035 SCHOOL CRAFT RD LIVONIA, MI 48150	PHONE: (734) 432-3036 FAX: (734) 432-3013 TOLL FREE: (888) 390-7473	

U

UCARE MINNESOTA

ILLINOIS
INDIANA
IOWA
KANSAS
MICHIGAN
MINNESOTA
NEBRASKA
NORTH DAKOTA
OHIO
SOUTH DAKOTA
WISCONSIN

2000 SUMMER ST NE
MINNEAPOLIS, MN 55413
PO BOX 52
MINNEAPOLIS, MN 55440-0052
PHONE: (612) 676-6500
FAX: (612) 676-6501
TOLL FREE: (800) 203-7225
WEB: WWW.UCARE.ORG

UGS — *SEE ALSO UNIFIED GROUP SERVICES*

UHC — *SEE ALSO UNITED HEALTHCARE*

UHP HEALTHCARE

CALIFORNIA

3405 W IMPERIAL HWY
INGLEWOOD, CA 90303-2299
PHONE: (310) 671-3465
FAX: (310) 673-9176
TOLL FREE: (800) 838-8347
WEB: WWW.UHPHEALTHCARE.COM

UICI — *SEE ALSO MEGA LIFE & HEALTH*

NATIONAL

1331 W MEMORIAL RD STE 112
OKLAHOMA CITY, OK 73114
PO BOX 548801
OKLAHOMA CITY, OK 73154
PHONE: (405) 848-0179
FAX: (405) 841-8758
TOLL FREE: (800) 725-7887
WEB: WWW.UICIOKC.COM

9151 BLVD 26
NORTH RICHLAND HILLS, TX 76180
PO BOX 982017
NORTH RICHLAND HILLS, TX 76182-8017
PHONE: (800) 733-8880
FAX: (817) 255-8101
TOLL FREE: (800) 527-5504
IN-STATE: (800) 733-1110
WEB: WWW.MIDWESTLIFE.COM

ADDITIONAL COMMENTS: NATIONAL EXCEPT MAINE, NEW HAMPSHIRE, NEW YORK, SOUTH DAKOTA, VERMONT

ULLICO FAMILY OF COMPANIES — *SEE ALSO UNION LABOR LIFE INSURANCE CO*

UMA REVIEWS

NATIONAL

1400 RENAISSANCE DR STE 300
PARK RIDGE, IL 60068-1336
PHONE: (847) 390-6606
FAX: (847) 390-8622
TOLL FREE: (800) 345-8622
WEB: WWW.UMACREVIEWS.COM

UNDERWRITERS SAFETY & CLAIMS

NATIONAL

1700 EASTPOINT PKY
LOUISVILLE, KY 40223
PO BOX 23790
LOUISVILLE, KY 40223
PHONE: (502) 244-1343
FAX: (502) 244-1411
TOLL FREE: (800) 678-1536
WEB: WWW.USCKY.COM

UNICARE HEALTH PLANS OF THE MIDWEST

NATIONAL

7025 ALBERTPICK RD 5TH FL
SCHAUMBURG, IL 60168
PO BOX 4458
CHICAGO, IL 60680
TOLL FREE: (877) 864-2273
WEB: WWW.UNICARE.COM

ILLINOIS
INDIANA
NEVADA
TEXAS
VIRGINIA

225 N MICHIGAN AVE
CHICAGO, IL 60440
PO BOX 805107
CHICAGO, IL 60680-4112
PHONE: (312) 297-6000
TOLL FREE: (877) 864-2273
WEB: WWW.UNICARE.COM

U

UNICARE LIFE AND HEALTH INSURANCE

NATIONAL	233 S WACKER DR STE 3900 CHICAGO, IL 60606	PHONE: (312) 234-7000 FAX: (312) 234-8005 TOLL FREE: (877) 864-2273	
	3200 GREENFIELD RD DEARBORN, MI 48120 PO BOX 4479 DEARBORN, MI 48126	PHONE: (313) 336-5550 FAX: (313) 594-5047 TOLL FREE: (800) 843-8184	E-MAIL: UNICARE@WELLPOINT.COM WEB: WWW.UNICARE.COM
	WELLPOINT SERVICE CENTER TWO GREENWAY PLZ STE 500 HOUSTON, TX 77036 PO BOX 833933 RICHARDSON, TX 75083	PHONE: (972) 599-6000 FAX: (713) 479-4288 TOLL FREE: (800) 333-3304 IN-STATE: (888) 697-3790	WEB: WWW.UNICARE.COM
CALIFORNIA	3179 TEMPLE AVE STE 200 POMONA, CA 91768-3249 PO BOX 6007 LOS ANGELES, CA 90067-0007	PHONE: (800) 678-4465 TOLL FREE: (877) 864-2273	WEB: WWW.UNICARE.COM

UNIFIED GROUP SERVICES — *UGS*

NATIONAL	PO BOX 10 PENDLETON, IN 46064	FAX: (765) 608-6689 TOLL FREE: (800) 291-5837	WEB: WWW.UGSWEB.COM

UNIFIED LIFE INSURANCE CO

KANSAS	PO BOX 25326 OVERLAND PARK, KS 66225-5326	PHONE: (913) 685-2233 FAX: (913) 685-2204 TOLL FREE: (800) 237-4463	WEB: WWW.UNIFIEDLIFE.COM

UNIGARD INSURANCE CO — *NATIONAL MERIT INSURANCE*

WASHINGTON	3015 112TH AVE NE STE 200 BELLEVUE, WA 98004	PHONE: (888) 592-7283 FAX: (877) 292-7283	WEB: WWW.NATIONALMERIT.COM

UNIGARD INSURANCE GROUP

CALIFORNIA	2260 DOUGLAS BLVD STE 100 ROSEVILLE, CA 95661-4210 PO BOX 13430 SACRAMENTO, CA 95813-4430	PHONE: (916) 783-2930 FAX: (916) 783-7531 OR (916) 783-2948 TOLL FREE: (800) 627-6320	WEB: WWW.UNIGARD.COM
IDAHO *NEVADA* *UTAH*	10653 RIVERFRONT PKWY STE 280 SOUTH JORDAN, UT 84095-3530	PHONE: (801) 446-7841 FAX: (801) 446-7851 TOLL FREE: (800) 777-4485 IN-STATE: (800) 662-6522	WEB: WWW.UNIGARD.COM

UNION BANKERS — *CONSTITUTION LIFE INSURANCE*

NATIONAL	401 N BAYLEN ST PENSACOLA, FL 32501 PO BOX 1985 PENSACOLA, FL 32591	PHONE: (850) 432-1700 FAX: (850) 432-7733 TOLL FREE: (800) 789-6364	WEB: WWW.CHCSERVICES.COM

UNION CENTRAL INSURANCE & INVESTMENTS

NATIONAL	1876 WAYCROSS RD CINCINNATI, OH 45240 PO BOX 40888 CINCINNATI, OH 45240-9858	PHONE: (513) 595-2200 FAX: (513) 595-2559 TOLL FREE: (800) 825-1551	WEB: WWW.UNIONCENTRAL.COM

UNION FIDELITY INSURANCE CO — *GE FINANCIAL ASSURANCE*

NATIONAL	500 VIRGINIA DR FT WASHINGTON, PA 19034 PO BOX 8121 FT WASHINGTON, PA 19034	PHONE: (267) 468-3000 FAX: (267) 468-6979 TOLL FREE: (800) 626-6557 IN-STATE: (800) 205-5648	WEB: WWW.GEFN.COM

U

UNION HEALTH SERVICE, INC

ILLINOIS	1634 W POLK ST CHICAGO, IL 60612-4352	PHONE: (312) 829-4224 FAX: (312) 423-4326	WEB: WWW.UNIONHEALTH.ORG

UNION INSURANCE COMPANY

NATIONAL	11201 DOUGLAS AVE DES MOINES, IA 50322 PO BOX 1594 DES MOINES, IA 50306-1594	PHONE: (515) 278-3000 FAX: (515) 278-3458 TOLL FREE: (800) 235-2942	WEB: WWW.CWGINS.COM

UNION LABOR LIFE INSURANCE CO — *ULLICO FAMILY OF COMPANIES*

NATIONAL	1625 EYE ST NW WASHINGTON, DC 20006	PHONE: (202) 682-0900 FAX: (202) 962-8904 TOLL FREE: (800) 431-5425	WEB: WWW.ULLICO.COM

UNION NATIONAL LIFE INSURANCE CO — *SEE ALSO UNITED INSURANCE CO OF AMERICA*

LOUISIANA	PO BOX 3638 BATON ROUGE, LA 70821-3638	PHONE: (877) 710-5081 FAX: (225) 231-7474 TOLL FREE: (800) 765-0550 IN-STATE: (800) 765-0550

UNION OF POSTAL WORKERS — *SEE ALSO NATIONAL RURAL LETTER CARRIERS' ASSOCIATION*

UNION STANDARD INSURANCE CO

ARKANSAS	10810 EXECUTIVE CTR DR STE 205 LITTLE ROCK, AR 72221-4320 PO BOX 21720 LITTLE ROCK, AR 72221-1720	PHONE: (501) 954-7888 FAX: (501) 954-9888 TOLL FREE: (800) 666-2452	WEB: WWW.USIC.COM

UNION STANDARD INSURANCE GROUP

NATIONAL	122 W CARPENTER FWY STE 350 IRVING, TX 75039-2094 PO BOX 152180 IRVING, TX 75015-2180	PHONE: (972) 719-2400 FAX: (866) 256-8744 TOLL FREE: (800) 444-0049	WEB: WWW.USIC.COM

UNITED AMERICAN INSURANCE CO

NATIONAL	3700 S STONEBRIDGE MCKINNEY, TX 75070-5934 PO BOX 8080 MCKINNEY, TX 75070-8080	PHONE: (972) 529-5085 FAX: (972) 569-3688	WEB: WWW.UNITEDAMERICAN.COM

UNITED COASTAL INSURANCE CO

NATIONAL	233 MAIN ST NEW BRITAIN, CT 06050-4204 PO BOX 2350 NEW BRITAIN, CT 06050	PHONE: (860) 223-5000 FAX: (860) 229-1111	WEB: WWW.ACSTAR.COM

UNITED COMMERCIAL TRAVELERS OF AMERICA

NATIONAL	632 N PARK ST COLUMBUS, OH 43215-8619 PO BOX 159019 COLUMBUS, OH 43215-8619	PHONE: (614) 228-3276 FAX: (614) 228-0365 TOLL FREE: (800) 848-0123	WEB: WWW.UCT.ORG

UNITED EQUITABLE GROUP

ILLINOIS	9833 WOODS DR SKOKIE, IL 60077 PO BOX 1091 SKOKIE, IL 60076-8091	PHONE: (847) 583-4600 FAX: (847) 583-9011 TOLL FREE: (800) 831-8330

UNITED FARM FAMILY MUTUAL INSURANCE

INDIANA	FARM BUREAU 1104 BOYD BLVD LA PORTE, IN 46350	PHONE: (219) 326-6624 FAX: (219) 362-7622 TOLL FREE: (800) 656-9550 IN-STATE: (800) 866-1160	WEB: WWW.INFARMBUREAU.COM
	1560 W LOGANSPORT RD PERU, IN 46970	PHONE: (765) 473-5559 FAX: (765) 472-1317	WEB: WWW.INFARMBUREAU.COM
	225 S EAST ST INDIANAPOLIS, IN 46202-4058 PO BOX 1250 INDIANAPOLIS, IN 46206-1250	PHONE: (317) 692-7200 FAX: (317) 692-7185 TOLL FREE: (800) 723-3276	WEB: WWW.INFARMBUREAU.COM

UNITED FIRE & CASUALTY

ALABAMA, COLORADO, FLORIDA, ILLINOIS, INDIANA, IOWA, KANSAS, LOUISIANA, MICHIGAN, MINNESOTA, MISSISSIPPI, MISSOURI, NEBRASKA, NORTH DAKOTA, OKLAHOMA, SOUTH DAKOTA, TEXAS, UTAH, WISCONSIN, WYOMING

118 2ND AVE SE CEDAR RAPIDS, IA 52401 PO BOX 73909 CEDAR RAPIDS, IA 52407-3909	PHONE: (319) 399-5700 FAX: (319) 399-5400 TOLL FREE: (800) 343-9131	WEB: WWW.UNITEDFIREGROUP.COM

UNITED FOOD & COMMERCIAL WORKERS' TRUST FUND

NATIONAL	SOUTHERN CALIFORNIA 6425 KATELLA AVE CYPRESS, CA 90630-5246 PO BOX 6010 CYPRESS, CA 90630-0010	PHONE: (714) 220-2297 FAX: (714) 828-6573

UNITED HEALTH CARE — *SEE ALSO DENTAL BENEFIT PROVIDERS*

UNITED HEALTHCARE — *UHC*

NATIONAL	CLAIMS SERVICE CENTER PO BOX 30555 SALT LAKE CITY, UT 84130-0555	FAX: (801) 233-9580 TOLL FREE: (877) 842-3210 IN-STATE: (877) 844-4999	WEB: WWW.MYUHC.COM
	CLAIMS SERVICE CENTER PO BOX 659735 SAN ANTONIO, TX 78265-9735	PHONE: (210) 694-6850 FAX: (210) 694-6868 TOLL FREE: (800) 842-0174	WEB: WWW.MYUHC.COM
	CLAIMS SERVICE CENTER PO BOX 740800 ATLANTA, GA 30374-0800	FAX: (801) 567-5498 TOLL FREE: (877) 842-3210	WEB: WWW.MYUHC.COM
	CLAIMS SERVICE CENTER PO BOX 981502 EL PASO , TX 79998	FAX: (915) 255-6777 TOLL FREE: (877) 842-3210	WEB: WWW.MYUHC.COM
	UNITED HEALTHGROUP CORPORATE OFFICE 9900 BREN ROAD EAST MINNETONKA, MN 55343	TOLL FREE: (800) 328-5979	WEB: WWW.UNITEDHEALTHGROUP.COM OR WWW.MYUHC.COM

DELAWARE
DISTRICT OF COLUMBIA
MARYLAND
VIRGINIA
WEST VIRGINIA

800 OAK ST
FREDERICK, MD 21703

PHONE: (301) 294-5057
FAX: (301) 360-8644
TOLL FREE: (800) 544-2853

WEB: WWW.MAMSI.COM

UNITED HEALTHCARE CLAIMS DIVISION — *SEE ALSO AARP HEALTHCARE OPTIONS*

UNITED HEALTHCARE/ BRONSON HEALTH PLANS/ABA PHP — *SEE ALSO PHYSICIANS HEALTH PLAN OF SOUTHWEST MICHIGAN*

UNITED HERITAGE LIFE INSURANCE CO

ARIZONA
ARKANSAS
CALIFORNIA
COLORADO
IOWA
KANSAS
MINNESOTA
MISSOURI
MONTANA
NEBRASKA
NEVADA
SOUTH DAKOTA
TEXAS
UTAH
WASHINGTON
WYOMING

707 E UNITED HERITAGE CT
MERIDIAN, ID 83642-3527
PO BOX 7777
MERIDIAN, ID 83680-7777

PHONE: (208) 493-6100
FAX: (800) 240-9734
TOLL FREE: (800) 657-6351

E-MAIL: HERITAGE@UNITEDHERITAGE.COM
WEB: WWW.UNITEDHERITAGE.COM

UNITED INSURANCE CO OF AMERICA — *UNION NATIONAL LIFE INSURANCE CO*

ILLINOIS
LOUISIANA

ONE E WACKER DR
CHICAGO, IL 60601-4305
PO BOX 4325
BATON ROUGE, LA 70821-4325

PHONE: (312) 661-4500
FAX: (312) 424-5620
TOLL FREE: (800) 777-8467

WEB: WWW.UNITRIN.COM

UNITED MEDICAL RESOURCES, INC

NATIONAL

5151 PFEIFFER RD ML 400
CINCINNATI, OH 45242-4805
PO BOX 145804
CINCINNATI, OH 45250-5804

PHONE: (513) 619-3000
FAX: (513) 619-3010
TOLL FREE: (800) 436-3100

WEB: WWW.UMR.COM

UNITED NATIONAL GROUP — *DIAMOND STATE INSURANCE CO*

NATIONAL

THREE BALA PLZ E STE 300
BALA CYNWYD, PA 19004

PHONE: (610) 664-1500
FAX: (610) 660-8882

E-MAIL: CLAIMSINFO@UNITEDNET.COM
WEB: WWW.UNITEDNAT.COM

UNITED SECURITY LIFE AND HEALTH INSURANCE CO OF ILLINOIS

ILLINOIS

10275 W HIGGINS RD
ROSE EMOND, IL 60018

PHONE: (847) 298-1400
FAX: (847) 298-1407
TOLL FREE: (800) 875-4422

E-MAIL: INFO@USLOFIL.COM
WEB: WWW.UNITEDSECURITYLIFEANDHEALTH.COM

UNITED STATES LIFE INSURANCE CO — *AIG AMERICAN GENERAL*

NATIONAL

3600 RTE 66
NEPTUNE, NJ 07754
PO BOX 1580
NEPTUNE, NJ 07754-1581

PHONE: (732) 922-7000
FAX: (732) 922-7136
TOLL FREE: (800) 346-7692

WEB: WWW.AGAC.COM

UNITED TEACHER ASSOCIATES INSURANCE CO

NATIONAL

5508 PARKCREST DR
AUSTIN, TX 78755
PO BOX 26580
AUSTIN, TX 78755-0580

PHONE: (512) 451-2224
FAX: (888) 670-0146
TOLL FREE: (800) 880-8824

E-MAIL: CUSTOMERSERVICE@UTAIC.COM
WEB: WWW.UTAIC.COM

U

UNITED TRANSPORTATION UNION INSURANCE ASSOCIATION

NATIONAL	14600 DETROIT AVE CLEVELAND, OH 44107-4207	PHONE: (216) 228-9400 FAX: (216) 228-0411 TOLL FREE: (800) 558-8842	WEB: WWW.UTU.ORG

UNITY HEALTH INSURANCE

WISCONSIN	840 CAROLINA ST SAUK CITY, WI 53583 PO BOX 610 SAUK CITY, WI 53583	PHONE: (608) 643-249[illegible] FAX: (608) 643-2564 TOLL FREE: (800) 362-3308	E-MAIL: CUSTOMERSERVICE@UNITYHEALTH.COM WEB: WWW.UNITYHEALTH.COM

UNIVERA HEALTHCARE, INC. — *EXCELLUS BCBSRA*

NEW YORK	205 PARK CLUB LN BUFFALO, NY 14221-5239	PHONE: (716) 847-1480 FAX: (716) 857-4499 TOLL FREE: (800) 427-8490	E-MAIL: CUSTOMERSERVICE@UNIVERAHEALTHCARE.COM WEB: WWW.UNIVERAHEALTHCARE.ORG OR WWW.UNIVERAHEALTHCARE.COM

UNIVERSAL — *SEE ALSO CAICO*

UNIVERSAL CARE

CALIFORNIA	1600 E HILL ST SIGNAL HILL, CA 90755-3612 PO BOX 93122 LONG BEACH, CA 90809-3122	PHONE: (562) 424-6200 FAX: (562) 981-5801 TOLL FREE: (800) 635-6668	E-MAIL: CLAIMSINQUIRY@UNIVERSALCARE.COM WEB: WWW.UNIVERSALCARE.COM

UNIVERSAL UNDERWRITERS GROUP

NATIONAL	6900 NORTH DALLAS PKY STE 800 PLANO, TX 75024	PHONE: (972) 422-3339 FAX: (972) 461-6075 TOLL FREE: (800) 622-6262	WEB: WWW.UNIVERSALUNDERWRITERS.COM
	7045 COLLEGE BLVD OVERLAND PARK, KS 66211-1551 PO BOX 2904 SHAWNEE MISSION, KS 66201-1304	PHONE: (913) 339-1000 FAX: (877) 331-1700 TOLL FREE: (800) 821-7803	WEB: WWW.UNIVERSALUNDERWRITERS.COM

UNIVERSITY HEALTH SERVICES — *SEE ALSO HARVARD UNIVERSITY GROUP HEALTH PROGRAM*

UNIVERSITY OF UTAH HEALTH PLANS — *SEE ALSO UUHP*

UNUM PROVIDENT

NATIONAL	2211 CONGRESS ST PORTLAND, ME 04122-0002	PHONE: (207) 575-2211 TOLL FREE: (800) 223-5937	WEB: WWW.UNUMPROVIDENT.COM

UNUMPROVIDENT — *SEE ALSO COLONIAL SUPPLEMENTAL INSURANCE*

US HEALTHGROUP — *NATIONAL FOUNDATION LIFE INSURANCE COMPANY*

TEXAS	3100 BURNETT PLZ 801 CHERRY ST UNIT 33 FORT WORTH, TX 76102-7825	PHONE: (817) 878-3480 TOLL FREE: (800) 221-9039	E-MAIL: INFO@ASCENTASSURANCE.COM WEB: WWW.USHEALTHGROUP.COM

US LIABILITY INSURANCE GROUP

NATIONAL	190 S WARNER RD WAYNE, PA 19087-2191	PHONE: (610) 688-2535 FAX: (610) 688-4391 TOLL FREE: (800) 523-5545	WEB: WWW.USLI.COM

US SPECIALTY INSURANCE

TEXAS	13403 NW FWY HOUSTON, TX 77040-6006	PHONE: (713) 744-3700 FAX: (713) 744-9675 TOLL FREE: (888) 688-0775	E-MAIL: INVESTORRELATIONS@HCCH.COM WEB: WWW.HCCH.COM

USAA LIFE INSURANCE CO

NATIONAL

9800 FREDERICKSBURG RD
SAN ANTONIO, TX 78288-0346
PO BOX 659464
SAN ANTONIO, TX 78265

PHONE: (210) 498-8000
FAX: (877) 435-7099 OR (800) 531-8877
TOLL FREE: (800) 531-8000

WEB: WWW.USAA.COM

USI RISK MANAGEMENT SERVICES

NATIONAL

840 GUESSNER STE 600
HOUSTON, TX 77024
PO BOX 218060
HOUSTON, TX 77218-8060

PHONE: (281) 496-3400
TOLL FREE: (800) 583-0255

WEB: WWW.USITX.COM OR WWW.USI.BIZ

UTICA NATIONAL INSURANCE GROUP

NATIONAL

180 GENESEE ST
NEW HARTFORD, NY 13413
PO BOX 530
UTICA, NY 13503-0530

PHONE: (315) 734-2000
FAX: (315) 734-2680
TOLL FREE: (800) 274-1914

E-MAIL: WEBMASTER@UTICANATIONAL.COM
WEB: WWW.UTICANATIONAL.COM

UUHP — *UNIVERSITY OF UTAH HEALTH PLANS*

UTAH

CLAIMS DEPARTMENT
PO BOX 45180
SALT LAKE CITY, UT 84145

PHONE: (801) 587-6447
FAX: (801) 587-6433
TOLL FREE: (888) 271-5870

WEB: WWW.UUHSC.UTAH.EDU/UHEALTHPLAN

VALERO CLAIMS MANAGEMENT

NATIONAL

ONE VALERO WY
SAN ANTONIO, TX 78249
PO BOX 696080
SAN ANTONIO, TX 78269

PHONE: (210) 592-2302
FAX: (210) 345-2302
TOLL FREE: (800) 678-9355

VALLEY HEALTH ADMINISTRATORS

PENNSYLVANIA

800 PLZ DR 230
BELLE VERNON, PA 15012

PHONE: (724) 379-4011
FAX: (724) 379-4354
TOLL FREE: (877) 264-8258

WEB: WWW.VALUHEALTH.COM

VANLINER INSURANCE CO

NATIONAL

ONE PREMIER DR
FENTON, MO 63026
PO BOX 26352
FENTON, MO 63026-1552

PHONE: (636) 343-9889
FAX: (636) 326-0403
TOLL FREE: (800) 325-3619

WEB: WWW.VANLINER.COM

VFS INSURANCE GROUP — *SEE ALSO TRIUMPHE CASUALTY CO*

VIRGINIA MUTUAL INSURANCE CO

VIRGINIA

4480 COX RD
GLEN ALLEN, VA 23060-6718
PO BOX 2460
GLEN ALLEN, VA 23058-2460

PHONE: (804) 346-1900
FAX: (804) 346-1995
TOLL FREE: (800) 394-8642

E-MAIL: CUSTSVC@VAMUTUALINS.COM
WEB: WWW.VAMUTUALINS.COM

VISION SERVICE PLAN — *VSP*

NATIONAL

3333 QUALITY DR
RANCHO CORDOVA, CA 95670-7985
PO BOX 997100
SACRAMENTO, CA 95899-7100

PHONE: (916) 851-5000
FAX: (916) 851-5152
TOLL FREE: (800) 852-7600

WEB: WWW.VSP.COM

VISTA HEALTHCARE

FLORIDA

1340 CONCORD TERRACE
SUNRISE, FL 33233

PHONE: (954) 858-3000
FAX: (850) 668-3133

WEB: WWW.HPSE.COM

VIVA HEALTH

ALABAMA	1222 14TH AVE S BIRMINGHAM, AL 35205-3853	PHONE: (205) 939-1718 FAX: (205) 939-1748	WEB: WWW.VIVAHEALTH.COM

VOLUNTARY PLAN ADMINISTRATORS — *SEE ALSO VPA, INC*

VPA, INC — *VOLUNTARY PLAN ADMINISTRATORS*

NATIONAL	24025 PARK SORRENTO STE 200 CALABASAS, CA 91302-4007 PO BOX 9444 CALABASAS, CA 91372-0830	PHONE: (818) 591-2772 FAX: (818) 591-7664 TOLL FREE: (800) 473-9761	WEB: WWW.VPAINC.COM

VSP — *SEE ALSO VISION SERVICE PLAN*

VYTRA HEALTH PLANS — *H I P*

NEW YORK	395 N SERVICE RD MELVILLE, NY 11747-3171	PHONE: (631) 694-4000 FAX: (631) 719-0911 TOLL FREE: (800) 406-0806 IN-STATE: (800) 926-9530	E-MAIL: GENERAL@VYTRA.COM WEB: WWW.VYTRA.COM

WACHOVIA INSURANCE SERVICES, INC

NATIONAL	65 WILLOWBROOK BLVD WAYNE, NJ 07470 PO BOX 927 WAYNE, NJ 07470	PHONE: (973) 890-18[illegible]8 FAX: (973) 890-7841 TOLL FREE: (800) 726-1989	WEB: WWW.WACHOVIA.COM/FUISAATLANTIC

WAKELY & ASSOCIATES — *STATE MUTUAL*

NATIONAL	PO BOX 10846 CLEARWATER, FL 33757-8846	PHONE: (727) 584-8128 FAX: (727) 559-8679 TOLL FREE: (877) 872-5500	E-MAIL: ADMINISTRATOR@WAKELYINC.COM WEB: WWW.WAKELYINC.COM

WARD NORTH AMERICA

CALIFORNIA	PO BOX 2422 TUSTIN, CA 92781-2422	PHONE: (714) 544-0980 FAX: (714) 544-1979 TOLL FREE: (800) 677-3313	E-MAIL: GBETTS@WARDCLAIMS.COM WEB: WWW.WARDNA.COM

WARD NORTH AMERICA, INC

ALASKA	PO BOX 101600 ANCHORAGE, AK 99501	PHONE: (907) 561-1725 FAX: (907) 562-6595	WEB: WWW.WARDNA.COM

WAS — *WILTON ADJUSTMENT SERVICES, INC*

ALASKA	335 6TH AVE FAIRBANKS, AK 99701-5059 PO BOX 70350 FAIRBANKS, AK 99707	PHONE: (907) 456-4342 FAX: (907) 456-4949	E-MAIL: WASFRBK@ALASKA.COM WEB: WWW.WILTONALASKA.COM
	625 E 34TH AVE STE 400 ANCHORAGE, AK 99503 PO BOX 92670 ANCHORAGE, AK 99509-2670	PHONE: (907) 276-3311 FAX: (907) 276-7877	E-MAIL: WASANCH@ALASKA.NET WEB: WWW.WILTONALASKA.COM

WASATCH CREST MUTUAL

ARIZONA *UTAH*	215 S STATE STE 300 SALT LAKE CITY, UT 84111	PHONE: (801) 972-7501 FAX: (801) 972-7630 IN-STATE: (800) 331-1686	

WATSON WYATT WORLDWIDE

NATIONAL	901 N GLEBE RD ARLINGTON, VA 22203	PHONE: (202) 715-7000 FAX: (202) 715-8585	WEB: WWW.WATSONWYATT.COM

W

WAUSAU BENEFITS

NATIONAL	115 W SAUSAU AVE WAUSAU, WI 54401-2875 PO BOX 8013 WAUSAU, WI 54402-8013	PHONE: (715) 841-2000 FAX: (715) 841-7569 TOLL FREE: (866) 881-0800	WEB: WWW.WAUSAUBENEFITS.COM

WAUSAU INSURANCE

ALABAMA	4425 ALEXANDER DR STE 100 ALPHARETTA, GA 30022-3741	TOLL FREE: (800) 943-1113	WEB: WWW.WAUSAU.COM
ALASKA *ARIZONA*	12725 SW MILLIKAN WY STE 500 BEAVERTON, OR 97005	PHONE: (503) 626-4100 FAX: (603) 334-0307 TOLL FREE: (800) 424-0054	WEB: WWW.WAUSAU.COM
ARIZONA	105 DECKER COURT STE 500 IRVING, TX 75062-2272	PHONE: (972) 650-1955 FAX: (603) 334-0304 TOLL FREE: (800) 634-1955	WEB: WWW.WAUSAU.COM
CALIFORNIA	12725 SW MILLIKAN WY STE 500 BEAVERTON, OR 97005	PHONE: (503) 626-4100 FAX: (603) 334-0307 TOLL FREE: (800) 424-0054	WEB: WWW.WAUSAU.COM
COLORADO	11225 COLLEGE BLVD STE 300 OVERLAND PARK, KS 66210-2770	TOLL FREE: (800) 255-6740	WEB: WWW.WAUSAU.COM
CONNECTICUT *DELAWARE* *DISTRICT OF COLUMBIA*	251 SALINA MEADOWS PKY STE 260 NORTH SYRACUSE, NY 13212	PHONE: (315) 461-0092 FAX: (315) 461-3700 OR (603) 334-8145 TOLL FREE: (800) 468-3000	WEB: WWW.WAUSAU.COM
FLORIDA	101 SOUTHHALL LN STE 160 MAITLAND, FL 32794-5290 PO BOX 945290 MAITLAND, FL 32794	FAX: (603) 334-8143 TOLL FREE: (800) 231-6165	WEB: WWW.WAUSAU.COM
GEORGIA	4425 ALEXANDER DR STE 100 ALPHARETTA, GA 30022-3741	TOLL FREE: (800) 943-1113	WEB: WWW.WAUSAU.COM
HAWAII	12725 SW MILLIKAN WY STE 500 BEAVERTON, OR 97005	PHONE: (503) 626-4100 FAX: (603) 334-0307 TOLL FREE: (800) 424-0054	WEB: WWW.WAUSAU.COM
IDAHO	PO BOX 58 BOISE, ID 83707	FAX: (208) 376-9937 TOLL FREE: (800) 324-9139	WEB: WWW.WAUSAU.COM
ILLINOIS	1431 OPUS PL STE 300 DOWNERS GROVE, IL 60515-1169	PHONE: (630) 719-9700 FAX: (630) 719-0600 TOLL FREE: (800) 835-0060	WEB: WWW.WAUSAU.COM
INDIANA	8440 WOODFIELD CROSSING STE 400 INDIANAPOLIS, IN 46240 PO BOX 1187 INDIANAPOLIS, IN 46206-1187	PHONE: (800) 782-2794 FAX: (603) 334-8151 TOLL FREE: (800) 266-2800	WEB: WWW.WAUSAU.COM
IOWA *KANSAS*	11225 COLLEGE BLVD STE 300 OVERLAND PARK, KS 66210-2770	TOLL FREE: (800) 255-6740	WEB: WWW.WAUSAU.COM
KENTUCKY	8440 WOODFIELD CROSSING STE 400 INDIANAPOLIS, IN 46240 PO BOX 1187 INDIANAPOLIS, IN 46206-1187	PHONE: (800) 782-2794 FAX: (603) 334-8151 TOLL FREE: (800) 266-2800	WEB: WWW.WAUSAU.COM
LOUISIANA	105 DECKER COURT STE 500 IRVING, TX 75062-2272	PHONE: (972) 650-1955 FAX: (603) 334-0304 TOLL FREE: (800) 634-1955	WEB: WWW.WAUSAU.COM
MARYLAND	251 SALINA MEADOWS PKY STE 260 NORTH SYRACUSE, NY 13212	PHONE: (315) 461-0092 FAX: (315) 461-3700 OR (603) 334-8145 TOLL FREE: (800) 468-3000	WEB: WWW.WAUSAU.COM

MICHIGAN	Workers Comp, Self-Insured	8440 WOODFIELD CROSSING STE 400 INDIANAPOLIS, IN 46240 PO BOX 1187 INDIANAPOLIS, IN 46206-1187	PHONE: (800) 782-2794 FAX: (603) 334-8151 TOLL FREE: (800) 266-2800	WEB: WWW.WAUSAU.COM
MINNESOTA	Workers Comp, Self-Insured	GRAND OAK ONE OFFICE CENTER 2854 HIGHWAY 55 STE 200 EAGAN, MN 55121	PHONE: (651) 365-8053 FAX: (603) 334-0317 TOLL FREE: (800) 862-6079	WEB: WWW.WAUSAU.COM
MISSISSIPPI	Workers Comp, Self-Insured	101 SOUTHHALL LN STE 160 MAITLAND, FL 32794-5290 PO BOX 945290 MAITLAND, FL 32794	FAX: (603) 334-8143 TOLL FREE: (800) 231-6165	WEB: WWW.WAUSAU.COM
MISSOURI	Workers Comp, Self-Insured	11225 COLLEGE BLVD STE 300 OVERLAND PARK, KS 66210-2770	TOLL FREE: (800) 255-6740	WEB: WWW.WAUSAU.COM
MONTANA	Workers Comp, Self-Insured	700 SW HAGGINS STE 250 MISSOULA, MT 59803	PHONE: (406) 543-4933 FAX: (800) 258-9081 TOLL FREE: (866) 890-3312	WEB: WWW.WAUSAU.COM
NEBRASKA	Workers Comp, Self-Insured	11225 COLLEGE BLVD STE 300 OVERLAND PARK, KS 66210-2770	TOLL FREE: (800) 255-6740	WEB: WWW.WAUSAU.COM
NEVADA	Workers Comp, Self-Insured	12725 SW MILLIKAN WY STE 500 BEAVERTON, OR 97005	PHONE: (503) 626-4100 FAX: (603) 334-0307 TOLL FREE: (800) 424-0054	WEB: WWW.WAUSAU.COM
NEW JERSEY	Workers Comp, Self-Insured	251 SALINA MEADOWS PKY STE 260 NORTH SYRACUSE, NY 13212	PHONE: (315) 461-0092 FAX: (315) 461-3700 OR (603) 334-8145 TOLL FREE: (800) 468-3000	WEB: WWW.WAUSAU.COM
NEW MEXICO	Workers Comp, Self-Insured	105 DECKER COURT STE 500 IRVING, TX 75062-2272	PHONE: (972) 650-1955 FAX: (603) 334-0304 TOLL FREE: (800) 634-1955	WEB: WWW.WAUSAU.COM
NEW YORK	Workers Comp, Self-Insured	251 SALINA MEADOWS PKY STE 260 NORTH SYRACUSE, NY 13212	PHONE: (315) 461-0092 FAX: (315) 461-3700 OR (603) 334-8145 TOLL FREE: (800) 468-3000	WEB: WWW.WAUSAU.COM
NORTH CAROLINA	Workers Comp, Self-Insured	4425 ALEXANDER DR STE 100 ALPHARETTA, GA 30022-3741	TOLL FREE: (800) 943-1113	WEB: WWW.WAUSAU.COM
NORTH DAKOTA	Workers Comp, Self-Insured	GRAND OAK ONE OFFICE CENTER 2854 HIGHWAY 55 STE 200 EAGAN, MN 55121	PHONE: (651) 365-8053 FAX: (603) 334-0317 TOLL FREE: (800) 862-6079	WEB: WWW.WAUSAU.COM
OHIO	Workers Comp, Self-Insured	8440 WOODFIELD CROSSING STE 400 INDIANAPOLIS, IN 46240 PO BOX 1187 INDIANAPOLIS, IN 46206-1187	PHONE: (800) 782-2794 FAX: (603) 334-8151 TOLL FREE: (800) 266-2800	WEB: WWW.WAUSAU.COM
OKLAHOMA	Workers Comp, Self-Insured	105 DECKER COURT STE 500 IRVING, TX 75062-2272	PHONE: (972) 650-1955 FAX: (603) 334-0304 TOLL FREE: (800) 634-1955	WEB: WWW.WAUSAU.COM
OREGON	Workers Comp, Self-Insured	12725 SW MILLIKAN WY STE 500 BEAVERTON, OR 97005	PHONE: (503) 626-4100 FAX: (603) 334-0307 TOLL FREE: (800) 424-0054	WEB: WWW.WAUSAU.COM
PENNSYLVANIA	Workers Comp, Self-Insured	251 SALINA MEADOWS PKY STE 260 NORTH SYRACUSE, NY 13212	PHONE: (315) 461-0092 FAX: (315) 461-3700 OR (603) 334-8145 TOLL FREE: (800) 468-3000	WEB: WWW.WAUSAU.COM
SOUTH CAROLINA	Workers Comp, Self-Insured	101 SOUTHHALL LN STE 160 MAITLAND, FL 32794-5290 PO BOX 945290 MAITLAND, FL 32794	FAX: (603) 334-8143 TOLL FREE: (800) 231-6165	WEB: WWW.WAUSAU.COM
SOUTH DAKOTA	Workers Comp, Self-Insured	GRAND OAK ONE OFFICE CENTER 2854 HIGHWAY 55 STE 200 EAGAN, MN 55121	PHONE: (651) 365-8053 FAX: (603) 334-0317 TOLL FREE: (800) 862-6079	WEB: WWW.WAUSAU.COM

W

TENNESSEE	4425 ALEXANDER DR STE 100 ALPHARETTA, GA 30022-3741	TOLL FREE: (800) 943-1113	WEB: WWW.WAUSAU.COM
TEXAS	105 DECKER COURT STE 500 IRVING, TX 75062-2272	PHONE: (972) 650-1955 FAX: (603) 334-0304 TOLL FREE: (800) 634-1955	WEB: WWW.WAUSAU.COM
UTAH	12725 SW MILLIKAN WY STE 500 BEAVERTON, OR 97005	PHONE: (503) 626-4100 FAX: (603) 334-0307 TOLL FREE: (800) 424-0054	WEB: WWW.WAUSAU.COM
VERMONT	251 SALINA MEADOWS PKY STE 260 NORTH SYRACUSE, NY 13212	PHONE: (315) 461-0092 FAX: (315) 461-3700 OR (603) 334-8145 TOLL FREE: (800) 468-3000	WEB: WWW.WAUSAU.COM
VIRGINIA	4425 ALEXANDER DR STE 100 ALPHARETTA, GA 30022-3741	TOLL FREE: (800) 943-1113	WEB: WWW.WAUSAU.COM
WASHINGTON	12725 SW MILLIKAN WY STE 500 BEAVERTON, OR 97005	PHONE: (503) 626-4100 FAX: (603) 334-0307 TOLL FREE: (800) 424-0054	WEB: WWW.WAUSAU.COM
WEST VIRGINIA	4425 ALEXANDER DR STE 100 ALPHARETTA, GA 30022-3741	TOLL FREE: (800) 943-1113	WEB: WWW.WAUSAU.COM
WISCONSIN	11800 W PARK PL MILWAUKEE, WI 53224-3009 PO BOX 245037 MILWAUKEE, WI 53224-9537	PHONE: (414) 577-2100 TOLL FREE: (800) 537-2350	WEB: WWW.WAUSAU.COM
WYOMING	11225 COLLEGE BLVD STE 300 OVERLAND PARK, KS 66210-2770	TOLL FREE: (800) 255-6740	WEB: WWW.WAUSAU.COM

WBI — *SEE ALSO WESTERN BENEFITS, INC*

WEA TRUST

WISCONSIN	45 NOB HILL RD MADISON, WI 53713 PO BOX 7338 MADISON, WI 53707-7338	PHONE: (608) 276-4000 FAX: (608) 276-9119 TOLL FREE: (800) 279-4000	WEB: WWW.WEATRUST.COM

WELBORN HEALTH PLANS

INDIANA	421 CHESTNUT ST EVANSVILLE, IN 47713	PHONE: (812) 426-6600 FAX: (812) 426-9476 TOLL FREE: (800) 521-0265	WEB: WWW.WELBORNHEALTHPLANS.COM

WELFARE & PENSION ADMIN SERV

NATIONAL	2815 SECOND AVE STE 300 SEATTLE, WA 98121-3209 PO BOX 34203 SEATTLE, WA 98124	PHONE: (206) 441-7574 FAX: (206) 441-9110 TOLL FREE: (800) 331-6158 IN-STATE: (800) 732-1121	E-MAIL: INFO@WPAS-INC.COM WEB: WWW.WPAS-INC.COM

WELFARE AND PENSION FUND — *SEE ALSO AUTOMOBILE MECHANICS LOCAL NO 701*

WELFARE PLAN — *SEE ALSO CALIFORNIA FIELD IRONWORKERS TRUST FUND*

WELL CARE HEALTH PLANS — *STAY WELL*

FLORIDA	8735 HENDERSON D TAMPA, FL 33634	PHONE: (813) 290-6200 FAX: (813) 262-2802 TOLL FREE: (800) 799-3081	WEB: WWW.WELLCARE.COM

WELL POINT, INC — *ANTHEM BLUE CROSS BLUE SHIELD*

NATIONAL	120 MONUMENT CIR INDIANAPOLIS, IN 46204	PHONE: (317) 532-6000 FAX: (408) 885-4425	WEB: WWW.WELLPOINT.COM

WELLCHOICE INSURANCE OF NEW JERSEY

NEW JERSEY
1333 BRUNSWICK AVE
LAWRENCEVILLE, NJ 08648
PHONE: (888) 476-6936
TOLL FREE: (888) 438-8624
WEB: WWW.WELLCHOICENJ.COM OR WWW.IMPERIALBLUE.COM

WELLMARK BLUE CROSS BLUE SHIELD — *SEE ALSO BLUE CROSS BLUE SHIELD*

WELLMARK BLUE CROSS BLUE SHIELD OF SOUTH DAKOTA

SOUTH DAKOTA
1601 W MADISON ST
SIOUX FALLS, SD 57104-5710
PHONE: (605) 373-7200
FAX: (605) 373-7497
TOLL FREE: (800) 831-4818
WEB: WWW.WELLMARK.COM

WELLPATH

NORTH CAROLINA
SOUTH CAROLINA

PO BOX 7102
LONDON, KY 40742
FAX: (701) 250-5391
TOLL FREE: (800) 470-4523
WEB: WWW.WELLPATHONLINE.COM

2801 SLATER RD STE 200
MORRISVILLE, NC 27560
TOLL FREE: (800) 935-7284
WEB: WWW.WELLPATHONLINE.COM

WESLEY MEDICAL CENTER — *HCA*

KANSAS
550 N HILLSIDE ST
WICHITA, KS 67214-4910
PO BOX 403101
ATLANTA, GA 30384-3101
PHONE: (316) 962-2000
FAX: (316) 962-7931
TOLL FREE: (866) 656-8778
WEB: WWW.HCAHEALTHCARE.COM

WEST AMERICAN INSURANCE

NATIONAL
9450 SEWARD RD
FAIRFIELD, OH 45014-5456
PHONE: (513) 603-2250
FAX: (513) 603-3168
TOLL FREE: (800) 843-6446
WEB: WWW.OCAS.COM

WEST BEND MUTUAL INSURANCE CO

ILLINOIS
INDIANA
IOWA
MINNESOTA
WISCONSIN

1900 S 18TH AVE
WEST BEND, WI 53095
PHONE: (262) 334-5571
FAX: (262) 338-5188
E-MAIL: DIRECTCONNECT@WBMI.COM
WEB: WWW.WESTBENDMUTUAL.COM

WEST CARE — *SEE ALSO COLORADO PREFERRED PHYSICIAN ORGANIZATION*

WESTCHESTER TEAMSTERS HEALTH & WELFARE — *TEAMSTERS ALLIED BENEFIT*

NATIONAL
160 S CENTRAL AVE
ELMSFORD, NY 10523
PHONE: (914) 592-9330
FAX: (914) 592-1519
WEB: WWW.TEAMSTERSLOCAL.COM

WESTERN AMERICAN INSURANCE COMPANY

TEXAS
2175 N GLENVILLE DR
RICHARDSON, TX 75082
PHONE: (972) 699-2770
FAX: (972) 699-2788
WEB: WWW.WALIC.COM

WESTERN BENEFITS, INC — *WBI*

CALIFORNIA
KENTUCKY
OREGON
UTAH
WASHINGTON

CLACKAMAS BUSINESS PLZ
14835 SE 82ND DR
CLACKAMAS, OR 97015
PO BOX 22185
PORTLAND, OR 97269
PHONE: (503) 968-2360
FAX: (503) 968-2817
TOLL FREE: (800) 277-8579
WEB: WWW.WESTERNBENEFITSINC.COM

WESTERN MUTUAL INSURANCE CO — *WESTERN PETROLEUM MARKETERS TRUST*

ARIZONA
IDAHO
MONTANA
NEVADA
NEW MEXICO
UTAH
WASHINGTON

4393 S RIVERBOAT RD
TAYLORSVILLE, UT 84123-2503
PO BOX 572450
SALT LAKE CITY, UT 84157-2450

PHONE: (801) 263-8000
FAX: (801) 263-1189
TOLL FREE: (800) 748-5340

WEB: WWW.WESTERNMUTUALINSURANCE.COM

WESTERN NATIONAL MUTUAL INSURANCE CO

MINNESOTA
NORTH DAKOTA
SOUTH DAKOTA
WASHINGTON
WISCONSIN

5350 W 78TH ST
EDINA, MN 55439
PO BOX 1463
MINNEAPOLIS, MN 55440-1463

PHONE: (952) 835-5350
FAX: (952) 921-3153
TOLL FREE: (800) 862-6070

E-MAIL: INFO@WNINS.COM
WEB: WWW.WNINS.COM

WESTERN PETROLEUM MARKETERS TRUST — *SEE ALSO WESTERN MUTUAL INSURANCE CO*

WESTERN RESERVE GROUP

INDIANA *OHIO*	1685 CLEVELAND RD WOOSTER, OH 44691-2335 PO BOX 36 WOOSTER, OH 44691-0036	PHONE: (330) 262-9060 FAX: (800) 392-7092 TOLL FREE: (800) 362-0426	WEB: WWW.WRG-INS.COM

WESTERN TEAMSTERS — *SEE ALSO GROUP BENEFIT ADMINISTRATORS — SEE ALSO NORTHWEST ADMINISTRATORS — SEE ALSO ROBERT F MAY CO — SEE ALSO SOUTHWEST ADMINISTRATORS*

WESTERN WORLD INSURANCE GROUP

NEW JERSEY	400 PARSON'S POND DR FRANKLIN LAKES, NJ 07417-2600	PHONE: (201) 847-8600 FAX: (201) 847-1010	WEB: WWW.WESTERNWORLD.COM

WESTFIELD INSURANCE

ILLINOIS	2325 DEAN ST STE 100 ST CHARLES, IL 60175	PHONE: (630) 587-1400 FAX: (630) 587-1500 TOLL FREE: (800) 414-4759	WEB: WWW.WESTFIELDGRP.COM
	7210 N VILLA LAKE DR STE 2 PEORIA, IL 61614 PO BOX 3499 PEORIA, IL 61612-3499	PHONE: (309) 693-7400 FAX: (309) 693-7414 TOLL FREE: (800) 757-9248	WEB: WWW.WESTFIELDGRP.COM
INDIANA	FORTUNE PK BLDG 3905 VINCENNES RD STE 201 INDIANAPOLIS, IN 46268	PHONE: (317) 879-1079 FAX: (317) 879-0287 TOLL FREE: (800) 243-0213	WEB: WWW.WESTFIELDGRP.COM
	4220 EDISON LAKE PKY STE 200 MISHAWAKA, IN 46546	PHONE: (800) 489-1220 FAX: (574) 243-0760	WEB: WWW.WESTFIELDGRP.COM
	7221 ENGLE RD STE 220 FT WAYNE, IN 46804	PHONE: (260) 432-3595 FAX: (260) 432-4989 TOLL FREE: (800) 243-0216	WEB: WWW.WESTFIELDGRP.COM
KENTUCKY	TWO PARAGON CENTRE 6040 DUTCHMANS LN STE 320 LOUISVILLE, KY 40205	PHONE: (502) 451-4198 FAX: (502) 451-4457 TOLL FREE: (800) 757-9245	WEB: WWW.WESTFIELDGRP.COM
MICHIGAN	38695 SEVEN MILE RD STE 110 LIVONIA, MI 48152	PHONE: (734) 542-9170 FAX: (734) 542-9270 TOLL FREE: (800) 243-0237	WEB: WWW.WESTFIELDGRP.COM

MICHIGAN — CONTINUED	5537 GLENWOOD HILLS PKWY STE 210 GRAND RAPIDS, MI 49512	PHONE: (616) 949-6500 FAX: (616) 949-6954 TOLL FREE: (800) 243-0247	WEB: WWW.WESTFIELDGRP.COM
MINNESOTA	800 NORMAN CENTER DR STE 310 MINNEAPOLIS, MN 55437	PHONE: (952) 831-6446 FAX: (952) 831-4015 TOLL FREE: (800) 757-9244	WEB: WWW.WESTFIELDGRP.COM
OHIO	2000 POLARIS PKY COLUMBUS, OH 43240	PHONE: (614) 848-6174 FAX: (614) 848-6184 TOLL FREE: (800) 472-9527	WEB: WWW.WESTFIELDGRP.COM
	955 WINDHAM CT STE 3 BOARDMAN, OH 44512	PHONE: (330) 726-4255 FAX: (330) 726-4270 TOLL FREE: (800) 358-7779	WEB: WWW.WESTFIELDGRP.COM
	ONE PARK CIR WESTFIELD CENTER, OH 44251	PHONE: (330) 887-6677 FAX: (330) 887-6678 TOLL FREE: (800) 552-9144	E-MAIL: WESTFIELDCENTERSERVICEOFFICE@WESTFIELD.COM WEB: WWW.WESTFIELDGRP.COM

WEYCO, INC

NATIONAL	PO BOX 30132 LANSING, MI 48909-7632	PHONE: (517) 349-7010 FAX: (517) 349-8555 TOLL FREE: (800) 748-0003	E-MAIL: INFO@WEYCO.COM WEB: WWW.WEYCO.COM

WHILSHIRE AND COMPANY — *SEE ALSO OCCIDENTAL FIRE & CASUALTY CO OF NORTH CAROLINA*

WICHITA NATIONAL LIFE INSURANCE CO

ARKANSAS *OKLAHOMA*	711 SW D AVE LAWTON, OK 73501 PO BOX 1709 LAWTON, OK 73502-1709	PHONE: (580) 353-5776 FAX: (580) 353-6482 TOLL FREE: (800) 522-1625	WEB: WWW.WNLIC.COM

WILLIAM C EARHART COMPANY, INC

MONTANA	3140 NE BROADWAY PORTLAND, OR 97232	PHONE: (503) 282-5581 TOLL FREE: (800) 547-1314	WEB: WWW.WCEARHART.COM

WILLIS GROUP LIMITED

ALABAMA	STE 400 ONE GALLERIA TOWER 13355 NOEL RD DALLAS, TX 75240	PHONE: (972) 385-9800 FAX: (972) 386-6337	WEB: WWW.WILLIS.COM
ARIZONA	US WEST 11202 N TATUM BLVD PHOENIX, AZ 85028-0000	PHONE: (602) 787-6000 FAX: (602) 787-8040 TOLL FREE: (800) 933-6385	WEB: WWW.WILLIS.COM
COLORADO	STE 400 ONE GALLERIA TOWER 13355 NOEL RD DALLAS, TX 75240	PHONE: (972) 385-9800 FAX: (972) 386-6337	WEB: WWW.WILLIS.COM
GEORGIA	11TH FL ONE GLEN LAKE 1 GLEN LAKE PKY ATLANTA, GA 30328	PHONE: (404) 224-5000 FAX: (404) 224-5001 TOLL FREE: (877) 725-9674	WEB: WWW.WILLIS.COM
HAWAII	US WEST 11202 N TATUM BLVD PHOENIX, AZ 85028-0000	PHONE: (602) 787-6000 FAX: (602) 787-8040 TOLL FREE: (800) 933-6385	WEB: WWW.WILLIS.COM
KANSAS	STE 400 ONE GALLERIA TOWER 13355 NOEL RD DALLAS, TX 75240	PHONE: (972) 385-9800 FAX: (972) 386-6337	WEB: WWW.WILLIS.COM
KENTUCKY	11TH FL ONE GLEN LAKE 1 GLEN LAKE PKY ATLANTA, GA 30328	PHONE: (404) 224-5000 FAX: (404) 224-5001 TOLL FREE: (877) 725-9674	WEB: WWW.WILLIS.COM

W

LOUISIANA		STE 400 ONE GALLERIA TOWER 13355 NOEL RD DALLAS, TX 75240	PHONE: (972) 385-9800 FAX: (972) 386-6337	WEB: WWW.WILLIS.COM
MARYLAND		11TH FL ONE GLEN LAKE 1 GLEN LAKE PKY ATLANTA, GA 30328	PHONE: (404) 224-5000 FAX: (404) 224-5001 TOLL FREE: (877) 725-9674	WEB: WWW.WILLIS.COM
MISSISSIPPI		STE 400 ONE GALLERIA TOWER 13355 NOEL RD DALLAS, TX 75240	PHONE: (972) 385-9800 FAX: (972) 386-6337	WEB: WWW.WILLIS.COM
NEW HAMPSHIRE *TENNESSEE*		11TH FL ONE GLEN LAKE 1 GLEN LAKE PKY ATLANTA, GA 30328	PHONE: (404) 224-5000 FAX: (404) 224-5001 TOLL FREE: (877) 725-9674	WEB: WWW.WILLIS.COM
TEXAS		STE 400 ONE GALLERIA TOWER 13355 NOEL RD DALLAS, TX 75240	PHONE: (972) 385-9800 FAX: (972) 386-6337	WEB: WWW.WILLIS.COM
VIRGINIA		11TH FL ONE GLEN LAKE 1 GLEN LAKE PKY ATLANTA, GA 30328	PHONE: (404) 224-5000 FAX: (404) 224-5001 TOLL FREE: (877) 725-9674	WEB: WWW.WILLIS.COM

WILSON MUTUAL INSURANCE

WISCONSIN		3330 STAHL RD SHEBOYGAN, WI 53081 PO BOX 1340 SHEBOYGAN, WI 53082-1340	PHONE: (920) 458-3359 FAX: (866) 633-9220 TOLL FREE: (800) 242-7708	E-MAIL: CUSTOMERSERV@WILSONMUTUAL.COM WEB: WWW.WILSONMUTUAL.COM

WILTON ADJUSTMENT SERVICES, INC — *SEE ALSO WAS*

WISCONSIN NATIONAL LIFE INSURANCE CO — *PROTECTIVE LIFE CO*

NATIONAL		2801 HWY 280 S BIRMINGHAM, AL 35223-2479 PO BOX 2606 BIRMINGHAM, AL 35202-6686	PHONE: (205) 879-9230 FAX: (205) 268-3684 TOLL FREE: (800) 955-4304 IN-STATE: (800) 866-3555

WISCONSIN PHYSICIANS SERVICE — *SEE ALSO WPS HEALTH INSURANCE*

WOLVERINE MUTUAL INSURANCE CO

INDIANA *MICHIGAN* *WISCONSIN*		ONE WOLVERINE WY DOWAGIAC, MI 49047 PO BOX 530 DOWAGIAC, MI 49047-0530	PHONE: (269) 782-3851 FAX: (888) 298-4516 TOLL FREE: (800) 733-3320	WEB: WWW.WOLVERINEMUTUAL.COM

WOODMEN OF THE WORLD

NATIONAL		1700 FARNAM ST OMAHA, NE 68102	PHONE: (402) 342-1890 FAX: (402) 271-7852 TOLL FREE: (800) 225-3108	WEB: WWW.WOODMEN.COM

WORKERS COMP FUND — *SEE ALSO ADVANTAGE INSURANCE CO*

WORKFORCE SAFETY & INSURANCE

NORTH DAKOTA		1600 ECENTRY AVE STE ONE BISMARCK, ND 58506 PO BOX 5585 BISMARCK, ND 58506-5585	PHONE: (701) 328-3800 FAX: (701) 328-3820 TOLL FREE: (800) 777-5033	E-MAIL: NDWSI@STATE.ND.US WEB: WWW.WORKFORCESAFETY.COM

WORKMEN'S CIRCLE

CALIFORNIA
FLORIDA
MASSACHUSETTS
MICHIGAN
NEW JERSEY
NEW YORK
OHIO

		45 E 33RD ST 4TH FL NEW YORK, NY 10016-5336	PHONE: (212) 889-6800 FAX: (212) 532-7518 TOLL FREE: (800) 922-2558	WEB: WWW.CIRCLE.ORG

WORKMEN'S INSURANCE GROUP

CALIFORNIA	714 W OLYMPIC BLVD STE 800 LOS ANGELES, CA 90015-1472 PO BOX 54845 LOS ANGELES, CA 90054-4845	PHONE: (213) 747-6492 FAX: (213) 747-4699 TOLL FREE: (800) 697-6117	WEB: WWW.WAIC.COM

WORLD INSURANCE CO

NATIONAL	11808 GRANT ST OMAHA, NE 68164-3603 PO BOX 2558 OMAHA, NE 68103-2558	PHONE: (402) 496-8000 FAX: (402) 496-8199 TOLL FREE: (800) 786-7557	WEB: WWW.WORLDINSCO.COM OR WWW.WEBMED.COM

WPS HEALTH INSURANCE — *WISCONSIN PHYSICIANS SERVICE*

WISCONSIN	1717 W BROADWAY MADISON, WI 53713 PO BOX 8190 MADISON, WI 53708-8190	PHONE: (608) 221-4711 FAX: (608) 223-3626	WEB: WWW.WPSIC.COM

WPS WISCONSIN PHYSICIAN SERVICES — *SEE ALSO EPIC LIFE INSURANCE CO*

ZENITH ADMINISTRATORS, INC

NATIONAL	2001 W CAMELBACK RD STE B350 PHOENIX, AZ 85015-3466	PHONE: (602) 248-8434 FAX: (602) 248-8301 TOLL FREE: (800) 553-2801	WEB: WWW.ZENITHADM.COM
	104 S FREYA STE 220 SPOKANE, WA 99202-4867	PHONE: (509) 534-5625 FAX: (509) 534-5910 TOLL FREE: (800) 522-2403	WEB: WWW.ZENITHTPA.COM
	221 MAIN ST 2ND FL SAN FRANCISCO, CA 94105-1909	PHONE: (415) 546-7800 FAX: (415) 546-0600 TOLL FREE: (800) 388-0508	WEB: WWW.ZENITHTPA.COM
	5565 STERRETT PL STE 210 COLUMBIA, MD 21044	PHONE: (410) 884-1445 FAX: (410) 997-3657 TOLL FREE: (800) 235-5805	WEB: WWW.ZENITHTPA.COM
ALASKA	201 QUEEN ANNE AVE N STE 100 SEATTLE, WA 98109	PHONE: (206) 282-4100 FAX: (206) 285-1701	WEB: WWW.ZENITHTPA.COM
ARIZONA	2001 W CAMELBACK RD STE B350 PHOENIX, AZ 85015-3466	PHONE: (602) 248-8434 FAX: (602) 248-8301 TOLL FREE: (800) 553-2801	WEB: WWW.ZENITHADM.COM
CALIFORNIA	2001 W CAMELBACK RD STE B350 PHOENIX, AZ 85015-3466	PHONE: (602) 248-8434 FAX: (602) 248-8301 TOLL FREE: (800) 553-2801	WEB: WWW.ZENITHADM.COM
	6801 E WASHINGTON BLVD COMMERCE, CA 90040-1905 PO BOX 22041 COMMERCE, CA 90022-2041	PHONE: (323) 722-7171	

COLORADO	2001 W CAMELBACK RD STE B350 PHOENIX, AZ 85015-3466	PHONE: (602) 248-8434 FAX: (602) 248-8301 TOLL FREE: (800) 553-2801	WEB: WWW.ZENITHADM.COM
	8700 TURNPIKE DR STE 200 WESTMINSTER, CO 80031	PHONE: (303) 430-1118 FAX: (303) 430-0224	WEB: WWW.ZENITHTPA.COM
ILLINOIS	541 N FAIRBANKS CT STE 2600 CHICAGO, IL 60611	PHONE: (312) 649-1200 FAX: (312) 649-1245	WEB: WWW.ZENITHTPA.COM
	5420 W SOUTHERN AVE STE 407 INDIANAPOLIS, IN 46241	PHONE: (317) 248-3924 FAX: (317) 248-3279	WEB: WWW.ZENITHTPA.COM
	2100 N MAYFAIR RD STE 100 MILWAUKEE, WI 53226	PHONE: (414) 476-1220 FAX: (414) 476-2997	WEB: WWW.ZENITHTPA.COM
INDIANA	5420 W SOUTHERN AVE STE 407 INDIANAPOLIS, IN 46241	PHONE: (317) 248-3924 FAX: (317) 248-3279	WEB: WWW.ZENITHTPA.COM
KANSAS	3100 BROADWAY STE 108 KANSAS CITY, MO 64111	PHONE: (816) 756-0173 FAX: (816) 531-6518 TOLL FREE: (866) 756-0414	WEB: WWW.ZENITHTPA.COM
KENTUCKY	5420 W SOUTHERN AVE STE 407 INDIANAPOLIS, IN 46241	PHONE: (317) 248-3924 FAX: (317) 248-3279	WEB: WWW.ZENITHTPA.COM
LOUISIANA	2450 SEVERN AVE STE 517 METAIRIE, LA 70001-1237	PHONE: (504) 831-1544 FAX: (504) 831-1894 TOLL FREE: (800) 638-4855	WEB: WWW.ZENITHTPA.COM
MASSACHUSETTS	33 EASTLAND ST SPRINGFIELD, MA 01109-2348	PHONE: (413) 733-0177 FAX: (413) 733-3325 TOLL FREE: (800) 634-2700	WEB: WWW.ZENITHTPA.COM
MICHIGAN	2001 W CAMELBACK RD STE B350 PHOENIX, AZ 85015-3466	PHONE: (602) 248-8434 FAX: (602) 248-8301 TOLL FREE: (800) 553-2801	WEB: WWW.ZENITHADM.COM

MICHIGAN — CONTINUED	5420 W SOUTHERN AVE STE 407 INDIANAPOLIS, IN 46241	PHONE: (317) 248-3924 FAX: (317) 248-3279	WEB: WWW.ZENITHTPA.COM
	6011 W SAINT JOSEPH STE 401 LANSING, MI 48917	PHONE: (517) 323-9250 FAX: (517) 323-1093	WEB: WWW.ZENITHTPA.COM
MINNESOTA	2520 PILOT KEONEV RD STE 325 MINDOTA HEIGHTS, MN 55120	PHONE: (651) 256-1900	WEB: WWW.ZENITHTPA.COM
	750 TORREY BLDG 314 W SUPERIOR ST DULUTH, MN 55802	PHONE: (218) 727-6668 FAX: (218) 727-5697	WEB: WWW.ZENITHTPA.COM
	2100 N MAYFAIR RD STE 100 MILWAUKEE, WI 53226	PHONE: (414) 476-1220 FAX: (414) 476-2997	WEB: WWW.ZENITHTPA.COM
MISSISSIPPI	2450 SEVERN AVE STE 517 METAIRIE, LA 70001-1237	PHONE: (504) 831-1544 FAX: (504) 831-1894 TOLL FREE: (800) 638-4855	WEB: WWW.ZENITHTPA.COM
MISSOURI	8700 TURNPIKE DR STE 200 WESTMINSTER, CO 80031	PHONE: (303) 430-1118 FAX: (303) 430-0224	WEB: WWW.ZENITHTPA.COM
	4260 SHORELINE DR STE 170 EARTH CITY, MO 63045	PHONE: (314) 344-8899 FAX: (314) 344-4407 TOLL FREE: (800) 556-1742	WEB: WWW.ZENITHTPA.COM
NEBRASKA	8700 TURNPIKE DR STE 200 WESTMINSTER, CO 80031	PHONE: (303) 430-1118 FAX: (303) 430-0224	WEB: WWW.ZENITHTPA.COM
NEVADA	8700 TURNPIKE DR STE 200 WESTMINSTER, CO 80031	PHONE: (303) 430-1118 FAX: (303) 430-0224	WEB: WWW.ZENITHTPA.COM
NEW MEXICO	2001 W CAMELBACK RD STE B350 PHOENIX, AZ 85015-3466	PHONE: (602) 248-8434 FAX: (602) 248-8301 TOLL FREE: (800) 553-2801	WEB: WWW.ZENITHADM.COM
OHIO	5420 W SOUTHERN AVE STE 407 INDIANAPOLIS, IN 46241	PHONE: (317) 248-3924 FAX: (317) 248-3279	WEB: WWW.ZENITHTPA.COM

OKLAHOMA	2001 W CAMELBACK RD STE B350 PHOENIX, AZ 85015-3466	PHONE: (602) 248-8434 FAX: (602) 248-8301 TOLL FREE: (800) 553-2801	WEB: WWW.ZENITHADM.COM
SOUTH DAKOTA	8700 TURNPIKE DR STE 200 WESTMINSTER, CO 80031	PHONE: (303) 430-1118 FAX: (303) 430-0224	WEB: WWW.ZENITHTPA.COM
TEXAS	2001 W CAMELBACK RD STE B350 PHOENIX, AZ 85015-3466	PHONE: (602) 248-8434 FAX: (602) 248-8301 TOLL FREE: (800) 553-2801	WEB: WWW.ZENITHADM.COM
	9555 W SAM HOUSTON PKY S STE 400 HOUSTON, TX 77099-2132	PHONE: (713) 219-1200 FAX: (713) 219-1299	WEB: WWW.ZENITHADM.COM
UTAH	8700 TURNPIKE DR STE 200 WESTMINSTER, CO 80031	PHONE: (303) 430-1118 FAX: (303) 430-0224	WEB: WWW.ZENITHTPA.COM
WASHINGTON	201 QUEEN ANNE AVE N STE 100 SEATTLE, WA 98109	PHONE: (206) 282-4100 FAX: (206) 285-1701	WEB: WWW.ZENITHTPA.COM
WISCONSIN	2100 N MAYFAIR RD STE 100 MILWAUKEE, WI 53226	PHONE: (414) 476-1220 FAX: (414) 476-2997	WEB: WWW.ZENITHTPA.COM
WYOMING	8700 TURNPIKE DR STE 200 WESTMINSTER, CO 80031	PHONE: (303) 430-1118 FAX: (303) 430-0224	WEB: WWW.ZENITHTPA.COM

ZENITH INSURANCE CO

NATIONAL	21255 CALIFA ST WOODLAND HILLS, CA 91367-5005	PHONE: (818) 713-1000 FAX: (818) 710-1860 TOLL FREE: (800) 448-4356	E-MAIL: WOODLANDHILLS@THEZENITH.COM WEB: WWW.THEZENITH.COM

ZENITH INSURANCE COMPANY

CALIFORNIA	4309 HACIENDA DR STE 200 PLEASANTON, CA 94588-2730 PO BOX 8002 PLEASANTON, CA 94588-8602	PHONE: (925) 460-0600 FAX: (925) 463-1864 OR (925) 460-5169 TOLL FREE: (800) 395-1124	E-MAIL: PLEASANTON@THEZENITH.COM WEB: WWW.THEZENITH.COM
	7440 NORTH PALM STE 103 FRESNO, CA 93711	PHONE: (559) 432-6660 FAX: (559) 436-8839 TOLL FREE: (800) 508-9910	E-MAIL: FRESNO@THEZENITH.COM WEB: WWW.THEZENITH.COM
	7676 HAZARD CENTER DR STE 1200 SAN DIEGO, CA 92108-2807	PHONE: (619) 299-6252 FAX: (619) 299-8465 TOLL FREE: (800) 533-6212	E-MAIL: SANDIEGO@THEZENITH.COM WEB: WWW.THEZENITH.COM

ZENITH, THE

FLORIDA	1390 MAIN ST SARASOTA, FL 34236	PHONE: (941) 906-2000 FAX: (941) 362-6035 TOLL FREE: (800) 226-2324	E-MAIL: SARASOTA@THEZENITH.COM WEB: WWW.THEZENITH.COM

FLORIDA — CONTINUED	Workers Comp	3504 LAKE LYNDA DR STE 200 ORLANDO, FL 32817	PHONE: (407) 206-8200 FAX: (407) 618-8586 TOLL FREE: (800) 999-3242	E-MAIL: ORLANDO@THEZENITH.COM WEB: WWW.THEZENITH.COM
ILLINOIS	Workers Comp	2105 W WHITE OAKS DR SPRINGFIELD, IL 62704	PHONE: (217) 726-2900 FAX: (217) 546-9521 TOLL FREE: (800) 733-0468	E-MAIL: ILLINOIS@THEZENITH.COM WEB: WWW.THEZENITH.COM
NORTH CAROLINA	Workers Comp	900 W TRADE ST STE 600 CHARLOTTE, NC 28202	PHONE: (704) 567-7400 FAX: (704) 567-7440 TOLL FREE: (800) 200-2667	E-MAIL: NORTHCAROLINA@THEZENITH.COM WEB: WWW.THEZENITH.COM
PENNSYLVANIA	Workers Comp	TWO VALLEY SQ STE 301 BLUE BELL, PA 19422-2717	PHONE: (215) 591-2900 FAX: (215) 654-1689 TOLL FREE: (877) 311-0703	E-MAIL: PENNSYLVANIA@THEZENITH.COM WEB: WWW.THEZENITH.COM
TEXAS	Workers Comp	1101 CAPITOL OF TEXAS HWY S BLDG J AUSTIN, TX 78746	PHONE: (512) 306-1700 FAX: (512) 327-7145 TOLL FREE: (800) 841-3987	E-MAIL: AUSTIN@THEZENITH.COM WEB: WWW.THEZENITH.COM

ZURICH NORTH AMERICA

NATIONAL	Main Office	13810 FNB PKY OMAHA, NE 68154-9877 PO BOX 542003 OMAHA, NE 68154-8003	PHONE: (402) 963-5000 FAX: (402) 963-5329 TOLL FREE: (800) 228-9283	WEB: WWW.ZURICHNA.COM
ALABAMA	Workers Comp, Self-Insured	PO BOX 20791 ATLANTA, GA 30320-0791	PHONE: (404) 851-3200 FAX: (404) 851-3601 TOLL FREE: (800) 241-7570	E-MAIL: USZ_CARECENTER@ZURICHNA.COM WEB: WWW.ZURICHNA.COM
	Self-Insured	SOUTHEAST CLAIM CENTER PO BOX 30729 TAMPA, FL 33630-3729	PHONE: (813) 873-2055 FAX: (800) 333-8004 TOLL FREE: (800) 239-4781	E-MAIL: USZ_CARECENTER@ZURICHNA.COM WEB: WWW.ZURICHNA.COM
ALASKA	Workers Comp, Self-Insured	PO BOX 7774 SAN FRANCISCO, CA 94120-7774	PHONE: (415) 538-7100 FAX: (415) 538-7150 TOLL FREE: (800) 701-4926	E-MAIL: USZ_CARECENTER@ZURICHNA.COM WEB: WWW.ZURICHNA.COM
	Workers Comp, Self-Insured	WESTERN CLAIM CENTER 3249 QUALITY DR STE 300 RANCHO CORDOVA , CA 95670 PO BOX 981030 WEST SACRAMENTO, CA 95798	PHONE: (916) 635-1113 FAX: (800) 547-2487 TOLL FREE: (800) 239-4829	E-MAIL: USZ_CARECENTER@ZURICHNA.COM WEB: WWW.ZURICHNA.COM
ARIZONA	Workers Comp, Self-Insured	PO BOX 92566 LOS ANGELES, CA 90009-2566	PHONE: (818) 227-1700 FAX: (818) 227-1740 TOLL FREE: (800) 338-3160	E-MAIL: USZ_CARECENTER@ZURICHNA.COM WEB: WWW.ZURICHNA.COM
	Workers Comp, Self-Insured	WESTERN CLAIM CENTER 3249 QUALITY DR STE 300 RANCHO CORDOVA , CA 95670 PO BOX 981030 WEST SACRAMENTO, CA 95798	PHONE: (916) 635-1113 FAX: (800) 547-2487 TOLL FREE: (800) 239-4829	E-MAIL: USZ_CARECENTER@ZURICHNA.COM WEB: WWW.ZURICHNA.COM
ARKANSAS	Workers Comp, Self-Insured	PO BOX 20791 ATLANTA, GA 30320-0791	PHONE: (404) 851-3200 FAX: (404) 851-3601 TOLL FREE: (800) 241-7570	E-MAIL: USZ_CARECENTER@ZURICHNA.COM WEB: WWW.ZURICHNA.COM
	Workers Comp, Self-Insured	26 CENTURY BLVD STE 710 N NASHVILLE, TN 37214 PO BOX 305010 NASHVILLE, TN 37229-5010	PHONE: (615) 872-1300 FAX: (615) 872-1303 TOLL FREE: (800) 366-8366	E-MAIL: USZ_CARECENTER@ZURICHNA.COM WEB: WWW.ZURICHNA.COM
	Workers Comp, Self-Insured	SOUTHWEST CLAIM CENTER PO BOX 610787 DALLAS, TX 75261-0787	FAX: (866) 689-8972 TOLL FREE: (866) 828-6816	E-MAIL: USZ_CARECENTER@ZURICHNA.COM WEB: WWW.ZURICHNA.COM
CALIFORNIA	Workers Comp, Self-Insured	PO BOX 7774 SAN FRANCISCO, CA 94120-7774	PHONE: (415) 538-7100 FAX: (415) 538-7150 TOLL FREE: (800) 701-4926	E-MAIL: USZ_CARECENTER@ZURICHNA.COM WEB: WWW.ZURICHNA.COM
	Workers Comp, Self-Insured	PO BOX 92566 LOS ANGELES, CA 90009-2566	PHONE: (818) 227-1700 FAX: (818) 227-1740 TOLL FREE: (800) 338-3160	E-MAIL: USZ_CARECENTER@ZURICHNA.COM WEB: WWW.ZURICHNA.COM

CALIFORNIA — CONTINUED	WESTERN CLAIM CENTER 3249 QUALITY DR STE 300 RANCHO CORDOVA , CA 95670 PO BOX 981030 WEST SACRAMENTO, CA 95798	PHONE: (916) 635-1113 FAX: (800) 547-2487 TOLL FREE: (800) 239-4829	E-MAIL: USZ_CARECENTER@ZURICHNA.COM WEB: WWW.ZURICHNA.COM
COLORADO	PO BOX 20048 KANSAS CITY, MO 64195-0048	PHONE: (913) 345-8600 FAX: (913) 345-1582 TOLL FREE: (800) 777-9005	E-MAIL: USZ_CARECENTER@ZURICHNA.COM WEB: WWW.ZURICHNA.COM
	SOUTHWEST CLAIM CENTER PO BOX 610787 DALLAS, TX 75261-0787	FAX: (866) 689-8972 TOLL FREE: (866) 828-6816	E-MAIL: USZ_CARECENTER@ZURICHNA.COM WEB: WWW.ZURICHNA.COM
CONNECTICUT	NORTHEAST CLAIM CENTER PO BOX 4030 ROCKY HILL, CT 06067-4030	PHONE: (860) 257-6500 FAX: (800) 887-1335 TOLL FREE: (800) 239-4559	E-MAIL: USZ_CARECENTER@ZURICHNA.COM WEB: WWW.ZURICHNA.COM
	PO BOX 55217 BOSTON, MA 02205-5217	PHONE: (978) 738-8700 FAX: (978) 738-8760 TOLL FREE: (800) 818-5835	E-MAIL: USZ_CARECENTER@ZURICHNA.COM WEB: WWW.ZURICHNA.COM
DELAWARE	MID ATLANTIC CLAIM CENTER EXPRESS PO BOX 28777 BALTIMORE, MD 21240	PHONE: (410) 527-3060 FAX: (800) 404-9987 TOLL FREE: (800) 239-6851	E-MAIL: USZ_CARECENTER@ZURICHNA.COM WEB: WWW.ZURICHNA.COM
	PO BOX 13761 PHILADELPHIA, PA 19104-3761	FAX: (856) 985-2960 TOLL FREE: (800) 257-8134	E-MAIL: USZ_CARECENTER@ZURICHNA.COM WEB: WWW.ZURICHNA.COM
DISTRICT OF COLUMBIA	MID ATLANTIC CLAIM CENTER EXPRESS PO BOX 28777 BALTIMORE, MD 21240	PHONE: (410) 527-3060 FAX: (800) 404-9987 TOLL FREE: (800) 239-6851	E-MAIL: USZ_CARECENTER@ZURICHNA.COM WEB: WWW.ZURICHNA.COM
	PO BOX 13761 PHILADELPHIA, PA 19104-3761	FAX: (856) 985-2960 TOLL FREE: (800) 257-8134	E-MAIL: USZ_CARECENTER@ZURICHNA.COM WEB: WWW.ZURICHNA.COM
FLORIDA	PO BOX 628210 ORLANDO, FL 32862-8210	PHONE: (407) 660-9096 FAX: (407) 660-0339 TOLL FREE: (800) 340-8602	E-MAIL: USZ_CARECENTER@ZURICHNA.COM WEB: WWW.ZURICHNA.COM
	SOUTHEAST CLAIM CENTER PO BOX 30729 TAMPA, FL 33630-3729	PHONE: (813) 873-2055 FAX: (800) 333-8004 TOLL FREE: (800) 239-4781	E-MAIL: USZ_CARECENTER@ZURICHNA.COM WEB: WWW.ZURICHNA.COM
GEORGIA	PO BOX 20791 ATLANTA, GA 30320-0791	PHONE: (404) 851-3200 FAX: (404) 851-3601 TOLL FREE: (800) 241-7570	E-MAIL: USZ_CARECENTER@ZURICHNA.COM WEB: WWW.ZURICHNA.COM
	SOUTHEAST CLAIM CENTER PO BOX 30729 TAMPA, FL 33630-3729	PHONE: (813) 873-2055 FAX: (800) 333-8004 TOLL FREE: (800) 239-4781	E-MAIL: USZ_CARECENTER@ZURICHNA.COM WEB: WWW.ZURICHNA.COM
HAWAII	PO BOX 7774 SAN FRANCISCO, CA 94120-7774	PHONE: (415) 538-7100 FAX: (415) 538-7150 TOLL FREE: (800) 701-4926	E-MAIL: USZ_CARECENTER@ZURICHNA.COM WEB: WWW.ZURICHNA.COM
	WESTERN CLAIM CENTER 3249 QUALITY DR STE 300 RANCHO CORDOVA , CA 95670 PO BOX 981030 WEST SACRAMENTO, CA 95798	PHONE: (916) 635-1113 FAX: (800) 547-2487 TOLL FREE: (800) 239-4829	E-MAIL: USZ_CARECENTER@ZURICHNA.COM WEB: WWW.ZURICHNA.COM
IDAHO	PO BOX 7774 SAN FRANCISCO, CA 94120-7774	PHONE: (415) 538-7100 FAX: (415) 538-7150 TOLL FREE: (800) 701-4926	E-MAIL: USZ_CARECENTER@ZURICHNA.COM WEB: WWW.ZURICHNA.COM
	WESTERN CLAIM CENTER 3249 QUALITY DR STE 300 RANCHO CORDOVA , CA 95670 PO BOX 981030 WEST SACRAMENTO, CA 95798	PHONE: (916) 635-1113 FAX: (800) 547-2487 TOLL FREE: (800) 239-4829	E-MAIL: USZ_CARECENTER@ZURICHNA.COM WEB: WWW.ZURICHNA.COM
ILLINOIS	CENTRAL CLAIM CENTER EXPRESS PO BOX 512000 INDIANAPOLIS, IN 46251-2000	PHONE: (317) 587-7500 FAX: (800) 282-7538 TOLL FREE: (800) 239-0283	E-MAIL: USZ_CARECENTER@ZURICHNA.COM WEB: WWW.ZURICHNA.COM

ILLINOIS — CONTINUED	Workers Comp, Self-Insured, Main Office	1400 AMERICAN LN (T2/8TH FL) SCHAUMBURG, IL 60196-1056 PO BOX 66941 CHICAGO, IL 60666-0941	PHONE: (847) 413-5669 FAX: (847) 240-8172 TOLL FREE: (800) 695-6575	E-MAIL: USZ_CARECENTER@ZURICHNA.COM WEB: WWW.ZURICHNA.COM
INDIANA *IOWA*	Workers Comp, Self-Insured	CENTRAL CLAIM CENTER EXPRESS PO BOX 512000 INDIANAPOLIS, IN 46251-2000	PHONE: (317) 587-7500 FAX: (800) 282-7538 TOLL FREE: (800) 239-0283	E-MAIL: USZ_CARECENTER@ZURICHNA.COM WEB: WWW.ZURICHNA.COM
IOWA	Workers Comp, Self-Insured, Main Office	1400 AMERICAN LN (T2/8TH FL) SCHAUMBURG, IL 60196-1056 PO BOX 66941 CHICAGO, IL 60666-0941	PHONE: (847) 413-5669 FAX: (847) 240-8172 TOLL FREE: (800) 695-6575	E-MAIL: USZ_CARECENTER@ZURICHNA.COM WEB: WWW.ZURICHNA.COM
KANSAS	Workers Comp, Self-Insured	PO BOX 20048 KANSAS CITY, MO 64195-0048	PHONE: (913) 345-8600 FAX: (913) 345-1582 TOLL FREE: (800) 777-9005	E-MAIL: USZ_CARECENTER@ZURICHNA.COM WEB: WWW.ZURICHNA.COM
KANSAS *KENTUCKY*	Workers Comp, Self-Insured	CENTRAL CLAIM CENTER EXPRESS PO BOX 512000 INDIANAPOLIS, IN 46251-2000	PHONE: (317) 587-7500 FAX: (800) 282-7538 TOLL FREE: (800) 239-0283	E-MAIL: USZ_CARECENTER@ZURICHNA.COM WEB: WWW.ZURICHNA.COM
KENTUCKY	Workers Comp, Self-Insured	PO BOX 20791 ATLANTA, GA 30320-0791	PHONE: (404) 851-3200 FAX: (404) 851-3601 TOLL FREE: (800) 241-7570	E-MAIL: USZ_CARECENTER@ZURICHNA.COM WEB: WWW.ZURICHNA.COM
	Workers Comp, Self-Insured	26 CENTURY BLVD STE 710 N NASHVILLE, TN 37214 PO BOX 305010 NASHVILLE, TN 37229-5010	PHONE: (615) 872-1300 FAX: (615) 872-1303 TOLL FREE: (800) 366-3366	E-MAIL: USZ_CARECENTER@ZURICHNA.COM WEB: WWW.ZURICHNA.COM
LOUISIANA	Workers Comp, Self-Insured	PO BOX 619507 DALLAS, TX 75261-9507	PHONE: (214) 866-1500 FAX: (214) 866-1676 TOLL FREE: (866) 828-5816	E-MAIL: USZ_CARECENTER@ZURICHNA.COM WEB: WWW.ZURICHNA.COM
	Workers Comp, Self-Insured	SOUTHWEST CLAIM CENTER PO BOX 610787 DALLAS, TX 75261-0787	FAX: (866) 689-8972 TOLL FREE: (866) 828-5816	E-MAIL: USZ_CARECENTER@ZURICHNA.COM WEB: WWW.ZURICHNA.COM
MAINE	Workers Comp, Self-Insured	NORTHEAST CLAIM CENTER PO BOX 4030 ROCKY HILL, CT 06067-4030	PHONE: (860) 257-6500 FAX: (800) 887-1335 TOLL FREE: (800) 239-4559	E-MAIL: USZ_CARECENTER@ZURICHNA.COM WEB: WWW.ZURICHNA.COM
	Workers Comp, Self-Insured	PO BOX 55217 BOSTON, MA 02205-5217	PHONE: (978) 738-8700 FAX: (978) 738-8760 TOLL FREE: (800) 818-5835	E-MAIL: USZ_CARECENTER@ZURICHNA.COM WEB: WWW.ZURICHNA.COM
MARYLAND	Workers Comp, Self-Insured	MID ATLANTIC CLAIM CENTER EXPRESS PO BOX 28777 BALTIMORE, MD 21240	PHONE: (410) 527-3060 FAX: (800) 404-9987 TOLL FREE: (800) 239-5851	E-MAIL: USZ_CARECENTER@ZURICHNA.COM WEB: WWW.ZURICHNA.COM
	Workers Comp, Self-Insured	PO BOX 13761 PHILADELPHIA, PA 19104-3761	FAX: (856) 985-2960 TOLL FREE: (800) 257-3134	E-MAIL: USZ_CARECENTER@ZURICHNA.COM WEB: WWW.ZURICHNA.COM
MASSACHUSETTS	Workers Comp, Self-Insured	NORTHEAST CLAIM CENTER PO BOX 4030 ROCKY HILL, CT 06067-4030	PHONE: (860) 257-6500 FAX: (800) 887-1335 TOLL FREE: (800) 239-4559	E-MAIL: USZ_CARECENTER@ZURICHNA.COM WEB: WWW.ZURICHNA.COM
	Workers Comp, Self-Insured	PO BOX 55217 BOSTON, MA 02205-5217	PHONE: (978) 738-8700 FAX: (978) 738-8760 TOLL FREE: (800) 818-5835	E-MAIL: USZ_CARECENTER@ZURICHNA.COM WEB: WWW.ZURICHNA.COM
MICHIGAN	Workers Comp, Self-Insured	CENTRAL CLAIM CENTER EXPRESS PO BOX 512000 INDIANAPOLIS, IN 46251-2000	PHONE: (317) 587-7500 FAX: (800) 282-7538 TOLL FREE: (800) 239-0283	E-MAIL: USZ_CARECENTER@ZURICHNA.COM WEB: WWW.ZURICHNA.COM
MINNESOTA	Workers Comp, Self-Insured	PO BOX 20048 KANSAS CITY, MO 64195-0048	PHONE: (913) 345-8600 FAX: (913) 345-1582 TOLL FREE: (800) 777-9005	E-MAIL: USZ_CARECENTER@ZURICHNA.COM WEB: WWW.ZURICHNA.COM
	Workers Comp, Self-Insured	CENTRAL CLAIM CENTER EXPRESS PO BOX 512000 INDIANAPOLIS, IN 46251-2000	PHONE: (317) 587-7500 FAX: (800) 282-7538 TOLL FREE: (800) 239-0283	E-MAIL: USZ_CARECENTER@ZURICHNA.COM WEB: WWW.ZURICHNA.COM

MISSISSIPPI	Casualty/Liability	PO BOX 20791 ATLANTA, GA 30320-0791	PHONE: (404) 851-3200 FAX: (404) 851-3601 TOLL FREE: (800) 241-7570	E-MAIL: USZ_CARECENTER@ZURICHNA.COM WEB: WWW.ZURICHNA.COM
	Casualty/Liability	26 CENTURY BLVD STE 710 N NASHVILLE, TN 37214 PO BOX 305010 NASHVILLE, TN 37229-5010	PHONE: (615) 872-1300 FAX: (615) 872-1303 TOLL FREE: (800) 366-8366	E-MAIL: USZ_CARECENTER@ZURICHNA.COM WEB: WWW.ZURICHNA.COM
MISSOURI	Casualty/Liability	PO BOX 20048 KANSAS CITY, MO 64195-0048	PHONE: (913) 345-8600 FAX: (913) 345-1582 TOLL FREE: (800) 777-9005	E-MAIL: USZ_CARECENTER@ZURICHNA.COM WEB: WWW.ZURICHNA.COM
MISSOURI MONTANA	Casualty/Liability	CENTRAL CLAIM CENTER EXPRESS PO BOX 512000 INDIANAPOLIS, IN 46251-2000	PHONE: (317) 587-7500 FAX: (800) 282-7538 TOLL FREE: (800) 239-0283	E-MAIL: USZ_CARECENTER@ZURICHNA.COM WEB: WWW.ZURICHNA.COM
MONTANA	Casualty/Liability	PO BOX 7774 SAN FRANCISCO, CA 94120-7774	PHONE: (415) 538-7100 FAX: (415) 538-7150 TOLL FREE: (800) 701-4926	E-MAIL: USZ_CARECENTER@ZURICHNA.COM WEB: WWW.ZURICHNA.COM
	Casualty/Liability	WESTERN CLAIM CENTER 3249 QUALITY DR STE 300 RANCHO CORDOVA , CA 95670 PO BOX 981030 WEST SACRAMENTO, CA 95798	PHONE: (916) 635-1113 FAX: (800) 547-2487 TOLL FREE: (800) 239-4829	E-MAIL: USZ_CARECENTER@ZURICHNA.COM WEB: WWW.ZURICHNA.COM
MONTANA NEBRASKA	Casualty/Liability	PO BOX 20048 KANSAS CITY, MO 64195-0048	PHONE: (913) 345-8600 FAX: (913) 345-1582 TOLL FREE: (800) 777-9005	E-MAIL: USZ_CARECENTER@ZURICHNA.COM WEB: WWW.ZURICHNA.COM
NEBRASKA	Casualty/Liability	CENTRAL CLAIM CENTER EXPRESS PO BOX 512000 INDIANAPOLIS, IN 46251-2000	PHONE: (317) 587-7500 FAX: (800) 282-7538 TOLL FREE: (800) 239-0283	E-MAIL: USZ_CARECENTER@ZURICHNA.COM WEB: WWW.ZURICHNA.COM
NEVADA	Casualty/Liability	PO BOX 7774 SAN FRANCISCO, CA 94120-7774	PHONE: (415) 538-7100 FAX: (415) 538-7150 TOLL FREE: (800) 701-4926	E-MAIL: USZ_CARECENTER@ZURICHNA.COM WEB: WWW.ZURICHNA.COM
	Casualty/Liability	PO BOX 92566 LOS ANGELES, CA 90009-2566	PHONE: (818) 227-1700 FAX: (818) 227-1740 TOLL FREE: (800) 338-3160	E-MAIL: USZ_CARECENTER@ZURICHNA.COM WEB: WWW.ZURICHNA.COM
	Casualty/Liability	WESTERN CLAIM CENTER 3249 QUALITY DR STE 300 RANCHO CORDOVA , CA 95670 PO BOX 981030 WEST SACRAMENTO, CA 95798	PHONE: (916) 635-1113 FAX: (800) 547-2487 TOLL FREE: (800) 239-4829	E-MAIL: USZ_CARECENTER@ZURICHNA.COM WEB: WWW.ZURICHNA.COM
NEW HAMPSHIRE	Casualty/Liability	NORTHEAST CLAIM CENTER PO BOX 4030 ROCKY HILL, CT 06067-4030	PHONE: (860) 257-6500 FAX: (800) 887-1335 TOLL FREE: (800) 239-4559	E-MAIL: USZ_CARECENTER@ZURICHNA.COM WEB: WWW.ZURICHNA.COM
	Casualty/Liability	PO BOX 55217 BOSTON, MA 02205-5217	PHONE: (978) 738-8700 FAX: (978) 738-8760 TOLL FREE: (800) 818-5835	E-MAIL: USZ_CARECENTER@ZURICHNA.COM WEB: WWW.ZURICHNA.COM
NEW JERSEY	Casualty/Liability	NORTHEAST CLAIM CENTER PO BOX 4030 ROCKY HILL, CT 06067-4030	PHONE: (860) 257-6500 FAX: (800) 887-1335 TOLL FREE: (800) 239-4559	E-MAIL: USZ_CARECENTER@ZURICHNA.COM WEB: WWW.ZURICHNA.COM
	Casualty/Liability	PO BOX 905 NEWARK, NJ 07101-0905	PHONE: (973) 394-5100 FAX: (973) 394-5262 TOLL FREE: (800) 255-3612	E-MAIL: USZ_CARECENTER@ZURICHNA.COM WEB: WWW.ZURICHNA.COM
NEW MEXICO	Casualty/Liability	PO BOX 7774 SAN FRANCISCO, CA 94120-7774	PHONE: (415) 538-7100 FAX: (415) 538-7150 TOLL FREE: (800) 701-4926	E-MAIL: USZ_CARECENTER@ZURICHNA.COM WEB: WWW.ZURICHNA.COM
	Casualty/Liability	PO BOX 20048 KANSAS CITY, MO 64195-0048	PHONE: (913) 345-8600 FAX: (913) 345-1582 TOLL FREE: (800) 777-9005	E-MAIL: USZ_CARECENTER@ZURICHNA.COM WEB: WWW.ZURICHNA.COM
	Casualty/Liability	SOUTHWEST CLAIM CENTER PO BOX 610787 DALLAS, TX 75261-0787	FAX: (866) 689-8972 TOLL FREE: (866) 828-6816	E-MAIL: USZ_CARECENTER@ZURICHNA.COM WEB: WWW.ZURICHNA.COM

NEW YORK	Workers Comp, Self-Insured	NORTHEAST CLAIM CENTER PO BOX 4030 ROCKY HILL, CT 06067-4030	PHONE: (860) 257-6500 FAX: (800) 887-1335 TOLL FREE: (800) 239-4559	E-MAIL: USZ_CARECENTER@ZURICHNA.COM WEB: WWW.ZURICHNA.COM
	Workers Comp, Self-Insured	PO BOX ZZ JAMAICA, NY 11430-00ZZ	FAX: (631) 845-2530 TOLL FREE: (800) 396-6677	E-MAIL: USZ_CARECENTER@ZURICHNA.COM WEB: WWW.ZURICHNA.COM
NORTH CAROLINA	Workers Comp, Self-Insured	MID ATLANTIC CLAIM CENTER EXPRESS PO BOX 28777 BALTIMORE, MD 21240	PHONE: (410) 527-3060 FAX: (800) 404-9987 TOLL FREE: (800) 239-6851	E-MAIL: USZ_CARECENTER@ZURICHNA.COM WEB: WWW.ZURICHNA.COM
	Workers Comp, Self-Insured	PO BOX 195008 CHARLOTTE, NC 28219-5008	PHONE: (704) 553-0360 FAX: (704) 551-3402 TOLL FREE: (800) 808-6412	E-MAIL: USZ_CARECENTER@ZURICHNA.COM WEB: WWW.ZURICHNA.COM
NORTH DAKOTA	Workers Comp, Self-Insured	PO BOX 20048 KANSAS CITY, MO 64195-0048	PHONE: (913) 345-8600 FAX: (913) 345-1582 TOLL FREE: (800) 777-9005	E-MAIL: USZ_CARECENTER@ZURICHNA.COM WEB: WWW.ZURICHNA.COM
	Workers Comp, Self-Insured	CENTRAL CLAIM CENTER EXPRESS PO BOX 512000 INDIANAPOLIS, IN 46251-2000	PHONE: (317) 587-7500 FAX: (800) 282-7538 TOLL FREE: (800) 239-0283	E-MAIL: USZ_CARECENTER@ZURICHNA.COM WEB: WWW.ZURICHNA.COM
OHIO	Workers Comp, Self-Insured	MID ATLANTIC CLAIM CENTER EXPRESS PO BOX 28777 BALTIMORE, MD 21240	PHONE: (410) 527-3060 FAX: (800) 404-9987 TOLL FREE: (800) 239-6851	E-MAIL: USZ_CARECENTER@ZURICHNA.COM WEB: WWW.ZURICHNA.COM
	Workers Comp, Self-Insured	PO BOX 13761 PHILADELPHIA, PA 19104-3761	FAX: (856) 985-2960 TOLL FREE: (800) 257-8134	E-MAIL: USZ_CARECENTER@ZURICHNA.COM WEB: WWW.ZURICHNA.COM
	Workers Comp, Main Office	PO BOX 1880 PITTSBURG, PA 15230-1880	FAX: (412) 928-0107 TOLL FREE: (800) 888-8765	E-MAIL: USZ_CARECENTER@ZURICHNA.COM WEB: WWW.ZURICHNA.COM
OKLAHOMA	Workers Comp, Self-Insured	PO BOX 619507 DALLAS, TX 75261-9507	PHONE: (214) 866-1500 FAX: (214) 866-1676 TOLL FREE: (866) 828-6816	E-MAIL: USZ_CARECENTER@ZURICHNA.COM WEB: WWW.ZURICHNA.COM
	Workers Comp, Self-Insured	SOUTHWEST CLAIM CENTER PO BOX 610787 DALLAS, TX 75261-0787	FAX: (866) 689-8972 TOLL FREE: (866) 828-6816	E-MAIL: USZ_CARECENTER@ZURICHNA.COM WEB: WWW.ZURICHNA.COM
OREGON	Workers Comp, Self-Insured	PO BOX 7774 SAN FRANCISCO, CA 94120-7774	PHONE: (415) 538-7100 FAX: (415) 538-7150 TOLL FREE: (800) 701-4926	E-MAIL: USZ_CARECENTER@ZURICHNA.COM WEB: WWW.ZURICHNA.COM
	Workers Comp, Self-Insured	WESTERN CLAIM CENTER 3249 QUALITY DR STE 300 RANCHO CORDOVA , CA 95670 PO BOX 981030 WEST SACRAMENTO, CA 95798	PHONE: (916) 635-1113 FAX: (800) 547-2487 TOLL FREE: (800) 239-4829	E-MAIL: USZ_CARECENTER@ZURICHNA.COM WEB: WWW.ZURICHNA.COM
PENNSYLVANIA	Workers Comp, Self-Insured	MID ATLANTIC CLAIM CENTER EXPRESS PO BOX 28777 BALTIMORE, MD 21240	PHONE: (410) 527-3060 FAX: (800) 404-9987 TOLL FREE: (800) 239-6851	E-MAIL: USZ_CARECENTER@ZURICHNA.COM WEB: WWW.ZURICHNA.COM
	Workers Comp, Self-Insured	PO BOX 13761 PHILADELPHIA, PA 19104-3761	FAX: (856) 985-2960 TOLL FREE: (800) 257-8134	E-MAIL: USZ_CARECENTER@ZURICHNA.COM WEB: WWW.ZURICHNA.COM
	Workers Comp, Main Office	PO BOX 1880 PITTSBURG, PA 15230-1880	FAX: (412) 928-0107 TOLL FREE: (800) 888-8765	E-MAIL: USZ_CARECENTER@ZURICHNA.COM WEB: WWW.ZURICHNA.COM
RHODE ISLAND	Workers Comp, Self-Insured	NORTHEAST CLAIM CENTER PO BOX 4030 ROCKY HILL, CT 06067-4030	PHONE: (860) 257-6500 FAX: (800) 887-1335 TOLL FREE: (800) 239-4559	E-MAIL: USZ_CARECENTER@ZURICHNA.COM WEB: WWW.ZURICHNA.COM
	Workers Comp, Self-Insured	PO BOX 55217 BOSTON, MA 02205-5217	PHONE: (978) 738-8700 FAX: (978) 738-8760 TOLL FREE: (800) 818-5835	E-MAIL: USZ_CARECENTER@ZURICHNA.COM WEB: WWW.ZURICHNA.COM
SOUTH CAROLINA	Workers Comp, Self-Insured	MID ATLANTIC CLAIM CENTER EXPRESS PO BOX 28777 BALTIMORE, MD 21240	PHONE: (410) 527-3060 FAX: (800) 404-9987 TOLL FREE: (800) 239-6851	E-MAIL: USZ_CARECENTER@ZURICHNA.COM WEB: WWW.ZURICHNA.COM

SOUTH CAROLINA — CONTINUED		PO BOX 195008 CHARLOTTE, NC 28219-5008	PHONE: (704) 553-0360 FAX: (704) 551-3402 TOLL FREE: (800) 808-6412	E-MAIL: USZ_CARECENTER@ZURICHNA.COM WEB: WWW.ZURICHNA.COM
SOUTH DAKOTA		PO BOX 20048 KANSAS CITY, MO 64195-0048	PHONE: (913) 345-8600 FAX: (913) 345-1582 TOLL FREE: (800) 777-9005	E-MAIL: USZ_CARECENTER@ZURICHNA.COM WEB: WWW.ZURICHNA.COM
		CENTRAL CLAIM CENTER EXPRESS PO BOX 512000 INDIANAPOLIS, IN 46251-2000	PHONE: (317) 587-7500 FAX: (800) 282-7538 TOLL FREE: (800) 239-0283	E-MAIL: USZ_CARECENTER@ZURICHNA.COM WEB: WWW.ZURICHNA.COM
TENNESSEE		PO BOX 20791 ATLANTA, GA 30320-0791	PHONE: (404) 851-3200 FAX: (404) 851-3601 TOLL FREE: (800) 241-7570	E-MAIL: USZ_CARECENTER@ZURICHNA.COM WEB: WWW.ZURICHNA.COM
		26 CENTURY BLVD STE 710 N NASHVILLE, TN 37214 PO BOX 305010 NASHVILLE, TN 37229-5010	PHONE: (615) 872-1300 FAX: (615) 872-1303 TOLL FREE: (800) 366-8366	E-MAIL: USZ_CARECENTER@ZURICHNA.COM WEB: WWW.ZURICHNA.COM
TEXAS		PO BOX 619507 DALLAS, TX 75261-9507	PHONE: (214) 866-1500 FAX: (214) 866-1676 TOLL FREE: (866) 828-6816	E-MAIL: USZ_CARECENTER@ZURICHNA.COM WEB: WWW.ZURICHNA.COM
		SOUTHWEST CLAIM CENTER PO BOX 610787 DALLAS, TX 75261-0787	FAX: (866) 689-8972 TOLL FREE: (866) 828-6816	E-MAIL: USZ_CARECENTER@ZURICHNA.COM WEB: WWW.ZURICHNA.COM
UTAH		WESTERN CLAIM CENTER 3249 QUALITY DR STE 300 RANCHO CORDOVA , CA 95670 PO BOX 981030 WEST SACRAMENTO, CA 95798	PHONE: (916) 635-1113 FAX: (800) 547-2487 TOLL FREE: (800) 239-4829	E-MAIL: USZ_CARECENTER@ZURICHNA.COM WEB: WWW.ZURICHNA.COM
		PO BOX 20048 KANSAS CITY, MO 64195-0048	PHONE: (913) 345-8600 FAX: (913) 345-1582 TOLL FREE: (800) 777-9005	E-MAIL: USZ_CARECENTER@ZURICHNA.COM WEB: WWW.ZURICHNA.COM
VERMONT		NORTHEAST CLAIM CENTER PO BOX 4030 ROCKY HILL, CT 06067-4030	PHONE: (860) 257-6500 FAX: (800) 887-1335 TOLL FREE: (800) 239-4559	E-MAIL: USZ_CARECENTER@ZURICHNA.COM WEB: WWW.ZURICHNA.COM
		PO BOX 55217 BOSTON, MA 02205-5217	PHONE: (978) 738-8700 FAX: (978) 738-8760 TOLL FREE: (800) 818-5835	E-MAIL: USZ_CARECENTER@ZURICHNA.COM WEB: WWW.ZURICHNA.COM
		PO BOX 13761 PHILADELPHIA, PA 19104-3761	FAX: (856) 985-2960 TOLL FREE: (800) 257-8134	E-MAIL: USZ_CARECENTER@ZURICHNA.COM WEB: WWW.ZURICHNA.COM
VIRGINIA		MID ATLANTIC CLAIM CENTER EXPRESS PO BOX 28777 BALTIMORE, MD 21240	PHONE: (410) 527-3060 FAX: (800) 404-9987 TOLL FREE: (800) 239-6851	E-MAIL: USZ_CARECENTER@ZURICHNA.COM WEB: WWW.ZURICHNA.COM
		PO BOX 13761 PHILADELPHIA, PA 19104-3761	FAX: (856) 985-2960 TOLL FREE: (800) 257-8134	E-MAIL: USZ_CARECENTER@ZURICHNA.COM WEB: WWW.ZURICHNA.COM
		PO BOX 1880 PITTSBURG, PA 15230-1880	FAX: (412) 928-0107 TOLL FREE: (800) 888-8765	E-MAIL: USZ_CARECENTER@ZURICHNA.COM WEB: WWW.ZURICHNA.COM
WASHINGTON		PO BOX 7774 SAN FRANCISCO, CA 94120-7774	PHONE: (415) 538-7100 FAX: (415) 538-7150 TOLL FREE: (800) 701-4926	E-MAIL: USZ_CARECENTER@ZURICHNA.COM WEB: WWW.ZURICHNA.COM
		WESTERN CLAIM CENTER 3249 QUALITY DR STE 300 RANCHO CORDOVA , CA 95670 PO BOX 981030 WEST SACRAMENTO, CA 95798	PHONE: (916) 635-1113 FAX: (800) 547-2487 TOLL FREE: (800) 239-4829	E-MAIL: USZ_CARECENTER@ZURICHNA.COM WEB: WWW.ZURICHNA.COM
WEST VIRGINIA		MID ATLANTIC CLAIM CENTER EXPRESS PO BOX 28777 BALTIMORE, MD 21240	PHONE: (410) 527-3060 FAX: (800) 404-9987 TOLL FREE: (800) 239-6851	E-MAIL: USZ_CARECENTER@ZURICHNA.COM WEB: WWW.ZURICHNA.COM

WEST VIRGINIA — CONTINUED	Workers Comp, Self-Insured	PO BOX 13761 PHILADELPHIA, PA 19104-3761	FAX: (856) 985-2960 TOLL FREE: (800) 257-8134	E-MAIL: USZ_CARECENTER@ZURICHNA.COM WEB: WWW.ZURICHNA.COM
WISCONSIN	Workers Comp, Self-Insured	CENTRAL CLAIM CENTER EXPRESS PO BOX 512000 INDIANAPOLIS, IN 46251-2000	PHONE: (317) 587-7500 FAX: (800) 282-7538 TOLL FREE: (800) 239-0283	E-MAIL: USZ_CARECENTER@ZURICHNA.COM WEB: WWW.ZURICHNA.COM
	Workers Comp, Self-Insured, Main Office	1400 AMERICAN LN (T2/8TH FL) SCHAUMBURG, IL 60196-1056 PO BOX 66941 CHICAGO, IL 60666-0941	PHONE: (847) 413-5669 FAX: (847) 240-8172 TOLL FREE: (800) 695-6575	E-MAIL: USZ_CARECENTER@ZURICHNA.COM WEB: WWW.ZURICHNA.COM
	Workers Comp	PO BOX 3193 MILWAUKEE, WI 53201-3193	PHONE: (262) 798-8920 FAX: (262) 798-8883 TOLL FREE: (800) 631-6074	E-MAIL: USZ_CARECENTER@ZURICHNA.COM WEB: WWW.ZURICHNA.COM
WYOMING	Workers Comp, Self-Insured	WESTERN CLAIM CENTER 3249 QUALITY DR STE 300 RANCHO CORDOVA , CA 95670 PO BOX 981030 WEST SACRAMENTO, CA 95798	PHONE: (916) 635-1113 FAX: (800) 547-2487 TOLL FREE: (800) 239-4829	E-MAIL: USZ_CARECENTER@ZURICHNA.COM WEB: WWW.ZURICHNA.COM
	Workers Comp, Self-Insured	PO BOX 20048 KANSAS CITY, MO 64195-0048	PHONE: (913) 345-8600 FAX: (913) 345-1582 TOLL FREE: (800) 777-9005	E-MAIL: USZ_CARECENTER@ZURICHNA.COM WEB: WWW.ZURICHNA.COM

State-by-State Index

NATIONAL

NATIONAL — CONTINUED

NATIONAL — CONTINUED

State-By-State Index

NATIONAL — CONTINUED

ALABAMA

ALASKA

ARIZONA — CONTINUED

ARKANSAS

BRITISH COLUMBIA

CALIFORNIA

CALIFORNIA — CONTINUED

CANADA

COLORADO

CONNECTICUT

DELAWARE

DELAWARE — CONTINUED

DISTRICT OF COLUMBIA

FLORIDA

GEORGIA

GUAM

HAWAII

IDAHO

ILLINOIS

ILLINOIS — CONTINUED

INDIANA

IOWA

KANSAS

KENTUCKY

LOUISIANA

LOUISIANA — CONTINUED

MAINE

MANITOBA

MARYLAND

MICHIGAN — CONTINUED

MINNESOTA

MISSISSIPPI

MISSOURI

MISSOURI — CONTINUED

MONTANA

NEVADA — CONTINUED

NEW BRUNSWICK

NEW HAMPSHIRE

NEW JERSEY

NEW MEXICO

NEW YORK

NEW ZEALAND

NEWFOUNDLAND

NORTH CAROLINA

NORTH DAKOTA

NOVA SCOTIA

NOVA SCOTIA — CONTINUED

OHIO

OKLAHOMA

ONTARIO

OREGON

OREGON — CONTINUED

PENNSYLVANIA

PRINCE EDWARD ISLAND

PUERTO RICO

QUEBEC

RHODE ISLAND

SASKATCHEWAN

SOUTH CAROLINA

SOUTH CAROLINA — CONTINUED

SOUTH DAKOTA

TENNESSEE

TENNESSEE — CONTINUED

TEXAS

VERMONT — CONTINUED

VIRGIN ISLANDS

VIRGINIA

WASHINGTON

WEST VIRGINIA

State-By-State Index

WEST VIRGINIA — CONTINUED

WISCONSIN

WYOMING

Appendix A: Abbreviations

State and Province Abbreviations

Alabama	AL
Alaska	AK
American Samoa	AS
Arizona	AZ
Arkansas	AR
California	CA
Colorado	CO
Connecticut	CT
Delaware	DE
District of Columbia	DC
Federated States of Micronesia	FM
Florida	FL
Georgia	GA
Guam	GU
Hawaii	HI
Idaho	ID
Illinois	IL
Indiana	IN
Iowa	IA
Kansas	KS
Kentucky	KY
Louisiana	LA
Maine	ME
Marshall Islands	MH
Maryland	MD
Massachusetts	MA
Michigan	MI
Minnesota	MN
Mississippi	MS
Missouri	MO
Montana	MT
Nebraska	NE
Nevada	NV
New Hampshire	NH
New Jersey	NJ
New Mexico	NM
New York	NY
North Carolina	NC
North Dakota	ND
Northern Mariana Islands	MP
Ohio	OH
Oklahoma	OK
Oregon	OR
Palau	PW
Pennsylvania	PA
Puerto Rico	PR
Rhode Island	RI
South Carolina	SC
South Dakota	SD
Tennessee	TN
Texas	TX
Utah	UT
Vermont	VT
Virgin Islands	VI
Virginia	VA
Washington	WA
West Virginia	WV
Wisconsin	WI
Wyoming	WY

Canadian Provinces

Alberta	AB
British Columbia	BC
Manitoba	MB
New Brunswick	NB
Newfoundland and Labrador	NL
Nova Scotia	NS
Northwest Territories	NT
Nunavut	NU
Ontario	ON
Prince Edward Island	PE
Quebec	QC
Saskatchewan	SK
Yukon	YT

Geographic Directional Abbreviations

North	N
East	E
South	S
West	W
Northeast	NE
Southeast	SE
Southwest	SW
Northwest	NW

Regional Abbreviations

All Regions	NATL
Central Region	CR
Eastern Region	ER
Northeast Region	NE
Southern Region	SR
Western Region	WR

Abbreviations for Steeet Designators

Street Suffix or Suffix Abbrev.	USPS Suffix Abbrev
allee	aly
alley	aly
ally	aly
anex	anx
annex	anx
annx	anx
arcade	arc
av	ave
aven	ave
avenu	ave
avenue	ave
avn	ave
avnue	ave
bayoo	byu
bayou	byu
beach	bch
bend	bnd
bluf	blf
bluff	blf
bluffs	blf
bot	btm
bottm	btm
bottom	btm
boul	blvd
boulevard	blvd
boulv	blvd
branch	br
brdge	brg
bridge	brg
brnch	br
brook	brk
brooks	brk
burg	bg
burgs	bg
bypa	byp
bypas	byp
bypass	byp
byps	byp
camp	cp
canyn	cyn
canyon	cyn
cape	cpe
causeway	cswy
causway	cswy
cen	ctr
cent	ctr
center	ctr
centers	ctr
centr	ctr
circ	cir
circl	cir
circle	cir
crcles	cir
clf	clfs
cliff	clfs
cliffs	clfs
club	clb
cmp	cp
cnter	ctr
cntr	ctr
cnyn	cyn
corner	cor
corners	cors
course	crse
court	ct
courts	cts
cove	cv
coves	cv
crcl	cir
circle	cir
crecent	cres
creek	crk
crest	cres
crescent	cres
cresent	cres
crossing	xing
crscent	cres
crsent	cres
crsnt	cres
crssng	xing
dale	dl
dam	dm
div	dv
divide	dv
driv	dr
drive	dr
drives	dr
drv	dr
dvd	dv
estate	est
estates	est
ests	est
exp	expy
expr	expy
express	expy
expressway	expy
expw	exp
extension	ext
extn	ext
extnsn	ext
exts	ext
falls	fls
ferry	fry
field	fld
fields	flds
flat	flt
flats	flt
flts	flt

Street Suffix or Suffix Abbrev.	USPS Suffix Abbrev
ford	frd
fords	frd
forest	frst
forests	frst
forg	frg
forge	frg
forges	frg
fork	frk
forks	frks
fort	ft
freeway	fwy
freewy	fwy
frry	fry
frt	ft
frway	fwy
frwy	fwy
garden	gdns
gardens	gdns
gardn	gdns
gateway	gtwy
Gatewy	gtwy
gatway	gtwy
gdn	gdns
glen	gln
glens	gln
grden	gdns
grdn	gdns
grdns	gdns
green	grn
greens	grn
grov	grv
grove	grv
gtway	gtwy
harb	hbr
harbor	hbr
harbors	hbr
harbr	hbr
haven	hvn
havn	hvn
height	hts
heights	hts
highway	hwy
highwy	hwy
hill	hl
hills	hls
hiway	hwy
hiwy	hwy
hllw	holw
hollow	holw
holws	holw
hrbor	hbr
ht	hts
hway	hwy
inlet	inlt
island	is

Street Suffix or Suffix Abbrev.	USPS Suffix Abbrev
islands	iss
isles	isle
islnd	is
islnds	iss
jction	jct
jctn	jct
jctns	jct
jcts	jct
junction	jct
junctn	jct
juncton	jct
key	ky
keys	ky
knl	knls
knol	knls
knoll	knls
knolls	knls
kys	ky
lake	lk
lakes	lks
landing	lndg
lane	ln
lanes	ln
ldge	ldg
light	lgt
lights	lgt
lndng	lndg
loaf	lf
lock	lcks
locks	lcks
lodg	ldg
lodge	ldg
loops	loop
manor	mnr
manors	mnr
mdw	mdws
meadow	mdws
meadows	mdws
medows	mdws
mill	ml
mills	mls
mission	msn
missn	msn
mnrs	mnr
mnt	mt
mntain	mtn
mntn	mtn
mntns	mtn
mount	mt
mountain	mtn
mountin	mtn
mssn	msn
mtin	mtn
neck	nck
orchard	orch

Appendix A

Street Suffix or Suffix Abbrev.	USPS Suffix Abbrev
orchrd	orch
ovl	oval
parks	park
parkway	pky
parkwy	pky
paths	path
pikes	pike
pine	pnes
pines	pnes
pkway	pky
pkwy	pky
pkwys	pky
place	pl
plain	pln
plaines	plns
plaza	plz
plza	plz
point	pt
points	pt
port	prt
ports	prt
prarie	pr
prk	park
prr	pr
prts	prt
pts	pt
rad	radl
radial	radl
radiel	radl
ranches	rnch
rapid	rpds
rapids	rpds
rdge	rdg
rdgs	rdg
rds	rd
rest	rst
ridge	rdg
ridges	rdg
river	riv
rivr	riv
rnchs	rnch
road	rd
roads	rd
route	rt
rpd	rpds
rvr	riv
shoal	shl
shoals	shls
shoar	shr
shoars	shrs
shore	shr
shores	shrs
spng	spg
spngs	spgs
spring	spg

Street Suffix or Suffix Abbrev.	USPS Suffix Abbrev
springs	spgs
sprng	spg
sprngs	spgs
spurs	spur
sqr	sq
sqre	sq
squ	sq
square	sq
squares	sq
station	sta
statn	sta
stn	sta
str	st
strav	stra
strave	stra
straven	stra
stravenue	stra
stravn	stra
stream	strm
street	st
streets	st
streme	strm
strt	st
strvn	stra
strvnue	stra
sumit	smt
sumitt	smt
summit	smt
terr	ter
terrace	ter
tpk	tpke
trace	trce
traces	trce
track	trak
tracks	trak
trail	trl
trailer	trlr
trails	trl
trk	trak
trks	trak
trlrs	trlr
trls	trl
trnpk	tpke
tunel	tunl
tunls	tunl
tunnel	tunl
tunnl	tunl
turnpike	tpke
turnpk	tpke
union	un
unions	un
valley	vly
valleys	vly
vally	vly
vdct	via

Street Suffix or Suffix Abbrev.	USPS Suffix Abbrev
viadct	via
viaduct	via
view	vw
views	vw
vill	vlg
villag	vlg
village	vlg
ville	vl
villg	vlg
villiage	vlg
vist	vis
vista	vis
vlg	vlg
vlgs	vlg
vlly	vly
vlys	vly
vst	vis
vsta	vis
vws	vw
walks	walk
ways	way
well	wls
wells	wls
wy	way

USPS Approved Envelope Addressing Formats

Appendix B: E-mail and Website Addresses

NOTE: FOR MULTIPLE LISTINGS UNDER A COMPANY, REFER TO CHAPTER 9, THE DIRECTORY, FOR CORRECT E-MAIL/WEBSITE BY STATE.

E-MAIL ADDRESSES

21ST CENTURY INSURANCE GROUP	INETCLAIMS@21ST.COM
ABC HEALTH PLAN	INFORMATION@ABCHEALTHPLAN.ORG
ACCESS ADMINISTRATORS, INC.	CS@AHS-ACCESS.COM
ACSTAR INSURANCE COMPANY	INFO@ACSTARINS.COM
ADMINISTRATION SERVICES, INC.	ASI@ADMIN-SERV.COM
ADMINISTRATIVE SERVICES, INC	INFO@ADMINSERV.COM
ADVANCE INSURANCE COMPANY	FEEDBACK@ADVANCEINSURANCE.COM
AFFINITY HEALTH PLAN	MEMBER@AFFINITYPLAN.ORG
AFLAC	AK@AFLAC.COM
AIG CLAIM SERVICES, INC	AIGH@AIGHAWAII.COM
AIM MUTUAL INSURANCE COMPANY	CLAIMS@AIMMUTUAL.COM
ALABAMA FINANCIAL POTENTIAL CENTRES, INC.	MSNOW@ALSTC.COM
ALASKA NATIONAL INSURANCE COMPANY	ANCHORAGE@ALASKANATIONAL.COM
ALASKA NATIONAL INSURANCE COMPANY	SANFRANSICO@ALASKANATIONAL.COM
ALASKA NATIONAL INSURANCE COMPANY	SEATTLE@ALASKANATIONAL.COM
ALEA NORTH AMERICA INSURANCE COMPANY	ROCKYHILL@ALEAGROUP.COM
ALICARE	GENERALINFO@ALICARE.COM
ALOHA CARE OF HAWAII	CUSTOMERSERVICE@ALOHACAREHAWAII.ORG
AMERIBEN SOLUTIONS	INFO@AMERIBEN.COM
AMERICAN COMMERCE INSURANCE CO	CUSTOMERSERVICE@ACILINK.COM
AMERICAN HARDWARE MUTUAL INSURANCE CO	MINNETONKABRANCH@MOTORISTSGROUP.COM
AMERICAN HARDWARE MUTUAL INSURANCE COMPANY	COLUMBUSBRANCH@MOTORISTGROUP.COM
AMERICAN HARDWARE MUTUAL INSURANCE COMPANY	INDIANAPOLIS.BRANCH@MOTORISTSGROUP.COM
AMERICAN INCOME LIFE INSURANCE CO	CONTACTUS@AILINS.COM
AMERICAN LIFECARE	INFO@AMERICANLIFECARE.COM
AMERICAN MAYFLOWER	AML1@GECAPITAL.COM
AMERICAN RE-INSURANCE	INFO@AMRE.COM
AMERICAN SOUTHERN INSURANCE CO.	INFO@AMSOU.COM
AMERICAN WHOLE HEALTH NETWORKS, INC	CONTACTUSI@AWHINC.COM
ARAG GROUP	SERVICE@ARAGGROUP.COM
ARCTIC ADJUSTERS, INC.	INFO@ARCTICADJUSTERS.COM
ARGUS SERVICES CORP	ARGUS1@AIRMAIL.NET
ASSOCIATED ADJUSTERS	INFO@ASSOCIATED-ADJUSTERS.COM
ASSOCIATION & SOCIETY INSURANCE CORP	CUSTSVC@ASICORPORATION.COM
ASSURE CARE	INFO@ASSURECARE.COM
ASSURITY LIFE INSURANCE	INFO@ASSURITY.COM
AULTCARE	AULTCARE@AULTMANS.COM
AV-MED HEALTH PLAN	MEMBERS@AVMED.ORG
BALBOA INSURANCE GROUP	INFO@BALBOAINSURANCE.COM
BANKERS INDEPENDENT INSURANCE CO	INFO@BIIC.COM
BANKERS INSURANCE GROUP	INFO@BANKERSINSURANCE.COM
BCI INSURANCE SERVICES	INFO@BCI-INS.COM
BEAR RIVER MUTUAL INSURANCE CO	SERVICES1@BRMUTUAL.COM
BEHAVIOR HEALTH SYSTEMS	INFO@BHS-INC.COM
BELOIT MEMORIAL HOSPITAL	WEBMASTER@BELOITMEMORIALHOSPITAL.ORG

BENEFICIAL LIFE INSURANCE CO. .... CUSTSERVE@BENFINANCIAL.COM
BENEFIT & RISK MANAGEMENT SERVICES .... INFO@BRMS-ONLINE.COM
BENEFIT ADMINISTRATIVE SYSTEMS, LTD .... ADMIN@BENADMINSYS.COM
BENEFIT PLAN ADMINISTRATORS, INC .... BPA@BPATPA.COM
BENEFIT PLANNERS, INC .... SERVICE@BENPLAN.COM
BENICOMP, INC .... BENICOMP@BENICOMP.COM
BENICORP INSURANCE CO .... CLAIMS@BENICORP.COM
BERKSHIRE LIFE INSURANCE CO OF AMERICA .... CUSTOMERSERVICE@BERKSHIRELIFE.COM
BLUE CROSS AND BLUE SHIELD OF ALABAMA .... WEBINPUT@BCBSAL.ORG
BLUE CROSS BLUE SHIELD OF KANSAS .... CSC@BCBSKS.COM
BLUE CROSS BLUE SHIELD .... GENERAL@BCBSMT.COM
BLUE CROSS BLUE SHIELD .... INFO@ARKBLUECROSS.COM
BLUE CROSS BLUE SHIELD .... NEREGIONCS@ARKBLUECROSS.COM
BLUE CROSS BLUE SHIELD .... SERVICEWNY@HEALTHNOW.COM
BLUE CROSS BLUE SHIELD .... UTGENDEV@REGENCE.COM
BLUE CROSS BLUE SHIELD .... WEBMASTER@BCBSAZ.COM
BLUEGRASS FAMILY HEALTH .... WEBMASTER@BGFH.COM
BMI - HEALTH PLANS .... BMI@BMI-HEALTHPLANS.COM
BOSTON MUTUAL LIFE INSURANCE CO .... CLIENTSERVICES@BOSTONMUTUAL.COM
BUSINESS MENS INSURANCE CO .... BMI@BMICOS.COM
CABINET FOR HEALTH SERVICE OF KENTUCKY .... CHS.DMSWEB@KY.GOV
CALCO, INC .... CAL@CALCOINCTPA.COM
CANADA LIFE ASSURANCE CO .... INFO@CANADALIFE.COM
CANAL INSURANCE CO .... INFO@CANAL-INS.COM
CANON COCHRAN MANAGEMENT SERVICES, INC .... CCMSI@CCMSI.COM
CAPITAL BLUE CROSS .... WEBMASTER@CAPBLUECROSS.COM
CAPITAL DISTRICT PHYSICIANS' HEALTH PLAN, INC .... INFO@CDPHP.COM
CAROLINA CASUALTY INSURANCE CO, INC .... INFO@CAROLINAS.COM
CBA, INC .... SERVICE@CBAVT.COM
CBCA ADMINISTRATORS, INC .... INFO@CBCA.COM
CBSA .... CBSA@CBSAINC.COM
CCMSI-MIDLAND LLC .... CCMSI@CCMSI.COM
CELINA INSURANCE GROUP .... HELPDESK@CELINAINSURANCE.COM
CENTRAL INSURANCE CO .... CLAIMS@CENTRAL-INSURANCE.COM
CENTRAL PENNSYLVANIA TEAMSTERS HEALTH & WELFARE FUND .... HEALTHANDWELFARE@CENTRALPATEAMSTERS.COM
CENTRAL RESERVE LIFE INSURANCE CO OF NORTH AMERICA .... CLAIMS@CENTRALRESERVE.COM
CHC .... CHC_CLAIMS@CHC-INC.COM
CHEROKEE NATIONAL LIFE FINANCIAL CORP .... CUSTOMER_SERVICE@CNLF.COM
CHURCH MUTUAL INSURANCE CO .... CLAIMS@CHURCHMUTUAL.COM
CINCINNATI INSURANCE CO .... CINCINNATI_LIFE@CINFIN.COM
CITIZENS SECURITY LIFE INSURANCE CO .... INMILLS@CITIZENSECURITYLIFE.COM
CNA .... CNA_HELP@CNA.COM
CNIC HEALTH SOLUTIONS .... CUSTOMERSERVICE@CNICHS.COM
COMBINED BENEFITS ADMINISTRATORS .... CBAFRESNO@SBCGLOBAL.NET
COMMERCIAL TRAVELERS MUTUAL INSURANCE CO .... CUSTSVC@COMMERCIALTRAVELERS.COM
COMPREHENSIVE BENEFITS ADMINISTRATOR, INC .... CUSTOMERSERVICE@CBAVT.COM
COMPUSYS, INC .... COMPUSYS@COMPUSYSUT.COM
CONTINENTAL GENERAL INSURANCE CO .... BENEFITS@CONTINENTALGENERAL.COM
CONTRA COSTA HEALTH PLAN .... CCHP@HSD.CO.CONTRA-COSTA.CA.US
CORNERSTONE BENEFITS, LLC .... INFO@CORNERSTONEBENEFITS.COM
CRAWFORD & CO .... BR00658_CA@US.CRAWCO.COM
CRAWFORD & CO .... CA@US.CRAWCO.COM
CT PIPE TRADES BENEFIT FUNDS ADMINISTRATORS, INC .... CONNECTICUTPIPETRADES@AOL.COM
CUNNINGHAM LINDSEY, INC .... PGILBERT@CL-INA.COM
DELTA DENTAL .... ASKDELTA@DELTADENTALIL.COM
DELTA DENTAL .... BENEFITSERVICES@DELTADENTALID.COM
DELTA DENTAL .... CMS@DELTA.ORG
DELTA DENTAL .... CSSTEAM@DELTAMASS.COM
DELTA DENTAL .... CUSTOMERSERVICE1@DDPKY.COM
DELTA DENTAL .... JOBS@DELTADENTALVA.COM
DELTA DENTAL .... NEDELTA@NEDELTA.COM
DESTINY HEALTH .... CUSTOMERCARE.COM

DIMENSION HEALTH	INFO@DIMENSIONHEALTH.COM
DINA DENTAL PLAN	DINAPLAN@BELLSOUTH.NET
DISABILITY MANAGEMENT SERVICES, INC	DMS.INQUIRY@DI-MGMT.COM
EBPA, INC	SERVICE@EBPANH.COM
EMIA	WEBMASTER@EDUCATORSMUTUAL.COM
EMPLOYEE BENEFIT CONSULTANTS	ALBUQUERQUE@EBCTPA.COM
EMPLOYEE BENEFIT CONSULTANTS	APPLETON@EBCTPA.COM
EMPLOYEE BENEFIT CONSULTANTS	CLEVELAND@EBCTPA.COM
EMPLOYEE BENEFIT CONSULTANTS	DESMOINES@EBCTPA.COM
EMPLOYEE BENEFIT CONSULTANTS	FINDLAY@EBCTPA.COM
EMPLOYEE BENEFIT CONSULTANTS	LOUISVILLE@EBCTPA.COM
EMPLOYEE BENEFIT CONSULTANTS	MILWAUKEE@EBCTPA.COM
EMPLOYEE SECURITY, INC.	BSACKS@ESIINC.NET
EMPLOYER PLAN SERVICES, INC	MARKETING@EPSIBENEFITSINC.COM
EMS ADMINISTRATIVE SERVICES	INFO@EMSADMIN.COM
EQUITABLE LIFE & CASUALTY INSURANCE CO	INFO@EQUILIFE.COM
EQUITABLE PLAN SERVICES, INC.	INFO@EPSTPA.COM
ERIN GROUP ADMINISTRATORS, INC	MARKETING@EGA-INC.COM
ESSEX INSURANCE CO	ESSEX@MARKELINSURANCE.COM
FCE BENEFIT	TXOFFICE@FCEBENEFIT.COM
FOREIGN SERVICE BENEFIT PLAN / MUTUAL OF OMAHA	AFSPA@AFSPA.ORG
FRINGE BENEFIT COORDINATORS	INFO@FBC-INC.COM
GAB ROBINS NORTH AMERICA	ANSWER@GABROBINS.COM
GAB ROBINS NORTH AMERICA	ANSWERS@GABROBINS.COM
GAINSCO	CLAIMS@GAINSCO.COM
GEICO DIRECT	R4NETSERVE@GEICO.COM
GENESIS HEALTHCARE	INFO@GENESISHCC.COM
GERBER LIFE INSURANCE CO	INFO@GERBERLIFE.COM
GILSBAR, INC.	GILSBAR@GILSBAR.COM
GOLDEN RULE INSURANCE CO.	FS@GOLDENRULE.COM
GREAT DIVIDE INSURANCE CO	NICMARKETING@NAUTILUS-INS.COM
GREAT WEST CASUALTY CO	Z.MARKETING@GWCCNET.COM
GREENTREE ADMINISTRATORS	PROVIDER@GREENTREEADMIN.COM
GROUP HEALTH COOPERATIVE	INFO@GHC.ORG
GROUP HEALTH PLAN	INFO-GHP@CVTV.COM
GROUP SERVICES & ADMINISTRATION, INC	GSAOKC@EARTHLINK.NET
GUIDEONE INSURANCE	ARLINGTONBRANCH@GUIDONE.COM
HARVARD PILGRIM HEALTH CARE, INC	PROVIDER_CALLCENTER@HPHC.ORG
HARVARD UNIVERSITY GROUP HEALTH PROGRAM	MSERVICE@UHS.HARDVARD.EDU
HEALTH AGENCIES OF THE WEST, INC	INFO@HEALTHAGENCIES.COM
HEALTH ECONOMICS GROUP, INC.	MEDICAL@HEGINC.COM
HEALTH NET	SERVICE@HEALTHNET.COM
HEALTH PLAN ADMINISTRATORS, INC	AGENTSUPPORT@HPA-INC.COM
HEALTH SERVICES BENEFITS ADMINISTRATORS	WEBMASTER@HSBA.COM
HEALTHPLEX, INC	INFO@HEALTHPLEX.COM
HELLER ASSOCIATES	CLAIMS@HELLERTPA.COM
HERITAGE INSURANCE MANAGERS, INC.	INFO@HERITAGE-INS.COM
HOLYOKE MUTUAL INSURANCE CO	INFO@HOLYOKEMUTUAL.COM
HORIZON BLUE CROSS BLUE SHIELD OF NEW JERSEY	HORIZONBLUE.COM
IBEW	IVPD_06@IBEW.ORG
IBEW	IVPD_08@IBEW.ORG
ILLINOIS MUTUAL LIFE INSURANCE CO.	INFO@ILLINOISMUTUAL.COM
INDIANAPOLIS LIFE	CORPCOM@INDIANAPOLISLIFE.COM
INDIANAPOLIS LIFE	CORPCOM@INDINANAPOLIS.COM
INTEGRITY MUTUAL INSURANCE CO	ISALES@IMICO.COM
INTRACORP	YOURCIGNALIFESERVICECENTER@CIGNA.COM
IOWA MUTUAL INSURANCE GROUP	CLAIM@IOWAMUTUAL.COM
JAS, INC.	JAS@JASBENEFITS.COM
JMH HEALTH PLAN	PROVIDERSERVICES@JMHHP.COM
JP FARLEY CORP	BENEFITS@JPFARLEY.COM
KEMPTON GROUP	SERVICE@KEMPTONGROUP.COM
LANDMARK HEALTH CARE INC.	INFO@LMHEALTHCARE.COM

LBA HEALTH PLANS	CUSTOMERCARE@LBAX.COM
LEWER AGENCY, INC	CLAIMS@LEWER.COM
LEXINGTON INSURANCE CO	LEXINGTONINS@AIG.COM
LOOMIS CO	INFO@LOOMISCO.COM
LOOMIS CO	LASVEGAS@LOOMISCO.COM
LOOMIS CO	RGITLAN@LOOMISCO.COM
MANAGED CARE CONSULTANTS, INC (MCC)	CUSTOMER_SERVICE@MCCNEVADA.COM
MANHATTAN INSURANCE GROUP	CS@MANHATTANLIFE.COM
MANHATTEN INSURANCE GROUP AND COMPANIES	CS@MANHATTENLIFE.COM
MANULIFE FINANCIAL	GCSC@MARITIMELIFE.CA
MASS HEALTH	MAINQUIRIES@UNISYS.COM
MASS MUTUAL FINANCIAL GROUP	MCYBULSKI@MASSMUTUAL.COM
MBA	CLAIMS@MBA.TO
M-CARE ADMINISTRATION	CUSTSERV@MCARE.ORG
MEDEX GLOBAL GROUP, INC	INFO@MEDEXASSIST.COM
MEDICAID OFFICE / UNISYS	ANN.CKOHLER@DHS.STATE.NJ.US
MEDICAID OFFICE	CARE.LINE@NCMAIL.NET
MEDICAID OFFICE	COMM@DSS.STATE.VA.US
MEDICAID OFFICE	CONTACT@HHSC.STATE.TX.US
MEDICAID OFFICE	DHRHELP@DHR.STATE.MD.US
MEDICAID OFFICE	DHSSINFO@STATE.DE.US
MEDICAID OFFICE	FELLERG@IDHW.STATE.ID.US
MEDICAID OFFICE	INFO@DHHS.STATE.SC.US
MEDICAID OFFICE	INFO@DHS.CAHWNET.GOV
MEDICAID OFFICE	MAINQUIRIES@UNISYS.COM
MEDICAID OFFICE	MEDICAID@HEALTH.STATE.NY.US
MEDICAID OFFICE	MEDMAN@WVHHR.ORG
MEDICAID OFFICE	PGE.DSS@PO.STATE.CT.US
MEDICAID OFFICE	PROVREP@ALXIX.SLG.EDS.COM
MEDICAID OFFICE	WEBMASTER@DHFS.STATE.WI.US
MEDICAID OFFICE	WEBMASTER@HEALTHSTATE.AK.US
MEDICAID OFFICE	DHSMED@STATE.ND.US
MEDICAID OFFICE	GAYLE@STATE.TN.US/TENNCARE/
MEDICARE - PART A INTERMEDIARIES	MEDICARE@BCBSKS.COM
MEDICARE - PART A INTERMEDIARIES	MEDICARE_A@CAREFIRST.COM
MEDICARE - PART A INTERMEDIARIES	RIVERBENDGBA@BCBST.COM
MEDICARE - PART A INTERMEDIARIES	VERITUSMEDICARE@HIGHMARK.COM
MEDICARE - PART B CARRIERS	ALMEDICARE@BCBSAL.ORG
MEDICARE - PART B CARRIERS	MEDICARE@BCBSKS.COM
MEDICARE - PART B CARRIERS	NHICMEDICARE@EDS.COM
MEDICARE - PART B CARRIERS	TLWHITE@ARKBLUECROSS.COM
MEDICARE - PART B CARRIERS	UT.MEDICAREGENERAL@REGENCE.COM
MEDICARE - PART B CARRIERS	VERITUSMEDICARE@HIGHMARK.COM
MEDICARE REGIONAL HOME HEALTH INTERMEDIARIES	ALMEDICARE@BCBSAL.ORG
MEDSAVE USA	INFO@MEDSAVEUSA.COM
MERITAIN HEALTH	INFO@MERITAIN.COM
MERITAIN HEALTH	INFO@NAHP.COM
MGIS COMPANIES	INFO@MGIS.COM
MICHIGAN EMPLOYEE BENEFIT SERVICES	CUSTSERV@MEBS.COM
MID-AMERICAN BENEFITS, INC	CLAIMS@MID-AMERICANBENEFITS.COM
MIDLAND CO	SERVICECENTER@AMIG.COM
MUTUAL ASSURANCE ADMINISTRATORS	CLAIMS@MAA-TPA.COM
MUTUAL OF OMAHA	INDIVIDUALSERVICE@MUTUALOFOMAHA.COM
MUTUAL SAVINGS LIFE INSURANCE CO	INFO@MSLDEC.COM
MYERS STEVENS	INFO@MYERS-STEVENS.COM
NATIONAL AMERICAN INSURANCE CO OF CALIFORNIA	WEBMASTER@NAICC.COM
NATIONAL GUARDIAN LIFE INSURANCE GROUP	NGL@NGLIC.COM
NATIONAL INDEMNITY CO	CLAIMS@NATIONALINDEMNITY.COM
NORTH CAROLINA MUTUAL LIFE INSURANCE CO	INFO@NCMUTUALLIFE.COM
NORTH POINTE INSURANCE CO	CLAIMS@HPIC.COM
NORTHERN ADJUSTERS, INC	NEWCLAIM@NADJ.COM
NORTHWEST ADMINISTRATORS	SEATTLE.PERSONNEL@NWADMIN.COM

OHIO CASUALTY GROUP............LEXINGTON.CLAIMS@OCAS.COM
ONE BEACON INSURANCE............INFO@ONEBEACON.COM
OPTIMA HEALTH PLAN............MEMBERS@OPTIMAHEALTH.COM
OSF HEALTH PLANS............MEMBER@OSFHEALTHCARE.ORG
OXFORD LIFE INSURANCE CO............INFO@OXFORDLIFE.COM
PEER REVIEW ORGANIZATIONS............RPOCHTER@IFMC.ORG
PENNSYLVANIA LIFE INSURANCE CO............ASKPENN@PENNLIFE.COM
PENNSYLVANIA LUMBERMEN'S MUTUAL INSURANCE CO............INFO@PALUMBERMENS.COM
PENNSYLVANIA NATIONAL MUTUAL CASUALTY INSURANCE CO............COMMUNICATIONS@PNAT.COM
PEOPLE BEFORE PROFITS............INFO@PBP.ORG
PHARMACIST MUTUAL............INFO@PHMIC.COM
PHILADELPHIA CONTRIBUTIONSHIP COMPANIES............INFO@CONTRIBUTIONSHIP.COM
PHYSICIANS HEALTH PLAN OF NORTHERN INDIANA, INC............CUSTSVC@PHPNI.COM
PIA............INFO@PIA-INC.COM
PREFERRED MUTUAL INSURANCE CO............INFO@PMINSCO.COM
PRESBYTERIAN HEALTH PLAN............INFO@PHS.ORG
PRIMARY HEALTH NETWORK, INC............SERVICE@PRIMARYHEALTH.COM
QBE REINSURANCE CO............CLAIMS@QBEUSA.COM
RESERVE NATIONAL INSURANCE CO............CUSTOMERSERVICE@RESERVENATIONAL.COM
RIVERBEND GOVERNMENT BENEFITS ADMINISTRATOR............RIVERBENDGBA@BCBST.COM
ROBERT PLAN CORP............DRIVEIN@RPC.COM
SECURE DENTAL............CLAIMS@SECUREDENTAL.COM
SECURITY HEALTH PLAN OF WISCONSIN, INC............SHPCSWEB@MFIDCLIN.EDU
SECURITY NATIONAL LIFE INSURANCE CO............CONTACT@SECURITYNATIONAL.COM
SELECT HEALTH............WEBMASTER@IHC.COM
SELMAN & CO............CUSTOMERSERVICE@SELMAN.CC
SEQUOIA INSURANCE CO............KENK@SEQUOIAINS.COM
SHEFFIELD OLSON & MCQUEEN, INC............CUSTOMERSERVICE@SOMI.COM
SONS OF NORWAY............CBS@SOFN.COM
STERLING BENEFIT SOLUTIONS............BENEFITS@AMERICANSTERLING.COM
STRATEGIC RESOURCE COMPANY............SRCMOREINFO@STRATEGIC-RESOURCE.COM
TBG ADMINISTRATIVE SERVICES............WEBSITE@TBGASI.COM
TEACHERS PROTECTIVE MUTUAL LIFE INSURANCE CO............TPM@TPMINS.COM
TEAMSTER LOCAL 731............IBTLU731@AOL.COM
TENCO SERVICES, INC............CLAIMS@TENCO.COM
TEXAS WORKERS' COMPENSATION COMMISSION............CUSTOM.RELATIONS@TWCC.STATE.TX.US
THREE RIVERS BENEFIT CORP............TRBCLAIMS@CABLEONE.NET
THRIVENT FINANCIAL FOR LUTHERANS............MAIL@THRIVENT.COM
TIC INTERNATIONAL CORP............TIC@TICI.COM
TOA REINSURANCE COMPANY OF AMERICA............INFO@TOARE.COM
TOTAL BENEFIT SERVICES............TBS@TOTALBENEFITSERVICES.COM
TOTAL HEALTH CARE, INC............THE@THC-ONLINE.COM
TR PAUL, INC............CUSTSER@TRPAUL.COM
TRAVELERS PROTECTIVE ASSOCIATION OF AMERICA............SUPPORT@TPAHQ.ORG
TRICARE............QUESTIONS@TMA.OSD.MIL
TRI-TEC EMPLOYEE BENEFITS, INC............TRI-TEC@TRI-TECEMP.COM
TUCKER ADMINISTRATORS, INC............TUCKER@TUCKERADMINISTRATORS.COM
UNICARE LIFE AND HEALTH INSURANCE............UNICARE@WELLPOINT.COM
UNITED HERITAGE LIFE INSURANCE CO............HERITAGE@UNITEDHERITAGE.COM
UNITED NATIONAL GROUP............CLAIMSINFO@UNITEDNET.COM
UNITED SECURITY LIFE AND HEALTH INSURANCE CO OF ILLINOIS............INFO@USLOFIL.COM
UNITED TEACHER ASSOCIATES INSURANCE CO............CUSTOMERSERVICE@UTAIC.COM
UNITY HEALTH INSURANCE............CUSTOMERSERVICE@UNITYHEALTH.COM
UNIVERA HEALTHCARE, INC............CUSTOMERSERVICE@UNIVERAHEALTHCARE.COM
UNIVERSAL CARE............CLAIMSINQUIRY@UNIVERSALCARE.COM
US HEALTHGROUP............INFO@ASCENTASSURANCE.COM
US SPECIALTY INSURANCE............INVESTORRELATIONS@HCCH.COM
UTICA NATIONAL INSURANCE GROUP............WEBMASTER@UTICANATIONAL.COM
VIRGINIA MUTUAL INSURANCE CO............CUSTSVC@VAMUTUALINS.COM
VYTRA HEALTH PLANS............GENERAL@VYTRA.COM
WAKELY & ASSOCIATES............ADMINISTRATOR@WAKELYINC.COM
WARD NORTH AMERICA............GBETTS@WARDCLAIMS.COM

WAS.......WASANCH@ALASKA.NET
WAS.......WASFRBK@ALASKA.COM
WELFARE & PENSION ADMIN SERV.......INFO@WPAS-INC.COM
WEST BEND MUTUAL INSURANCE CO.......DIRECTCONNECT@WBMI.COM
WESTERN NATIONAL MUTUAL INSURANCE CO.......INFO@WNINS.COM
WESTFIELD INSURANCE.......WESTFIELDCENTERSERVICEOFFICE@WESTFIELD.COM
WEYCO, INC.......INFO@WEYCO.COM
WILSON MUTUAL INSURANCE.......CUSTOMERSERV@WILSONMUTUAL.COM
WORKFORCE SAFETY & INSURANCE.......NDWSI@STATE.ND.US
ZENITH INSURANCE CO.......WOODLANDHILLS@THEZENITH.COM
ZENITH INSURANCE COMPANY.......FRESNO@THEZENITH.COM
ZENITH INSURANCE COMPANY.......PLEASANTON@THEZENITH.COM
ZENITH INSURANCE COMPANY.......SANDIEGO@THEZENITH.COM
ZENITH, THE.......AUSTIN@THEZENITH.COM
ZENITH, THE.......ILLINOIS@THEZENITH.COM
ZENITH, THE.......NORTHCAROLINA@THEZENITH.COM
ZENITH, THE.......ORLANDO@THEZENITH.COM
ZENITH, THE.......PENNSYLVANIA@THEZENITH.COM
ZENITH, THE.......SARASOTA@THEZENITH.COM
ZURICH NORTH AMERICA.......USZ_CARECENTER@ZURICHNA.COM

Website Addresses

21ST CENTURY INSURANCE GROUP.......WWW.21ST.COM
A & I BENEFIT PLAN ADMINISTRATORS.......WWW.AIBPA.COM
AAA INSURANCE CO.......WWW.AAASOUTH.COM
AAA MID-ATLANTIC INSURANCE GROUP.......WWW.AAA.COM OR WWW. AAAMIDATLANTIC.COM
AAA OF MISSOURI.......WWW.AAAMISSOURI.COM
AARP HEALTHCARE OPTIONS.......WWW.AARPHEALTHCARE.COM
ABAS.......WWW.ABASTPA.COM
ABC HEALTH PLAN.......WWW.ABCHEALTHPLAN.ORG
ABETON.......WWW.ABETON.COM
ABPA.......WWW.ABPA-TPA.COM
ACADEMY LIFE INSURANCE.......WWW.ACADEMYLIFE.COM
ACADIA INSURANCE.......WWW.ACADIAINSURANCE.COM
ACCESS ADMINISTRATORS, INC.......WWW.AHS-ACCESS.COM
ACCIDENT FUND INSURANCE COMPANY OF AMERICA.......WWW.ACCIDENTFUND.COM
ACCORDANT HEALTH SERVICES, INC.......WWW.ACCORDANT.NET
ACE USA WORKERS' COMPENSATION.......WWW.ESIS.COM
ACH.......WWW.ACHONLINE.COM
ACMG, INC.......WWW.ACMG-INC.COM
ACORDIA NATIONAL.......WWW.ACORDIANATIONAL.COM
ACS BENEFIT SERVICES.......WWW.ACSBENEFITSERVICESINC.COM
ACSTAR INSURANCE COMPANY.......WWW.ACSTARINS.COM
ACUITY.......WWW.ACUITY.COM
ADMINISTRATION SERVICES, INC.......WWW.ADMIN-SERV.COM
ADMINISTRATION SYSTEMS RESEARCH CORP.......WWW.ASRCORP.COM
ADMINISTRATIVE CONCEPTS, INC.......WWW.ADMINCONCEPTS.COM
ADMINISTRATIVE ENTERPRISES, INC.......WWW.AEIAZ.BIZ
ADMINISTRATIVE SERVICES, INC.......WWW.ADMINSERV.COM
ADMIRAL INSURANCE CO.......WWW.ADMIRALINS.COM
ADVANCE INSURANCE COMPANY.......WWW.ADVANCEINSURANCE.COM
ADVANTAGE INSURANCE COMPANY.......WWW.WCFGROUP.COM
AEGON MARKETING.......WWW.STONEBRIDGELIFE.COM
AETNA DENTAL.......WWW.AETNA.COM
AETNA U.S. HEALTHCARE.......WWW.AETNA.COM
AFFINITY HEALTH PLAN.......WWW.AFFINITYPLAN.ORG
AFFORDABLE BENEFIT ADMINISTRATORS, INC.......WWW.BENEFITSABA.COM
AFLAC NEW YORK.......WWW.AFLACNY.COM
AFLAC.......WWW.AFLAC.COM
AGENCY SERVICES, INC.......WWW.AGENCYSERVICES.COM
AGIA, INC.......WWW.AGIA.COM

AGRI SERVICES AGENCY	WWW.DAILYLEA.COM
AHI-HEALTHLINK	WWW.AHI-HEALTHLINK.COM
AHI-HEALTHLINK	WWW.MAA-TPA.COM
AIG CLAIM SERVICES, INC	WWW.AIG.COM
AIG CLAIM SERVICES, INC	WWW.AIGCS.COM
AIG CLAIM SERVICES, INC	WWW.AIGHAWAII.COM
AIG CLAIM SERVICES	WWW.AIGCS.COM
AIM MUTUAL INSURANCE COMPANY	WWW.AIMMUTUAL.COM
ALABAMA FINANCIAL POTENTIAL CENTRES, INC	WWW.ALSTC.COM
ALAMANCE INSURANCE CO	WWW.BURLINGTONINSURANCE.COM
ALASKA NATIONAL INSURANCE COMPANY	WWW.ALASKANATIONAL.COM
ALASKA TIMBER INSURANCE EXCHANGE	WWW.ATIE-INS.COM
ALEA NORTH AMERICA INSURANCE COMPANY	WWW.ALEAGROUP.COM
ALFA INSURANCE CORP	WWW.ALFAINS.COM
ALICARE	WWW.ALICARE.COM
ALLEGIANCE BENEFIT PLAN MANAGEMENT, INC.	WWW.ABPMTPA.COM
ALLIANZ INSURANCE COMPANY	WWW.AIC-ALLIANZ.COM
ALLIANZ LIFE INSURANCE CO OF NORTH AMERICA	WWW.ALLIANZLIFE.COM
ALLIED ADMINISTRATORS, INC	WWW.ALLIEDADMINISTRATORS.COM
ALLIED BENEFIT SYSTEMS, INC	WWW.ALLIEDBENEFIT.COM
ALLIED INSURANCE CO	WWW.ALLIEDINSURANCE.COM
ALLIED NATIONAL	WWW.ALLIEDNATIONAL.COM
ALLSTATE INSURANCE CO	WWW.ALLSTATE.COM
ALOHA CARE OF HAWAII	WWW.ALOHACAREHAWAII.ORG
ALTERNATIVE RISK MANAGEMENT LIMITED	WWW.ALTRISK.COM
ALTICOR	WWW.ALTICOR.COM
AMERAPLAN, INC	WWW.AMERAPLAN.COM
AMERIBEN SOLUTIONS	WWW.AMERIBENIECGROUP.COM
AMERICA FIRST INSURANCE CO	WWW.AMERICAFIRST-INS.COM
AMERICA FIRST INSURANCE	WWW.AMERICAFIRST-INS.COM
AMERICAN ADMINISTRATIVE GROUP	WWW.AAGCORPORATE.COM
AMERICAN ADMINISTRATORS GROUP	WWW.ICONBA.COM
AMERICAN BENEFITS MANAGEMENT	WWW.AMERICANBENEFITS.ORG
AMERICAN COMMERCE INSURANCE CO	WWW.ACILINK.COM
AMERICAN COMMERCIAL BARGE LINES	WWW.ACBL.NET
AMERICAN COMMUNITY MUTUAL INSURANCE CO	WWW.AMERICAN-COMMUNITY.COM
AMERICAN EMPIRE SURPLUS LINES INSURANCE CO	WWW.AESLIC.COM
AMERICAN FAMILY INSURANCE	WWW.AMFAM.COM
AMERICAN FAMILY MUTUAL INSURANCE	WWW.AMFAM.COM
AMERICAN FIDELITY ASSURANCE CO	WWW.AF-GROUP.COM
AMERICAN GENERAL LIFE & ACCIDENT INSURANCE CO	WWW.AIGAG.COM
AMERICAN GROUP ADMINISTRATORS	WWW.AMGROUPADMIN.COM
AMERICAN GUARANTY LIFE INSURANCE COMPANY	WWW.TDI.STATE.TX.US
AMERICAN HARDWARE MUTUAL INSURANCE CO	WWW.AMERICANHARDWAREINS.COM
AMERICAN HARDWARE MUTUAL INSURANCE COMPANY	WWW.MOTORISTSGROUP.COM
AMERICAN INCOME LIFE INSURANCE CO	WWW.AILINS.COM
AMERICAN LIFECARE	WWW.AMERICANLIFECARE.COM
AMERICAN MAYFLOWER	WWW.GEFINANCIALSERVICE.COM
AMERICAN MEDICAL & LIFE INSURANCE CO	WWW.AMLICO.COM
AMERICAN MEDICAL SECURITY	WWW.EAMS.COM
AMERICAN MINING INSURANCE CO, INC	WWW.CGHINSURANCE.COM
AMERICAN NATIONAL INSURANCE CO	WWW.ANICO.COM
AMERICAN NATIONAL PROPERTY & CASUALTY CO	WWW.ANPAC.COM
AMERICAN POLICY HOLDERS LIQUIDATING TRUST	WWW.AIMMUTUAL.COM
AMERICAN PROGRESSIVE LIFE & HEALTH INSURANCE CO	WWW.UAFC.COM
AMERICAN PUBLIC LIFE INSURANCE CO	WWW.AMPUBLIC.COM
AMERICAN RE-INSURANCE	WWW.AMRE.COM
AMERICAN REPUBLIC INSURANCE CO	WWW.AMERICANREPUBLIC.COM
AMERICAN RESOURCES INSURANCE CO	WWW.ARIC.CC
AMERICAN SENTINEL INSURANCE CO	WWW.AMERICANSENTINEL.CC
AMERICAN SOUTHERN INSURANCE CO	WWW.AMSOU.COM
AMERICAN SPECIALTY HEALTH INCORPORATED	WWW.ASHCOMPANIES.COM

AMERICAN TRUST ADMINISTRATORS, INC .... WWW.ATAAMERICA.COM
AMERICAN UNDERWRITERS LIFE INSURANCE CO .... WWW.IAI-ONLINE.COM
AMERICAN UNITED LIFE INSURANCE COMPANY .... WWW.AUL.COM
AMERICAN UNITED LIFE INSURANCE COMPANY .... WWW.CNLF.COM
AMERICAN WHOLE HEALTH NETWORKS, INC .... WWW.ALIGNIS.COM OR WWW.AMERICANWHOLEHEALTH.COM
AMERICAN YOUTH STUDENTS & SPORTS INSURANCE .... WWW.STUDENTPLANS.NET
AMERICAS INSURANCE CO .... WWW.OMNIWHITTINGTON.COM
AMERICHOICE CLAIMS CENTER .... WWW.AMERICHOICE.COM
AMERICHOICE CLAIMS CENTER .... WWW.UNITEDHEALTHGROUP.COM
AMERICO FINANCIAL LIFE & ANNUITY INSURANCE CO .... WWW.AMERICO.COM
AMERIGROUP CORPORATION .... WWW.AMERIGROUPCORP.COM
AMERIHEALTH ADMINISTRATORS .... WWW.AMERIHEALTHPA.COM
AMERISURE COMPANIES .... WWW.AMERISURE.COM
AMERISURE INSURANCE COMPANY .... WWW.AMERISURE.COM
AMERITAS ACACIA COMPANIES .... WWW.AMERITASACACIA.COM
AMICA MUTUAL INSURANCE .... WWW.AMICA.COM
AMTRUST SOUTH .... WWW.THECOVENANTGROUP.NET
ANTHEM BLUE CROSS AND BLUE SHIELD .... WWW.ANTHEM.COM
ANTHEM BLUE CROSS AND BLUE SHIELD .... WWW.ANTHEM.COM OR WWW.WELLPOINT.COM
A-PLUS BENEFITS .... WWW.APLUSBENEFITS.COM
ARAG GROUP .... WWW.ARAGGROUP.COM
ARCTIC ADJUSTERS, INC .... WWW.ARCTICADJUSTERS.COM
ARGONAUT CENTRAL INSURANCE COMPANY .... WWW.ARGONAUTCENTRAL.COM
ARGONAUT INSURANCE COMPANY .... WWW.ARGONAUTGROUP.COM
ARGONAUT INSURANCE COMPANY .... WWW.ARGONAUTINSURANCE.COM
ARGUS SERVICES CORP .... WWW.ARGUSSERVICES.NET
ARIZONA FOUNDATION FOR MEDICAL CARE .... WWW.AZFIMC.COM
ARIZONA PHYSICIANS, IPA, INC .... WWW.MYAPIPA.COM
ARIZONA PIPE TRADES .... WWW.AZPIPE.ORG
ARKANSAS BEST CORP .... WWW.CHOICEBENEFITS.COM
ARKANSAS BLUE CROSS / BLUE SHIELD .... WWW.ARKBLUECROSS.COM
ARNETT HEALTH PLANS .... WWW.ARNETTPLANS.COM
ARTHUR J GALLAGAR & CO .... WWW.AJG.COM
ASSOCIATED ADJUSTERS .... WWW.ASSOCIATED-ADJUSTERS.COM
ASSOCIATED PLAN ADMINISTRATORS .... WWW.ASSOCIATEDPLAN.COM
ASSOCIATION & SOCIETY INSURANCE CORP .... WWW.ASICORPORATION.COM
ASSUMPTION MUTUAL LIFE INSURANCE CO .... WWW.ASSUMPTION.CA
ASSURANT HEALTH .... WWW.ASSURANTHEALTH.COM OR WWW.ASSURANTEMPLOYEEBENEFITS.COM
ASSURANT HEALTH .... WWW.HEALTH.US.FORTIS.COM
ASSURANT SOLUTIONS .... WWW.ASSURANTSOLUTIONS.COM
ASSURE CARE .... WWW.ASSURECARE.COM
ASSURITY LIFE INSURANCE .... WWW.ASSURITY.COM
ATLANTIC MUTUAL / CENTENNIAL INSURANCE CO .... WWW.ATLANTICMUTUAL.COM
ATLANTIC MUTUAL .... WWW.ATLANTICMUTUAL.COM
ATLANTIC SOUTHERN INSURANCE COMPANY .... WWW.ATLANTICSOUTHERN.COM
ATRIUM HEALTH PLAN & BLUE CROSS/BLUE SHIELD WISCONSIN .... WWW.ATRIUMHEALTHPLAN.COM
ATTENTA .... WWW.ATTENTA.COM
AULTCARE .... WWW.AULTCARE.ORG
AUSTIN MUTUAL INSURANCE CO .... WWW.AUSTININSURANCEGROUP.NET
AUTOMATED BENEFITS SERVICES, INC .... WWW.ABS-TPA.COM
AUTOMOBILE CLUB INSURANCE CO .... WWW.AAA-CALIF.COM
AVALON BENEFIT SERVICES .... WWW.AVALONBENEFITS.COM
AV-MED HEALTH PLAN .... WWW.AVMED.COM
AXA CORPORATE SOLUTIONS REINSURANCE CO .... WWW.AXA.COM
BABB, INC .... WWW.BABBINC.COM
BADGER MUTUAL INSURANCE CO .... WWW.BADGERMUTUAL.COM
BALBOA INSURANCE GROUP .... WWW.BALBOAINSURANCE.COM
BANKERS FIDELITY LIFE INSURANCE .... WWW.BFLIC.COM
BANKERS INDEPENDENT INSURANCE CO .... WWW.BANKERSINSURANCE.COM
BANKERS INSURANCE GROUP .... WWW.BANKERSINSURANCE.COM
BANKERS LIFE & CASUALTY CO .... WWW.BANKERSLIFE.COM
BCI INSURANCE SERVICES .... WWW.BCI-INS.COM

BCS FINANCIAL CORP/BCS INSURANCE CO	WWW.BCSIGROUP.COM
BEAR RIVER MUTUAL INSURANCE CO	WWW.BEARRIVERMUTUAL.COM
BEECH STREET CORP	WWW.BEECHSTREET.COM
BEHAVIOR HEALTH SYSTEMS	WWW.BHS-INC.COM
BEHAVIORAL HEALTHCARE OPTIONS	WWW.BEHAVIORALHEALTHCAREOPTIONS.COM
BELOIT MEMORIAL HOSPITAL	WWW.BELOITMEMORIALHOSPITAL.ORG
BENEFICIAL LIFE INSURANCE CO	WWW.BENEFICIALFINANCIALGROUP.COM
BENEFIT & RISK MANAGEMENT SERVICES	WWW.BRMS-ONLINE.COM
BENEFIT ADMINISTRATIVE SYSTEMS, LTD	WWW.BENADMINSYS.COM
BENEFIT ASSISTANCE CORPORATION	WWW.BACWV.COM
BENEFIT CLAIMS PAYORS, INC	WWW.DHSNYU.COM
BENEFIT CONSULTANTS, INC	WWW.BCI-STL.COM
BENEFIT PLAN ADMINISTRATORS, INC	WWW.BPATPA.COM
BENEFIT PLAN SERVICES, INC	WWW.BPSTPA.COM
BENEFIT PLANNERS, INC	WWW.BENPLAN.COM
BENEFIT SUPPORT, INC	WWW.BENEFITSUPPORT.ORG
BENEFIT SYSTEMS & SERVICES, INC	WWW.BENEFIT-SYS.COM
BENEFITSOURCE, INC	WWW.BENEFITSOURCEINC.COM
BENESIGHT	WWW.BENESIGHT.COM
BENICOMP, INC	WWW.BENICOMP.COM
BENICORP INSURANCE CO	WWW.BENICORP.COM
BERKLEY INSURANCE CO	WWW.WRBERKLEY.COM
BERKLEY RISK SERVICES	WWW.DENTALLIABILITY.COM
BERKSHIRE HATHAWAY HOMESTATE CO	WWW.BH-HC.COM
BERKSHIRE HATHAWAY HOMESTATE COMPANIES	WWW.BH-HC.COM
BERKSHIRE LIFE INSURANCE CO OF AMERICA	WWW.THEBERKSHIRE.COM
BEST LIFE AND HEALTH INSURANCE CO	WWW.BESTLIFE.COM
BITUMINOUS INSURANCE CO	WWW.BITUMINOUSINSRUANCE.COM
BITUMINOUS INSURANCE CO	WWW.BITUMINOUSINSURANCE.COM
BLUE CROSS BLUE SHIELD OF KANSAS	WWW.BCBSKS.COM
BLUE CROSS BLUE SHIELD OF MINNESOTA	WWW.BLUECROSSMN.COM
BLUE CROSS BLUE SHIELD OF MISSISSIPPI	WWW.BCBSMS.COM
BLUE CROSS BLUE SHIELD OF TEXAS	WWW.BCBSTX.COM
BLUE CROSS BLUE SHIELD OF WYOMING	WWW.WYOMINGBLUE.COM
BLUE CROSS BLUE SHIELD	WWW.ARKBLUECROSS.COM
BLUE CROSS BLUE SHIELD	WWW.BCBSAL.COM OR WWW.BCBSAL.ORG
BLUE CROSS BLUE SHIELD	WWW.BCBSAZ.COM
BLUE CROSS BLUE SHIELD	WWW.BCBSDE.COM
BLUE CROSS BLUE SHIELD	WWW.BCBSFL.COM
BLUE CROSS BLUE SHIELD	WWW.BCBSGA.COM
BLUE CROSS BLUE SHIELD	WWW.BCBSIL.COM
BLUE CROSS BLUE SHIELD	WWW.BCBSKC.COM
BLUE CROSS BLUE SHIELD	WWW.BCBSLA.COM
BLUE CROSS BLUE SHIELD	WWW.BCBSMA.COM
BLUE CROSS BLUE SHIELD	WWW.BCBSMI.COM
BLUE CROSS BLUE SHIELD	WWW.BCBSMT.COM
BLUE CROSS BLUE SHIELD	WWW.BCBSNC.COM
BLUE CROSS BLUE SHIELD	WWW.BCBSNE.COM
BLUE CROSS BLUE SHIELD	WWW.BCBSNM.COM
BLUE CROSS BLUE SHIELD	WWW.BCBSOK.COM
BLUE CROSS BLUE SHIELD	WWW.BCBSRI.COM
BLUE CROSS BLUE SHIELD	WWW.BCBST.COM
BLUE CROSS BLUE SHIELD	WWW.BCBSTX.COM
BLUE CROSS BLUE SHIELD	WWW.BCBSVT.COM
BLUE CROSS BLUE SHIELD	WWW.BCBSWNY.COM
BLUE CROSS BLUE SHIELD	WWW.BCIDAHO.COM
BLUE CROSS BLUE SHIELD	WWW.BCNBSMI.COM
BLUE CROSS BLUE SHIELD	WWW.BCNEPA.COM
BLUE CROSS BLUE SHIELD	WWW.BLUECROSSWISCONSIN.COM
BLUE CROSS BLUE SHIELD	WWW.CAREFIRST.COM
BLUE CROSS BLUE SHIELD	WWW.CRUZAZUL.COM
BLUE CROSS BLUE SHIELD	WWW.EMPIREBLUE.COM

BLUE CROSS BLUE SHIELD ..... WWW.EXCELLUSBCBS.COM
BLUE CROSS BLUE SHIELD ..... WWW.HIGHMARK.COM
BLUE CROSS BLUE SHIELD ..... WWW.HMSA.COM
BLUE CROSS BLUE SHIELD ..... WWW.IBX.COM
BLUE CROSS BLUE SHIELD ..... WWW.ID.REGENCE.COM
BLUE CROSS BLUE SHIELD ..... WWW.OR.REGENCE.COM
BLUE CROSS BLUE SHIELD ..... WWW.PREMERA.COM
BLUE CROSS BLUE SHIELD ..... WWW.SOUTHCAROLINABLUES.COM
BLUE CROSS BLUE SHIELD ..... WWW.SSSPR.COM
BLUE CROSS BLUE SHIELD ..... WWW.UT.REGENCE.COM
BLUE CROSS BLUE SHIELD ..... WWW.WA.REGENCE.COM
BLUE CROSS BLUE SHIELD ..... WWW.WELLMARK.COM
BLUE CROSS CANADA ..... WWW.AB.BLUECROSS.CA
BLUE CROSS CANADA ..... WWW.MB.BLUECROSS.CA
BLUE CROSS CANADA ..... WWW.USEBLUE.COM OR WWW.MEDAZIE.BLUECROSS.CA
BLUE CROSS OF CALIFORNIA ..... WWW.BLUECROSSCA.COM
BLUE SHIELD OF CALIFORNIA ..... WWW.MYLIFEPATH.COM
BLUECHOICE HEALTH PLAN ..... WWW.BLUECHOICESC.COM
BLUEGRASS FAMILY HEALTH ..... WWW.BGFH.COM
BMI - HEALTH PLANS ..... WWW.BMI-HEALTHPLANS.COM
BMI HEALTH PLANS ..... WWW.BMI-HEALTHPLANS.COM
BMI -HEALTH PLANS ..... WWW.BMI-HEALTHPLANS.COM
BOILERMAKERS NATIONAL FUNDS ..... WWW.BOILERMAKERS.ORG
BOLLINGER, INC ..... WWW.BOLLINGERINSURANCE.COM
BOON-CHAPMAN BENEFIT ADMINISTRATORS ..... WWW.BOONCHAPMAN.COM
BOSTON MUTUAL LIFE INSURANCE CO ..... WWW.BOSTONMUTUAL.COM
BRADFORD FINANCIAL CENTER ..... WWW.BRADFORDFINANCIALCENTER.COM
BRETHREN MUTUAL INSURANCE CO ..... WWW.BMICONLINE.COM
BRISTOL WEST INSURANCE GROUP ..... WWW.BRISTOLWEST.COM
BROADSPIRE ..... WWW.CHOOSEBROADSPIRE.COM
BROADSPIRE ..... WWW.KEMPERSERVICES.COM
BROKERAGE CONCEPTS, INC ..... WWW.BCITPA.COM
BROOKSHIRE BROTHERS, LTD ..... WWW.BROOKSHIREBROTHERS.COM
BROTHERHOOD MUTUAL INSURANCE CO ..... WWW.BROTHERHOODMUTUAL.COM
BROWN & BROWN ..... WWW.CALSURANCE.COM
BSI NORTH AMERICAN ..... WWW.BSICONNECT.COM
BUSINESS COUNCIL OF NEW YORK STATE, INC ..... WWW.BCNYS.ORG
BUSINESS MENS INSURANCE CO ..... WWW.BMICO.COM
C AND O EMPLOYEES' HOSPITAL ASSOCIATION ..... WWW.CFW.COM/~COEHA
C L FRATES AND COMPANY ..... WWW.CLFRATES.COM
CABINET FOR HEALTH SERVICE OF KENTUCKY ..... WWW.CHFS.KY.GOV/DMS
CAI INSURANCE AGENCY, INC ..... WWW.CAIINSURANCE.COM
CAICO ..... WWW.CAICOPR.COM
CALIFORNIA BENEFITS DENTAL PLAN ..... WWW.GEFINANCIALBENEFITS.COM
CALIFORNIA CAPITAL INSURANCE COMPANY ..... WWW.CIGINSURANCE.COM
CALIFORNIA CASUALTY INSURANCE CO ..... WWW.CALCAS.COM
CALIFORNIA CASUALTY INSURANCE CO ..... WWW.CALIFORNIACASUALTY.COM
CALIFORNIA CASUALTY INSURANCE ..... WWW.CALIFORNIACASUALTY.COM
CALIFORNIA CASULTY MANAGEMENT CO ..... WWW.CALCAS.COM
CALIFORNIA FIELD IRONWORKERS TRUST FUND ..... WWW.IRONWORKERBENNY.COM
CAM ADMINISTRATIVE SERVICES, INC ..... WWW.CAMADS.COM
CAMBRIDGE INTEGRATED SERVICES GROUP, INC ..... WWW.CAMBRIDGEINTEGRATED.COM
CAMBRIDGE INTEGRATED SERVICES GROUP, INC ..... WWW.CAMBRIDGEWORLDWIDE.COM
CAMERON MUTUAL INSURANCE CO ..... WWW.CAMERON-INSURANCE.COM
CANADA LIFE ASSURANCE CO ..... WWW.CANADALIFE.COM
CANAL INSURANCE CO ..... WWW.CANAL-INS.COM
CANON COCHRAN MANAGEMENT SERVICES, INC ..... WWW.CCMSI.COM
CAPE HEALTH PLAN ..... WWW.CAPEHEALTH.COM
CAPITAL BLUE CROSS ..... WWW.CAPBLUECROSS.COM
CAPITAL CITY INSURANCE CO, INC ..... WWW.CAPITALCITYINSURANCE.COM
CAPITAL DISTRICT PHYSICIANS' HEALTH PLAN, INC ..... WWW.CDPHP.COM
CAPITOL ADMINISTRATORS ..... WWW.CAPITOL-SE.COM

CAPITOL INDEMNITY CORP .... WWW.CAPITOLINDEMNITY.COM
CARDAY ASSOCIATES, INC. .... WWW.CARDAYASSOCIATES.COM
CARE CHOICES HMO .... WWW.CARECHOICES.COM
CAREMARK, INC. .... WWW.CAREMARK.COM
CARESOURCE .... WWW.CSMG-ONLINE.COM
CARITEN HEALTHCARE .... WWW.CARITEN.COM
CAROLINA BENEFIT ADMINISTRATORS LLC .... WWW.CBAOFSC.COM
CAROLINA CARE PLAN, INC .... WWW.CAROLINACAREPLAN.COM
CAROLINA CASUALTY INSURANCE CO, INC .... WWW.CAROLINACAS.COM
CATHOLIC KNIGHTS .... WWW.CATHOLICKNIGHTS.ORG
CBA, INC .... WWW.CBAVT.COM
CBCA ADMINISTRATORS, INC .... WWW.CBCA.COM
CBCA .... WWW.CBA.COM
CBSA .... WWW.CBSAINC.COM
CCMSI-MIDLAND LLC .... WWW.CCMSI.COM
CCN .... WWW.CCNUSA.COM
CDS GROUP HEALTH .... WWW.CDSGROUPHEALTH.COM
CELINA INSURANCE GROUP .... WWW.CELINAINSURANCEGROUP.COM
CELTIC INSURANCE CO .... WWW.CELTIC-NET.COM
CENTRAL BENEFITS ADMINISTRATORS .... WWW.CENTRALBENEFITS.COM
CENTRAL INSURANCE CO .... WWW.CENTRAL-INSURANCE.COM
CENTRAL PENNSYLVANIA TEAMSTERS HEALTH & WELFARE FUND .... WWW.CENTRALPATEAMSTERS.COM
CENTRAL RESERVE LIFE INSURANCE CO OF NORTH AMERICA .... WWW.CENTRALRESERVE.COM OR WWW.CERESGP.COM
CENTRAL SECURITY LIFE INSURANCE COMPANY .... WWW.CSLIC.COM
CENTRAL STATES FUNDS .... WWW.CENTRALSTATESFUNDS.ORG
CENTRAL STATES HEALTH & LIFE INSURANCE CO OF OMAHA .... WWW.CSO.COM
CENTRAL VALLEY HEALTH AND WELFARE TRUST .... WWW.CVTRUST.ORG
CENTRE SOLUTIONS .... WWW.CENTRESOLUTIONS.COM
CENTURION LIFE INSURANCE .... WWW.WELLSFARGO.COM
CHC .... WWW.COLONIALHEALTHCARE.COM
CHEROKEE NATIONAL LIFE FINANCIAL CORP .... WWW.CNLF.COM
CHILDREN'S MERCY FAMILY HEALTH PARTNERS .... WWW.FHP.ORG
CHINESE COMMUNITY HEALTH PLAN .... WWW.CCHPHMO.COM
CHRISTIANA CARE HEALTH PLANS .... WWW.CHRISTIANACARE.ORG
CHUBB GROUP OF INSURANCE COMPANIES .... WWW.CHUBB.COM
CHURCH MUTUAL INSURANCE CO .... WWW.CHURCHMUTUAL.COM
CHURCHILL ADMINISTRATIVE PLANS, INC .... WWW.MULTIPLAN.COM
CIGNA CORPORATION .... WWW.CIGNA.COM
CIGNA HEALTH CARE .... WWW.CIGNA.COM
CIGNA HEALTHCARE .... WWW.CIGNA.COM
CIGNA HEALTHCARE .... WWW.CIGNA.COM OR WWW.MYCIGNA.COM
CIGNA INTERNATIONAL EX PATRIOTS BENEFITS .... WWW.CIGNA.COM
CIGNA LIFE OF CANADA .... WWW.CIGNA.COM
CINCINNATI EQUITABLE INSURANCE CO .... WWW.CINCINNATIEQUITABLE.COM
CINCINNATI INSURANCE CO .... WWW.CINFIN.COM
CITIZENS INSURANCE CO .... WWW.ALLMERICA.COM
CITIZENS SECURITY LIFE INSURANCE CO .... WWW.CITIZENSFINANCIALCORP.COM
CITY OF LOS ANGELES WORKERS' COMPENSATION DIVISION .... WWW.CITYOFLOSANGELES.ORG
CITY OF MESA EMPLOYEE BENEFITS .... WWW.CITYOFMESA.ORG
CIVIL SERVICE EMPLOYEES INSURANCE CO .... WWW.CSE-INSURANCE.COM
CIVIL SERVICE EMPLOYEES INSURANCE GROUP .... WWW.CSE-INSURANCE.COM
CLAIM MANAGEMENT SERVICES .... WWW.CMSINS.COM
CLEAR CARE CORPORATION .... WWW.CLEARCARECORP.COM
CMS CAP MANAGEMENT SYSTEMS .... WWW.TENETHEALTH.COM
CNA .... WWW.CNA.COM
CNIC HEALTH SOLUTIONS .... WWW.CNICHS.COM
COALITION AMERICA, INC .... WWW.COALITIONAMERICA.COM
COLONIAL SUPPLEMENTAL INSURANCE .... WWW.COLONIALLIFE.COM
COLONIAL-PENN LIFE INSURANCE .... WWW.COLONIALPENN.COM
COLUMBIA UNITED PROVIDERS .... WWW.CUPHEALTH.COM
COLUMBUS LIFE INSURANCE CO .... WWW.COLUMBUSLIFE.COM
COMBINED BENEFITS ADMINISTRATORS .... WWW.COMBINEDBENEFITSADMINISTRATORS.COM

COMBINED INSURANCE ... WWW.COMBINED.COM
COMBINED LIFE INSURANCE CO OF NEW YORK ... WWW.COMBINEDNY.COM
COMMERCE BENEFITS GROUP, THE ... WWW.COMMERCEBENFITSGROUP.COM
COMMERCE INSURANCE CO, INC, THE ... WWW.COMMERCEINSURANCE.COM
COMMERCIAL TRAVELERS MUTUAL INSURANCE CO ... WWW.COMMERCIALTRAVELERS.COM
COMMONWEALTH ADMINISTRATORS ... WWW.CATPA.COM
COMMUNITY HEALTH PLAN ... WWW.MYCHP.COM
COMP CAROLINA ... WWW.COMPCAROLINA.COM
COMPANION LIFE INSURANCE CO ... WWW.COMPANIONLIFE.COM
COMPBENEFITS ... WWW.COMPBENEFITS.COM
COMPREHENSIVE BENEFITS ADMINISTRATOR, INC ... WWW.CBAVT.COM
COMPUSYS, INC ... WWW.CSERISA.COM
CONCENTRA, INC ... WWW.CONCENTRA.COM
CONCORD GROUP INSURANCE CO ... WWW.CONCORDGROUPINSURANCE.COM
CONNECTICARE INC & AFFILIATES ... WWW.CONNECTICARE.COM
CONSECO ... WWW.CONSECO.COM
CONSOLIDATED ASSOCIATION OF RAILROAD EMPLOYEES CARE ... WWW.CAREHEALTHPLAN.COM
CONSOLIDATED HEALTH PLANS ... WWW.CONSOLIDATEDHEALTHPLAN.COM
CONSUMER HEALTH NETWORK ... WWW.CHN.COM
CONTINENTAL AMERICAN INSURANCE GROUP ... WWW.CAIG-INS.COM
CONTINENTAL GENERAL INSURANCE CO ... WWW.CONTINENTALGENERAL.COM
CONTINENTAL GENERAL INSURANCE ... WWW.CONTINENTALGENERAL.COM
CONTINENTAL LIFE INSURANCE CO OF BRENTWOOD TN ... WWW.CONTLIFE.COM
CONTINENTAL WESTERN GROUP ... WWW.CWGINS.COM
CONTRA COSTA HEALTH PLAN ... WWW.CONTRACOSTAHEALTHPLAN.ORG
COOK & CO, INC ... WWW.COOKANDCOMPANY.COM
CO-OP INSURANCE COOPERATIVES ... WWW.CO-OPINSURANCE.COM
COOPERATIVA DE SEGUROS ... WWW.COSVI.COM
CORE MANAGEMENT RESOURCES ... WWW.COREMRG.COM
CORESOURCE ... WWW.CORESOURCE.COM
CORNERSTONE BENEFITS, LLC ... WWW.CORNERSTONEBENEFITS.COM
CORPORATE BENEFITS SERVICE, INC ... WWW.CORBENSER.COM
CORPORATE SYSTEMS ADMINISTRATION, INC ... WWW.CSABENEFITS.COM
CORVEL CORP - MANAGE CARE ... WWW.CORVEL.COM
CORVEL CORP ... WWW.CORVEL.COM
COTTAGE HEALTH SYSTEM ... WWW.SBCH.ORG
COTTON STATES INSURANCE COMPANIES ... WWW.COTTONSTATESINSURANCE.COM
COUNTRY INSURANCE AND FINANCIAL SERVICES ... WWW.COUNTRYFINANCIAL.COM
COUNTRY-WIDE MANAGEMENT SERVICES ... WWW.CWI.COM
COUNTY OF LOS ANGELES DEPT OF HUMAN RESOURCES ... DHR.LACOUNTY.INFO/
COVENANT ADMINISTRATORS / MUTUAL TRUST GROUP ... WWW.THECOVENANTADMINISTRATORS.NET
COVENANT ADMINISTRATORS ... WWW.COVENANTADMINISTRATORS.NET
COVENTRY HEALTH CARE & SOUTH CARE ... WWW.CHCGA.COM
COVENTRY HEALTH CARE / COVENTRY ONE ... WWW.CHCKANSAS.COM
COVENTRY HEALTH CARE ... WWW.CHCDE.COM
COVENTRY HEALTH CARE ... WWW.CHCIOWA.COM
COVENTRY HEALTH CARE ... WWW.CHCLOUISIANA.COM
COVENTRY HEALTH CARE ... WWW.CHCNEBRASKA.COM
COX INSURANCE GROUP, INC ... WWW.COXINSURANCEGROUP.COM
CRAWFORD & CO ... WWW.CRAWFORDANDCOMPANY.COM
CRUM & FORSTER INSURANCE ... WWW.CFINS.COM
CT PIPE TRADES BENEFIT FUNDS ADMINISTRATORS, INC ... WWW.CONNECTICUTPIPETRADES.COM
CUMBERLAND INSURANCE GROUP ... WWW.CUMBERLANDGROUP.COM
CUNA MUTUAL GROUP ... WWW.CUNAMUTUAL.COM
CUNNINGHAM LINDSEY US, INC ... WWW.CUNNINGHAMLINDSEY.COM
CUNNINGHAM LINDSEY, INC ... WWW.CUNNINGHAMLINDSEY.COM
CWI BENEFITS MANAGEMED ... WWW.CWIBENEFITS.COM
CYPRESS BENEFIT ADMINISTRATORS ... WWW.CYPRESSBENEFIT.COM
CYPRESS INSURANCE CO ... WWW.BH-HC.COM
DAIRYLAND INSURANCE CO ... WWW.SENTRY.COM
DAKOTACARE ... WWW.DAKOTACARE.COM
DC CHARTERED HEALTH PLAN, INC ... WWW.CHARTER-HEALTH.COM

DEAN HEALTH PLAN	WWW.DEANCARE.COM
DEEP SOUTH SURPLUS OF TEXAS	WWW.DEEP-SOUTH.COM
DEFINITY HEALTH & UNITED HEALTH PLAN	WWW.DEFINITYHEALTH.COM
DEFINITY HEALTH / UNITED HEALTH CARE	WWW.DEFINITYHEALTH.COM
DEFINITY HEALTH / UNITED	WWW.DEFINITYHEALTH.COM
DEFINITY HEALTH	WWW.DEFINITYHEALTH.COM
DELTA DENTAL OF CALIFORNIA & PMI	WWW.DELTADENTALCA.ORG
DELTA DENTAL	WWW.DELTADENTAL.COM
DELTA DENTAL	WWW.DELTADENTALAR.COM
DELTA DENTAL	WWW.DELTADENTALAZ.COM
DELTA DENTAL	WWW.DELTADENTALCA.ORG
DELTA DENTAL	WWW.DELTADENTALCO.COM
DELTA DENTAL	WWW.DELTADENTALHI.ORG
DELTA DENTAL	WWW.DELTADENTALIA.COM
DELTA DENTAL	WWW.DELTADENTALID.COM
DELTA DENTAL	WWW.DELTADENTALIL.COM
DELTA DENTAL	WWW.DELTADENTALINS.COM
DELTA DENTAL	WWW.DELTADENTALKS.COM
DELTA DENTAL	WWW.DELTADENTALKY.COM
DELTA DENTAL	WWW.DELTADENTALMASS.COM
DELTA DENTAL	WWW.DELTADENTALMN.ORG
DELTA DENTAL	WWW.DELTADENTALMO.COM
DELTA DENTAL	WWW.DELTADENTALNC.ORG
DELTA DENTAL	WWW.DELTADENTALNJ.COM
DELTA DENTAL	WWW.DELTADENTALNM.COM
DELTA DENTAL	WWW.DELTADENTALOK.ORG
DELTA DENTAL	WWW.DELTADENTALRI.COM
DELTA DENTAL	WWW.DELTADENTALSD.COM
DELTA DENTAL	WWW.DELTADENTALTN.COM
DELTA DENTAL	WWW.DELTADENTALVA.COM
DELTA DENTAL	WWW.DELTADENTALWA.COM
DELTA DENTAL	WWW.MIDATLANTICDELTADENTAL.COM
DELTA DENTAL	WWW.NEDELTA.COM
DELTA DENTAL	WWW.ODSCOMPANIES.COM
DELTA HEALTH SYSTEMS	WWW.DELTAHEALTHSYSTEMS.COM
DENTAL BENEFIT PROVIDERS	WWW.DBP.COM
DENTAL HEALTH ALLIANCE	WWW.DHA.COM
DENTAL NETWORK OF AMERICA	WWW.DNOA.COM
DENTAL SOURCE OF MISSOURI AND KANSAS	WWW.DENSOURCE.COM
DENVER HEALTH MEDICAL PLAN	WWW.DENVERHEALTH.ORG
DEPARTMENT OF WATER & POWER CITY OF LOS ANGELES	WWW.LADWP.COM
DESTINY HEALTH	WWW.DESTINYHEALTH.COM
DETROIT & VICINITY TROWEL TRADES	WWW.DVTT.ORG
DIMENSION HEALTH	WWW.DIMENSIONHEALTH.COM
DINA DENTAL PLAN	WWW.DINADENTAL.COM
DIRECTCARE AMERICA	WWW.DIRECTCAREAMERICA.COM
DISABILITY MANAGEMENT SERVICES, INC	WWW.DISABILITYMANAGEMENTSERVICES.COM
DIVERSIFIED GROUP ADMINISTRATORS	WWW.DGATPA.COM
DIVERSIFIED GROUP BROKERS/DIVERSIFIED ADMINISTRATION	WWW.DGB-ONLINE.COM
DMBA	WWW.DMBA.COM
DONEGAL MUTUAL INSURANCE CO	WWW.DONEGALGROUP.COM
DUNN-EDWARDS CORP	WWW.DUNN-EDWARDS.NET
EBA&M	WWW.EBAM.COM
EBMS	WWW.EBMS.COM
EBMS	WWW.EBMSTPA.COM
EBPA, INC	WWW.EBPANH.COM
EBS	WWW.MCS/EBS.COM
EFG COMPANIES	WWW.EFGCOMPANIES.COM
ELECTRIC INSURANCE CO	WWW.ELECTRICINSURANCE.COM
ELI LILLY & CO	WWW.LILLY.COM
EMC INSURANCE	WWW.EMCINSURANCE.COM
EMC NATIONAL LIFE CO	WWW.EMCNATIONALLIFE.COM

EMI	WWW.EMI-TPA.COM
EMIA	WWW.EDUCATORSMUTUAL.COM
EMPLOYEE BENEFIT CONSULTANTS	WWW.EBCTPA.COM
EMPLOYEE BENEFIT SERVICES	WWW.EBSOFLA.COM
EMPLOYEE BENEFIT SERVICES	WWW.KEYBENEFIT.COM
EMPLOYEE BENEFIT SYSTEMS	WWW.EBS-TPA.COM
EMPLOYEE SECURITY, INC	WWW.YOURONLINEBENEFITS.COM
EMPLOYER PLAN SERVICES, INC	WWW.EPSIBENEFITSINC.COM
EMPLOYERS COMPENSATION INSURANCE CO.	WWW.EIG.COM
EMPLOYERS COMPENSATION INSURANCE CO.	WWW.EIGWC.COM
EMPLOYERS COMPENSATION INSURANCE	WWW.FREMONTEMPLOYERS.COM
EMPLOYERS INSURANCE COMPANY OF NEVADA	WWW.EMPLOYERSINGO.COM
EMPLOYERS INSURANCE GROUP	WWW.EIGWC.COM
EMS ADMINISTRATIVE SERVICES	WWW.EMSADMIN.COM
ENTERPRISE GROUP PLANNING	WWW.EGP-INC.COM
EPIC LIFE INSURANCE CO	WWW.EPICLIFE.COM
EPOCH GROUP	WWW.EPOCHGRP.COM
EQUITABLE LIFE & CASUALTY INSURANCE CO.	WWW.EQUILIFE.COM
EQUITABLE PLAN SERVICES, INC	WWW.EPSTPA.COM
ERIE INSURANCE GROUP	WWW.ERIEINSURANCE.COM
ERIN GROUP ADMINISTRATORS, INC	WWW.EGA-INC.COM
ESIS	WWW.ESIS.COM
ESSEX INSURANCE CO	WWW.ESSEX@MARKELINSURANCE.COM
EVEREADY INSURANCE CO.	WWW.EVEREADYINSURANCE.COM
EVEREST HEALTHPLAN ADMINISTRATORS	WWW.EVHEALTH.COM
EVEREST REINSURANCE HOLDING	WWW.EVERESTRE.COM
EVOLUTIONS HEALTHCARE SYSTEMS	WWW.EHPPO.COM
EXCESS REINSURANCE UNDERWRITERS AGENCY, INC	WWW.EXCESSRE.COM
EXCLUSIVE HEALTHCARE, INC	WWW.MUTUALOFOMAHA.COM
FAIRMONT SPECIALTY GROUP	WWW.FAIRMONTSPECIALTY.COM
FALLON COMMUNITY HEALTH PLAN, INC	WWW.FCHP.ORG
FAMILY HEALTH PARTNERS	WWW.FHP.ORG
FARM BUREAU FINANCIAL SERVICES	WWW.FBFS.COM
FARM BUREAU INSURANCE	WWW.AFBIC.COM
FARM BUREAU INSURANCE	WWW.FARMBUREAUINSURANCE-MI.COM
FARM BUREAU INSURANCE	WWW.FBINSURANCE.COM
FARM BUREAU INSURANCE	WWW.FLORIDAFARMBUREAU.COM
FARM BUREAU INSURANCE	WWW.GFB.ORG
FARM BUREAU INSURANCE	WWW.IDFBINS.COM
FARM BUREAU INSURANCE	WWW.INFARMBUREAU.COM
FARM BUREAU INSURANCE	WWW.KYFBINS.COM
FARM BUREAU INSURANCE	WWW.LAFBINS.COM
FARM BUREAU INSURANCE	WWW.MOFB.COM
FARM BUREAU INSURANCE	WWW.MSFBINS.COM
FARM BUREAU INSURANCE	WWW.MWFBI.COM
FARM BUREAU INSURANCE	WWW.NCFBINS.COM
FARM BUREAU INSURANCE	WWW.OKFARMINSURANCE.COM
FARM BUREAU INSURANCE	WWW.SCFBINS.COM
FARM BUREAU INSURANCE	WWW.TXFB.ORG
FARM BUREAU INSURANCE	WWW.TXFB-INS.COM
FARM BUREAU INSURANCE	WWW.VAFB.COM
FARM FAMILY CASUALTY	WWW.FARMFAMILY.COM
FARM FAMILY LIFE & CASUALTY INSURANCE	WWW.FARMFAMILY.COM
FARMERS ALLIANCE MUTUAL INSURANCE	WWW.FAMI.COM
FARMERS INSURANCE EXCHANGE	WWW.FARMERSINSURANCE.COM
FARMERS INSURANCE	WWW.FARMERINSURANCE.COM
FARMERS INSURANCE	WWW.FARMERS.COM
FARMERS INSURANCE	WWW.FARMERSINSURANCE.COM
FBD CONSULTING, INC	WWW.FBDCONSULT.COM
FCE BENEFIT	WWW.FCEBENEFIT.COM
FEDERAL EXPRESS FREIGHT EAST	WWW.FEDEX.COM
FEDERATED MUTUAL INSURANCE CO	WWW.FEDERATEDINSURANCE.COM

FIC INSURANCE GROUP	WWW.FAMILYLIFEINS.COM
FIDELIO INSURANCE CO	WWW.FIDELIODENTAL.COM
FIDELITY SECURITY LIFE INSURANCE CO.	WWW.FSLINS.COM
FIREMAN'S FUND INSURANCE CO	WWW.FIREMANSFUND.COM
FIRST ADMINISTRATORS, INC	WWW.FIRSTADMINISTRATORS.COM
FIRST ADVANTAGE DENTAL	WWW.FIRSTADVANTAGEDENTAL.COM
FIRST CHICAGO INSURANCE CO	WWW.FIRSTCHICAGOINSURANCE.COM
FIRST CHOICE HEALTH NETWORK	WWW.FCHN.COM
FIRST COMMUNITY HEALTH PLAN INC	WWW.FIRSTCOMM.ORG
FIRST HEALTH CCN	WWW.FIRSTHEALTH.COM
FIRST HEALTH SERVICES CORP	WWW.ALASKA.FHSC.COM
FIRST HEALTH	WWW.FIRSTHEALTH.COM
FIRST INSURANCE CO OF HAWAII	WWW.FICOH.COM
FIRST UNITED AMERICAN LIFE INSURANCE CO.	WWW.UNITEDAMERICAN.COM
FIRSTCARE	WWW.FIRSTCARE.COM
FISERV / BPI RISK MANAGEMENT	WWW.BENPLAN.COM
FISERV HEALTH BENESIGHT	WWW.BENESIGHT.COM
FISERV HEALTH-KANSAS	WWW.FISERVHEALTH.COM
FLEX CORP	WWW.FLEXCORP125.COM
FLORIDA COMBINE LIFE	WWW.BCBSFL.COM
FLORIDA HEALTH CARE PLAN, INC	WWW.FHCP.COM
FLORISTS MUTUAL INSURANCE	WWW.HORTICA-INSURANCE.COM
FMH BENEFITS	WWW.F-M-H.COM
FOREIGN SERVICE BENEFIT PLAN / MUTUAL OF OMAHA	WWW.AFSPA.ORG
FOX-EVERETT, INC	WWW.FOXEVERETT.COM
FREMONT INSURANCE CO	WWW.FMIC.COM
FRINGE BENEFIT COORDINATORS	WWW.FBC-INC.COM
GAB ROBINS NORTH AMERICA	WWW.GABROBINS.COM
GAB ROBINS NORTH AMERICA	WWW.GABROBINSNA.COM
GAINSCO	WWW.GAINSCO.COM
GALLAGHER BENEFIT ADMINISTRATORS, INC	WWW.GALLAGHERBENEFITS.COM
GARMI, INC	WWW.GARMI.COM
GATES MCDONALD HEALTH PLUS	WWW.GMCDHEALTHPLUS.COM
GATEWAY HEALTH PLAN	WWW.GATEWAYHEALTHPLAN.COM
GCAN INSURANCE CO	WWW.GCAN.COM
GE INSURANCE SOLUTIONS	WWW.ERCGROUP.COM
GE INSURANCE SOLUTIONS	WWW.GEINSURANCESOLUTIONS.COM
GEHA	WWW.GEHA.COM
GEICO DIRECT	WWW.GEICO.COM
GENERAL CASUALTY COMPANY OF WISCONSIN	WWW.GENERALCASUALTY.COM
GENERAL CASUALTY	WWW.GENERALCASUALTY.COM
GENESIS HEALTHCARE	WWW.GENESISHCC.COM
GERBER LIFE INSURANCE CO	WWW.GERBERLIFE.COM
GERLING GLOBAL REINSURANCE CORPORATION OF AMERICA	WWW.GERLING.COM
GHI	WWW.GHI.COM
GILSBAR, INC	WWW.GILSBAR.COM
GLOBE LIFE & ACCIDENT INSURANCE CO	WWW.GLOBEONTHEWEB.COM
GMAC INSURANCE	WWW.GMACINSURANCE.COM
GMP EMPLOYERS RETIREE TRUST	WWW.GMPTRUST.COM
GOLDEN EAGLE INSURANCE	WWW.GOLDENEAGLECORP.COM
GOLDEN EAGLE INSURANCE	WWW.GOLDENEAGLE-INS.COM
GOLDEN RULE INSURANCE CO	WWW.GOLDENRULE.COM
GOODVILLE MUTUAL CASUALTY, INC	WWW.GOODVILLE.COM
GOTHAM INSURANCE CO	WWW.NYMAGIC.COM
GRAIN DEALERS MUTUAL INSURANCE CO	WWW.GRAINDEALERS.COM
GRAMERCY INSURANCE CO	WWW.GRAMERCYINSURANCE.COM
GRAND VALLEY HEALTH PLAN	WWW.GVHP.COM
GRANGE INSURANCE ASSOCIATION	WWW.GRANGE.COM
GRANGE INSURANCE GROUP	WWW.GRANGE.COM
GRANGE MUTUAL CASUALTY CO	WWW.GRANGEINSURANCE.COM
GRANGE MUTUAL INSURANCE CO	WWW.GRANGEINSURANCE.COM
GRAY INSURANCE CO	WWW.GRAYINSCO.COM

GREAT AMERICAN INSURANCE CO .... WWW.GREATAMERICANINSURANCE.COM
GREAT DIVIDE INSURANCE CO........ WWW.NAUTILUSINSGROUP.COM
GREAT LAKES HEALTH PLAN........ WWW.GLHP.COM
GREAT WEST CASUALTY CO .... WWW.GWCCNET.COM
GREAT WEST HEALTHCARE........ WWW.GREATWEST.COM
GREAT WEST HEALTHCARE........ WWW.GREATWEST.COM/PROVIDERS OR WWW.MYGREATWEST.COM
GREAT WEST HEALTHCARE........ WWW.GREATWESTHEALTHCARE.COM
GREAT WEST HEALTHCARE........ WWW.GREATWESTHEALTHCARE.COM OR WWW. MYGREATWESTHEALTHCARE.COM
GREAT WEST HEALTHCARE........ WWW.MYGREATWEST.COM
GREAT WEST LIFE........ WWW.GWI.CA
GREATER NEW YORK MUTUAL INSURANCE CO........ WWW.GNY.COM
GREENTREE ADMINISTRATORS .... WWW.GREENTREEADMIN.COM
GROCERS INSURANCE .... WWW.GROCINS.COM
GROUP & PENSION ADMINISTRATORS........ WWW.GPATPA.COM
GROUP BENEFIT SERVICES, INC .... WWW.GBSIO.NET
GROUP DEKKO LLC .... WWW.DEKKO.COM
GROUP HEALTH COOPERATIVE .... WWW.GHC.ORG
GROUP HEALTH COOPERATIVE .... WWW.GHC-HMO.COM
GROUP HEALTH COOPERATIVE .... WWW.GROUP-HEALTH.COM
GROUP HEALTH MANAGERS........ WWW.IHGHM.COM
GROUP HEALTH PLAN .... WWW.GHP.COM
GROUP INSURANCE SERVICE CENTER........ WWW.GISCINC.COM
GUARANTEE TRUST LIFE .... WWW.GTLIC.COM
GUARDIAN LIFE INSURANCE CO OF AMERICA........ WWW.GLIC.COM
GUARDIAN LIFE INSURANCE CO OF AMERICA........ WWW.GUARDIANLIFE.COM
GUARDIAN LIFE INSURANCE CO OF AMERICA........ WWW.GUARDIANLIFE.COM OR WWW.GLIC.COM
GUIDEONE INSURANCE .... WWW.GUIDEONE.COM
GULF GUARANTY EMPLOYEE BENEFIT SERVICES, INC........ WWW.GGEBS.COM
GULFCO LIFE INSURANCE CO .... WWW.GULFCOLIFE.COM
GUY CARPENTER........ WWW.GUYCARP.COM
HANOVER INSURANCE CO .... WWW.ALLMERICA.COM
HANOVER INSURANCE CO .... WWW.ALLMERICA.COM OR HANOVER.COM
HANOVER INSURANCE CO .... WWW.HANOVER.COM
HANOVER INSURANCE GROUP .... WWW.HANOVER.COM
HARLEYSVILLE INSURANCE........ WWW.HARLEYSVILLEGROUP.COM
HARRINGTON BENEFIT SERVICES, INC........ WWW.FISERVHEALTH-HARRINGTON.COM
HARRINGTON BENEFIT SERVICES, INC........ WWW.HARRINGTONBENEFITS.COM
HARTFORD INSURANCE CO .... WWW.THEHARTFORD.COM
HARTFORD MUTUAL INSURANCE CO........ WWW.HARTFORDMUTUAL.COM
HARTFORD, THE .... WWW.THEHARTFORD.COM
HARVARD PILGRIM HEALTH CARE, INC........ WWW.HARVARDPILGRIM.ORG
HARVARD PILGRIM HEALTH CARE, INC........ WWW.HPHC.ORG
HARVARD UNIVERSITY GROUP HEALTH PROGRAM .... WWW.UHS.HARVARD.EDU
HAWKEYE SECURITY INSURANCE........ WWW.HAWKEYESECURITY-INS.COM
HCC BENEFITS CORPORATION .... WWW.HCCLIFE.COM
HCH ADMINISTRATORS, INC........ WWW.HCHADMIN.COM
HEALTH ADVANTAGE HMO PARTNERS .... WWW.HEALTHADVANTAGE-HMO.COM
HEALTH AGENCIES OF THE WEST, INC........ WWW.HEALTHAGENCIES.COM
HEALTH ALLIANCE PLAN OF MICHIGAN........ WWW.HAP.ORG
HEALTH ALLIANCE .... WWW.HEALTHALLIANCE.ORG
HEALTH BENEFIT TRUST FUND LOCAL 94 .... WWW.LOCAL94.COM
HEALTH CARE ADMINISTRATORS, INC........ WWW.ARNETTPLAN.COM
HEALTH ECONOMICS GROUP, INC........ WWW.HEGINC.COM
HEALTH FIRST........ WWW.HEALTH-FIRST.ORG
HEALTH FUTURE, LLC........ WWW.HEALTHFUTURE.ORG
HEALTH GROUP LLC, THE........ WWW.THCG.ORG
HEALTH INSURANCE PLAN OF GREATER NEW YORK .... WWW.HIPUSA.COM
HEALTH NET........ WWW.HEALTHNET.COM
HEALTH NET........ WWW.HEALTHNETFEDERALSERVICES.COM
HEALTH NETWORK AMERICA, INC .... WWW.HEALTHNETWORKAMERICA.COM
HEALTH NEW ENGLAND .... WWW.HNE.COM
HEALTH PARTNERS CENTRAL MINNESOTA CLINICS/PHARRMACY........ WWW.HEALTHPARTNERS.COM

HEALTH PARTNERS	WWW.HEALTHPART.COM
HEALTH PARTNERS	WWW.HEALTHPARTNERS.COM
HEALTH PLAN ADMINISTRATORS, INC	WWW.HPA-INC.COM
HEALTH PLAN OF NEVADA, INC	WWW.SIERRAHEALTH.COM OR WWW.HEALTHPLANOFNEVADA,COM
HEALTH PLAN SERVICES	WWW.HEALTHPLAN.COM
HEALTH PLAN, THE	WWW.HEALTHPLAN.ORG
HEALTH PLUS OF MICHIGAN	WWW.HEALTHPLUS.COM
HEALTH SERVICES BENEFITS ADMINISTRATORS	WWW.HSBA.COM
HEALTH SPECIAL RISK, INC	WWW.HEALTHSPECIALRISK.COM
HEALTH SYSTEMS INTERNATIONAL	WWW.US-HSI.COM
HEALTHCARE PARTNERS MEDICAL GROUP, INC	WWW.HEALTHCAREPARTNERS.COM
HEALTHCARE SOLUTIONS GROUP, INC	WWW.HSG.COM
HEALTHCARE USA OF MISSOURI LLC	WWW.CHCHCUSA.COM
HEALTHCOMP	WWW.HEALTHCOMP.COM
HEALTHFIRST TPA, INC	WWW.HFTPA.COM
HEALTHLINK, INC	WWW.HEALTHLINK.COM
HEALTHNET OREGON	WWW.HEALTHNET.COM
HEALTHNOW NY, INC	WWW.HEALTHNOWNY.COM
HEALTHPLEX, INC	WWW.HEALTHPLEX.COM
HEALTHSPRING	WWW.HEALTHSPINGOFALABAMA.COM
HEALTHSPRING	WWW.MYHEALTHSPRING.COM
HEART OF AMERICA HEALTH PLAN	WWW.HOAHP.COM
HELLER ASSOCIATES	WWW.HELLERTPA.COM
HELMSMAN MANAGEMENT SERVICES, INC	WWW.LIBERTYMUTUAL.COM/HELMSMAN
HERITAGE INSURANCE MANAGERS, INC	WWW.HERITAGE-INS.COM
HILB ROGAL & HOBBS COMPANY / HRH	WWW.HRH.COM
HIP HEALTH PLAN OF NEW YORK	WWW.HIPUSA.COM
HMA, INC	WWW.HMA-INC.COM
HOLYOKE MUTUAL INSURANCE CO	WWW.HOLYOKEMUTUAL.COM
HOMETOWN HEALTH PLAN	WWW.HOMETOWNHEALTH.COM
HORACE MANN COMPANIES	WWW.HORACEMANN.COM
HORIZON BLUE CROSS BLUE SHIELD OF NEW JERSEY	WWW.HORIZON-BCBSNJ.COM
HOSPITAL BENEFITS, INC	WWW.HBIFLM.COM
HOTEL & RESTAURANT EMPLOYEES INT'L UNION WELFARE PENSION FUNDS	WWW.HEREIUFUND.COM
HOUSING AUTHORITY INSURANCE GROUP	WWW.HOUSINGCENTER.COM
HOUSTON CASULTY COMPANY	WWW.HCCH.COM
HUMAN RESOURCE BENEFIT ADMINISTRATORS	WWW.HRBENEFITS.NET
HUMANA DENTAL SERVICES	WWW.HUMANADENTAL.COM
HUMANA, INC	WWW.HUMANA.COM
IBA HEALTH PLANS / IBA PHP	WWW.IBAHEALTHPLANS.COM
IBEW	WWW.4IBEW.COM
IBEW	WWW.IBEW.ORG
IBEW	WWW.IBEW10TH.ORG
IBEW	WWW.IBEW11TH.ORG
IBEW	WWW.IBEW6TH.ORG
IBEW	WWW.IBEW8TH.ORG
IBEW	WWW.IBEWNINTHDISTRICT.ORG
ICW GROUP	WWW.ICWGROUP.COM
IDS LIFE OF NEW YORK	WWW.AMERIPRISEINTERNATIONAL.COM
IFG CO	WWW.BURLINGTONINSURANCE.COM
ILLINOIS MUTUAL LIFE INSURANCE CO	WWW.ILLINOISMUTUAL.COM
ILWU/PMA COASTWISE CLAIMS OFFICE	WWW.ILW.ORG
IMA OF KANSAS	WWW.IMACORP.COM
IMT INSURANCE CO	WWW.IMTINS.COM
INDEPENDENCE BLUE CROSS	WWW.IBX.COM
INDEPENDENT HEALTH	WWW.INDEPENDENTHEALTH.COM
INDIANA INSURANCE / REGIONAL AGENCY MARKET	WWW.INDIANA-INS.COM
INDIANA INSURANCE	WWW.INDIANA-INS.COM
INDIANA INSURANCE	WWW.LIBERTYRAM.COM OR INDIANA-INS.COM
INDIANA TEAMSTERS HEALTH BENEFIT & FUND	WWW.LOCAL135.COM
INDIANAPOLIS LIFE	WWW.INDIANAPOLISLIFE.COM
INDIVIDUAL ASSURANCE COMPANY	WWW.IAC-GROUP.COM

INDUSTRIAL ALLIANCE PACIFIC INSURANCE AND FINANCIAL SERVICES .... WWW.IAPLIFE.COM
INDUSTRIAL RISK INSURERS .... WWW.INDUSTRIALRISK.COM
INFINITY INSURANCE COMPANIES .... WWW.INFINITYAUTO.COM
INFINITY INSURANCE COMPANIES .... WWW.INFINITY-GROUP.COM OR WWW.INFINITY-AUTO.COM
INFINITY INSURANCE COMPANIES .... WWW.INFINITY-INSURANCE.COM
ING .... WWW.ING.COM
INSURANCE & RISK MANAGEMENT .... WWW.EMPLOYEEPLANSLLC.COM
INSURANCE MANAGEMENT ADMINISTRATORS OF LOUISIANA .... WWW.IMALA.COM
INSURANCE SERVICING GROUP .... WWW.BANKAMERICA.COM
INSURERS ADMINISTRATIVE CORP / IAC .... WWW.IACUSA.COM
INTEGRITY BENEFIT NETWORK .... WWW.IBNTPA.COM
INTEGRITY MUTUAL INSURANCE CO .... WWW.INTEGRITYINSURANCEOM.COM
INTER VALLEY HEALTH PLAN .... WWW.IVHP.COM
INTER-AMERICAS INSURANCE .... WWW.IAI-ONLINE.COM
INTRACORP .... WWW.CIGNA.COM
INTRACORP .... WWW.INTRACORP.COM
INVESTORS HERITAGE LIFE INSURANCE CO .... WWW.INVESTORSHERITAGE.COM
IOWA MUTUAL INSURANCE GROUP .... WWW.IOWAMUTUAL.COM
ISLAND INSURANCE CO, LTD .... WWW.ISLANDINSURANCE.COM
J P FARLEY CORPORATION .... WWW.JPFARLEY.COM
JAS, INC .... WWW.JASBENEFITS.COM
JEFFERSON PILOT FINANCIAL .... WWW.JPFINANCIAL.COM
JEFFERSON PILOT FINANCIAL .... WWW.JPFINANCIALCOM
JEWELERS MUTUAL INSURANCE CO. .... WWW.JEWELERSMUTUAL.COM
JFP BENEFIT MANAGEMENT .... WWW.JFPBENEFITMANAGEMENT.COM
JLT SERVICES CORP .... WWW.JLTSERVICES.COM
JM FAMILY ENTERPRISES .... WWW.JMFAMILY.COM
JMH HEALTH PLAN .... WWW.JMHHP.COM
JOHN DEERE HEALTH / UNITED HEALTH .... WWW.JOHNDEEREHEALTH.COM
JOHN DEERE HEALTH/UNITED HEALTH .... WWW.JOHNDEEREHEALTH.COM
JOHN DEERE HEALTH .... WWW.JOHNDEEREHEALTH.COM
JOHN MUIR MEDICAL CENTER .... WWW.JOHNMUIRHEALTH.COM
JP FARLEY CORP .... WWW.JPFARLEY.COM
K & K INSURANCE GROUP .... WWW.KANDKINSURANCE.COM
KAISER PERMANENTE .... WWW.KAISERPERMANENTE.ORG
KAISER PERMANENTE .... WWW.KAISERPERMANENTE.ORG OR WWW.KP.ORG
KAISER PERMANENTE .... WWW.KP.ORG
KANAWHA INSURANCE CO .... WWW.KMGAMERICA.COM
KANSAS CITY LIFE INSURANCE CO .... WWW.KCLGROUPBENEFITS.COM
KEENAN & ASSOCIATES .... WWW.KEENANASSOC.COM
KEMPER AUTO & HOME .... WWW.UNITRIN.COM
KEMPER AUTO AND HOME .... WWW.KEMPERAUTO&HOME.COM
KEMPER AUTO AND HOME .... WWW.KEMPERAUTOANDHOMEINSURANCE.COM
KEMPER AUTO AND HOME .... WWW.KEMPERINSURANCE.COM ORWWW.KEMPERAUTOANDHOME.COM
KEMPER INSURANCE COMPANIES .... WWW.KEMPERINSURANCE.COM
KEMPTON GROUP .... WWW.KEMPTONGROUP.COM
KEYSTONE HEALTH PLAN CENTRAL .... WWW.CAPBLUECROSS.COM
KEYSTONE MERCY HEALTH PLAN .... WWW.KMHP.COM
KHS .... WWW.KHSONLINE.COM
KIPP & COMPANY .... WWW.KIPPCO.COM
KITSAP PHYSICIANS SERVICE .... WWW.KPSHEALTHPLANS.COM
KLAIS & CO .... WWW.KLAIS.COM
KPS HEALTH PLAN .... WWW.KPSHEALTHPLANS.COM
KROGER .... WWW.KROGER.COM
LANCER CORP .... WWW.LANCERCORP.COM
LANDMARK HEALTH CARE INC .... WWW.LANDMARKHEALTHCARE.COM
LAWRENCE E. SMITH & ASSOCIATES, INC .... WWW.LESMITH.NET
LBA HEALTH PLANS .... WWW.DOCFIRST.COM
LEMARS MUTUAL INSURANCE CO OF IOWA .... WWW.LEMM.COM
LEWER AGENCY, INC .... WWW.LEWER.COM
LEXINGTON INSURANCE CO .... WWW.LEXINGTONINSURANCE.COM
LIBERTY INTERNATIONAL UNDERWRITERS .... WWW.LIBERTYIU.COM

LIBERTY LIFE INSURANCE CO	WWW.LIBERTYLIFE.COM
LIBERTY MUTUAL	WWW.LIBERTYMUTUAL.COM
LIBERTY NORTHWEST	WWW.LIBERTYNORTHWEST.COM
LIFE AT THE SOUTH	WWW.LIFE-SOUTH.COM
LIFE INSURANCE CO OF ALABAMA	WWW.LICOA.COM
LIFE OF THE SOUTH SERVICE CO	WWW.LIFE-SOUTH.COM
LIFEWELL HEALTH PLANS	WWW.LWHP.COM
LIFEWISE HEALTH PLAN OF OREGON	WWW.LIFEWISEOR.COM
LINECO	WWW.LINECO.ORG
LITITZ MUTUAL INSURANCE COMPANY	WWW.LITITZMUTUAL.COM
LOCAL 1014 HEALTH AND WELFARE	WWW.LOCAL1014.ORG OR WWW.LOCAL1014MEDICAL.ORG
LOCAL 338 HEALTH & WELFARE FUND	WWW.LOCAL338.COM
LOCAL 365 UAW WELFARE FUND	WWW.COMPREHENSIVE-BENEFIT.COM
LOCAL 802 MUSICIANS HEALTH BENEFIT	WWW.LOCAL802AFM.ORG
LOMA LINDA UNIVERSITY ADVENTIST HEALTH SCIENCES CENTER	WWW.LLUMC.EDU
LOOMIS CO	WWW.LOOMISCO.COM
LOVELACE HEALTH PLAN, INC	WWW.LOVELACEHEALTHPLAN.COM
LWP CLAIMS SOLUTIONS, INC	WWW.LWPCLAIMS.COM
MADISON NATIONAL LIFE INSURANCE CO, INC	WWW.MADISONLIFE.COM
MAGNA CARTA COMPANIES	WWW.MCARTA.COM
MAGNA CARTA	WWW.MCARTA.COM
MAILHANDLERS BENEFIT PLAN	WWW.MHBP.COM
MAKSIN MANAGEMENT CORP	WWW.MAKSIN.COM
MANAGED CARE CONSULTANTS, INC (MCC)	WWW.MCCNEVADA.COM
MANAGED HEALTH, INC	WWW.HEALTHNY.COM
MANHATTAN INSURANCE GROUP	WWW.MANHATTANLIFE.COM
MANHATTEN INSURANCE GROUP & COMPANIES	WWW.MANHATTENLIFE.COM
MANHATTEN INSURANCE GROUP AND COMPANIES	WWW.MANHATTENLIFE.COM
MANHATTEN LIFE INSURANCE COMPANY	WWW.MANHATTENLIFE.COM
MANPOWER, INC	WWW.MANPOWER.COM OR WWW.USMANPOWER.COM OR WWW.MANPOWERPROFESSIONAL.COM
MANULIFE FINANCIAL	WWW.MANULIFE.COM
MARICOPA INTEGRATED SYSTEM HEALTHCARE	WWW.UPH.ORG
MARKEL WEST	WWW.MARKELCORP.COM
MARRIOTT INTERNATIONAL, INC	WWW.MARRIOTT.COM
MARSH	WWW.MARSH.COM
MARTIN'S POINT HEALTH CARE	WWW.MARTINSPOINT.ORG
MASS HEALTH	WWW.MASS.GOV/DMA
MASS MUTUAL FINANCIAL GROUP	WWW.MASSMUTUAL.COM
MBA	WWW.CMI-MBA.COM
MBA	WWW.MBA.TO
M-CARE ADMINISTRATION	WWW.MCARE.ORG
MEADOWBROOK INSURANCE GROUP	WWW.MEADOWBROOK.COM
MEDAVANT HEALTHARE SOLUTIONS	WWW.MEDAVANT.COM
MEDEX GLOBAL GROUP, INC	WWW.MEDEXASSIST.COM
MEDICAID OFFICE / UNISYS	WWW.STATE.NJ.US/HUMANSERVICES/DMAHS
MEDICAID OFFICE	HTTP://HEALTH.UTAH.GOV/MEDICAID/
MEDICAID OFFICE	HTTP://WWW.STATE.SD.US/SOCIAL/MEDICAL/INDEX.HTM
MEDICAID OFFICE	WWW.ADSA.DSHS.WA.GOV
MEDICAID OFFICE	WWW.AHCCCS.STATE.AZ.US
MEDICAID OFFICE	WWW.ASSIST.DHHS.DELAWARE.GOV
MEDICAID OFFICE	WWW.CHCPF.STATE.CO.US
MEDICAID OFFICE	WWW.CO.RAMSEY.MN.US
MEDICAID OFFICE	WWW.COMMUNITYHEALTH.STATE.GA.US
MEDICAID OFFICE	WWW.DCHEALTH.DC.GOV
MEDICAID OFFICE	WWW.DFSWEB.STATE.WY.US
MEDICAID OFFICE	WWW.DHFS.STATE
MEDICAID OFFICE	WWW.DHH.STATE.LA.US
MEDICAID OFFICE	WWW.DHHS.STATE.NC.US/DMA
MEDICAID OFFICE	WWW.DHHS.STATE.NH.US
MEDICAID OFFICE	WWW.DHHS.STATE.SC.US OR WWW.SCDHHS.GOV
MEDICAID OFFICE	WWW.DHR.STATE.ME.US
MEDICAID OFFICE	WWW.DHS.STATE.IA.US

MEDICAID OFFICE .... WWW.DHS.STATE.RI.US
MEDICAID OFFICE .... WWW.DMAS.VIRGINIA.GOV
MEDICAID OFFICE .... WWW.DOM.STATE.MS.US
MEDICAID OFFICE .... WWW.DPHHS.MT.GOV
MEDICAID OFFICE .... WWW.DPW.STATE.PA.US
MEDICAID OFFICE .... WWW.DSS.STATE.CT.US
MEDICAID OFFICE .... WWW.EMOMED.COM
MEDICAID OFFICE .... WWW.FLORIDAHEALTHSTAT.COM
MEDICAID OFFICE .... WWW.HEALTHANDWELFARE.IDAHO.GOV
MEDICAID OFFICE .... WWW.HEATLH.STATE.NY.US
MEDICAID OFFICE .... WWW.HFS.ILLINOIS.GOV\
MEDICAID OFFICE .... WWW.HHS.STATE.NE.US
MEDICAID OFFICE .... WWW.HHSC.STATE.TX.US
MEDICAID OFFICE .... WWW.HSS.STATE.AK.US
MEDICAID OFFICE .... WWW.IN.GOV/FSSA/HEALTHCARE/
MEDICAID OFFICE .... WWW.JFS.OHIO.GOV/OHP
MEDICAID OFFICE .... WWW.MASS.GOV/MASSHEALTH
MEDICAID OFFICE .... WWW.MEDICAID.STATE.AL.US
MEDICAID OFFICE .... WWW.MEDICAID.STATE.AR.US
MEDICAID OFFICE .... WWW.MEDI-CAL.CA.GOV
MEDICAID OFFICE .... WWW.MED-QUEST.US
MEDICAID OFFICE .... WWW.MICHIGAN.GOV/MDCH
MEDICAID OFFICE .... WWW.NVAGING.NET
MEDICAID OFFICE .... WWW.OHCA.STATE.OK.US
MEDICAID OFFICE .... WWW.OREGON.GOV
MEDICAID OFFICE .... WWW.OVHA.STATE.VT.US
MEDICAID OFFICE .... WWW.SRSKANSAS.ORG
MEDICAID OFFICE .... WWW.STATE.ME.US OR WWW.STATE.MAINE.GOV/DHHS/BMS
MEDICAID OFFICE .... WWW.STATE.ND.US/HUMANSERVICES
MEDICAID OFFICE .... WWW.STATE.NM.US/HSD/MAD
MEDICAID OFFICE .... WWW.STATE.TN.US/TENNCARE/
MEDICAID OFFICE .... WWW.WVDHHR.ORG
MEDICAL ASSOCIATES HEALTH PLANS AND HEALTH CHOICES .... WWW.MAHEALTHCARE.COM
MEDICAL NETWORK OF COLORADO SPRINGS .... WWW.MYMEDNET.COM
MEDICAL PROTECTIVE COMPANY, THE .... WWW.GEMEDICALPROTECTIVE.COM
MEDICAL PROTECTIVE COMPANY, THE .... WWW.MEDPRO.COM
MEDI-CAL .... WWW.MEDI-CAL.CA.GOV
MEDICARE - DMERC CARRIERS .... WWW.ADMINASTAR.COM
MEDICARE - DMERC CARRIERS .... WWW.CIGNAGOVERMENTSERVICES.COM
MEDICARE - DMERC CARRIERS .... WWW.PALMETTOGBA.COM
MEDICARE - DMERC CARRIERS .... WWW.UMD.NYCPIC.COM
MEDICARE - PART A INTERMEDIARIES .... WWW.ANTHEM.COM
MEDICARE - PART A INTERMEDIARIES .... WWW.ANTHEMBCBSNH.COM
MEDICARE - PART A INTERMEDIARIES .... WWW.ARKMEDICARE.COM
MEDICARE - PART A INTERMEDIARIES .... WWW.BCBSAL.COM
MEDICARE - PART A INTERMEDIARIES .... WWW.BCBSNE.COM
MEDICARE - PART A INTERMEDIARIES .... WWW.BCBSOK.COM
MEDICARE - PART A INTERMEDIARIES .... WWW.EMPIREMEDICARE.COM
MEDICARE - PART A INTERMEDIARIES .... WWW.FLORIDAMEDICARE.COM
MEDICARE - PART A INTERMEDIARIES .... WWW.GEORGIAMEDICARE.COM
MEDICARE - PART A INTERMEDIARIES .... WWW.HIGHMARKMEDICARESERVICES.COM
MEDICARE - PART A INTERMEDIARIES .... WWW.KANSASMEDICARE.COM
MEDICARE - PART A INTERMEDIARIES .... WWW.MEDICARE.BCBSMT.COM
MEDICARE - PART A INTERMEDIARIES .... WWW.MEDICARE.GOV
MEDICARE - PART A INTERMEDIARIES .... WWW.MEDICAREAZ.COM
MEDICARE - PART A INTERMEDIARIES .... WWW.MEDICAREWY.COM
MEDICARE - PART A INTERMEDIARIES .... WWW.NORIDIAN.COM
MEDICARE - PART A INTERMEDIARIES .... WWW.NORIDIANMEDICARE.COM
MEDICARE - PART A INTERMEDIARIES .... WWW.PALMETTOGBA.COM
MEDICARE - PART A INTERMEDIARIES .... WWW.RIVERBENDGBA.COM
MEDICARE - PART A INTERMEDIARIES .... WWW.TRAILBLAZERHEALTH.COM
MEDICARE - PART A INTERMEDIARIES .... WWW.TRIPLES-MED.ORG

MEDICARE - PART A INTERMEDIARIES	WWW.TRISPAN.COM
MEDICARE - PART A INTERMEDIARIES	WWW.UGSMEDICARE.COM
MEDICARE - PART A INTERMEDIARIES	WWW.VERITUSMEDICARE.COM
MEDICARE - PART B CARRIERS	WWW.ARKMEDICARE.COM
MEDICARE - PART B CARRIERS	WWW.CAHABAGBA.COM
MEDICARE - PART B CARRIERS	WWW.CIGNAGOVERMENTSEVICES.COM
MEDICARE - PART B CARRIERS	WWW.FLORIDAMEDICARE.COM
MEDICARE - PART B CARRIERS	WWW.KANSASMEDICARE.COM
MEDICARE - PART B CARRIERS	WWW.MEDICARE.BCBSMT.COM
MEDICARE - PART B CARRIERS	WWW.MEDICARE.GOV
MEDICARE - PART B CARRIERS	WWW.MEDICARENHIC.COM
MEDICARE - PART B CARRIERS	WWW.NORIDIANMEDICARE.COM
MEDICARE - PART B CARRIERS	WWW.PALMETTOGBA.COM
MEDICARE - PART B CARRIERS	WWW.REGENCE.COM
MEDICARE - PART B CARRIERS	WWW.TRAILBLAZERHEALTH.COM
MEDICARE - PART B CARRIERS	WWW.TRIPLES-MED.ORG
MEDICARE - PART B CARRIERS	WWW.UMD.NYCPIC.COM
MEDICARE - PART B CARRIERS	WWW.VERITUSMEDICARE.COM
MEDICARE - PART B CARRIERS	WWW.WPSIC.COM
MEDICARE REGIONAL HOME HEALTH INTERMEDIARIES	WWW.ANTHEM.COM
MEDICARE REGIONAL HOME HEALTH INTERMEDIARIES	WWW.CAHABAGBA.COM
MEDICARE REGIONAL HOME HEALTH INTERMEDIARIES	WWW.PALMETTOGBA.COM
MEDICARE REGIONAL HOME HEALTH INTERMEDIARIES	WWW.UGSMEDICARE.COM
MEDICO INSURANCE COMPANY	WWW.GOMEDICO.COM
MEDIVERSAL, INC	WWW.MEDIVERSAL.COM
MEDMARC INSURANCE GROUP	WWW.MEDMARC.COM
MED-PAY, INC	WWW.MED-PAY.COM
MEDSAVE USA	WWW.MEDSAVEUSA.COM
MEIJER, INC	WWW.MEIJER.COM
MENNONITE MUTUAL AID	WWW.MMA-ONLINE.ORG
MERCER ADMINISTRATION	WWW.ONLINEBENEFITSACCESS.COM
MERCHANTS INSURANCE GROUP	WWW.MERCHANTSGROUP.COM
MERCURY CASUALTY CO	WWW.MERCURYINSURANCE.COM
MERCURY INSURANCE GROUP	WWW.MERCURYINSURANCE.COM
MERCURY INSURANCE GROUP	WWW.MERCURYINSURANCEGROUP.COM
MERCY HEALTH PLANS OF MISSOURI	WWW.MERCYHEALTHPLANS.COM
MERCYCARE INSURANCE CO	WWW.MERCYHEALTHSYSTEM.ORG
MERITAIN HEALTH	WWW.MERITAIN.COM
MERITAIN HEALTH	WWW.NAHP.COM
METLIFE AUTO & HOME	WWW.METLIFE.COM
METLIFE DENTAL	WWW.METLIFE.COM/DENTAL
METROPOLITAN LIFE INSURANCE CO	WWW.METLIFE.COM
MGIS COMPANIES	WWW.MGIS.COM
MHNET	WWW.MHNET.COM
MICHIGAN EMPLOYEE BENEFIT SERVICES	WWW.MEBS.COM
MICHIGAN MILLERS MUTUAL INSURANCE	WWW.MIMILLERS.COM
MID-AMERICAN BENEFITS, INC	WWW.MID-AMERICANBENEFITS.COM
MID-CONTINENT GROUP	WWW.MCG-INS.COM
MIDDLESEX INSURANCE	WWW.DAIRYLAND-INSURANCE.COM
MIDDLESEX MUTUAL ASSURANCE CO	WWW.MIDDLESEXMUTUAL.COM
MIDLAND CO	WWW.AMIG.COM
MIDLAND NATIONAL LIFE INSURANCE CO	WWW.MIDLANDNATIONAL.COM
MIDWEST SECURITY ADMINISTRATORS	WWW.MIDWESTSECURITY.COM
MIDWEST SECURITY INSURANCE CO.	WWW.MIDWESTSECURITY.COM
MILLERS CAPITAL INSURANCE CO	WWW.MILLERSINSURANCE.COM
MOLINA HEALTHCARE	WWW.MOLINAHEALTHCARE.COM
MONTGOMERY INSURANCE	WWW.MONLIFE.COM
MONTGOMERY MUTUAL INSURANCE CO.	WWW.MONTGOMERY-INS.COM
MONUMENTAL LIFE INSURANCE CO	WWW.MONLIFE.COM
MONY LIFE INSURANCE COMPANY	WWW.MONY.COM
MOUNTAIN STATE BLUE CROSS BLUE SHIELD	WWW.MSBCBS.COM
MOUNTAIN STATES ADMINISTRATIVE SERVICES	WWW.MYMSAS.COM

M-PLAN .... WWW.MPLAN.COM
MS ADMINISTRATORS .... WWW.MSADMIN.COM
MULTI LINES INSURANCE .... WWW.UNITRINMLI.COM
MUTUAL ASSURANCE ADMINISTRATORS .... WWW.MAA-TPA.COM
MUTUAL OF AMERICA .... WWW.MUTUALOFAMERICA.COM
MUTUAL OF ENUMCLAW INSURANCE CO .... WWW.MUTUALOFENUMCLAW.COM
MUTUAL OF OMAHA .... WWW.MUTUALOFOMAHA.COM
MUTUAL OF OMAHA .... WWW.MUTUALOFOMAHACOMPANY.COM
MUTUAL SAVINGS LIFE INSURANCE CO .... WWW.MSLDEC.COM
MYERS STEVENS .... WWW.MYERS-STEVENS.COM
NALC HEALTH BENEFIT PLAN .... WWW.NALC.ORG/DEPART/HBP
NAMIC .... WWW.NAMIC.ORG
NATIONAL AMERICAN INSURANCE CO OF CALIFORNIA .... WWW.NAICC.COM
NATIONAL AMERICAN INSURANCE CO .... WWW.NAICO.COM
NATIONAL CLAIMS ADMINISTRATIVE SOURCES .... WWW.NCAS.COM
NATIONAL CONTINENTAL PROGRESSIVE CASUALTY INSURANCE CO .... WWW.PROGRESSIVE.COM
NATIONAL FARMERS UNION PROPERTY & CASUALTY CO .... WWW.NFUIC.COM
NATIONAL FOUNDATION LIFE INSURANCE CO .... WWW.USHEALTHGROUP.COM
NATIONAL GRANGE MUTUAL INSURANCE CO .... WWW.MSAGROUP.COM
NATIONAL GUARDIAN LIFE INSURANCE CO .... WWW.NATIONALGUARDIAN.COM
NATIONAL GUARDIAN LIFE INSURANCE GROUP .... WWW.NGLIC.COM
NATIONAL INDEMNITY CO .... WWW.NATIONALINDEMNITY.COM
NATIONAL MUTUAL BENEFIT .... WWW.NMBLIFE.COM
NATIONAL RURAL LETTER CARRIERS' ASSOCIATION .... WWW.MUTUALOFOMAHA.COM
NATIONAL SECURITY INSURANCE CO .... WWW.NATIONALSECURITYINSURANCE.COM
NATIONWIDE AGRA BUSINESS .... WWW.NATIONWIDEAGRABUSINESS.COM
NATIONWIDE HEALTH PLANS .... WWW.NATIONWIDEHEALTHPLANS.COM
NATIONWIDE INSURANCE .... WWW.NATIONWIDE.COM
NATIONWIDE MUTUAL INSURANCE CO .... WWW.NATIONWIDE.COM
NEIGHBORHOOD HEALTH PARTNERSHIP .... WWW.MYNHP.COM
NEIGHBORHOOD HEALTH PLAN .... WWW.NHP.ORG
NEW ERA LIFE INSURANCE CO .... WWW.NEWERALIFE.COM
NEW JERSEY MANUFACTURERS INSURANCE CO .... WWW.NJM.COM
NEW LONDON COUNTY MUTUAL INSURANCE CO .... WWW.NLCINSURANCE.COM
NGS AMERICAN, INC .... WWW.NGS-AMERICAN.COM
NLC .... WWW.SUMMITINSURANCE.COM
NOITU INSURANCE TRUST FUND .... WWW.NOITU.ORG
NORTH AMERICA ADMINISTRATORS, LP .... WWW.NAA-LP.COM
NORTH CAROLINA MUTUAL LIFE INSURANCE CO .... WWW.NCMUTUALLIFE.COM
NORTH POINTE INSURANCE CO .... WWW.NPIC.COM
NORTHEAST INSURANCE CO .... WWW,PRESERVER.COM
NORTHERN ADJUSTERS, INC .... WWW.NADJ.COM
NORTHLAND INSURANCE CO .... WWW.NORTHLANDINS.COM
NORTHWEST ADMINISTRATORS .... WWW.NWADMIN.COM
NORTHWEST TEXAS HEALTHCARE SYSTEM .... WWW.NWTEXASHEALTHCARE.COM
NOVA HEALTHCARE ADMINISTRATORS .... WWW.INDEPENDANTHEALTH.COM
NY LIFE ADMINISTRATION CORP .... WWW.NEWYORKLIFELTC.COM
OAK AGENCY .... WWW.CALLOAK.COM
ODS COMPANIES .... WWW.ODSCOMPANIES.COM
OHIO BUREAU OF WORKERS' COMPENSATION .... WWW.OHIOBWC.COM
OHIO CASUALTY GROUP .... WWW.OCAS.COM
OHIO MUTUAL INSURANCE GROUP .... WWW.OMIG.COM
OHIO NATIONAL FINANCIAL SERVICE .... WWW.OHIONATIONAL.COM
OLD AMERICAN INSURANCE CO .... WWW.OAIC.COM
OLD GUARD-WESTFIELD INSURANCE .... WWW.WESTFIELDGRP.COM
OLD REPUBLIC INSURANCE CO .... WWW.OLDREPUBLIC.COM
OLD REPUBLIC INTERNATIONAL .... WWW.OLDREPUBLIC.COM
OLD UNITED LIFE INSURANCE CO .... WWW.OLDUNITED.COM
OMNICARE HEALTH PLAN .... WWW.OMNICAREHEALTHPLAN.COM
ONE BEACON INSURANCE .... WWW.ONEBEACON.COM
OPTICARE OF UTAH, INC .... WWW.OPTICAREOFUTAH.COM
OPTIMA HEALTH PLAN .... WWW.OPTIMAHEALTH.COM

OPTIMUM REINSURANCE CO .... WWW.OPTIMUMRE.COM
ORAL HEALTH SERVICES .... WWW.COMPBENEFITS.COM
OSF HEALTH PLANS .... WWW.OSFHEALTHPLANS.COM
OXFORD HEALTH PLANS .... WWW.OXFORDHEALTH.COM
OXFORD HEALTH PLANS .... WWW.UNITEDHEALTHGROUP.COM
OXFORD LIFE INSURANCE CO .... WWW.OXFORDLIFE.COM
P5 HEALTH SERVICES WWW.P5HEALTH.COM
PACIFIC BLUE CROSS .... WWW.PAC.BLUECROSS.CA
PACIFIC SOURCE HEALTH PLANS .... WWW.PACIFICSOURCE.COM
PACIFICARE HEALTH SYSTEMS, INC .... WWW.PACIFICARE.COM
PAN AMERICAN LIFE INSURANCE CO .... WWW.PANAMERICANLIFE.COM
PARAGON BENEFITS, INC .... WWW.PARAGONBENEFITS.COM
PARAMOUNT HEALTH CARE .... WWW.PARAMOUNTHEALTHCARE.COM
PARTNER REINSURANCE COMPANY OF THE U.S. .... WWW.PARTNERRE.COM
PARTNERS MUTUAL INSURANCE CO .... WWW.PARTNERSMUTUAL.COM
PARTNERS NATIONAL HEALTH PLANS .... WWW.PARTNERSHEALTH.COM
PATH MARK STORES, INC .... WWW.PATHMARK.COM
PAWTUCKET MUTUAL INSURANCE COMPANY .... WWW.PAWMUT.COM
PEARL & ASSOCIATES .... WWW.PEARLINS.COM
PEER REVIEW ORGANIZATIONS .... WWW.GMCF.ORG
PEER REVIEW ORGANIZATIONS .... WWW.HCE.ORG
PEER REVIEW ORGANIZATIONS .... WWW.IFMC.ORG
PEER REVIEW ORGANIZATIONS .... WWW.IPRO.ORG
PEER REVIEW ORGANIZATIONS .... WWW.MASSPRO.ORG
PEERLESS INSURANCE CO .... WWW.PEERLESS-INS.COM
PEERLESS INSURANCE .... WWW.PEERLESS-INS.COM
PEHP .... WWW.PEHP.ORG
PEKIN INSURANCE CO .... WWW.PEKININSURANCE.COM
PEMCO INSURANCE CO .... WWW.PEMCO.COM
PENINSULA INSURANCE CO .... WWW.PENINSULAINSURANCE.COM
PENN TREATY AMERICAN COMPANIES .... WWW.PENNTREATY.COM
PENN WESTERN BENEFITS, INC .... WWW.PENNWESTERN.COM
PENN-AMERICA INSURANCE CO .... WWW.PENN-AMERICA.COM
PENNSYLVANIA LIFE INSURANCE CO .... WWW.PENNLIFE.COM
PENNSYLVANIA LUMBERMEN'S MUTUAL INSURANCE CO .... WWW.PALUMBERMENS.COM
PENNSYLVANIA MILLERS INSURANCE CO .... WWW.PENNMILLERS.COM
PENNSYLVANIA NATIONAL MUTUAL CASUALTY INSURANCE CO .... WWW.PENNNATIONALINSURANCE.COM
PEOPLE BEFORE PROFITS .... WWW.POSTMASTERS.ORG/PBP.ASP
PERSONALCARE HEALTH MANAGEMENT .... WWW.PERSONALCAREHMO.ORG
PHARMACIST MUTUAL .... WWW.PHMIC.COM
PHCO .... WWW.PHCO.ORG
PHILADELPHIA AMERICAN LIFE .... WWW.NEWERALIFE.COM
PHILADELPHIA BENEFITS CORP .... WWW.PHILABENEFITS.COM
PHILADELPHIA CONTRIBUTIONSHIP COMPANIES .... WWW.CONTRIBUTIONSHIP.COM
PHILLIPS ADMINISTRATIVE SERVICES .... WWW.PAS-BENEFITS.COM
PHOENIX LIFE INSURANCE CO .... WWW.PHOENIXWM.COM
PHYSICIANS HEALTH PLAN OF MID MICHIGAN .... WWW.PHPMM.ORG
PHYSICIANS HEALTH PLAN OF NORTHERN INDIANA, INC .... WWW.PHPIN.COM
PHYSICIANS HEALTH PLAN OF SOUTHWEST MICHIGAN .... WWW.PHPIBA.COM
PHYSICIANS HEALTH SERVICES OF NEW YORK, INC .... WWW.HEALTH.NET
PHYSICIANS HEALTH SERVICES OF NEW YORK, INC .... WWW.PHSHMO.COM
PHYSICIANS PLUS INSURANCE CORP .... WWW.PPLUSIC.COM
PIA .... WWW.PIA.CLAIMS.COM
PICA GROUP SERVICES, INC .... WWW.PICAGROUP.COM
PIMA HEALTH SYSTEM .... WWW.PIMAHEALTHSYSTEM.ORG
PINNACLE RISK MANAGEMENT SERVICES .... WWW.PINNACLERISK.COM
PINNACLE WEST CAPITOL CORP .... WWW.PINNACLEWEST.COM
PITNEY BOWES, INC .... WWW.PITNEYBOWES.COM
PPOM/FLORA MIDWEST .... WWW.PPOM.COM
PREFERRED CARE .... WWW.PREFERREDCARE.ORG
PREFERRED HEALTH SYSTEMS INSURANCE CO .... WWW.PHSYSTEMS.COM
PREFERRED MUTUAL INSURANCE CO .... WWW.PMINSCO.COM

PREFERRED ONE.....WWW.PREFERREDONE.COM
PRESBYTERIAN HEALTH PLAN.....WWW.PHS.ORG
PRESERVER GROUP, THE.....WWW.PRESERVER.COM
PRIMARY HEALTH NETWORK, INC.....WWW.PRIMARYHEALTH.COM
PRINCIPAL FINANCIAL GROUP.....WWW.PRINCIPAL.COM
PRINCIPLE FINANCIAL GROUP.....WWW.PRINCIPLE.COM
PRODUCER'S EXCHANGE BENEFIT SERVICES, INC.....WWW.PEBSI.COM
PROFESSIONAL ADMINISTRATORS, INC.....WWW.PROFADMIN.COM
PROFESSIONAL BENEFIT ADMINISTRATORS, INC.....WWW.PBACLAIMS.COM
PROGRESSIVE CASUALTY INSURANCE CO.....WWW.PROGRESSIVE.COM
PROGRESSIVE DIVERSIFIED INSURANCE CO.....WWW.PROGRESSIVE.COM
PRONATIONAL INSURANCE CO.....WWW.PROINSURANCE.COM
PROTECTIVE INSURANCE CO.....WWW.BALDWINANDLYONS.COM
PROVIDENCE HEALTH PLANS.....WWW.PROVIDENCE.ORG/HEALTHPLANS
PROVIDENCE MUTUAL FIRE INSURANCE CO.....WWW.PROVIDENCEMUTUAL.COM
PROVIDENT AMERICAN INSURANCE CO.....WWW.PROVIDENTAMERICAN.COM
PROVIDENT NATION WIDE.....WWW.NATIONWIDEPROVIDENT.COM
PUBLIC EMPLOYEES RETIREMENT SYSTEM.....WWW.OPERS.ORG
PUBLIC SERVICE MUTUAL INSURANCE CO.....WWW.MCARTA.COM
PYRAMID LIFE.....WWW.PYRAMIDLIFE.COM
QBE REINSURANCE CO.....WWW.QBE.COM
QUALCARE, INC.....WWW.QUALCARE-USA.COM
QUALCHOICE HMO.....WWW.QCPE.COM
QUALITY IMPROVEMENT ORGANIZATION.....WWW.SDFMC.ORG
REGIONAL MEDICAL ADMINISTRATORS, INC.....WWW.REGIONALMEDICALADMINISTRATOR.COM
RELIABLE LIFE INSURANCE CO.....WWW.UNITRIN.COM
RELIANCE STANDARD LIFE INSURANCE CO.....WWW.RSLI.COM
REPUBLIC GROUP, THE.....WWW.REPUBLICGROUP.COM
REPUBLIC INDEMNITY CO OF AMERICA.....WWW.REPUBLICINDEMNITY.COM
REPUBLIC WESTERN INSURANCE CO.....WWW.REPWEST.COM
RESERVE NATIONAL INSURANCE CO.....WWW.RESERVENATIONAL.COM
RITE AID CORP.....WWW.RITEAID.COM
RIVERBEND GOVERNMENT BENEFITS ADMINISTRATOR.....WWW.RIVERBENDGBA.COM
RLI CORP.....WWW.RLICORP.COM
RMSCO, INC.....WWW.RMSCOINC.COM
ROBERT F MAY COMPANY.....WWW.WESTERNTEAMSTERS.COM
ROBERT PLAN CORP.....WWW.RPC.COM
ROCKWOOD CASUALTY INSURANCE CO.....WWW.ROCKWOODCASUALTY.COM
ROCKY MOUNTAIN HEALTH PLANS.....WWW.RMHP.ORG
ROYAL & SUNALLIANCE.....WWW.ROYALSUNALLIANCE-USA.COM
ROYAL & SUNALLIANCE.....WWW.RSAUSA.COM
ROYAL NEIGHBORS OF AMERICA.....WWW.ROYALNEIGHBORS.ORG
ROYAL STATE GROUP.....WWW.ROYALSTATE.COM
RURAL MUTUAL INSURANCE CO.....WWW.RURALINS.COM
S & S HEALTHCARE STRATEGIES.....WWW.S&SHEALTHCARE.COM
SAFECO INSURANCE CO OF AMERCIA.....WWW.SAFECO.COM
SAFECO INSURANCE.....WWW.SAFECO.COM
SAFEGUARD HEALTH ENTERPRISES, INC.....WWW.SAFEGUARD.NET
SAFETY NATIONAL CASUALTY CORP.....WWW.SNCC.COM
SAGAMORE HEALTH NETWORK.....WWW.SAGAMOREHN.COM
SAIF CORP.....WWW.SAIF.COM
SAMBA.....WWW.SAMBAPLANS.COM
SCAN HEALTH PLAN.....WWW.SCANHEALTHPLAN.COM
SCOTT & WHITE HEALTH PLAN.....WWW.SW.ORG
SEABRIGHT INSURANCE.....WWW.SBIC.COM
SEABRIGHT INSURANCE.....WWW.SEABRIGHT.COM
SECURE DENTAL.....WWW.SECURECAREDENTAL.COM
SECURE HEALTH PLANS.....WWW.SHPG.COM
SECURIAN.....WWW.SECURIAN.COM
SECURITY HEALTH PLAN OF WISCONSIN, INC.....WWW.SECURITYHEALTH.ORG
SECURITY LIFE INSURANCE CO OF AMERICA.....WWW.SECURITYLIFE.COM
SECURITY NATIONAL LIFE INSURANCE CO.....WWW.SECURITYNATIONAL.COM

SEIBELS BRUCE GROUP........WWW.SEIBELS.COM
SEIU LOCAL 36 BENEFIT FUNDS........WWW.SEIU36.COM
SELECT HEALTH........WWW.IHC.COM
SELECTIVE INSURANCE CO........WWW.SELECTIVEINSURANCE.COM
SELECTIVE INSURANCE COMPANY OF AMERICA........WWW.SELECTIVEINSURANCE.COM
SELF FUNDING ADMINISTRATORS........WWW.SELF-FUNDING-ADMIN.COM
SELF INSURED BENEFIT ADMINISTRATORS........WWW.SIBATPA.COM OR WWW.BOUCHARDINSURANCE.COM
SELF INSURED SERVICES CO........WWW.CB-SISCO.COM
SELMAN & CO........WWW.SELMAN.CC
SENECA........WWW.SENECAINSURANCE.COM
SENTRY DAIRYLAND........WWW.SENTRY.COM
SENTRY INSURANCE MUTUAL CO........WWW.SENTRYINSURANCE.COM
SENTRY SELECT INSURANCE CO........WWW.SENTRYINSURANCE.COM
SEQUOIA INSURANCE CO........WWW.SEQUOIAINS.COM
SERVICE INSURANCE CO........WWW.SERVICEINSURANCECO.COM
SERVICE LIFE & CASUALTY........WWW.SERVICE-INS-GROUP.COM
SHASTA ADMINISTRATIVE SERVICES........WWW.SHASTAADMIN.COM
SHEFFIELD OLSON & MCQUEEN, INC........WWW.SOMI.COM
SHELBY INSURANCE CO........WWW.VESTA.COM
SHELTER INSURANCE COMPANIES........WWW.SHELTERINSURANCE.COM
SHENANDOAH LIFE INSURANCE CO........WWW.SHENLIFE.COM
SIERRA HEALTH & LIFE INSURANCE CO, INC........WWW.SIERRAHEALTH.COM
SIERRA PROVIDENCE HEALTH NETWORK........WWW.SPHN.COM
SIGNET STAR REINSURANCE CO........WWW.WRBERKLEY.COM
SMITH ADMINISTRATORS........WWW.SMITHADMIN.COM
SOCIETY INSURANCE........WWW.SOCIETYINSURANCE.COM
SOMPO JAPAN INSURANCE COMPANY OF AMERICA........WWW.SOMPO-JAPAN-US.COM
SONS OF NORWAY........WWW.SONSOFNORWAY.COM
SOUTHEASTERN INDIANA HEALTH ORGANIZATION........WWW.SIHO.ORG
SOUTHERN GROUP ADMINISTRATORS, INC........WWW.SOGROUP.COM
SOUTHERN TRUST INSURANCE CO........WWW.STINS.COM
SOUTHWEST ADMINISTRATORS........WWW.SWADMIN.COM
SOUTHWEST BUSINESS CORP........WWW.SWBC.COM
SOUTHWEST LIFE AND HEALTH........WWW.FIRSTCARE.COM
SPECTERA........WWW.SPECTERA.COM
SRC SERVICES, INC........WWW.SRC-WEB.COM
STANDARD INSURANCE CO........WWW.STANDARD.COM
STANDARD LIFE & ACCIDENT INSURANCE CO........WWW.SLAICO.COM
STANDARD MUTUAL INSURANCE CO........WWW.STANDARDMUTUAL.COM
STANTON GROUP........WWW.STANTON-GROUP.COM
STATE AUTOMOBILE MUTUAL INSURANCE CO........WWW.STATEAUTO.COM
STATE COMPENSATION INSURANCE FUND........WWW.SCIF.COM
STATE FARM INSURANCE CO........WWW.STATEFARM.COM
STATE NATIONAL INSURANCE CO, INC........WWW.STATENATIONAL.COM
STATE OF ALASKA WORKERS' COMP DIVISION........WWW.LABOR.STATE.AK.US
STATE OF NEW YORK INSURANCE DEPT LIQUIDATION BUREAU........WWW.NYLB.ORG
STERLING BENEFIT SOLUTIONS........WWW.STERLINGBENEFITSOLUTIONS.COM
STERLING........WWW.STERLINGPLANS.COM
STONEBRIDGE INSURANCE CO........WWW.PLANPLUS.COM
STRATEGIC RESOURCE COMPANY........WWW.SRC-WEB.COM
SUMMA CARE HEALTH PLAN........WWW.SUMMACARE.COM
SUN LIFE ASSURANCE CO OF CANADA........WWW.SUNLIFE.CA
SUN LIFE FINANCIAL........WWW.SUNLIFE-USA.COM
SUPERIOR INSURANCE SERVICE........WWW.SUPERIORINSURANCESERVICE.COM
SWISS RE LIFE & HEALTH AMERICA, INC........WWW.SWISSRE.COM
SWISS REASSURANCE........WWW.SWISSRE.COM
T I G SPECIALTY INSURANCE........WWW.TIGSPECIALTY.COM
TARRANT HEALTH SERVICES........WWW.TXHEALTHCARE.COM
TBG ADMINISTRATIVE SERVICES........WWW.TBGASI.COM
TEACHERS PROTECTIVE MUTUAL LIFE INSURANCE CO........WWW.TPMINS.COM
TEAMSTERS BENEFIT TRUST........WWW.TBTFUND.ORG
TEAMSTERS........WWW.TEAMSTER.ORG

Appendix B

TENCO SERVICES, INC .... WWW.TENCO.COM
TENNESSEE FARMERS INSURANCE CO .... WWW.TENNESSEEFARMERS.COM
TEXAS WORKERS' COMPENSATION COMMISSION .... WWW.TDI.STATE.TX.US
THE HARTFORD INSURANCE CO .... WWW.THEHARTFORD.COM
THE HEALTH PLAN .... WWW.HEALTHPLAN.ORG
THOMAS M. MURPHY & ASSOCIATES, INC .... WWW.TMMANDA.COM
THREE RIVERS BENEFIT CORP .... WWW.THREERIVERSBENEFIT.COM
THRIVENT FINANCIAL FOR LUTHERANS .... WWW.THRIVENT.COM
TIAA CREF .... WWW.TIAA-CREF.ORG
TIC INTERNATIONAL CORP .... WWW.TICI.COM
TOA REINSURANCE COMPANY OF AMERICA .... WWW.TOARE.COM
TOPA INSURANCE CO .... WWW.TOPAINS.COM
TOTAL BENEFIT SERVICES .... WWW.TOTALBENEFITSERVICES.COM
TOTAL DENTAL ADMINISTRATOR OF UTAH .... WWW.TOTALDENTALADMIN.COM
TOTAL HEALTH CARE, INC .... WWW.TOTALHEALTHCAREONLINE.COM
TOTAL HEALTH CHOICE .... WWW.THC-ONLINE.COM
TOWER LIFE INSURANCE CO .... WWW.TOWERLIFE.COM
TR PAUL, INC .... WWW.TRPAUL.COM
TRANS HEALTH .... WWW.THICARE.COM
TRANSAMERICA ASSURANCE CO .... WWW.TRANSAMERICA.COM OR WWW. MYTRANSAMERICA.COM
TRANSAMERICA ASSURANCE CO .... WWW.TRRANSAMERICA.COM
TRAVELERS INSURANCE .... WWW.STPAULSTRAVELERS.COM
TRAVELERS INSURANCE .... WWW.STPAULTRAVELERS.COM
TRAVELERS INSURANCE .... WWW.TRAVELERS.COM
TRAVELERS INSURANCE .... WWW.TRAVELERS.COM OR WWW.STPAULTRAVELERS.COM
TRAVELERS PROTECTIVE ASSOCIATION OF AMERICA .... WWW.TPAHQ.ORG
TRICARE FOR LIFE WWW.TRICARE4U.COM
TRICARE .... WWW.HEALTHNETFEDERALSERVICES.COM
TRICARE .... WWW.TRICARE.OSD.MIL
TRICARE .... WWW.TRIWEST.COM
TRI-TEC EMPLOYEE BENEFITS, INC .... WWW.TRI-TECEMP.COM
TRIUMPHE CASUALTY CO .... WWW.TRIUMPHECASUALTY.COM
TRUSTMARK INSURANCE .... WWW.TRUSTMARKINS.COM
TUCKER ADMINISTRATORS, INC .... WWW.TUCKERADMINISTRATORS.COM
TUFTS HEALTH PLAN .... WWW.TUFTSHEALTHPLAN.COM
UCARE MINNESOTA .... WWW.UCARE.ORG
UHP HEALTHCARE .... WWW.UHPHEALTHCARE.COM
UICI .... WWW.MIDWESTLIFE.COM
UICI .... WWW.UICIOKC.COM
UMA REVIEWS .... WWW.UMACREVIEWS.COM
UNDERWRITERS SAFETY & CLAIMS .... WWW.USCKY.COM
UNICARE HEALTH PLANS OF THE MIDWEST .... WWW.UNICARE.COM
UNICARE LIFE AND HEALTH INSURANCE .... WWW.UNICARE.COM
UNIFIED GROUP SERVICES .... WWW.UGSWEB.COM
UNIFIED LIFE INSURANCE CO .... WWW.UNIFIEDLIFE.COM
UNIGARD INSURANCE CO .... WWW.NATIONALMERIT.COM
UNIGARD INSURANCE GROUP .... WWW.UNIGARD.COM
UNION BANKERS .... WWW.CHCSERVICES.COM
UNION CENTRAL INSURANCE & INVESTMENTS .... WWW.UNIONCENTRAL.COM
UNION FIDELITY INSURANCE CO .... WWW.GEFN.COM
UNION HEALTH SERVICE, INC .... WWW.UNIONHEALTH.ORG
UNION INSURANCE COMPANY .... WWW.CWGINS.COM
UNION LABOR LIFE INSURANCE CO .... WWW.ULLICO.COM
UNION STANDARD INSURANCE CO .... WWW.USIC.COM
UNION STANDARD INSURANCE GROUP .... WWW.USIC.COM
UNITED AMERICAN INSURANCE CO .... WWW.UNITEDAMERICAN.COM
UNITED COASTAL INSURANCE CO .... WWW.ACSTAR.COM
UNITED COMMERCIAL TRAVELERS OF AMERICA .... WWW.UCT.ORG
UNITED FARM FAMILY MUTUAL INSURANCE .... WWW.INFARMBUREAU.COM
UNITED FIRE & CASUALTY .... WWW.UNITEDFIREGROUP.COM
UNITED HEALTHCARE .... WWW.MAMSI.COM
UNITED HEALTHCARE .... WWW.MYUHC.COM

UNITED HEALTHCARE.......WWW.UNITEDHEALTHGROUP.COM OR WWW.MYUHC.COM
UNITED HERITAGE LIFE INSURANCE CO.......WWW.UNITEDHERITAGE.COM
UNITED INSURANCE CO OF AMERICA.......WWW.UNITRIN.COM
UNITED MEDICAL RESOURCES, INC.......WWW.UMR.COM
UNITED NATIONAL GROUP.......WWW.UNITEDNAT.COM
UNITED SECURITY LIFE AND HEALTH INSURANCE CO OF ILLINOIS.......WWW.UNITEDSECURITYLIFEANDHEALTH.COM
UNITED STATES LIFE INSURANCE CO.......WWW.AGAC.COM
UNITED TEACHER ASSOCIATES INSURANCE CO.......WWW.UTAIC.COM
UNITED TRANSPORTATION UNION INSURANCE ASSOCIATION.......WWW.UTU.ORG
UNITY HEALTH INSURANCE.......WWW.UNITYHEALTH.COM
UNIVERA HEALTHCARE, INC.......WWW.UNIVERAHEALTHCARE.ORG OR WWW.UNIVERAHEALTHCARE.COM
UNIVERSAL CARE.......WWW.UNIVERSALCARE.COM
UNIVERSAL UNDERWRITERS GROUP.......WWW.UNIVERSALUNDERWRITERS.COM
UNUM PROVIDENT.......WWW.UNUMPROVIDENT.COM
US HEALTHGROUP.......WWW.USHEALTHGROUP.COM
US LIABILITY INSURANCE GROUP.......WWW.USLI.COM
US SPECIALTY INSURANCE.......WWW.HCCH.COM
USAA LIFE INSURANCE CO.......WWW.USAA.COM
USI RISK MANAGEMENT SERVICES.......WWW.USITX.COM OR WWW.USI.BIZ
UTICA NATIONAL INSURANCE GROUP.......WWW.UTICANATIONAL.COM
UUHP.......WWW.UUHSC.UTAH.EDU/UHEALTHPLAN
VALLEY HEALTH ADMINISTRATORS.......WWW.VALUHEALTH.COM
VANLINER INSURANCE CO.......WWW.VANLINER.COM
VIRGINIA MUTUAL INSURANCE CO.......WWW.VAMUTUALINS.COM
VISION SERVICE PLAN.......WWW.VSP.COM
VISTA HEALTHCARE.......WWW.HPSE.COM
VIVA HEALTH.......WWW.VIVAHEALTH.COM
VPA, INC.......WWW.VPAINC.COM
VYTRA HEALTH PLANS.......WWW.VYTRA.COM
WACHOVIA INSURANCE SERVICES, INC.......WWW.WACHOVIA.COM/FUISAATLANTIC
WAKELY & ASSOCIATES.......WWW.WAKELYINC.COM
WARD NORTH AMERICA, INC.......WWW.WARDNA.COM
WARD NORTH AMERICA.......WWW.WARDNA.COM
WAS.......WWW.WILTONALASKA.COM
WATSON WYATT WORLDWIDE.......WWW.WATSONWYATT.COM
WAUSAU BENEFITS.......WWW.WAUSAUBENEFITS.COM
WAUSAU INSURANCE.......WWW.WAUSAU.COM
WEA TRUST.......WWW.WEATRUST.COM
WELBORN HEALTH PLANS.......WWW.WELBORNHEALTHPLANS.COM
WELFARE & PENSION ADMIN SERV.......WWW.WPAS-INC.COM
WELL CARE HEALTH PLANS.......WWW.WELLCARE.COM
WELL POINT, INC.......WWW.WELLPOINT.COM
WELLCHOICE INSURANCE OF NEW JERSEY.......WWW.WELLCHOICENJ.COM OR WWW.IMPERIALBLUE.COM
WELLMARK BLUE CROSS BLUE SHIELD OF SOUTH DAKOTA.......WWW.WELLMARK.COM
WELLPATH.......WWW.WELLPATHONLINE.COM
WESLEY MEDICAL CENTER.......WWW.HCAHEALTHCARE.COM
WEST AMERICAN INSURANCE.......WWW.OCAS.COM
WEST BEND MUTUAL INSURANCE CO.......WWW.WESTBENDMUTUAL.COM
WESTCHESTER TEAMSTERS HEALTH & WELFARE.......WWW.TEAMSTERSLOCAL.COM
WESTERN AMERICAN INSURANCE COMPANY.......WWW.WALIC.COM
WESTERN BENEFITS, INC.......WWW.WESTERNBENEFITSINC.COM
WESTERN MUTUAL INSURANCE CO.......WWW.WESTERNMUTUALINSURANCE.COM
WESTERN NATIONAL MUTUAL INSURANCE CO.......WWW.WNINS.COM
WESTERN RESERVE GROUP.......WWW.WRG-INS.COM
WESTERN WORLD INSURANCE GROUP.......WWW.WESTERNWORLD.COM
WESTFIELD INSURANCE.......WWW.WESTFIELDGRP.COM
WEYCO, INC.......WWW.WEYCO.COM
WICHITA NATIONAL LIFE INSURANCE CO.......WWW.WNLIC.COM
WILLIAM C EARHART COMPANY, INC.......WWW.WCEARHART.COM
WILLIS GROUP LIMITED.......WWW.WILLIS.COM
WILSON MUTUAL INSURANCE.......WWW.WILSONMUTUAL.COM
WOLVERINE MUTUAL INSURANCE CO.......WWW.WOLVERINEMUTUAL.COM

Appendix B

WOODMEN OF THE WORLD .... WWW.WOODMEN.COM
WORKFORCE SAFETY & INSURANCE .... WWW.WORKFORCESAFETY.COM
WORKMEN'S CIRCLE .... WWW.CIRCLE.ORG
WORKMEN'S INSURANCE GROUP .... WWW.WAIC.COM
WORLD INSURANCE CO .... WWW.WORLDINSCO.COM OR WWW.WEBMED.COM
WPS HEALTH INSURANCE .... WWW.WPSIC.COM
ZENITH ADMINISTRATORS, INC .... WWW.ZENITHADM.COM
ZENITH ADMINISTRATORS, INC .... WWW.ZENITHTPA.COM
ZENITH INSURANCE CO .... WWW.THEZENITH.COM
ZENITH INSURANCE COMPANY .... WWW.THEZENITH.COM
ZENITH, THE .... WWW.THEZENITH.COM
ZURICH NORTH AMERICA .... WWW.ZURICHNA.COM